Java Web Development Illuminated

Kai Qian
Southern Polytechnic State University

Richard Allen
Georgia Tech Research Institute

Mia Gan
Georgia Institute of Technology

Robert Brown
Southern Polytechnic State University

JONES AND BARTLETT PUBLISHERS
Sudbury, Massachusetts
BOSTON TORONTO LONDON SINGAPORE

World Headquarters
Jones and Bartlett Publishers
40 Tall Pine Drive
Sudbury, MA 01776
978-443-5000
info@jbpub.com
www.jbpub.com

Jones and Bartlett Publishers
Canada
6339 Ormindale Way
Mississauga, Ontario L5V 1J2
CANADA

Jones and Bartlett Publishers
International
Barb House, Barb Mews
London W6 7PA
UK

Jones and Bartlett's books and products are available through most bookstores and online booksellers. To contact Jones and Bartlett Publishers directly, call 800-832-0034, fax 978-443-8000, or visit our website www.jbpub.com.

Substantial discounts on bulk quantities of Jones and Bartlett's publications are available to corporations, professional associations, and other qualified organizations. For details and specific discount information, contact the special sales department at Jones and Bartlett via the above contact information or send an email to specialsales@jbpub.com.

ISBN-13: 978-0-7637-3423-7
ISBN-10: 0-7637-3423-3

Library of Congress Cataloging-in-Publication Data
Java Web development illuminated / Kai Qian ... [et al.].
p. cm.
Includes bibliographical references and index.
ISBN-13: 978-0-7637-3423-7 (pbk.)
ISBN-10: 0-7637-3423-3 (pbk.)
1. Java (Computer program language) 2. Web site development. I. Qian, Kai.
QA76.73.J38J3858 2006
005.13'3—dc22
2006003577

6048

Production Credits
Acquisitions Editor: Tim Anderson
Production Director: Amy Rose
Production Editor: Tracey Chapman
Editorial Assistant: Laura Pagluica
Production Assistant: Jamie Chase
Manufacturing Buyer: Therese Connell
Marketing Manager: Andrea DeFronzo
Composition: Northeast Compositors
Test Design: Kristin O. Ohlin
Cover Design: Anne Spencer
Cover Image: © Robert Sarosiek/ShutterStock, Inc.
Printing and Binding: Malloy, Inc.
Cover Printing: Coral Graphics

Printed in the United States of America
10 09 08 07 06 10 9 8 7 6 5 4 3 2 1

Acknowledgments

It is a great pleasure for us to acknowledge the very supportive and helpful assistance and contributions of our editors and staff: Tim Anderson, Tracey Chapman, Jamie Chase, and Laura Pagluica.

We would like to express our thanks to those who reviewed and contributed to this book. These include John J. Ulmer, Purdue University, Michael Crowley, University of Southern California, and Dunren Che, Southern Illinois University at Carbondale. We would also like to thank Warren Sheaffer, Chair of the Computer Science Department at Saint Paul College, Jorge Díaz-Herrera, Dean of College of the Computer and Information Systems at Rochester Institute of Technology, and Mike Murphy, Dean of Computing and Software Engineering at Southern Polytechnic State University for their support.

We would like to thank everyone else who helped in writing this book.

Finally, we give thanks to our families for their support and encouragement. Specifically, Richard Allen thanks his wonderful, loving wife Kelly, and his children, Brighton and Brooke, for their support, patience, and understanding.

Preface

Audience of This Book

This book introduces the fundamental concepts, design, and development of Web applications in Java. The book is meant to be used as a textbook for a one-semester course in Java Web application design, programming, and development at the junior, senior, or graduate level for computer science, information technology, information systems, or other related fields. Any advanced courses on Web application and development can use this book as a text because it covers some advanced Web application topics such as Web enterprise applications, SOAP, and Web services. It is also a good self-study reference book for Web developers.

As prerequisites, we assume that the readers are familiar with Java object-oriented programming language basics, and have had some exposure to Web applications.

Features

Throughout the book, we have attempted to promote effective teaching and learning of the topics by providing many example labs with step-by-step guidelines. This book also provides the instructor and students with an extensive variety of end-of-chapter learning materials that include self-review multiple choice questions with keys, exercises, and programming assignments and projects. All the examples have been tested. All the supporting software is open source or free to use, including Apache Tomcat,

J2EE, JDK1.4 or JDK 1.5, and Apache Axis. Students can download and install on their own computer all necessary software for lab practices in this book without any cost. The source code for all practice labs and the instruction slides are available on the Internet.

Contents of this book

The text is organized in three major parts:

- Basics (Chapters 1–2)
- Java Web server components (Chapters 3–6)
- Java SOAP and Web Services components (Chapters 7–8)

Here is a brief summary of the topics covered in each chapter:

Chapter 1: Web Application Concepts

This chapter introduces students to the concepts and evolution of Web applications. HTTP protocol is introduced. Then Web application architectures and Web servers are discussed.

Finally, the J2EE platform is introduced.

Chapter 2: XML Basics

This is a foundation chapter for the rest of the book. The concepts of XML are introduced, including the XML document, its definition specifications (Document Type Definition [DTD], and XML Schema), and XML applications. Additionally, this chapter explains how to parse and process XML documents in Java using the Simple API for XML (SAX), Document Object Model (DOM), and JDOM.

Chapter 3: Java Servlets

Java Servlets are widely used in Java Web applications to handle business logic, flow control, request validation, authentication, job dispatch, and other processes. This chapter covers the Java Servlet API in detail including step-by-step tutorials on building, deploying, and using Java Servlet components. Many Java Servlet practice examples are demonstrated.

Chapter 4: JavaServer Pages (JSP)

This chapter covers JSP Basics, JSP syntax, the JSP Expression Language (EL), JSP Custom Tags, JSP XML Syntax Documents, JavaBean components, and JSP integration with Java Servlets. Many JSP Web application examples and the integration of JSP with Java Servlets are demonstrated.

Chapter 5: Case Study: MVC Architecture for Web Applications

This chapter is a case study of a comprehensive Web application or online shopping developed using Java Servlet, JSP, JavaBean, and JDBC technologies. First, we teach students the typical Web application design pattern—Model-View-Controller (MVC). Next, we give a tutorial on the Java DataBase Connectivity (JDBC) protocols that support persistent data for the online Web applications. Finally, we provide a complete online store application to show how to integrate all technologies we have introduced thus far.

Chapter 6: Enterprise JavaBeans (EJB)

We describe the Java enterprise technology that is called EJB. EJB supports Web-based enterprise applications. We discuss all EJB types: stateless session bean, stateful session bean, Bean Managed Persistence entity bean (BMP), Container Managed Persistence entity bean (CMP), and Message Driven Bean (MDB). In this chapter, we build a comprehensive Web enterprise application that integrates all Java Web components and Java enterprise bean components. The deployment of an enterprise application with Web components and EJB components on the J2EE platform is also demonstrated.

Chapter 7: SOAP

SOAP is a protocol for packaging and exchanging data between Web services in the form of an XML document. SOAP is the foundation of modern Web services. In this chapter, we cover the SOAP message specification and message structure including its envelope, header, body, data encoding, message styles, and SOAP applications.

Chapter 8: Web Services

This chapter discusses the SOAP-based Web services approach to the Service-Oriented Architecture concept including the Web Services Description Language (WSDL), Universal Description, Discovery, and Integration (UDDI), and Java APIs for programming Web services such as the SOAP with Attachment API for Java (SAAJ), the Java API for XML-based RPC (JAX-RPC), and the Java API for XML Registries (JAXR). The deployment of Java Web services on the J2EE platform is also discussed. Many Java Web services examples are given.

Instructors Materials

The following ancillaries are available online at http://www.jbpub.com/catalog/0763734233/supplements.

- Answers to the end-of-chapter exercises
- A set of lecture outlines in PowerPoint format
- Source code and solutions for all programs to the examples and Practice Labs sections
- Test items for each chapter

Contacting the Authors

We have checked the technical details of this book. Almost all application examples are tested. Despite our best efforts, there may still be some errors. If you find any technical errors in this book, please contact us at kqian@spsu.edu.

Contents

About the Authors

Kai Qian, PhD, is a professor of Computer Science and Software Engineering at Southern Polytechnic State University. Dr. Qian has written a book and many papers on distributed computing and has taught Java enterprise application development for many years.

Richard L. Allen is a Research Engineer for Georgia Tech Research Institute in Atlanta, Georgia, where he has worked since 2002. His expertise and work at Georgia Tech encompass Web-based distributed systems written in Java. Richard has a Master of Science degree in Software Engineering.

Mia Gan is a systems analyst for the Office of Information Technology at Georgia Institute of Technology. She has a Master's degree in Computer Information Systems. Her expertise is in client/server and Web-based application development and database application development.

Bob Brown is an instructor at Southern Polytechnic State University, where he has been teaching Web development and computer security for more than five years. He is a candidate for the PhD. Brown has a 30-year career in management of technology, including eleven years with direct involvement in Web technologies.

CHAPTER 1

Web Application Concepts

Objectives of This Chapter

- Describe the evolution of Web applications
- Introduce the basics of HTTP protocol
- Introduce the Web application architectures
- Introduce the basics of Java Web technologies and applications

1.1 History

The Internet and the World Wide Web (WWW), sometimes collectively referred to as the Web, have revolutionized the way that companies conduct business and even the way that humans communicate. Today, one can buy nearly anything on the Web, one can manage all of one's financial accounts on the Web, companies readily conduct critical business meetings over the Web, greater portions of the population get their daily news and information from the Web, and many humans would rather communicate via e-mail or instant messaging than talk on the phone. If you are reading this book and you have never used the Web, then you are most certainly a rarity.

The Internet is a global network of computer networks that join together millions of government, university, and private computers. This network provides a mechanism for communication where any type of data (text, images, video, etc.) can be exchanged between linked computers. These computers can be physically located on opposite sides of the globe, yet the data can be exchanged in a matter of seconds. Although often used interchangeably, the terms Internet and WWW are not the same thing. The Internet is the worldwide network of computers (and other devices like cell phones), but the WWW refers to all the information sources that a Web browser can access, which include all the global publicly available Web sites plus FTP (File Transfer Protocol) sites, USENET newsgroups, etc. E-mail is not considered to be part of the WWW, but is a technology that is made possible by the Internet.

The Web had its very early beginnings in the early 1960s when some visionaries saw great potential value in allowing computers to share information on research and development in scientific and military fields. In 1962, Joseph Carl Robnett Licklider at the Massachusetts Institute of Technology (MIT) first proposed a global network of computers. Later that year he started working at the Defense Advanced Research Projects Agency (DARPA), then called the Advanced Research Projects Agency (ARPA), to develop his idea. From 1961 through 1964, Leonard Kleinrock, while working on a PhD thesis at MIT, and later while working at the University of California at Los Angeles (UCLA), developed the concept of packet switching, which is the basis for Internet communications today. In 1965 while at MIT, Lawrence Roberts and Thomas Merrill used Kleinrock's packet switching theory to successfully connect a computer in Massachusetts with a computer in California over dial-up telephone lines—the first Wide Area Network (WAN).

In 1966, Roberts started working at DARPA on plans for the first large-scale computer network called ARPANET, at which time he became aware of work done by Donald Davies and Roger Scantlebury of National Physical Laboratory (NPL) and Paul Baran of RAND Corporation that coincided with the packet switching concept developed by Kleinrock at MIT. Coincidentally, the early work of the three groups (MIT, NPL, and RAND) had proceeded in parallel without any knowledge of each other. The word *packet* was actually adopted for the ARPANET proposal from the work at NPL. DARPA awarded the contract for bringing ARPANET online to BBN Technologies of Massachusetts. Bob Kahn headed the work at BBN, which in 1969 brought ARPANET (later called the Internet, in 1974) online at 50 kilobits per second (kbps), connecting four major computers at universities in the southwestern United States—UCLA, Stanford Research Institute, University of California at Santa Barbara, and University of Utah.

ARPANET quickly grew as more sites were connected. In 1970, the first host-to-host protocol for ARPANET was developed called Network Control Protocol (NCP). In 1972, Ray Tomlinson of BBN developed e-mail for ARPANET. In 1973, Vinton Cerf of Stanford and Bob Kahn of DARPA began to develop a replacement for NCP, which was later called Transmission Control Protocol/Internet Protocol (TCP/IP). ARPANET was transitioned to TCP/IP by 1983. TCP/IP is still used today as the Internet's underlying protocol for connecting computers and transmitting data between them over the network.

The original Internet was not very user-friendly so only researchers and scientists used it at that time. In 1991, the University of Minnesota developed the first user-friendly interface to the Internet called Gopher. Gopher became very popular because it allowed noncomputer scientist types to easily use the Internet. Earlier, in 1989, Tim Berners-Lee and others at the European Laboratory for Particle Physics (CERN) in Switzerland proposed a new protocol for information distribution on the Internet, which was based on hypertext, a system of embedding links in text to link to other text. This system was invented before Gopher but took longer to develop. Berners-Lee eventually created the Hypertext Transfer Protocol (HTTP)[1] and the Hypertext Markup Language (HTML),[2] coined the term "World Wide Web," developed the first Web browser and Web server, and helped found the World Wide Web Consortium (W3C),[3] which is a large umbrella organization that currently manages the development of HTTP, HTML, and other Web technologies.

1.2 Web Architecture

The majority of the traffic on the Internet today is the transmission of HTTP messages. Most Internet users have applications on their computers called Web browsers (typically Microsoft Internet Explorer, Netscape, or Mozilla). The Web browser is a user interface that is programmed to know how to send HTTP messages to, and receive HTTP messages from, a remote Web server. The Web browser establishes a TCP/IP connection with the Web server and sends it an HTTP request message. The Web server is programmed to know how to handle HTTP request messages to obtain data (text, images, movies, etc.) from the server and send it back to the Web browser, or process data that

[1]The HTTP specification can be found at `http://www.ietf.org/rfc/rfc2616.txt`. The HTTP specification is maintained by multiple groups including the Internet Engineering Task Force (IETF) and the World Wide Web Consortium (W3C). See also, `http://www. w3.org/Protocols/`.

[2]The HTML specification can be found at `http://www.w3.org/TR/html4/`. The World Wide Web Consortium (see footnote 3) is the organization that maintains the HTML specification.

[3]W3C is an international consortium of organizations devoted to leading the World Wide Web to its full potential by developing common protocols that promote its evolution and ensure its interoperability. Its Web site is located at `http://www.w3.org`.

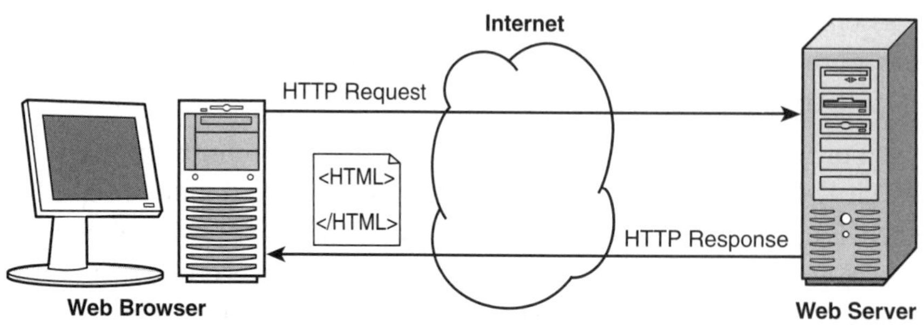

Figure 1.1

Typical Interaction Between Web Browser and Web Server

is submitted to the Web server from the Web browser (e.g., a username and password required for login). Internet users typically use Web browsers to simply get Web pages from the Web server in the form of HTML documents (see Figure 1.1). The Web browser is programmed to know how to process the HTML document that it receives from the Web server, and display the results to the user via a graphical interface. Once the Web browser receives the HTTP response message from the Web server, the TCP/IP connection between the Web browser and Web server is closed.

1.2.1 Uniform Resource Identifier (URI) / Uniform Resource Locator (URL)

Web browsers always initiate TCP/IP connections with the Web server, never vice versa. The Web browser identifies with which Web server to make a connection and what is being requested of the Web server with a Uniform Resource Locator (URL). A URL is a classification of Uniform Resource Identifier (URI) that identifies a resource by its location. URI is a more general term that encompasses all types of Web identifier schemes. The terms URL and URI are often used interchangeably, but the term URL is meant to specify a type of URI that identifies the location of a resource, as opposed to identifying a resource by name, independent of location, as is done with a Uniform Resource Name (URN).

A URI is simply the address that you type into the address field of your browser, such as `http://www.w3c.org`. URIs are composed of several parts—scheme, authority, path, query, fragment. The following illustrates the division of the parts of a URI.

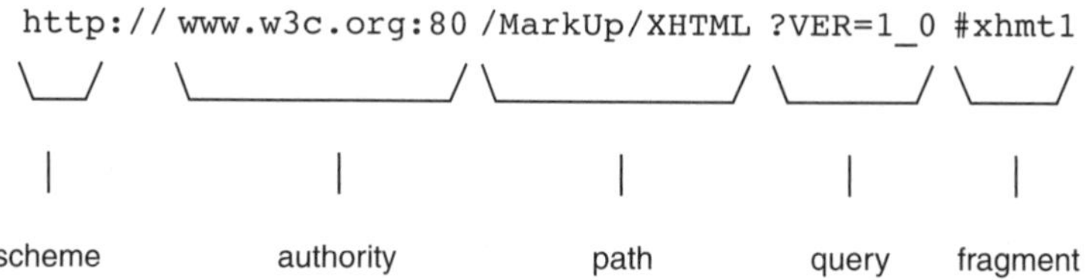

- **Scheme** identifies the application-level protocol. Examples are http, ftp, news, mailto, file, telnet. The :// following the scheme separates the scheme from the authority.
- **Authority** is the host name or IP address of the Web server and an optional port number. The standard port for HTTP is 80, which most all computers already recognize, so it can be omitted. If the Web server is listening for connections to a different port, like 8080, then the port will need to be specified.
- **Path** is a directory path to the resource. The concept of directory used here is the same as used with file systems. The ? (question mark) after the path is used to separate the query from the rest of the URI and is not necessary if there is no query.
- The optional **query** is information that is to be interpreted by the Web server. It is used to provide additional information that is not included in the path or to submit text data to the Web server. The query can contain multiple name-value pairs separated by an & (ampersand) symbol). Each name is separated from its associated value by an = (equal sign).
- The optional **fragment** is used to identify a location within a document. This part is actually used by the Web browser, not the Web server, to bring the client to a specific location in a document. The # (pound symbol) is used to separate the fragment from the rest of the URI.

1.2.2 Hypertext Transfer Protocol (HTTP)

HTTP is a stateless protocol that supports requests followed by responses (request-response message exchange pattern). Previously we described the use of HTTP between a Web browser and a Web server; however, HTTP messages are also commonly exchanged between Web servers or other applications that do not require human interaction such as a Web browser. The HTTP protocol does not require the use of a Web browser; it simply describes how data can be exchanged over a network that uses TCP/IP (e.g., the Internet). By default, HTTP uses TCP/IP connections on port 80 of a computer, but other ports can and often are used. An HTTP transaction begins with a request from the client and ends with a response from the server.

An HTTP request message consists of three parts: 1) a line defining the HTTP method, the URI requested, and HTTP version used; 2) a list of HTTP request headers; 3) the entity body. An example HTTP request message is given here.

```
POST /catalog/prices HTTP/1.1[CRLF]
Host: www.somesite.com[CRLF]
Connection: close[CRLF]
Accept-Encoding: gzip[CRLF]
Accept: text/plain; text/html[CRLF]
Accept-Language: en-us,en[CRLF]
Accept-Charset: ISO-8859-1,utf-8[CRLF]
User-Agent: Mozilla/5.0 Gecko/20041107 Firefox/1.0[CRLF]
Referer: http://web-sniffer.net/[CRLF]
```

```
Content-Length: 16[CRLF]
Content-Type: application/x-www-form-urlencoded[CRLF]
[CRLF]
productId=ABC123[CRLF]
```

The [CRLF] tags in the message above represent the carriage return/linefeed characters. They normally would not be seen, however they are significant in an HTTP message so they are displayed here. CRLF characters are used to separate each line of the header and the header from the entity body. The message header includes every line before the first blank line (the line above with only a CRLF). The first blank line defines where the message header ends and the entity body begins.

Each line of the HTTP request message that occurs after the first line and before the blank line is called an HTTP request header. HTTP request headers contain useful information about the client environment and the entity body, such as the type of Web browser being used, languages for which the browser is configured, and the length of the entity body. The first line of the HTTP request message contains the HTTP method (`GET`), the URI (`/catalog/prices`), and the protocol/version (`HTTP/1.1`). The HTTP method tells the Web server something about how the message is structured and what the client expects the Web server to do. The latest version of HTTP is version 1.1. The HTTP 1.1 specification defines the methods in Table 1.1. The `GET` and `POST` methods are the most widely used.

Table 1.1 HTTP 1.1 Request Methods

Method	Description
GET	Simply retrieves the data identified by the URL
HEAD	Like GET, but only retrieves the HTTP headers
POST	Used to submit data to the Web server in the entity body Sometimes data is also submitted to a Web server by adding a query string to the URL; however, this is not how the GET method was intended to work. A query string added to a URL for a GET is only intended to help identify the data to be retrieved from the Web server and sent in an HTTP response message back to the client. The POST method is typically used with HTML forms.
OPTIONS	Used to query a Web server about the capabilities it provides
PUT	Stores the entity body at the location specified by the URL
DELETE	Deletes a document from the Web server that is identified by the URL
TRACE	Used to trace the path of a request through firewalls and proxy servers for debugging network problems

An HTTP response message also contains three parts as does the request message: 1) a line defining the version of the protocol used, a status code to identify if the request was successful, and a description; 2) a list of HTTP response headers; 3) the entity body. An example HTTP response message is given here.

```
HTTP/1.1 200 OK[CRLF]
Date: Sun, 13 Mar 2005 22:07:43 GMT[CRLF]
Server: Apache/2.0.49[CRLF]
Last-Modified: Sun, 17 Oct 2004 00:26:16 GMT[CRLF]
Content-Length: 70[CRLF]
Keep-Alive: timeout=15, max=99[CRLF]
Connection: Keep-Alive[CRLF]
Content-Type: text/html;charset=UTF-8[CRLF]
[CRLF]
<html>[CRLF]
<head>[CRLF]
<title>Example</title>[CRLF]
</head>[CRLF]
<body>[CRLF]
Hello World[CRLF]
</body>[CRLF]
</html>[CRLF]
```

As with the HTTP request message example, this example shows the `[CRLF]` characters even though they would normally not be visible. The message header is separated from the entity body by a blank line. Every line after the first line and before the first blank line is called an HTTP response header. The HTTP response headers contain useful information such as the length and type of data in the entity body, the type of server that processed the request, and information that can be used by the Web browser to determine how long it can cache the data. The entity body of the message may contain both text and binary data. In this case, it contains HTML code, which will be processed by the Web browser and displayed to the user. The status code in this example is `200` and the description is `OK`. This indicates to the client that the request was successful. The HTTP success codes are in the 200s, HTTP redirect codes are in the 300s, and HTTP error codes are in the 400s and 500s. An HTTP redirect is when the Web server responds with an indication that the Web browser should take some action, typically to request a different URL. Some common HTTP error codes and descriptions that you may have seen displayed by your Web browser when surfing the Web are `404 Not found` (the resource requested was not found), and `500 Internal Error` (the Web server encountered an error).

1.2.3 Web Application Architecture

Web servers evolved over the years from serving up static content such as predefined HTML pages and images to serving up dynamic content where the actual content that is sent back to the browser

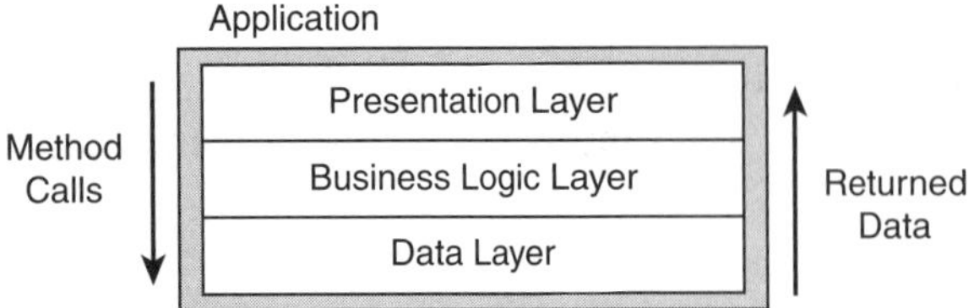

Figure 1.2
Layers of Application Code

is generated on the fly when the HTTP request is made. Additionally, Web servers have evolved to execute server-side programs that perform some business process related activity in response to a request, such as transferring money from a savings account to a checking account. The programs developed to execute business processes in response to Web requests are commonly called Web applications. Web applications have given businesses a mechanism to provide services online to the entire world 24 hours a day, 7 days a week, with little overhead cost. Such exposure has the potential to greatly expand the customer base of a business and the number of business transactions processed in a given time period, which leads to increased revenue for the business. Consequently, Web applications have rapidly grown in popularity. In this section we discuss a few of the many types of architectures that are used for developing Web applications. First, we clarify some terminology.

Most software systems can be partitioned into separate physical tiers and logical layers, where each part handles a different responsibly. The words *tier* and *layer* are often used interchangeably when discussing software architectures. For this discussion, we use the word *tier* to mean a physical partition. In other words, different tiers reside on different computers. We use the word *layer* to mean a logical partition. Logical layers may or may not reside on different tiers.

It is considered good practice to design and develop software applications with different logical layers (see Figure 1.2). Each layer interacts only with its neighboring layers. For instance, in Figure 1.2, the presentation layer only interacts with the business logic layer, the business logic layer interacts with both the presentation layer and the data layer, and the data layer interacts only with the business logic layer. The best practice is to let upper layers make calls to lower layers, but not vice versa. This reduces coupling because each layer only *knows* (is coupled to) one other layer—the layer below. In Figure 1.2, the presentation layer *knows* about the business logic layer because it makes calls to it, but the business logic layer does not *know* about the presentation layer. Additionally, the business logic layer *knows* about the data layer, but the data layer does not *know* about the business logic layer. In other words, procedure calls flow down to lower layers, but they should not flow back up. The only thing flowing up the layers is data returned from method calls.

Applications designed with this type of layered separation are easier to understand, easier to maintain, easier to scale, and provide the opportunity for the application code to be distributed on separate computers and networked together. When the application layers are well separated and loosely coupled, they can be modified or one of the layers may even completely be rewritten without incurring changes to the others. Additionally, this separation reduces the complexity for the developer because his or her focus can be concentrated on one responsibility of the application without having to think much about the other responsibilities.

Distributing application code to different physical tiers is sometimes a good idea and at other times a bad idea. Two of the major disadvantages to separating an application into different tiers are the complex and latent effects caused by having to pass commands across the network. If all of the code is executed on one computer, one does not need to write or use network code, integrate or maintain various computers, etc. One can also more easily take steps to optimize the code to improve performance. However, the advantages of monolithic applications dissipate when increasing the users of the application and it is necessary to maintain the application on the user's computer. Granted, some applications have to be run on the user's computer, but if one wants to distribute and maintain the application to users en masse, and it is a monolithic application, then the workload, and thus the cost, can drastically increase. Every time a new user is added, it is necessary to make sure that the user's computer is powerful enough to handle the application and to install and maintain the application on that computer. If there are thousands or even millions of users, then be prepared to hire a lot of new employees.

Web applications are by nature distributed applications. They have at least two physical tiers—the client computer with the Web browser and the computer hosting the Web server. The client computer is typically maintained by the user, so right away that cost is saved. However, as mentioned earlier, the addition of tiers increases the complexity and the latency of the application. No full-featured Web application will run as fast as it would if it were designed and implemented on a single computer as long as that computer was powerful enough to handle it. Unless the Web application is run on a network that you fully control, there is not much that can be done about network latency between your server and the client's computer. To improve network latency, the customer would typically need to obtain a faster Internet connection (again, another cost transferred to the customer). However, since most of the application code executes on computers that you fully control (your Web servers), then you can do something about the throughput of your application. You can optimize the code or enhance the processing power of the server by using more powerful processors, increasing the number of processors, using faster hard drives, and/or increasing the RAM. With Web applications, there are typically many clients to only a few servers, so spending money on the few servers will not be as expensive as upgrading all the user's computers.

Tiers and layers typically fall into one of three categories: *presentation*, *business logic*, and *data*. The presentation tier/layer handles presenting data to the user and accepting user inputs. Today this is often a graphical user interface. The business logic tier/layer handles the business processing, and the data tier/layer is used to persist data created at runtime. A typical data tier of today is a relational database, which, as the word *tier* indicates, typically resides and therefore executes on a separate computer from the rest of the system. As Web applications and other distributed software applications have become larger, more complex, and have needed to handle significantly more processing, distributing the layers to separate computers to improve performance has become more important. Distributing layers to different tiers can certainly hurt performance if it is not done correctly, and it definitely increases complexity, but it is sometimes demanded by usage. There just are not single servers powerful enough to handle complex transactions at millions of hits per hour such as some Web sites encounter. The processing has to be distributed to multiple servers. This also provides a maintenance benefit because a server can be brought down to upgrade the software or make repairs while the other servers handle the processing load.

The layers of an application can be distributed to different computers in a number of ways, which fall into one of essentially three different types of architectures—two-tier architecture, three-tier architecture, and *n*-tier architecture. Each tier is usually a different computer, but sometimes it is only a different process on the same computer. For instance, with a multiprocessor computer, one process can be executed simultaneously with others on the same computer. These three different architectures are briefly described in the following sections.

Two-Tier Architecture

A two-tier architecture is the simplest and consists only of two computers—a client and a server. The client in this architecture is commonly referred to as a "fat client" because it handles a significant portion of the processing. In a two-tier architecture, the client tier usually hosts both the presentation layer and the business layer, while the server hosts the data layer (see Figure 1.3). Actually, part of the data layer often resides on the client to provide an interface to the database. This layer is often called an *integration layer* because it serves to integrate the client with the server, in this case, the business logic layer with the data layer.

Although this architecture is the simplest, it has several drawbacks. One drawback is that the client computers must be powerful enough to handle the processing required by both the presentation layer and the business layer. A second drawback is that the business layer usually needs to make a large amount of calls to the data layer, which resides on a different computer. As the amount of clients on the network increases, the amount of network traffic significantly increases because all those clients are making many network calls to the data tier. A third drawback is that upgrading the clients to new versions of the software can become labor-intensive. The business layer usually incurs

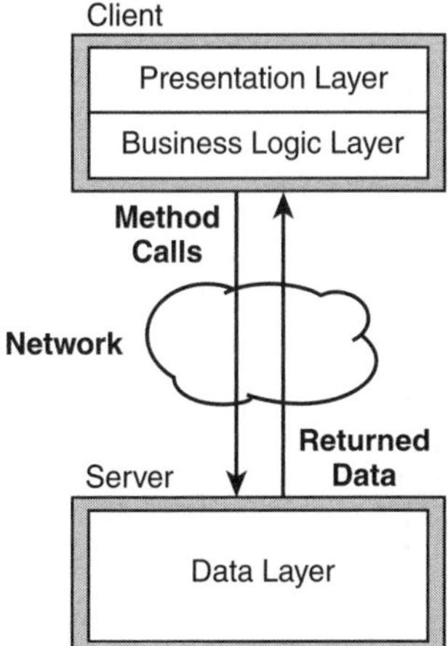

Figure 1.3
Two-Tier Architecture

the most changes over the lifetime of a system. Since the business layer is on the client and there can be any number of clients, system administrators are dealt a significant burden. This process can be automated, but experience has shown that upgrading clients is usually more complex than automated upgrades can completely handle. For instance, often some clients may not be able to be upgraded at the same time as others or require an upgrade to a different version.

Three-Tier Architecture

The three-tier architecture consists of three computers—a client, a business server, and a database server. In general, the client handles the presentation layer, the business server handles the business layer, and the database server handles the data layer. Figure 1.4 shows two possible alternatives for this architecture. The one on the left has all of the presentation logic on the client, while the Web application on the right has some of the presentation logic on the server. The Web application also has an integration layer that contains data access code. This is the architecture that most Web applications use today.

The logical layers of the system can be distributed a number of ways. The presentation code of a Web application is basically always divided. In a typical Web application, the presentation (HTML and Cascading Style Sheets) is essentially constructed on a Web server and the Web browser just displays it to the user. The Web browser will often process some minor logic written in scripting languages such as JavaScript or JScript to manipulate the HTML (called Dynamic HTML or DHTML), but the majority of the logic that structures how the presentation will appear to the end user occurs on the server. Web

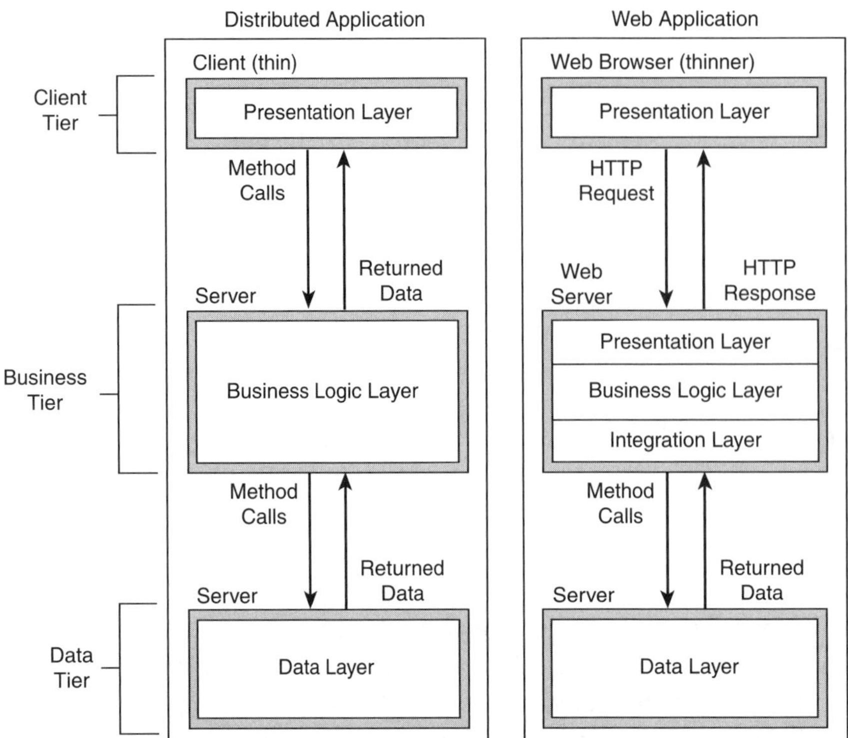

Figure 1.4
Three-Tier Architecture

browsers are able to handle some fairly heavyweight processing by downloading and executing programs such as Java Applets, Microsoft ActiveX controls, and Macromedia Flash, but even in these cases, the server ends up doing a significant amount of the work. In a typical Web application architecture, the Web browser is considered a "thin client" because very little processing is handled by it.

The three-tier architecture solves many of the problems of the two-tier architecture by separating the presentation layer from the business layer. The business layer can now reside on one or a few computers that are strictly maintained and controlled by the system administrators and developers. In the three-tier architecture only one or a few business servers are communicating with one or a few database servers, reducing the network traffic. Since the presentation layer does not need to make many calls to the business layer, the amount of clients can grow to a measurable degree without significantly impacting network traffic and, thus, performance. Since the business layer now resides on its own computer, the processing power of the overall system has been improved. Additionally, the business server and database server can be upgraded without affecting the clients or drastically increasing the cost of the system. There are many more clients in a system than there are servers. If all the clients needed to be upgraded to improve the performance of the overall system (as would be necessary in a two-tier architecture), then the cost impact would be tremendous.

n-Tier Architecture

Many Web applications today are moving to *n*-tier architectures. These architectures break down the application into even more tiers. This additional segregation typically occurs within the presentation layer and the business layer, but can also happen in the data layer. The logic of the application is divided into clearly separable responsibilities, and each is executed on a different computer or processor. This allows the Web application to be very scalable. Additional computers can be added as demands increase. Development and maintenance responsibilities can also be divided among business units. This increased division of responsibilities has lead to the concept of service-oriented architectures where different functional units of a business process are actually hosted on different Web sites. Not only are layers of the system distributed to different computers, but those computers may reside anywhere in the world and be maintained by some other organization. Service-oriented architectures and one popular implementation, Web services, are discussed in Chapter 8.

It is also common to add additional business servers and database servers that divide up and process incoming requests and/or act as a failover mechanism if servers go down unexpectedly or need to be brought down for maintenance. This is how Web sites such as Google, Yahoo, and eBay are online 24 hours a day, 7 days a week, 365 days a year.

1.3 J2EE Architecture

The first real widespread solution to dynamic Web-based applications was Common Gateway Interface (CGI). CGI provides a fairly simple way for Web applications to accept input from a Web browser, query a database, and return some dynamic results back to the Web browser for display to the user. In CGI, a Web server, in response to a specific URL, starts a server-side process to handle the request. The program that executes in the process can be written in any language but is typically written in Perl or C. The Web server passes the request data to the program when it is started, and the Web server reads the response from the program through standard output (`stdout`). A new process is executed for each new request and each process has its own runtime environment including memory allocation and environment variables. This solution did not scale well, because the great number of processes that had to be executed in response to many requests would heavily burden the system, often causing system crashes. Alternative CGI implementations such as FastCGI and Apache's `mod_perl` helped, but they did not compare to the solutions that came next.

Both Microsoft and Netscape developed proprietary solutions, ISAPI and NSAPI, respectively, that loaded with the same process as the Web server and serviced multiple requests without creating new processes. The problems with these solutions were that the code was specific to a platform and could not easily be moved to another environment (in order to upgrade to a better solution), the processes were accessed by multiple requests so there was more potential for a rogue program to corrupt data used by other requests. Since the programs ran in the same process as the Web server, a bug in the code could easily bring down the entire server.

The next solution presented by Microsoft was Active Server Pages (ASP), widely used today and part of .NET, Microsoft's latest development platform. ASP combines HTML with server-side code in files that are compiled and executed on the server. These ASP pages can access other server-side code that presents itself as a Microsoft COM or .NET component. Resultant HTML code is dynamically generated from the HTML placed in the ASP page and shipped back to the Web browser. This solution has turned out to be fairly efficient, but the drawbacks are there tends to be much HTML intermixed with scripting code that results in messy code that can be very difficult to maintain, and the code that is written is tied to the Microsoft platform, on both the server and the operating system.

The first Java solution to dynamic Web applications was Java Servlets. A Java Servlet is a server-side program that services HTTP requests and returns HTTP responses. Java Servlets use a threading model to process multiple requests, requiring fewer resources than independent processes, thereby improving performance. Also, since Java Servlets are written in Java, they are completely object-oriented, independent of the underlying platform, less prone to memory leaks, and they run in a virtual machine that imposes security constraints to help minimize rogue programs wreaking havoc on the system.

Java and Java Servlets became popular for Web application programming nearly overnight, it seemed, and now they are one of the most used technologies for Web application development. Since the creation of Java Servlets, Java has expanded greatly into the field of enterprise Web application development, such that it now provides a full suite of technologies for Web development called the Java 2 Platform, Enterprise Edition (J2EE). The J2EE API specifications are managed by Sun Microsystems and developed under the Java Community Process (JCP),[4] which includes participation from a variety of leading industry developers such as IBM, Oracle, SAP, BEA, and Macromedia, to name a few. J2EE is a standard for component-based design, development, assembly, and deployment of *n*-tier distributed applications. It offers a reusable component model, a security model, transaction control, and support for Web services. Many vendors provide implementations of the J2EE standard so the application can be moved to a different vendor implementation with little or no changes. Therefore, the J2EE standard provides the ability to choose a vendor based upon things such as pricing, performance, hardware requirements, support services, etc. (something not allowed by .NET applications, which require one server vendor, Microsoft).

---

[4]JCP is an open organization, sponsored by Sun Microsystems, of active members and nonmember public input that guides the development and approval of specifications for new Java technology. Their Web site is located at `http://www.jcp.org`.

The J2EE platform uses a distributed multi-tiered application model that is illustrated in Figure 1.5. The model consists of four distinct tiers—the client tier, the Web tier, the business tier, and the enterprise information systems (EIS) tier. The client tier runs on the user's computer and handles some of the presentation logic. The EIS tier represents back-end enterprise systems such as mainframe transaction processors, enterprise resource planning (ERP), message-oriented-middleware (MOM), Web services, and database systems. The Web tier and business tier may reside on the same computer or separate computers, depending on the needs of the system. The Web and business tiers provide an execution environment for J2EE application code that handles presentation, business, and integration logic. Since the Web and business tiers in J2EE do not have to reside on the same computer, the system can actually be expanded to include multiple Web and business tiers, hence the term *n-tier*.

The many components of the J2EE model include the Java Applet, the Java Application Client, Java Servlets, JavaServer Pages (JSP), custom JSP tag libraries, session Enterprise Java Beans (EJB), and entity EJBs. Figure 1.5 illustrates every J2EE component and the tier in which it resides. Java Servlets, JSPs, and tag libraries execute on the Web tier in a runtime environment called the *Web Container*. EJBs execute on the business tier in a runtime environment called the *EJB Container*. These containers provide life cycle management for the components, various services such as security and transaction management, and a suite of useful APIs. A *J2EE application server* is the combination of a Web container and an EJB container. The suite of APIs provided by J2EE is listed on the left side of the J2EE application server depicted in Figure 1.5. The bottom six APIs (Java IDL, JDBC, RMI-IIOP, JNDI, JAXP, and JAAS) are provided by the Java 2 Standard Edition. The entire J2EE API is much too large to cover in this book. We cover only the most used APIs, which are listed and briefly described below.

- **Java Database Connectivity (JDBC)** provides connectivity to relational databases.
- **Java Naming and Directory Interface (JNDI)** provides access to naming and directory services. JNDI is not covered in detail in this book, but is used in some of the examples.
- **Java API for XML Parsing (JAXP)** provides support for parsing XML documents into memory, as well as performing XSLT transformations on XML documents to convert them to another form.
- **Java Servlets** provide a simple way to extend the functionality of a Web server in order to access enterprise information systems and provide dynamic content to users.
- **JavaServer Pages (JSP)** are similar to Active Server Pages. They allow mixing Java code, scripting, and custom tags with HTML and XML to produce dynamic Web content.
- **Enterprise Java Beans (EJB)** are components that are meant to simplify the developers' work in developing enterprise level applications by providing built-in services like transaction management and persistence management.

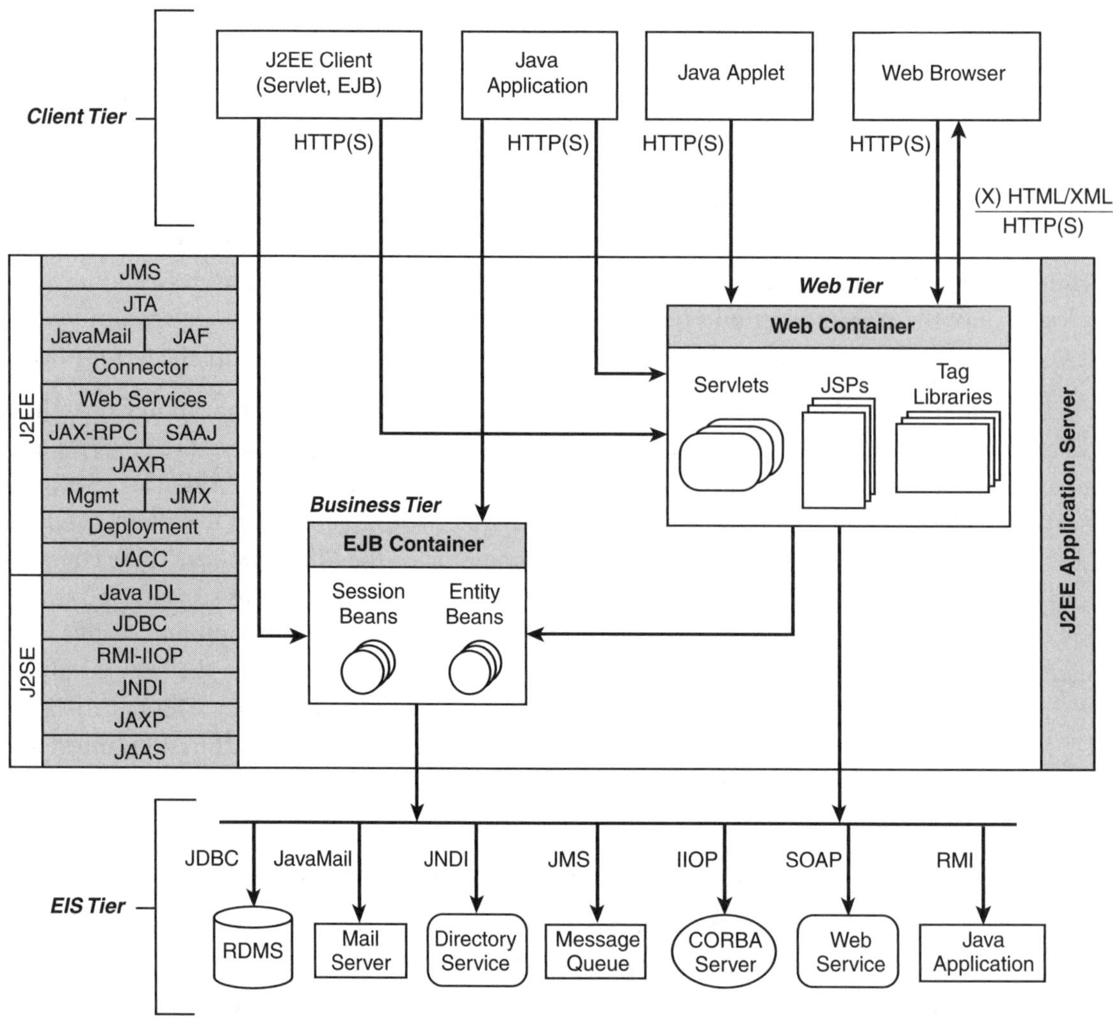

Figure 1.5
J2EE Architecture and APIs

- **SOAP with Attachments API for Java (SAAJ)** is an API that allows creation, manipulation, sending, and receiving SOAP messages.
- **Java API for XML-based RPC (JAX-RPC)** provides facilities for serializing Java objects into a SOAP message and deserializing XML from a SOAP message into Java objects so that Java developers can invoke remote Web services by simply making method calls on remote objects.

- **Java API for XML Registries (JAXR)** provides access to XML-based registries, including UDDI registries.

If some of these API descriptions do not make sense to you right now, you will understand them by the time you are done with this book. If you would like to learn more about the J2EE APIs that are not covered in this book, start with the J2EE tutorial provided by Sun Microsystems at `http://java.sun.com/j2ee/1.4/docs/tutorial/doc/index.html`. There are also links to more J2EE documentation, including the specifications for all of the APIs, at `http://java.sun.com/j2ee/1.4/docs/index.html`.

1.4 Self-Review Questions

1. HTTP works on top of TCP/IP.

a. True

b. False

2. HTTP is a stateless protocol that supports

a. HTTP requests only

b. HTTP responses only

c. Both

3. URN is a classification of Uniform Resource Identifier (URI) that identifies a resource by its location.

a. True

b. False

4. URL is a classification of Uniform Resource Identifier (URI) that identifies a resource by its name.

a. True

b. False

5. `POST` method is typically used for an HTTP form request.

a. True

b. False

6. Which two methods are most often used in an HTTP request?

a. `GET` and `POST`

b. `GET` and `PUT`

c. HEAD and GET

d. HEAD and DELETE

7. A two-tier Web architecture consists of

a. Client and database server

b. Web client and Web server

8. A three-tier Web architecture consists of

a. Web client, business server, and database server

b. Interfaces, services, and utilities

9. In a three-tier Web application, the business server and the database server must be two separate servers.

a. True

b. False

10. HTTP is the only protocol used in any Web application.

a. True

b. False

11. Http, ftp, news, mailto, file, telnet are protocol schema that may be used in a URI.

a. True

b. False

12. A fat client handles business processes and a thin client handles only the request interface.

a. True

b. False

1.5 Keys to the Self-Review Questions

1. a 2. c 3. b 4. b 5. a 6. a 7. b 8. a 9. b 10. b 11. a 12. a

1.6 References

Allamaraju, Subrahmanyam, Karl Avedal, Richard Brodett, Dan O'Connor, Jason Diamond, and John Griffin MacHolden. *Professional Java Server Programming J2EE Edition*. Birmingham, UK: Wrox Press Ltd., 2000.

Armstrong, Eric, Jennifer Ball, Stephanie Bodoff, Debbie Bode Carson, Ian Evans, Dale Green, Kim Haase, and Eric Jendrock. *The J2EE 1.4 Tutorial.* Santa Clara, CA: Sun Microsystems. 2004, http://java.sun.com/j2ee/1.4/docs/tutorial/doc/index.html (accessed February 2005).

Berners-Lee, T., R. Fielding, and L. Masinter. *Uniform Resource Identifier (URI): Generic Syntax.* Network Working Group, 2005. http://www.gbiv.com/protocols/uri/rfc/rfc3986.html (accessed February 2005).

Boutell.Com, Inc. "The New WWW FAQs." Boutell.com. http://www.boutell.com/newfaq/ (accessed February 2005).

Fielding, R., J. Gettys, J. Mogul, H. Frystyk, L. Masinter, P. Leach, and T. Berners-Lee. *Hypertext Transfer Protocol*—HTTP/1.1. The Internet Society, 1999. http://www.ietf.org/rfc/rfc2616.txt (accessed February 2005).

Howe, Walt. "A Brief History of the Internet." Walt Howe. http://www.walthowe.com/navnet/history.html (accessed September 17, 2004).

Lenier, Barry M., Vinton G. Cerf, David D. Clark, Robert E. Kahn, Leonard Kleinrock, Daniel C. Lynch, Jon Postel, Larry G. Roberts, and Stephen Wolff. *A Brief History of the Internet*, version 3.32. Internet Society. http://www.isoc.org/internet/history/brief.shtml (accessed February 2005).

Shannon, Bill. "Final Release." *Java 2 Platform, Enterprise Edition Specification*, v1.4. Santa Clara, CA: Sun Microsystems, 2003. http://java.sun.com/j2ee/j2ee-1_4-fr-spec.pdf (accessed February 2005).

CHAPTER 2

XML Basics

Objectives of This Chapter

- Introduce XML concepts
- Introduce the technologies for describing XML—DTD and XML Schema
- Discuss how to parse XML in Java using SAX, DOM, and JAXP
- Introduce two alternative APIs to SAX and DOM—JDOM and dom4j
- Introduce XSL Transformations and how to process XSLT in Java
- Give some step-by-step examples of parsing and manipulating XML in Java

2.1 Overview

XML is the eXtensible Markup Language. An XML document will look very familiar to anyone who has worked with HTML; it has the same structure of tags, elements, and attributes. As does HTML, XML has its roots in the standard generalized markup language, SGML. Also XML adds meaning to text by "marking it up" to provide more information than the text alone can convey. In fact, XML grew out of the phenomenal success of HTML and its application to the World Wide Web.

They look similar and have a common ancestry, but XML is different from HTML in two very important ways. First, although it is called the "extensible markup language," XML is really a meta-markup language. That is, it is a language for defining markup languages. This is an incredibly powerful concept. HTML is defined and standardized by the World Wide Web Consortium. Adding a new tag to HTML involves going through the standards process, which can take years. XML has no such limitation. XML specifies a syntax and structure, but the designer of an XML application specifies the tag set and the semantics of the tags.

The second difference is that the semantics of HTML are limited to describing the logical structure of a document and providing hints about how parts of the document should be displayed. In contrast, XML can define the semantics of data in a very general way.

Consider the following HTML fragment:

```
<h1>Paul Clifford</h1>
<p style="text-align: center;">Edward George Bulwer-Lytton</p>
<p>It was a dark and stormy night...</p>
```

This tells an HTML browser or other display agent to format the first line as a top-level heading, to display Bulwer-Lytton's name in a centered paragraph below the heading, and to begin a new paragraph with the text in the third line.

Now look at how we might use XML to convey similar information:

```
<?xml version="1.0" encoding="iso-8859-1" ?>
<book>
  <book-title>Paul Clifford</book-title>
  <author>Edward George Bulwer-Lytton</author>
  <year>1830</year>
  <price>5.50</price>
  <text>
   <chapter>
    <para>It was a dark and stormy night...</para>
   </chapter>
  </text>
</book>
```

There are many more tags, but there is also is much more semantic information. Not only that, the information is easily interpreted by a human reader. You know that we are dealing with a book with the title *Paul Clifford*. You know the author, year, and price, and something about how the text is arranged.

It is easy to interpret the same information programmatically, too. The success of HTML drove the development of parsers for SGML-like markup. There are a number of tools available for dealing with XML documents that allow the programmer to concentrate on the data, not the markup. The XML of the example could be transformed into HTML for display just by the application of a style sheet. No programming at all would be necessary. We look at some of these tools later in the chapter.

The great promise of XML is true portability of data. The boundaries of data items are clearly defined, and if the element names are chosen carefully, a great deal of semantic information travels with the data. Anyone who has ever tried to work with fixed format or delimited data files will appreciate the value of this. This technique can be applied to any kind of information that can be represented as plain text.

Because of the promise of portability across applications and across organizational boundaries, XML was adopted very quickly for Web applications. Whether you are working with Web services, using directory services, creating news feeds, or just working with data, you will be sure to encounter XML. Even the latest Web markup language, XHTML, is really an XML application that serves as Web markup.

As you can see, an XML document is composed of *elements* consisting of beginning and ending tags. The tags are bounded by angle-brackets (less-than and greater-than signs) and enclose text and possibly other elements. That makes the overall structure of an XML document a tree. As in HTML, there is one and only one root element. In the example, it is `<book>`. In order to include information about more than one book in a single XML document, a new root element, perhaps `<book-collection>`, would have to be defined. This new element would enclose the collection of `<book>` elements.

The tags in the example are not defined in any standard. They were chosen by the application designer to represent information about a book and its contents.

XML is a powerful and flexible tool, but it is important to recognize that it is not a magic solution to the difficult problems of describing the semantics of data and portability of data among applications. At first glance, the `<price>` element seems simple and straightforward. Looking a little deeper, we realize that we do not know the currency nor whether the price is wholesale or retail. XML provides a mechanism for applying *attributes* to elements. Attributes can work as adjectives, so we can answer those two questions this way:

```
<price currency="usd" type="retail">5.50</price>
```

That tells us more about the price, but now to exchange data among two applications using this document, the applications must agree on the meaning of the attributes *currency* and *type* and the values *usd* and *retail.* XML can encode an enormous amount of semantic information, but applications that exchange data using XML must have a common understanding of the encoded semantics.

One other characteristic of the example deserves mention. To reinforce that XML is not HTML, we deliberately avoided using tags that are defined in HTML. We used `<para>` instead of `<p>` for paragraphs and `<book-title>` instead of `<title>` for the title information. However, there are no reserved tags. When designing XML applications, it is not necessary to avoid the HTML tag names. It may even be preferable to use the HTML tags when a tag such as `<p>` for paragraph conveys precisely the same meaning in HTML and an XML application. Even when meanings are very different, such as `<table>` for a piece of furniture and `<table>` for a layout structure of rows and columns, name collisions can be resolved by assigning element names to namespaces as described in a following section.

XHTML is HTML 4.01 restructured to conform to the syntax required of XML documents. The biggest differences are that the case sensitivity of XML was accommodated by requiring that all tag and attribute names be lowercase, that tags are required to be closed, that attributes must have values, and that attribute values are required to be in quotes.

The World Wide Web Consortium has provided three distinct definitions for XHTML. The strict definition omits deprecated elements and attributes. The transitional definition includes many of the deprecated elements and attributes, and the frameset definition is the transitional definition with the addition of frames.

2.2 XML Documents

We have been referring to the combination of text and XML markup as an XML document. The XML standards refer to a markup language designed in XML as an XML *application.* The phrase *XML application* can also refer to the totality of markup language definition, formal specifications, marked up data, and processing programs. In this chapter, we refer to data marked up using a particular markup language definition as an *XML document.* We call a specific markup language an *application* or *language definition* depending on the context and also use *application* for the whole of language definition, marked up data, and processing programs.

2.2.1 The Document Prolog

We saw from the example that an XML document is introduced with a prolog that includes an `<?xml ?>` document declaration and consists of elements formed of tags enclosing data and other elements. The XML document declaration has the properties *version, encoding,* and *standalone.* The current XML version is 1.0 and it is good practice to include the version number in every XML document declaration. That will allow XML documents to be parsed correctly even if there is a major change in the XML specification. The encoding property specifies the character set used to encode the document. Good practice dictates that the encoding also be specified. The standalone property is a hint to XML processing programs that no other files will need to be loaded. Here are example XML document declarations:

```
<?xml version="1.0" encoding="iso-8859-1"?>
<?xml version="1.0" encoding="iso-8859-1" standalone="yes"?>
```

If an XML document is defined by a document type declaration, the DTD itself or more usually, a pointer to the DTD, is also included in the prolog. DTDs are discussed in Section 2.3.

XML parsers are required to process documents encoded in UTF-8 and UTF-16. The XML specification lists more than a dozen other character encodings that XML parsers should recognize. Parsers are not prohibited from recognizing other encodings. The examples in this book will all use ISO-8859-1, the Western Latin-1 character set. Through the use of Unicode, XML documents can be rendered in any language, including languages that do not use the Latin alphabet.

2.2.2 Elements and Element Names

XML documents are composed of *elements.* An element consists of an opening tag, which is a name and possibly other information enclosed in angle brackets, element data, and a closing tag. The closing tag begins with an angle bracket and a slash and has the same name as the opening tag. An XML element looks like this:

```
<author>Edward George Bulwer-Lytton</author>
```

XML tag names are more properly called *element names.* Element names must begin with a letter or underscore and may contain letters, numbers, hyphens, underscores, and periods. *Letters* are defined by the encoding character set, and may include accented letters, non-Latin letters, and even ideographs. The colon is also a valid XML name character, but it should only be used with namespace prefixes, which are described in Section 2.2. Element names are case sensitive. Element names may not include character entities; character entities are described later in this chapter. Separator characters are the white space characters (space, tab, and new line), the equal sign, and quotation marks. In Latin encodings, the quotation marks are the apostrophe and the straight double-quote.

Element names are enclosed in angle brackets < and >. There must be no whitespace between the opening angle bracket and the element name. Whitespace, including new lines, is allowed after the name part. This allows elements with attributes to be spaced out in a way that makes them easy to read.

The XML standard does not limit the length of element names. In practice, very long names will make markup cumbersome and very short names may be so cryptic as to reduce the usefulness of having human-readable markup.

XML element contents are limited to characters in the encoding character set. In particular, they may not contain arbitrary binary data. If binary data must be associated with an XML document, the application designer must provide a link to an external binary source. Best practice is to specify a URL in an attribute of the appropriate element.

Although element contents are limited to characters in the encoding character set, character entities allow other characters to be represented. Character entities are described below.

There are two major differences between HTML and XML that could cause problems for people used to working with HTML. XML element names are case-sensitive, but HTML before XHTML 1.0 is not case-sensitive. That has caused some people to be inconsistent in the use of case. Because XML is case-sensitive, element names of different case will be interpreted as distinct names and will likely cause a document not to be well formed. Also, XML elements always require closing tags. Someone with experience in coding HTML may have developed the habit of omitting some closing tags. Omitting closing tags in XML will cause a document not to be well formed. An element that does not enclose content may be empty, i.e., may have a closing tag immediately following the opening tag. If the design of the XML application is such that a particular element may never enclose content, it may be made self-closing by including a slash before the ending angle bracket in the opening (and only) tag. For example, the semantics of the line break tag in XHTML are such that it may never enclose content. It is made self-closing by representing it as `<br />`.

2.2.3 Attributes

Sometimes an element name alone does not convey all the information needed about the contents of the element. Elements may have attributes that modify the element. If we think of element names as nouns, the attributes are the adjectives. In an earlier example, we modified a `<price>` element by adding two attributes:

```
<price currency="usd" type="retail">5.50</price>
```

An attribute consists of a name and value pair. In the example, the names are *currency* and *type*. Attribute values must consist of text in the character set used to encode the XML document. As element contents, attribute values may not be binary strings nor characters outside the set of characters in the document encoding.

Binary material such as images or sounds may be referenced from an XML document by including a (text) pointer to the binary material in the XML. Current practice is to use a Uniform Resource Identifier (URI) for the link and make it an attribute of the appropriate object. A well-known example is the XHTML `<img />` element whose `src` attribute points to binary image data. The designer of an XML application can include other attributes that further describe the binary data. For example:

```
<picture content-type="image/jpeg"
         source="http://webdev.spsu.edu/images/noclowns.gif"
         h="140px" w="140px"/>
```

XML tools do not process the binary data; it is up to the supporting application to understand the syntax and semantics of any binary data and to process it appropriately.

Attribute names may not be duplicated within a single element. The following is incorrect:

```
<book author="Halliday" author="Resnick">                  Incorrect
```

Although an attribute name may not be repeated for a single element, the attribute value string could be multivalued, e.g., `author="Halliday, Resnick"`. However, doing so defeats the objective of using a general purpose parser to extract the individual semantic elements of an XML document because the parser will extract a multivalued item with no indication that there are multiple values.

2.2.4 Attribute or Element?

The restriction that an attribute name may not be repeated leads to the question of how to decide whether a particular data item should be an attribute or an element. One approach is to think of elements as nouns and attributes as adjectives. If an item of data names something, it should probably be an element. If it modifies some object, it might qualify as an attribute. Earlier we made `currency` and `type` attributes of a `price` element because both `currency` and `type` modify `price`. One might let `color` be an attribute of `car` because it modifies the car object: `<car color="red">`.

Attributes should be atomic; if it is possible to subdivide a data value, such as dividing a name into surname and given names, use elements.

```
<name>
  <surname>Bulwer-Lytton</surname>
  <forename>Edward</forename>
  <forename>George</forename>
</name>
```

One possible exception to requiring compound values to be elements rather than attributes is when a compound value can be considered to be a data type. In XML when defined by a schema, dates are members of a specific data type, and thus are candidates for use as attribute values.

Another consideration is that attributes should not be multivalued for the reasons given earlier. If a data item can occur two or more times, make it an element and instantiate multiple instances of the element. It would be better to recast the previous example as:

```
<book>
  <author>Halliday</author>
  <author>Resnick</author>
</book>
```

With this structure, an XML parser can treat each data item as an atomic value. XML preserves the order of elements, so if there is an ordering over the names of authors in the examples above, it is implied by the order in which the elements are given.

One particularly useful application of attributes is to attach a unique identifier to an instance of an element, such as `<employee employee-number="12345">`. By specifying that employee-number is of type ID in the document definition, a validating parser can be required to guarantee that it is not duplicated within a single XML document. The identifying attribute can be used in queries to select a specific instance of an element.

2.2.5 XML Syntax

Every XML document is a collection of elements. An XML element consists of a named tag and possibly contents enclosed by a beginning and ending tag. The rules for forming XML names are discussed above. Regardless of whether an element encloses content, every element must be closed. Elements can be closed with an ending tag following data: `<author>Halliday</author>`. A closing tag is allowed even when nothing is enclosed: `<awards></awards>`. Finally, elements that can never contain data may be made self-closing. The XHTML line break element, `<br />`, was used earlier as an example of a self-closing tag.

The opening tag of an XML element may have attributes. Attributes are name and value pairs that carry additional information about the element they modify. Attribute names are formed using the same rules as XML element names. Attribute values are required to be present; for every name, there must be a value. Attribute values are separated from attribute names by an equal sign and must be enclosed in quotation marks. For ASCII and Latin encodings, that means the use of the straight double quote or the apostrophe.

An XML document has one and only one instance of one and only one root element. Its opening tag usually immediately follows the document prolog, and its closing tag is usually the last thing in the document. (The exceptions are XML comments and XML processing instructions, which are not elements and so may occur outside the root element.) Other elements are nested inside the root element. Elements may not overlap.

XML comments are enclosed in a string that begins with `<!--` and ends with `-->`. XML comments may not contain a string of two consecutive dashes, and may not be nested.

Comments are used to record human-readable information about XML documents. They are not part of the structure or semantics of an XML document. Comments may appear anywhere that text may appear in an XML document. Since comments are not elements, they may also appear before the opening tag of the root element or after its closing tag. Comments may not appear within a tag.

XML parsers are not required to return comments. For that reason, comments should never be used to encode application information. Instead, define and use appropriate XML elements, or use XML processing instructions as described below.

It is common in HTML to define special comment contents that have meaning to the application that will process the HTML file. Examples are Internet Explorer's conditional comments and the comments used by the Apache server for Server-Side Includes. XML provides the XML processing instruction for this purpose. An XML processing instruction begins with <? and ends with ?>. The beginning <? must be followed immediately by a legal XML name, called the *target*, that identifies the type of processing that is wanted. Any name other than case-insensitive combinations of XML (xml, XmL, etc.) may be used as a target. A common processing instruction seen in XHTML is that for the PHP processor: `<?php ?>`. The syntax and semantics of text enclosed within an XML processing instruction are determined by the application that processes the contents.

The characters left angle bracket (less-than sign) and ampersand are illegal in XML text because they introduce markup and entity references, respectively. Five character entities are predefined by XML, among them `<` for the left angle bracket and `&` for the ampersand. In general, entity names are XML names, in this case `lt` and `amp`, and entity references are entity names preceded by an ampersand and followed by a semicolon. Entity references are placeholders; XML parsers replace entity references with the entities they represent.

The five predefined character entities are:

```
&lt;	<
&gt;	>
&amp;	&
&quot;	"
&apos;	'
```

The quote and apostrophe entities solve the problem of getting quotes or apostrophes inside attribute names. Either of the two following examples is legal XML:

```
<book distributor="Bob's Books">
<book distributor='Bob&apos;s Books'>
```

Character entities substitute a single character for the placeholder in the parsed XML text. The predefined character entities are part of a larger class of character entities. The other character entity types are numbered character entities and named character entities.

Although XML documents may be represented in virtually any character encoding, internal processing is done in Unicode. Numbered character entities are predefined in the sense that the designer need not do anything to enable their use. A numbered character entity reference consists of an ampersand, a pound sign (#), a number, and a semicolon. The number represents a code point (character position) in the Unicode set, and so Unicode itself defines the numbered character entities. So, `à` represents the letter *a* with grave accent: à. Unicode code points can also be written as hexadecimal numbers by following the pound sign with the letter *x*. So `à` can also be used to represent à. Numbered character entities address the problem of representing characters for which no keyboard combination exists in the context of document generation, or which cannot be displayed by the editor in use. Charts of Unicode code points are online at `http://www.unicode.org`.

Named character entities address the problem that it is difficult and error-prone to look up Unicode code points. It is much easier to write `à` than to look up and enter `à`. Reading documents with named character entities is even easier than writing them, provided the names have been well chosen. However, only the five character entities listed above are predefined by XML. An XML application designer must define any named character entities to be used, or borrow a definition developed by others. We discuss defining one's own character entities in Section 2.3. The other alternative is to re-use a previously defined set of character entities. ISO 8879 defines hundreds of character entities in the form of parameter entities that can be included with XML application DTDs. Parameter entities are discussed in Section 2.3.

Character entities are not allowed in XML names; they may only be used in XML text. Character entities are part of a larger class of general entities. Besides the character entities, there are mixed-content entities and unparsed entities. Character entities represent a single character and can be used only in text, not in element or attribute names. Mixed-content entities can contain both text and markup.

Both character entities and mixed-content entities are parsed by XML parsers. Unparsed entities are not. Unparsed entities provide a way of referring to binary data or other data that should not be interpreted by an XML parser. Mixed-content entities are covered in Section 2.3.

The last syntactic element we discuss is the `CDATA` (character data) section. The predefined character entities can be used to escape left angle brackets and ampersands to prevent them from being interpreted as markup. If a large amount of text that would otherwise be interpreted as markup must be included in an XML document, escaping each markup character with an entity reference becomes difficult. Enclosing text and possibly markup in a `CDATA` section instructs the XML parser not to attempt to parse it.

A `CDATA` section begins with the markup `<![CDATA[` and ends with `]]>`. A `CDATA` section may contain any characters except the `CDATA` ending sequence. The following two fragments are equivalent:

```
<para>Consider the following HTML:</para>
&lt;h1&gt;Paul Clifford&lt;/h1&gt;
&lt;p&gt;Edward George Bulwer-
Lytton&lt;/p&gt;
&lt;p&gt;It was a dark and stormy
night... &lt;/p&gt;
```

```
<para>Consider the following HTML:</para>
<![CDATA[
<h1>Paul Clifford</h1>
<p>Edward George Bulwer-Lytton</p>
<p>It was a dark and stormy night...</p>
]]>
```

In the example on the left, markup introducers have been replaced by character entities in the section of HTML that is to be reproduced as is. In the example on the right, the entire HTML fragment was escaped by enclosing it in a CDATA section. In XHTML, CDATA sections are frequently used to enclose JavaScript or other material that is neither text nor markup, and for which the semantics of strings such as < and -- are different from the XML semantics.

2.2.6 Well-Formed Documents

XML documents are tree structures. This is illustrated by the following XML document and a graphical representation of its structure.

Listing 2.1 Sample XML Document

```
<employee id="12345">
  <name>
    <surname>Smith</surname>
    <forename>John</forename>
    <forename>Robert</forename>
  </name>
  <department id="9350" />
  <projects>
    <project>Mars Lander</project>
    <project>Butter Applicator</project>
  </projects>
</employee>
```

Listing 2.2 Illustration of Tree Structure for Listing 2.1

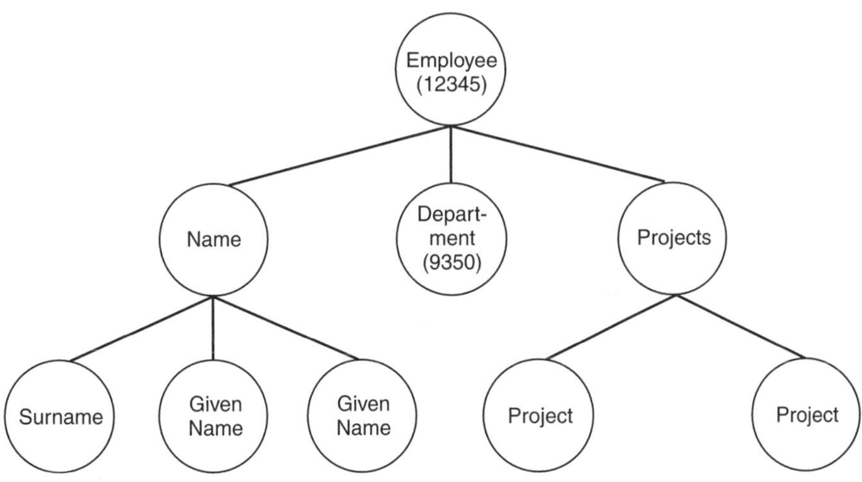

An XML document is well formed if it obeys the syntax rules of XML. Some of the rules of XML syntax are discussed above. Here are some of the rules that could easily be violated accidentally:

- Element and attribute names must be legal XML names.

- Markup characters < and & must be escaped as character entities when used in text.
- Every element must be closed.
- Attributes must have values (there can be no keyword-only attributes).
- Attribute values must be delimited with quotation marks.
- Every element except the root element must be the child of exactly one element (elements may not overlap).
- Comments must be properly formed; in particular, a comment may not contain the string `"--"`.

There are many other syntax rules, but a simple and carefully constructed XML document that obeys the rules just given will generally be well formed.

An important difference between XML and HTML is that XML parsers are required to report errors of form. If an XML document is not well formed, the error must be reported. XML parsers may not replace missing quotes, close unclosed tags, or silently rearrange overlapping tags based on an assumption about the intended meaning. Check that a document is well formed by loading it into a Web browser that contains an XML parser, or by using a standalone parser tool. If the document loads, it is well formed. If not, the error message will often point directly to the problem.

The fact that a document is well formed means only that it conforms to the syntax rules of XML. In the next section we look at two ways to define the structure and content of an XML application. Validating parsers can then be used to examine an XML document in light of a document definition as well as checking the document's syntax.

2.2.7 Namespaces

XML application designers may choose their own element names. It is often desirable to include XML from two or more sources in an XML document. The element name `<table>` is used by XHTML to refer to a display structure composed of rows and columns. A furniture catalog might use the same element name to refer to a piece of furniture. We use XML to define mathematical equations in MathML and graphics in SVG. eXtensible Stylesheet Language Transformation (XSLT), which we will use for reformatting documents, is XML. It would seem that name collisions among elements of an XML document instance would almost be unavoidable.

The solution to name collisions in XML is XML Namespaces (`http://www.w3.org/TR/REC-xml-names/`). An XML Namespace is declared by adding an `xmlns` attribute to an element, where the value of the `xmlns` attribute is a unique URI. The element where the namespace is declared, and all its child elements, inherit the unique namespace. Usually, namespaces are declared on the root element of a document so that any other elements in the document can use the declaration, or inherit it, depending on how it is defined. However, it is sometimes convenient to define a namespace deeper in the document to prevent it from being available outside that element. Namespace declarations do not affect elements that are not nested inside the element where the namespace is declared.

XML Namespace declarations may also be defined by attaching a suffix to the `xmlns` attribute. (A suffix is a colon followed by a name, e.g., `:xsd`.) One can associate XML elements and attributes in the document with a namespace declared via a suffix by attaching prefixes to element and attribute names. (A prefix is name followed by a colon, e.g., `xsd:`.) The prefixes link the XML element or attribute with the namespace declared with a suffix of the same name. This is called *qualifying* an element. For instance, after qualifying the two `<table>` elements given above we could get `<xhtml:table>` and `<furniture:table>`. Now these two elements are clearly distinct. Thus, if we use them both in the same XML document, we will know they are not the same. The namespace declarations for these elements might look like the following.

```
<html xmlns:xhtml="http://www.w3.org/1999/xhtml">
<catalog xmlns:furniture="http://www.acmefurniture.org/mynames">
```

However, since namespace declarations affect only nested elements, the two example declarations above would not really solve the problem of name collisions unless the `<catalog>` element were a child of the `<html>` element. It is often more useful to declare two or more namespaces on the root element of a document, such as:

```
<html xmlns:xhtml="http://www.w3.org/1999/xhtml"-
      xmlns:furniture="http://www.acmefurniture.org/mynames">
```

With this definition, the `<html>` element has both the `xhtml` and `furniture` namespaces available. However, it also means that every element name in the document has to be qualified. Often, the majority of element names will be from one namespace, with just a few from others. A *default namespace* can be defined by omitting the qualifier from one of the `xmlns` attributes.

```
<html xmlns="http://www.w3.org/1999/xhtml"-
      xmlns:furniture="http://www.acmefurniture.org/mynames">
```

This definition makes the XHTML namespace the default namespace. Unqualified elements and attributes (names without prefixes) fall under the default namespace. For example, if an XML document had the `html` element declaration given above as the root element, then all elements of the XML document named `<table>` are assumed to be defined by the "`http://www.w3.org/1999/xhtml`" namespace and all elements named `<furniture:table>` are defined by the "`http://www.acmefurniture.org/mynames`" namespace. Valid XML requires the root element of an XML document to be qualified, but other elements need not be. Best practice is to make sure that all elements in an XML document are qualified, either by the default namespace or explicitly by a prefix.

Support for namespaces has to be built into the application that processes the XML. It is up to application processing programs to recognize namespaces, map the namespace URI to the identifying prefix, and process elements correctly depending upon their namespace. Most Web browsers, which understand XHTML, will process `<table>` elements, but will ignore elements named `<furniture:table>` because most Web browsers do not understand XML namespaces and thus ignore undefined tags. Browsers usually display the contents of such elements, however.

The significance of the URI that is the value of an `xmlns` attribute is that it is, by definition, unique. Even though the URI will frequently take the form of a URL, there need not be, and usually will not be a defining document at the location named by the URL. In fact, there need not be anything there at all. Typing the URL of the XHTML namespace, `http://w3.org/1999/xhtml/`, into a browser's address bar will produce a simple text page explaining XHTML and providing several links. The significance of the URI is that it is a globally unique name for a particular namespace. The existence of a globally unique name allows the writer of an XML document to choose an arbitrary prefix for the namespace for a particular document instance, avoiding another possible source of name collisions. The `xmlns` attribute provides the link between the globally unique name and the local prefix. Applications should recognize the global name and use the local prefix to identify elements associated with that global name.

Although there need not be a definition at a URL used in an `xmlns` attribute, that fact is so astonishing to some people that it has become the practice to put something there. The simple Web page at the XHTML namespace URL is an example. The desire to put a machine-readable specification at a URL referred to in an `xmlns` specification is complicated by the question of what sort of specification to choose. Some examples are a Document Type Definition, an XML schema, or even a program to process the elements of a namespace. This complication is resolved by using a second level of indirection. An `xmlns` URL can point to a Web page containing XHTML, text, and Resource Directory Description Language (RDDL) elements. Browsers will ignore the RDDL elements because they are not a part of XHTML, but will display their contents. Programs searching for formal document definitions can ignore the XHTML and process the RDDL elements. A discussion of RDDL is beyond the scope of this chapter. The fundamental idea is to provide a link to something that defines the type of resource (DTD, schema, or something else) and a link to the resource itself.

2.3 DTD and XML Schema

An XML parser will tell whether a document is well formed. A well-formed document conforms to the syntax rules of XML, but it is not necessarily valid in the context of a particular application. A well-formed XML document describing an invoice is probably not valid in the context of an application dealing with a catalog of books.

If no formal document model is defined for an XML document, the document must still be well formed, but there are no limits on the element names used, the structure or contents of the elements, or the use of attributes. While there are many general purpose XML processors, programs used in specific applications likely make assumptions about a document model and may fail or produce unexpected results if those assumptions are not fulfilled. Ad hoc definition of XML documents is workable for small applications within a single organization. It is possible to validate simple XML documents against informal specifications by inspection. Validation by inspection is error prone even for short documents. For a book-length document or a complex document containing machine-readable data, it is virtually impossible to guarantee that there are no missing or extraneous elements. Furthermore, as document complexity grows, it is possible, or even likely, that ambiguities will occur in the informal specification.

For complex documents or documents that will be used across organizational boundaries, a more formal definition of validity is needed. There are two standard methods to formally define the structure and content of an XML document. The first to be developed and widely used was the Document Type Definition (DTD), which is a legacy of XML's link to SGML, and is included in the XML specification. The second, called XML Schema, was developed primary because of the weaknesses in DTD. DTDs were originally developed for documents whose primary purpose was to exchange simple text data, and still serve well in that context. HTML and XHTML both have definitions written using DTD (see `http://www.w3.org/TR/html401/struct/global.html#idx-document_type_declaration-3` and `http://www.w3.org/TR/html/#dtds`). XML Schema provides the finer grained control needed for documents that are used to exchange machine-processed data. There are three different XML Schema documents that describe XHTML (see `http://www.w3.org/TR/xhtml1-schema/`). In the discussion that follows, the term *instance document* refers to a particular XML document with particular content that is to be validated by comparing its form and content to a formal specification, either a DTD or an XML schema.

2.3.1 Document Type Definitions (DTDs)

A DTD is a formal, machine-readable specification that defines the structure of an XML document and provides some information about the required content. Given a DTD, a validating parser can determine not only that the document is well-formed XML, but also that it conforms to the specifications for the application as set out in the DTD. Not all XML parsers are validating parsers. We used the Xerces parser from the Apache Group to test the examples in this chapter. The XML parser built into Internet Explorer does some validation, but is tolerant of errors.

DTDs provide for declaring elements, attribute lists, entities, and notations. A DTD is a sequence of declarations enclosed in a DOCTYPE declaration or stored separately and referred to from a DOCTYPE. Declarations begin with the opening delimiter sequence `<!` and end with `>`. The opening delimiter must be immediately followed by one of the four keywords `ELEMENT`, `ATTLIST`, `ENTITY`, or `NOTATION`.

An element declaration consists of <!ELEMENT, a case-sensitive element name, a content description, and the closing delimiter.

```
<!ELEMENT element_name content_description>
```

The simplest element declarations are those where the element contains only text content, or where the element contains only other elements in a defined order. In the example below, the <memo> element contains only other elements, and the <body> contains only text.

```
<?xml version="1.0" encoding="iso-8859-1"?>
<!DOCTYPE memo [
  <!ELEMENT memo (from, to, date, body)>
  <!ELEMENT from (#PCDATA)>
  <!ELEMENT to  (#PCDATA)>
  <!ELEMENT date (#PCDATA)>
  <!ELEMENT body (#PCDATA)>
]>
<memo>
  <from>Boss</from>
  <to>Troops</to>
  <date>15 April 1951</date>
  <body>The buck stops here.</body>
</memo>
```

In the example, parentheses serve as grouping operators and commas serve as "and" operators. The notation (#PCDATA) means parsed character data. The enclosing parentheses are required. The XML parser will parse the data, replacing any entity names with their declarations and pass the data to the application.

Xerces is a toolkit for XML processing from the Apache Software Foundation. Xerces contains tools for validating documents against DTDs, and one of the sample programs included in the distribution can be used directly as a validation tool. If the text of the example is stored in a file named memo_dtd.xml, it can be validated as:

```
dom.Writer -v memo_dtd.xml
```

The intended purpose of dom.Writer is to read its input as XML and list it to the standard output. The -v option requests validation. Since both the DTD and the body of the XML document are syntactically correct, the dom.Writer program just lists the input file. If a syntax error is introduced into either the DTD part or the XML part of the example, dom.Writer produces an error message.

Here is the power of formal specification, even for simple documents: we designed the <memo> XML document without a <subject> element. If someone "corrected" that by including the line

<subject>Making Changes</subject>, the document would no longer validate. A program written to process <memo> documents might fail in an obscure way if a required element were missing or an unexpected element were present. The validating parser used by dom.Writer produces two error messages, one stating that <subject> is not declared and another stating that a <memo> element must contain from, to, date, and body elements, in that order. Since parsing is an essential part of an XML application, the application designer can choose to use a validating parser and detect such errors any time a nonconforming document is read. Another alternative is to parse without validation for ordinary processing and choose to validate only if there are problems. In either case, the ability to validate XML depends upon a formal specification of the document.

In the example, the document type declaration is embedded in the prolog of the XML document. This is an *internal subset* DTD. It is often useful to have the DTD and a prototype document in the same file during development, but the real value of a DTD is to be able to use it as a standard against which instance documents are validated. In that case, it is desirable to store the DTD separately from the instances of the XML documents. Such a DTD is an *external subset* DTD. An external subset DTD is specified in the DOCTYPE declaration using the SYSTEM keyword.

```
<!DOCTYPE memo SYSTEM "http://webdev.spsu.edu/~bbrown/memo.dtd" >
```

In that case, the DTD definition would be stored in its own file, and the XML document would look like the following example:

```
<?xml version="1.0" encoding="iso-8859-1" ?>
<!DOCTYPE memo SYSTEM "http://webdev.spsu.edu/~bbrown/memo.dtd" >
<memo>
  <from>Boss</from>
  <to>Troops</to>
  <date>15 April 1951</date>
  <body>The buck stops here.</body>
</memo>
```

It is also possible to declare a DTD as PUBLIC rather than SYSTEM. In that case, a unique name will be specified in the URI area and an external mechanism must be used to map the name to a URI. A URI may also be supplied following the DTD unique name, and in practice that is what is actually used. The example below shows the DOCTYPE specification for HTML 4.01 Transitional.

```
<!DOCTYPE HTML PUBLIC "-//W3C//DTD HTML 4.01 Transitional//EN"
     "http://www.w3.org/TR/html4/loose.dtd">
```

Most XML applications that use DTDs will use SYSTEM DTDs. An XML document may have both an external subset DTD and an internal subset. If both are present, they must not conflict.

The operators and keywords available for declaring content descriptions are:

, (comma)	ordered list (and operator)
|	or operator
( )	content grouping
?	the preceding item may occur zero or one time
+	the preceding item may occur one or more times
*	the preceding item may occur zero or more times
#PCDATA	parsed character data
EMPTY	the element may not contain content
ANY	the element may contain any content defined in the DTD

Note that the occurrence indicators are the same as those used in regular expressions.

The DTD in the example used only commas, parentheses, and #PCDATA. If one wanted to allow one or more <to> elements in the memo document, all that is necessary is to place a plus sign (one or more occurrences) after the element name to in the definition of memo. If an element name is unqualified, exactly one occurrence is required. The definition of memo now looks like this:

```
<!ELEMENT memo (from, to+, date, body)>
```

Exploring the expressive power of the DTD grammar further requires making our sample document a little more complex. Suppose that our model of a memo must allow it to be addressed to entire departments or to one or more named individuals. We can easily define <department> and <name>; the problem is how to require the <to> element to contain any number of <department> or <name> elements, in any order, but at least one. The solution is to combine grouping and the OR operator with the plus operator. Here is a fragment of the revised DTD:

```
<!ELEMENT memo (from, to+, date, body)>
<!ELEMENT to (name | department)>
<!ELEMENT name (#PCDATA)>
<!ELEMENT department (#PCDATA)>
```

The second line specifies that the <to> element may contain either <name> or <department> and the first line specifies that there must be at least one and possibly more <to> elements. The last two lines define the two new elements as #PCDATA. We would also have to change the XML to use the <to> element with either <name> or <department> like this:

```
<to><department>Troops</department></to>
```

or the document will no longer validate.

We now extend the application to allow <name> or <department> to be selected from a database using point-and-click. The department element remains text data, but names in the database have the structure that there must be one surname and zero or more given names. The definition for the department element does not change, but <name> and its subelements now look like this:

```
<!ELEMENT name (surname, forename*)>
<!ELEMENT surname (#PCDATA)>
<!ELEMENT forename (#PCDATA)>
```

The asterisk modifier allows <forename> to occur zero or more times, allowing no given names, one, or more than one. If at least one given name were required, we would change the asterisk to a plus.

Selecting names by point-and-click no longer allows free-text addressing of memos. If the <to> element must be allowed to contain a name from the database, a department from the database, or a free-text name, the definition must be further extended to allow #PCDATA. Here is the extended definition:

```
<!ELEMENT to (#PCDATA | name | department)* >
```

We have made <to> a mixed element; it can contain both text and subelements. For mixed elements, the declaration for #PCDATA is required to be the first. The asterisk modifier, zero or more elements, is also required. This means that it is possible for a <to> element to be empty.

The EMPTY keyword specified that an element may not have content. The <br /> element of XHTML is an example of an element that would be declared EMPTY. The ANY keyword allows an element to have any content, including both character data and other elements. However, the other elements must be defined in the DTD. Use of ANY is primarily for development; it is poor practice to include it in a production DTD.

So far, our DTD has declared neither attributes nor entities. We will change date from an element to an attribute and add a priority attribute with possible values of high, medium, and low, and a default priority of medium. Attributes are declared with an <!ATTLIST > declaration. The declaration contains the element name for which the attributes are being declared followed by a list of attribute declarations. Each declaration includes the attribute name, a data type specification, and a default definition that tells whether the attribute is required and, if not, what action the parser should take. It is customary to group attribute lists after the element declarations.

```
<!ATTLIST memo date CDATA #REQUIRED
    priority (high | medium | low) "medium" >
```

The date attribute is required and is of type CDATA, character data. The #REQUIRED keyword means the attribute must be present and contain a value for the instance document to be valid. Nothing in the DTD forces it to be a valid date. The XML application can help by supplying a system date, but an XML instance document would be declared valid by this DTD if there is anything at all in the date attribute.

The priority attribute is an enumerated type. The values must be legal XML names and are enclosed in parentheses and separated by vertical bars. Only the values listed may be used; anything else is an error that will be detected when the instance document is validated against the DTD. The quoted string "`medium`" in the requirement specification says that the priority attribute is optional, and that if it is omitted, the XML parser should supply the default value of `medium`.

Attribute declarations provide somewhat more control over the data types of attributes than is possible with element contents. The available data type definitions and their meanings are:

`CDATA`	Character data
(enumerated list)	A literal list of permitted values
`ID`	A legal XML name that is unique in the instance document
`IDREF, IDREFS`	An ID or list of IDs of other elements
`NMTOKEN, NMTOKENS`	One or a list of legal XML name tokens
`ENTITY, ENTITIES`	One or a list of external unparsed entities
`NOTATION`	A previously declared notation name

The most commonly used data type definition is `CDATA`, although it offers essentially no control over the value given in the instance document. An enumerated list gives all of the permitted values. The `priority` example above is an enumerated list. The `ID` data type refers to a legal XML name unique in the instance document. Attributes of type `ID` are often named `id`, but that is not a requirement. One element can have only one attribute of type `ID`. Because the `ID` data type is an XML name, numbers alone cannot be used as values for attributes of type `ID`. The type `IDREF` is a reference (or list of references) to the `ID` of another element in the instance document. If a list of `IDREFS` is given, the items are separated by whitespace.

The type `NMTOKEN` is an XML name token. Name tokens are similar to XML names with the exception that the requirement that the first character be a letter or underscore is removed, so numbers are valid XML name tokens. Name tokens may not contain whitespace, so when a single value is wanted in an attribute `NMTOKEN` is a better choice than `CDATA`.

The `ENTITY` type requires the name of an external unparsed entity or a whitespace-separated list of external unparsed entity names. Entities are discussed below. The `NOTATION` type is rarely used and is not discussed here.

The attribute default definitions and their meanings are:

`#REQUIRED`	The attribute is required to be present
`#IMPLIED`	The attribute is optional
(quoted string)	Optional and defaults to the string value given
`#FIXED` (quoted string)	Always the value given in the quoted string

The `#FIXED` definition provides an immutable value for the attribute. The attribute need not be present, and will default to the specified value. However, if it is present, if must have the value given in the quoted string.

General and unparsed entities are also declared in the DTD. A general entity is similar to the XML predefined entities except that the replacement string is not limited to a single character. A common example is to use general entities to allow a short string, the entity name, to substitute for a longer string. A more useful application of general entities is to replace a string that may change from time to time with a surrogate. When a change is needed, only the definition must be changed; otherwise, one would have to search all possible instance documents to find and replace the value. For example, for a certain set of documents, one might define `&monarch;` to be replaced by "Queen Elizabeth." In the future, changing the definition to "King Charles" would cause the new value to be substituted any time an instance document is parsed.

We will declare an entity for the convenience of the memo-writer. This declaration will cause `&boss;` to be replaced by the string "Harry S Truman" wherever it occurs in the document text by adding the following to our DTD:

```
<!ENTITY boss "Harry S Truman" >
```

Entity definitions are not limited to short strings. Sets of navigation elements or legal boilerplate can be declared in an entity definition. This allows necessary changes to be made in one place rather than many. Entities can contain markup as well as text, with the restriction that entity replacement must not be able to cause an otherwise well-formed document to fail to be well formed. For example, an entity definition may not contain an opening element tag without the corresponding closing tag. Another way to say this is to say that the entity text must be well formed with the exception that it need not have a single root element.

External entities are pointers to text and markup which is well-formed XML with the exception that they need not have a single root element. They allow a collection of text and possibly markup to be defined once and used from many places. External entities are declared with the SYSTEM keyword and a URL pointing to the item to be retrieved.

```
<!ENTITY nav_bar SYSTEM "http://webdev/spsu.edu/nav_bar.xml">
```

Validating parsers are required to retrieve the external entity, but parsers that check only for well-formed documents are not. For Web applications, other approaches such as server-side includes may be a better solution.

External unparsed entities are external references to data other than well-formed XML documents. An external unparsed entity may point to a source program in which symbols that are used for markup in XML have entirely different meanings, or to binary data such as a picture or sound file. External unparsed entities do not require XML processors to do anything in particular with the files to which they point, and they introduce an unnecessary second level of indirection. Better practice is to provide a pointer to the external data directly in an attribute and design the overall application to process the external data as appropriate. An example of the latter approach is the `src=` attribute in the XHTML `<img />` element. The Web browser must know how to deal with image files, but the parser does not.

DTD entity definitions may not themselves include entity instances. A special entity type, the parameter entity, allows definition of special entities that may be used in entity declarations within the DTD, but may not be used in instance documents. Parameter entities are useful for writing complex DTDs, and especially for modularizing DTDs. They are not discussed here.

Here, all together, is the DTD we have built up in this section, along with a small instance document that is valid according to the DTD.

```
<?xml version="1.0" encoding="iso-8859-1" ?>
<!DOCTYPE memo [
  <!ELEMENT memo (from, to+, body) >
  <!ELEMENT from (#PCDATA)>
  <!ELEMENT to (#PCDATA | name | department)* >
  <!ELEMENT name (surname, forename*) >
  <!ELEMENT surname (#PCDATA) >
  <!ELEMENT forename (#PCDATA) >
  <!ELEMENT department (#PCDATA) >
  <!ELEMENT body (#PCDATA)>
  <!ATTLIST memo date CDATA #REQUIRED
        priority (high | medium | low) "medium" >
  <!ENTITY boss "Harry S Truman" >
]>
<memo date="15 April 1951">
  <from>&boss;</from>
  <to>
    <name>
  <surname>MacArthur</surname>
  </name>
  Troops
  </to>
  <body>The buck stops here.</body>
</memo>
```

This document can be validated, but part of the value of a DTD lies in separating it from the instance document so that the same DTD can be used to validate many instances of the document it models. Separation is accomplished by storing the DTD so that it is accessible to the parser and making a link to the DTD in the prolog of the instance document. The next example shows the DTD and the instance document as they would be stored separately.

```
<?xml version="1.0" encoding="iso-8859-1" ?>

<!ELEMENT memo (from, to+, body) >
<!ELEMENT from (#PCDATA)>
<!ELEMENT to (#PCDATA  name  department)* >
<!ELEMENT name (surname, forename*) >
<!ELEMENT surname (#PCDATA) >
<!ELEMENT forename (#PCDATA) >
<!ELEMENT department (#PCDATA) >
<!ELEMENT body (#PCDATA)>

<!ATTLIST memo date CDATA #REQUIRED
    priority (high  medium  low) "medium" >

<!ENTITY boss "Harry S Truman" >
```

```
<?xml version="1.0"
      encoding="iso-8859-1" ?>
<!DOCTYPE memo SYSTEM "memo.dtd" >
<memo date="15 April 1951">
  <from>&boss;</from>
  <to>
    <name>
      <surname>MacArthur</surname>
    </name>
    Troops
    </to>
  <body>
    The buck stops here.
    </body>
</memo>
```

The example assumes that the DTD is stored as "memo.dtd" in the same location as the XML instance document. The <!DOCTYPE > of the instance document now declares a SYSTEM DTD and specifies its location as a relative URL. For a DTD that is to apply to many instance documents that could be stored at different locations, an absolute URL would be needed.

This DTD specifies the structure of a simple memo, but it has two obvious shortcomings. First, nothing constrains the date attribute to be a valid date, and the element values are also unconstrained. Second, although the <to> element is required to be present, it may be empty.

2.3.2 XML Schema

DTDs are useful for validating that an XML document uses the correct markup language, meaning an XML document uses the correct tags, in the correct amount and the correct order. However, when it comes to validating that an XML document contains the correct type of data, DTDs fall short. DTDs have a very weak typing system that can only restrict XML elements to containing no data, other XML elements, or text data. DTDs do not support data types such as integers, decimals, booleans, dates, or enumerations. Using a DTD to specify that the data appear in a specific format is also impossible. For most applications, the following are basic needs for correctly processing data. For an application to correctly understand what a specific piece of data is, this data must be in a prescribed format (e.g., "1951-02-15" instead of "15 February 1951") with a specific data type and size (e.g., byte data must only contain digits and have a value between -128 and 127). DTDs do not provide a mechanism for specifying this level of detail. Additionally, because DTDs are a legacy of SGML and thus were developed before namespaces, DTDs do not support namespaces, which are very useful for categorizing and identifying data types. The final drawback to DTDs is that they use a different syntax than the XML documents they describe. It is very useful to have the document definitions look like the documents they are defining. Someone familiar with creating XML markup should be familiar with the mechanisms used for declaring the XML document definition. In response to these problems with DTD the World Wide Web Consortium developed XML Schema. The current version of XML Schema is 1.0, which is a W3C recommendation. Version 1.1 is in development.

Recall the simple memo document for which a DTD was developed in the preceding section. We will develop an XML Schema document that describes the same XML document. First, let us look at the memo document instance, changed to refer to an XML schema instead of a DTD. Note that in this text "Schema" with a capital "S" is used to refer to the XML Schema specification, while "schema" with a lowercase "s" is used to refer to a specific schema document. An XML **s**chema is a document that has been created to conform to the XML **S**chema specification.

```
<?xml version="1.0" encoding="iso-8859-1" ?>
<memo xmlns="http://webdev.spsu.edu/namespaces/memo"
      xmlns:xsi="http://www.w3.org/2001/XMLSchema-instance"
      xsi:schemaLocation="http://webdev.spsu.edu/namespaces/memo
                          memo.xsd">
  <from>Boss</from>
  <to>Troops</to>
  <date>15 April 1951</date>
  <body>The buck stops here.</body>
</memo>
```

With DTDs, the binding of document to definition occurred in the prolog. With XML schemas, the binding occurs in the form of attributes on the root element. The first attribute declares a namespace. XML documents without namespaces are common, but "retrofitting" a namespace into an XML design is very difficult. It is preferable to define and use a default namespace from the outset for all but very simple applications. Remember, the URI is only a name; nothing needs to be stored there. The second attribute binds the `xsi` namespace prefix to the name `http://www.w3.org/2001/XMLSchema-instance`.

The third attribute identifies the schema location. There are two whitespace-separated values in the attribute; the first is the namespace name and the second is the URI of the schema itself. In this case, we have used a relative URI.

If we were not using namespaces, we would bind the schema location to the instance document using `xsi:noNamespaceSchemaLocation`.

It is possible to validate an XML instance document against an XML schema without explicitly binding the schema to the document. Doing so requires identifying the schema to the parser by some other means, such as when the parser class is instantiated. Because a part of the motivation of XML is that it be self-documenting, it is better practice to make an explicit binding in each instance document.

The schema definition itself is longer than the equivalent DTD. That is because XML schemas separate description of the document structure from description of element and attribute contents. The example also includes some lines that are not strictly necessary because we wanted to call attention to them.

```
<xsd:schema
    xmlns:xsd="http://www.w3.org/2001/XMLSchema"
    xmlns:mmo="http://webdev.spsu.edu/namespaces/memo"
    targetNamespace="http://webdev.spsu.edu/namespaces/memo"
    elementFormDefault="qualified">
  <xsd:element name="memo">
    <xsd:complexType>
      <xsd:sequence>
        <xsd:element name="from" type="xsd:string"
                     minOccurs="1" maxOccurs="1" />
        <xsd:element name="to">
          <xsd:complexType mixed="true">
            <xsd:choice minOccurs="1" maxOccurs="unbounded">
              <xsd:element name="department" type="xsd:string"/>
              <xsd:element name="name" type="mmo:nameStructure"/>
            </xsd:choice>
          </xsd:complexType>
        </xsd:element>
        <xsd:element name="body" type="xsd:string"
                     minOccurs="1" maxOccurs="1" />
      </xsd:sequence>
      <xsd:attribute name="date" type="xsd:date" use="required" />
      <xsd:attribute name="priority" type="mmo:priorityValues"
                     default="medium" />
    </xsd:complexType>
  </xsd:element>

  <xsd:complexType name="nameStructure">
    <xsd:sequence>
      <xsd:element name="surname" type="xsd:string"
                   minOccurs="1" maxOccurs="1" />
      <xsd:element name="forename" type="xsd:string"
                   minOccurs="0" maxOccurs="unbounded" />
    </xsd:sequence>
  </xsd:complexType>

  <xsd:simpleType name="priorityValues">
    <xsd:restriction base="xsd:string">
      <xsd:enumeration value="high"/>
```

```
      <xsd:enumeration value="medium"/>
      <xsd:enumeration value="low"/>
    </xsd:restriction>
  </xsd:simpleType>
</xsd:schema>
```

The `xmlns` attribute of the schema definition binds the namespace prefix `xsd` to the name `http://www.w3.org/2001/XMLSchema`. The target namespace name is also given; it must match the `xmlns` attribute on the instance definition.

The `elementFormDefault` attribute set to "`qualified`" indicates that nested elements in the XML document instance must be namespace qualified. This means that one must be able to look at the XML document instance and associate the specific XML element with a namespace declared in the document. To be qualified, an XML element may fall under the default namespace or a namespace that is declared with a suffix appended to the `xmlns` attribute. If a suffix follows the `xmlns` attribute, then the elements in that namespace must have a prefix to be considered qualified. The default value for the `elementFormDefault` attribute is "`unqualified`," which is almost always the wrong choice. XML Schema also includes an attribute called `attributeFormDefault`, which is similar to `elementFormDefault` but is used to indicate that all attributes of an XML document must be qualified.

Elements are defined using the `<element>` tag, `<xsd:element>` in the example. Elements are given a name and a type with the corresponding attributes. They may also be given a default value with the `default` attribute, or assigned a constant value with the `fixed` attribute.

There are approximately 40 built-in atomic types in XML Schema, covering the categories of strings, numbers, dates and times, and a few miscellaneous types. Some of the more frequently used atomic types are listed.

`string`	Any Unicode character string.
`decimal`	A decimal number with an integer and fraction part.
`integer`	A counting number.
`date`	An ISO 8601 date, expressed as yyyy-mm-dd with optional time zone The time zone is "Z" for UTC or a positive or negative offset from UTC.
`dateTime`	A date as above, the letter "T" and a time in colon-separated hours, minutes, and seconds. Decimal fractions of a second and a time zone are optional. The time zone is specified as for a date and follows the seconds part.
`boolean`	True, false, 1, or 0. True and 1 are equivalent, as are false and 0.
`double`	A double-precision floating-point number expressed as an integer and fraction, optionally followed by a case-insensitive "e" and a decimal power of ten multiplier, e.g., 6.022e23.

The atomic types can be further specified by specifying constraints on their *facets* using the `<restriction>` element. The result is a `simpleType`. Depending upon how they are counted, there are about a dozen facets. The string type has a `length` facet that can be set to a fixed number using `length` or to a range using `minLength` and `maxLength`. The other facets applicable to string are `pattern`, `enumeration`, and `whitespace`. The `pattern` facet specifies an expression very similar to a regular expression, but adapted for Unicode. If the allowed values of a string are known, they can be set out using the `enumeration` facet. The `whitespace` facet controls whether `whitespace` in a string is preserved, converted to spaces, or collapsed to a single space.

The facets that can be controlled when defining types are:

`length`	String length
`minLength`	Minimum string length
`maxLength`	Maximum string length
`pattern`	String must match the specified pattern, similar to a regular expression
`enumeration`	The possible values are listed
`whitespace`	`preserve`, `replace`, or `collapse`
`minExclusive`	Minimum exclusive range of a number
`maxExclusive`	Maximum exclusive range of a number
`minInclusive`	Minimum inclusive range of a number
`maxInclusive`	Maximum inclusive range of a number
`totalDigits`	Total digits, exclusive of sign and decimal point
`fractionDigits`	Of total digits, how many must appear in the fraction part

In the `priorityValues` type in the example schema, a `string` type is declared by enumerating possible values. In the fragment below, a decimal type is declared by setting range and precision limits on the `decimal` atomic type.

```
<xsd:simpleType name="currencyValue">
  <xsd:restriction base="xsd:decimal">
    <xsd:minExclusive value="0"/>
    <xsd:maxInclusive value="1000"/>
    <xsd:fractionDigits value="2"/>
  </xsd:restriction>
</xsd:simpleType>
```

Simple types are derived from atomic types by restriction. Simple types may have neither attributes nor child elements. Complex types are data types that will contain child elements or have attributes.

The <memo> element is defined as complexType because it will contain other elements. This is an anonymous complex type; the memo type contains its own definition. It is also possible to define named complex types; the nameStructure type in the example schema is a named complex type.

Schemas provide a mechanism similar to inheritance in which user-defined types can be used as the base type for new type definitions, called *derived types.* The new definitions may be formed by further restricting the base type using <restriction> elements, or by extending the base type. In the latter case, an <extension> element is used to add new content to the base type.

Up to this point, we have considered types that contain text or types that contain other types. A complex type can be declared to be mixed, that is to contain both child elements and text nodes, by setting mixed="true" on its declaration. The <to> element in the example schema is mixed.

The child elements of the example and also the child <memo> are enclosed in a <sequence> element. (It is <xsd:sequence> in the schema because we qualified the schema namespace.) Using <sequence> requires that the child elements occur in the order specified, similar to the comma operator in DTDs. As with our first attempt at a DTD, all of the child elements are of type string and so may contain any legal characters of any length, just as with #PCDATA in a DTD. The maximum and minimum numbers of occurrences of each child element are specified by the minOccurs and maxOccurs attributes. These are really unnecessary in the example because the default is one, but they are shown to emphasize the greater control XML Schema provides.

We used <sequence> to define the child elements of memo. The possibilities for specifying child elements are listed below.

<all> Elements in the list may occur in any order; an element may be made optional by setting minOccurs to zero. The maxOccurs attribute must be one.

<choice> One of a list of choices must appear in the instance document. The maxOccurs attribute may be set higher than one to allow the choice to be repeated.

<sequence> The elements must appear in the order shown; minOccurs and maxOccurs can be used to allow optional or repeated elements.

XML Schema provides much finer control over data types than is possible with DTDs. However, schemas do not provide a way to declare general entities such as &boss; in the example memo. One possible solution is to declare fixed content for elements or attributes; another is to combine DTDs and schemas. Neither is completely satisfactory.

2.4 Parsing XML

One of the most important aspects of XML is the fact that XML documents are simply plain text that can be created and maintained with any common text editor. Other popular data storage formats are binary and proprietary to a specific vendor such that you need special programs to view and edit the data (e.g., Microsoft Word and Excel). Since XML is nonproprietary, text-based, and designed for easy processing by computer software, without much effort, an application to read and manipulate XML documents can be created. However, many programs for processing XML are freely available so writing your own is not necessary. Software programs that know how to read and manipulate XML documents are commonly called *XML parsers.* XML parsers read the XML data into computer memory and give either specific pieces of the data or the whole XML document.

When XML first gained popularity, many different XML parsers became available, each with their own interface. Since XML parsers typically have different performance characteristics or other qualities, it is common to want to test various parsers with an application before settling on a specific implementation. Unfortunately, the difference in interfaces among the various parsers requires a change in code each time a different parser is integrated. The software community grew tired of the effort required to change parsers, so standard XML parser APIs were created. The concept behind a "standard" XML parser API is simple—if all parsers implement a standard API, then an application can be coded to that interface and changing code when changing parsers is not required. Thus, XML parser APIs are not XML parsers, but rather a common API for parsers to implement.

The most popular XML parser APIs today are the Simple API for XML (SAX) and the Document Object Model (DOM). SAX was developed by a group of individuals on the XML-DEV mailing list (`http://www.xml.org/xml/xmldev.shtml`) starting in December 1997. The first version of SAX was released in May 1998, and quickly became a universally accepted de facto standard. The first official version of DOM, labeled DOM Level 1, was developed by the World Wide Web Consortium (W3C) and released in October 1998. DOM Level 1 is based on the first unofficial version of DOM, labeled DOM Level 0, which was used in the Netscape Navigator 3.0 and Internet Explorer 3.0 browsers. Netscape originally developed DOM Level 0 as a programmatic interface to HTML that was implemented in JavaScript (`http://www.mozilla.org/js/`) and first packaged with the Netscape Navigator 2.0 browser in October 1995. Now, the official DOM specification provides a programmatic interface to both HTML and XML. The primary difference between SAX and DOM is that SAX does not cache the parsed XML document in memory but DOM does. SAX sends events to registered listeners when it encounters data while parsing an XML document, but does not store the parsed data in memory. The listeners have to cache the data if they want to keep it. On the other hand, DOM parses the entire XML document into memory as a hierarchical object model—a tree structure of objects called *nodes.* All the tags and the text data they contain are encapsulated by node objects that can be randomly referenced multiple times until the tree structure is explicitly removed from memory. In general, SAX parsers tend to consume less memory and be faster than DOM parsers. However, DOM provides the benefit of being able to randomly access the parsed document. Both APIs have been implemented in several different programming languages including Java, C++, Perl, and Python. In the next two sections we discuss these two APIs.

2.4.1 Simple API for XML (SAX)

SAX was originally developed only for Java but quickly became the first widely accepted programmatic API for XML and now has implementations in several different languages, including Pascal, C++, Perl, and Python. The development of SAX is open-source and managed by David Megginson and David Brownell. The code is housed on `SourceForge.net` with a home page at `http://www.saxproject.org/`. At the time of this writing the latest version of SAX is 2.0.2, which can be downloaded from `http://sourceforge.net/projects/sax/`. Although SAX has been implemented in various languages, the official release of SAX is still published in Java.

SAX is an event-driven model where objects are provided with callback methods (sometimes called listeners) that the parser invokes as it reads data from an XML document. Access to the XML data is provided by a SAX parser in a serial fashion; once a piece of data is read and provided to a callback method that data is not read again. Keeping the data requires that code be written in the callback method to cache the data. If all of the data needs to be cached, then using a DOM parser is preferred. In fact, quite a few DOM parsers use this same method. They employ SAX to parse the XML document and then generate DOM objects that encapsulate the data passed to the callback methods. It is also fairly common to use SAX to create a custom object model of the XML document, because DOM does not always satisfy everyone's needs. However, SAX is typically used to read only specific pieces of the XML document into memory, not the whole document. For example, one may want to search one or more XML documents for a specific piece of data, such as a record of some kind, and display that data to a user.

Writing an application that uses a SAX parser consists mostly of writing the callback methods. SAX provides four interfaces with callback methods that can be passed to the parser, each serving a different purpose. These four interfaces are briefly described below.

- `org.xml.sax.ContentHandler`

  The SAX parser passes data (content) that it reads from the XML document to a registered implementation of the `ContentHandler` interface. The `ContentHandler` interface has methods that correspond to the types of data that is found in XML documents including XML elements (tags), namespace declarations, character data, whitespace, and processing instructions. The parser calls the appropriate method of the `ContentHandler` implementation each time it encounters a piece of data. The `ContentHandler` is the primary listener that will be implemented for most applications that use SAX; in fact, it may be the only listener to implement. The `ContentHandler` interface is discussed further in the next section.

- `org.xml.sax.ErrorHandler`

  A SAX parser does not throw exceptions if it encounters errors in the XML document it is parsing, instead it calls methods of the `ErrorHandler` listener. The `ErrorHandler` interface has the following three methods:

```
public void error(SAXParseException exception) throws SAXException;

public void fatalError(SAXParseException exception) throws SAXException;

public void warning(SAXParseException exception) throws SAXException;
```

The XML Recommendation from W3C states that XML parsers can generate two types of errors—*errors* and *fatal errors.* Errors should report conditions that are not fatal such as nonconformance with a DTD or XML schema. Fatal errors include conditions such as XML documents that are not well formed (e.g., start tag with no end tag) and should stop the processing of the XML parser. Warnings are not defined by the XML Recommendation from W3C, but are added by SAX to handle anything that does not fit into the error or fatal error categories.

- `org.xml.sax.DTDHandler`

  This interface is used when parsing an XML document with a DTD. A SAX parser provides very little information to an application about the DTD of an XML document. The `DTDHandler` interface contains only the following two methods:

```
public void notationDecl(String name, String publicId, String systemId)
    throws SAXException;

public voidunparsedEntityDecl(String name, String publicId,
                              String systemId, String notationName)
    throws SAXException;
```

  Among other things, an XML document may contain references to *unparsed entities* and *notations.* Unparsed entities allow an XML document to contain nontext objects, such as a binary image. Notations allow the format of the nontext objects to be identified so that the data can be processed correctly. XML parsers do not process unparsed entities (hence the name), so the job of processing the unparsed entity is left up to the application. However, to correctly process the data, an application needs the associated unparsed entity declaration and notation declaration from the DTD. SAX provides this information to the application via the `DTDHandler` interface. It is up to the application to cache the information about the DTD so that it can use it later when it encounters an XML type of entity, entities, or notation in the body of the XML document. If this all sounds somewhat confusing, do not worry because you are not likely to need to use the `DTDHandler` interface.

- `org.xml.sax.EntityResolver`

  The `EntityResolver` interface is very simple; it contains only one method:

```
public InputSource resolveEntity(String publicId, String systemId)
    throws SAXException, java.io.IOException
```

An XML document may contain references to data external of the document. External entities in XML are identified by a system identifier and, optionally, a public identifier. System identifiers are typically URIs and public identifiers are rarely used. When the SAX parser cannot resolve an external entity by a URL, then an `EntityResolver` should be provided. Cases where the SAX parser will not be able to find the external entity include a situation where the URI is a type other than a URL (e.g., a URN), or the external entity is read from a database or some other source. The `resolveEntity` method of the `EntityResolver` implementation must return an `org.xml.sax.InputSource` object that the parser can use to read the content of the external entity. The SAX `InputSource` object is used to encapsulate a `java.io.InputStream`, `java.io.Reader`, or URL. Later we present an example of how the `InputSource` is used.

SAX also provides the `org.xml.sax.helpers.DefaultHandler` class that implements all four event-handler interfaces similar to the way the Java library provides the `Adapter` classes for GUI event listeners. (As an aside, note that the adapter classes for GUI events in the Java library are *not* implementations of the well-known Adapter Pattern.) The `DefaultHandler` class and only the methods chosen can be implemented. The event-handler methods implemented by `DefaultHandler` have no functionality.

A class and an interface from SAX is generally used to initiate the parser of an XML document—`org.xml.sax.helpers.XMLReaderFactory` and `org.xml.sax.XMLReader`, respectively. Use the `XMLReaderFactory` class to create and return a concrete instance of `XMLReader`. The `XMLReader` instance that `XMLReaderFactory` returns can be specified by a system property[1] or a fully qualified class name. `XMLReaderFactory` contains two methods, both called `createXMLReader`. One takes in no parameters, looks up the `XMLReader` implementation class name from the system property `org.xml.sax.driver`, instantiates an instance of that class, and returns it. The other takes in a string identifying the fully qualified name of the `XMLReader` implementation class name, creates an instance of that class, and returns it.

The `XMLReader` implementation is used to actually parse the XML document. `XMLReader` contains `get` and `set` methods for each of the four SAX event-handler interfaces, e.g., `setContentHandler()`, `getContentHandler()`, etc. Register the implementations of the event-handler interfaces with the SAX parser by calling the appropriate set methods. Additionally, `XMLReader` contains `get` and `set` methods

[1]System properties in Java can be set from your code by calling `java.lang.System.setProperty(String key, String value)` or by passing them to the JVM from the command line using the following syntax: `java -D<propertyName>=<propertyValue>`, where `<propertyName>` is the name of the property and `<propertyValue>` is the value of the property.

for *features* and *properties*, e.g., `setFeature()`, `setProperty()`. These methods can be used to enable features and configure properties of those features for the specific SAX parser implementation being used. SAX requires parsers to support a standard set of features, which can be found at `http://www.saxproject.org/apidoc/org/xml/sax/package-summary.html#package_description`. Parser implementations can also provide their own specific features. For example, SAX is designed to validate an XML document using a DTD but not an XML schema, so some SAX parser implementations, such as Apache Xerces (`http://xml.apache.org/xerces2-j/`), allow schema validation with a feature to be specified, and the specific schema to validate against with a property. The list of features supported by the Xerces parser can be found at `http://xml.apache.org/xerces2-j/features.html`. An example that uses `XMLReaderFactory` and the Xerces `XMLReader` implementation to parse an XHTML document and validate it against the XHTML 1.0 Strict schema is given below.

Listing 2.3 Using the Xerces Implementation of SAX to Parse XHTML

```
package javawebbook.sax;

import org.xml.sax.ContentHandler;
import org.xml.sax.InputSource;
import org.xml.sax.SAXException;
import org.xml.sax.XMLReader;
import org.xml.sax.helpers.XMLReaderFactory;
import java.io.File;
import java.io.IOException;

public class SAXTest {
  public static void main(String[] args)
    throws ClassNotFoundException, IllegalAccessException,
           InstantiationException, SAXException, IOException {
    String xhtmlFileName = args[0];
    String contentHandlerClass = args[1];

    // Create an instance of the specified ContentHandler.
    // SAX will pass data it reads from the XML file to this handler.
    ContentHandler contentHandler = (ContentHandler)
      Class.forName(contentHandlerClass).newInstance();

    // Create an instance of the parser.
    XMLReader reader = XMLReaderFactory.createXMLReader();

    // This line registers the ContentHandler with the parser.
    reader.setContentHandler(contentHandler);

    // This line sets a SAX standard feature, which tells the parser
```

```
    // that we want to use XML qualified (prefixed)
    // names and attributes.
    reader.setFeature("http://xml.org/sax/features/namespace-prefixes", true);

    // This line sets a SAX standard feature, which tells the parser
    // to validate the XML document.
    reader.setFeature("http://xml.org/sax/features/validation", true);

    // This line sets a Xerces specific feature, which tells the
    // parser to validate the XML document against an XML schema.
    reader.setFeature("http://apache.org/xml/features/validation/schema", true);

    // This line tells the parser where the XML schema is located.
    reader.setProperty(
      "http://apache.org/xml/properties/schema/external-schemaLocation",
      "http://www.w3.org/2002/08/xhtml/xhtml1-strict.xsd");

    // Illustrate InputSource by using the URI to the file.
    String uri = "file:" + new File(xhtmlFileName).getAbsolutePath();
    InputSource input = new InputSource(uri);

    // Now parse the document.
    reader.parse(input);
  }
}
```

The `XMLReader` `setFeature` method accepts a URI and a `boolean` that turns the feature on (true) or off (false). All features are identified by URIs, usually URLs. The `setProperty` method accepts a URI and a `java.lang.Object`. The example above did not define the `ContentHandler` implementation. Instead, the main method just accepts a `ContentHandler` implementation class name, and an instance of that class is instantiated and used. Next we discuss how `ContentHandler` implementation can be created and used.

org.xml.sax.ContentHandler

`ContentHandler` is the primary SAX event handler that will be implemented, because it is the one that receives notifications on the data that the XML document contains, which is what we are most concerned about. The `ContentHandler` interface and a brief explanation of all its methods are given in the listing that follows.

Listing 2.4 The SAX `ContentHandler` Interface

```
package org.xml.sax;

public interface ContentHandler {
  /* This method is called before any other methods of this interface. It gives the
     application an object that can later be used within the methods below to get the
     location (line and column number) of the data (passed to a method below) in the source
     XML document that is being parsed. */
  public void setDocumentLocator (Locator locator);

  /* The startDocument() method is called after the setDocumentLocator() method and before
     any other methods to notify the application that the parser is starting to parse the
     document. The endDocument() method is called when the parser has finished parsing the
     document. */
  public void startDocument() throws SAXException;
  public void endDocument() throws SAXException;

  /* The startPrefixMapping() method is called before the startElement() method below, and
     the endPrefixMapping() element is called after the endElement() method below. The
     startPrefixMapping() method is given the prefix and URI for an XML namespace.
     This data can be used to associate a prefix used on an attribute or element value
     with its namespace URI. */
  public void startPrefixMapping(String prefix, String uri) throws SAXException;
  public void endPrefixMapping(String prefix) throws SAXException;

  /* The startElement() method is called when the parser encounters a start tag (e.g.,
     <html>), and the endElement() method is called when the parser encounters an end tag
     (e.g., </html>). The startElement() method provides information on the XML namespace of
     the tag and all of its attributes, as well as the value of the attributes. Attribute
     information is provided by the org.xml.sax.Attributes parameter. */
  public void startElement(String uri, String localName,
                           String qName, Attributes atts)
    throws SAXException;
  public void endElement(String uri, String localName, String qName)
    throws SAXException;

  /* This method is invoked when the parser encounters an element that contains text. It
     is called after the startElement() method and before the endElement() method for a
     specific XML element. It may be called multiple times for a single element because
```

```
     the parser may not have been able to pass all of the text in one method call.
     Therefore, you need to combine all of the text from each call to the characters()
     method between a specific call to startElement() and the associated call to
     endElement(). */
  public void characters(char ch[], int start, int length) throws SAXException;

  /* This method is called when the parser encounters whitespace between XML elements
     of the document. You rarely need to use this method. */
  public void ignorableWhitespace(char ch[], int start, int length) throws SAXException;

  /* The parser calls this method when it encounters an XML processing instruction. */
  public void processingInstruction(String target, String data) throws SAXException;

  /* This method is invoked whenever the parser skips (does not process) an XML entity. */
  public void skippedEntity(String name) throws SAXException;
}
```

A simple way to implement ContentHandler is to extend org.xml.sax.helpers.DefaultHandler and override only the methods that are wanted. Recall that DefaultHandler implements all four event-handler interfaces with methods that do nothing. As an example, we can create an XHTML file, and then parse the file using a ContentHandler to capture and output the content of the first paragraph (<p> tag). The XHTML file is given in the listing below.

Listing 2.5 The File test.xhtml

```
<html xmlns="http://www.w3.org/1999/xhtml">
  <head><title>XHTML Test</title></head>
  <body>
    <h1>Heading Content</h1>
    <p>First Paragraph Content</p>
    <p id="p2">Second Paragraph Content</p>
  </body>
</html>
```

The ContentHandler implementation is given in the following listing. To capture the content of the first paragraph we needed to override the startElement, characters, and endElement methods. The startElement method is called when the start tag is encountered (<p>). In the startElement method we check to make sure that we have not already found the first paragraph tag and that the tag encountered is a paragraph tag. If these checks pass, then we set flags to indicate that we have found the first paragraph tag and that we need to process the current tag. The characters method will be called after the `startElement` method. In the `characters` method we check the flag to see if we should process this content. If so, we append the characters to a buffer. We need to accumulate the characters in a buffer because the `characters` method may need to be called multiple times for a single tag in order for a parser to pass the entire text content of the tag to the application. Finally, in the `endElement` method we clear the flag that indicates the current tag should be processed, and we output the content that we captured. The `endElement` method is called after the `characters` method, when the end tag is encountered (</p>).

Listing 2.6 Example `ContentHandler` That Captures XHTML Paragraph Content

```
package javawebbook.sax;

import org.xml.sax.Attributes;
import org.xml.sax.SAXException;
import org.xml.sax.helpers.DefaultHandler;

public class ContentHandlerExample extends DefaultHandler {
  StringBuffer buffer = new StringBuffer();
  boolean foundTag = false;
  boolean processTag = false;

  public void startElement(String uri, String localName,
                           String qName, Attributes atts)
    throws SAXException {
    System.out.println("startElement() called for tag: " + localName);

    // Only process the first <p> tag that is found.
    if (!foundTag && localName.equals("p")) {
      foundTag = true;
      processTag = true;
    }
  }

  public void characters(char[] chars, int start, int length) throws SAXException {
    System.out.println("characters() called");

    // If we have found the first <p> tag and we are currently
    // processing it, then capture its text content.
    if (processTag) {
      buffer.append(chars, start, length);
    }
  }
```

```
  public void endElement(String uri, String localName, String qName) throws SAXException {
    System.out.println("endElement() called for tag: " + localName);

    if (processTag) {
      // When this method is called we are through processing the tag.
      processTag = false;
      System.out.println("Content of first paragraph: " + buffer.toString());
    }
  }
}
```

It is important to realize that the `startElement` method is called every time a start tag is encountered and the `endElement` method is called every time an end tag is encountered. Since XML elements can contain nested XML elements, the `startElement` method will be called for a nested start tag after the `startElement` method is called for its parent's start tag but before the `endElement` method is called for its parent's end tag. Listing 2.6 contains output statements at the top of each method to indicate when the method was called. We can test the code of Listing 2.6 by passing `javawebbook.sax.ContentHandlerExample` and `test.xhtml` (from Listing 2.5) to the `main` method of Listing 2.3, as follows.

```
java -classpath %CLASSPATH%;.
-Dorg.xml.sax.driver=org.apache.xerces.parsers.SAXParser
javawebbook.sax.SAXTest test.xhtml javawebbook.sax.ContentHandlerExample
```

On UNIX type systems `%CLASSPATH%` can be replaced with `$CLASSPATH`. Of course, the above command assumes that Xerces has already been downloaded, its `.jar` files have been placed in the `CLASSPATH` environment variable, and that `SAXTest` and `ContentHandlerExample` have already been compiled. If these conditions were true and the command above was executed, the output would be as follows.

```
startElement() called for tag: html
characters() called
startElement() called for tag: head
startElement() called for tag: title
characters() called
endElement() called for tag: title
endElement() called for tag: head
characters() called
startElement() called for tag: body
characters() called
startElement() called for tag: h1
characters() called
endElement() called for tag: h1
characters() called
```

```
startElement() called for tag: p
characters() called
endElement() called for tag: p
Content of first paragraph: First Paragraph Content
characters() called
startElement() called for tag: p
characters() called
endElement() called for tag: p
characters() called
endElement() called for tag: body
characters() called
endElement() called for tag: html
```

You may wonder why the `characters` method is called so many times. That is because the `characters` method is called for all text between the start and end tags, including whitespace. The XHTML of Listing 2.5 contains spaces before the `<body>`, `<h1>`, first `<p>`, second `<p>`, and `</body>` tags, and the last tag on each line has a carriage return behind it. There is no space between the `<head>` and `<title>` tags so the `characters` method is not called between these tags.

2.4.2 Document Object Model (DOM)

DOM is a tree-based model that is developed and maintained by the World Wide Web Consortium (W3C). As mentioned earlier, the difference between SAX and DOM is that with DOM, the entire XML document is parsed and cached in memory as a tree structure of objects called *nodes*. No part of the object model can be accessed until the entire document is parsed. The benefit of this model over SAX is that the entire document tree structure can be randomly accessed until it is removed from memory. The drawback is that large XML documents consume much memory and thus present a significant burden for the system. However, if an XML document needs to be randomly accessed, the document will either need to be parsed multiple times using SAX or a library that reads the entire document into memory, such as DOM.

DOM provides an object model for both HTML and XML documents that is platform-and-language independent. Like SAX, DOM is just an API that requires implementation. DOM has been implemented in many languages including Java, JavaScript (Java and JavaScript are *not* the same language), C++, Perl, and Python. The original DOM, referred to as DOM Level 0, was included with early versions of the Netscape and Internet Explorer browsers—originally just Netscape, then Microsoft joined in later. Actually Netscape had its own version implemented in JavaScript[2] and Internet Explorer developed something similar in JScript,[3] but with added functionality. At that time, the DOM was meant only to provide a programmatic interface to HTML

---

[2]Information on Netscape's/Mozilla's JavaScript can be found on the Web at `http://www.mozilla.org/js/`.

[3]Information on Microsoft's JScript, which is included with Internet Explorer, can be found on the Web at `http://msdn.microsoft.com/library/default.asp?url=/library/en-us/script56/html/js56jsoriJScript.asp`.

so that Web developers could write scripts that dynamically manipulate the content of a Web page (commonly referred to as DHTML—the D is for "dynamic"). Since the different browsers used their own versions of DOM, Web developers were burdened with needing to add control logic (if/else statements) that branched their scripting code for every possible peculiarity of every possible Web browser that might access their Web sites. Otherwise, their dynamic Web content might not work for some viewers. To resolve this problem, the W3C developed a new version of DOM, called DOM Level 1, which was intended as a standard API for all browser implementations (Netscape, Mozilla, Internet Explorer, Opera, etc.), as well as any other applications that used a programmatic interface to HTML or XML documents. The standard API has allowed Web developers to eliminate, in large part, the messy branching in their scripting code and still provide dynamic Web content that is cross-browser compatible. However, there are still quirky differences between the browsers that require special handling to make the script code cross-browser compatible.

The latest version of the document object model is DOM Level 3. Level 3 was released by the W3C as a Recommendation in April 2004 and is available on the Web at `http://www.w3.org/TR/DOM-Level-3-Core/`. The most popular version of the DOM in use today is DOM Level 2, which was released by the W3C as a Recommendation in November 2000 and is available on the Web at `http://www.w3.org/TR/DOM-Level-2-Core/`. Links to all of the DOM specifications can be found at `http://www.w3.org/DOM/DOMTR`. Because most browsers and parsers support DOM Level 2, that is the version we discuss in this chapter.

DOM Level 1, Level 2, and Level 3 all include a binding to Java. The binding describes an exception called `DOMException` that extends `java.lang.RuntimeException`, plus multiple interfaces for various objects, several of which extend an interface called `Node`. The DOM Level 2 specification packages all of these classes in the `org.w3c.dom` Java package, which can be downloaded from `http://www.w3.org/TR/2000/REC-DOM-Level2-Core-20001113/java-binding.zip`. An illustration of the DOM Level 2 class hierarchy is given in Figure 2.1.

DOM parsers generate a `Document` object as the result of parsing an XML document. The `Document` object represents an XML document instance and contains references to all other objects generated by the DOM parser. It is the root of the document tree structure. The `Document` interface has `get` methods that allow one to obtain references to the nodes of the tree and the XML document's DTD (represented by `DocumentType`), `create` methods for creating new objects that become part of the tree structure, and an `import` method for importing an external `Node` into the tree structure.

All XML elements in an XML document are parsed into `Element` objects. All other XML artifacts are parsed into their own types; for instance, XML attributes are encapsulated by the `Attr` type, comments by the `Comment` type, text by the `Text` type, CDATA sections by the `CDATASection` type, and so on. The common supertype for all XML artifacts is the `Node` type. There are `get` methods in `Document` that can

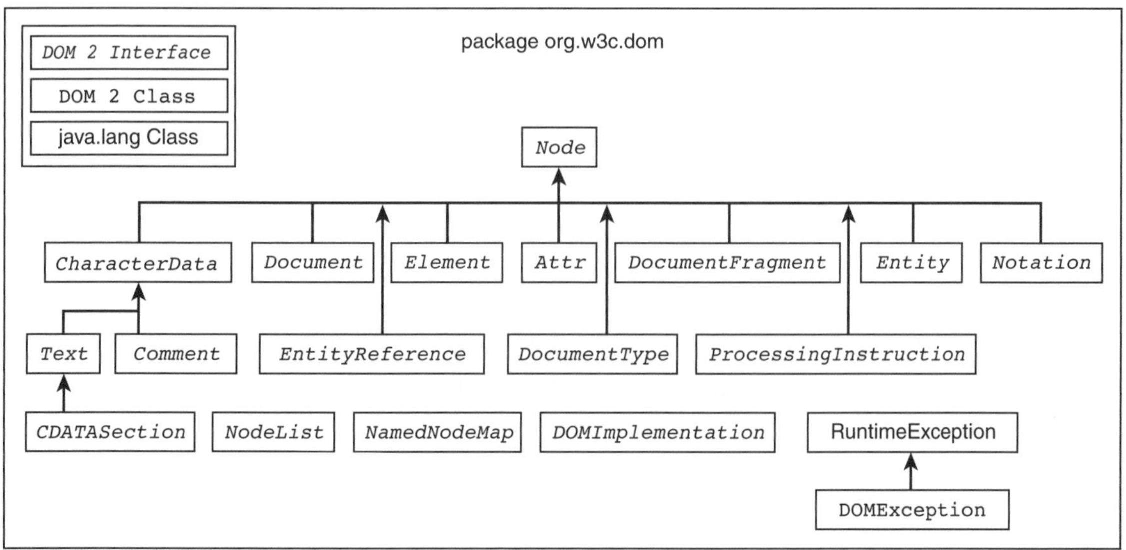

Figure 2.1
DOM Level 2 Classes (package org.w3c.dom)

be used to return all, or a subset of, the list of XML elements that were parsed into memory. This list of resulting elements is encapsulated in a `NodeList`. `NodeList` is simply an ordered collection of nodes with two methods—one method called `getLength()` that returns the total number of nodes in the collection and another method called `item(int index)` that returns the `Node` at a specified index. The `Node` at the specified index will be type `Element` because all XML elements are parsed into `Element` objects.

If we were to parse the XHTML file of Listing 2.5 using a DOM parser, we would obtain something similar to Figure 2.2.

The DOM parser generates a tree structure of linked `Node` objects that represent the XML document in memory. Note that even the text inside an XML element is encapsulated within a `Node` (see bottom row of Figure 2.2). The supertype for each of the objects in Figure 2.2 is `Node`. The nodes below a particular `Node` are called *children* of that `Node`. For instance, `Element` head and `Element` body are the children of `Element` html. `Element` html is called the *parent* of both `Element` head and body. The nodes on the same level as a `Node` are called the *siblings* of that node (`Element` body is a sibling of `Element` head). The nodes at the end of a branch (such as the entire bottom row of nodes in Figure 2.2) are called *leaves.*

The `Node` interface contains a list of constants that are used to identify the type of a particular `Node`. For example, in Figure 2.2 there are four different types of `Nodes`, each representing a different type

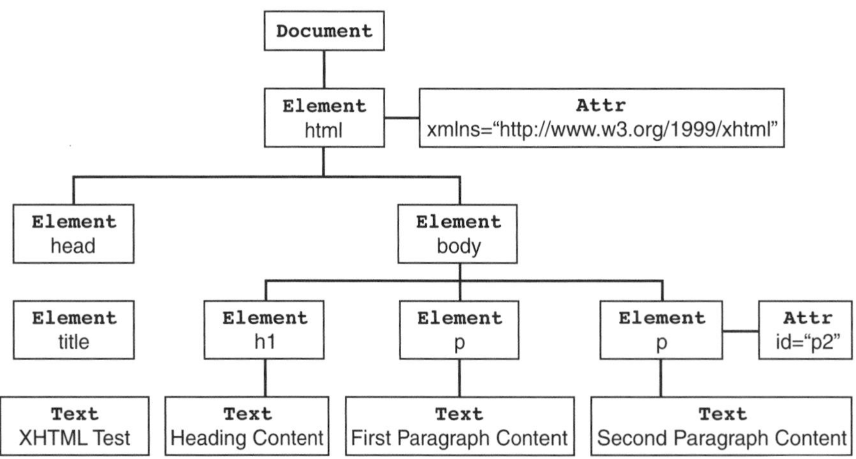

Figure 2.2
DOM Tree of a Parsed XHTML File

of artifact from the XML document—`Document`, `Element`, `Attr`, and `Text`. The `Element` type is associated with the `ELEMENT_NODE` constant within the `Node` interface, which is defined as the following.

```
public static final short ELEMENT_NODE;
```

If we had a reference to a `Node` (let us call it `myNode`) that we wanted to determine the type of, we can do the following.

```
boolean isElement = (myNode.getNodeType() == Node.ELEMENT_NODE);
```

Since the supertype for most of the DOM types is `Node`, the `Node` methods are used quite often when programming with DOM. The methods of the `Node` type can be grouped into the following categories.

- Methods to obtain/set type-specific information about the referenced `Node`. The information returned from these methods can be very different depending on the type of `Node` being accessed.

  `getNodeType()`, `getNodeName()`, `getNodeValue()`, `setNodeValue()`

- Methods to obtain/set the XML namespace information for the referenced `Node`

  `getLocalName()`, `getNamespaceURI()`, `getPrefix()`, `setPrefix()`

- Methods to reference the attributes of the `Node`

  `hasAttributes()`, `getAttributes()`

- A method to get a reference to the Node's parent Document

  getOwnerDocument()

- Methods for obtaining references to the Node's parent, siblings, and children

  getParentNode(), hasChildNodes(), getFirstChild(), getLastChild(), getChildNodes(), getPreviousSibling(), getNextSibling()

- Methods to add or remove children of the referenced Node

  appendChild(), replaceChild(), removeChild(), insertBefore()

- Other methods

  cloneNode(), normalize(), isSupported()

When you parse an XML document using DOM, you get a reference to an instance of the Document type, which implements Node. Calling getFirstChild() on the Document, will produce a reference to the top level XML element of the document, which is Element html in Figure 2.2. Calling getFirstChild() on that Node (Element html) produces a reference to Element head. For example, the following code, which uses the Xerces DOM parser, will output the content of the second paragraph if given Listing 2.5 as the XML document instance to parse.

Listing 2.7 Example Use of DOM Parser and DOM API

```
package javawebbook.dom;

import java.io.IOException;
import org.w3c.dom.Document;
import org.w3c.dom.Element;
import org.w3c.dom.Node;
import org.w3c.dom.NodeList;
import org.w3c.dom.Text;
import org.xml.sax.SAXException;
import org.apache.xerces.parsers.DOMParser;

public class DOMTest {
  public static void main(String[] args) throws IOException, SAXException {
    String xhtmlFileName = args[0];

    // Create the parser and parse the XML document.
    DOMParser parser = new DOMParser();
    parser.parse(xhtmlFileName);

    // Get the Document instance.
    Document document = parser.getDocument();
```

```
// Get the html Element. Because html is the root XML element
// of the XML document you can also access it using the
// getDocumentElement() method of the Document interface.
Node rootNode = document.getFirstChild();
Element htmlElement = (Element) rootNode;

// Get the body Element from the html Element, which like all
// Elements is a Node, so if we want to assign it to an Element
// reference we have to cast it.
NodeList childNodes = htmlElement.getChildNodes();
Element bodyElement = null;

// You might assume that the body Element would be the
// second Node in the list. If it weren't for the whitespace
// between the XML elements, this would be the case.
// Since there is whitespace between the XML elements,
// this whitespace is also parsed as Nodes. Therefore
// we'll just iterate through the list until we find the
// Node with a name equal to "body".
for (int i = 0; i < childNodes.getLength(); i++) {
  if (childNodes.item(i).getNodeName().equals("body")) {
    bodyElement = (Element) childNodes.item(i);
    break;
  }
}

// Get the second paragraph Element from the body Element.
childNodes = bodyElement.getChildNodes();
Element secondParagraphElement = null;
int count = 0;

for (int i = 0; i < childNodes.getLength(); i++) {
  if (childNodes.item(i).getNodeName().equals("p") && (++count == 2)) {
    secondParagraphElement = (Element) childNodes.item(i);
  }
}

// Get the Text Node from the second paragraph Element.
Text secondParagraphContent = (Text) secondParagraphElement.getFirstChild();

// Output the paragraph content. The getNodeValue() method will
// return null for most Node types including Elements because
// Elements do not contain text. For further information
```

```
      // read the JavaDoc for org.w3c.dom.Node that is included
      // with the Java Development Kit (JDK).
      System.out.println(secondParagraphContent.getNodeValue());
    }
}
```

The code of Listing 2.7 can be tested by passing "`test.xhtml`" (from Listing 2.5) to the `main` method as follows.

```
java -classpath %CLASSPATH%;. javawebbook.dom.DOMTest test.xhtml
```

The above command assumes that Xerces has already been downloaded and its `.jar` files placed in the `CLASSPATH` environment variable, and that `DOMTest` has been compiled. If these conditions were true and the above command were to be executed, output such as the following would be produced.

```
Second Paragraph Content
```

Two other useful DOM methods are defined in the `Document` interface as:

```
public Element getElementById(String elementId)
public NodeList getElementsByTagName(String tagname)
```

The `getElementById` method accepts the value of an XML attribute of type ID for an element in the `Document` and returns that `Element`, or null if no element is found with the specified ID value. For this method to work, the parser must know which attributes of the XML document are of type ID. ID is a type defined by XML. To inform the parser which elements are of type ID, the parser must validate the XML document against a DTD or XML schema. How that is done depends on the parser implementation. For Xerces, the `setFeature` and `setProperty` methods of `org.apache.xerces.parsers.DOMParser` can be called the same way `org.xml.sax.XMLReader` was called in the last section.

The `getElementsByTagName` method accepts the name of a tag and returns a `NodeList` of all the `Elements` in the `Document` that have that name. For example, in Listing 2.7, `document.getElementsByTagName("p")` could be called to get a list of all the paragraph `Elements` in the `Document`.

2.4.3 Java API for XML Processing (JAXP)

JAXP is an API that provides an abstraction layer to XML parser implementations (specifically implementations of DOM and SAX), and applications that process Extensible Stylesheet Language Transformations (XSLT). XSLT allows an XML document to be transformed into an XML document of another form or some other type of document such as HTML. The details of XSLT are discussed in a later section.

JAXP is not another XML parser API; it is a layer above the parser APIs that makes it easier to perform some vendor-specific tasks in a vendor-neutral fashion. JAXP employs the Abstract Factory design pattern to provide a *plugability* layer, which allows an implementation of DOM or SAX, or an application that processes XSLT to be plugged in. The primary classes of the JAXP plugability layer are `javax.xml.parsers.DocumentBuilderFactory`, `javax.xml.parsers.SAXParserFactory`, and `javax.xml.transform.TransformerFactory`. All of these classes are abstract, so an instance of them cannot be created. Instead, the specific factory is asked to create an instance of itself, and then that instance is used to create a `javax.xml.parsers.DocumentBuilder`, `javax.xml.parsers.SAXParser`, or `javax.xml.transform.Transformer`, respectively. `DocumentBuilder` abstracts the underlying DOM parser implementation, `SAXParser` abstracts the underlying SAX parser implementation, and `Transformer` abstracts the underlying XSLT processor. `DocumentBuilder`, `SAXParser`, and `Transformer` are also abstract classes; instances of them can only be obtained through their respective factory. The listing below illustrates how to use these classes.

Listing 2.8 Using the JAXP `DocumentBuilder`, `SAXParser`, and `Transformer`

```
package javawebbook.jaxp;

import java.io.File;
import java.io.IOException;
import javax.xml.parsers.DocumentBuilder;
import javax.xml.parsers.DocumentBuilderFactory;
import javax.xml.parsers.ParserConfigurationException;
import javax.xml.parsers.SAXParser;
import javax.xml.parsers.SAXParserFactory;
import javax.xml.transform.Result;
import javax.xml.transform.Source;
import javax.xml.transform.Transformer;
import javax.xml.transform.TransformerConfigurationException;
import javax.xml.transform.TransformerException;
import javax.xml.transform.TransformerFactory;
import javax.xml.transform.stream.StreamResult;
import javax.xml.transform.stream.StreamSource;
import org.w3c.dom.Document;
import org.xml.sax.SAXException;
import javawebbook.sax.ContentHandlerExample;

public class JAXPTest {
  public static void main(String[] args)
    throws ParserConfigurationException, IOException, SAXException,
           TransformerConfigurationException, TransformerException {
    File xmlFile = new File(args[0]);
    File xslFile = new File(args[1]);
    File xsltResultFile = new File(args[2]);

    // Obtain an instance of the DOM parser factory.
    DocumentBuilderFactory docBuilderFactory = DocumentBuilderFactory.newInstance();
    // Tell the factory that we want the parser to support XML namespaces.
    docBuilderFactory.setNamespaceAware(true);
```

```
    // Tell the factory that we want the parser to validate XML documents.
    // Note that this means validate against a DTD. To validate against
    // an XML schema you must use the setSchema() method. An example is
    // given in the labs at the end of this chapter.
    docBuilderFactory.setValidating(true);
    // Obtain an instance of the DOM parser abstraction.
    DocumentBuilder docBuilder = docBuilderFactory.newDocumentBuilder();
    // Parse the XML document using DOM.
    Document doc = docBuilder.parse(xmlFile);

    // Obtain an instance of the SAX parser factory.
    SAXParserFactory saxParserFactory = SAXParserFactory.newInstance();
    // Tell the factory that we want the parser to support XML namespaces.
    saxParserFactory.setNamespaceAware(true);
    // Tell the factory that we want the parser to validate XML documents.
    // Note that this means validate against a DTD. To validate against
    // an XML schema you must use the setSchema() method. An example is
    // given in the labs at the end of this chapter.
    saxParserFactory.setValidating(true);
    // Obtain an instance of the SAX parser abstraction.
    SAXParser saxParser = saxParserFactory.newSAXParser();
    // Parse the XML document using SAX and the DefaultHandler
    // from Listing 2.6.
    saxParser.parse(xmlFile, new ContentHandlerExample());

    // Obtain an instance of the XSLT Transformer factory.
    TransformerFactory transformerFactory = TransformerFactory.newInstance();
    // Create a JAXP Source for the XSLT file. Source is just an object
    // that acts as a source input for an XSLT Transformer.
    Source xslSource = new StreamSource(xslFile);
    // Obtain an instance of the XSLT processor abstraction.
    Transformer transformer = transformerFactory.newTransformer(xslSource);
    // Create a JAXP Source and Result for the input XML file and
    // the result of the XSLT transformation.
    Source xmlSource = new StreamSource(xmlFile);
    Result xsltResult = new StreamResult(xsltResultFile);
    // Perform the XSL transformation to translate the XML file
    // to another form.
    transformer.transform(xmlSource, xsltResult);
  }
}
```

In Listing 2.8 we used an instance of `java.io.File` as the source document passed to the DOM and SAX parsers; however, `DocumentBuilder` and `SAXParser` both accept a few other sources—a URI as a string, a `java.io.InputStream`, and an `org.xml.sax.InputSource`. That is correct. `DocumentBuilder` (used for parsing XML into DOM) accepts a SAX `InputSource`. `DocumentBuilder` happens to use several SAX classes, but this does not mean that the underlying implementation must use SAX to parse an XML document into an `org.w3c.dom.Document` instance.

`TransformerFactory` accepts an XSLT document when creating an instance of `Transformer`, and `Transformer` requires an XML source document and a place to put the result of the transformation. The input sources are specified as instances of the `javax.xml.transform.Source` interface and the output is specified as an instance of `javax.xml.transform.Result`. `Source` is similar to the SAX `InputSource`. Implementations of `Source` reside in the `javax.xml.transform.dom`, `javax.xml.transform.sax`, and `javax.xml.transform.stream` packages. These implementations are used to encapsulate a DOM `Node`, SAX `InputSource`, or Java `InputStream`, respectively. The `javax.xml.transform.stream.StreamSource` also accepts a `java.io.File`, a `java.io.Reader`, or a URL as a string. Implementations of `Result` also reside in the same packages alongside their respective `Source` implementations.

The underlying JAXP factory implementations (and thus the XML parser implementations and XSLT processor) that are used by setting system properties (or by a few other methods) can be specified.[4] The system property for the DOM parser factory is `javax.xml.parsers.DocumentBuilderFactory`. The system property for the SAX parser factory is `javax.xml.parsers.SAXParserFactory`. The system property for the XSLT processor is `javax.xml.transform.TransformerFactory`. Just call `System.setProperty()` or pass the property and value as a –D option to the virtual machine from the command line (`java -D<property>=<value>`).

JAXP is a very small API that provides a nice uniform interface to DOM and SAX parser implementations as well as XSLT processors. The current version of JAXP is 1.3 and is included with the J2SE version 5.0 (or version 1.5 depending on what you read; Java version numbers 5.0 and 1.5 are synonymous). J2EE version 1.4, which is the version covered by this book, requires support for JAXP version 1.2. J2SE version 1.4.2 includes JAXP version 1.1. There is not much difference between JAXP version 1.1 and 1.2—just new properties that must be supported by the parsers. As far as implementations go, J2SE 1.4.2 includes version 1.1.3 of the Apache Crimson XML parser, which supports DOM and SAX (`http://xml.apache.org/crimson/`), and version 2.4.1 of the Apache Xalan-J XSLT processor (`http://xml.apache.org/xalan-j/`). J2SE 5.0 includes version 2.6.2 of the Apache

---

[4]See the JAXP JavaDocs for information on the various ways that you can configure what XML parser implementations or XSL processor are used. The JavaDoc for `DocumentBuilderFactory` can be found on the Web at `http://java.sun.com/j2se/1.5.0/docs/api/javax/xml/parsers/DocumentBuilderFactory.html#newInstance()`. The JavaDoc for `SAXParserFactory` is at `http://java.sun.com/j2se/1.5.0/docs/api/javax/xml/parsers/SAXParserFactory.html#newInstance()`. The JavaDoc for `TransformerFactory` is at `http://java.sun.com/j2se/1.5.0/docs/api/javax/xml/transform/TransformerFactory.html#newInstance()`.

Xerces parser, which also supports both DOM and SAX (`http://xml.apache.org/xerces2-j/`), and version 2.6.0 of the Apache XSLTC compiling XSLT processor, which is part of Apache Xalan (`http://xml.apache.org/xalan-j/xsltc/`). Therefore, to write applications that perform XML parsing or XSL transformations all that is really needed is the J2SE (sometimes referred to as the JDK).

2.4.4 Alternatives to DOM: JDOM and dom4j

DOM has proven to be very useful, but it can be quite awkward to use. The W3C designed DOM to be independent of any programming language, and for that reason, it does not take advantage of the strengths of any particular language, such as Java. However, a few very good Java-based solutions for accessing, manipulating, and outputting XML do exist. Two of the most popular are JDOM (`http://jdom.org`) and dom4j (`http://dom4j.org`). This book does not cover these libraries in detail. Instead, this section gives a brief description of the libraries and code examples. More about the libraries can be found by visiting their respective Web sites.

Both JDOM and dom4j are open source projects, so they can be downloaded and used for free. Both APIs can be used with JAXP-compliant parsers such Xerces. The features of both projects are similar—they both developed a Java-specific API that takes advantage of built-in Java classes such as the Java collections; provides an object model to represent an XML tree in memory; is intuitive; is easy to use; integrates well with the JAXP, SAX, and DOM APIs; supports XPath (`http://www.w3.org/TR/xpath`) for navigating through XML documents; and is more efficient with a smaller memory footprint than DOM. The main difference between the two is that JDOM is built around concrete classes and dom4j is built around interfaces. This gives dom4j much greater flexibility with the side effect that it is more complex. With its greater flexibility, dom4j provides addition features over JDOM such as event-based processing for handling very large documents or streamed documents. The dom4j project also aims to be a more complete solution than JDOM, the goal of which is to solve only about 80% of the Java/XML problems.

The following listing illustrates how to do some things in JDOM.

Listing 2.9 Example JDOM Code

```
package javawebbook.jdom;

import java.io.File;
import java.io.IOException;
import java.util.List;
import org.jdom.Document;
import org.jdom.Element;
import org.jdom.Namespace;
import org.jdom.Parent;
import org.jdom.JDOMException;
import org.jdom.input.SAXBuilder;
```

```
import org.jdom.output.Format;
import org.jdom.output.XMLOutputter;
import org.jdom.transform.XSLTransformer;

public class JDOMTest {
  public static void main(String[] args) throws JDOMException, IOException {
    String xslFileName = args[1];

    // Create an XML document from scratch.
    // This builds: <books><book><title>My Book</title></book></books>
    Document myDoc = new Document();
    Element books = new Element("books");
    Element book = new Element("book");
    Element title = new Element("title");
    title.setText("My Book");
    book.addContent(title);
    books.addContent(book);
    myDoc.addContent(books);

    // Pretty-print XML to an OutputStream.
    XMLOutputter outp = new XMLOutputter(Format.getPrettyFormat());
    System.out.println("\nDocument build from scratch:");
    outp.output(myDoc, System.out);

    // Parse an XML document.
    SAXBuilder builder = new SAXBuilder();
    builder.setValidation(true);
    // Ignores ignorable whitespace so the in-memory object model
    // does not have mostly useless objects, like in DOM.
    builder.setIgnoringElementContentWhitespace(true);
    // Parse the XHTML file from Listing 2.5.
    Document doc = builder.build(new File("test.xhtml"));

    // Manipulate the document.

    // Get the root element of the document.
    Element root = doc.getRootElement();
    // Get all children of the root element.
    List allChildren = root.getChildren();
    Namespace ns = root.getNamespace();
    // Get all paragraph elements.
    List namedChildren = root.getChild("body", ns).getChildren("p", ns);
    // Get first paragraph element.
    Element firstChild = root.getChild("body", ns).getChild("p", ns);
    // Change the text content.
```

```
    firstChild.setText("This is the first paragraph");

    // Copy the document.
    Document docCopy = (Document) doc.clone();
    Element body = docCopy.getRootElement().getChild("body", ns);
    // Remove the first paragraph.
    Element firstP = (Element) body.getChild("p", ns).detach();
    // Copy first paragraph from original document.
    firstP = (Element) firstChild.clone();
    // Add the copy back. Since we didn't provide an index, the
    // copy will be appended to the end and won't be the first
    // paragraph anymore.
    body.addContent(firstP);
    // To move an element from one document to another you just
    // remove it from one and add it to the other.

    // Output the manipulated document.
    System.out.println("\nManipulated document:");
    outp.output(docCopy, System.out);

    // Process XSL Transform.
    XSLTransformer transformer = new XSLTransformer(new File(xslFileName));
    Document doc2 = transformer.transform(doc);
  }
}
```

The next listing illustrates how to do the same things in dom4j.

Listing 2.10 Example dom4j Code

```
package javawebbook.dom4j;

import java.io.File;
import java.io.IOException;
import java.io.UnsupportedEncodingException;
import java.util.List;
import javax.xml.transform.Transformer;
import javax.xml.transform.TransformerConfigurationException;
import javax.xml.transform.TransformerException;
import javax.xml.transform.TransformerFactory;
import javax.xml.transform.stream.StreamSource;
import org.dom4j.Document;
import org.dom4j.DocumentException;
import org.dom4j.DocumentHelper;
import org.dom4j.Element;
import org.dom4j.Namespace;
```

```
import org.dom4j.Node;
import org.dom4j.QName;
import org.dom4j.io.DocumentResult;
import org.dom4j.io.DocumentSource;
import org.dom4j.io.SAXReader;
import org.dom4j.io.OutputFormat;
import org.dom4j.io.XMLWriter;

public class dom4jTest {
  public static void main(String[] args)
    throws UnsupportedEncodingException, IOException,
           DocumentException, TransformerConfigurationException,
           TransformerException {
    String xslFileName = args[1];

    // Create an XML document from scratch.
    // This builds: <books><book><title>My Book</title></book></books>
    Document myDoc = DocumentHelper.createDocument();
    Element books = myDoc.addElement("books");
    Element book = books.addElement("book");
    Element title = book.addElement("title");
    title.addText("My Book");

    // Pretty-print XML to an OutputStream.
    OutputFormat format = OutputFormat.createPrettyPrint();
    XMLWriter writer = new XMLWriter(System.out, format);
    System.out.println("\nDocument build from scratch:");
    writer.write(myDoc);

    // Parse an XML document.
    SAXReader reader = new SAXReader();
    reader.setValidation(true);
    // Ignores ignorable whitespace so the in-memory object model
    // does not have mostly useless objects, like in DOM.
    reader.setStripWhitespaceText(true);
    // Parse the XHTML file from Listing 2.5.
    Document doc = reader.read(new File("test.xhtml"));

    // Manipulate the document.

    // Get the root element of the document.
    Element root = doc.getRootElement();
    // Get all children of the root element.
    List allChildren = root.elements();
```

```
    Namespace ns = root.getNamespace();
    // Get all paragraph elements.
    List namedChildren =
      root.element(new QName("body", ns)).elements(new QName("p", ns));
    // Get first paragraph element.
    Element firstChild =
      root.element(new QName("body", ns)).element(new QName("p", ns));
    // Change the text content.
    firstChild.setText("This is the first paragraph");

    // Copy the document.
    Document docCopy = (Document) doc.clone();
    Element body =docCopy.getRootElement().element(new QName("body", ns));
    // Remove the first paragraph.
    Element firstP = (Element) body.element(new QName("p", ns)).detach();
    // Copy first paragraph from original document.
    firstP = (Element) firstChild.clone();
    // Add the copy back. The copy won't be the first paragraph
    // anymore.
    body.add(firstP);
    // To move an element from one document to another you just
    // remove it from one and add it to the other.

    // Output the manipulated document.
    System.out.println("\nManipulated document:");
    writer.write(docCopy);

    // Process XSL Transform.
    TransformerFactory factory = TransformerFactory.newInstance();
    Transformer transformer =
      factory.newTransformer(new StreamSource(new File(xslFileName)));
    DocumentSource source = new DocumentSource(doc);
    DocumentResult result = new DocumentResult();
    transformer.transform(source, result);
    Document doc2 = result.getDocument();
  }
}
```

2.5 Transforming XML

Extensible Stylesheet Language Transformations (XSLT) are part of the XML Stylesheet Language (XSL). XSL Transformations provide a way to translate the semantic descriptions of an XML document to presentational descriptions. One reason to do this might be to display the XML document in a Web browser. Modern Web browsers, including Microsoft Internet Explorer 6 and Mozilla Firefox, include support for XSLT stylesheets.

XSL Transformations are only one part of the XML Stylesheet Language. The other part is XSL Formatting Objects, or XSL-FO. XSL-FO is a complete page layout specification suitable for describing pages for print or similar media.

XSL Transformations allow XML data to be reordered, permit the display of attributes, and allow elements to be displayed in an order other than that in which they are given in the XML document. XSL Transformations can add constant data to the result, including XHTML tags and CSS style specifications.

One use of XSL Transformations is reformatting XML documents for Web display, but there is much more that can be done with XSLT. Any linear output format can be produced using XSLT. The same XML document, with different XSLT stylesheets, can be displayed in a Web browser or converted to static XHTML, written as comma-separated values for importation into a spreadsheet, and written as a sequence of SQL INSERT statements for loading into a database. An important use of XSL Transformations is to produce XSL-FO specifications from XML documents.

A word of caution is needed. An XSL stylesheet need not select all elements and attributes of an XML document for display, and elements and attributes that are not selected are not shown in the displayed XHTML document. However, if the XSLT stylesheet is applied by the Web browser, the original XML document is the source document, and the entire XML document is transmitted to the browser and is visible using the browser's "view source" tool. If an XML document contains confidential information that is not to be visible to a Web browser's user, the XSL Transformation must be applied before the document is served by the Web server, or by the Web server while the document is being served. In that way, the browser will receive only XHTML markup containing only those elements selected for display by the XSLT stylesheet.

In addition to the security implications of serving XML to browsers, not all browsers handle XSLT markup equally well. The example below works under Microsoft Internet Explorer but fails with Mozilla Firefox. (A small change could correct the failure.) By performing transformations at the server, it becomes possible to know exactly what XHTML is presented to the browser, something that is essential when trying to support the widest variety of browsers.

A major feature of XSLT is the template. Writing an XSLT stylesheet involves writing templates for those elements that are to be a part of the output. The XSLT processor traverses the XML document tree looking for templates that match elements in the document. Templates can include XML element and attribute contents, other markup, such as XHTML tags, and other literal and computed values. Look at this XSLT stylesheet fragment:

```
<xsl:template match="department">
  <xsl:text>Department: </xsl:text>
```

```
  <xsl:value-of select="." />
  <br />
</xsl:template>
```

In an XML document that contained <department> elements, this fragment would output the word "Department" followed by a colon and a space, the contents of the <department> element, and the markup <br /> for each <department> element it encountered. Strictly speaking, the <xsl:text> tags enclosing "Department: " are not necessary; they prevent the XSLT processor from modifying the whitespace. The <br /> tag is XHTML markup; it is not in the xsl namespace, so it will be copied to the output just as any other text. (Markup included in an XSLT stylesheet cannot cause the stylesheet to fail to be well formed. The biggest implication of this is that opening and closing tags for included markup must match.)

The other important thing to notice in the example fragment is the <xsl:value-of > element. It can be used for computation, but is most often used to select elements or attributes of the input document for writing to output. The select attribute of <xsl:value-of > is an XPath expression that determines what value from the input document is to be written to the output. This section provides some XPath examples, but does not cover XPath in detail. In the example above, the dot indicates the element at the current point in the input document tree.

The default behavior of XSLT is to copy the element values and whitespace outside of elements to the output document. A template at the outermost level can be used to specify which inner elements are to be used, and in what order.

Let us return to our memo example. Here is a version of the sample memo with most of the options exercised.

```
<?xml version="1.0" encoding="iso-8859-1"?>
<!DOCTYPE memo SYSTEM "memo.dtd">
<?xml-stylesheet type="text/xsl" href="memo.xsl"?>
<memo date="15 April 1951">
  <from>&boss;</from>
  <to>
    <name>
      <surname>MacArthur</surname>
    </name>
    <name>
      <surname>Eisenhower</surname>
      <forename>Dwight</forename>
      <forename>David</forename>
    </name>
    <department>Senate</department>
    <department>House of Representatives</department>
    Troops
```

```
  </to>
  <body>The buck stops here. </body>
</memo>
```

An XSLT stylesheet to process this memo, or any memo described in the DTD or schema reviewed earlier, is given below. This stylesheet rewrites the memo for display in a Web browser; other stylesheets could be used to rewrite the memo for other purposes. One of the great advantages of XML with XSLT stylesheets is that the same document can be reformatted for many different purposes.

```
<xsl:stylesheet version="1.0" xmlns:xsl="http://www.w3.org/1999/XSL/Transform">
  <xsl:template match="memo">
    <html>
      <head>
        <title>Memo</title>
        <meta http-equiv="Content-Type"
              content="text/html; charset=iso-8859-1"/>
        <style type="text/css">
          <xsl:text>
            h1 {
              font-size: 120%;
              font-family: arial, sans-serif;
              text-align:center
            }
            td { vertical-align: top; }
          </xsl:text>
        </style>
      </head>
      <body style="background-color: #FFFFFF">
        <h1>Memorandum</h1>
        <table>
          <tr>
            <td>To:</td>
            <td>
              <xsl:value-of select="to/text()" />
              <br />
              <xsl:apply-templates select="to/department" />
              <xsl:apply-templates select="to/name" />
            </td>
          </tr>
          <tr>
            <td>From:</td>
```

```
            <td><xsl:value-of select="from" /></td>
          </tr>
          <tr>
            <td>Date:</td>
            <td><xsl:value-of select="@date" /></td>
          </tr>
          <tr>
            <td>Priority:</td>
            <td><xsl:value-of select="@priority" /></td>
          </tr>
        </table>
        <hr />
        <p><xsl:value-of select="body"/></p>
      </body>
    </html>
  </xsl:template>

  <xsl:template match="department">
    <xsl:value-of select="."/>
    <br />
  </xsl:template>

  <xsl:template match="name">
    <xsl:for-each select="forename">
      <xsl:value-of select="."/><xsl:text> </xsl:text>
    </xsl:for-each>
    <xsl:value-of select="surname"/>
    <br />
  </xsl:template>
</xsl:stylesheet>
```

We are rewriting the memo document for the Web. The following figure shows how it is displayed using Microsoft Internet Explorer 6.0. (As already mentioned, this example does not work with Mozilla Firefox, which complains that the entity `&boss;` is not defined.)

The first template of the stylesheet matches the "memo" element of the memo document; that is the top-level element. The next several lines are html markup that are copied directly to the output. These lines set up the head of the XHTML document, establish some CSS style specifications, and begin an XHTML table structure.

The next XSLT is the `<xsl:value-of select="to/text()" />` in the second table data cell of the first row. The XPath expression `to/text()` specifies selecting the text portion of the `<to>` element. (Recall that the `<to>` element can contain `<name>` and `<department>` elements as well as text; we want only the text at the moment.) The text part of <to> is followed by an XHTML line break tag.

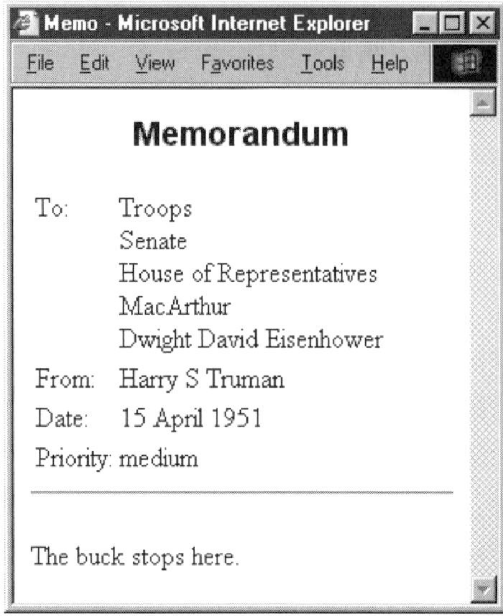

Next an <xsl:apply-templates> element applies the template for processing department elements. The XPath applies the department template to all department elements within the <to> element. There are two such elements, "Senate" and "House of Representatives." Iteration over the number of elements present is automatic. The actual department template is near the bottom of the stylesheet. It selects the value of the department element with the dot expression, then emits a line break.

The two <department> elements are physically together in the input file, but they need not have been. All <department> subelements of the <to> element will be copied to the output in the order of the input file, and intervening elements will be skipped, although we can and will come back and process them after the departments have been processed.

Another <xsl:apply-templates> applies a template to the <name> subelements of <to>. This template is a little more interesting. According to the DTD (and the schema), a name consists of exactly one surname and zero or more forenames. The template uses <xsl:for-each> to iterate over the <forename> elements, selecting each one and following it with a space. Finally, the surname is selected. In the case of MacArthur, only the surname is present in the input document, so that is all that is copied to the output. Eisenhower has two <forename> elements, and they are copied to the output in the order they appear in the input XML document.

The From: line of the formatted memo is selected from the <from> element, which contains the general entity &boss;. The XML parser will have performed entity replacement when the input XML document was parsed, so the entity value, "Harry S Truman," is placed in the From: line of the memo. Only validating parsers are required to retrieve the DTD, which may explain why this document does not work with Firefox.

Attributes are retrieved with the `@` operator, so the date can be placed in the output document with `<xsl:value-of select="@date" />`. We have not changed the context (location within the input XML document) so the context remains that of the <memo> element and the date attribute is available without the need for an XPath expression more complex than the attribute operator.

The last interesting element is the Priority: header. Refer to `memo.xml`; it does not contain a priority attribute, yet `<xsl:value-of select="@priority" />` has extracted a priority value of "medium" from the <memo> element. The answer lies in the DTD, which declared priority to be optional and assigned a default value of "medium." When the input document was parsed by the validating parser, not only was `&boss;` replaced with "Harry S Truman," a priority attribute was added to <catalog> and given the default value of "medium." It was this structure that was passed to the XSLT processor for selection and formatting of output. Finally, the stylesheet describes some more markup to close the XHTML table, write a horizontal rule, and copy the <body> subelement of <memo> to the output, enclosed in paragraph tags and followed by the ending markup for the XHTML.

XSLT is a full programming language, although designed for reformatting XML documents and itself expressed as XML. There are more than 50 XSLT elements and more than 200 attributes. The expressive power of XSLT is shown by the fact that the example used only five XSLT elements, several attributes, and some simple XPath expressions.

XPath expressions look a lot like directory path expressions for operating systems; that is not surprising because both describe a path through a tree structure. Absolute paths begin with a slash and start at the root element of the document. The XSLT processor traverses the input document in preorder fashion and keeps track of its current position. The current position is called the context node, and it is referred to with a period. Relative path specifications are relative to the context node and do not begin with a slash. For most applications of XSLT, absolute paths and paths relative to the current context will be enough. The example uses relative paths and the "." path only. Here are a few possible XPath specifications and their meanings:

`/`	The root of the document.
`.`	Contents of the current context node.
`to/text()`	Contents of the text node of the <to> element (relative to the context node).
`/memo/to/name`	All the <name> elements in the document.
`//surname`	All <surname> elements, even if at different levels.
`/memo/to/name[1]`	First <name> child element of /memo/to.
`/memo/to/name[last()]`	Last <name> child element of /memo/to.

`@date`	Contents of the date attribute of the current context element.
`/memo@date`	Contents of the date attribute of the `<memo>` element.

There is much more to XPath than this, including functions and operators. Generally you would need advanced XPath expressions only for very complex source documents.

We have already commented that XSLT is a full-fledged programming language. You can write very sophisticated transformations with only three or four of the 50-plus XSLT elements. The root element of an XSLT stylesheet must be a `<stylesheet>` element that binds a prefix (we used `xsl`) to the W3C name `http://www.w3.org/1999/XSL/Transform`. Using namespaces requires that a local prefix must also be bound to the local namespace name, as shown in the example in the Examples and Practice Labs in Section 2.6. Sophisticated results can be obtained using only the first three elements in the list below. We include the fourth and fifth elements in the example, although it could have been coded without them.

```
<xsl:value-of select="xpath_expression">
<xsl:template match="xpath_expression">
<xsl:apply-templates select="xpath_expression">
<xsl:for-each select="xpath_expression">
<xsl:text>any text<xsl:text>
```

The `<value-of>` element places an element or attribute value in the output stream; the element or attribute is chosen based on the XPath expression in the `select` attribute. Often the expression will be as simple as "." to represent the current context node.

The `<template>` element describes the action to take when an element in the tree matches the template's `match=` attribute. The XSLT processor starts at the root node of the XML document and does a preorder traversal of the tree described by the document. A preorder traversal means that the first subelement of the root is visited first, then its first subelement, and so on, depth first and left to right. It is the order of tree traversal, not the order of templates in the stylesheet, that determines when they are applied. Templates can be applied out of order, which implicitly inhibits in-order application. In the example, the first `<template>` element matches "memo." This template generates all the preparatory XHTML output, then explicitly calls the other templates at the appropriate place. By using explicit calls, the elements in the XML document are sent to the output in a different order. The example defines templates for `<name>` and `<department>`.

The `<apply-templates>` element directs the XSLT processor to apply any templates for which the template's `match` attribute matches the XPath expression in `<apply-templates>`. Explicitly applying a template inhibits automatic application. In the example, the templates for `to` and `department` were applied before the `<from>` element was reached, allowing the heading elements in the result document to appear in a different order than the elements in the XML input document.

Strictly speaking, the `<for-each>` element is not needed in this example. The XSLT processor will automatically iterate over elements as they are reached in traversing the XML document tree. It was included to show some more of the power of XSLT. By using a more complex XPath expression, <for-each> can iterate over elements that are not together in the XML tree, or even over collections of elements. Similarly, the <text> element is unnecessary for this simple example. Text and well-formed markup can be copied from the stylesheet to the output document simply by including them at the proper point in a template in the stylesheet. The <text> element can be used to preserve whitespace, and, by setting an attribute, can disable entity substitution in the output.

Another example XSLT stylesheet is given in the next section. It introduces the <sort> element, which can reorder collections of branches in the input document tree. In the example, a collection of books is sorted by author.

2.6 Examples and Practice Labs

This section provides some example DTD, XML Schema, and Java code for parsing and transforming XML documents.

2.6.1 Lab 1 Example Document Type Definition (DTD)

We start with an XML document describing a book; this is the example from the beginning of the chapter, modified slightly to reflect the material we have already covered.

```
<?xml version="1.0" encoding="iso-8859-1" ?>
<book isbn="123456789">
  <book-title>Paul Clifford</book-title>
  <author>
    <surname>Bulwer-Lytton</surname>
    <forename>Edward</forename>
    <forename>George</forename>
  </author>
  <year>1830</year>
  <price currency="usd" type="retail">5.50</price>
  <text>
    <chapter number="1">
      <chapter-title>Chapter 1</chapter-title>
      <para>It was a dark and stormy night...</para>
    </chapter>
  </text>
</book>
```

We can derive an informal description of a book from the example document. A book has a unique identifying number, its ISBN, a title, and one or more authors. All authors must have surnames, and may have one or more forenames. The book also has a year of publication and a price. The price has attributes of currency and type. Valid types are wholesale and retail. The text of a book is divided into one or more chapters, each of which has a unique chapter number and a chapter title. Each chapter consists of one or more paragraphs of text.

A DTD for the example document follows:

```
<?xml version="1.0" encoding="iso-8859-1" ?>
<!ELEMENT book (book-title, author, year, price, text)>
<!ELEMENT book-title (#PCDATA)>
<!ELEMENT author (surname, forename*)>
<!ELEMENT surname (#PCDATA)>
<!ELEMENT forename (#PCDATA)>
<!ELEMENT year (#PCDATA)>
<!ELEMENT price (#PCDATA)>
<!ELEMENT text (chapter+)>
<!ELEMENT chapter (chapter-title, para+)>
<!ELEMENT chapter-title (#PCDATA)>
<!ELEMENT para (#PCDATA)>
<!ATTLIST book isbn CDATA #REQUIRED>
<!ATTLIST price currency CDATA #REQUIRED
          type (retail | wholesale) #REQUIRED>
<!ATTLIST chapter number ID #REQUIRED>
```

The first element declaration is for the `book` element, the root element of the XML document. The list in parentheses is an ordered list of required subelements of `book`. The comma is the "and" operator. This list says that each of the five listed elements is required to be present, and in the order given. The declaration for `book-title` says the title may contain parsed character data. Book titles may contain any text legal in the document's encoding, and may contain parsed entities. Book titles may not contain subelements. One could not decide to insert a `<subtitle>` element without first changing the DTD. The `author` declaration requires a `surname` element and zero or more `forename` elements. The asterisk following `forename` modifies the declaration by specifying zero or more instances. The `ATTLIST` declarations declare attribute lists for elements. The `book` element has one attribute, `isbn`, and it can contain `CDATA`. The `CDATA` declaration allows any data in the character set of the document. In the example, nothing requires the `isbn` attribute to "look like" an ISBN. The `type` attribute of `price` can be only "retail" or "wholesale" because those are the only things declared in an enumerated list of allowed values. Coding `<price type="sale">` would cause a validation error.

The example document can be validated against the DTD shown by using a validating parser such as the Xerces parser.

2.6.2 Lab 2 Example XML Schema

A collector of old books has created an XML catalog document listing the title, author, date of publication, publisher, city, condition, and value. A fragment of the catalog looks as follows:

```
<?xml version="1.0" encoding="UTF-8" ?>
```

```
<catalog class="Miscellaneous Old Books">
  <book>
    <title>Paul Clifford</title>
    <author>
      <surname>Bulwer-Lytton</surname>
      <forename>Edward</forename>
      <forename>George</forename>
    </author>
    <year>1830</year>
    <publisher>Colburn</publisher>
    <city>London</city>
    <condition>Good</condition>
    <value currency="usd">58.00</value>
  </book>
</catalog>
```

An XML Schema is wanted to validate this document. No constraints are to be put on the text fields. Development of a constraint on the year is reserved as an exercise. The values of the books can be expressed in one of only three currencies—US dollars, British pounds, or Euros. The value must be greater than zero (in whatever currency that is used) and not greater than 1,000. (Otherwise, the book belongs in the "Rare and Antique Books" catalog instead.)

Here is a schema that provides a formal description of the catalog of books:

Listing 2.11 XML Schema for a Catalog of Books

```
<xsd:schema xmlns:xsd="http://www.w3.org/2001/XMLSchema"
    xmlns:cat="http://webdev.spsu.edu/namespaces/catalog"
    targetNamespace="http://webdev.spsu.edu/namespaces/catalog"
    elementFormDefault="qualified">
  <xsd:element name="catalog">
    <xsd:complexType>
      <xsd:sequence>
        <xsd:element name="book" type="cat:bookStructure"
                     maxOccurs="unbounded"/>
      </xsd:sequence>
      <xsd:attribute name="class" type="xsd:string" use="required"/>
    </xsd:complexType>
  </xsd:element>

  <xsd:complexType name="bookStructure">
   <xsd:sequence>
     <xsd:element name="title" type="xsd:string"/>
     <xsd:element name="author" type="cat:nameStructure"/>
     <xsd:element name="year" type="xsd:string"/>
     <xsd:element name="publisher" type="xsd:string"/>
```

```
      <xsd:element name="city" type="xsd:string"/>
      <xsd:element name="condition" type="xsd:string"/>
      <xsd:element name="value">
        <xsd:complexType>
          <xsd:simpleContent>
            <xsd:extension base="cat:currencyValue">
              <xsd:attribute name="currency" type="cat:currencyType"/>
            </xsd:extension>
          </xsd:simpleContent>
        </xsd:complexType>
      </xsd:element>
    </xsd:sequence>
  </xsd:complexType>

  <xsd:simpleType name="currencyType">
    <xsd:restriction base="xsd:string">
      <xsd:enumeration value="usd"/>
      <xsd:enumeration value="eur"/>
      <xsd:enumeration value="gbp"/>
    </xsd:restriction>
  </xsd:simpleType>

  <xsd:simpleType name="currencyValue">
    <xsd:restriction base="xsd:decimal">
      <xsd:minExclusive value="0"/>
      <xsd:maxInclusive value="1000"/>
      <xsd:fractionDigits value="2"/>
    </xsd:restriction>
  </xsd:simpleType>

  <xsd:complexType name="nameStructure">
    <xsd:sequence>
      <xsd:element name="surname" type="xsd:string"
                   minOccurs="1" maxOccurs="1"/>
      <xsd:element name="forename" type="xsd:string"
                   minOccurs="0" maxOccurs="unbounded"/>
    </xsd:sequence>
  </xsd:complexType>
</xsd:schema>
```

The approach taken to building this schema was to define the XML document, assuming the existence of specialized data types and structures when the XML Schema primitive types were not sufficient, then to define the needed types and structures. In a few cases, the example uses primitive types where user-defined types would serve better. You will define the necessary new types when you complete the exercises.

Before we look at the details of the example, we look at the namespaces used. The `xsd:` prefix is bound to the World Wide Web Consortium's XML Schema namespace name and the `cat:` prefix is bound to the name chosen for the book catalog. When using namespaces and changing `elementFormDefault` to "qualified," both of which are good practice, it is necessary to explicitly qualify the target namespace name in the XML schema.

The example defines two types and a structure. The `currencyType` is a `simpleType` used for the `currency` attribute of the `<value>` element. It is derived from the primitive `string` type by enumeration. Only the three values given are permitted in the `currency` attribute. The `currency` attribute could also have been given a default value or made required, and best practice would be to have done one or the other.

The `currencyValue` type is derived by restriction from the `decimal` primitive type. The problem specification stated that the value needed to be greater than zero. By setting `minExclusive` to zero, we say that value may be close to zero, but may not be equal to zero. The upper bound uses `maxInclusive`; the value may be anything up to and including 1,000. There is a limit of two on the fraction digits facet.

The `nameStructure` type is borrowed from the memo example earlier in the chapter.

2.6.3 Lab 3 SAX Example

In this example, we show how to use SAX within the context of JAXP. We create a simple XML schema based on Listing 2.11, which defines an XML document that contains a listing of books. We use this XML schema to create an XML file containing data about a few books. Then we write Java code to parse the XML file using SAX in order to find a book with a given ISBN.

This example required Java version 5.0 or later. If you don't have Java 5.0 installed on your computer, download it from the following URL and follow the installation instructions to get it installed on your computer. Note, you need the JDK, not the JRE: `http://java.sun.com/j2se/1.5.0/download.jsp`.

We begin by creating the XML schema file. Create the following listing in directory `javawebbook/jaxp/sax`.

Listing 2.12 javawebbook/jaxp/sax/books.xsd

```
<xsd:schema xmlns:xsd="http://www.w3.org/2001/XMLSchema"
    xmlns:bks="http://javawebbook.edu/namespaces/books"
    targetNamespace="http://javawebbook.edu/namespaces/books"
    elementFormDefault="qualified">
  <xsd:element name="books">
    <xsd:complexType>
      <xsd:sequence>
        <xsd:element name="book" type="bks:book"
                     minOccurs="0" maxOccurs="unbounded"/>
      </xsd:sequence>
    </xsd:complexType>
```

```
  </xsd:element>

  <xsd:complexType name="book">
    <xsd:sequence>
      <xsd:element name="title" type="xsd:string"/>
      <xsd:element name="author" type="bks:person"
                   minOccurs="0" maxOccurs="unbounded"/>
      <xsd:element name="pubDate" type="xsd:date"/>
      <xsd:element name="publisher" type="xsd:string"/>
    </xsd:sequence>
    <xsd:attribute name="isbn" type="xsd:string"/>
  </xsd:complexType>

  <xsd:complexType name="person">
    <xsd:sequence>
      <xsd:element name="surname" type="xsd:string"/>
      <xsd:element name="forename" type="xsd:string"/>
    </xsd:sequence>
  </xsd:complexType>
</xsd:schema>
```

The schema of Listing 2.12 defines the root element of the XML document as `books`, which contains zero or more complex types named `book`. The `book` type contains several elements and a single attribute called `isbn`, which is used to store the International Standard Book Number (ISBN) for a book. The child elements of the `book` type are defined as `string` types, a `date` type, and a `person` type, which is used to identify the authors of the book. The `person` type contains two elements that accept `string` types for a single surname and a single forename. This example does not allow multiple forenames such as Listing 2.11.

Next, create an instance of the XML document defined by Listing 2.12 by creating the following file in directory `javawebbook/jaxp/sax`.

Listing 2.13 javawebbook/jaxp/sax/books.xml

```
<?xml version="1.0" encoding="UTF-8"?>
<books xmlns="http://javawebbook.edu/namespaces/books">
  <book isbn="0201633612">
    <title>Design Patterns</title>
    <author>
      <surname>Gamma</surname>
      <forename>Erich</forename>
    </author>
    <author>
      <surname>Helm</surname>
      <forename>Richard</forename>
```

```
    </author>
    <author>
      <surname>Johnson</surname>
      <forename>Ralph</forename>
    </author>
    <author>
      <surname>Vlissides</surname>
      <forename>John</forename>
    </author>
    <pubDate>1995-01-15</pubDate>
    <publisher>Addison-Wesley Professional</publisher>
  </book>
  <book isbn="0321247140">
    <title>Design Patterns Explained: A New Perspective on Object-Oriented Design, 2nd
Edition</title>
    <author>
      <surname>Shalloway</surname>
      <forename>Alan</forename>
    </author>
    <author>
      <surname>Trott</surname>
      <forename>James</forename>
    </author>
    <pubDate>2004-10-12</pubDate>
    <publisher>Addison-Wesley Professional</publisher>
  </book>
  <book isbn="0596007124">
    <title>Head First Design Patterns</title>
    <author>
      <surname>Freeman</surname>
      <forename>Elisabeth</forename>
    </author>
    <author>
      <surname>Freeman</surname>
      <forename>Eric</forename>
    </author>
    <author>
      <surname>Bates</surname>
      <forename>Bert</forename>
    </author>
    <author>
      <surname>Sierra</surname>
      <forename>Kathy</forename>
    </author>
```

```
    <pubDate>2004-10-01</pubDate>
    <publisher>O'Reilly</publisher>
  </book>
</books>
```

Note that the italicized line of Listing 2.13 must be entered on a single line. Listing 2.13 contains information on three different books. Feel free to add more books to this document if you like. Note that the default namespace for the XML document is given in the opening `books` tag. Therefore all of the XML elements in the document are qualified as required by the XML schema in Listing 2.12.

Now let us create the Java code to process this XML document. We are going to parse this XML document using SAX. SAX does not provide an in-memory representation for the document as DOM does; however, we would like to be able to retain the information for the found book in memory. So the first Java code we should create is an object model containing the types defined by the XML schema of Listing 2.12. We do not need to retain the entire document in memory, only the single book we found; therefore, we will just create a `Person` type and a `Book` type. Create the following two listings in the directory `javawebbook/jaxp/sax`.

Listing 2.14 javawebbook/jaxp/sax/Person.java

```
package javawebbook.jaxp.sax;

public class Person {
  private String surname = null;
  private String forename = null;

  public String getSurname() {
    return surname;
  }

  public void setSurname(String surname) {
    this.surname = surname;
  }

  public String getForename() {
    return forename;
  }

  public void setForename(String forename) {
    this.forename = forename;
  }
}
```

The Person class is very simple, containing only a single surname and a single forename. The Book class given below contains an array of Persons to store all the authors of the book.

Listing 2.15 javawebbook/jaxp/sax/Book.java

```
package javawebbook.jaxp.sax;

import java.util.Calendar;

public class Book {
  private String isbn = null;
  private String title = null;
  private Person[] authors = null;
  private Calendar pubDate = null;
  private String publisher = null;

  public String getIsbn() {
    return isbn;
  }

  public void setIsbn(String isbn) {
    this.isbn = isbn;
  }

  public String getTitle() {
    return title;
  }

  public void setTitle(String title) {
    this.title = title;
  }

  public Person[] getAuthors() {
    return authors;
  }

  public void setAuthors(Person[] authors) {
    this.authors = authors;
  }

  public Calendar getPubDate() {
    return pubDate;
  }
```

```
  public void setPubDate(Calendar pubDate) {
    this.pubDate = pubDate;
  }

  public String getPublisher() {
    return publisher;
  }

  public void setPublisher(String publisher) {
    this.publisher = publisher;
  }
}
```

Now we can create the SAX-specific code. We start with the event handlers by creating a class that extends `org.xml.sax.helpers.DefaultHandler`. This class will look for a book with a given ISBN in the data that it receives from the SAX parser. Create the following listing in the directory `javawebbook/jaxp/sax`.

Listing 2.16 javawebbook/jaxp/sax/BookIsbnSearch.java

```
package javawebbook.jaxp.sax;

import java.text.DateFormat;
import java.text.ParseException;
import java.text.SimpleDateFormat;
import java.util.Calendar;
import java.util.Date;
import java.util.Set;
import java.util.LinkedHashSet;
import org.xml.sax.Attributes;
import org.xml.sax.SAXException;
import org.xml.sax.SAXParseException;
import org.xml.sax.helpers.DefaultHandler;

public class BookIsbnSearch extends DefaultHandler {
  private String isbn = null;
  private Book book = null;
  private Person author = null;
  private Set<Person> authors = new LinkedHashSet<Person>();
  private StringBuffer buffer = new StringBuffer();
  private DateFormat format = new SimpleDateFormat("yyyy-MM-dd");
  private boolean foundTag = false;
  private boolean processTag = false;

  public BookIsbnSearch(String isbn) {
    if (isbn == null) {
```

```
      throw new IllegalArgumentException("ISBN cannot be null.");
    }

    this.isbn = isbn;
  }

  public Book getSearchResult() {
    return this.book;
  }

  public void startElement(String uri, String localName,
                           String qName, Attributes atts)
    throws SAXException {

    if (!foundTag) {
      String isbnValue = null;

      // Search the list of attributes for the isbn attribute.
      for (int i = 0; i < atts.getLength(); i++) {
        if (atts.getLocalName(i).equals("isbn")) {
          isbnValue = atts.getValue(i);
        }
      }

      // If the element name is "book" and there is an "isbn"
      // attribute equal to our specified value, then we found the book.
      if (localName.equals("book") && isbn.equals(isbnValue)) {
        foundTag = true;
        book = new Book();
        book.setIsbn(isbnValue);
        processTag = true;
      }
    }else {
      // Clear the string buffer since we are starting a new tag.
      buffer.delete(0, buffer.length());

      // Create a new Person object for each author.
      if (localName.equals("author")) {
        author = new Person();
      }
    }
  }

  public void characters(char[] chars, int start, int length)
    throws SAXException {
```

```
    // If we have found the first <p> tag and we are currently
    // processing it, then capture its text content.
    if (processTag) {
      buffer.append(chars, start, length);
    }
  }

  public void endElement(String uri, String localName, String qName)
    throws SAXException {

    if (processTag) {
      if (localName.equals("title")) {
        book.setTitle(buffer.toString());
      }else if (localName.equals("surname")) {
        author.setSurname(buffer.toString());
      }else if (localName.equals("forename")) {
        author.setForename(buffer.toString());
      }else if (localName.equals("author")) {
        // There may be multiple authors, so collect them in a Set.
        authors.add(author);
      }else if (localName.equals("pubDate")) {
        Date pubDate = null;

        // Parse the date string into a Date object.
        try {
          pubDate = format.parse(buffer.toString());
        }catch (ParseException ex) {
          throw new SAXException("Failed to parse the pubDate: "
              + buffer.toString(), ex);
        }

        Calendar cal = Calendar.getInstance();
        cal.setTime(pubDate);
        book.setPubDate(cal);
      }else if (localName.equals("publisher")) {
        book.setPublisher(buffer.toString());
      }else if (localName.equals("book")) {
        // Set the collection of authors.
        book.setAuthors(authors.toArray(new Person[authors.size()]));

        // If we encounter the book end tag, then we are done
        // collecting information on the book.
        processTag = false;
      }
    }
  }
```

```
  // Handle any errors.

  public void warning(SAXParseException ex) throws SAXException {
    System.err.println("Warning!");
    ex.printStackTrace();
  }

  public void error(SAXParseException ex) throws SAXException {
    System.err.println("Error!");
    ex.printStackTrace();
  }

  public void fatalError(SAXParseException ex) throws SAXException {
    System.err.println("FatalError!");
    ex.printStackTrace();
  }
}
```

As it is titled, `BookIsbnSearch` essentially performs the search for us. Give it an ISBN when instantiating it, then give it to a SAX-compliant parser and have the parser parse an XML document that is compliant with the schema of Listing 2.12. If `BookIsbnSearch` finds a book with the specified ISBN, it will collect this information into an instance of `Book`. After the parsing has completed retrieve the book that `BookIsbnSearch` has found by calling `getSearchResult()`. If the search did not find the specified book, then `getSearchResult()` will return null.

Notice that we must look through the attributes for each `book` tag that is passed to `startElement()` to determine if the tag contains an `isbn` attribute with the specified ISBN value. Once we find the right tag we set a flag so the other methods—`characters()` and `endElement()`—know that they need to collect data. The data collected by the `characters()` method is set in the `Book` instance in the `endElement()` method. Recall that we must wait until the `endElement()` method is called before setting the data because the `characters()` method may be called multiple times for the data within a single element.

Next we need to create a class with a main method that accepts an ISBN and the document to search, and calls the SAX parser passing it an instance of `BookIsbnSearch`. Create the following listing in the directory `javawebbook/jaxp/sax`.

Listing 2.17 javawebbook/jaxp/sax/BookFinder.java

```
package javawebbook.jaxp.sax;

import java.text.DateFormat;
import java.text.SimpleDateFormat;
import java.io.File;
import java.io.IOException;
import javax.xml.XMLConstants;
```

```
import javax.xml.parsers.ParserConfigurationException;
import javax.xml.parsers.SAXParser;
import javax.xml.parsers.SAXParserFactory;
import javax.xml.validation.Schema;
import javax.xml.validation.SchemaFactory;
import org.xml.sax.SAXException;

public class BookFinder {
  public static void main(String[] args)
    throws SAXException, ParserConfigurationException, IOException {

    String xmlFileName = args[0];
    String isbn = args[1];

    Book book = findBookByIsbn(new File(xmlFileName), isbn);

    if (book == null) {
      System.out.println("No book found for ISBN: " + isbn);
      return;
    }

    DateFormat format = new SimpleDateFormat("MMMMM d, yyyy");
    System.out.println("Found the following book:");
    System.out.println("  ISBN: " + book.getIsbn());
    System.out.println("  Title: " + book.getTitle());

    for (int i = 0; i < book.getAuthors().length; i++) {
      System.out.println("  Author: "
          + book.getAuthors()[i].getSurname() + ", "
          + book.getAuthors()[i].getForename());
    }

    System.out.println("  Publish Date: "
        + format.format(book.getPubDate().getTime()));
    System.out.println("  Publisher: " + book.getPublisher());
  }

  public static Book findBookByIsbn(File xmlFile, String isbn)
    throws SAXException, ParserConfigurationException, IOException {
    // Create an instance of the specified ContentHandler.
    // SAX will pass data it reads from the XML file to this handler.
    BookIsbnSearch bookSearch = new BookIsbnSearch(isbn);

    // Obtain an instance of the SAX parser factory.
```

```
        SAXParserFactory saxParserFactory = SAXParserFactory.newInstance();
        // Tell the factory that we want the parser to support XML namespaces.
        saxParserFactory.setNamespaceAware(true);

        // Obtain the XML schema that we want to validate against.
        SchemaFactory schemaFactory =
            SchemaFactory.newInstance(XMLConstants.W3C_XML_SCHEMA_NS_URI);
        Schema schema =
            schemaFactory.newSchema(BookFinder.class.getResource("books.xsd"));

        // Tell the factory about the schema. This causes the parser
        // to validate the XML against this schema.
        saxParserFactory.setSchema(schema);

        // Obtain an instance of the SAX parser abstraction.
        SAXParser saxParser = saxParserFactory.newSAXParser();
        // Parse the XML document using SAX and BookIsbnSearch.
        saxParser.parse(xmlFile, bookSearch);

        return bookSearch.getSearchResult();
    }
}
```

`BookFinder` passes an instance of `BookIsbnSearch` to a SAX parser obtained from JAXP's `SAXParserFactory`, and then gets the found book from the `BookIsbnSearch` instance. If the book is null, then `BookFinder` outputs a message stating that no book was found matching the specified ISBN, otherwise the book information is output. Notice that `BookFinder` also sets a `Schema` object for the `books` schema on the `SAXParserFactory` before obtaining the SAX parser. This is how we indicate that we want the XML document to be validated against a schema in JAXP. It is simpler than what needs to be done if using the SAX API directly.

To test this code you first need to compile the Java classes, so open a command prompt, navigate to the directory above the javawebbook directory, and enter the following command.

```
javac -classpath . javawebbook\jaxp\sax\Person.java javawebbook\jaxp\sax\Book.java
javawebbook\jaxp\sax\BookIsbnSearch.java javawebbook\jaxp\sax\BookFinder.java
```

This command must be entered on a single line. On UNIX-type operating systems, just replace the backslashes (\) with forward slashes (/). After you have successfully compiled the code, test it by entering the following command.

```
java -classpath . javawebbook.jaxp.sax.BookFinder javawebbook\jaxp\sax\books.xml 0596007124
```

This command must also be entered on a single line. This searches for the book entitled Head First Design Patterns, which has the ISBN 0596007124. After running the program you should see output such as the following.

```
Found the following book:
  ISBN: 0596007124
  Title: Head First Design Patterns
  Author: Freeman, Elisabeth
  Author: Freeman, Eric
  Author: Bates, Bert
  Author: Sierra, Kathy
  Publish Date: October 1, 2004
  Publisher: O'Reilly
```

Next, try it with a bogus ISBN. You should see output similar to the following.

```
No book found for ISBN: 0000
```

To make sure that the validation is working properly we modify the XML document to add invalid data and then run the test again. Add the following `book` after the last `book` in the XML document.

```
<book isbn="0123456789">
  <title>My Book</title>
  <author>
    <surname>MeLastName</surname>
    <forename>MeFirstName</forename>
  </author>
  <pubDate>April 9, 2005</pubDate>
  <publisher>MyPub</publisher>
</book>
```

This `book` specifies the date for `pubDate` in an invalid format. XML Schema, by default, requires date types to be specified in the format 2005-01-31. If you run the test again, you should get a stack trace. If you give an ISBN to the program that is for one of the books other than the last invalid one you just added, then the program will find the book correctly, but still spit out a stack trace. This is because the validation error is not reported as a fatal error, so the parser does not stop processing. If you give the program the ISBN of the invalid book, then you will get additional stack traces and the program will not output that book because it will fail to parse the date string into a `Date` object when collecting the information into a `Book` object. The output in this case should look something like the following.

```
Error!
org.xml.sax.SAXParseException: http://www.w3.org/TR/xml-
schema-1#cvc-datatype-valid.1.2.1?April 9, 2005&dateTime
...
Error!
org.xml.sax.SAXParseException: http://www.w3.org/TR/xml-
schema-1#cvc-datatype-valid.1.2.1?April 9, 2005&dateTime
```

```
...
Error!
org.xml.sax.SAXParseException: http://www.w3.org/TR/xml-
schema-1#cvc-type.3.1.3?pubDate&April 9, 2005
...
Error!
org.xml.sax.SAXParseException: http://www.w3.org/TR/xml-
schema-1#cvc-type.3.1.3?pubDate&April 9, 2005
...
Exception in thread "main" java.text.ParseException: Unparseable date: "April 9, 2005"
        at javawebbook.jaxp.sax.BookIsbnSearch.endElement(BookIsbnSearch.java:100)
...
```

Most of the stack trace output was removed for brevity. The `org.xml.sax.SAXParseExceptions` are validation exceptions from the parser, while the `java.text.ParseException` is from the code in Listing 2.16. Understand that you can run the program through tests by modifying the XML file without having to recompile the Java code. You can play with the data and run several other tests if you like. For example, you could replace the `pubDate` for the last book with completely invalid data, such as XXXX, which will also give you validation errors.

2.6.4 Lab 4 DOM Example

This example requires you to have already completed the SAX example of Section 2.6.3. So if you have not, then work through that example first. In this example we use DOM to copy a list of books from one XML document to another. Both XML documents use the XML schema of Listing 2.12. For the destination XML document we use Listing 2.13, so copy Listing 2.13 from the `javawebbook/jaxp/sax` directory to `javawebbook/jaxp/dom`. Now we will create a list of book elements that we want to add to the destination XML document. Create the following listing in the directory `javawebbook/jax/dom`.

Listing 2.18 javawebbook/jaxp/dom/newbooks.xml

```
<?xml version="1.0" encoding="UTF-8"?>
<books xmlns="http://javawebbook.edu/namespaces/books">
  <book isbn="0321127420">
    <title>Patterns of Enterprise Application Architecture</title>
    <author>
      <surname>Fowler</surname>
      <forename>Martin</forename>
    </author>
    <pubDate>2002-11-05</pubDate>
    <publisher>Addison-Wesley Professional</publisher>
  </book>
  <book isbn="0849321425">
    <title>Software Architecture Design Patterns In Java</title>
    <author>
```

```
      <surname>Kuchana</surname>
      <forename>Partha</forename>
    </author>
    <pubDate>2004-04-22</pubDate>
    <publisher>Auerbach Publications</publisher>
  </book>
</books>
```

Listing 2.18 contains two books that will be added to the destination XML document. Now we just need to create the JAXP/DOM code that will add the books from the source XML document to the destination XML document and write out the result to the destination XML document file. Create the following listing in the directory `javawebbook/jaxp/dom`.

Listing 2.19 javawebbook/jaxp/dom/AddBooksTest.java

```java
package javawebbook.jaxp.dom;

import java.io.File;
import java.io.IOException;
import javax.xml.XMLConstants;
import javax.xml.parsers.DocumentBuilder;
import javax.xml.parsers.DocumentBuilderFactory;
import javax.xml.parsers.ParserConfigurationException;
import javax.xml.transform.Result;
import javax.xml.transform.Source;
import javax.xml.transform.Transformer;
import javax.xml.transform.TransformerConfigurationException;
import javax.xml.transform.TransformerException;
import javax.xml.transform.TransformerFactory;
import javax.xml.transform.dom.DOMSource;
import javax.xml.transform.stream.StreamResult;
import javax.xml.validation.Schema;
import javax.xml.validation.SchemaFactory;
import org.w3c.dom.Document;
import org.w3c.dom.Element;
import org.w3c.dom.Node;
import org.w3c.dom.NodeList;
import org.w3c.dom.Text;
import org.xml.sax.SAXException;

public class AddBooksTest {
  public static void main(String[] args)
    throws ParserConfigurationException, IOException, SAXException,
           TransformerConfigurationException, TransformerException {
    File xmlFileToAdd = new File(args[0]);
    File destXmlFile = new File(args[1]);
```

```
    // Obtain an instance of the DOM parser factory.
    DocumentBuilderFactory docBuilderFactory =
        DocumentBuilderFactory.newInstance();
    // Tell the factory that we want the parser to support XML namespaces.
    docBuilderFactory.setNamespaceAware(true);

    // Obtain the XML schema that we want to validate against.
    SchemaFactory schemaFactory =
        SchemaFactory.newInstance(XMLConstants.W3C_XML_SCHEMA_NS_URI);
    Schema schema = schemaFactory.newSchema(
        AddBookTest.class.getResource("../sax/books.xsd"));

    // Tell the factory about the schema. This causes the parser
    // to validate the XML against this schema.
    docBuilderFactory.setSchema(schema);

    // Obtain an instance of the DOM parser abstraction.
    DocumentBuilder docBuilder =
        docBuilderFactory.newDocumentBuilder();
    // Parse the XML document to add using DOM.
    Document booksToAdd = docBuilder.parse(xmlFileToAdd);
    // Parse the destination XML document using DOM.
    Document destDoc = docBuilder.parse(destXmlFile);

    addBooks(destDoc, booksToAdd);

    // In the following lines we use a JAXP Transformer to write
    // the resultant DOM to the destination XML file.

    // Obtain an instance of the XSL Transformer factory.
    TransformerFactory transformerFactory =
        TransformerFactory.newInstance();
    // Obtain an instance of the XSL processor abstraction.
    Transformer transformer =
        transformerFactory.newTransformer();
    // Create a JAXP Source for the DOM that we want to output.
    Source domSource = new DOMSource(destDoc);
    // Create a JAXP Result for the destination XML file.
    Result xmlResult = new StreamResult(destXmlFile);
    // Perform the XSL transformation to output the DOM to the
    // destination XML file.
    transformer.transform(domSource, xmlResult);

    System.out.println("Addition of books to " + args[1] + " successful");
}
```

```
  /** Adds the book elements in booksToAdd to destDoc */
  private static void addBooks(Document destDoc, Document booksToAdd) {
    // Get the books Element from the destination document.
    Element destBooksRoot = destDoc.getDocumentElement();
    // Get the books Element from the source document.
    Element srcBooksRoot = booksToAdd.getDocumentElement();
    // Get all of the book Elements from the source document.
    NodeList books = srcBooksRoot.getChildNodes();
    Node node = null;

    // Loop through the list of nodes. Note that this includes Text nodes
    // for whitespace between book Elements in the source Document. If
    // you do not want to include this whitespace in the destination
    // document, then you first need to check the value returned from
    // getNodeName() to see if it is equal to "book" before copying the
    // node.
    for (int i = 0; i < books.getLength(); i++) {
      // This line creates a copy of the node that is suitable for
      // adding to the destination Document. You cannot simply add
      // a node from one Document to another; you must import it.
      node = destDoc.importNode(books.item(i), true);
      destBooksRoot.appendChild(node);
    }
  }
}
```

Listing 2.19 parses the source XML document and the destination XML document (`newbooks.xml` and `books.xml`) into `Document` objects, then retrieves the list of book `Nodes` from the books `Element` of the source `Document` and imports them into the destination `Document`. In DOM you cannot simply take a `Node` from one `Document` and add it to another `Document`. You must either manually create a copy of the node yourself and then add the copy, or use the `Document.importNode()` method, as is done in Listing 2.19. The `importNode` method copies the specified node such that it is suitable for adding to the `Document` that did the import. You then must add it yourself, which can be done by appending it as a child to another `Node`, as is done in Listing 2.19. DOM Level 3, which is supported by J2SE 5.0, adds another method to the `Document` interface called `adoptNode()` that allows moving a `Node` from one `Document` to another. The `adoptNode` method works similarly to `importNode` except the `Node` is not copied, but is removed from the source `Document`. As with `importNode`, you must manually add the `Node` to the destination `Document` yourself after the method call completes.

To compile the example code, open a command prompt, navigate to the directory above javawebbook, and enter the following command. On a UNIX-type operating system just change the backslashes (\) to forward slashes (/).

```
javac -classpath . javawebbook\jaxp\dom\AddBooksTest.java
```

Now you can run the code by entering the following command from the same directory.

```
java -classpath . javawebbook.jaxp.dom.AddBookTest javawebbook\jaxp\dom\newbooks.xml
javawebbook\jaxp\dom\books.xml
```

Note that the previous command must be entered on a single line. When this command completes you should see output such as the following.

```
Addition of books to javawebbook\jaxp\dom\books.xml successful
```

Now, if you open `javawebbook/jaxp/dom/books.xml`, you should see the book elements from `new-books.xml` at the bottom of the file, as the following listing illustrates.

Listing 2.20 books.xml After AddBooksTest Is Executed

```
<?xml version="1.0" encoding="UTF-8"?>
<books xmlns="http://javawebbook.edu/namespaces/books">
  <book isbn="0201633612">
    <title>Design Patterns</title>
    <author>
      <surname>Gamma</surname>
      <forename>Erich</forename>
    </author>
    <author>
      <surname>Helm</surname>
      <forename>Richard</forename>
    </author>
    <author>
      <surname>Johnson</surname>
      <forename>Ralph</forename>
    </author>
    <author>
      <surname>Vlissides</surname>
      <forename>John</forename>
    </author>
    <pubDate>1995-01-15</pubDate>
    <publisher>Addison-Wesley Professional</publisher>
  </book>
  <book isbn="0321247140">
    <title>Design Patterns Explained: A New Perspective On Object-Oriented Design, 2nd
Edition</title>
    <author>
      <surname>Shalloway</surname>
      <forename>Alan</forename>
    </author>
    <author>
      <surname>Trott</surname>
```

```
      <forename>James</forename>
    </author>
    <pubDate>2004-10-12</pubDate>
    <publisher>Addison-Wesley Professional</publisher>
  </book>
  <book isbn="0596007124">
    <title>Head First Design Patterns</title>
    <author>
      <surname>Freeman</surname>
      <forename>Elisabeth</forename>
    </author>
    <author>
      <surname>Freeman</surname>
      <forename>Eric</forename>
    </author>
    <author>
      <surname>Bates</surname>
      <forename>Bert</forename>
    </author>
    <author>
      <surname>Sierra</surname>
      <forename>Kathy</forename>
    </author>
    <pubDate>2004-10-01</pubDate>
    <publisher>O'Reilly</publisher>
  </book>

  <book isbn="0321127420">
    <title>Patterns of Enterprise Application Architecture</title>
    <author>
      <surname>Fowler</surname>
      <forename>Martin</forename>
    </author>
    <pubDate>2002-11-05</pubDate>
    <publisher>Addison-Wesley Professional</publisher>
  </book>
  <book isbn="0849321425">
    <title>Software Architecture Design Patterns In Java</title>
    <author>
      <surname>Kuchana</surname>
      <forename>Partha</forename>
    </author>
    <pubDate>2004-04-22</pubDate>
    <publisher>Auerbach Publications</publisher>
  </book>
</books>
```

2.6.5 Lab 5 Example XSL Transformation

An XML schema for a catalog of old books was defined in Listing 2.11 of Section 2.6.2. In this example, we create an XML file that complies with that schema and contains a list of books. Then we use an XSLT stylesheet to translate that XML file into an XHTML file for display in a Web browser. We begin by creating the XML file. Create the following listing in the directory `javawebbook/jaxp/xslt`.

Listing 2.21 javawebbook/jaxp/xslt/catalog.xml

```
<?xml version="1.0" encoding="UTF-8" ?>
<catalog class="Miscellaneous Old Books">
  <book>
    <title>Cambriensis</title>
    <author>
      <surname>Fitzaubrey</surname>
      <forename>Edmund</forename>
    </author>
    <year>1808</year>
    <publisher>Phillips</publisher>
    <city>London</city>
    <condition>Good</condition>
    <value currency="usd">58.00</value>
  </book>
  <book>
    <title>Paul Clifford</title>
    <author>
      <surname>Bulwer-Lytton</surname>
      <forename>Edward</forename>
      <forename>George</forename>
    </author>
    <year>1830</year>
    <publisher>Colburn</publisher>
    <city>London</city>
    <condition>Good</condition>
    <value currency="usd">58.00</value>
  </book>
  <book>
    <title>The Appeal</title>
    <author>
      <surname>Galt</surname>
      <forename>John</forename>
    </author>
    <year>1818</year>
    <publisher>Constable</publisher>
    <city>Edinburgh</city>
```

```
    <condition>Good</condition>
    <value currency="usd">58.00</value>
  </book>
  <book>
    <title>Shakespearean Synopses</title>
    <author>
      <surname>McSpadden</surname>
      <forename>J.</forename>
      <forename>Walker</forename>
    </author>
    <year>1902</year>
    <publisher>Crowell</publisher>
    <city>New York</city>
    <condition>Good</condition>
    <value currency="usd">58.00</value>
  </book>
  <book>
    <title>Alice's Adventures in Wonderland</title>
    <author>
      <surname>Carroll</surname>
      <forename>Lewis</forename>
    </author>
    <year>1866</year>
    <publisher>Appleton</publisher>
    <city>New York</city>
    <condition>Good</condition>
    <value currency="usd">58.00</value>
  </book>
  <book>
    <title>Rubaiyat of Doc Sifers</title>
    <author>
      <surname>Riley</surname>
      <forename>James</forename>
      <forename>Whitcomb</forename>
    </author>
    <year>1897</year>
    <publisher>Century</publisher>
    <city>New York</city>
    <condition>Good</condition>
    <value currency="usd">58.00</value>
  </book>
  <book>
    <title>The Rime of the Ancient Mariner</title>
    <author>
      <surname>Coleridge</surname>
```

```
      <forename>Samuel</forename>
      <forename>Taylor</forename>
    </author>
    <year>1884</year>
    <publisher>Estes and Lauriat</publisher>
    <city>Boston</city>
    <condition>Good</condition>
    <value currency="usd">58.00</value>
  </book>
  <book>
    <title>The Castle of Otranto</title>
    <author>
      <surname>Walpole</surname>
      <forename>Horace</forename>
    </author>
    <year>1794</year>
    <publisher>Himbourg</publisher>
    <city>Berlin</city>
    <condition>Good</condition>
    <value currency="usd">58.00</value>
  </book>
</catalog>
```

Listing 2.21 contains a random list of old books. The condition and value of all the books were left the same because they are not used in this example. When this data is displayed in a Web browser, we want it to appear in a table with columns for the author's name, then the year in which the book was published, the title of the book, the name of the publisher, and finally the city. We also want the data to be sorted by the author's name, the author's name to be displayed in the format "lastname, firstname," and the title of the book to be italicized. Additionally, the `class` attribute of the `<catalog>` element should be used as both the XHTML `<title>` element and as a level one heading (`<h1>`). The XHTML file must also have a background color, set the font for the level one heading to Sans Serif, and center the level one heading text. An XSLT stylesheet that satisfies these requirements is given in the listing below. Create this listing in the directory `javawebbook/jaxp/xslt`.

Listing 2.22 javawebbook/jaxp/xslt/catalog.xsl

```
<xsl:stylesheet version="1.0"
    xmlns:xsl="http://www.w3.org/1999/XSL/Transform">
  <xsl:template match="catalog">
    <html>
    <head>
      <title><xsl:value-of select="@class"/></title>
      <meta http-equiv="Content-Type"
            content="text/html; charset=UTF-8"/>
      <style type="text/css">
```

```
      <xsl:text>
        h1 {
          font-size: 120%; font-family: arial, sans-serif;
          text-align:center
        }
      </xsl:text>
    </style>
    </head>
    <body style="background-color: #FFFFCC">
      <h1><xsl:value-of select="@class"/></h1>
      <table>
        <tr>
          <th>Author</th>
          <th>Year</th>
          <th>Title</th>
          <th>Publisher</th>
          <th>City</th>
        </tr>
        <xsl:apply-templates select="book">
          <xsl:sort select="author/surname" data-type="text"/>
          <xsl:sort select="author/forename" data-type="text"/>
        </xsl:apply-templates>
      </table>
    </body>
  </html>
</xsl:template>

<xsl:template match="book">
  <tr>
    <td>
      <xsl:value-of select="author/surname" />
      <xsl:text>,</xsl:text>
      <xsl:for-each select="author/forename">
        <xsl:text> </xsl:text>
        <xsl:value-of select="." />
      </xsl:for-each>
    </td>
    <td><xsl:value-of select="year" /></td>
    <td><em><xsl:value-of select="title" /></em></td>
    <td><xsl:value-of select="publisher" /></td>
    <td><xsl:value-of select="city" /></td>
  </tr>
```

```
  </xsl:template>
</xsl:stylesheet>
```

The `stylesheet` element of Listing 2.22 declares the version number and the XSLT namespace with a prefix of `xsl`. The prefix is important because markup within the `templates` of the XSLT stylesheet that is not a part of the stylesheet namespace is automatically copied to the output.

The first template matches `<catalog>`, the root element in the XML document. The first several lines in the template are XHTML markup that will be copied to the result tree. The resulting document will have a document-level stylesheet that modifies the `<h1>` element as required by the specification. The style specification is not markup, so it is enclosed in an `<xsl:text>` element. Both the XHTML title and the `<h1>` contents are provided with an `<xsl:value-of>` element that selects the `class` attribute of the `<catalog>` element. We know it is the `class` attribute of `<catalog>` because the context is a template that matches `catalog`.

Additional non-XSL markup sets up the table, which will be populated by data from the book catalog. When the table has been set up, `<xsl:apply-templates select="book">` applies the template for `<book>` to every instance of `<book>` in the source document. The `<xsl:apply-templates>` element contains two instances of `<xsl:sort>` to sort the `<book>` elements first on author's surname and then on the author's forename. After the template for `<book>` is applied to each instance, additional non-XSL markup closes the table and the XHTML document.

Within the template for the `<book>` element, the author's surname is selected by specifying a path relative to the book element. An `<xsl:text>` element provides the comma that follows the surname. This implies that the comma will be present even if there are no forenames. An `<xsl:for-each>` iterates over each occurrence of the author's forename. The `<xsl:value-of select=".">` outputs each forename in turn. The preceding `<xsl:text>` element places a space before each forename. Once the name has been constructed, the remainder of the `<book>` template is straightforward, emitting XHTML markup and the values of the appropriate elements.

Now that we have defined the XML data and the XSLT stylesheet to transform it, we create the Java code that will run the processor. Create the following listing in the directory `javawebbook/jaxp/xslt`.

Listing 2.23 javawebbook/jaxp/xslt/XSLTTest.java

```
package javawebbook.jaxp.xslt;

import java.io.File;
import java.io.IOException;
import javax.xml.transform.Result;
import javax.xml.transform.Source;
import javax.xml.transform.Transformer;
import javax.xml.transform.TransformerConfigurationException;
```

```
import javax.xml.transform.TransformerException;
import javax.xml.transform.TransformerFactory;
import javax.xml.transform.stream.StreamResult;
import javax.xml.transform.stream.StreamSource;
import org.xml.sax.SAXException;

public class XSLTTest {
  public static void main(String[] args)
    throws TransformerConfigurationException, TransformerException {
    File xmlFile = new File(args[0]);
    File xslFile = new File(args[1]);
    File xsltResultFile = new File(args[2]);

    // Obtain an instance of the XSL Transformer factory.
    TransformerFactory transformerFactory =
        TransformerFactory.newInstance();
    // Create a JAXP Source for the XSL file. Source is just an object
    // that acts as a source input for an XSL Transformer.
    Source xslSource = new StreamSource(xslFile);
    // Obtain an instance of the XSL processor abstraction.
    Transformer transformer =
        transformerFactory.newTransformer(xslSource);
    // Create a JAXP Source and Result for the input XML file and
    // the result of the XSLT transformation.
    Source xmlSource = new StreamSource(xmlFile);
    Result xsltResult = new StreamResult(xsltResultFile);
    // Perform the XSL transformation to translate the XML file
    // to another form.
    transformer.transform(xmlSource, xsltResult);
  }
}
```

Listing 2.23 is fairly simple. It uses JAXP to obtain a reference to an XSLT processor, then it applies the XSLT stylesheet to the XML file. To compile this code, open a command prompt, navigate to the directory above javawebbook, and enter the following command. On a UNIX-type operating system just change the backslashes (\) to forward slashes (/).

```
javac -classpath . javawebbook\jaxp\xslt\XSLTTest.java
```

Next, execute the program by entering the following command.

```
java -classpath . javawebbook.jaxp.xslt.XSLTTest javawebbook\jaxp\xslt\catalog.xml
javawebbook\jaxp\xslt\catalog.xsl javawebbook\jaxp\xslt\catalog.html
```

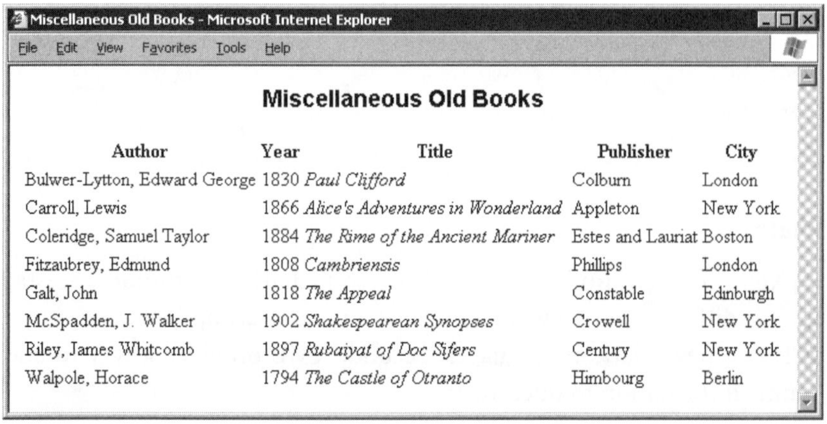

Miscellaneous Old Books - Microsoft Internet Explorer

File Edit View Favorites Tools Help

Miscellaneous Old Books

Author	Year	Title	Publisher	City
Bulwer-Lytton, Edward George	1830	*Paul Clifford*	Colburn	London
Carroll, Lewis	1866	*Alice's Adventures in Wonderland*	Appleton	New York
Coleridge, Samuel Taylor	1884	*The Rime of the Ancient Mariner*	Estes and Lauriat	Boston
Fitzaubrey, Edmund	1808	*Cambriensis*	Phillips	London
Galt, John	1818	*The Appeal*	Constable	Edinburgh
McSpadden, J. Walker	1902	*Shakespearean Synopses*	Crowell	New York
Riley, James Whitcomb	1897	*Rubaiyat of Doc Sifers*	Century	New York
Walpole, Horace	1794	*The Castle of Otranto*	Himbourg	Berlin

Figure 2.3

Catalog.html in a Web Browser

The previous command must be entered on a single line. When the program completes you should now have the file javawebbook/jaxp/xslt/catalog.html. If you open this file in a Web browser, it should look like the listing shown in Figure 2.3.

You can see that the books are sorted by author in the XHTML file, which they are not in the source XML file. You can play with sorting by changing the field by which the data is sorted. For example, if you wanted the data sorted by book title, change the lines with `xsl:sort` as the following code snippet indicates.

```
          <xsl:apply-templates select="book">
            <xsl:sort select="title" data-type="text"/>
<!-- Commented out sort by author name.
            <xsl:sort select="author/surname" data-type="text"/>
            <xsl:sort select="author/forename" data-type="text"/>
-->
          </xsl:apply-templates>
```

You can then run the example again without recompiling the Java code. When you view the XHTML file in the Web browser again you will see that the data is sorted by the book title. You could also sort by the year the book was published as the following code snippet indicates.

```
          <xsl:apply-templates select="book">
            <xsl:sort select="year" data-type="number"/>
<!-- Commented out sort by book title.
            <xsl:sort select="title" data-type="text"/>
-->
<!-- Commented out sort by author name.
```

```
        <xsl:sort select="author/surname" data-type="text"/>
        <xsl:sort select="author/forename" data-type="text"/>
-->
      </xsl:apply-templates>
```

2.7 Summary

XML is the eXtensible Markup Language. Although it shares a common ancestry with HTML, it is different in two ways. First, it is a meta-markup language: a language for defining new markup languages. Second, XML provides a way to add general semantic information to documents.

XML defines a general set of rules to which all XML documents must conform. Conforming documents are called *well formed.* Characteristics of an XML document that are specific to a particular application can be described in a document type definition (DTD) or an XML schema. A well-formed document that also conforms to a particular DTD or schema is *valid* in the context of the DTD or schema.

XML documents cannot contain binary data. Binary data is handled by including a link to the binary object, usually in the form of a URI, in the XML document, or by encoding binary data in a character format. It is up to the application processing the XML to understand the syntax and semantics of binary objects.

Information in an XML document may be contained in elements or attributes. Think of elements as nouns and attributes as adjectives. In general, attributes should be atomic and single-valued. Validating parsers can enforce uniqueness within an XML document for attributes of type ID.

Character entities provide a way for inserting characters that would otherwise be parsed as markup. They also provide a convenient way to include other characters that do not appear on a keyboard or cannot be displayed by the editor in use. XML predefines five character entities to avoid collisions with markup symbols. Numbered character entities are defined by their position within Unicode. Named character entities are defined in DTDs.

Document Type Definitions (DTDs) are one of two ways to declare a formal structure for a class of XML documents. Using a syntax derived from SGML, DTDs can declare elements, attributes, and entities. DTDs can define the structure of a document and are well suited for text-based XML applications such as publishing. However, DTDs provide almost no control over the content of elements and very little control over the content of attributes. This makes them less well suited to data-oriented applications of XML. DTDs are connected to XML documents by the <!DOCTYPE > declaration. A validating parser can compare an XML document against its DTD and report errors of validity.

XML schemas are one of several ways to use XML to describe XML documents. XML schemas became a World Wide Web Consortium recommendation in 2001, and thus are the preferred way of describing XML documents. XML schemas describe elements and attributes in a way that is similar to class definitions in object-oriented programming. There are more than 40 primitive data types that cover strings, numbers, dates and times, and several miscellaneous types. The primitive data types are made more specific by specifying some of more than a dozen facets. For example, the string data type can be specified to have a fixed length, or a variable length with upper and lower bounds, or to conform to a regular expression pattern. Unlike DTDs, XML schemas are namespace-aware. A validating parser can compare an XML instance document against its schema and report errors of validity, including violations of constraints on the primitive data types.

XSL Transformations (XSLT) provide a very powerful stylesheet capability for rewriting XML documents. XSLT stylesheets can add text and markup to the output, reorder or omit XML elements, and even sort elements from the input document before writing them to the output. The fundamental paradigm of XSLT is matching templates in the stylesheet against elements in the input document. The templates themselves specify how to transform the XML for presentation. XSLT is a complete programming language, expressed as XML. It has more than 50 elements and over 200 attributes. Although the XSLT transformation vocabulary is very rich, it is possible to write sophisticated transformations using only a small subset of XSLT. Modern Web browsers are XSLT-aware and can apply styles at the Web client. It may be better to apply XSLT transformations at the Web server for reasons of security and for support of the widest possible variety of browsers.

Two standard models are available for programming in Java with XML. The SAX model is an even model in which event messages are generated as the XML parser traverses a document tree. The DOM model builds up the entire tree in memory. Each model has advantages and shortcomings. The SAX model is conservative of memory, but the programmer may not have all the information about the document available when it is needed. In the DOM model, the entire document is available, but large documents can consume a lot of memory.

SAX and especially DOM are intended to be language-neutral. If you do not care about using language independent APIs and need functionality such as DOM provides, you may want to check out JDOM or dom4j, which are two libraries that are written specifically for Java. Since they are written specifically for Java, they provide a set of classes that make XML processing in Java easier than DOM by giving up language independence.

2.8 Self-Review Questions

1. What are two ways in which XML is different from HTML?
   a. XML is a meta-markup language, and the semantics of XML are not limited to describing the structure of a document.
   b. XML cannot be used on the Web, and XML documents are in binary form.
   c. Unlike XML, HTML can display binary items such as sounds and pictures, and XML documents cannot be displayed in a pleasing format.
2. What do the letters XML stand for?
   a. Extended Markup Language.
   b. Extensible Markup Language.
   c. Extra Markup Language.
3. What is the difference between a markup language and a meta-markup language?
   a. All meta-markup languages use an entirely different syntax.
   b. A markup language cannot be defined using a meta-markup language.
   c. The semantics of a markup language are predefined, but the semantics of a meta-markup language are not.
4. How many root elements may an XML document have?
   a. As many as necessary.
   b. Exactly one.
   c. Only one or two.
5. How are pictures and other binary data handled in XML?
   a. Binary data cannot be handled by XML.
   b. Through the use of attributes or unparsed entities.
   c. Through the use of unparsed entities.
6. Name any three of the requirements for an XML document to be well formed.
   a. Attributes cannot have values, only double quotes are legal, and comments may not contain two consecutive hyphens.
   b. There must be exactly one root element, all tags must be closed, and all element and attribute names must be legal XML names.
   c. Attributes must have values, only single quotes are legal, and names cannot start with an underscore.

7. What are character entities?
   a. Entities that replace exactly one character in an XML document.
   b. Entities that are exactly one character long in an XML document.
   c. Replacements for < and & only.
8. Give two reasons why character entities might be used in an XML document.
   a. To escape markup introducers and to include characters not available through the keyboard.
   b. To obscure URLs so they cannot be read, and to control vertical spacing in documents.
   c. To escape markup introducers and to allow JavaScript to be included in XML documents.
9. Why are namespaces needed in XML?
   a. To make names longer and more meaningful.
   b. To assist in interpreting the semantics of element names.
   c. To prevent namespace collisions when using two or more XML definitions.
10. What is the purpose of a default namespace?
    a. To allow one set of names in an instance document to be used without prefixes.
    b. To make the meanings of the element names clearer.
    c. To allow all names in an instance document to be used without prefixes.
11. How is an XML default namespace defined?
    a. By declaring it the default in the defining XML schema.
    b. By using the keyword "default" in the namespace definition of the instance document.
    c. By omitting the prefix in the namespace definition of the instance document.
12. What is required to be stored at the URI of a namespace specification?
    a. Nothing.
    b. The XML schema that describes the namespace.
    c. A text document that describes the namespace.
13. Describe how a choice of exactly one of a list of elements can be specified in a DTD.
    a. Using an enumeration.
    b. Placing a plus sign after the element name.
    c. Leaving the element name unqualified.

14. How are optional elements specified in a DTD?
    a. Using enumeration.
    b. Placing an asterisk or question mark after the element name.
    c. Placing an asterisk or a plus sign after the element name.
15. What are the content restrictions on a DTD attribute definition of type `ID`?
    a. Must be a legal XML name that is unique in the instance document.
    b. Must be a sequential number that is unique in the instance document.
    c. The attribute must be named "id".
16. Distinguish between an external parsed entity and an external unparsed entity.
    a. There are no external parsed entities; only unparsed entities may be external.
    b. An external parsed entity is processed by the XML parser and an unparsed entity is not.
    c. There are no external unparsed entities; everything must be processed by the XML parser.
17. What is a major difference between DTDs and XML schemas?
    a. XML schemas provide finer control over element and attribute content.
    b. XML schemas allow general entity definition.
    c. XML schemas allow validation of document structure, but DTDs do not.
18. In the context of an XML schema, what is a facet?
    a. A collection of predefined data types.
    b. A collection of user-defined data types.
    c. A characteristic of a data type that can be restricted.
19. Do all facets apply to all XML Schema data types?
    a. Yes.
    b. No.
20. Why must elements with attributes be declared as `complexType` in XML Schema?
    a. They don't; they can be simple types as long as they do not enclose other elements.
    b. Because two or more data types are potentially present.
    c. Because attribute values can be of `complexType`.
21. What is the difference between an anonymous complex type and a named complex type in XML Schema?
    a. Anonymous types are not allowed in XML.

   b. An anonymous type must be referred to by an ID, not a name.

   c. Anonymous complex types are defined in-line where they are used.

22. What are two reasons to consider applying XSL Transformations at the Web server rather than depending upon the browser to reformat the XML?

   a. The Web server is faster than the browser and the stylesheet can remain on the server.

   b. The document sent over the network will always be smaller if transformed first.

   c. Security of document elements and support for multiple browsers.

23. What is an advantage of holding information for display on the Web in an XML document and displaying it using an XSLT stylesheet?

   a. The display format can be changed by changing the stylesheet.

   b. Stylesheet support is uniform across browsers.

   c. Stylesheets are always included in the same file as the XML document.

24. What is a shortcoming of using cascading stylesheets (CSS) to display XML documents in Web browsers?

   a. Styles can only be applied to elements defined in XHTML.

   b. Data cannot be reordered, and all elements will be displayed.

   c. Placement of new lines in the display cannot be controlled and only the default fonts are available.

25. What is the major difference between the SAX model and the DOM model for programming with XML?

   a. SAX is event-driven and DOM is tree-structured.

   b. SAX builds the entire document in memory and DOM does not.

   c. SAX is language-neutral and DOM is applicable only to Java.

2.9 Keys to the Self-Review Questions

1. a 2. b 3. c 4. b 5. b 6. b 7. b 8. a 9. c 10. a 11. c 12. a 13. c 14. b 15. a 16. b 17. a 18. c 19. b 20. b 21. c 22. c 23. a 24. b 25. a

2.10 Exercises

1. Develop an XML document structure to define courses in a university. At a minimum, the structure should account for course name, course number, credit hours, section, starting and ending meeting times, room, and

professor. Account for the fact that a single course may have several sections taught simultaneously in different rooms by different professors. Your document structure should make use of both elements and attributes. Prepare an example document with several instances of courses in it and display your document using a Web browser. (Microsoft Internet Explorer has a built-in style for displaying XML.)

2. Describe how the "memo" DTD developed in Section 2.3 can be extended to allow important phrases in the body of the memo to be identified by enclosing them in `<important>` and `</important>` markup elements.

3. Describe how the "nameStructure" in the sample schemas can be extended so that `<name>` may have an optional `<prefix>` element for titles such as "Reverend" and an optional `<suffix>` element for generational qualifiers (such as "Jr.") or degrees.

4. Check the Web sites of one or two chain used car dealers and note what they provide on the Web about the cars they have for sale. Develop an XML document structure to describe used cars. Be sure to allow for at least one photograph of the car. Create at least three instances of "used car" and display your form in a browser such as Internet Explorer.

5. An application program uses an XML document to store simple configuration information. Users of the application can change configuration options using the program's toolbar options. The program saves configuration changes by rewriting the configuration file. Tell whether this program needs to include an XML parser and explain why or why not.

6. Consider the book catalog used in the examples. Does anything prevent this catalog from holding data for more than one copy of the same book? Explain why or why not. What changes, if any, would you recommend to someone who told you that multiple copies would have to be included frequently?

2.11 Programming Exercises

1. Write a document type definition for the university course data developed in Exercise 1 above. Validate the example document from Exercise 1 using your DTD and a validating parser such as the Xerces dom.Writer. If you needed to make changes to your document in order to get it to validate, explain what changes you needed to make and why they were necessary. (DecisionSoft provides a Web front end to the Xerces parsers at `http://tools.decisionsoft.com/schemaValidate.html`.)

2. Write an XML schema for your university course data and validate your data using the schema. Explain what areas of the document are defined more rigorously by the schema than by the DTD. Validate your document against the schema using a validating parser. If you had to make further changes to make your document validate, explain what they were and why they were necessary.
3. Write a CSS stylesheet to display your course list in a Web browser.
4. Write an XSL Transformation to convert your university course list for display in a Web browser. Courses should be listed in ascending order of course number. Meeting times for each course should be given from earliest to latest.
5. Write a Java program to read the book catalog document described in this chapter and output the total value of the book collection. (*Hint:* This is not as easy as it sounds; take a close look at the attribute of the `<value>` element. How will you address this difficulty?)
6. Write a Java program to check the university course document for time conflicts for professors and rooms. A time conflict exists if there is not at least fifteen minutes between the ending time of one class and the beginning time of the next. If your document did not contain time conflicts, introduce at least one professor time conflict and one room time conflict to test your program. If you needed to change your document to accomplish testing for time conflicts, explain what changes you needed to make and how the XML schema would need to be changed to accommodate those changes.
7. Modify the book catalog schema of the example in this chapter to restrict the `<year>` element to an inclusive range of 1760 to 1960.
8. Modify the book catalog schema to restrict the `<condition>` element to one of "Fine," "Good," "Fair," or "Poor."
9. Modify both the book catalog schema and the XSL stylesheet to allow books to have multiple authors. (*Hint:* Notice how multiple forenames are handled in the example.)

2.12 References

Applequist, D. K. *XML and SQL Developing Web Applications.* Reading, MA: Addison-Wesley, 2002.

Daconta, M. C., and A., Saganich *XML Development with Java 2.* Indianapolia, IN: Sams, 2000.

Gamma, E., R., Helm, R., Johnson, and J., Vlissides, *Design Patterns: Elements of Reusable Object-Oriented Software.* Boston: Addison-Wesley, 1995.

Harold, E. R., and W.S. Means, *XML in a Nutshell.* Sebastopol, CA: O'Reilly & Associates, 2002.

Hunter, D., et al. *Beginning XML.* Birmingham, UK: Wrox Press, Ltd., 2000.

Hunter, Jason. *JDOM AND XML PARSING: JDOM Makes XML Manipulation in Java Easier Than Ever.* http://www.oracle.com/technology/oramag/oracle/02-sep/o52jdom.html. (accessed March 2005).

Hunter, Jason. X Is for XQuery. http://www.oracle.com/technology.oramag/oracle/03-may/ 033devxml.html (accessed March 2005).

Monson-Haefel, Richard. *J2EE Web Services.* Boston: Addison-Wesley, 2004.

Ray, E. T. *Learning XML.* Sebastopol, CA: O'Reilly & Associates, 2001.

Programs

MetaStuff Ltd. 2004. dom4j, Quick Start Guide. http://dom4j.org/guide.html.

W3C Recommendation, February 4, 2004. Extensible Markup Language (XML) 1.0 (3rd ed.). http://www.w3.org/TR/REC-xml.

W3C Recommendation, 1999. Namespaces in XML. http://www.w3.org/TR/REC-xml-names.

W3C Recommendation, October 28, 2004. XML Schema Part 0: Primer Second Edition. http://www.w3.org/TR/xmlschema-0/.

W3C Recommendation, October 28, 2004. XML Schema Part 1: Structures Second Edition. http://www.w3.org/TR/xmlschema-1/.

W3C Recommendation, October 28, 2004. XML Schema Part 2: Datatypes Second Edition. http://www.w3.org/TR/xmlschema-2/.

W3C Recommendation, November 16, 1999. XSL Transformations Version 1.0. http://www.w3.org/TR/xslt.

CHAPTER 3

Java Servlets

Objectives of This Chapter

- Introduce concepts of Java Servlet Web components
- Support environments for Java Servlets
- Compare Servlet with CGI and Java applets
- Discuss the functionality of Java Servlets
- Discuss the Java Servlet API
- Discuss Java Servlet debugging
- Provide step-by-step tutorials on building, deploying, and using Java Servlet components

3.1 Overview

Java Servlet technology provides an HTTP-based request and response paradigm on Web servers. Java Servlets can handle generic service requests and respond to the client's requests. Applications of Java Servlets include embedded systems, wireless communication, and any other generic request/response application. We focus on Java Web HTTP Servlets that take HTTP requests, process them, and respond to the client with process results via HTTP.

In the first generation of Web applications, Web developers could provide only static Web pages for clients to browse using Web browsers. The second generation of Web applications provides dynamic Web pages with which clients can interact. Web page contents are based on input from clients. Online shopping, online student registrations, online surveys, and online job applications are some examples. Web applications require Web servers to handle the user's inputs, process requests through business rules, and stream the results to users.

The Common Gateway Interface (CGI) was a popular technology to generate dynamic HTTP Web contents in the middle 1990s. The CGI-based Perl and C programs were widely used for Web middleware applications at the time. Traditional CGI programs are not very efficient because a CGI program must spawn a new process to handle every new incoming request. If there are many requests, resources such as memory may be exhausted. Each process takes CPU time and memory space. Also, it is very time-consuming to create a dedicated process for each single request. CGI has many other restrictions in terms of platform dependency, security, and portability. CGI is being phased out and replaced by PHP, ASP.NET, Java Servlets, and JSP.

Java Servlet technology was introduced by Sun Microsystems in 1996 as an alternative to CGI. Java Servlets version 2.X is the current specification and is implemented in Tomcat 5.x. There are many Java-compliant Web servers on the market. Jakarta Tomcat is one of the most popular Java technology–based Web servers. A Java Servlet class is a class available in the Java Servlet API supported by `servlet-api.jar`. The program needs to instantiate a Servlet in order to provide services. The Java Virtual Machine (JVM) will not spawn any new processes for new requests; instead it will create a new thread to handle the new request. This is much more efficient because all threads will share the same memory space. Once a Servlet is loaded, it will stay in memory to handle multiple requests until the server is shut down or the Servlet is unloaded. This significantly reduces the costs of server resources.

Figure 3.1 shows the advantage of Java Servlet technology over CGI in terms of server resource utilization.

Java Servlets are written in Java and run on the Java Runtime Environment (JRE). CGI is written in Perl or other scripting languages. Java Servlets have many advantages.

- Efficiency: reduction of the time spent on creating new processes and initialization, as well as reduction of memory requirements.

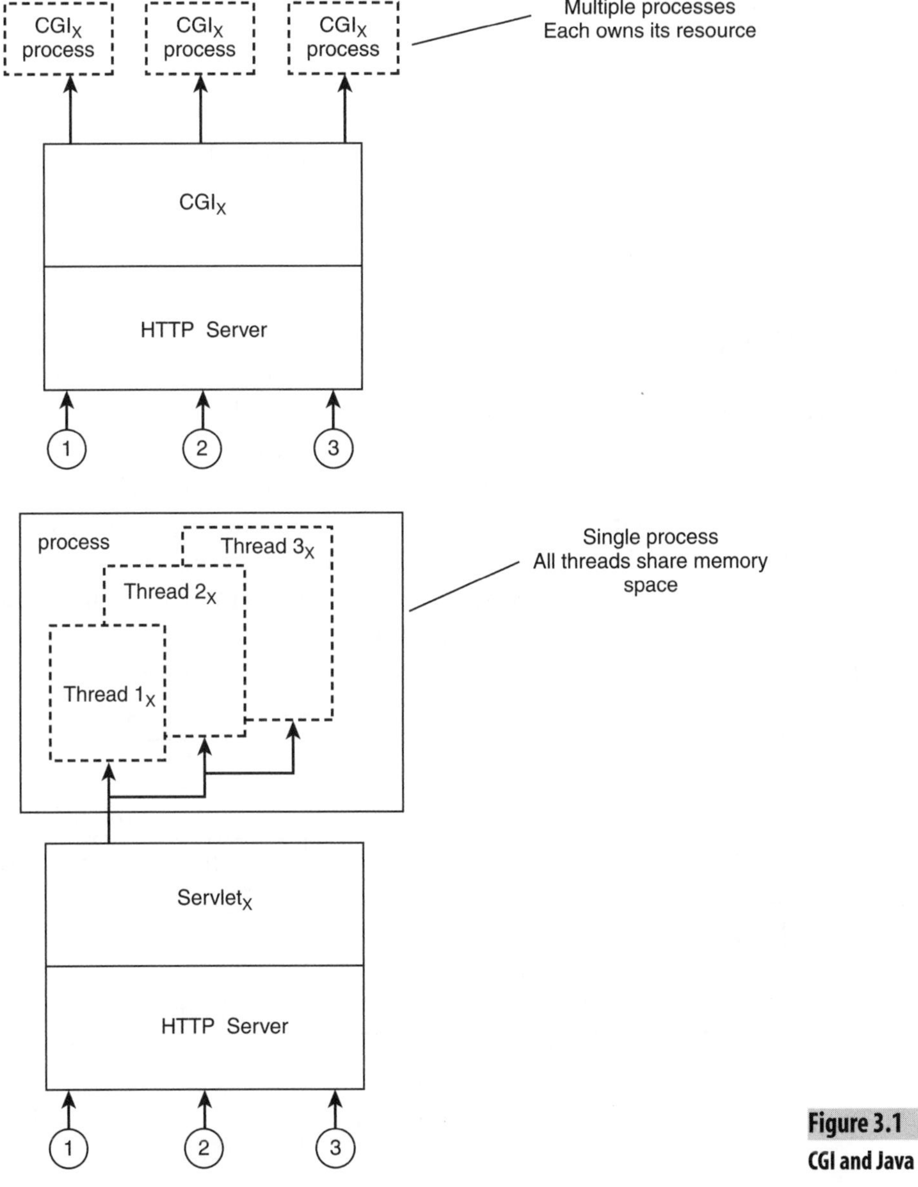

Figure 3.1
CGI and Java Servlet

- Convenience: all needed functionality is provided by the Servlets API.
- Portability: cross-platform, Write-Once-Run-Anywhere (WORA) code.
- Security: built-in security layers.
- Open source: free Servlet development kits available for download.
- Functionality: session tracking, data sharing, JDBC database connections and others.

The Java Servlet resembles a Java applet. A Java applet is an enhancement to a Web client and a Java Servlet is an addition to the Web server's functionality. A Java applet is embedded in an HTTP page and downloaded with the page from the Web server where the HTTP page resides. It is run by the client browser at the client site. A Java Servlet object is created on the Web server and runs on the server. An applet is called a Java client-side program and a Servlet is called a Java server-side program. A Servlet object is supported by a Servlet container, which is supported by an HTTP Web server. The Servlet container is responsible for managing the life cycle of a Servlet object. Functions of the Servlet container include taking input requests from clients, instantiating an instance of the Servlet class, passing the requests to the Servlet object and letting the Servlet object process the requests, and forwarding the results to clients. The results returned to the client by a Servlet Web component may be in a format of TEXT/HTML, TEXT/XML, TEXT/PLAIN, IMAGE/JPEG, or in another binary type of format. Figure 3.2 shows the concepts of Java applets and Java Servlets technology.

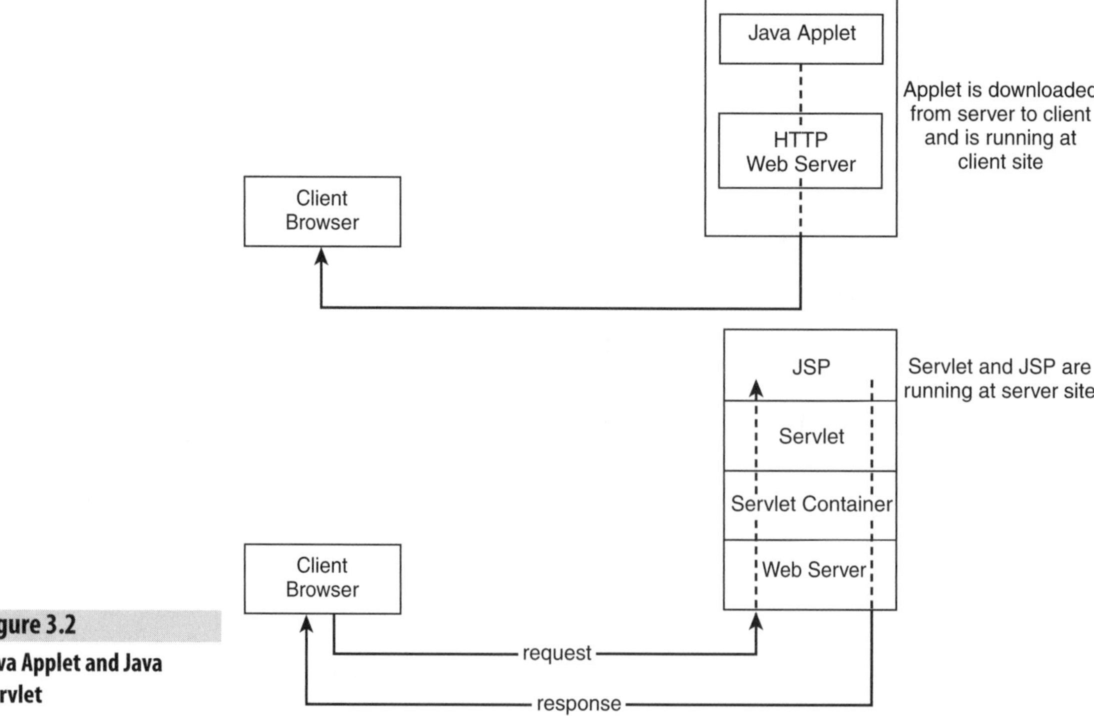

Figure 3.2
Java Applet and Java Servlet

A Servlet component can delegate the requests to its back-end tier such as a database management system, RMI, EAI, or other Enterprise Information System (EIS). In this case, the Servlet plays a role of the middle tier in a three-tier architecture. A Servlet is deployed as a middle tier just as other Web components such as JSP components. The Servlet Web components are always part of the Web application. For example, in J2EE, Servlet Web components and Java Server Pages (JSP) Web components can be deployed in a `.war` file; EJB components can be deployed in a `.jar` file. All together, an enterprise application can be deployed in an `.ear` file, which consists of `.jar` files and `.war` files. The Servlet components are building block components that always work together with other components such as JSP components, JavaBean components, Enterprise Java Bean (EJB) components, and Web service components.

A Servlet component is also a distributed component, which can provide services to remote clients and also access remote resources.

In the next section, you will learn the Java Servlet execution environments, including containers and the HTTP Web servers where the Java Servlet containers reside. The Java-compliant Tomcat Web server is introduced next. This Web server is also used for the JSP Web component.

3.2 Support Environments for Java Servlets

A Java Servlet application is supported by its Servlet container. The container may be an add-on Servlet container or stand-alone container that comes as part of a Web server. Since a Java Servlet itself is a Java class it also needs Java API support, specifically the Java Servlet API that is available in an archive file called `servlet-api.jar` in Tomcat.

The Apache Tomcat Web server is the official reference implementation of Servlet containers, supporting Servlets and JSP. Tomcat itself can be a stand-alone Web server and can also be an add-on Servlet/JSP engine/container for other Web servers. At the time of this writing, Tomcat 5.x is the newest edition that supports Servlet 2.4 and JSP 2.0.

The Tomcat Web server is an open-source Servlet container originally developed by Sun Microsystems. There are many other Web servers supporting Servlets and JSP, such as Sun's Java Web server and Macromedia's JRun, Caucho Resin, and Jetty. Many application servers, such as the Sun Java System Application Server, BEA WebLogic and IBM WebSphere, Oracle Application Server, Pramati Server, and JBoss, also support Servlets and JSP.

3.2.1 Web Server Configuration (`server.xml`)

An XML format file called `server.xml` is used to control and configure the behavior and setting of the Tomcat Web server. This file is located in the `conf` subdirectory of the Tomcat installation directory.

Some common changes needed in the configuration of Tomcat Web server may be:

1. resetting the server port number where the Servlet class or other Web component will listen for requests,

   ```
   <Connector port="80" ... />
   ```

   where 8080 is the initial port number. It is replaced by 80 to make it much more convenient for clients to access Servlets because 80 is the default HTTP port.

2. turning on the Servlet reloading so that the recompiled Servlet does not need to be reloaded:

   `<DefaultContext reloadable="true"/>` is inserted in the `Service` tag.

   The following is a sample of `server.xml`.

```
 . . .
 <Server port="8005" shutdown="SHUTDOWN" debug="0">
   . . .
   <Service name="Catalina">
      <Connector port="80" maxThreads="150" minSpareThreads="25"
        maxSpareThreads="75" enableLookups="false" redirectPort="8443"
        acceptCount="100" debug="0" connectionTimeout="20000"
        disableUploadTimeout="true" />
     <Engine name="Catalina" defaultHost="localhost" debug="0">
      <Host name="localhost" debug="0" appBase="webapps" unpackWARs="true"
               autoDeploy="true">
         . . .
         <DefaultContext reloadable="true" />
         <Context path="" docBase="ROOT" debug="0" />
    </Host>
   </Engine>
  </Service>
</Server>
```

3.2.2 Java Servlet Deployment Descriptor (web.xml)

An XML format file called `web.xml` in the WEB-INF subdirectory of the Web application directory is used to control and configure the behavior and setting of Java Servlets in a specific Web application. There is another serverwide `web.xml` in the same place as `server.xml`. The serverwide configurations will apply to all Web components on the server. As each application is deployed, this file is processed first, followed by the "`/WEB-INF/web.xml`" deployment descriptor from the application. The application-specific resource configurations should go in the "`/WEB-INF/web.xml`" in the application.

Here is a sample Web serverwide `web.xml` for Tomcat 5. Most of the time the serverwide `web.xml` configuration file does not need to be changed.

The following is an example of an application-specific `web.xml` for the `myServlet` class in the package "`myPackage`."

```
<?xml version="1.0" encoding="ISO-8859-1"?>

<!DOCTYPE web-app
    PUBLIC "-//Sun Microsystems, Inc.//DTD Web Application 2.3//EN"
    "http://java.sun.com/dtd/web-app_2_3.dtd">

<web-app>
  <display-name>Welcome to Tomcat</display-name>
  <description>Welcome to Tomcat</description>

    <servlet>
        <servlet-name>myServlet</servlet-name>
        <servlet-class>myPackage.myServlet</servlet-class>
        <init-param>
           <param-name>key1</param-name>
           <param-value>value1</param-value>
        </init-param>
        <init-param>
           <param-name>key2</param-name>
           <param-value>value2</param-value>
        </init-param>
    </servlet>

    <servlet-mapping>
        <servlet-name>myServlet</servlet-name>
        <url-pattern>/GetMyServlet</url-pattern>
    </servlet-mapping>
</web-app>
```

By this mapping you can use a custom URL `http://host/`*<yourWebAppName>*`/GetMyServlet` to access this Servlet component; otherwise you need to use `http://host/`*<yourWebAppName>*`/servlet/myPackage.myServlet`. The `<init-param>` initializes key/value pairs, which can be accessed by Servlet's `ServletConfig.getInitParameter()`.

3.2.3 Other Configurations

There are some other configurations such as `PATH`, `CLASSPATH`, `JAVA_HOME`, and `TOMCAT_HOME` environment settings. The environment variable `JAVA_HOME` is set to the Java installation directory and the environment variable *path* is set to `bin` subdirectory by command line or by Windows Control Panel => System Setting after installing JSDK. The environment variable `TOMCAT_HOME` is set to the

Tomcat installation directory and the environment variable `CLASSPATH` needs to point to `install_dir/common/lib/servlet-api.jar` and `install_dir/common/lib/jsp-api.jar` in order to make Java API of Servlet and JSP available. Often the current working directory "." needs to be included in the `CLASSPATH`. The detail settings are shown in Section 3.5, Examples and Lab Practice.

3.3 Basics of Java Servlets

Both Java Servlet technology and Java Server Pages (JSP) technology are very popular in Web applications. JSP is an extension of the Servlet and is discussed in the next chapter. The Java Servlet is a server-side Web component that takes an HTTP request from a client, handles it, talks to a database, talks to a JavaBean component, and responds with an HTTP response or dispatches the request to other Servlets or JSP components. Servlets can dynamically produce text-based HTML markup contents and binary contents based on the client's request. Because a Servlet is a Web component, it needs to be deployed in a Servlet-supporting Web server with its deployment descriptor.

3.3.1 Java Servlet architecture

A Java `Servlet` is just a typical Java class that extends an abstract class `HttpServlet`.

The `HttpServlet` class extends another abstract class, `GenericServlet`. The `GenericServlet` class implements three interfaces: `javax.servlet.Servlet`, `javax.servlet.ServletConfig`, and `java.io.Serializable`.

The following is a detailed discussion of the Java `HttpServlet` API class and interface hierarchy.

1. `public interface` **`Servlet`**

   The `Servlet` interface provides Servlet life cycle method and Servlet configuration information access methods. The life cycle methods are called in this sequence: The Servlet is loaded, then initialized with the `init()` method; the calls from clients to the `service()` method are handled; the Servlet is taken out of service, then destroyed with the `destroy()` method, then garbage collected. It also provides the `getServletConfig()` method, which the Servlet can use to get any startup information, and the `getServletInfo()` method to get basic information, such as the Servlet version. The following list shows the often-used methods in this interface:

   ```
   public void init(ServletConfig config) throws ServletException
   ```

   ```
   //Called by the servlet container when the servlet is loaded.
   ```

```
public void service(ServletRequest req, ServletResponse res)
     throws ServletException, java.io.IOException
```

```
//Called by the Servlet container to let Servlet respond to a request.
```

```
public void destroy()
```

```
//Called by the Servlet container when the Servlet is unloaded
```

```
public ServletConfig getServletConfig()
```

```
//Returns a Servlet object with initialization and startup parameters of this
//Servlet.
```

```
//The init() method can use this object to get the Servlet configuration
//information.
```

2. `public interface ServletConfig`

   The `ServletConfig` interface provides many methods for the Servlet to get Servlet configuration initialization information, which is set in `web.xml`.

   The following list shows the often-used methods in this interface:

```
public String getInitParameter(String name)
```

```
//Returns the value of the named initialization parameter defined in web.xml, or
//null if the name does not exist.
```

```
public ServletContext getServletContext()
```

```
//Returns a reference to the ServletContext in the Web application scope
```

   The `ServletContext` interface keeps one context per Web application. It has the following methods:

```
public String getInitParameter(String name)
```

```
//Returns a String containing the value of the named context-wide initialization
//parameter, or null if the parameter does not exist.
```

```
public Enumeration getInitParameterNames()
```

```
//Returns the names of the context's initialization parameters as an Enumeration of
//String.
```

```
public Enumeration getAttributeNames()
```

```
//Returns an Enumeration containing the attribute names available within this
//Servlet context.
```

```
public Object getAttribute(String name)

//Returns the Servlet container attribute with the given name, or null.

public void setAttribute(String name, Object object)

//Binds an object to a given attribute name in this Servlet context.

public void removeAttribute(java.lang.String name)

//Removes the attribute with the given name from the Servlet context.
```

3. `public abstract class GenericServlet extends Object implements Servlet, ServletConfig, java.io.Serializable`

   In addition to the methods derived from all the interfaces, it implements this class also and adds a few methods such as:

```
public void init() throws ServletException

//A convenience method that can be overridden so that there's no need to call
//super.init(config).
```

4. `public abstract class HttpServlet extends GenericServlet implements java.io.Serializable`

   The HttpServlet provides an abstract class to be subclassed to create an HTTP Servlet object. A subclass of HttpServlet must override at least one method, usually one of the following: doGet() for HTTP get requests and doPost() for HTTP post requests. The serializable interface provides the mechanism to implement Servlet session tracking, such as Servlet cookies. The hierarchy is shown in Figure 3.3. Not all methods are listed in the figure. We focus on the HttpServlet class because all Web application Servlets must be subclasses of HttpServlet class. Figure 3.3 shows the HttpServlet class hierarchy.

The doGet() and doPost() methods are two widely used methods provided by the HttpServlet class. There are two basic HTTP request types in HTTP: get or post. The get request is commonly used to retrieve data or images from a Web server and the post request is commonly used to send form data to the Web server. get and post methods can be used alternately in some cases such as submitting an HTTP form. Although get is basically used for reading, it can also include some short data along with the request. The get-type request is the default type. It can also be made by clicking on a hyperlink that points to the Servlet. The set-type request is also URL bookmarkable if it is used as part of a URL. It is better to use the post method if the contents of the request are very large or need to be kept confidential.

The following is an example of an HTTP form that makes a request to an HTTP Servlet.

```
<html xmlns = "http://www.w3.org/1999/xhtml">
<head>
```

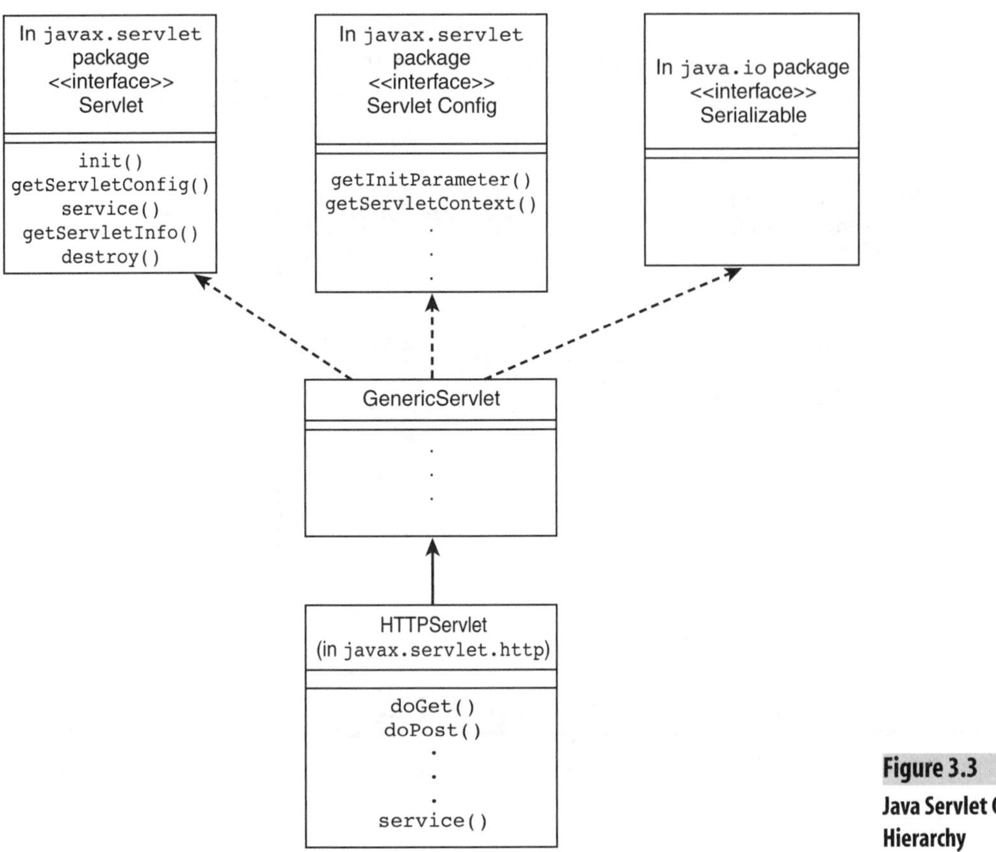

Figure 3.3
Java Servlet Class Hierarchy

```
   <title>Processing post requests with data</title>
</head>

<body>
   <form action = " /conv/conversion" method = "post">

      <p><label>
         Convert from Feet to Meters.
         Enter the feet value in the field.
         <br /><input type = "text" name = "feet" />
         <input type = "submit" value = "Submit" />
      </p></label>

   </form>
</body>
</html>
```

The `POST` method type is specified in this form request to a Servlet named *conversion* as the action attribute of the form tag. The Servlet class name is not necessarily the same as this name because the deployment descriptor may map a virtual name to the actual Servlet class name. The HTTP form that invokes the Servlet conversion is shown here. This Web application's root directory is `conv`.

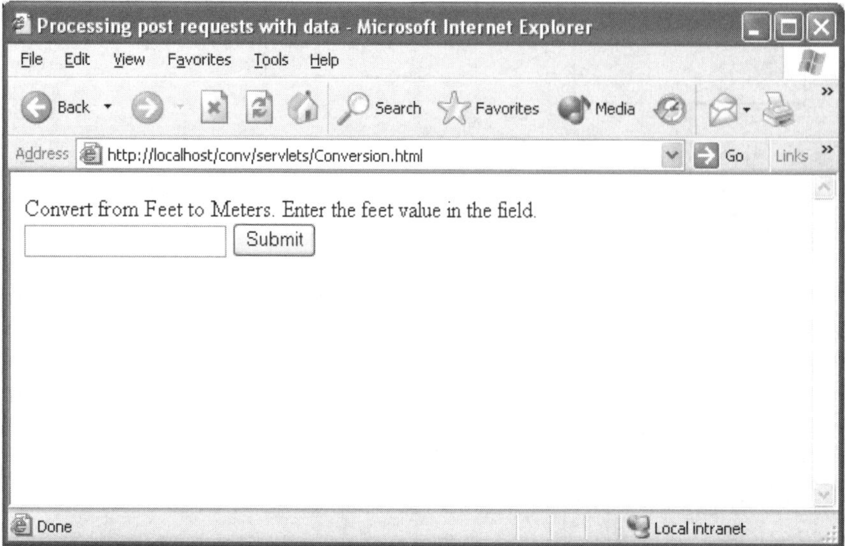

3.3.2 Servlet Life Cycle

A Servlet has a life cycle just as a Java applet does. The life cycle is managed by the Servlet container. There are three methods in the Servlet interface that each Servlet class must implement. They are `init()`, `service()`, and `destroy()`. Figure 3.4 shows the flowchart of the life cycle of a Servlet class.

All of them are invoked by the Servlet container. The `init()` method is called only once. The Servlet object can be instantiated either by the `web.xml` Servlet configuration file (<load-on-startup/> in its `servlet` tag of the `web.xml` file), or by its first request access. The `init()` method is called by the Servlet container right after the Servlet object is loaded. Some routine processes such as database connection can be specified in the `init()` method so that the connection time can be significantly reduced. Otherwise, these functions must be performed for each HTTP Servlet request, which may require substantial time. All subsequent requests are handled by `service()` method. If an application Servlet is a generic Servlet instead of an HTTP Servlet, the `service()` method must be specified. The `service()` method is called by the Servlet container once per request. If the request to the Servlet is an HTTP request, then the `service()` method will forward the request to either the `doPost()` method or `doGet()` method, respectively, according to the HTTP request types.

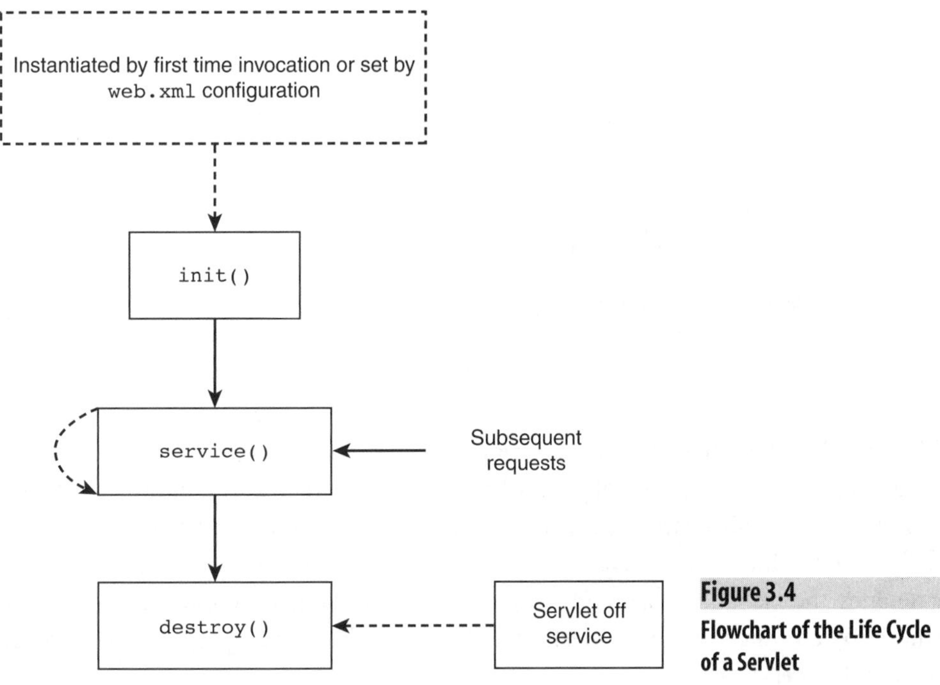

Figure 3.4
Flowchart of the Life Cycle of a Servlet

The following fragment shows an example of `init()` and `destroy()` methods.

```
public class MyServlet extends HttpServlet {
   private Connection DBconn = null;
   private String dbURL;
   private String URL = "jdbc:odbc:";

   public void init( ServletConfig config )
      throws ServletException
   {
      super.init( config );
      dbURL = config.getInitParameter("database");
      URL = URL + dbURL;
      try {
         Class.forName( "sun.jdbc.odbc.JdbcOdbcDriver" );
         DBconn =
            DriverManager.getConnection( URL, "", "" );
      }
      catch ( Exception e ) {
         e.printStackTrace();
         DBconn = null;
```

```
        }
    } ...

        public void destroy()
        {
            try {
            if DBConn != Null)
            {  DBConn.close();
            }
          catch   (Exception e) {
                e. printStackTrace();
            }
        }
```

The `init()` method has a `ServletConfig` parameter. The Servlet can read its initialization arguments through the `ServletConfig` object, which has all initialization parameter values configured in `web.xml` file. In this example, the `init()` method reads the init parameter called *database* that is defined in the following `web.xml` and assigns the string `myDatabase` to variable `dbURL`. The `init()` concatenates the `URL` and `dbURL` and uses it to make a database connection. This connection can be shared by all other Servlet requests. The following is an example of `web.xml` configuration for the Servlet `MyServlet`.

```
<web-app>
...
<servlet>
  <servlet-name>MyServlet</servlet-name>
  <servlet-class>Myservlet</servlet-class>
  <init-param>
    <param-name>database</param-name>
    <param-value>MyDatabase</param-value>
  </init-param>
</servlet>
...
</web-app>
```

The `service()` method can be customized to handle a generic Servlet request or it can forward the request to the `doGet()` or `doPost()` method for an HTTP Servlet request. If an HTTP request specifies a `post`-type request, then `doPost()` will respond to this request and process it. The `destroy()` method is called only once when the Servlet is unloaded, and all its resources will be released.

3.3.3 Processing of HTTP Requests and Responses

This section focuses on how a Servlet receives an HTTP request and processes it, then returns the result in an HTTP response object. As mentioned before, `doGet()` and `doPost()` are the two most often used methods for an HTTP Servlet to retrieve and respond to the request. Selection of `doGet()` or `doPost()` depends on the HTTP request type. The following are the prototypes of these two methods.

```
void doPost( HttpServletRequest request, HttpServletResponse response )
        throws ServletException, IOException;

void doPost( HttpServletRequest request, HttpServletResponse response )
        throws ServletException, IOException;
```

We first take a look at the two parameters of `doGet()` and `doPost()`.

1. `public abstract interface` **`HttpServletRequest`** `extends ServletRequest`

   This interface has many methods. The important ones are shown here:

   ```
   public Cookie[] getCookies()

   //Returns an array containing the entire Cookie objects the browser sent with this
   //request. This method will be discussed again in the Servlet Cookie section.

   public String getQueryString()

   //Returns the query string that is contained in the HTTP request URL after the path.
   public HttpSession getSession(boolean create)

   //Returns the current HttpSession of this request or, if necessary, creates a new
   //session for the request. Use true to create a new session, or use false to return
   //the current HttpSession.

   public String getRequestedSessionId()

   //Returns the session ID specified by the client.
   ```

   The following methods are inherited from the `ServletRequest` interface:

   ```
   public void setAttribute(java.lang.String key,java.lang.Object o)

   //Stores an attribute in the context of this request. Attributes are reset when the
   //request is switched.

   public Object getAttribute(String name)

   //Returns the value of the named attribute as an Object.

   public String getParameter(String name)

   //Returns the value of a request parameter or null if the parameter does not exist.
   ```

2. `public abstract interface` **`HttpServletResponse`** `extends ServletResponse`

   Some of its important methods are listed here.

```
public abstract void addCookie(Cookie cookie)

//Adds the specified cookie to the response.

public abstract String encodeURL(String url)

//Encodes the URL by including the session ID in it, or, if encoding is not needed,
//returns URL unchanged.

public abstract String encodeRedirectURL(String url)

//Encodes the specified URL for use in the sendRedirect method.

public abstract void sendError(int sc) throws IOException

//Sends an error response to the client using the specified status code and a
//default message.

public abstract void sendRedirect(String location) throws IOException

//Sends a redirect response to the client using the specified redirect location URL.
//The location may point to a static or dynamic resource.
```

The following methods are inherited from `ServletResponse` interface.

```
public ServletOutputStream getOutputStream()throws java.io.IOException

//Returns a ServletOutputStream for writing binary data in the response. The Servlet
//container does not encode the binary data.

public PrintWriter getWriter()throws java.io.IOException

//Returns a PrintWriter object that can send character text to the client.
```

`HttpServletRequest` and `HttpServletResponse` are the two interfaces that provide the Servlet with full access to all information from the request and the response sent back to the client. When the `doGet()` or `doPost()` is called the Servlet container passes in the `HttpServletRequest` and `HttpServletResponse` objects.

The `HttpServletRequest` interface comes with a number of very useful methods. The method `String getParameter(String name)` returns the value of a parameter as part of GET- or POST-type requests. In the Servlet `Conversion`, `request.getParameter("feet")` returns the value that the client inputs in the *feet* text field of the HTML form. The types of the component parameters can be a radio button, check box, combo box, etc. The method `HttpSession getsession(Boolean create)` returns an `HttpSession` object, which can be shared by all Web components within the client's current session. There are many other methods, such as `getParameters()`, which returns all parameter names, and `getCookies()`, which returns Cookie objects used to identify the client of the Servlet.

The HttpServletResponse interface comes with some useful methods.

The setContextType(String type) method is used to tell the client browser the MIME type of the response. It can be "text/html," "text/xml," or others.

The PrintWriter getWriter() method is widely used to return a text output stream for sending text data to clients. The ServletOutputStream getOutputStream() method is used to return a byte output stream for sending binary data such as music or images to clients. There are also some other methods such as addcookie(Cookie cookie).

The following is a simple Servlet that takes an input of feet units from an HTML page and converts it to meter units in the metric system.

```
import java.util.*;
import java.text.*;
import javax.servlet.*;
import javax.servlet.http.*;
import java.io.*;

public class Conversion extends HttpServlet {

// process "post" request from client
   protected void doPost( HttpServletRequest request,
      HttpServletResponse response )
         throws ServletException, IOException
   {
      String feet = request.getParameter( "feet" );
  Double feetNum = Double.valueOf(feet);
  Double meters = 0.3048;
  Double metersHeight = feetNum*meters;
         response.setContentType( "text/html" );
         PrintWriter out = response.getWriter();
  DecimalFormat decimalFormatter = new DecimalFormat("0.000");
  String mtrs = decimalFormatter.format(metersHeight);

// send HTML document to client

      out.println( "<html>" );

// head section of document
      out.println( "<head>" );
      out.println(
         "<title>Processing get requests with data</title>" );
      out.println( "</head>" );
```

```
// body section of document
      out.println( "<body>" );
      out.println( "<h1>"+feet+" ft = " + mtrs + " meters<br
                   />" );
      out.println( "Thanks!</h1>" );
      out.println( "</body>" );

      // end HTML document
      out.println( "</html>" );
      out.close();
// close stream to complete the page
   }
}
```

Let us take a look how the Servlet dynamically produces HTML content. The `response` object's method `setContentType()` specifies the type of content in text/html format rather than some other format such as image/gif, etc. The `response` object's method `getWriter()` gets a reference `out` pointing to a `PrintWriter` object to let the Servlet send HTML contents to the client. The rest of the `out.println()` statements just append the HTML contents to the outgoing page one line per statement.

Here is the output HTTP page dynamically generated by this Servlet. You can see that the header title specified in the `head` tag on the top of the page and the output result in the body section are displayed in the Z of "h1."

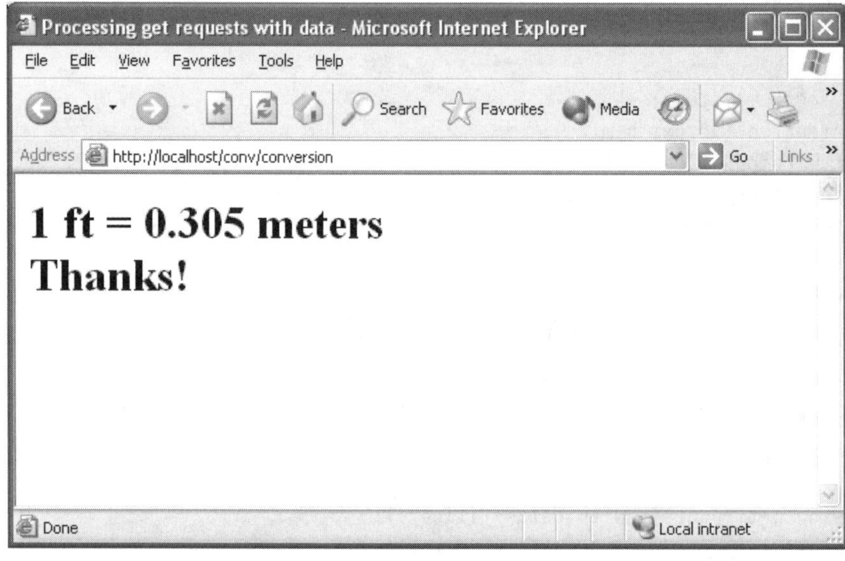

3.4 Communications with HTTP Servlets

3.4.1 Communication from Clients to HTTP Servlets

The typical way for a Web client to call an HTTP Servlet on a Web server is to use an HTTP form. The HTTP Servlet can be specified in the action attribute of the `<form>` tag. The default request type is the `GET` method. The `POST` method can also be specified in the method attribute.

For GET-type HTTP requests, `http://`*<host>*`/`*<servletName>* can also be directly typed in the URL location field of the browser if no parameter values need to be passed. If some parameter values need to be passed with the request, type `http://`*<host>*`/`*<servletName>*`?`*<parameterName>*`=`*<value>* (example: `http://localhost:8080/conv/conversion?feet=100`). There may be more than one pair of *<parameter name>*/*<value>* pairs that are separated by "&." The "?" indicates the beginning of the query string. Another way is to have a hyperlink tag in an HTML file so you can access the Servlet by clicking on the link. You can attach a query string to the *<servletName>* in the hyperlink tag.

```
<A HREF="http://<host>/<servletName>Click me to get Servlet</A>
```

A POST request cannot be bookmarked since it cannot be typed in the URL address field of any browser.

3.4.2 The Ways for Servlets to Communicate with Other Web Components

We have discussed a number of ways for a Web client to access an HTTP Servlet. We will discuss the communication between HTTP Servlets, between Servlets and other Web server components such as JSP and JavaBeans, and from Servlets to Web clients. The details of communications with JSP and JavaBeans will be discussed in the following chapters.

It is not realistic that a Web application has only one single Java HTTP Servlet. The Servlet Web component plays a role of traffic control dispatcher to forward a request with data to other Web components to process. Many components need to work together to accomplish a real-world application.

There are four Web component scopes: `page`, `request`, `session`, and `application`. Web components can share and delegate the data within request, session, or application scopes. There may be many requests in one client session and there may be many client sessions in the Web application. The following is a partial fragment of an HTTP Servlet class to explain how a Servlet dispatches a request to another Web component with shared data.

```
. . .
MyObject myObject = new MyObject(...)
request.setAttribute("myData", myObject);
        RequestDispatcher rd;
        rd = getServletContext().getRequestDispatcher(targetURL);
        rd.forward(request, response);
. . .
```

where `targetURL` may be another Servlet object or a JSP object.

This short fragment involves a lot of interfaces and classes. The `RequestDispatcher` interface in `javax.servlet` API package has two methods: `forward()` and `include()`.

```
public void forward(ServletRequest request, ServletResponse response)
                    Throws ServletException, java.io.IOException;
```

This method forwards the current request to another resource (servlet, JSP, HTML page, etc.). The control is shifted to the target.

```
public void include(ServletRequest request, ServletResponse response)
                    Throws ServletException, java.io.IOException;
```

This method includes another resource in the current Servlet's output. The current Servlet is still in charge.

The `HttpServlet` class implements `ServletConfig` interface, which has a method called `getServletContext()`. An `HttpServlet` can call this method to obtain a `ServletContext` object. By the method `getRequestDispatcher()` of the `ServletContext` a `RequestDispatcher` object can be obtained. Finally, the `HttpServlet` forwards the control to the target Web component with the request and response objects where the attribute data is attached. The `targetURL` servlet or JSP object can retrieve the `myObject` by `request.getAttribute("`*`myData`*`")` where *`myData`* is the name of the attribute and *`myObject`* is the value of this attribute.

In some cases a Servlet needs to let another Servlet or JSP component within the same session take over control and pass on some data to it. This can be done by passing the `HttpSession` object instead of request object since the scope of `HttpSession` is the whole session instead of the current request only.

```
. . .
MyObject myObject = new MyObject(. . .)
HttpSession session = request.getSession();
session.setAttribute("myData", myObject);
        RequestDispatcher rd;
        rd = getServletContext().getRequestDispatcher(targetURL);
        rd.forward(request, response);
. . .
```

If a Servlet needs to talk to another Servlet or another Web component outside the current session, the Servlet object must obtain a `ServletContext` and attach the data by setting its attributes as follows.

```
. . .
MyObject myObject = new MyObject(. . .)
getServletContext().setAttribute("myData", myObject);
        RequestDispatcher rd;
        rd = getServletContext().getRequestDispatcher(targetURL);
        rd.forward(request, response);
. . .
```

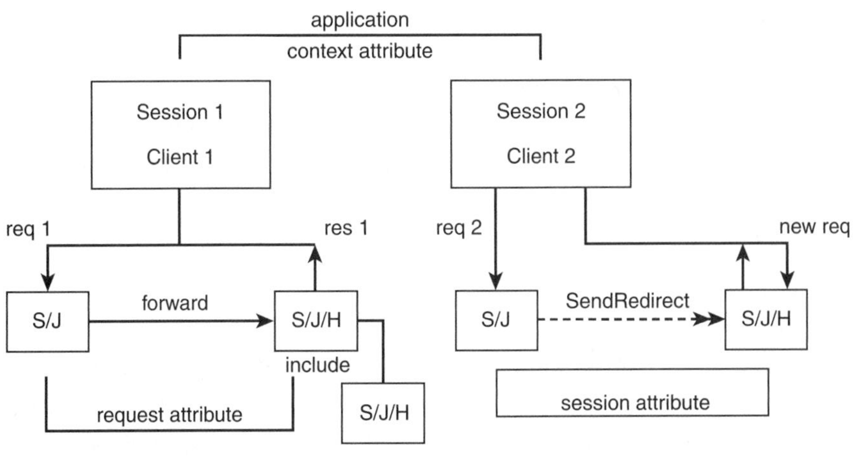

Figure 3.5
Attribute Scopes in Servlet

Figure 3.5 depicts the concepts of data sharing between many pages in the same request, between many requests in the same session, and between many client sessions in the same Web application.

A Servlet can include the output of another Web component such as a Servlet, JSP, or HTML page as part of its own output, such as:

```
RequestDispatcher rd;
        rd = getServletContext().getRequestDispatcher(targetURL);
        rd.include(request, response);
```

The `targetURL` has all access to the request object. The `targetURL` can be static HTML content, another Servlet with parameter/value pairs separated by a "?", or another JSP.

A Servlet can also send a temporary redirect response to the client using the specified redirect URL pointing to another Java Web component or HTML page by invoking the `sendRedirect()` method. The signature of the `sendRedirect` method is

```
public void sendRedirect(String URL) throws java.io.IOException;
```

Two example code snippets follow.

```
response.sendRedirect(www.yahoo.com);
    response.sendRedirect(http://<host>/servlet/<servletName>?<param>=<value>);
```

The first statement just redirects the client to a new Web page without passing any parameters. The second statement redirects the request to another Servlet with a <param>/<value> pair.

The `sendRedirect()` method of the `HttpServletResponse` interface and the `forward()` method of `HttpServletRequest` play a similar role in transferring the control from one Java Web component to the other. There are many differences between these two mechanisms: the forwarded URL cannot be bookmarked, but the sendRedirected URL can; the target of the forward method is within the same request scope, but the target of the `sendRedirect()` method will result in a different request in the same session. Note that `sendRedirect()` always takes a round trip to the client and redirects the client to make a new request to the target. The information of the source Servlet is lost unless a query string is passed appended to the `targetURL`. Always use the `forward()` method unless it is impossible, such as when the target is located on another Web server out of the current context.

3.4.3 Web Client Session Tracking

We discussed how a Servlet talks to other Web components such as HTTP Servlets, JSP, and HTML pages in Web applications by using the `forward()`, `sendRedirect()`, and `include()` methods. Also, we discussed data sharing between the Web components when the flow control is shifted from one component to another component on the Web server. In this section we focus on how a Servlet keeps track of a client session.

An HTTP proposal is a stateless protocol that takes requests from Web clients and responds with a file. It does not memorize what has happened in the past. FTP and Telnet protocols know the client states, such as users, connections, and disconnections, but HTTP does not. A client session consists of a series of conversations between the client and Web applications on the Web server over a period of time. There is often a requirement for a Web application on the server to keep track of all data from the beginning of the client session all the way to the end of the session. Such requirements occur in online shopping applications, for example.

There are two mechanisms to handle the client session tracking. One is to save the client identification and session information on the server side once the Servlet receives a request from the client. The other is to save the client information on the client browser at the client side for subsequent request use.

Hidden Form Fields

The hidden form field is a form field that does not appear on the GUI, but it can carry the user input data just as any other input field. Data can be passed via a hidden form field in a static or dynamic HTML page in an HTML form.

```
<input type ="HIDDEN" name="myId" value="1234" />
```

Once the request is sent to the Servlet, the hidden data is attached to the request. The Servlet can use `request.getParameter("myId")` in the `doGet()` or `doPost()` method to obtain the ID for this specific client where the request is an `HttpServletRequest` object as the first parameter of these two methods.

URL Rewriting

As done before in the GET-type request, a query string with param/value pairs can be attached to the URL address with a "?" as a separator. In the same way, we can attach a token or identifier to the URL of the Servlet or other targets.

```
<a href = "http://<host>/servlet/myServlet?myId=1234">_URL Rewriting Link Request </a>
```

Follow this link to invoke the target Servlet myServlet. The invocation of `request.getParameter("myId")` in the `doGet()` or `doPost()` method will get the ID for this specific client where the `request` is an `HttpServletRequest` object as the first parameter of these two methods. A session identifier in the URL can also be sent in URL rewriting. For example, a developer can write the following code:

```
out.println("<a href =" + response.encodeURL("Servlet1") + ">Click here
           </a>");
```

This will result in a URL that may look similar to:

```
http://<host>/servlet/Servlet1;jsessionid=ABC123
```

where ABC123 is produced by the `encodeURL()` method of `HttpServletResponse`.

Both of these two mechanisms of session tracking require that the clients identify themselves so that the Servlets can distinguish different sessions from different clients. The session identification data are stored on the server.

The disadvantages of the above mechanisms are the privacy issue and amount of data that can be passed on.

Servlet Cookie

Cookies are text files that store sets of param/value pairs. The Servlet at the server site generates the cookie based on the client's HTTP request (see Figure 3.6). The cookie is created on the server site and sent back to the client along with the `HttpServletResponse object`. The cookie is stored at the client's browser. A subsequent request from the same client to the same server will send the cookie to the Servlet to be recognized as the identification of the client. As long as the client does not invalidate the cookie, the

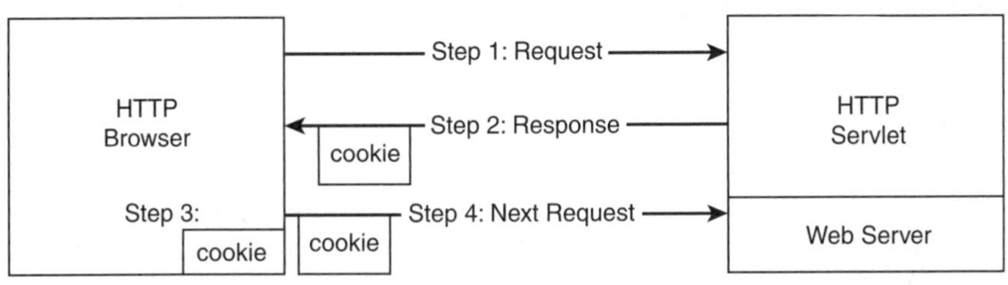

Figure 3.6
Servlet Cookie

Servlet is always able to identify the client. The cookie is widely used in user authentication, e-commerce, e-advertisements, and custom home page generation.

The following is an example of a Servlet class that generates cookies. This Servlet retrieves a username from the username parameter in the form request and creates a cookie with a "name/uname" pair; sets the expiration time of the cookie to five minutes; and sends the cookie with the response object back to the client's browser. The browser saves the cookie and returns it to the server on subsequent transactions.

```
import javax.servlet.*;
import javax.servlet.http.*; //class Cookie is available here
import java.io.*;
import java.util.*;

public class CookieServlet1 extends HttpServlet {

   void doPost( HttpServletRequest request,
      HttpServletResponse response )
         throws ServletException, IOException
   {
      String uname = request.getParameter( "username" );
      Cookie cookie = new Cookie( "name", uname );
      Cookie.setMaxAge(5*60); //The cookie will expire in 5 minutes.
      response.addCookie( cookie );

      response.setContentType( "text/html" );
      PrintWriter out = response.getWriter();
      . . .
      out.println( "  . . . " );
     . . .
      }
 }
```

There is another Servlet that reads the cookies from clients. When the same client accesses the following Servlet, the Servlet can retrieve the cookie from the request object and process it.

```
public class CookieServlet1 extends HttpServlet {

 void doGet( HttpServletRequest request,
      HttpServletResponse response )
         throws ServletException, IOException
   {  . . .
      Cookie cookies[] = request.getCookies();  // get cookies
      response.setContentType( "text/html" );
      PrintWriter out = response.getWriter();
```

```
      . . .
            // get the name of each cookie
         for ( int i = 0; i < cookies.length; i++ )
            out.println( cookies[ i ].getName() +
               cookies[ i ].getValue() + "<br />" );
      . . .

   }
}
```

Cookies can last much longer than a single session as long as the cookie is not invalidated and not yet expired.

HttpSession Object in Session Tracking

Using `HttpSession` API in session management is quite straightforward. It may be the best option in most cases for session tracking. The `HttpSession` object can hold a session ID that can be used to identify whether the requests are within the same session so that they can share the same data. Each `HttpSession` object represents a single user HTTP session.

The `HttpServletRequest` interface provides some useful methods such as:

```
HttpSession getSession(Boolean create)
//If create is True, then a new HttpSession object is created and returned. If create is
//False, then the current HttpSession object is returned.
```

The `HttpSession` interface has a number of useful methods:

```
setAttribute(String key, Object value);
// sets a key/value pair in the HttpSession object

Object getAttribute(String name)
// gets the value of the key in the HttpSession object

String getId()
// returns the unique ID assigned to this session

ServletContext getServletContext)
// returns application context of the servlet

Boolean isNew()
// returns true if the session is new and client does not know it yet

Void invalidate()
// invalidates the session

void setMaxInactiveInterval(int seconds)
// The session will be invalidated in the given number of seconds if no subsequent query
// comes within the interval.
```

Other methods such as getMaxInactiveInterval(), getlastAccessTime(), getCreationTime(), and getLastAccessedTime() can also be used to access the session information.

Let us look at a simple online shopping cart example. The online shopping server must know who the owner of the shopping cart is because every user needs to make many requests to different Servlets and pages before checking out. The server needs to keep track of items put in the shopping cart. There may be many users shopping on the same site at the same time.

```
public class ShoppingServlet extends HttpServlet {

      void doPost( HttpServletRequest request,
                   HttpServletResponse response )
         throws ServletException, IOException
   {

      // Get the user's session object.
      // Create a session (true) if one does not exist.
      HttpSession session = request.getSession( true );
      . . .
      // ShoppingCart may be a vector class holding many items
      ShoppingCart cart =
                   (ShoppingCart)session.getAttribute("usercart");

      if (cart == null){
      cart = new ShoppingCart();

      session.setAttribute( "usercart", cart );
      . . .
      //user adds items to the shoppingCart
      cart.add(item-name, item);
      . . .
      //display new added items
      response.setContentType( "text/html" );
      PrintWriter out = response.getWriter();
      . . .
    }
}

public class CheckoutServlet extends HttpServlet {

void doPost( HttpServletRequest request, HttpServletResponse response )
             throws ServletException, IOException
   {
```

```
        . . .
        shoppingCart = (ShoppingCart)session.getAttribute("cart");
        . . .
        session.invalidate(); //Invalidate the session after the checkout.
        . . .
        PrintWriter out = response.getWriter();
        response.setContentType( "text/html" );
        . . .
        out.println( . . . );
        . . .
    }
}
```

By using session tracking management, the server knows whose shopping cart it is processing and knows what items this user's shopping cart has so far.

In the lab section we present a complete Servlet example of session tracking implementation.

3.4.4 Debugging Servlets

Debugging Servlets is not an easy job. The best solution to fix a runtime logic error is to plug in the Tomcat Servlet container to JBuilder, Eclipse, or VisualAge, or just use an intergrated debugger in the IDE such as Sun One Studio, BEA WebLogic, or IBM WebSphere so that these IDE tools can be used to debug and test.

First, we look at some simple high-level debugging techniques we can apply without any other development tool supports. Since a Java HTTP Servlet is running at the server site and the results are sent back to the client, we can debug either by checking the generated dynamic pages at the client site or by checking the error status at the server site.

- Check the generated HTML source code by View Source from the Web browser menu. Some simple HTML errors can be easily located that help to locate the Servlet error.
- Use the `sendError(int sc)` method of `HttpServletResponse` to send an error response to the client with the specified status code and a default message.
- Use the `out.println()` method to print debugging messages on the client page.
- Use the `jdb` Java debug utility to debug the Servlet. You must start Tomcat in debug mode by running the `Catalina.bat` startup file in the `bin` directory of the Tomcat installation directory so that a new separate window is not opened. This is a low-level debugging mode. The detailed debugging environment setting can be found in the Tomcat User's Guide.

- Use the `void log(String message)` method of `HttpServlet` to write debug information into the log file in the `Tomcat` installation directory.
- Use `System.out.println()` or `System.err.println()` to write error messages. The error messages will be displayed on the server console if `Tomcat` is started in developer mode.
- Check the request data and response data separately. Determine whether clients have sent the right data or the Servlets responded with the right data. You can have separate classes to detect these problems.

3.5 Examples and Lab Practice

What follows are a number of labs that will help you better understand the concepts of Java Servlets. Lab 1 shows the detailed steps to download and install the Servlet execution environments and their configurations. Lab 2 gives a simple Servlet application that converts a temperature from Fahrenheit to Celsius. Lab 3 depicts how one Servlet can collaborate with other Servlets to accomplish a task. Lab 4 uses a simple example in Java Servlet session tracking showing how to distinguish different sessions during a Web application. All the labs have been tested in Tomcat 5 with Servlet 2.4. Because of the platform-independence feature of Java technology, the labs can be implemented on any platform. We implemented them on Windows XP.

3.5.1 Lab 1: Tomcat 5 Installation and Configuration

Tomcat 5 supports Java Servlet 2.4 and JSP 2.0. Tomcat can be used as a stand-alone Web server or an add-on Servlet container to another Web server. In this lab you will learn how to download Sun JDK 1.5 and Apache Jakarta Tomcat 5.0 and how to configure the Servlet environment including `server.xml` and `web.xml`.

We focus on the MS Windows XP system in this section. This software can also be installed on Linux or other Unix systems.

1. Download and install the Java SDK 1.5.

   Go to `http://java.sun.com/j2se/1.5.0/download.jsp` to download JDK1.5 and install it in `c:\java\jdk1.5.0`.

2. Download and install Tomcat 5.0 (or latest version).

   Go to `http://jakarta.apache.org/site/binindex.cgi` to download `Jakarta-tomcat-5.0.x.zip` file and install it in `c:\jakarta-tomcat5`. The download link is shown below.

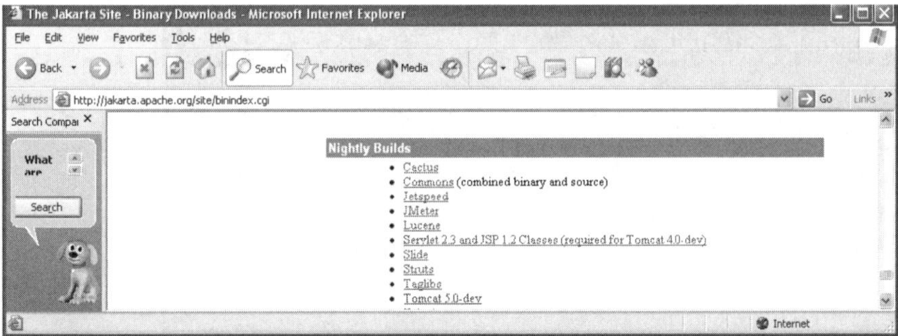

3. Environment configurations:

   a. Set PATH environment variable.

      Use the command line: `set path=C:\Java\jdk1.5.0\bin`, or use Windows: Start → Control Panel → System where you will see:

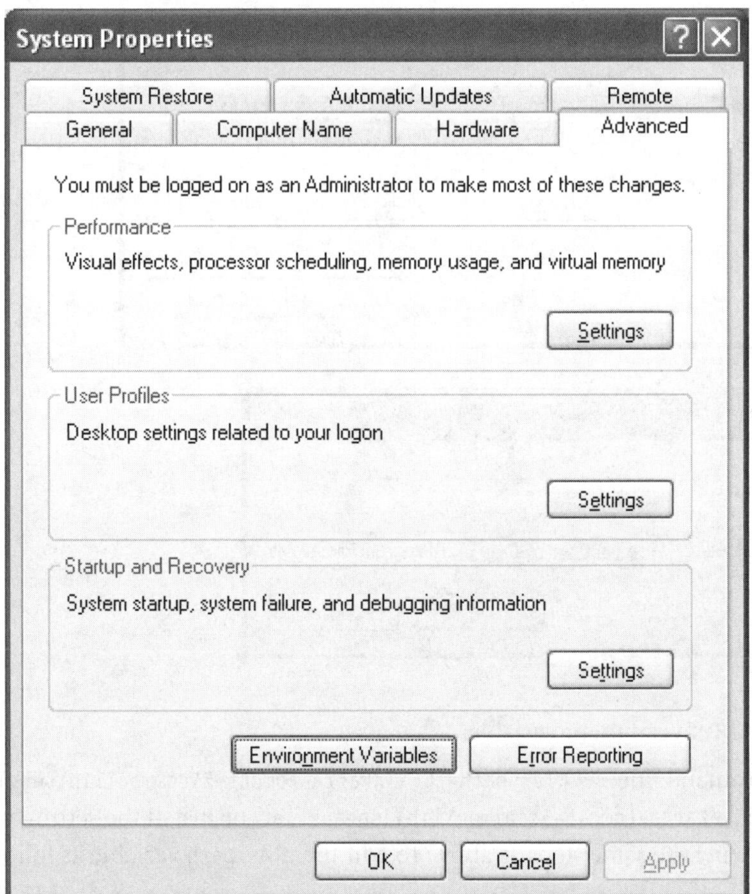

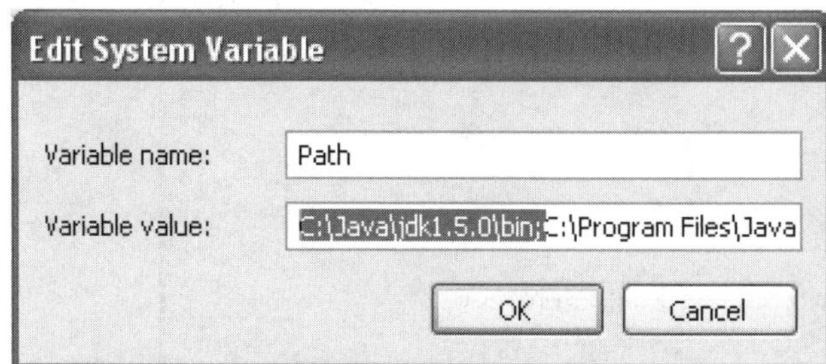

b. Set `CLASSPATH` environment variable.

On the command line: set `Classpath= C:\jakarta-tomcat-5\common\lib\servlet-api.jar;C:\jakarta-tomcat-5\common\lib\jsp-api.jar`, or install the setting via Windows following the same steps as above to edit the `classpath` variable as follows.

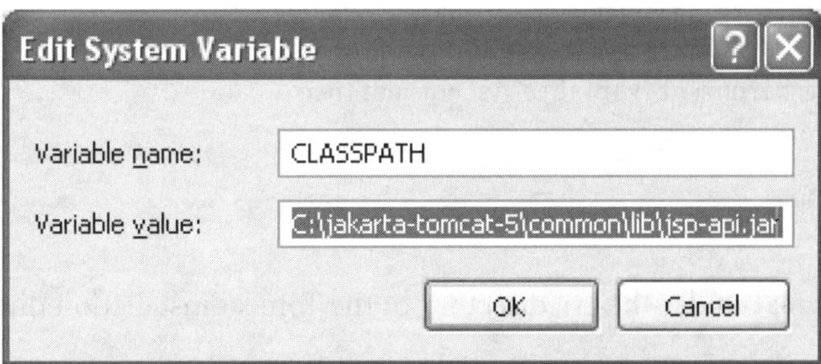

The CLASSPATH can also be set in the setclasspath.bat file that comes with Tomcat 5.x.

4. Configure the server.xml:

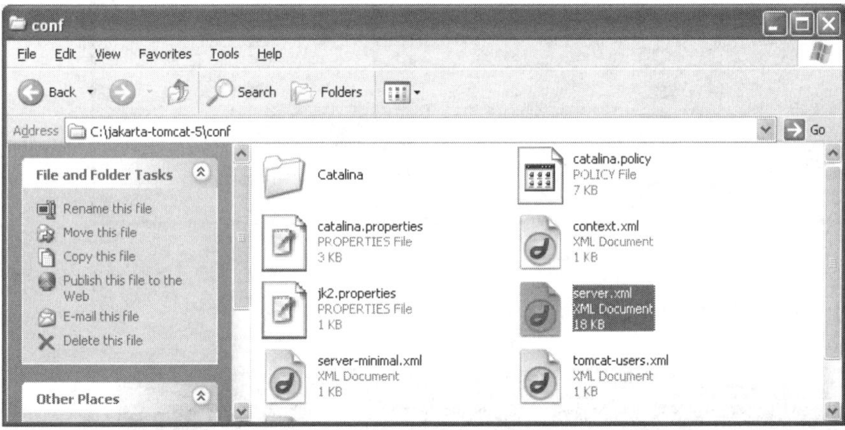

Insert the following two lines in bold into server.xml to set the JAVA_HOME and TOMCAT_HOME.

```
. . .
rem ---------------------------------------------------------------------------
rem Set CLASSPATH and Java options
rem
rem $Id: setclasspath.bat,v 1.7 2004/07/26 15:34:31 yoavs Exp $
rem ---------------------------------------------------------------------------

set CATALINA_HOME=C:\jakarta-tomcat-5
set JAVA_HOME=C:\Java\jdk1.5.0
```

```
rem Make sure prerequisite environment variables are set
if not "%JAVA_HOME%" == "" goto gotJavaHome
echo The JAVA_HOME environment variable is not defined
goto exit
. . .
```

5. Start Tomcat server.

   Double-click `startup.bat` under the `bin` directory of the Tomcat installation directory.

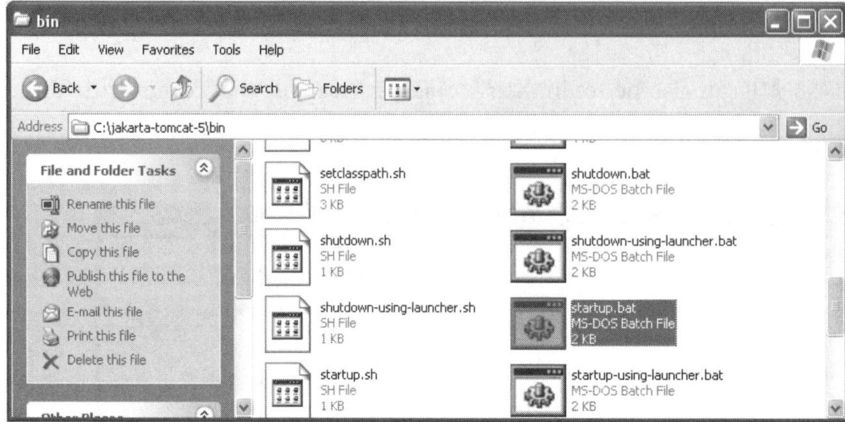

Now Tomcat is up running.

```
Tomcat
Aug 20, 2004 10:58:43 AM org.apache.catalina.core.ApplicationContext log
INFO: ContextListener: contextInitialized()
Aug 20, 2004 10:58:43 AM org.apache.catalina.core.ApplicationContext log
INFO: SessionListener: contextInitialized()
Aug 20, 2004 10:58:43 AM org.apache.catalina.core.ApplicationContext log
INFO: ContextListener: contextInitialized()
Aug 20, 2004 10:58:43 AM org.apache.catalina.core.ApplicationContext log
INFO: SessionListener: contextInitialized()
Aug 20, 2004 10:58:43 AM org.apache.coyote.http11.Http11Protocol start
INFO: Starting Coyote HTTP/1.1 on http-80
Aug 20, 2004 10:58:43 AM org.apache.jk.common.ChannelSocket init
INFO: JK2: ajp13 listening on /0.0.0.0:8009
Aug 20, 2004 10:58:43 AM org.apache.jk.server.JkMain start
INFO: Jk running ID=0 time=0/31  config=C:\jakarta-tomcat-5\conf\jk2.properties
Aug 20, 2004 10:58:44 AM org.apache.catalina.startup.Catalina start
INFO: Server startup in 3515 ms
```

6. Test the Tomcat HTTP server.

Browse the default Web page of the Tomcat 5.x at the URL `http://localhost`.

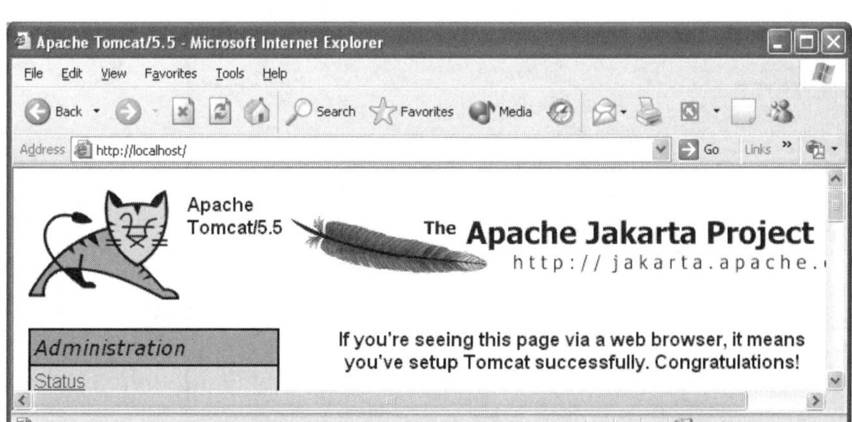

3.5.2 Lab 2: A Simple HTTP Servlet Development and Deployment

The following screens show the directory structure for the temperature conversion Web application. The root directory is named `conv`. The HTML files and JSP files are placed here. WEB-INF directory is also here.

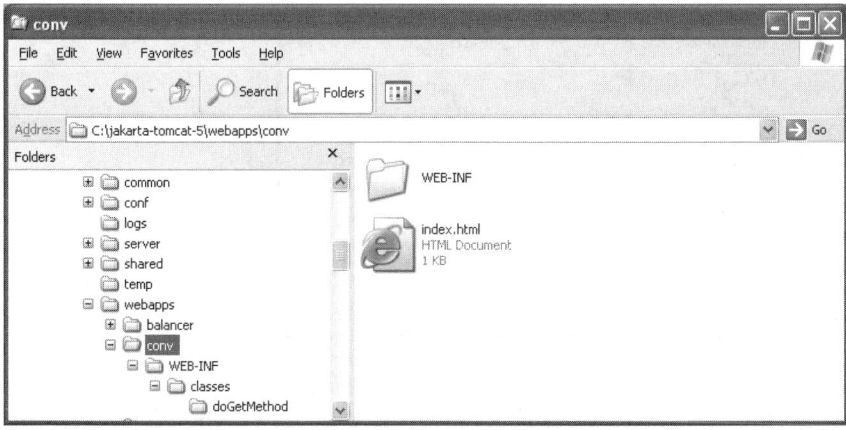

The Servlet deployment descriptor file `web.xml` is placed in the WEB-INF directory. The `classes` directory holds Servlet packages and class files.

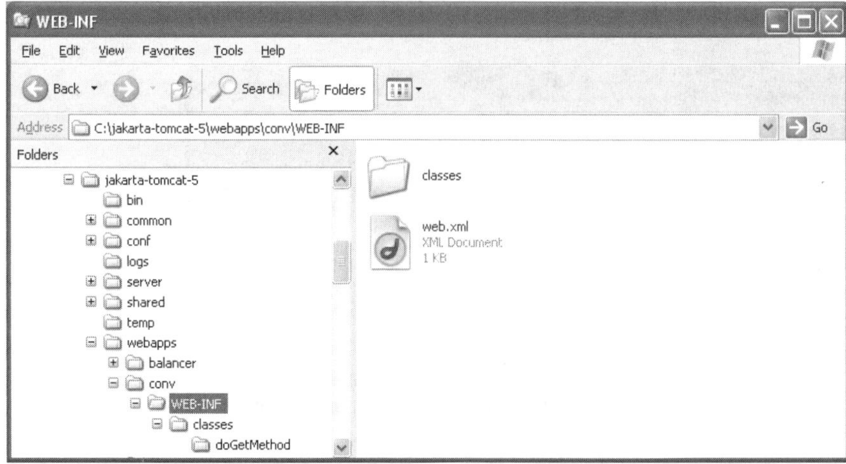

In the `doGetMethod` subdirectory you can find the Servlet class file `TestServlet` class. The `doGetMethod` directory serves as the package for the `TestServlet` class. It can be created automatically by using a **javac –d** command on the command line or can be created manually.

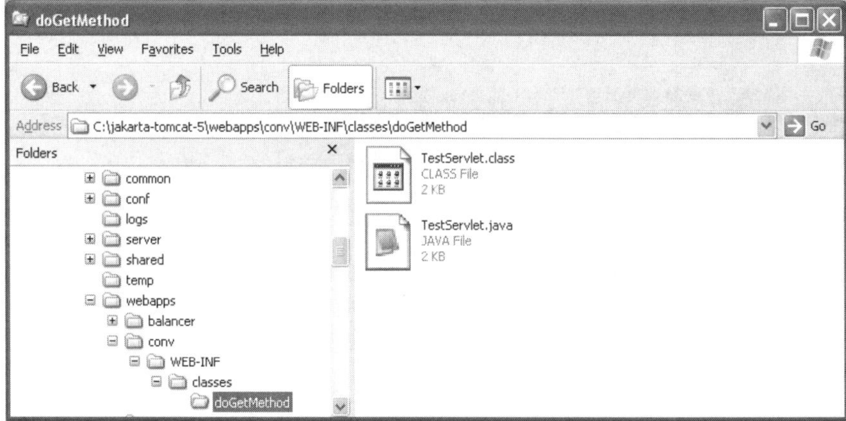

What follows is the `index.html` file that makes the HTTP request to the Servlet. The `action` attribute of the `form` tag specifies the name of the Servlet that will respond this request. The request type is not shown because the `get` method request type is the default. The text field input parameter is named as "temperature" and will be processed by the Servlet.

```
<!DOCTYPE HTML PUBLIC "-//W3C//DTD HTML 4.0 Transitional//EN">

<html>
<head>
</head>

<body>

<h3>Please enter Fahrenheit temperature:</h3><p>

<form action="/conv/test">
Temperature(F) : <input type="text" name="temperature"><br><br>
<input type="submit" value="Submit">
</form>

</body>
</html>
```

Next, we look at the Servlet web.xml deployment descriptor file that is placed in the WEB-INF subdirectory of the application root directory. The TestServlet class is in the DoGetMethod package so that doGetMethod.TestServlet is specified in the <servlet-class> tag that has its Servlet name as testServlet. In the <servlet-mapping> tag the Servlet name is mapped to a URL-pattern name "/test" that can be used as a virtual URL path name for this Servlet. It makes things much easier. For example, we can make a query by simply typing the address http://*<host>*/*<application-root>*/test?temperature=32 in the browser URL location field to access this servlet. Here the "/test" plays a role of virtual URL-pattern path name to the Servlet destination and conv is the Web application root directory.

```
<?xml version="1.0" encoding="ISO-8859-1"?>

<!DOCTYPE web-app
    PUBLIC "-//Sun Microsystems, Inc.//DTD Web Application 2.3//EN"
    "http://java.sun.com/dtd/web-app_2_3.dtd">

<web-app>

  <servlet>
    <servlet-name>testServlet</servlet-name>
    <servlet-class>doGetMethod.TestServlet</servlet-class>
  </servlet>

  <servlet-mapping>
    <servlet-name>testServlet</servlet-name>
    <url-pattern>/test</url-pattern>
```

```
  </servlet-mapping>

</web-app>
```

The following is the source code of the `TestServlet` Servlet class. This Servlet simply takes an input value of Fahrenheit temperature from the parameter "temperature" in the form request of `index.html` or from a query string of a URL address and converts it to a Celsius temperature, and then renders the converted result to the client. If the input from the client is invalid data, and then an exception is thrown and a status code 500 is sent back to the client to give an error message.

```
import java.io.*;
import java.net.*;
import javax.servlet.*;
import javax.servlet.http.*;
import java.text.DecimalFormat;

public class TestServlet extends HttpServlet
{
      public void doGet(HttpServletRequest req,
HttpServletResponse res) throws javax.servlet.ServletException, java.io.IOException
      {
        String temperature = req.getParameter("temperature");
            DecimalFormat twoDigits = new DecimalFormat("0.00");

            try
            {
              double tempF = Double.parseDouble(temperature);
              String tempC = twoDigits.format((tempF -32)*5.0/9.0);

              PrintWriter out = res.getWriter();
              out.println("<html>");
              out.println("<head>");
              out.println("</head>");
              out.println("<body>");
              out.println("<h3>" + temperature + " Fahrenheit is
                 converted to " + tempC + " Celsius</h3><p>");
              out.println("</body>");
              out.println("</html>");
            }
            catch(Exception e)
            {

              res.sendError(HttpServletResponse.SC_INTERNAL_SERVER_ERROR,
```

```
                "There was an input error");
            }
        }
}
```

Now let us run this Servlet example. Type `http://localhost/conv` to access the `index.html`. You do not need to type "`index.html`" in the URL address because it is the default HTTP home page. The page is shown below.

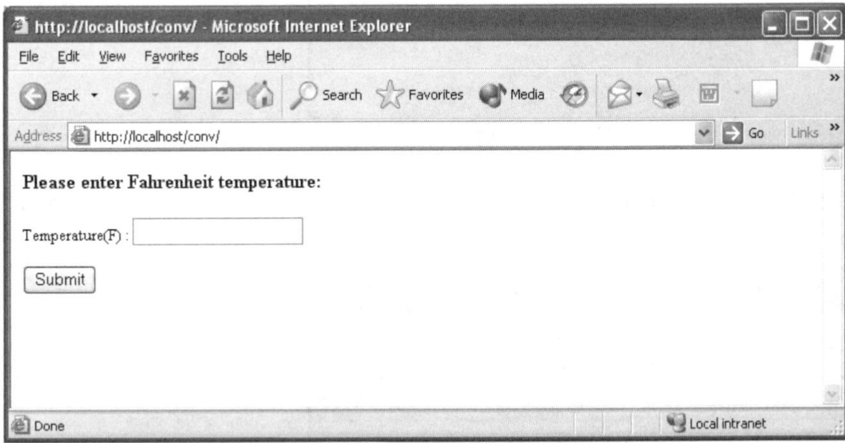

Type 32 in the Fahrenheit temperature input text field of this page.

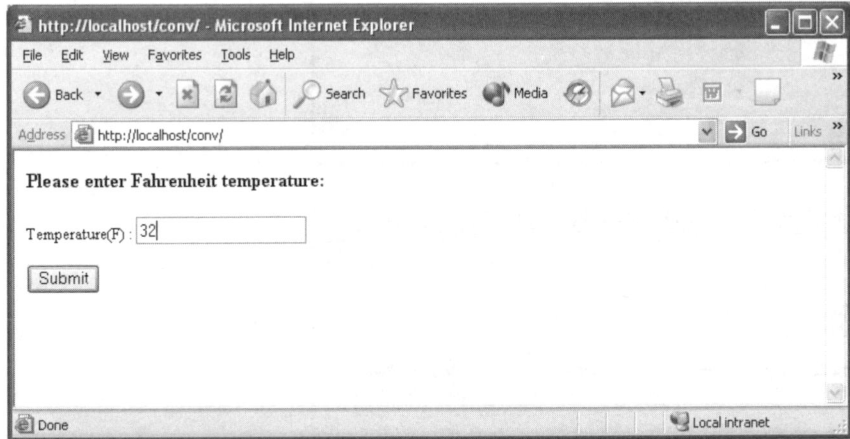

When you submit the page, you will see the following page dynamically generated by the Servlet. The 32 degree value in Fahrenheit is converted to 0 degrees in Celsius.

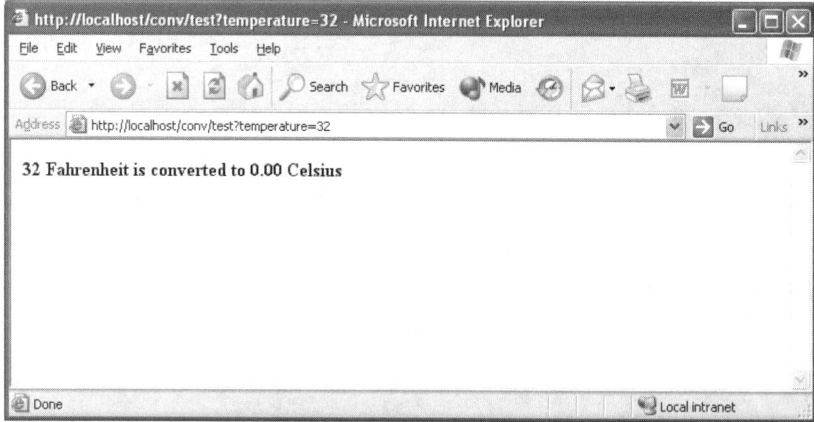

If you type invalid data such as a character string, you will get an error status message in the response page as follows:

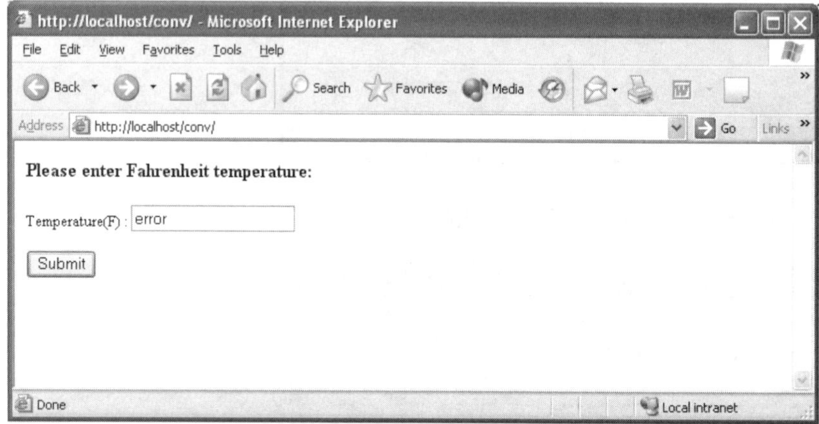

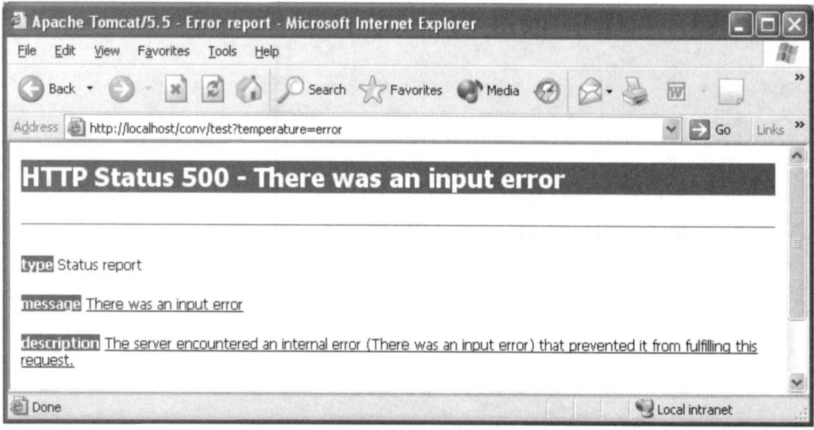

3.5.3 Lab 3: A Servlet Forwards the Control to Another Servlet

In Lab 3 you will see how a Servlet takes requests from clients and forwards the requests to another Servlet or other Web components based on certain conditions. The most important role a Servlet plays in any Web application is front-end decision making or traffic control. The complex business logic processing and GUI presentation are usually done by other Java Web components such as JSP, Enterprise JavaBeans, and JavaBeans.

First, create a Web application root directory called `forwardMethod` under the `webapps` directory and place the `index.html` file under this newly created directory.

The `index.html` is almost identical to the one in Lab 1 except that it targets a different Servlet where `/forwardMethod` is the root and `/test` is the URL-pattern name for the Servlet `TestServlet` in `/forwrdMethod/test`.

```
<!DOCTYPE HTML PUBLIC "-//W3C//DTD HTML 4.0 Transitional//EN">
<html>
<head>
     <title>doGetMethod</title>
</head>
<body>
<h3>Please enter the number of tempareture(F):</h3><p>
<form action="/forwardMethod/test">
Temperature(F) : <input type="text" name="temperature"><br><br>
<input type="submit" value="Submit">
</form>
</body>
</html>
```

What follows is the `web.xml` file for this application. Place this file under the WEB-INF subdirectory of the application root directory `forwardMethod`. Notice that there are two Servlet classes, `TestServlet` and `ForwardServlet`. The `<servlet>` tags always precede the `<servlet-mapping>` tags. Both of these two classes are in the `forwardMethod` package. Both of them get new Servlet names and URL-pattern names through mapping.

```
<?xml version="1.0" encoding="ISO-8859-1"?>

<!DOCTYPE web-app
    PUBLIC "-//Sun Microsystems, Inc.//DTD Web Application 2.3//EN"
    "http://java.sun.com/dtd/web-app_2_3.dtd">

<web-app>

  <servlet>
```

```
    <servlet-name>testServlet</servlet-name>
    <servlet-class>forwardMethod.TestServlet</servlet-class>
  </servlet>

  <servlet>
    <servlet-name>forwardServlet</servlet-name>
    <servlet-class>forwardMethod.ForwardedServlet</servlet-class>
  </servlet>

  <servlet-mapping>
    <servlet-name>testServlet</servlet-name>
    <url-pattern>/test</url-pattern>
  </servlet-mapping>

  <servlet-mapping>
    <servlet-name>forwardServlet</servlet-name>
    <url-pattern>/forward</url-pattern>
  </servlet-mapping>

</web-app>
```

Two Servlet classes are generated either in the *classes* subdirectory by **javac –d *.java** if all Java files are in the `classes` directory, or by **javac *.java** in the `forwardMethod` subdirectory of `classes` directory if all Java source files are available in the `forwardMethod` directory. The source code is listed here: The first Servlet forwards the request to the second Servlet, and the second Servlet receives the forwarded request. First, let us take a look at the `TestServlet` that forwards the request to another `Forwarded` Servlet. The first Servlet checks the validation of the data. If the data is valid, then the converted temperature is sent back to the client. Otherwise this `TestServlet` will forward the same request to the second Servlet `Forwarded` to generate a custom error page. This Servlet takes both `get` and `post` requests by adding `doPost(req, res)` in the body of the `doGet()` method.

The two most important statements in this class are

```
req.setAttribute("temperature", temperature);
req.getRequestDispatcher("/forward").forward(req, res);
```

In the first statement, the value of the temperature is stored in a request attribute called "temperature". In the second statement the Servlet gets the `requestDispatcher` reference pointing to the second Servlet by its URL name and then forwards the request and response objects to the second Servlet.

```
package forwardMethod;

import java.io.*;
import java.net.*;
import javax.servlet.*;
```

```
import javax.servlet.http.*;
import java.text.DecimalFormat;

public class TestServlet extends HttpServlet
{
     public void doGet(HttpServletRequest req, HttpServletResponse res) throws
     javax.servlet.ServletException, java.io.IOException
     {
          doPost(req, res);
     }
     public void doPost(HttpServletRequest req, HttpServletResponse res) throws
     javax.servlet.ServletException, java.io.IOException
     {
          String temperature = req.getParameter("temperature");
            DecimalFormat twoDigits = new DecimalFormat("0.00");

            try
            {
            double tempF = Double.parseDouble(temperature);
            String tempC = twoDigits.format((tempF -32)*5.0/9.0);

            PrintWriter out = res.getWriter();
            out.println("<html>");
            out.println("<head>");
            out.println("</head>");
            out.println("<body>");
            out.println("<h3>" + temperature + " Fahrenheit
            is converted to " + tempC + " Celsius</h3><p>");
            out.println("</body>");
            out.println("</html>");
            }
            catch(Exception e)
            {
                req.setAttribute("temperature", temperature);
                req.getRequestDispatcher("/forward").forward(req, res);
              return;
            }
     }
}
```

The following is the second Servlet, `ForwardedServlet`, that gets the value of the `temperature` attribute with the `req.getAttribute("temperature")` method and includes it as part of the error message sent back to the client. You can see that this attribute of the request is shared by these Servlets because they are in the same session.

```
package forwardMethod;

import java.io.*;
import java.net.*;
import java.util.*;
import javax.servlet.*;
import javax.servlet.http.*;

public class ForwardedServlet extends HttpServlet
{
     public void doGet(HttpServletRequest req, HttpServletResponse res) throws
                      javax.servlet.ServletException, java.io.IOException
     {
          doPost(req, res);
     }
     public void doPost(HttpServletRequest req, HttpServletResponse res) throws
                       javax.servlet.ServletException, java.io.IOException
     {
            try
            {
            String temp = (String) req.getAttribute("temperature");

            PrintWriter pw = res.getWriter();
            pw.println("<html>");
            pw.println("<head>");
            pw.println("</head>");
            pw.println("<body>");
            pw.println("<h3>" + "Input " + temp + " is not valid! </h3><p>");
            pw.println("</body>");
            pw.println("</html>");
            }
            catch(Exception e)
            {
            }
     }
}
```

You can run this application using any Internet browser as follows. You can attach a query string after the URL address and a "?" such as this: `http://localhost/forwardMethod/-index.html?temperature=56`.

Even the `index.html` in this string can be omitted since it is the default home page name.

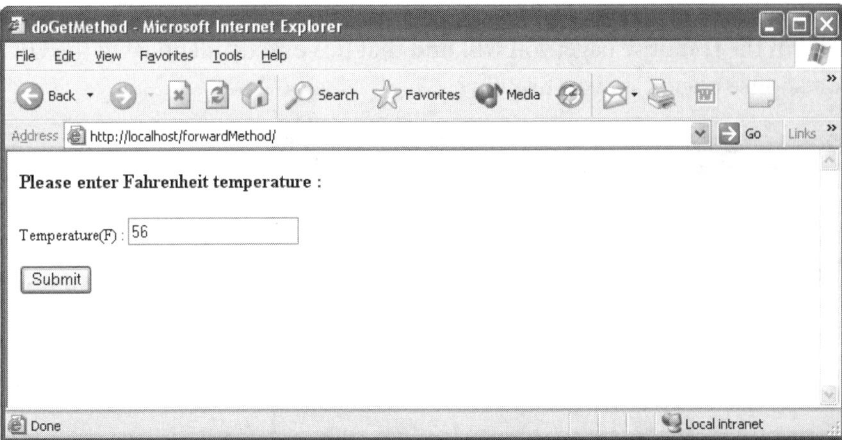

The next screen shows the response from the first Servlet.

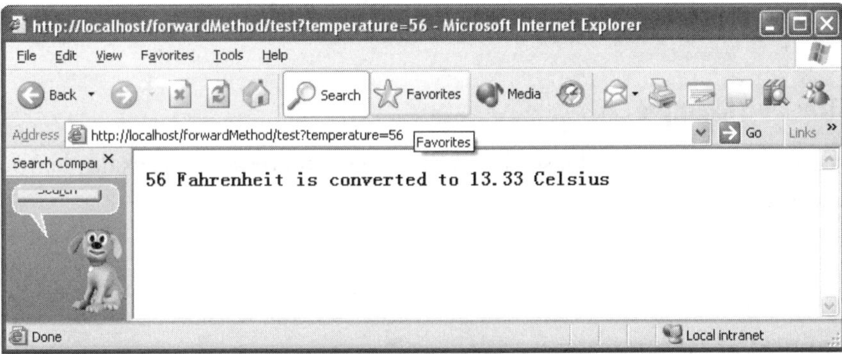

You may type in an invalid input as follows.

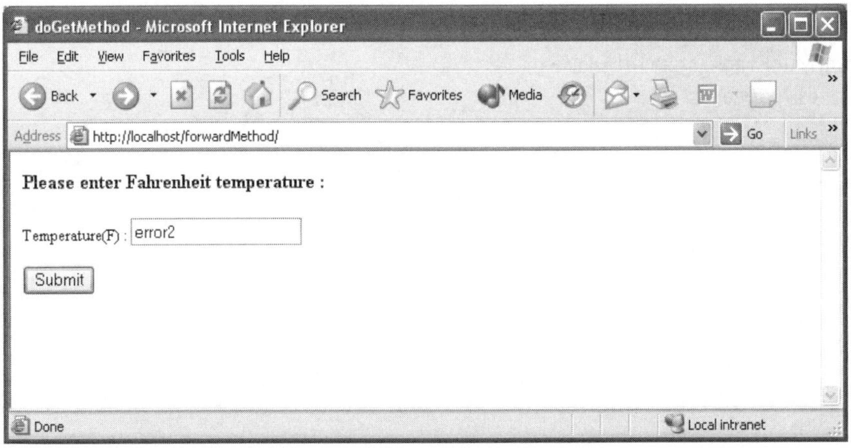

The next screen shows the error pages generated from the `Forwarded` Servlet (the second Servlet). Pay attention to the URL address in the response page; you will find that it is exactly identical to the URL address of the valid input response page. Can you tell why?

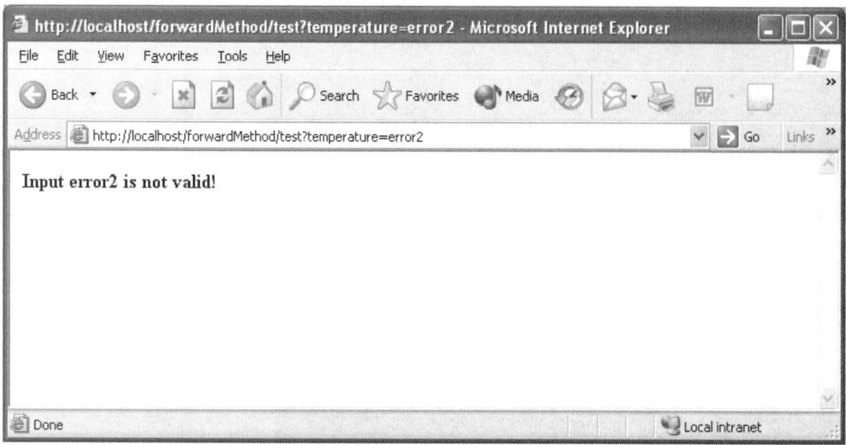

3.5.4 Lab 4: A Session-Tracking Example

This session-tracking lab demonstrates the Servlet session tracking control by a simple example. You can see when the new session starts and the session terminates.

```
<web-app>

  <servlet>
    <servlet-name>SessionTracking</servlet-name>
    <servlet-class>servlet.session.SessionTracking</servlet-class>
  </servlet>

  <servlet-mapping>
    <servlet-name>SessionTracking</servlet-name>
    <url-pattern>/test</url-pattern>
  </servlet-mapping>

</web-app>
```

```
package servlet.session;
```

```
import java.io.*;
import java.util.*;
import javax.servlet.*;
import javax.servlet.http.*;

public class SessionTracking extends HttpServlet
{
    public void service(HttpServletRequest req, HttpServletResponse res) throws
javax.servlet.ServletException, java.io.IOException
    {
        PrintWriter out = res.getWriter();
          HttpSession session = req.getSession(true);
          Integer counter = (Integer)session.getAttribute("sessionCounter");

          if(session.isNew())
          {
              counter = new Integer(1);
              session.setMaxInactiveInterval(10);
          }
          else
          {
              counter = new Integer(counter.intValue() + 1);
          }

          session.setAttribute("sessionCounter", counter);

          out.println("<html>");
          out.println("<head>");
          out.println("</head>");
          out.println("<body>");
          out.println("<h1>Session Tracking : </h1>");
          out.println("You have visited this page <b>" + counter + "</b> times. <p>");
          out.println("<h3>Session Data:</h3>");
          out.println("New Session: " + session.isNew());
          out.println("<br>Session ID: " + session.getId());
          out.println("</body>");
          out.println("</html>");
    }
}
```

Test session Servlet:

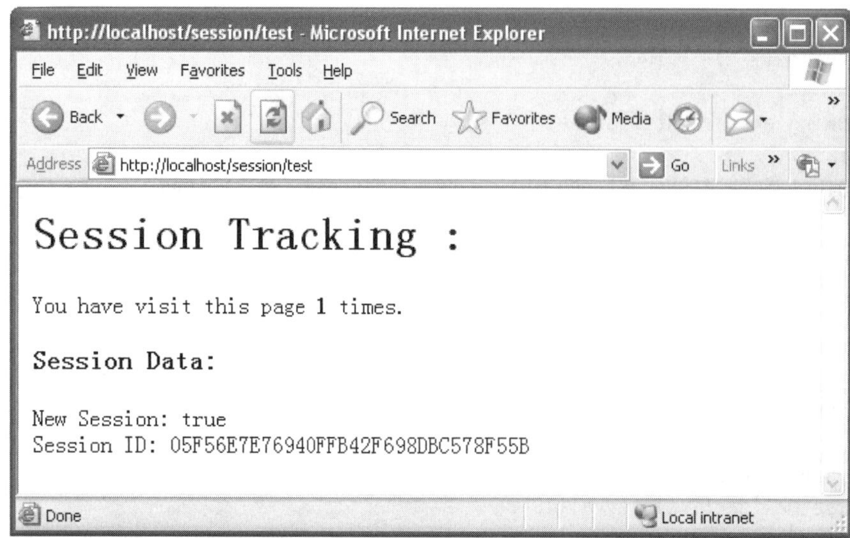

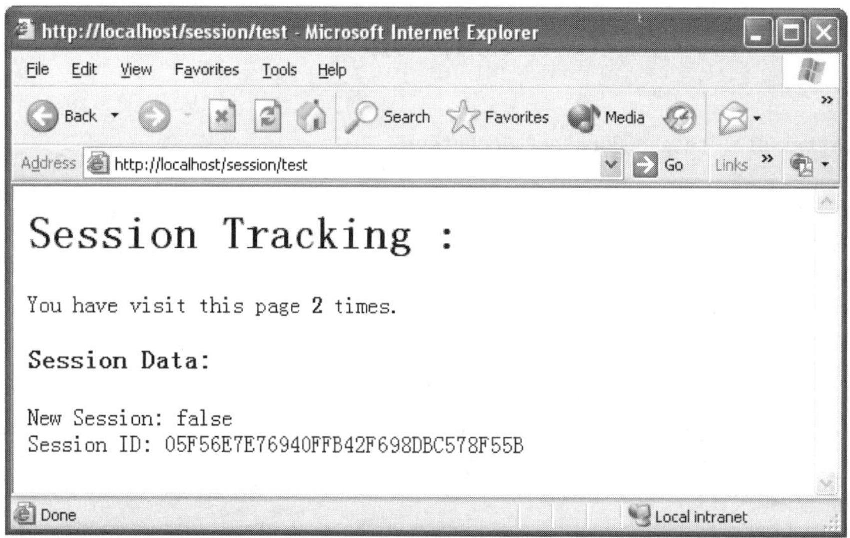

3.6 Summary

Java Servlets are a key component of server-side Java Web application development. A Java HTTP Servlet is a pluggable, lightweight component that can be deployed to any Java-compliant Web server on any platform. It is an extension to a Web server to enhance the server's functionality. It is also part of J2EE and can integrate with other Java Web components such as JSP, JavaBeans, Enterprise JavaBeans, and Web services.

In this chapter we explored the Servlet runtime environment, configuration, container, life cycle, API, and class hierarchy. We also showed how a Web client sends a request to a Servlet and how a Servlet gets the request and processes it. We examined how a Servlet can dispatch the request to another Servlet or other Web component to cooperate to complete the job, and how to dynamically generate HTML content and send it back to the client.

We know the strengths and weaknesses of the Servlet. Although Servlets are very powerful Web application tools, it may be hard for an HTML designer to write Servlet code. The Java code and HTML page generation are intertwined. JSP technology, an extension to Java Servlets, may be a better tool for this purpose.

3.7 Self-Review Questions

1. Which of the following methods is not defined in the Servlet interface `init()`?

   a. `service()`

   b. `finalize()`

   c. `destroy()`

   d. `init()`

2. By default, how many instances of a Servlet are created by a Servlet Container?

   a. One.

   b. One per request.

   c. One per session.

   d. None of the above.

3. Servlets are widely used to produce static HTML pages.

   a. True

   b. False

4. An HTTP Servlet is a server-side Java applet that generates dynamic HTML contents.

   a. True

   b. False

5. Which of the following methods are defined by the `RequestDispatcher` interface?

   a. `dispatch()`

   b. `include()`

   c. `redirect()`

   d. `forward()`

6. Which of the following method types is the default HTTP request type?

   a. POST

   b. GET

   c. HTTP

7. Which of the following URL addresses can be bookmarked?

   a. GET-type request.

   b. POST-type request.

   c. `include()` method.

   d. `forward()` method.

8. Which of the following objects are passed to a Servlets `service()` method?

   a. `ServletRequest`

   b. `ServletResponse`

   c. `HttpServletRequest`

   d. `HttpServletResponse`

9. The `include()` method of the `RequestDispatch` interface can shift the control to the target URL specified as its argument.

   a. True

   b. False

10. The `server.xml` file in Tomcat is used to configure an HTTP Servlet so that it will have a virtual name.

    a. True

    b. False

11. The `web.xml` file in the WEB-INF subdirectory in Tomcat can be used to do Servlet mapping for a Servlet.

    a. True

    b. False

12. The attribute object of an HTTP request can be shared by all requests in the same session.

    a. True

    b. False

13. The attribute object of an HTTP session can be shared by all sessions in the same Web application.

    a. True

    b. False

14. The `init()` method is invoked at what time?

    a. When the Servlet is loaded.

    b. When the Servlet is invoked the first time.

    c. Whenever the Servlet is accessed.

15. The `forward()` method will result in

    a. A new request.

    b. A new session.

    c. none of the above.

16. The `include()` method will result in

    a. A new request.

    b. A new session.

    c. none of the above.

17. The `sendRedirect()` method will result in

    a. A new request.

    b. A new session.

    c. none of the above.

18. The `getServletContext()` method is defined in

    a. Servlet interface.

    b. ServletConfig interface.

19. `HttpServlet` directly implements or extends

    a. `javax.servlet.Servlet.`

    b. `javax.servlet.GenericServlet.`

    c. `javax.servlet.ServletConfig.`

20. Who passes the `HttpServletRequest` object and `HttpServletResponse` object to `doGet()` and `doPost()`?

    a. Servlet container.

    b. Programmer.

    c. Servlet deployment descriptor.

3.8 Keys to the Self-Review Questions

1. b 2. a 3. b 4. a 5. b,d 6. b 7. a,c 8. a,b 9. b 10. b 11. b 12. b 13. b 14. a,b 15. c 16. c 17. a 18. b 19. b 20. a

3.9 Exercises

1. What is a Servlet?
2. How does a Servlet work?
3. What is the Servlet container?
4. What is the HTTP request and HTTP response?
5. Which classes does the `HttpServlet` class extend?
6. Which interfaces does the `HttpServlet` class implement?
7. What is an HTTP session?
8. How many different ways are there to implement session tracking?

9. Why is session tracking important?
10. What file is the deployment descriptor for an HTTP Servlet? Where is it located in Tomcat?
11. What file is the configuration for the Tomcat server? Where is it located in Tomcat?
12. How many different methods are there to shift the control from one Servlet to another?
13. How many different ways are there for a Web client to access an HTTP Servlet?
14. What is a URL query string?
15. How can two pages or Servlets share data in the same session?
16. How can two sessions share the data in the same Web application?
17. What are the advantages of Servlet technology?
18. What are the disadvantages of Servlet technology?
19. Should we override `service()` method?
20. Can a POST-type URL address be bookmarked?

3.10 Programming Exercises

1. Develop an HTTP Servlet that displays the current date and time.
2. Develop a Web services component using HTTP Servlets that provide services of a simple calculator. The calculator has the functionality to perform addition, subtraction, multiplication, and division of two real numbers. It can also detect a zero divisor in the division operation and return an error message.
3. Develop an HTTP Servlet application for an online guest book registration. If it is a new user, put him/her in the book; otherwise reply to the user with a message. This application involves two Servlets, one handles registration and the other handles the message generation. The `forward()` method is used.
4. Implement cookie technology in a Servlet Web application of an online survey. Use the `doGet()` method to get the preference in the first visit and use the `doPost()` to report the preference in the next visit.
5. Rewrite exercise 3 using `HttpSession` object management.

3.11 References

1. Apache Software Foundation Jakarta Project. "The Apache Jakarta Tomcat 5 Servlet/JSP Container." http://jakarta.apache.org/tomcat/tomcat-5.0-doc/default-servlet.html.

2. Hall, Marty and Larry Brown. *Core Servlets and JavaServer Pages.* 2nd ed. Upper Saddle River, NJ: Prentice Hall, 2004.

3. Sun Technologies. "Debugging JSP and Servlets." http://java.sun.com/developer/Books/javaserverpages/ProJSP/Chap19.pdf.

4. Sun Technologies. "Java 2 Platform Enterprise Edition, v 1.4, API Specification." http://java.sun.com/j2ee/1.4/docs/api/.

5. Sun Technologies. "Java Servlet Technology." http://java.sun.com/products/servlet/.

6. Sun Technologies. "Java Software FAQ Index." http://java.sun.com/docs/faqindex.html.

7. Sun Technologies. "JSR-000154 Java Servlet 2.4 Specification." http://www.jcp.org/aboutJava/communityprocess/first/jsr154/index.html.

8. Sun Technologies. "Servlet API." http://java.sun.com/products/servlet/2.1/api/javax.servlet.http.HttpServlet.html.

CHAPTER 4

Java Server Pages (JSP)

Objectives of This Chapter

- Introduce concepts of JSP Web components
- Compare JSP with Servlets
- Discuss JSP syntax, EL
- Discuss the integrations with JSP
- Discuss the Standard Tag Library, Custom Tag Library
- Discuss JSP debugging and testing
- Provide step-by-step tutorials on building, deploying, and using JSP components

4.1 Overview

The Java Server Pages (JSP) technology allows Web developers to generate static and dynamic HTTP contents. The JSP is just like ordinary Web pages with some additional embedded Java code. For example, a simplest JSP page can just be a simple HTML page with a `.jsp` extension.

```
<HTML>
<BODY>
<H1> This is a simplest JSP page <H1>
</BODY>
<HTML>
```

This is the simplest JSP page without any embedded Java code. It can be treated just as an HTML page. Of course, almost all JSP pages have embedded Java code. This allows access to server-side data and implements business logic. Java Server Pages are an extension of Java Servlet technology. JSP can not work without Servlet container support. When a Web server receives a JSP request from a client, the JSP engine converts the JSP page into Java Servlet code and compiles it into Servlet classes. The generated Servlet code is run on the Java Servlet container and finally sends the results back to the Web client. The advantage of JSP is that it separates the HTTP presentation authoring and business logic process coding. JSP focuses on the data presentation while the other Web components such as Servlets, JavaBeans, custom tags, and EJB take care of business logic processing.

With the JSP support, two different type developers, Web page designers and Java code programmers, can work on different aspects of the same Web application and incorporate static contents and dynamic elements such as JSP action tags and JSP scripting elements. These JSP tags and JSP elements can easily access shared data, forward flow controls to other Web components, and include the outputs of other Web components. It greatly reduces coding compared with Java Servlet technology. Some of the detailed work is done by the JSP API and the JSP/Servlet container so that developers do not need to know all the details of the corresponding Servlet interfaces, classes, and methods. JSP also makes the tag library extensible so that developers can develop their own reusable custom tags.

The new features of JSP 2.0 such as Expression Language (EL) make Web server page authoring even easier. JSP provides a more consistent way for Web developers to access different types of data such as implicit server objects, JavaBeans, Servlets, and even other remote distributed data.

JSP plays a role very similar to Microsoft ASP.NET and PHP in Web application development. ASP.NET only works on MS Windows platforms. JSP is a platform-independent technology that almost all platforms and Web servers use. JSP is extensible in that it supports a custom tag library; ASP does not. Also, JSP supports many more component technologies such as JavaBean components, EJB components, tag components, and Web components.

Now we know the difference between JSP and ASP.NET. How about the choice between Servlets and JSP?

Both Servlets and JSP can produce Web-dynamic contents via HTTP. Servlets handle flow control processing in the middle tier of three-tier Web application architectures. Examples where Servlets are the preferred choice are authentication, dispatching requests, and database connections. Servlet technology is the Java server programming language.

JSP is a text-document-based technology that supports two formats: JSP standard format and HTML/XML format. JSP is suitable to handle data presentation and Web page authoring. In the Model-View-Controller (MVC) architecture, JSP plays the role of View to present data to clients; Servlets play the role of Controller to take client requests, get request parameters, analyze the requests, make decisions based on the request, and transfer flow controls to other Web components. Servlets and JSP need to work together with other Web components in a real-world Web application.

4.2 JSP Basics

4.2.1 JSP Life Cycle

JSP is a Web-server-side programming technology based on Servlet technology. The JSP specification is built on top of the Servlet API. Any JSP page is translated into a Java Servlet by a JSP engine at runtime so that the JSP life cycle is determined by Servlet technology. The JSP engine is a JSP specification implementation that comes with Web servers that implement JSP. Tomcat is one example. When a request comes to a JSP page, it may come from a client browser or come from another Web component such as a Servlet or JSP. The Web server asks the JSP engine to check whether the JSP page has been accessed before or modified since its last access. If this is the case, the JSP engine will

1. Parse the JSP document to translate into a Servlet Java file,
2. Compile the Servlet Java file into a class file.

Then the Servlet container loads the Servlet class for execution and sends the results back to the client.

Figure 4.1 shows the JSP page translation, compilation, and execution on the Web server. Otherwise the Servlet container just loads the Servlet class and executes it. The JSP life cycle is very similar to the Servlet life cycle in that it consists of initialization, execution, and termination.

JSP Initialization

The `jspInit()` method is executed first after the JSP is loaded. If the JSP developer needs to perform any JSP-specific initialization such as database connections, this method can be specified at the beginning. We have not discussed any JSP scripting elements yet.

`<%! . . . %>` is a JSP declaration element that is used to declare variables or methods. The `jspInit()` is called only once during any JSP component life time.

```
<%! public void jspInit(){ . . . }   %>
```

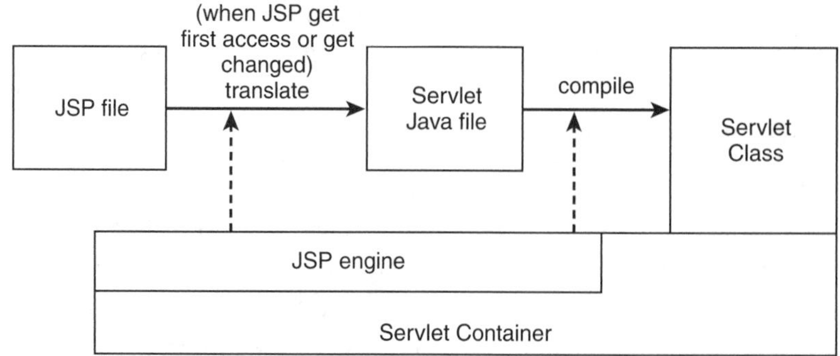

Figure 4.1
Process of a JSP page

JSP Execution

`public _service (HttpServletRequest req, HttpServletResponse res)` is a JSP service method that is the same as the `service()` method of a Servlet class. This method never needs to be customized. All Java code defined in scripting elements are inserted in this method by the JSP engine.

JSP Termination

```
<%! public void jspDestroy(){ . . . } %>
```

This method allows developers to specify resource cleanup jobs such as database disconnections.

4.2.2 First Simple Interactive JSP Example

Let us look at our first simple interactive JSP example named `helloJsp.jsp`. In this Hello User example, the HTML page takes a username from an HTML form and sends a request to a JSP page, and the JSP page generates a dynamic HTML page based on the data that comes with the request. Basically, this JSP page takes a username input from a Web client and generates a dynamic page to greet the user. The request may come from a Web form page request or from a query string following a URL of this JSP page. First, examine the Web form HTML file named `index.html` placed in the `JSP` directory that is this Web application `root` directory under `webapps`.

```
<html>
<head>
     <title>Demo1</title>
</head>
<body>
<h3>Please enter the user name :</h3><p>
```

```
<form action="/jsp/helloJsp.jsp">
UserName : <input type="text" name="userName"><br><br>
<input type="submit" value="Submit">
</form>
</body>
</html>
```

The `index.html` in the URL of the browser does not need to be specified, because `index.html` is the default HTML name for Tomcat.

This HTML takes a string of a user name from the HTML form and submits a request to `helloJsp.jsp` as specified in the action attribute of the HTML form. For example, a user types SPSU in the form and pushes the Submit button.

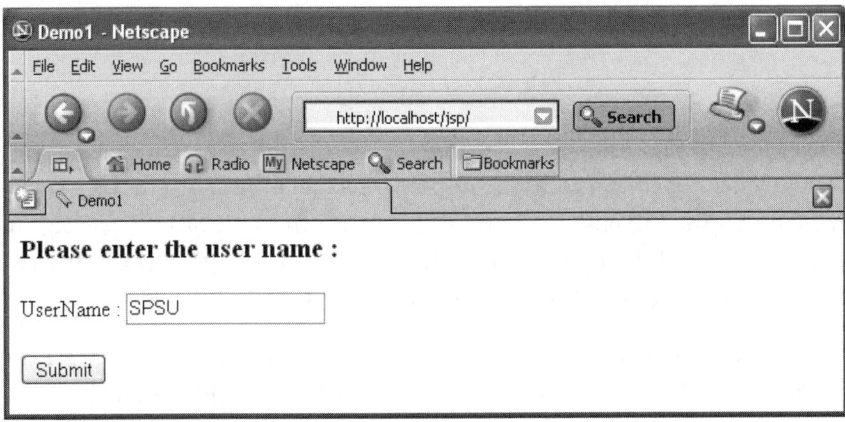

The `helloJsp.jsp` receives the HTML request from the client and generates a dynamic HTML page as follows.

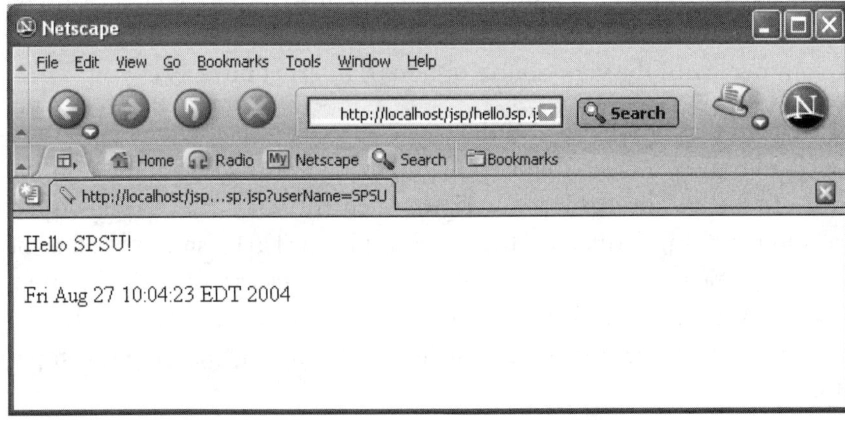

The page `helloJsp.jsp` is placed in the same directory as `index.html` and `WEB-INF`. You can find a number of HTML tags you have used before. All HTML tags can be used in a JSP page because JSP is an extension of HTML. A JSP file can be placed anywhere an HTML file can be placed.

```
<%@ page import="java.util.*" info = " This is a simplest JSP with Java code embedded"
contentType = "text/html"  %>
<%! Date today; %>
<html>
    <%-- This is a Simplest JSP (comment from JSP tag -- %>
<body>
    <!-- This is a simplest JSP (Comment from HTML tag -->
    Hello <%= request.getParameter("userName")   %>!
<br>
    <% today = new Date(); %>
    <%= today %>
</body>
</html>
```

The first line is a JSP directive element tag (`<%@ . . . %>`) that directs the JSP engine to set the page structure. It will not result in any Servlet code, just as the import directive in Java or `#include` directive in C. This directive element tells the JSP engine to import all classes in the `java.util` package to allow use of the `Date` class and tells the JSP engine that content type of this page is `text/html` not `text/xml` or some other Multipurpose Internet Mail Extension (MIME) type.

The second line is a JSP declaration element `<%! . . . %>` that tells the JSP engine to insert the enclosed Java code into the generated Servlet Java source code somewhere outside of any method. Variable declarations or method declarations may be placed here. A `Date` class variable (class reference) is declared here. Of course there can be an in-line variable declaration with its assignment statement instead of the two separate scripting elements in the above JSP example.

There are two different comments here: `<%-- . . . %>` is a JSP comment scripting element that stays on the server while `<!-- . . . -->` is a regular HTML comment that is sent back to the client. The client can view the HTML comment with the view-source option of Internet browsers.

Everything not within JSP element tags will be sent to the client browser as literal data. The word "Hello" is displayed on the client browser screen followed by the string returned from the next JSP expression scripting element and the "!". The expression scripting element `<%= . . . %>` will display values of the enclosed expression in string format. In this JSP example, the `helloJsp.jsp` obtains the parameter input string by the `getParameter()` method of `HttpServletRequest` object. The input string either comes from the input text field of the request form or the URL query string of this JSP address. The `"userName"` of the `getParameter()` method matches the `"userName"` text input component name in the HTML form.

The next JSP scripting element is scriptlet, which is simply a Java Servlet code fragment. It is inserted into the `service()` method of the generated Servlet code. Here, JSP instantiates a new instance of `Date` class and the current date is displayed in the next expression scripting element.

In this JSP there are two types of JSP constructs: directive elements and scripting elements (including expression scripting, declaration scripting, and scriptlets scripting). Soon we will discuss another type of constructor, the action tag element.

The following screen shots show the directory structure of this JSP Web application on Tomcat. The `index.html` and `helloJsp.jsp` files are placed in the JSP subdirectory of `webapps` directory.

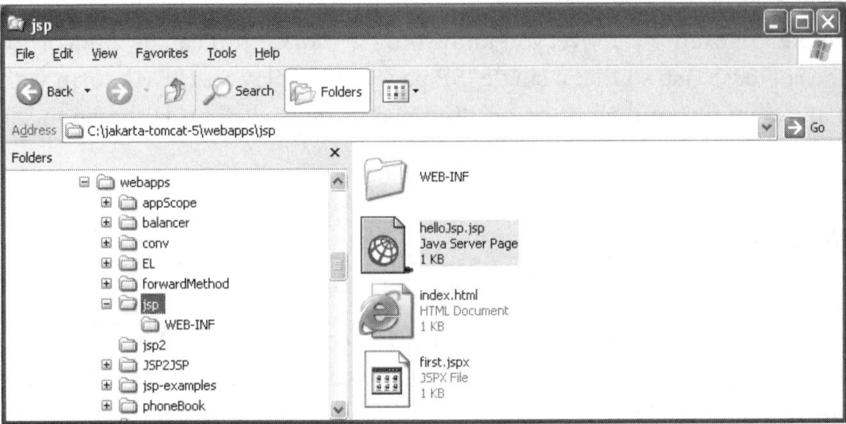

You can use the view option of the browser to view the source HTML code generated by JSP. You can see the HTML comments but not the JSP comments.

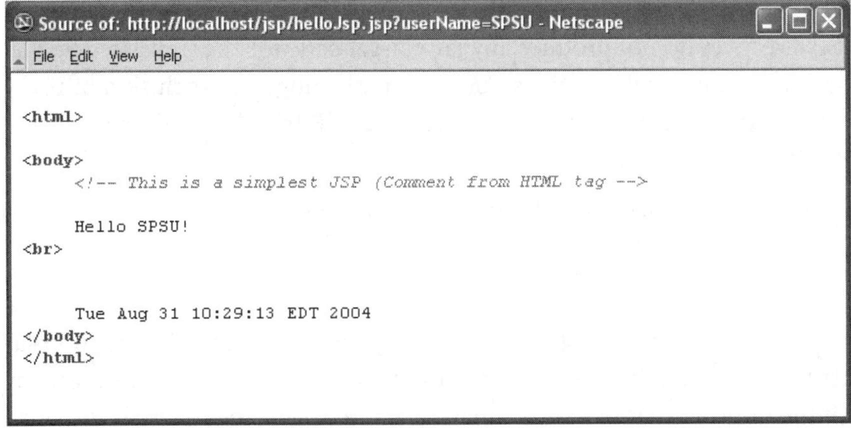

We can also use JSP expression language of JS P 2.0 to rewrite the `helloJsp.jsp` as follows:

```
<%@ page isELIgnored = "false" %>
<html>
<body>
    Hello, ${param['userName']}!
</body>
</html>
```

where "*userName*" is the parameter name defined in the HTML file.

The expression language makes data access much easier. You can use the expression `${param['userName']}` instead of `<%= request.getParameter("userName") %>` to get the *userName* parameter on the HTML form. From the simple JSP example above, you know the JSP works. You can even incorporate the `index.html` into the `helloJsp.jsp` so that a single JSP page can display an HTML form with which a user can interact and then respond with the result to clients by itself. This is shown in the following sections.

4.3 JSP Standard Syntax

Besides HTML tag elements, JSP provides four basic categories of constructors (markup tags): directives, scripting elements, standard actions, and comments. You can author a JSP page either in JSP standard syntax format or in a pure XML document format. We will discuss JSP standard syntax formats at this time because it generates HTML pages and it is widely used in Java Web applications. The JSP XML format document complies with the XML specification and can be used for data interchange. We discuss the XML format later.

4.3.1 JSP Directives

A JSP directive instructs the JSP engine to configure the structure of the Servlet that is generated from the JSP pages. The JSP directives do not produce any Java target code for the translated Servlet class. The JSP directives only affect the Servlet settings, such as page settings and inclusion of packages, classes, and custom tag libraries. JSP directives are processed at JSP translation time instead of execution time. The general syntax of a JSP directive is:

```
<%@ directive attribute1="value1" attribute2="value2" . . . attributen="valuen" %>
```

JSP Page Directive

The JSP page directive directs the JSP engine to specify the page setting during the Servlet translation time. It has many attributes. Some attributes have their default values. All the attributes may have only one value except the import attribute, which may have multiple values. Here is the summary of all attributes of page directive. The value of the attribute must be enclosed in a pair of quotation marks. The values in bold indicate the default values. The often used attributes are listed at the top of following list.

`contentType="`**`text/html`**`"`	specifies the response type, which may be text/xml, text/plain, wml, or other MIME types.
`import="`*`packages.class`*`"`	imports API packages, full qualified classes separated by a comma. The default import packages are java.lang.*, javax.servlet.*, javax.servlet.jsp.*, and javax.servlet.http.*.
`session="`**`true`**` | false"`	specifies the session participation of the JSP page. It affects the availability of the session object in this page.
`errorPage="`*`URL`*`"`	specifies the error handling page to handle exceptions in the current page.
`isErrorPage="true | `**`false`**`"`	designates the current page to be an error-handling page for another page. The URL of this page is referenced in the `errorPage` attribute of the other JSP page.
`isThreadSafe="`**`true`**` | false"`	controls the way the Servlet handles the multithreads. If a false value is assigned, the Servlet will take only one request at a time; otherwise, the programmer needs to take care of multi-thread synchronization.
`info="`*`message`*`"`	describes the page and is accessed by Servlet `getServlet Info()`.
`extends="`*`packages.class`*`"`	designates the super class of the Servlet class that is translated from the JSP.
`Language="`**`Java`**`"`	specifies the scripting language used in JSP.
`isELIgnored="true | `**`false`**`"`	specifies whether the JSP engine enables the Expression Language (EL) or not
`buffer="`*`n kb`*` | none"`	specifies the buffer size for Servlet *out* object.
`autoflush="`**`true`**` | false"`	The *out* object will be flushed automatically if *true* is set. If the *buffer* attribute is set to none, then the *true* value must be set.
`pageEncoding="`***`ISO-8859-1`***`"`	Specifies the character encoding for the JSP page. **UTF-8** is another possible encoding and may influence date display in locales where not all characters of the month names are included in ISO-8859-1.

JSP Include Directive

The JSP include directive instructs the JSP engine to include the actual contents of another file that may be a static HTML page, text file, or JSP file. The included file may declare methods or variables. The included file is inserted into the current page at translation time. People refer to this include directive as a static include. The syntax of the include directive is:

```
<%@ include file=<relative path>/<file name> %>
```

A banner page, heading page, copyright page, or a footnote page is a perfect example of a file to be included in a JSP page.

JSP Taglib Directive

The taglib directive is used to include a custom tag library so that the JSP can make use of the tags defined in the tag library. There are two types of tags: standard tags and user-defined custom tags. JSP developers can encapsulate complex and often-used server-side tasks in custom tags for reuse purposes. This is similar to standard tags such as the JSP useBean action tag that we will introduce. Each self-defined tag must have three components:

- a tag handler class that specifies the behavior of the new defined tag.
- a Tag Library Descriptor (TLD) XML file with an extension .tld that describes all tags in the tag library. It maps the tag names to their tag handler classes in the library.
- a JSP page that uses the user-defined tag.

The syntax of the taglib directive is:

```
<%@ taglib uri="<taglib.tld>" prefix="<p_name>"   %>
```

where the Uniform Resource Identifier (URI) attribute specifies the absolute or relative URI to the TLD file. For example, you can use a custom tag in the following way:

```
<p_name:myTag> . . . </p_name:myTag>
```

where myTag is defined in taglib.tld with the prefix p_name. The detailed taglib specification and its application examples are given in Section 4.6.

4.3.2 JSP Scripting Elements

There are three scripting elements in JSP syntax. All of them are Java code.

Declaration Element

The JSP declaration element defines page-scope variables to store information or defines supporting methods that the rest of a JSP page may need. Declaration elements do not produce outputs. The declaration content must be a valid Java statement or multiple statements separated by semicolons.

The contents of the declaration scripting element will be translated into Servlet Java code and inserted into the body of the translated corresponding Servlet code somewhere outside of any methods. Its syntax is:

```
<%!  Java Code  %>
```

For example, you can define page scope primitive or class variables as:

```
<%! int i=0; Double d; %>
```

Methods can also be declared by declaration scripting elements. For example, the JSP life cycle methods `jspInit()` and `jspDestroy()` can be declared as follows:

```
<%! Connection conn %>
. . .
<%! public void jspInit() {
{
        try
        {
                Class.forName("oracle.jdbc.driver.OracleDriver");
                conn = java.sql.DriverManager.getConnection(
                        "jdbc:oracle:oci9:myDB","scott","tiger");
        }
        catch (Exception e)
        {
        . . .}
}
    }
%>
```

This JSP method will be part of the `init()` method of the Servlet after JSP translation. It will be called when the object of the corresponding Servlet class is instantiated. It is called only once so that it can save resources such as database connection cost in the above example.

```
<%! public void jspDestroy() {
      try
        {
                if (conn != null) conn.close();
        }
        catch (java.sql.SQLException e)
        {
        . . .}
    }
%>
```

The `jspDestroy()` method will be part of the `destroy()` method of the Servlet. When the Servlet instance ends, it clears up all resources the JSP has acquired.

Expression Scripting Elements

In JSP, the results of an expression evaluation are always converted to a string and directly included in the output page. Typically, expressions are used to display simple values of variables or return values of shared data by invoking a bean's getter methods. The JSP expression syntax is given here. The predefined JSP objects such as request, response, and session can also be used within the expression element to make the expression as simple as possible.

```
<%=  expr  %>  // No semicolon
```

```
<%=   i * j + k %>
<%=  myBean.getSalary() %>
<%=  request.getRemoteHost() %>
```

The three simple examples above show how to output a value of a numerical expression, property of a JavaBean, and the remote host name of the client who sent the request to this JSP page.

Scriptlet Element

JSP scriptlets are embedded within `<% ... %>` tags. They are executed at runtime. The syntax is

```
<%  Java code %>
```

The scriptlets are inserted into the `_jspService()` method of the translated Servlet code that is invoked by the Servlet `service()` method. This Java code is executed when the request is serviced by the JSP page. Any valid Java code can be placed within a scriptlet element, and it is not limited to one line of source code. For example, the following displays the counter during execution of a loop, combining the use of the expressions element and the scriptlets element:

```
<% for (int i=1; i<=4; i++) { %>
     The counter is now <% =  i %>
<% } %>
```

4.3.3 JSP Standard Actions

JSP standard action elements simplify the access actions to other Web components such as Servlet, JSP, or JavaBean.

JSP Forward Action

```
<jsp:forward  page="another page" />
```

This action forwards the request to another page, i.e., an internal redirect. For example, it forwards the control from the current page to `second.jsp`.

```
. . .
<jsp:forward page='second.jsp'/>
. . .
```

JSP Include Action

In addition to the JSP page include directive that includes a page at the JSP translation time, JSP also supports an action that can dynamically include a page at runtime.

```
<jsp:include page = "<jsp or html page>" flush="true | false" />
```

If the flush attribute is set to true, the included page will update when the JSP is updated. Remember that the include directive only copies the contents once and never changes afterward because it is static. The purpose of an include action is to include the other page to be part of the current page. It is used for such actions as conditionally including other pages at runtime.

JSP JavaBean Actions

JavaBean Components JavaBean technology is a component-based technology that allows the Web designer to make maximum reuse of an existing Java class. JSP provides a number of JSP JavaBean action elements to free JSP page designers from complex Java Servlet programming or JSP scripting constructs. A JavaBean is a wrapper for business logic and data processing. Any Java class can be converted to a JavaBean class as long as it satisfies the JavaBean convention (design pattern). You can easily create and initialize beans and set and get the values of their properties. A simple bean named Book is given below. It has a default constructor `Book()`; all properties are not public, each writable property has a `setXXX()` public method where `XXX` is the name of the property; each readable property has a `getXXX()` public method. A Boolean property is accessed using `isXXX()` that returns a Boolean value of `XXX` property and `setXXX()` that assigns a Boolean value to `XXX` property. The JSP actions can only call `set` and `get` methods. Other JSP scriptlets can call other methods. The bean class file is placed in Tomcat `WEB-INF/classes` along with the Servlet class. For example, the following `Book` JavaBean class is stored in `<ROOT>/WEB-INF/classes/shopping/` directory. Each JavaBean class must have its package just as the `shopping` package for the `Book` class in the example. The full coverage of component technology is beyond the scope of this book.

```
package shopping;
public class Book {
  String Title;
  String isbn;
  float price;
```

```
  int quantity;
  public Book() {
    title="";
    isbn="";
    price=0;
    quantity=0;
  }
  public void setTitle(String name) {
    title=name;
  }
  public String getTitle() {
    return title;
  }
  public void setIsbn(String id) {
    isbn=id;
  }
  public String getIsbn() {
    return isbn;
  }
  public void setPrice(float p) {
    price=p;
  }
  public float getPrice() {
    return price;
  }
  public void setQuantity(int q) {
    quantity=q;
  }
  public int getQuantity() {
    return quantity;
  }
}
```

`jsp:useBean` Action Element The `jsp:useBean` action instantiates an instance of the bean class if there is not an existing one or creates a reference to an existing one. It also specifies the visibility and accessibility scope of this bean. The other Web components in JSP can reference this bean object by its ID. Its syntax is given as:

```
<jsp:useBean id="name" class="<package>.<Java bean class>"
             scope=". . .">
```

The ID is the access name of this bean. The scope attribute defines the visibility of this bean.

- page Only active in the page, default scope
- request Active for the current request

- session Active for the current session
- application Active for the current application

After you get a reference to a bean you can use `jsp:setProperty` action and `jsp:getProperty` action to modify and retrieve the bean properties. Once you have a bean reference, you can also modify its properties by calling the bean's `getXXX()` or `setXXX()` methods explicitly in a scriptlet element. Note that the class specified for the bean must be in the server's regular class path. For example, in Tomcat, this class and all the classes it uses should go in the `classes` directory or be in a `.jar` file in the `lib` directory. You can also incorporate Java code into the body of a `jsp:useBean` tag so that the incorporated code will be executed when the bean is instantiated for the first time. If the instance exists already, the code will be ignored.

```
<jsp:useBean ...>
  Java code
</jsp:useBean>
```

`jsp:setProperty` Action You use `jsp:setProperty` to assign values to properties of a bean. You can either use `jsp:setProperty` after, but outside of, a `jsp:useBean` element or within the body of `jsp:useBean` action element.

Option 1:

```
<jsp:useBean id="myBook" ... />
...
<jsp:setProperty name="myBook" property="price" ... />
```

In this case, the `jsp:setProperty` is executed regardless of whether a new bean was instantiated or an existing bean was found.

Option 2:

```
<jsp:useBean id="myBook" ... >
  ...
  <jsp:setProperty name="myBook" property="price" ... />
</jsp:useBean>
```

In this case, the `jsp:setProperty` is executed only if a new object is instantiated, i.e., no existing bean object yet exists. The following action sets `myBook's` `price` property to 31.99.

```
<jsp:setProperty name="myBook"  property="price" value = "31.99" />
 param="<param-name"] />
```

The required "name" attribute is the ID of the bean specified in the `<jsp:useBean>` action tag.

The required "property" attribute specifies the property you want to set. You can also assign a `"*"` to the property if all request parameter names match bean property names. It will set all corresponding properties of the bean with the values of request parameters either from the request form or request string. The "value" attribute specifies the value for the property. The String type value will be converted to the correct type for the property.

You can also associate the bean properties with the input parameters. The next example shows that the bookPrice input parameter in the request form or query string is associated with the price property of the myBook bean.

```
<jsp:setProperty name="myBook"  property="price" param="bookPrice" />
```

You can also associate all properties with input request parameters using the "*" wildcard character. Assume that there are four input request parameters whose names match four property names: title, isbn, price, and quantity. Whatever data you input to the parameters will be assigned to the properties with the same names. This is one of the most useful JavaBean features.

```
<jsp:setProperty name="myBook"  property="*" />
```

You cannot use both value and param at the same time, but it is allowed to use neither. If you use neither param nor value, that indicates that a parameter name matches the property name. JSP will take the input from the parameter that has the same name as the property name. The jsp:setProperty action is much more powerful than the setXXX() methods in that it can automatically convert String type data to the required data type of the bean property and set multiple properties using only one single command.

jsp:getProperty Action Element This element retrieves the value of a bean property, converts it to a string, and inserts it into the JSP outputs. The two required attributes are name—the ID of a bean defined via jsp:useBean—and property—the property whose value should be inserted. The following is an example.

```
<jsp:useBean id='myBook'
               class='shopping.Book'
               scope='session' >
...
```

The next action can find the number of copies of myBook, which may reference a specific book at any time.

```
<jsp:getProperty name="myBook" property="quantity" />
```

To return the price of the same book:

```
    <jsp:getProperty name="myBook" property="price" />

</jsp:useBean>
```

The following is a simple complete application example using all the syntax we discussed so far in Section 4.3. The form.jsp takes username input on the form request, saves the input in a JavaBean, and redirects to response.jsp. The response.jsp JSP page retrieves the username from the bean, and finally responds to the user with a message, "Hello, <*user name*>." This is the form.jsp.

```
<%@ page import=user.NameBean" %>
<jsp:useBean id="myBean" scope="request" class="user.NameBean" />
<jsp:setProperty name="myBean" property="*" />

<html>
<body>
<form method="get">
<input type="text" name="userName" size="20">
<br>
<inpt type="submit" value="Submit">
</form>
<% if (request.getParameter("userName") != null) { %>
<%@ include file="response.jsp" %>
<% } %>
</body>
</html>
```

The following is the *NameBean* JavaBean file.

```
Package user;
Public class NameBean {
   String userName;
  Public NameBean(){ userName=null; }
  Public void setUserName(String name) { userName=name; }
  Public String getUserName() { return userName; }
}
```

The following is the `response.jsp` file.

```
<h1>Hello, <jsp:getproperty name="myBean" property="username" /><h1>
```

Of course, a simple EL notation can be used to replace the `jsp:getProperty` action in this file. The EL notation will be discussed later.

`jsp:plugin` Action Element The `jsp:plugin` action can insert a Java applet client-side component into a server-side JSP page component. It downloads Java plug-in software (if necessary) and a client-side component such as applet and executes the client-side component. The syntax is as follows.

```
<jsp:plugin type="applet" code="MyApplet.class" width="400" height="200">
. . .
<!-- Parameter lists passed on the current JSP -->

  <jsp:param name="username" value="Smith" />
  ...
</jsp:plugin>
```

The `<jsp:plugin>` element can display an applet object or a bean object in the client Web browser, using a Java plug-in that is part of the browser or downloaded from a specified URL. When the JSP file sends an HTML response to the client, the `<jsp:plugin>` element is replaced by an `<object>` element in HTML specification. In general, the attributes to the `<jsp:plugin>` element specify whether the object is a bean or an applet, locate the code that will be run, position the object in the browser window, specify the URL from which to download the plug-in software, and pass parameter names and values to the object.

4.3.4 JSP Comments

You can always include HTML comments in JSP pages so that users can view these comments with the browser's view option on the HTML source. If you do not want users to see your comments, embed them within a JSP comment tag:

```
<%-- comment for server side only --%>
```

A useful feature of JSP is that the JSP comment can be used to selectively block out scriptlets or tags from compilation. Thus, comments can play a significant role during the debugging and testing process.

4.3.5 JSP Predefined Objects

JSP provides very useful built-in implicit objects that greatly simplify Web page authoring and data sharing between pages, requests, and sessions in a Web application. JSP developers can not only easily access JSP built-in parameters of implicit objects but also associate user-defined objects with attributes of implicit objects to pass them on to other Web components for data sharing.

The Scopes of JSP Predefined (Implicit) Objects

As a convenience feature, JSP supports predefined objects that can be used within scriptlets and expressions. Web page authors may use these predefined objects instead of creating their own, similar objects. These objects simplify accessing underlying Java Servlet classes or interfaces.

Before discussion of the implicit JSP objects, let us review the concept of scope accessibilities: page, request, session, and application. The application scope represents the current Web application in which an application object can be shared by all clients in different sessions as long as they are accessing the same application. The session scope object is only shared by all requests within the same session. One session ties with one client most of the time. Its lifetime can also be controlled by a timer setting or by a session invalidation code. A request object can be shared among pages as long as they are handling the same request. For example, one page can forward the request and response objects to another page so that the second page will be able to share the request with the first page. The page scope is the default scope and is not sharable.

Often Used JSP Implicit Objects:

JSP container makes a set of implicit objects automatically available to JSP developers. The following list explains the usages of these objects.

- `request`: an `HttpServletRequest` object passed to a Servlet. The accessibility of this request object is request scope. It can be used to access the request parameters, type, and header information. An example is `request.getParameter("username")`.
- `response`: an `HttpServletResponse` object used by a Servlet. The scope of this object is within this page. It can be used to set the response headers and status.
- `out`: a buffered `JspWriter` object that writes into the output stream. It can only be used by a scriptlet element. An example is `out.println()`. The scope is page.
- `pageContext`: an access point to all page attributes. Some of its methods are `getSession()`, `getRequest()`, `getResponse()`, `getOut()`. The scope is this page only.
- `application`: represents the `ServletContext` obtained from the servlet configuration object. You can set an attribute by `application.setAttribute(key,value)` and get the attribute value by `application.getAttribute(key)`. The application object has application scope.
- `config`: represents the `ServletConfig` for the JSP. The JSP initialization parameters can be read via it. It has a page scope.
- `page`: synonym for the `"this"` operator. Not often used by page authors.
- `session`: an `HttpSession` object with session scope. `session.setAttribute( key, data)`; `session.getAttribute( key)`, and `session.getId()` are examples.

These implicit objects are only visible within the system-generated `_jspService()` method. They are not visible within methods you define yourself.

4.4 Expression Language (EL)

A new feature of JSP technology version 2.0 is the Expression Language (EL). The EL is a simple and very powerful notation that makes it easier for the JSP page author to write code for accessing application data such as data stored in JavaBean components and attribute data of `pageContext`, request, session, and application. EL uses a shorthand notation of `${ expr } instead of <%= expr %>`.

Let us use the `Book` JavaBean class in the `shopping` package as we have seen before.

```
package shopping;
public class Book {
  . . .
  float price;
```

```
  public Book() {
    . . .
    price= 0;
      }
  . . .
  public void setPrice(float p) {
    price=p;
  }
  public float getPrice() {
    return price;
  }
  . . .
}
```

After you specify

```
<jsp:useBean id="myBook" class="shopping.Book" scope="session"  />
```

you can use

```
${myBook.price}
```

to get the value of the *price* property of the bean instead of using the following scripting elements:

```
<%@ page import="shopping.Book" @>
<% Book myBook = new Book(); %>
. . .
<%= myBook.getPrice() %>
```

You can also use `${myBook.price}` to replace the following JSP action elements:

```
<jsp:getProperty name="myBook" property="price" />
```

If the *myBook.price* does not exist, the expression just returns a null value rather than throwing an exception.

The Expression Language also simplifies access to collection type data: request parameters, cookies, etc. It supports the conditional expression `${test? Opt1, opt2}` that is an alternative to a scriptlet element. It also supports automatic type conversion. In addition to the above, another useful feature of EL is the nested notation, such as `${student.address.state}` where *state* is a property of the *address* class and *address* is a property of the *student* class. EL can retrieve data but can never set any data because EL is an expression language only. Figure 4.2 summarizes the ways in which JSP accesses JavaBeans, and other objects.

4.4.1 General Syntax for Bean Access

`${expr1.expr2}` or `${expr1["expr2"]}` where *expr1* is the bean reference and *expr2* is the property of the bean.

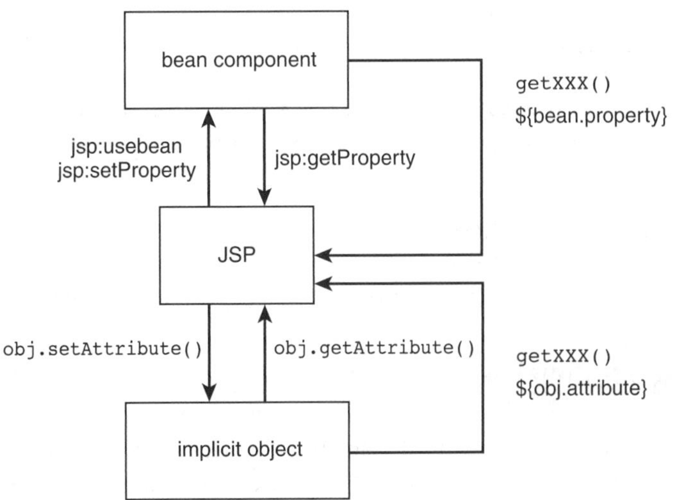

Figure 4.2
JSP Access to Other Resources

4.4.2 Syntax for Collection Data Access

The syntax is `${expr1[expr2]}` where *expr1* is a reference to an array or a list and *expr2* is an integer index. For example, `${myList[2]}` returns a value at the 3rd position of this list.

`${expr1[expr2]}` or `${expr1.expr2}` where *expr1* is a map and *expr2* is the key of the map that the value of this key is returned. For example, `${myMap["Smith"]}` returns the phone number of Smith if the *myMap* consists of pairs of name/phone.

4.4.3 Syntax for Shared Data Access in JSP Contexts

JSP always searches for data in the scope order of page, request, session, and application unless you provide a specific scope prefix such as `pageScope`, `requestScope`, `sessionScope`, `applicationScope`, `param`, `header`, or `cookie`. For example, `${param['userName']}` is the equivalent EL notation to `<%=request.getParameter("userName") %>`.

`${pageContext.session.id}` returns an ID number of the session the page belongs to.

Let us take a look at an example of a session-scoped attribute that can be shared during the session. The attribute `myAttribute` is set by a fragment:

```
HttpSession session = request.getSession();
```

```
session.setAttribute("myAttribute", obj1);
// obj1 is an object reference pointing to an object.
```

In a JSP file you can access this `obj1` by `${session.myAttribute}` if there is no attribute named *`myAttribute`* in *`pageScope`* or *`requestScope`* or you can explicitly specify this by a scope prefix as `${sessionScope.myAttribute}`.

```
<% session.setAttribute ("name", "Mary"); %>
$sessionScope.name} <%-- returns Mary --%>
<%= session.getAttribute("name"); %><%-- this is an equivalent scripting expression --%>
```

4.5 Integrations with JSP

In any real-world Java Web application, a JSP page must work together with other Java Web components such as Java Servlets, JavaBeans, or other JSP pages on the same Web server container. It may also need to work together with remote components such as EJBs in enterprise applications. The Model-View-Controller (MVC) model is a typical design pattern for decomposition of a Web application into Servlet, JSP, and JavaBeans. We will discuss the details of the MVC model in the next chapter. In this section we focus on the interactions between JSP and other Java Web components.

4.5.1 Integration of Servlet with JSPs

A Servlet can play the role of front-end reception in a Web application. It accepts complicated requests from clients, validates the requests, calculates some pre-results, stores the preliminary results in sharable objects such as implicit objects or JavaBeans, makes decisions, and transfers control to other Web components such as JSPs to let them create response outputs. There are a number of ways a Servlet component can communicate with a JSP component.

- A servlet component can store data in an implicit object as its attribute and the JSP can retrieve the data via the attribute of that object. For example, assume that the Servlet and JSP are in the same request scope. The Servlet stores the data in an attribute of the request object such as:

  ```
  request.setAttribute(key, data);
  ```

  Then the JSP can retrieve the data by:

  ```
  <% data= (class type)request.getAttribute(key); %>
  ```

- A Servlet stores a bean in the scope of application by:

  ```
  getServletContext().setAttribute(key, data);
  ```

  Or stores a bean in the scope of session by:

  ```
  request.getSession()setAttribute(key, data);
  ```

- A Servlet can also instantiate an instance of the JavaBean class and initialize it by:

  ```
  Data data = new Data(); // where Data is a bean class
  ```

  A JSP can get this shared bean by `jsp:usebean` action as

  ```
  <jsp:useBean id="key" class="<class>" scope="application or
   session" />
  ```

- A Servlet can attach data as a query string of a get method request and pass it to a JSP.

  In the Servlet:

  ```
  String url ="/<url>.target.jsp?key=data";
  RequestDispatcher rd =
  getServletContext().getRequestDispatcher(url);
  rd.forward(request, response);
  ```

  In the JSP:

  ```
  <% request.getParameter(key); %> or ${param(key)}
  ```

  will get the data of the key.

4.5.2 Integration of JSP with Other JSPs

The ways a Servlet talks to a JSP discussed above can also be used to allow a JSP to talk to another JSP because Servlet code is equivalent to JSP scriptlets in a JSP page. In addition, a JSP page can easily forward or dispatch control to other JSP pages, or easily include other JSP dynamic pages or HTML static pages based on the conditions.

- JSP `jsp:forward` action can forward control to another JSP such as

  ```
     <% String target
  if (hour<12) { target =" am.jsp";} else target={
             target = pm.jsp;}%>
  <jsp:forward page="<%= target %>" />
  ```

- JSP `jsp:include` action can insert an HTML page, plain text document, or output of JSP or Servlet into the current JSP output in `<jsp:include page="<target page>" />`

- JSP `jsp:useBean` action can instantiate a new instance of JavaBean class if needed and also set the properties of the bean object and visibility scope of this bean to be shared by other Web components in the same application. Figure 4.3 shows the possible integrations and communications between multiple JSPs.

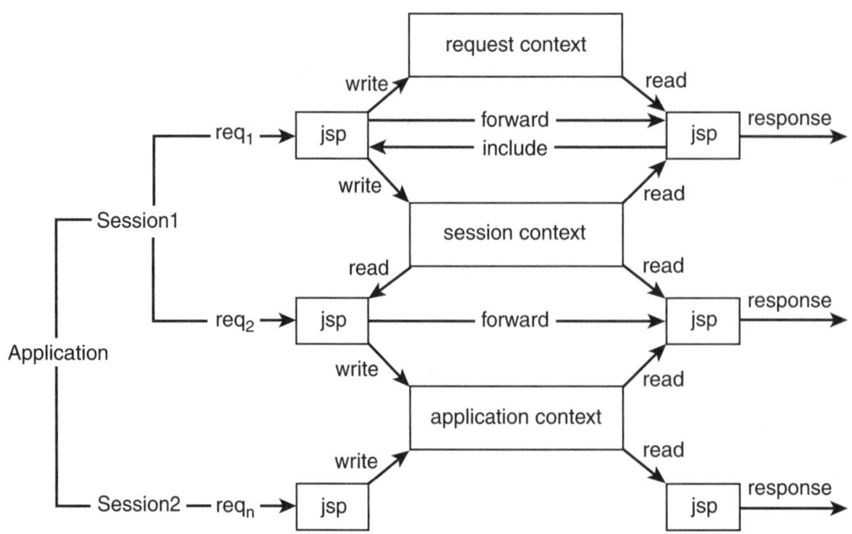

Figure 4.3
JSP Integrations

4.6 Custom Tag Library

JSP technology provides a custom tag library feature that allows JSP developers to define their own reusable custom tags. The new user-defined tags are stored in tag libraries called `taglibs`. The advantages of custom tags are as follows:

- Separate HTML page authoring from Java programming
- Encapsulate complex Java code behind the tag interface that makes it easy to reuse
- Easy to maintain because any change of tag implementation will not result in any change of the tag application

In order to make custom tags work, there must be an XML descriptor file to map the tag to its implementation class file (called the tag handler class). There must also be a Java tag handler class. Of course, the custom-defined tag is used in a JSP file. Figure 4.4 shows the relations among these three files. In this section we present a simple user-defined tag that just displays a greeting word, "Welcome!" In the examples and Lab practice section, there is a more realistic tag with a tag attribute that formats any numerical number to a precision of two digits after the decimal point. Some tags may even have their own tag body.

4.6.1 Tag Implementation Class

First, we discuss the `WelcomeTag` tag handler class that just displays "Welcome!" The file is saved in `webapps\tagLib\myLib\WelcomeTag.java` in Tomcat where `taglib` is the root directory of this Web application.

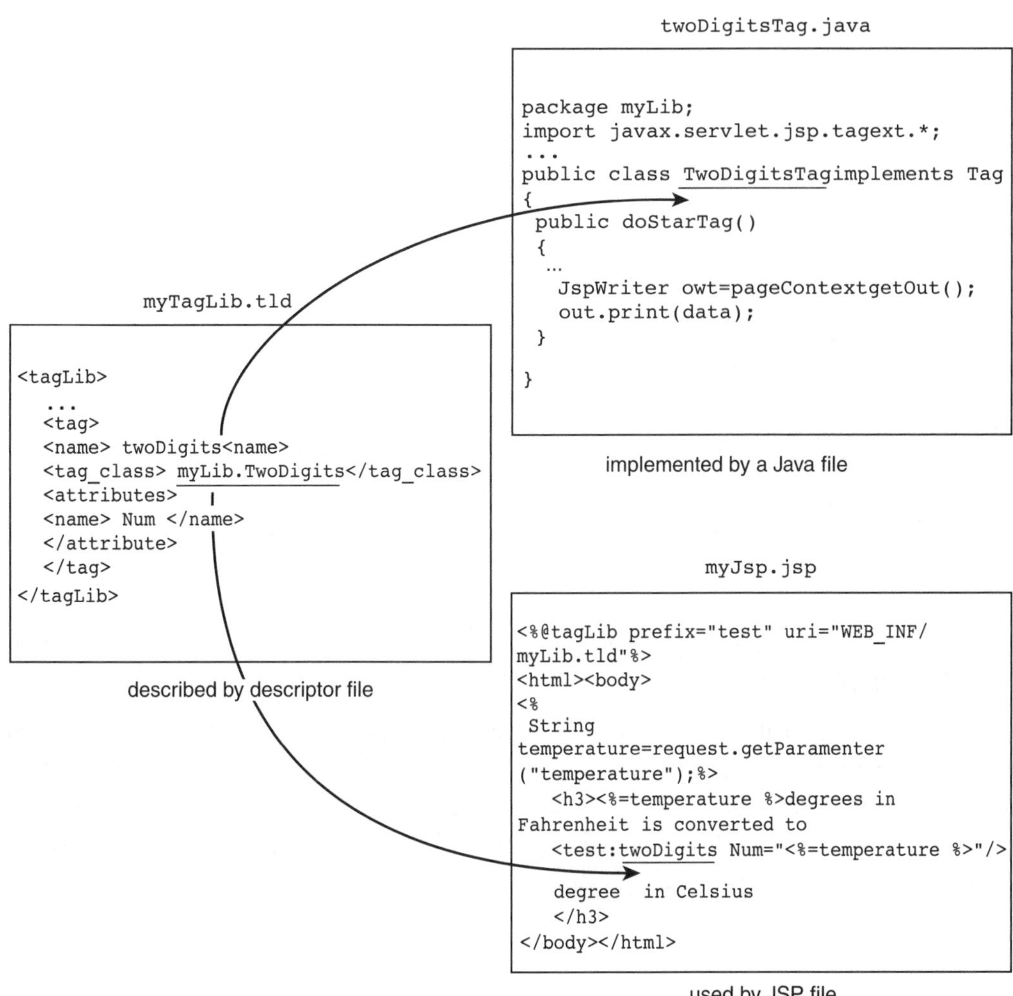

Figure 4.4
Custom Tag Library

```
package myLib;

import javax.servlet.jsp.*;
import javax.servlet.jsp.tagext.*;
import java.io.*;

public class WelcomeTag implements TagSupport
{
   public int doStartTag() throws JspException
```

```
    {
        try
        {
            JspWriter out = pageContext.getOut();
            out.print(" Welcome! ");
        }
        catch(Exception e)
        {
           throw new JspException("error");
        }
        return SKIP_BODY;
    }

    public int doEndTag() throws JspException
    {
        return EVAL_PAGE;
    }

}
```

The container invokes the `doStartTag()` when the start tag is encountered. It is processed in the same way as the Java Simple API for XML parser (SAX) handles XML tag elements.

Next, we look at the application of this `welcome` tag used in the `webapps\tagLib\myFirst.jsp`. This JSP specifies the location of the `myLib.tld` file that maps the definition of the `Welcome` custom tag to its `WelcomeTag` tag handler class file. The prefix attribute in the `taglib` directive plays a role of "namespace." When this `myFirst.jsp` file is browsed the word "Welcome!" is displayed on the browser screen.

```
<%@ taglib prefix="test" uri="/WEB-INF/myLib.tld" %>

<html><body>
<test:welcome/>
</body></html>
```

The `webapps\tagLib\WEB-INF\myLib.tld` defines the `welcome` tag and maps the `welcome` tag name to its tag handler class, `myLab.Welcome.class`.

```
<!DOCTYPE taglib
    PUBLIC "-//Sun Microsystems, Inc.//DTD JSP Tag Library 1.2//EN"
     "http://java.sun.com/j2ee/dtd/web-jsptaglibrary_1_2.dtd">

<taglib>
     <!-- INFO ABOUT THIS LIBRARY -->
          <tlib-version>1.0</tlib-version>
          <jsp-version>1.2</jsp-version>
```

```
        <short-name>myLib</short-name>

    <!-- GREET TAG -->
    <tag>
        <name>welcome</name>
        <tag-class>myLib.WelcomeTag</tag-class>
        <body-content>empty</body-content>
    </tag>
</taglib>
```

4.7 JSP XML Syntax Documents

A JSP page can use either regular JSP syntax, such as all of the JSP syntax we discussed so far, or an XML syntax. The latter one is called a JSP XML document. It must be well formed according to the XML standards.

Why is the JSP XML syntax document needed? An XML document can be manipulated by any XML-aware tools and can interchange information with other applications. An XML document can also be validated against its Document Type Definition (DTD). The XML syntax also eases JSP page authoring for page designers because any XML document can be used as a JSP document and XML syntax elements can be used in a JSP standard page as well.

First, look at a simple JSP XML document named `first.jspx`. The extension `.jspx` is the default extension for a JSP XML document supported by JSP 2.0 specification. Otherwise, a `<jsp:root>` tag must be at the top level of the JSP XML document.

```
<html xmlns:jsp="http://java.sun.com/JSP/Page" version="2.0">
<jsp:text>
See the template text here
<body><h1>Hello World!</h1>
</body>
</jsp:text>
</html>
```

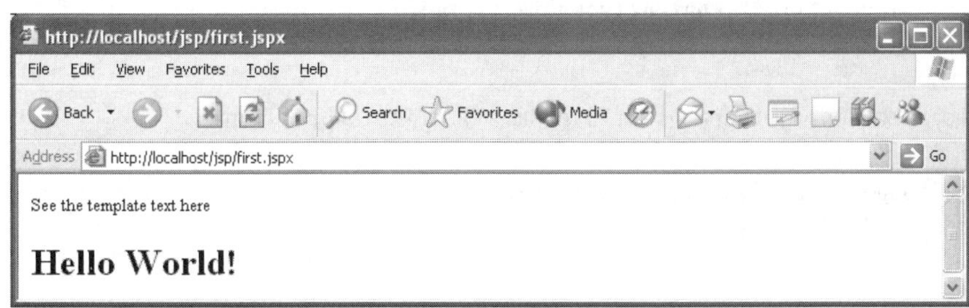

Here the <jsp:text> is a tag to enclose all template text in the generated outputs. This JSP XML only displays messages. Let us look at the next JSP XML document, `second.jspx`, that interacts with clients.

```
<html xmlns:jsp="http://java.sun.com/JSP/Page" version="2.0">
<jsp:directive.page import="java.util.*" />
<jsp:text>
<body>
     Hello <jsp:expression> request.getParameter("username")   </jsp:expression>!
<br>
     <jsp:scriptlet> Date today = new Date(); </jsp:scriptlet>
     <jsp:expression> today </jsp:expression>
</br>
</body>
</jsp:text>
</html>
```

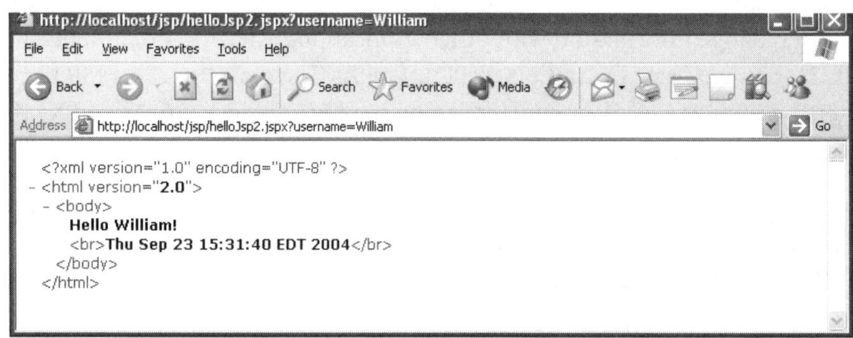

If you add an attribute `contentType="text/html"` in this `.jspx` file as follows, you will see a page displayed in HTML format instead of XML document format.

```
<html xmlns:jsp="http://java.sun.com/JSP/Page" version="2.0">

<jsp:directive.page import="java.util.*" contentType="text/html"/>
<jsp:text>
<body>
     Hello <jsp:expression> request.getParameter("username") </jsp:expression>!
<br />
     <jsp:scriptlet> Date today = new Date(); </jsp:scriptlet>
     <jsp:expression> today </jsp:expression>
</body>
</jsp:text>
</html>
```

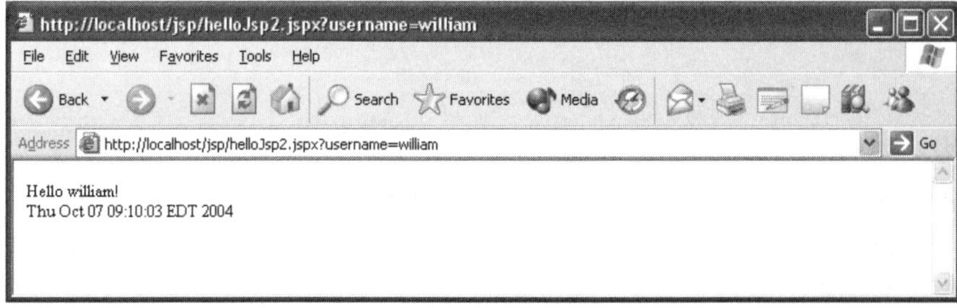

You have seen some JSP action tags in the previous section. The JSP XML document tag uses the following syntax:

```
<prefix:tag-name> body </prefix:tag-name>
```

instead of using syntax of <% such as <%, <%=, <%!, <%@ tags.

A JSP tag can have a start tag, a tag body, and an end tag. If a tag does not need a body, it can have its shorthand notation as

```
<prefix:tag-name/>
```

The `<jsp:forward>`, `<jsp:include>`, `<jsp:usebean>`, `<jsp:setProperty>`, and `<jsp:getproperty>` standard JSP action tag element tags already comply with this syntax format.

The following table lists all other JSP standard syntax and its alternative JSP XML syntax.

Elements	JSP Standard Syntax	JSP XML Syntax
Declarations	<%! ..%>	<jsp:declaration> .. </jsp:declaration>
Directives	<%@ include .. %>	<jsp:directive.include .. />
	<%@ page *attributes* %>	<jsp:directive.page *attributes* />
	<%@ taglib .. %>	<html xmlns:prefix="*tag library URL*" >
Expressions	<%= ..%>	<jsp:expression> .. </jsp:expression>
Scriptlets	<% ..%>	<jsp:scriptlet> .. </jsp:scriptlet>
Comments	<%--.. --%>	<!-- .. -->

4.8 JSP Debugging and Testing

JSP debugging is even more difficult than Servlet debugging in that the tester not only needs to know Servlets, but also needs to understand about JSP itself and JSP connections with other Web components. The conceptual confusion between client and server-side code may still be there. Make debugging easier by designing a modular application that allows each component to be tested.

4.8.1 Compilation Errors

A JSP file is translated into a Servlet Java class file when it is accessed the first time or it has been changed since it was last used. Compilation errors can come from JSP elements such as page directives, scripting elements, action elements, or EL expression notations. There are two types of compilation errors: translation errors from JSP to the Servlet Java file generated by the JSP engine (Tomcat Jasper) and compilation errors from the Servlet Java file to the Servlet class file generated by the Java compiler. The first phase errors may be caused by misspelling of JSP keywords or omitting required attributes in the JSP elements so that the JSP engine is unable to produce its Servlet Java file. The second phase errors may be caused by Java syntax problems. There is an easy way to distinguish these two types of errors by just checking the generation of the Servlet Java file for the JSP. If the Servlet file is not generated at all, then it indicates that the errors are located in JSP syntax rather than in Java syntax.

4.8.2 Run-Time Errors

There are two major types of run-time errors during the Servlet class run-time. One throws exceptions and the other does not throw an exception but produces unexpected results. For the exception errors, check the detail exception messages to locate and fix the bugs.

For the business logic errors (for example, the JSP does not get the right data or does not display the data in a correct format), you can apply the techniques we discussed in the Debugging Servlets section of the last chapter. The following list includes some often used techniques:

1. Using `System.out.println()` statement.
2. Using `log()` method of `ServletContext` to store the hint messages in the log file in the Tomcat installation directory on the server.
3. Using comments:
   a. Using Java comments, `// . . .` for single-line comment and `/* . . . */` for multiple-line comments, to temporarily remove a section of Java code. If the problem is gone, then the commented part is the source of the error. The comments can be placed within the scriptlet element such as `<% /* . . . */ %>`.

   b. Using JSP comments to locate the errors when JSP is translated into a Servlet Java file. Comments must be placed in the JSP template portion such as `<%-- <% . . . . %> --%>`.

c. Using HTML comments to hide everything inside the HTML comments. This cannot remove the code temporarily such as JSP comments and Java comments.

4. The ultimate solution is to use IDE debugger tools such as VisualAge, JBuilder, Visual Café, Forte, and others.

4.9 Examples and Lab Practice

You will have a number of labs with which to practice. These will help you better understand about the concepts of JSP and its applications. Lab 1 shows how a Servlet talks to a JSP in a conference registration example. Lab 2 gives a simple application that shows how multiple JSP pages (including a JSP error page) work together. Lab 3 depicts how to use a custom tag library to define a two-decimal-digits format tag that can be reused in any JSP application. Lab 4 demonstrates a programming language survey example that uses the scoped data between requests in the same session. Lab 5 demonstrates a comprehensive example of a phone book management application that applies most of the JSP elements discussed in this chapter. All source code of the labs can be found online.

4.9.1 Lab 1: Integration of a Servlet with JSP

In this conference registration example, a Servlet class `DispatchServlet` (with a `"Dispatch"` URL-pattern name defined in `web.xml`) plays a controller role that takes inputs of attendee name and status (student or faculty) on an HTML request form, calculates the registration fee according to the status, and redirects the control to a JSP (`output.jsp`) by Servlet RequestDispatcher's forward (`req`, `res`) method. The JSP is responsible for generating a confirmation page with the attendee name and the conference registration fee. The diagram illustrates the interactions between the HTML request form page, the Java Servlet component, and the JSP component.

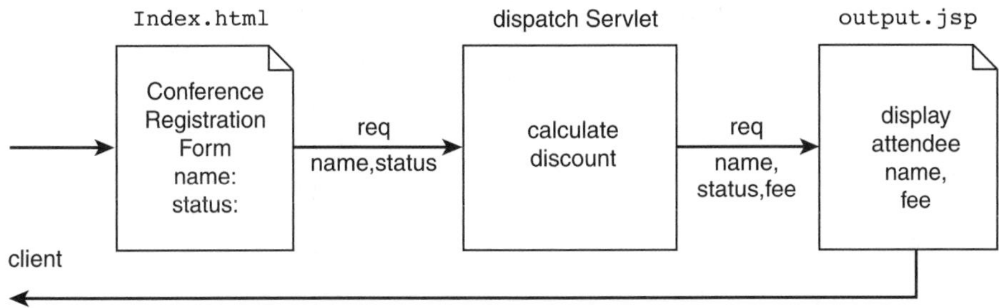

The following screen shots show the interaction between a conference attendee and this Web application with Servlet and JSP integration. John registers for the conference with a student status and gets a 50% discount from the regular $500 registration fee. Kai registers for the conference with a faculty status and gets no discount.

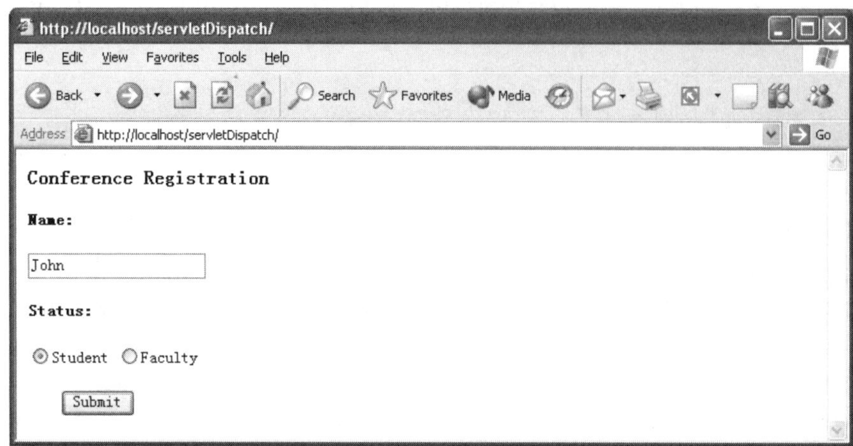

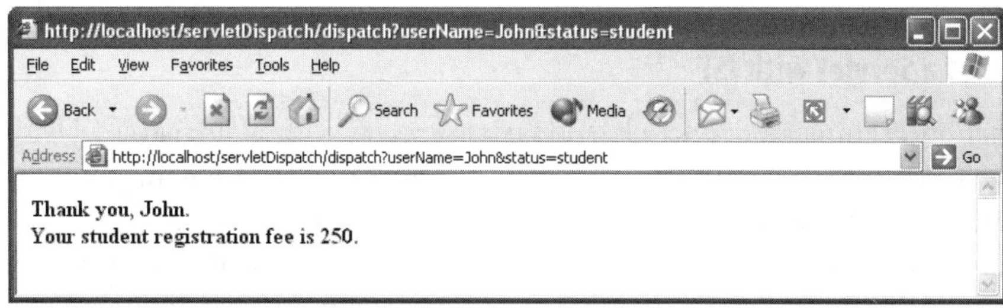

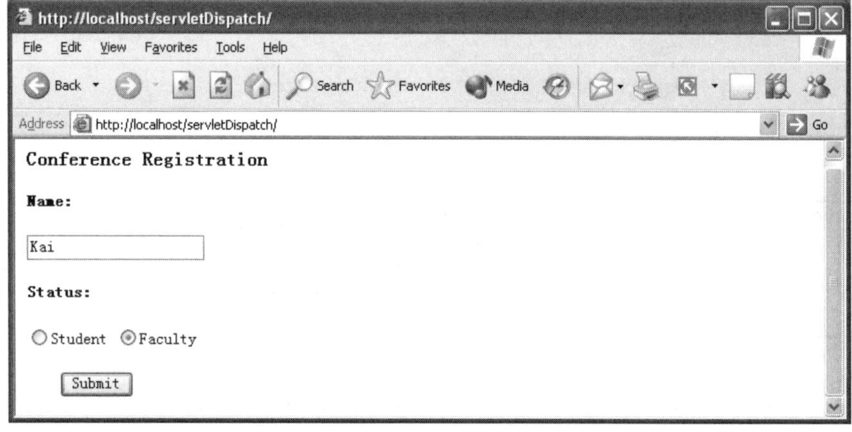

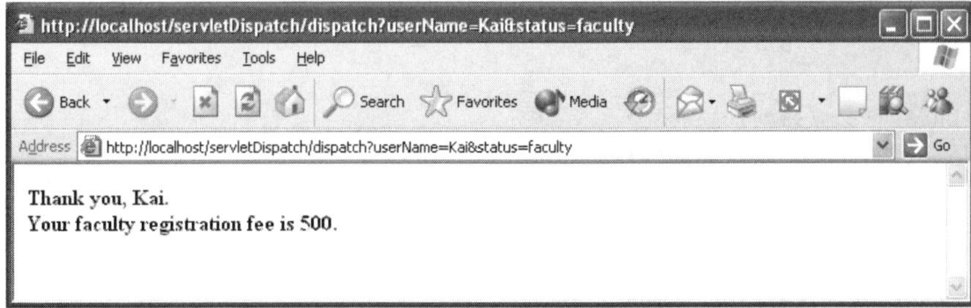

This Web application is called `servletDispatch` in Tomcat.

`C:\jakarta-tomcat-5\webapps\servletDispatch\index.html` is a default HTML request form file.

```
<html>
<head>
    <title></title>
</head>

<body>
    <h3> Conference Registration </h3>

    <form action="/servletDispatch/dispatch">

    <h4> Name: </h4>
         <input type="text" name="userName">
    <h4> Status: </h4>
         <input type=radio name="status" value="student">Student
         <input type=radio name="status" value="faculty">Faculty <p>
         <input type=submit value="Submit">
     </form>
</body>
</html>
```

The file `C:\jakarta-tomcat-5\webapps\servletDispatch\WEB-INF\web.xml` specifies the Servlet name as `dispatchServlet` and its class file `servletDispatch.DispatchServlet.class`, and maps the `dispatchServlet` Servlet name to its URL-pattern name, `dispatch`.

```
<?xml version="1.0" encoding="ISO-8859-1"?>

<!DOCTYPE web-app
    PUBLIC "-//Sun Microsystems, Inc.//DTD Web Application 2.3//EN"
    "http://java.sun.com/dtd/web-app_2_3.dtd">
```

```
<web-app>

  <servlet>
    <servlet-name>dispatchServlet</servlet-name>
    <servlet-class>servletDispatch.DispatchServlet</servlet-class>
  </servlet>

  <servlet-mapping>
    <servlet-name>dispatchServlet</servlet-name>
    <url-pattern>/dispatch</url-pattern>
  </servlet-mapping>

</web-app>
```

The file `C:\jakarta-tomcat-5\webapps\servletDispatch\WEB-INF\classes\servletDispatch\DispatchServlet.java` is the Servlet source code. It takes inputs of attendee name and status (student or faculty) on an HTML request form, calculates the registration fee according to the status (a 50% discount applies to student attendees, based on a regular $500 registration fee), and transfers the control to the `output.jsp`.

```
package servletDispatch;

import java.io.*;
import java.net.*;
import java.util.*;
import javax.servlet.*;
import javax.servlet.http.*;

public class DispatchServlet extends HttpServlet
{
     public void doGet(HttpServletRequest req, HttpServletResponse res) throws
javax.servlet.ServletException, java.io.IOException
     {
          String status = req.getParameter("status");
                int orgFee = 500;

          if(status != null && status.equals("student") )
          {
                       int studentFee = 500 / 2;
               req.setAttribute("regFee", "" + studentFee);
               req.getRequestDispatcher("/output.jsp").forward(req,
                                           res);
               return;
```

```
            }
            else if(status != null && status.equals("faculty") )
            {
                      int facultyFee = 500;
                      req.setAttribute("regFee", "" + facultyFee);
            req.getRequestDispatcher("/output.jsp").forward(req, res);
                      return;
            }
      }
}
```

The file `C:\jakarta-tomcat-5\webapps\servletDispatch\output.jsp` is the JSP file that retrieves the request and response objects from the Servlet component, obtains the attendee name and status from the parameters of the request implicit object, gets a registration fee from the `reFee` attributes of the request object, and displays the results to clients.

```
<html>
<head>
    <title></title>
</head>
<body>
    <H3> Thank you, <%=request.getParameter("userName") %>.<br>
    Your <%=request.getParameter("status") %> registration fee is
    <%=request.getAttribute("regFee") %>.
    </H3>
</body>
</html>
```

4.9.2 Lab 2: A Form Request Application with Integrations of Multiple JSP Pages

In this simple example, you will practice integrations of multiple JSP pages by JSP forwarding or including actions. A user types in his/her name in the front-end HTML form `index.html` as follows.

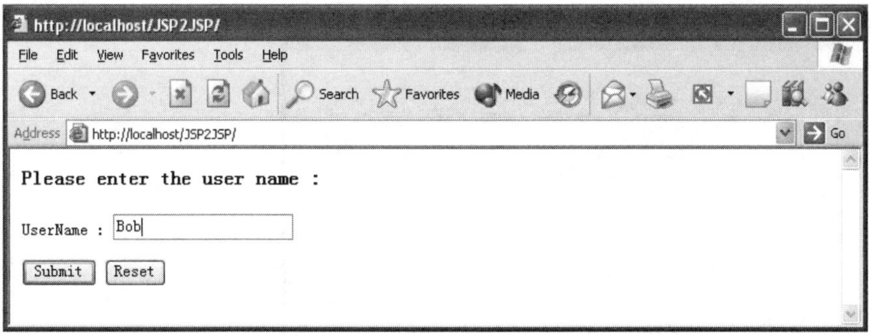

The request is sent to the `test.jsp` that checks the presence of the user name. If a user name is there, the `test.jsp` includes a greeting page `helloJSP.jsp` and the `index.html` to prompt for a user name again.

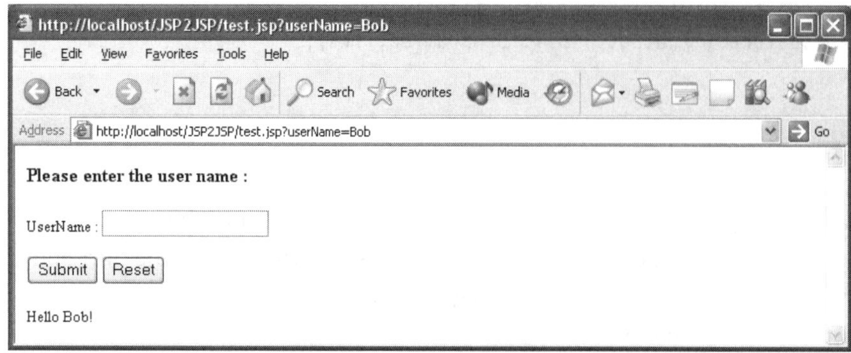

If the user did not type anything in the prompt and submits the request form, then `test.jsp` forwards it to an `errorJSP` page that displays an error message and includes the `index.html` to prompt for user input again.

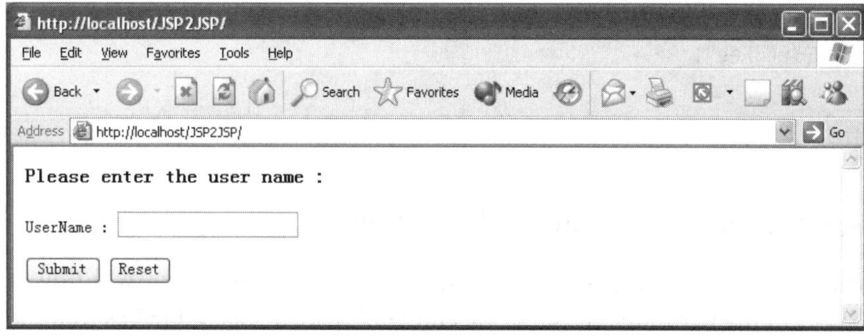

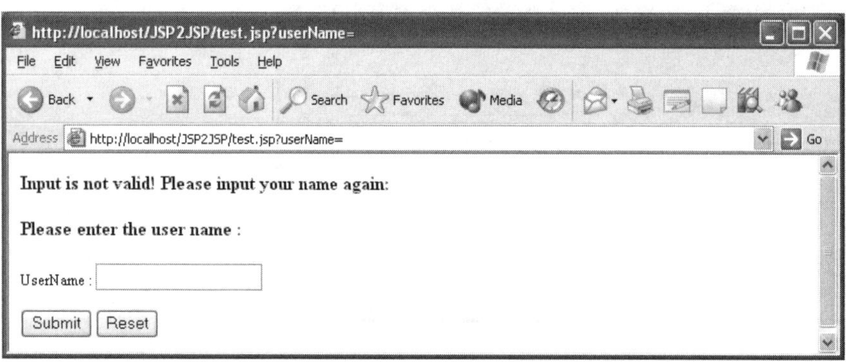

The next diagram illustrates the JSP page interactions in this application.

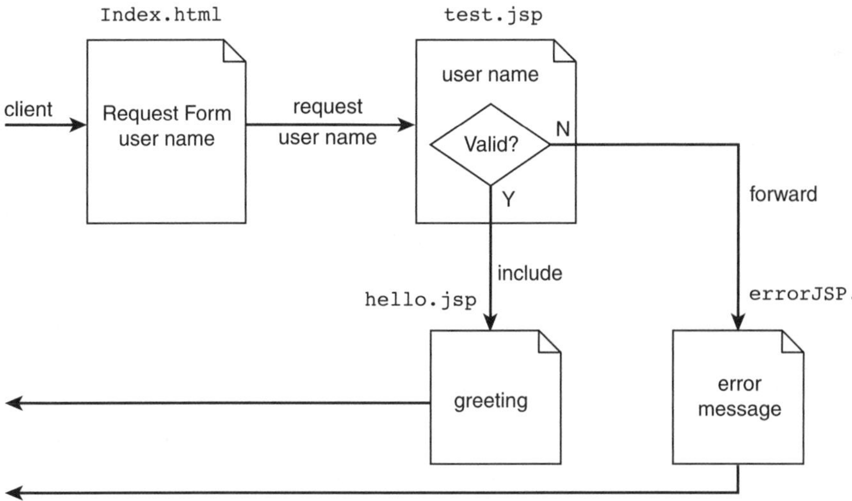

The file C:\jakarta-tomcat-5\webapps\JSP2JSP\index.html is the front-end form request HTML page shown as below.

```
<html>
<head>
     <title></title>
</head>
<body>

<h3>Please enter the user name :</h3><p>
<form action="test.jsp">
UserName : <input type="text" name="userName"><br><br>
<input type="submit" value="Submit">
<input type="reset" value="Reset">
</form>

</body>
</html>
```

The file C:\jakarta-tomcat-5\webapps\JSP2JSP\test.jsp either forwards the control to an error page or includes a response page, depending on conditions of the parameters.

```
<html>
<head>
     <title></title>
</head>
```

```
<body>

<%
    if (!request.getParameter("userName").equals( "" ))
{
%>
    <%@ include file="index.html" %>
    <jsp:include page="helloJsp.jsp" />
<%
}
    else
{
%>
    <jsp:forward page="errorJSP.jsp" />
<%
}
%>

</body>
</html>
```

The file `C:\jakarta-tomcat-5\webapps\JSP2JSP\helloJsp.jsp` is a greeting page that just says "Hello <*your name*>!".

```
<html>
<body>
     Hello <%=request.getParameter("userName")%>!
</body>
</html>
```

The file `C:\jakarta-tomcat-5\webapps\JSP2JSP\errorJSP.jsp` is a page to display an error message and also include the front `index.html` to prompt user again.

```
<html>
    <head>
    </head>
    <body>
       <h3>Input is not valid! Please input your name again:</h3>
       <%@ include file="index.html" %>
    </body>
</html>
```

4.9.3 Lab 3: Application of a Custom Tag Library for a Two-Decimal-Digits Format Tag

This practice lab shows detailed steps to develop a custom tag named `twoDigits` that takes a real number attribute and formats it into a precision of two decimal digits after the decimal point.

Because this type of format processing is often required at the JSP level, it is very convenient to have such a tag ready in the tag library for the JSP designer to use instead of using Java scriptlets to doing detail coding.

This tag is specified in the `webapps\tagLib\WEB-INF\testLib.tld` tag library definition file as follows. The tag handler class is also specified in this `tld` file. This Web application root directory is `taglib`.

```
<!DOCTYPE taglib
        PUBLIC "-//Sun Microsystems, Inc.//DTD JSP Tag Library 1.2//EN"
     "http://java.sun.com/j2ee/dtd/web-jsptaglibrary_1_2.dtd">

<taglib>

     <!-- INFO ABOUT THIS LIBRARY -->
          <tlib-version>1.0</tlib-version>
          <jsp-version>1.2</jsp-version>
          <short-name>testLib</short-name>
     <tag>
          <name>twoDigits</name>
          <tag-class>testLib.TwoDigitsTag</tag-class>
          <body-content>empty</body-content>
          <description></description>
          <attribute>
               <name>num</name>
               <required>true</required>
               <rtexprvalue>true</rtexprvalue>
          </attribute>
     </tag>

</taglib>
```

The following is the `webapps\tagLib\converter.jsp` file that uses the `twoDigits` tag. The first bold line specifies the prefix named `test` and its tag library `uri` identifier. The next bold line shows the application of the tag. This `twoDigits` tag has one String type attribute named `num`, and the output of this tag becomes a part of output of the JSP that is displayed to clients.

```
<%@ taglib prefix="test" uri="/WEB-INF/testLib.tld" %>

<html><body>

<h3>Please enter Fahrenheit temperature : </h3><p>

<form>
Temperature(F) : <input type="text" name="temperature"><br><br>
<input type="submit" value="Submit">
```

```
</form>

<%
    String temperature = request.getParameter("temperature");
    if(temperature != null && (!temperature.equals("")))
    {
         double tempF = Double.parseDouble(temperature);
         String tempC = "" + (tempF -32)*5.0/9.0;

%>
    <h3> <%= temperature %> degrees in Fahrenheit is converted to
         <test:twoDigits num="<%= tempC %>" />
         degrees in Celsius
    </h3>
    <%
    }
    %>

</body></html>
```

The `twoDigits` tag-handler class is given in the file `webapps\tagLib\WEB-INF\classes\testLib\TwoDigitsTag.java`. There are many ways to implement a tag handler. It can implement a Tag interface or extend a `TagSupport` class. In this example, we implement it by Tag interface so we need to override all the abstract methods in this interface. The implementation is given in the `doStartTag()` method. When the `twoDigits` tag is encountered, this method is called back by the container to start handling the tag. Since this tag has an attribute, there is a `setNum()` method for the attribute `field num`. There is no need to take care of the body of the tag since this tag does not have a body.

```
package testLib;

import javax.servlet.jsp.*;
import javax.servlet.jsp.tagext.*;
import java.text.DecimalFormat;

public class TwoDigitsTag implements Tag
{
   private PageContext pageContext;
   private Tag parentTag;

   //initialization part
   public void setPageContext(PageContext pageContext)
   {
      this.pageContext = pageContext;
```

```
    }

    public void setParent(Tag parentTag)
    {
       this.parentTag = parentTag;
    }

    public Tag getParent()
    {
       return this.parentTag;
    }

    //A String that holds the user attributes private String num;

    //The setter method that is called by the container
    public void setNum(String num){ this.num = num; }

   //actual tag handling code
    public int doStartTag() throws JspException
    {
       try
       {
           DecimalFormat twoDigits = new DecimalFormat("0.00");
           double d1 = Double.parseDouble(num);
           String s1 = twoDigits.format(d1);

           JspWriter out = pageContext.getOut();
           out.print(s1);
       }
       catch(Exception e)
       {
          throw new JspException("error");
       }
       return SKIP_BODY;
    }

    public int doEndTag() throws JspException
    {
       return EVAL_PAGE;
    }
       public void release()//clean up the resources (if any)
    {
    }
}
```

Here is a sample execution result. Web clients browse the `index.html` and input the Fahrenheit temperature.

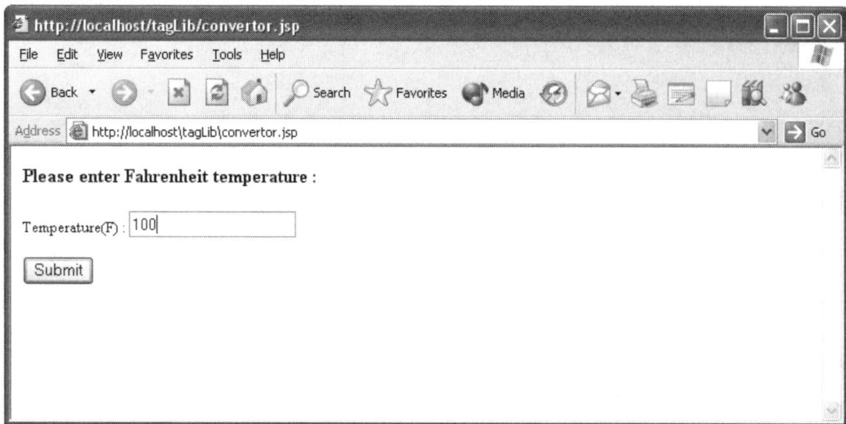

The `converter.jsp` responds with a converted Celsius number with two decimal digits after the decimal point by the `twoDigits` tag.

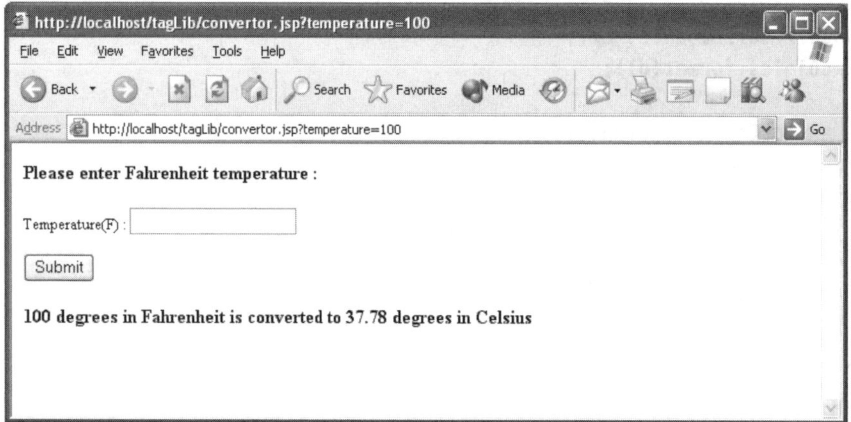

4.9.4 Lab 4: A Survey of Programming Language Preference with Java Scoped Objects

This survey lab shows the implementation of Java objects in an application scope. This Web application conducts an online programming language preference survey on C# and Java. Every user who takes the survey will result in a new session. After a specific session is over, the summary data should stay in order for the survey to continue. Because the survey is online, clients can access this Web application everywhere. For example, one participant, Mary, received a survey result of two for Java and one for C# by accessing the URL at the IP address shown below.

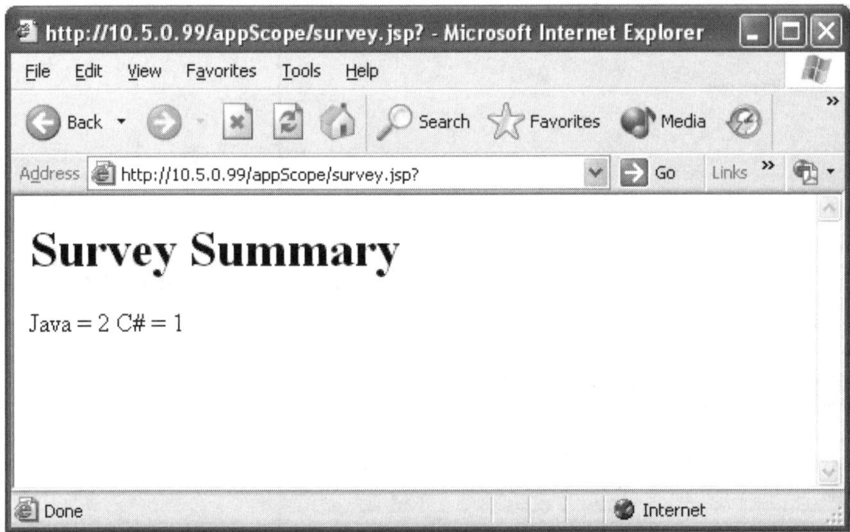

Another participant, John, took the survey and chose Java as his preference.

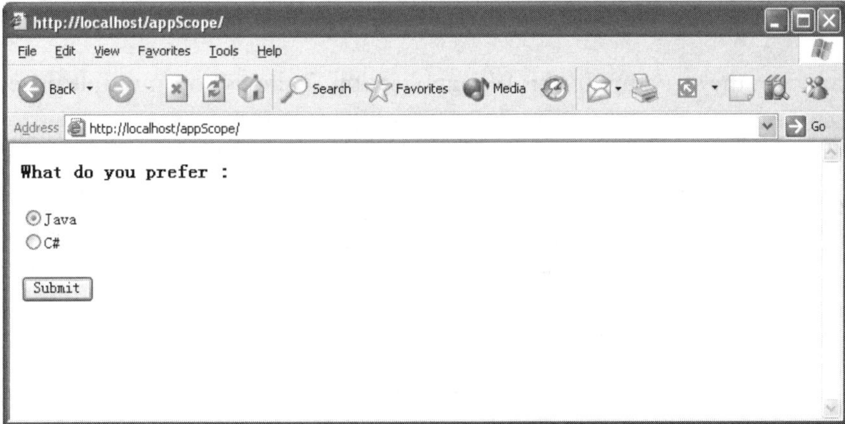

Then, John received a confirmation message and is promoted for further action to view the poll.

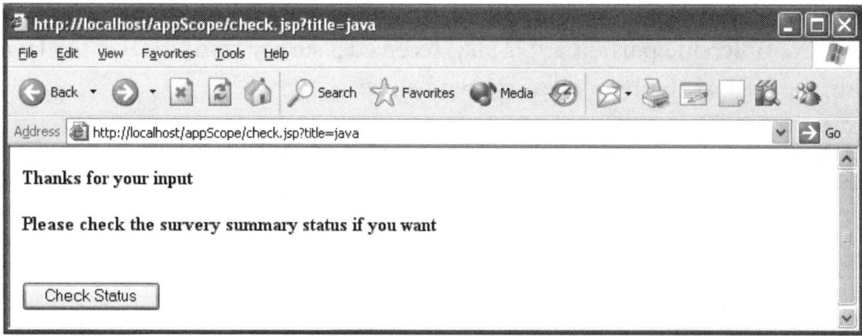

John responded with the Check Status button and the Survey Summary showed an updated poll result with three Java votes instead of two.

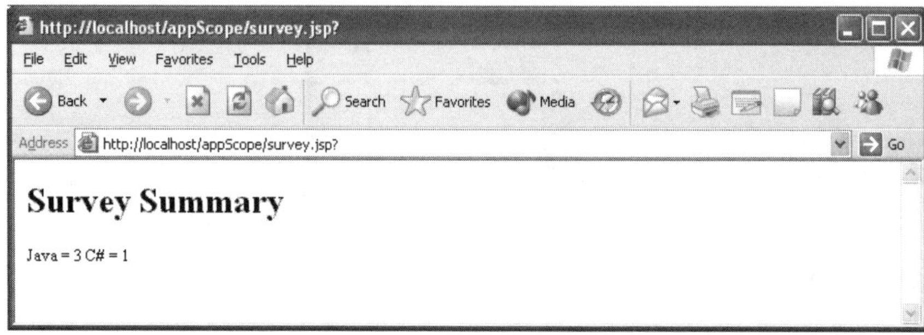

The following diagram illustrates the structure of this Web application. It shows how multiple pages share a JavaBean component.

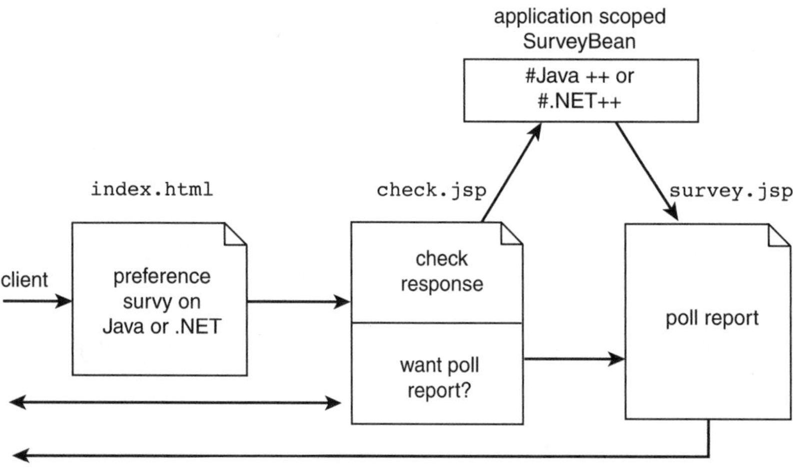

The following is the index.html of this appScope Web application named C:\jakarta-tomcat-5\webapps\appScope\index.html. It takes the user inputs and passes them on to check.jsp to process the poll.

```
<html>
    <head>
        <title></title>
    </head>

    <body>

        <form action="/appScope/check.jsp">
        <h3>What do you prefer :</h3>
        <input type=radio name="title" value="java">Java <br>
        <input type=radio name="title" value="c">C# <p>
        <input type=submit value="Submit">
        </form>

    </body>
</html>
```

The SurveyBean is given as follows:

```
package appScope;

public class SurveyBean
{
    private int javaQuality = 0;
    private int csQuality = 0;

    public int getJavaQuality()
    {
        return javaQuality;
    }
    public int getCsQuality()
    {
        return csQuality;
    }
    public void setQuality(String bookTitle)
    {
        try
        {
            if (bookTitle.equals("java"))
            {
                javaQuality++;
            }
```

```
            if (bookTitle.equals("c"))
            {
                csQuality++;
            }
        }catch(Exception e){e.printStackTrace();}
    }
}
```

The file C:\jakarta-tomcat-5\webapps\appScope\check.jsp retrieves the request parameters and saves the values in an application-scoped JavaBean named "appScope.SurveyBean", then transfers control to survey.jsp to report the updated poll results if the user chooses to check the status.

```
<html>
<body>
    <jsp:useBean id="survey" class="appScope.SurveyBean" scope="application"/>
    <jsp:setProperty name="survey" property="quality"
                 value='<%= request.getParameter("title")%>' />

    <form action="/appScope/survey.jsp">
     <h3> Thanks for your input <h3>
     <h3> Please check the survery summary status if you want <h3> <br>

    <input type=submit value="Check Status">
</body>
</html>
```

The file C:\jakarta-tomcat-5\webapps\appScope\survey.jsp retrieves the data from the application-scoped JavaBean and reports the Survey Summary as follows.

```
<HTML>
<HEAD>
    <TITLE>Survey Summary</TITLE>
</HEAD>
    <jsp:useBean id="survey" class="appScope.SurveyBean" scope="application"/>

<BODY>
    <H1>Survey Summary</H1>
    Java = <jsp:getProperty name="survey" property="javaQuality" />
    C# = <jsp:getProperty name="survey" property="csQuality" />

<BODY>
</HTML>
```

4.9.5 Lab 5: A Comprehensive Example of Phone Book Management

This is a more comprehensive JSP lab. Many JSP techniques are used in this example including standard tag library, custom tag library, Expression Language, JavaBeans, and many others. Basically, this phonebook Web application presents a phone book in a drop-down combo list for clients to look up. When a user selects Mary Smith, her phone number, 770-444-1101, is shown as the demo below. All the interaction is taken care of by the index.jsp itself. A single JSP file can take inputs and responds with results and continues this way. This application is named phonebook in the Web application root directory.

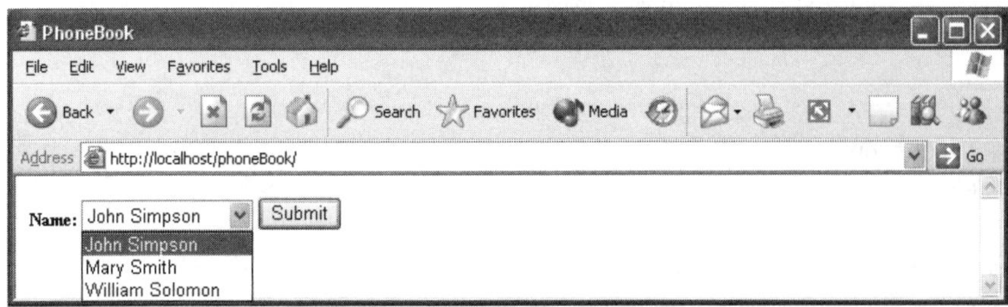

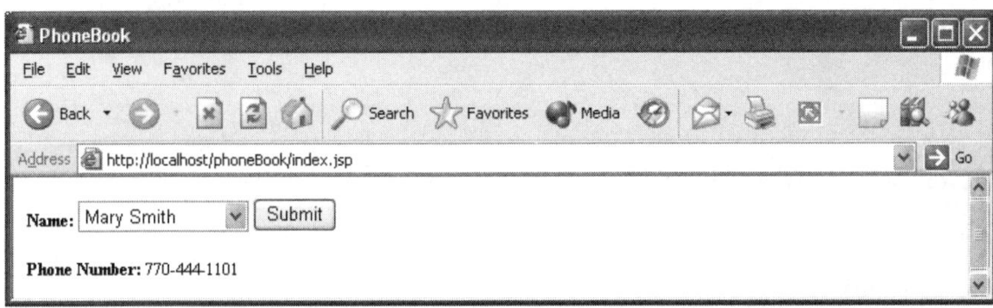

The file C:\jakarta-tomcat-5\webapps\phoneBook\index.jsp uses two tag libraries. One is the core Java Standard Tag Library (*JSTL*) with the prefix "standard," and the other is the custom-defined functions.tld with a prefix "f."

The core JSTL provides many useful tags such as set, forEach, when, choose, and if. Standard tags are used for iteration over the phone book JavaBean to find the phone number of a given name.

```
<%@ page isELIgnored = "false" %>
<%@ page contentType="text/html; charset=UTF-8" %>
<%@ taglib uri="http://java.sun.com/jsp/jstl/core" prefix="standard" %>
<%@ taglib uri="/WEB-INF/functions.tld" prefix="f" %>
<html>
<head><title>PhoneBook</title></head>
<body bgcolor="white">

<jsp:useBean id="phoneBook" scope="application" class="mypbk.MyPhoneBook"/>

<form name="phoneBookForm" action="index.jsp" method="post">
<standard:set var="selectedName" value="${param.names}" />
<standard:set var="selectedFlag" value="${!empty selectedName}" />
```

```
<b>Name:</b>
<select name=names>
<standard:forEach var="name" items="${phoneBook.names}" >
  <standard:choose>
      <standard:when test="${selectedFlag}">
      <standard:choose>
      <standard:when test="${f:equals(selectedName,name)}" >
           <option selected>${name}</option>
      </standard:when>
      <standard:otherwise>
           <option>${name}</option>
      </standard:otherwise>
  </standard:choose>
      </standard:when>
      <standard:otherwise>
      <option>${name}</option>
      </standard:otherwise>
  </standard:choose>
</standard:forEach>
</select>
<input type="submit" name="Submit" value="Submit">
</form>

<standard:if test="${selectedFlag}" >
  <jsp:setProperty name="phoneBook" property="selectedName" value="${selectedName}" />
  <b>Phone Number: </b>${phoneBook.selectedNumber}
</standard:if>

</body>
</html>
```

The file `webapps\phoneBook\WEB-INF\functions.tld` defines a custom-defined tag `"equals"` that is implemented in the `MyPhoneBook` class.

```
<?xml version="1.0" encoding="UTF-8" ?>

<taglib xmlns="http://java.sun.com/xml/ns/j2ee"
    xmlns:xsi="http://www.w3.org/2001/XMLSchema-instance"
    xsi:schemaLocation="http://java.sun.com/xml/ns/j2ee web-jsptaglibrary_2_0.xsd"
    version="2.0">
    <description>A tag library that defines a function.</description>
    <tlib-version>1.0</tlib-version>
    <short-name>FunctionTagLibrary</short-name>
    <uri>/FunctionLibrary</uri>
  <function>
```

```
    <name>equals</name>
    <function-class>mypbk.MyPhoneBook</function-class>
    <function-signature>boolean equals( java.lang.String, java.lang.String )</function-
signature>
  </function>
</taglib>
```

The file `webapps\phoneBook\WEB-INF\classes\mypbkmyPhoneBook.java` in the package `mypbk` is a JavaBean file that complies with the JavaBean conventions. It is also the `equals` tag handler class, where the method `equals` is defined.

```
package mypbk;

import java.util.*;
import java.text.DateFormat;

public class MyPhoneBook {
    HashMap phoneBooks;
    ArrayList names;
    String selectedNumber;
    String selectedName;
    String phoneBookInfo[][] = {{"Mary Smith", "770-444-1101"},
                                {"John Simpson", "770-444-1102"},
                                {"William Solomon", "770-444-1103"}};

    public MyPhoneBook() {

        phoneBooks = new HashMap();
        names = new ArrayList();

        for (int i = 0; i < phoneBookInfo.length; i++) {
            phoneBooks.put(phoneBookInfo[i][0], phoneBookInfo[i][1]);
            names.add(phoneBookInfo[i][0]);
        }
        Collections.sort(names);
        selectedNumber = null;
        selectedNumber = null;
    }

    public static boolean equals(String l1, String l2) {
        return l1.equals(l2);
    }

    public Collection getNames() {
        return names;
```

```
    }

    public void setSelectedName(String displayName) {
        this.selectedName = displayName;
        this.selectedNumber = (String) phoneBooks.get(displayName);
    }

    public String getSelectedNumber() {
        return selectedNumber;
    }

    public String getSelectedName() {
        return selectedName;
    }
}
```

4.10 Summary

JSP technology is an extension of Java Servlet technology. JSP allows Web designers and Web application programmers to generate dynamic Web contents and it simplifies the Web server-side programming by providing powerful constructs in tag-scripting form instead of code programming. The biggest advantage of JSP over Servlets is that it enables Web page designers who are not familiar with Java coding to design interactive and dynamic Web pages. JSP technology is also platform-independent and extensible in order to work with other technologies such as JavaBeans, Enterprise JavaBeans (EJB), and Web Services. WYSIWYG is another advantage in using JSP because many IDE tools can be used for authoring JSP as long as they support HTML.

The key components or constructs of JSP are JSP directives; scripting elements including include, expression, scriptlets; and JSP actions, tag library, Expression Language. The custom tag library is another important feature that other technologies such as ASP do not support.

Directive elements specify overall page settings and configurations; directive elements do not produce outputs. JSP expression scripting elements enable an expression to be evaluated and converted into a string that is part of the JSP template text. It produces output. JSP declaration scripting elements allow JSP designers to declare variables and methods. JSP scriptlets can insert Java Servlet code in the JSP to enable it to interact with components in JSP or components outside the JSP. JSP actions encapsulate predefined tags such as JavaBean creation and enable access and control transferring such as `<jsp:forward>` and `<jsp:include>`.

The custom tag library enables Java programmers to create new tags that encapsulate complex Java coding that will be reused by the JSP designer. For a complex application or for a large software development team, there is a need to reuse the components in order to reduce costs and to increase productivity. This makes custom tags good choices. For small projects or small development teams there may be no need to have custom tags available, so sciptlets or JavaBeans may be a better choice. In addition, JSP also supports implicit (predefined) objects that can be shared in the scopes of page, request, session, and application by setting or getting the attribute of objects.

The new feature of EL is a big plus for JSP. It makes it much easier to access any implicit object, JavaBean, and other data when compared to traditional expression scripting.

Comparing JSP and Servlets, the request/response mechanism and life cycle are same. It is recommended to use Servlets if only a small portion of generated contents is fixed-template data.

4.11 Self-Review Questions

1. Which of the following is the attributes of a JSP page directive?

   a. `isELIgnored`

   b. `isErrorPage`

   c. `isThreadSafe`

   d. All of above

2. How many scopes are there for a JavaBean or a JSP implicit object?

   a. One

   b. Two

   c. Three

   d. Four

3. JSP is widely used to produce static HTML pages.

   a. True

   b. False

4. A JSP can do anything an HTML page can do.
   a. True
   b. False
5. Are JSP comments and HTML comments the same?
   a. Yes
   b. No
6. The JSP include directive `<%@ include file= "file name"   %>` will include the file at run time.
   a. True
   b. False
7. A `jspInit()` method can be specified in the JSP declaration directive element.
   a. True
   b. False
8. Which of the following are not JSP construct elements?
   a. JSP directive
   b. JSP action
   c. JSP scripting
   d. JSP tag
   e. None
9. Which of the following can have a Java statement?
   a. JSP scriptlets
   b. JSP expression
   c. JSP declaration
   d. JSP directive
10. EL supports nested dot notation so that it can evaluate a property of an object that is a property of another object.
    a. True
    b. False

11. All JSP JavaBean action elements can be substituted by a corresponding EL expression.

    a. True

    b. False

12. The attribute object of an HTTP request can be shared by all requests in the same session.

    a. True

    b. False

13. A `<jsp:forward>` action can also forward a control to a static HTML page.

    a. True

    b. False

14. A JSP file is compiled at the time:

    a. when the JSP is changed.

    b. when the JSP is accessed the first time.

    c. whenever the Servlet is accessed.

15. The `<jsp:forward>` action will result in

    a. a new request.

    b. a new session.

    c. none of the above.

16. The `<jsp:include>` action will result in

    a. a new request.

    b. a new session.

    c. none of the above.

17. Any Java class can be converted to a JavaBean.

    a. True

    b. False

18. `<jsp:setProperty>` can pass request parameters to JavaBean properties by specifying a "*" for its property attributes if the names match.

    a. True

    b. False

19. JSP translation into its Servlet Java file is done by
    a. JSP engine.
    b. Servlet container.
    c. Web server.
20. `<jsp:param>` specifies the key/value pairs that can be passed to the include, forward, and plug-in actions.
    a. True
    b. False

4.12 Keys to the Self-Review Questions

1. d 2. d 3. b 4. a 5. b 6. b 7. a 8. e 9. a 10. a 11. b 12. b 13. a
14. a,b 15. c 16. c 17. a 18. a 19. a 20. a

4.13 Exercises

1. What is a JSP?
2. How does a JSP page work?
3. What is the JSP engine?
4. What is the JSP directive element?
5. What is a JSP action element? How many different types are there?
6. What is a JSP scripting element? How many different types are there?
7. What is a JSP implicit object?
8. How many different ways are there to include another JSP file into the JSP file itself?
9. How many different ways are there for a JSP to share data with another JSP or other Web components?
10. How many different ways are there for a JSP to access a JavaBean?
11. Can we say that a JSP is an HTML or an HTML is a JSP?
12. How many different ways are there to transfer the flow control from one JSP to another Web component?
13. How many different ways are there for a Web client to access a JSP?
14. What is a custom tag? How does it work?

15. How can two JSP pages share data in the same session or in the same application?
16. How many different ways are there to instantiate a JavaBean instance?
17. What are the advantages of JSP technology?
18. What are the disadvantages of JSP technology?
19. What is the guideline when selecting the various techniques among Java scriptlets, JavaBeans, EL, and TLD?
20. Can JSP Expression Language be used to set a variable?

4.14 Programming Exercises

1. Develop a JSP page that displays the current date and time.
2. Develop a Web services component by JSP that provides services of a simple calculator. The calculator has the functionality to perform addition, subtraction, multiplication, and division of two real numbers. It can also detect a zero divisor in a division operation.
3. Develop a Web JSP application for an online guest book registration. If it is a new user, put him/her in the book; otherwise reply to the user with a message. This application involves two JSP pages where one handles registration and the other handles the message generation. The `jsp:forward` action is used.
4. Develop a simple Web application on a Tomcat server that includes an HTML page that takes a Fahrenheit temperature from clients and submits the request to a Servlet. The Servlet validates the request:
    a. If the input is empty or not a numerical data, it then forwards it to an error JSP page to report the error.
    b. If the input is valid, it then translates it into a Celsius temperature and displays it to the client via a JSP.
5. Develop a JSP Web application to conduct an alumni survey for a university football program. There are only two radio buttons (Yes and No) and one submit push button (Poll and Report) on the interface that alumni can use to evaluate the achievement of the football program. The Poll and Report button will display the percentage of positive responses and negative responses.

4.15 References

1. ASF. The Apache Jakarta Tomcat 5 Servlet/JSP Container.
2. Hall, Marty, and Larry Brown. *Core Servlets and JavaServer Pages: Volume 1: Core Technologies.* 2nd ed. Toms River, NJ: Prentice Hall, 2004.
3. Sun Industries. "Java 2 Platform Enterprise Edition, v 1.4, API Specification." http://java.sun.com/j2ee/1.4/docs/api/.
4. Sun Industries. "JSR-000154 Java Servlet 2.4 Specification." http://www.jcp.org/aboutJava/communityprocess/first/jsr154/index.html.
5. Sun Industries. "Java Servlet Technology." http://java.sun.com/products/servlet/.
6. Sun Industries. "Java Software FAQ Index." http://java.sun.com/reference/faqs/index.html.
7. Sun Industries. "JSR-000152 JavaServer Pages™ 2.0 Specification." http://www.jcp.org/aboutJava/communityprocess/first/jsr152/index3.html.
8. Mark Wutka. *Using Java Server Pages and Servlets.* Indianapolis, IN: Que, 2000.

CHAPTER 5

Case Study: MVC Architecture for Web Applications

Objectives of This Chapter

- Introduce concepts of MVC design architecture
- Demonstrate the Java implementation of MVC architecture
- Introduce concepts of JDBC
- Provide step-by-step tutorials on MVC design and development

5.1 Overview

Software architecture is the overall structure of a software system. Software architecture specifies the modular decompositions and the connections between the modules to divide and conquer a complex system. A good software architecture will also capture the non-functional requirements of a software system. There are many architectural styles that can be applied to the software architecture design in the software design phase. Master/slave, pipe/filter, repository, interpreter, implicit invocation, object-oriented, multitier, component-based, and MVC are popular architectural styles. This chapter discusses the MVC architecture, which is a very popular architecture for the middle tier (Web server) of a three-tier Web application. A single software system may need to have many architectural styles working together.

The detailed design is the process after the architectural design in the design phase. The design blueprint provides the basis for the software code development. A good software design can reduce the cost and production cycle time of software production and make the product easy to maintain, more portable, reliable, secure, efficient, and have a longer lifetime.

The Model-View-Controller (MVC) object-oriented architecture originally came from Smalltalk-80 as a methodology to separate the user interface presentation from the underlying data. The MVC is very similar to the Presentation-Abstraction-Control (PAC) model. The purpose of MVC is to decompose the whole system into three subsystems (modules). It is also called a component-based architectural style, because each module can be implemented by software components: data components, presentation components, input controls, control dispatch, and business process components. Each module in the MVC architecture has its own responsibility. It allows project team members with different expertise to work more efficiently in their own areas. For example, graphic professionals can work on the presentation of the GUI interface module; programmer professionals can work on input processing such as authentication, flow logic, and job dispatching in the Controller module; and data processing and database professionals can focus on the Model module to provide all the data the Web application needs. The connections between modules are also well defined in MVC. The Controller takes the inputs and does the authorization and authentication checking, dispatches requests to the corresponding module or submodule in the Model by instantiating new instances of data sources in the Model module and calling the methods provided by the data source objects. The data source forwards the controls to a specific representation module and lets that module be in charge of rendering the data retrieved from the data source objects. The data Model module may generate events to notify the Model listeners when the data are changed. The View module listens to the data Model module as its event listener. When such an event occurs, the View module needs to update its presentation views. Because the MVC architecture is object-oriented, each module may consist of a number of components. MVC does not restrict an application to a single view and controller. Typically for Java technology, most designers would like to have multiple JSP pages in a View module, multiple JavaBeans in a Model module, and a necessary number of Servlet classes in a Controller module. Generally, one JavaBean needs to have a corresponding database table to support it. We will discuss Java Data Base Connectivity (JDBC) in this chapter to show how the database supports the JavaBean in MVC. Because we have already introduced Java Servlet, JSP, and JavaBean technologies, this is a good time to explore the Java implementation of MVC architecture. (Some of the practice examples in the last chapter have applied this principle but it was not emphasized.)

5.2 MVC Basics

5.2.1 MVC Type-1 Architecture

Figure 5.1 illustrates the principle of MVC Module-1 architecture that is widely used in the design of simple Web server applications. It combines the Controller and the View module into a single module to take care of input and output processing; the remaining tasks are handled in the Data Model module. In a Java implementation, the front module is implemented using JSP technology and the back-end module is implemented with JavaBean technology. JSP on the Web server accepts requests, instantiates the required JavaBeans, and generates HTML pages for response. We know that each JavaBean object will usually have a relational table to support it.

Here is a simple MVC-1 Web application example implemented by JSP and JavaBeans. There are two JSP pages in the front module of this MVC-1 architecture: `mvc-1.jsp` and `hello.jsp`. As we discussed before, there may be many components working together in a single module. There is one JavaBean in the data module, the `myBean` JavaBean class. We look at the front module first.

```
// mvc-1.jsp

<%@ page import= "myPackage.*" %>
<jsp:useBean id="myBean" class="myPackage.MyBean" scope="request"/>
<jsp:setProperty name="myBean" property="*"/>
```

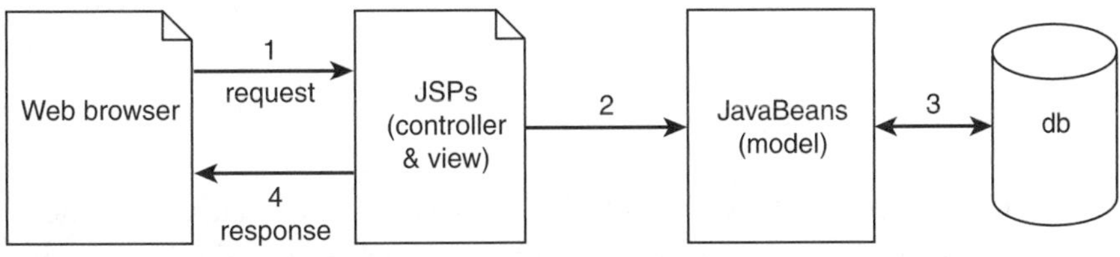

Figure 5.1
Overall MVC-1 Architecture

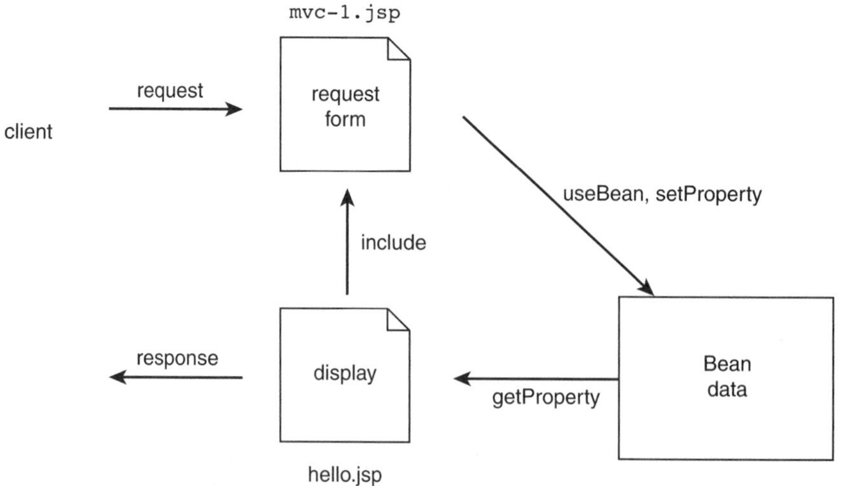

Figure 5.2
Java MVC-1 Architecture of the Simple Example

```
<html>
<body>
<form method="get">
<input type="text" value="userName">
<input type="submit" value="Submit">
</form>
<%
   if ${param['username']} != null) {
%>
<%@ include file = "hello.jsp" %>
<%
    }
%>

</body>
</html>
```

This module first creates a new instance of `myPackage.MyBean` JavaBean class with the `<jsp:useBean>` action tag. Then it takes user input from the request form and assigns the input value to the bean property by the `<jsp:setProperty name="myBean" property="*"/>` action tag. If there is an input string (rather than nothing), the module will include another page, `hello.jsp`, to render the output. The `hello.jsp` page shown below simply uses an Expression Language notation `${myBean.userName}` to get the data from the JavaBean in the end module where the data is set by the first `mvc-1.jsp` page. It is clear that the front-end module of MVC-1 does both input processing and the result presentation and the back-end module does all the business logic and data processing.

```
//hello.jsp

<b>
  Hello ${myBean.userName}!
</b>
```

The following `MyBean.java` shows a JavaBean declaration that complies with the JavaBean convention.

Every JavaBean has a default public constructor and it has all properties in private. It provides public methods to read from or write to its private properties. The names of methods meet the convention pattern in the formats of `getXXX()` and `setXXX()` where *XXX* is the name of its property. It must implement the `serializable` interface to have its persistent state. The following fragment shows the `MyBean` JavaBean used in this example.

```
// MyBean.java

package myPackage;
import java.io.*;

public class MyBean implements serializable {

  private String userName;

  public void MyBean(){
  userName= null;}

  public void setUserName(String userName) {
    this.userName = userName;
  }

  public String getUserName() {
    return this.userName;
  }
```

There is no data table associated with the JavaBean in this example, because it is not our focus at this time. It is presented in a case study example provided in this chapter.

5.2.2 MVC Type-2 Architecture

The MVC type-2 architecture is a better fit for more complex Web application design. It has a dedicated controller module that is in charge of user request processing such as authorization and

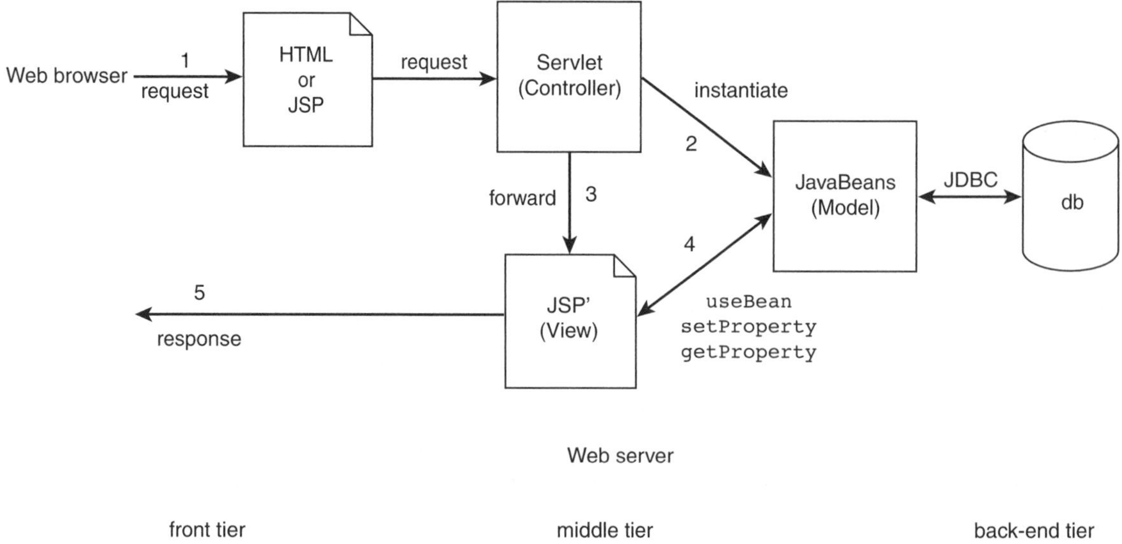

Figure 5.3
MVC-2 Architecture

authentication, deciding flow control dispatching such as selection of presentation views, as well as selection and instantiation of data models. The controller module is programming-centric-oriented, because there may be complex logic controls in a large application. There may be many classes working together in the Controller module. Java Servlet is a typical technology used in the controller module for process-intensive tasks. There is no processing logic in the presentation View module. The View module is only responsible for retrieving any data objects that are created by the Servlets and for generating dynamic contents to clients. There may be many View pages in a View module. The View module is page-centric-oriented. The clean separation of presentation from data processing and request processing results in a clear division of the roles and responsibilities of developers and page graphics designers in a development team. The more complex the application is, the more benefits the MVC type-2 architecture will bring.

Figure 5.3 shows a typical MVC type-2 architecture used in the middle tier (Web server) of a Web application.

5.2.3 A Simple MVC-2 Example

Figure 5.4 illustrates a simple implementation of an MVC architecture where there is only one Java class in each of the three modules. The `MyBean` JavaBean class plays the role of `model`, `MyServlet` Servlet class plays the role of Controller, and the `fromServlet` JSP plays the role of View in the MVC architecture. The figure shows the architecture diagram of this Web application. This example emphasizes the MVC so the user input interfaces are omitted. The `myServlet` Servlet sets a username

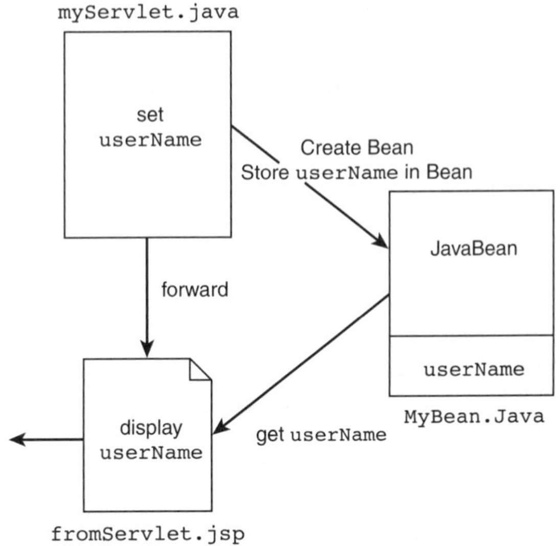

Figure 5.4
A Simple Example of MVC Architecture

and stores this name in a JavaBean named `myBean`, then transfers the control to a JSP page named `fromServlet.jsp`, which retrieves the username from the `myBean` and displays it on a Web page.

`MyBean` is a JavaBean class responsible for storing and providing data for business processing. This data JavaBean has one `userName` private property and two public methods to read from and write to this property.

```
// MyBean.java

package myPackage;

public class MyBean {

  private String userName;

  public MyBean(){
  username="";}

  public void setUserName(String userName) {
    this.userName = userName;
  }

  public String getUserName() {
    return this.userName;
  }
}
```

The `MyServlet` Servlet class in the Controller module sets the `userName` property of `myBean` by hard coding, stores this bean as an attribute (`beanInfo`) of the session implicit object, and dispatches the control to `fromServlet.jsp` of the View module in the MVC architecture.

```
//MyServlet.java

import java.io.*;
import javax.servlet.*;
import javax.servlet.http.*;
import myPackage.MyBean;

public class MyServlet extends HttpServlet {
    public void service(HttpServletRequest request,
            HttpServletResponse response)
            throws ServletException, IOException {

        MyBean myBean = new MyBean();
        myBean.setUserName("Kai");
        HttpSession session = request.getSession();
        session.setAttribute("beanInfo", myBean);
        RequestDispatcher rd;
        rd =getServletContext().getRequestDispatcher("/fromServlet.jsp");
        rd.forward(request, response);
    }
}
```

The `fromServlet.jsp` in the View module just retrieves the `userName` property stored in `myBean` with the `beanInfo` ID and displays the `userName` on the resulting page.

```
//fromServelt.jsp

<jsp:useBean id="beanInfo" class="myPackage.MyBean" scope="session"/>

<html>
<body>
<b>
  Hello <jsp:getProperty name="beanInfo" property="userName"/>
</b>
</body>
</html>
```

Or you can use JSP EL notation in the JSP file as follows.

```
<html>
<body>
```

```
<b>
  Hello ${beanInfo.userName}!
</b>
</html>
</body>
```

The JavaBeans in the MVC-1 and MVC-2 examples above are standalone JavaBeans without any support from database tables. JavaBeans in real-world applications are backed up by database tables most of time. Java Database Connectivity (JDBC) technology is widely used to support JavaBean component implementations.

5.3 JDBC

5.3.1 Overview

Java Database Connectivity (JDBC) is a standard that describes how to connect and talk to a database from within a Java application or applet. JDBC is a layer of abstraction that allows users to choose between databases. It provides cross-DBMS connectivity to a wide range of SQL databases. It allows access to virtually any SQL database engine with the single JDBC API. This standard allows database applications such as Java applications, Java applets, Servlets, or EJB to be written without the concern for the underlying details of a particular database. The JDBC API provides Java programmers with a uniform interface with a wide range of relational databases.

All Java database-related classes and interfaces are packaged together in the API package of `java.sql` that includes both the JDBC interfaces and the JDBC driver manager. A JDBC driver is a set of Java classes that implements the JDBC interfaces and translates vendor-neutral JDBC calls to vendor-specific DBMS commands, allowing JDBC to talk to any specific SQL database. JDBC drivers are provided by database vendors. A JDBC driver can be installed by downloading. The JDBC driver must register with the JDBC driver-manager. The JDBC driver-manager will connect to a given database upon requests from a Java application or Java applet. Figure 5.5 shows the connection of Java to a database by JDBC drivers.

5.3.2 JDBC API

The JDBC API provides a set of interfaces and classes for Java programmers to make a connection to a given database via the JDBC driver-manager, prepare a SQL statement, make the query or update requests by the prepared SQL statement, obtain the results and save them in the `resultSet`, and review the data in the `resultSet`. We can summarize any JDBC operation into the following steps:

1. Connection
   a. Load and register the driver

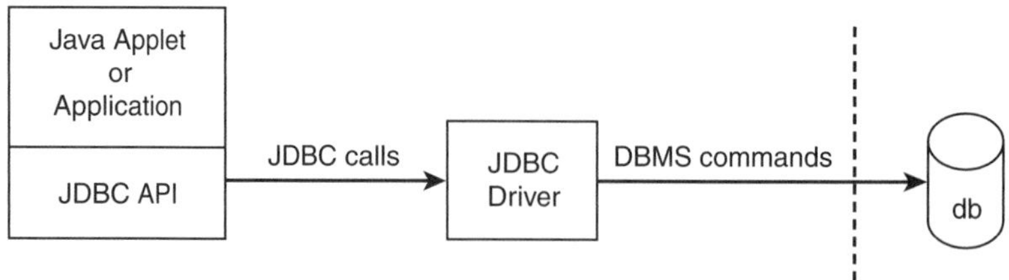

Figure 5.5
JDBC Driver

`Class.forName("oracle.jdbc.driver.OracleDriver");` or

```
DriverManager.registerDriver(new oracle.jdbc.driver.OracleDriver());
```

b. Connect to the database

```
Connection conn = DriverManager.getConnection("jdbc.oracle:thin", "Scott",
"Tiger");
// thin driver is a pure Java driver that can be downloded for a Java applet to use.
// jdbc.oracle:thin is the URL for this JDBC connection.
```

2. SQL statement

a. Prepare a SQL statement (query or update)

```
Statement st  = conn.createStatement();
```

b. Access SQL database by executing the SQL statement

`ResultSet rs = st.executeQuery( sql-query-statement);` or

```
Int count = st.executeUpdate(sql-update-stament);
```

For example, the sql-query-statement may look like:

```
select * from customers;
```

3. Processing of returned results

a. Obtain metadata

```
  ResultSetMetaData md = rs.getMetaData();
String colName=md.getColumnName(i)
```

b. Navigate the query `ResultSet`

```
while(rs.next()){
```

```
String name =  rs.getString(colName);
. . . }
```

By default, the result set cursor points to the row before the first row of the result set. A call to `next()` gets the first result set row. If there are no more rows unchecked, `next()` will return a false value. You can navigate the cursor by calling one of the following `ResultSet` methods:

`beforeFirst()`	(default position) puts the cursor before the first row of the result set.
`first()`	positions the cursor on the first row of the result set.
`last()`	positions the cursor before the last row of the result set.
`afterLast()`	positions the cursor beyond the last row of the result set.
`absolute(pos)`	positions the cursor at the row number position where `absolute(1)` is the first row and `absolute(-1)` is the last row.
`relative(pos)`	positions the cursor at a row relative to its current position where `relative(1)` moves the row cursor forward one row.

4. Close database connection

   a. Close the connection to release the resource:

   ```
   Con.close();
   ```

5.3.3 JDBC Drivers

A JDBC driver is a program that processes JDBC calls from any Java application and translates them to fit specific requirements of certain data sources. JDBC drivers simplify the Java database access activities just like any other types of drivers such as printer drivers, network drivers, scanner drivers, and so on. The JDBC drivers themselves may be written purely in Java or partially in Java, db-independent or db-dependent, network protocol-specific or nonnetwork protocol-specific, fat or thin, Java applet-supported or Java application only.

Type-1 JDBC Driver

The JDBC-ODBC bridge-type driver translates Java JDBC code to ODBC binary code (C++), which, in turn, translates it into DBMS commands for the target database. This type of driver must be installed at the client site and cannot be downloaded via network, because it is not written purely in Java. This driver is not very efficient due to the overhead of the additional layer. Only Java applications, not Java applets, can use this type of driver. If there is an ODBC driver available at the client site, this driver can be a good choice because the ODBC driver is an open-database-connection

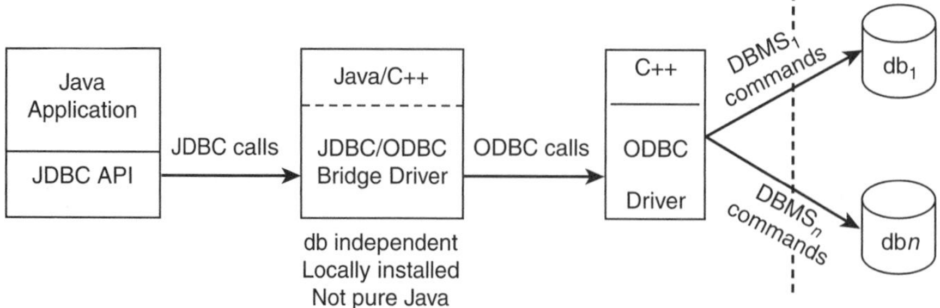

Figure 5.6
Type-1 JDBC Driver

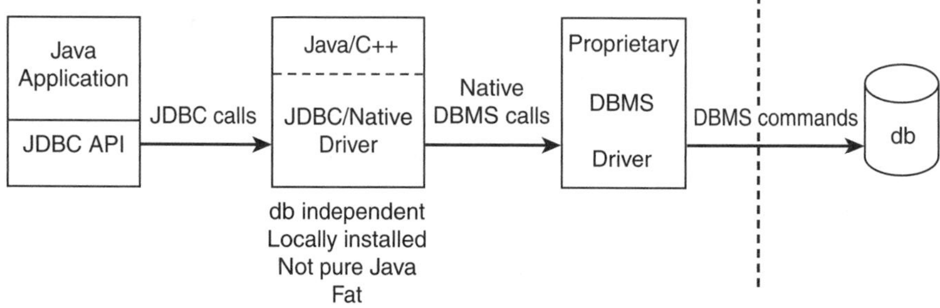

Figure 5.7
Type-2 JDBC Driver

driver that can access many vendor databases. The type-1 driver allows access to any ODBC data source from a Java application, but not from a Java applet. The name of the driver class is `sun.jdbc.odbc.JdbcOdbcDriver`. In Figure 5.6 a JDBC/ODBC driver takes JDBC calls and translates them to ODBC calls, and an ODBC driver (supporting many vendor databases), in turn, translates the ODBC calls to database-specific calls.

Type-2 JDBC Driver

The native-API, partly Java driver type uses Java code to call native (non-Java) code to a DBMS-specific API, `jdbc:oracle:oci` for `oracle.jdbc.driver. OracleDriver` is an example of the type of driver Oracle provides. The vertical dash line in Figure 5.7 indicates the division of the client site and the server site.

This type of driver can make use of existing DBMS-specific drivers; therefore, it is more efficient than a type-1 driver. Due to the use of native code on the client and because the driver is DBMS-specific, a Java applet cannot use this type of driver. This type also requires prior installation of client software. Compared with the type-4 driver, this type of driver is called a fat driver.

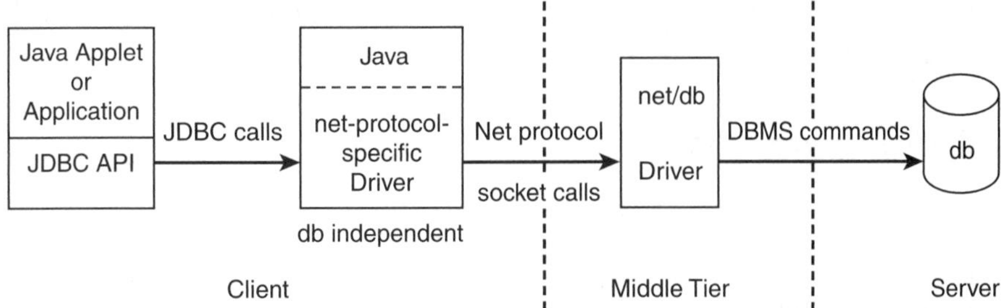

Figure 5.8
Type-3 JDBC Driver

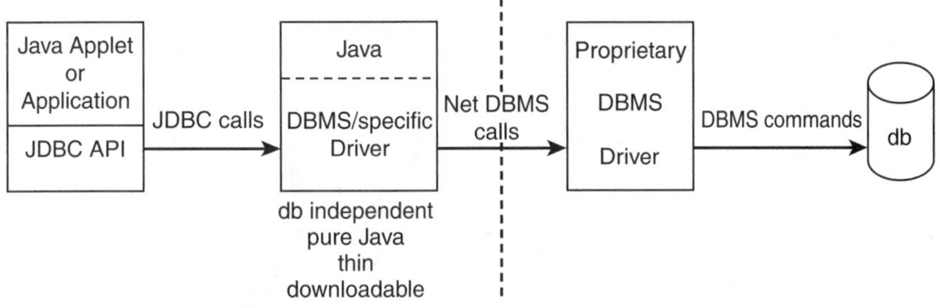

Figure 5.9
Type-4 JDBC Driver

Type-3 JDBC Driver

This net-protocol pure Java driver type translates JDBC calls into a DBMS-independent network protocol that is then translated to a specific DBMS protocol by the middleware.

This driver type uses pure Java client software; it can, therefore, be downloaded automatically by Java applets. The client driver is DBMS-independent, but it needs middle-tier support. This type of driver is similar to a server-side driver because part of it resides on a middleware server, as shown in Figure 5.8.

Type-4 JDBC Driver

The DBMS-protocol pure Java driver type translates JDBC calls into a network protocol that is used directly by the DBMS.

The advantage of this type is that it uses pure Java client software; it can, therefore, be downloaded automatically by Java applets. This type of driver is platform-independent and is a thin driver, jdbc:oracle:thin for oracle.jdbc.driver. OracleDriver is an example of the type of driver Oracle provides. The disadvantage is that the driver is vendor-specific.

5.3.4 JDBC Application Examples

Example 1

This simple Java program illustrates how JDBC works with a database. The JDBC driver used in this example is a type-1 JDBC/ODBC bridge driver because the ODBC driver is available in MS Windows. The customer data table is built in the db1.mdb MS Access database. The schema of the table consists of three columns: OrderID, CustomerID, and Phone. Only three rows of customer data are stored in the table. The mydsn data source is mapped to the db1.mdb. The next two screens show the database table and data source configurations.

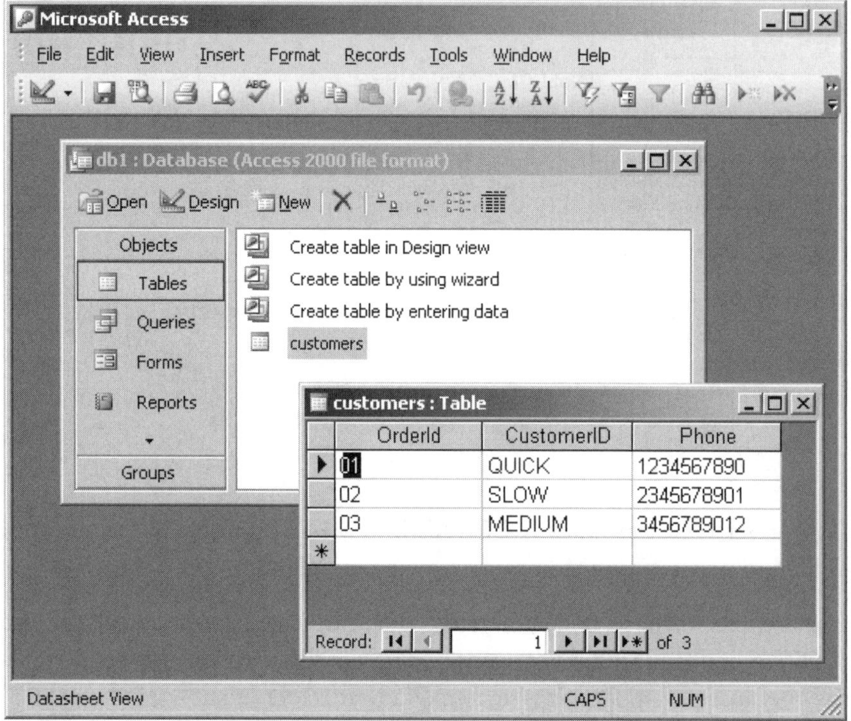

The next screen shows the ODBC Microsoft Data Source named mydsn which maps to db1.mdb. The customers table is part of this database. The JDBC/ODBC driver connects this ODBC data source to save data to the customers table of the db1.mdb database or to retrieve data from the table.

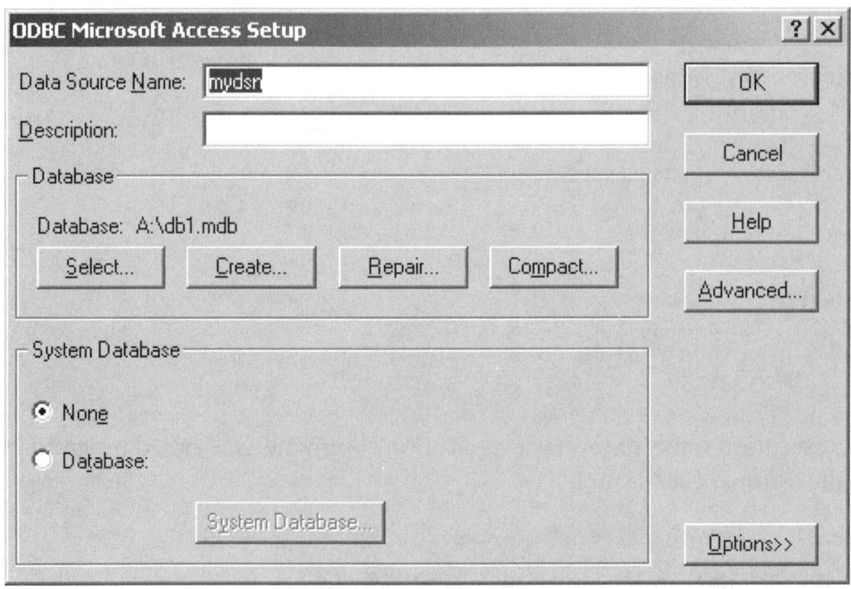

The following is the code list of the `simple.java` program.

```
import java.sql.*;
public class simple{
     public static void main(String argv[]) throws Exception {
          int numCols;

          String url = "jdbc:odbc:mydsn";
          String query = "select * from Customers" ;

      //All JDBC operations must have exception handlings

     try{
          //load JDBC/ODBC driver
            Class.forName("sun.jdbc.odbc.JdbcOdbcDriver");
            // connect to MS Access data source mydsn
          Connection con = DriverManager.getConnection(
                          url, "", "");
            //Make a JDBC select query statement specified above
          Statement stmt = con.createStatement();
          ResultSet rs = stmt.executeQuery(query);
            //Get the total numbers of columns in the table
          numCols = rs.getMetaData().getColumnCount();
            //Look over each row in the table
```

```
          while(rs.next()){
               for(int i=1; i<=numCols; i++){
          System.out.print(rs.getString(i) + "|");}
               System.out.println();
     }
      //Close resultSet, statement, and connection
     rs.close();
      stmt.close();
      con.close();}
     catch(SQLException ex){
          System.out.println("Exceptions");}
     }
}
```

The next screen shows the execution result of this Java application command-line-based program. It displays information on all customers in the table.

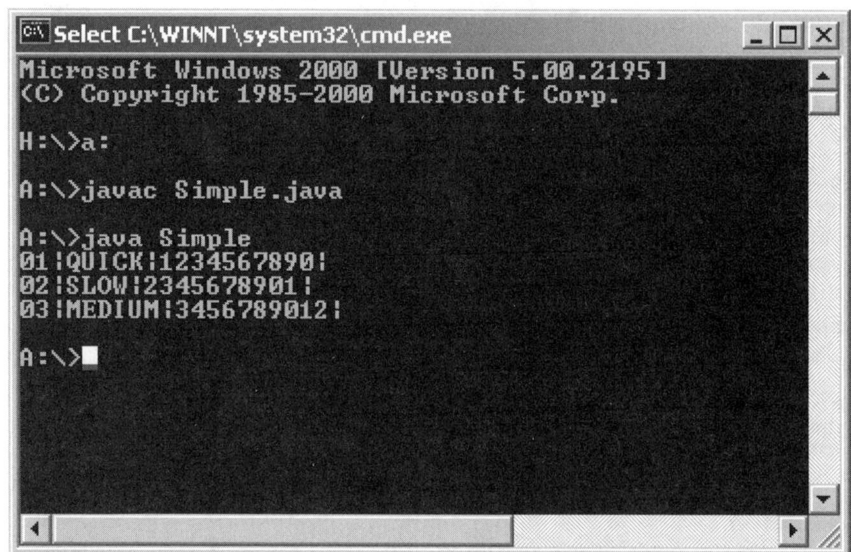

Example 2

The following Java Windows-based application example shows a JDBC application with GUI interfaces. It operates on the same database as the last example except that the GUI interface provides a mechanism for the user to make a query to find the information of a specific customer.

```
//QueryTest.java

import java.awt.*;
   import java.awt.event.*;
   import javax.swing.*;
```

```
import java.sql.*;

 public class QueryTest extends JFrame implements ActionListener{
   private JTextField t1, t2, t3;
   JButton b1;
   Connection con;
   String url = "jdbc:odbc:mydsn";

    public QueryTest()
    { //Construct a Windows frame
      super("Query Test");
      Container c = getContentPane();
      c.setLayout(new FlowLayout());

      try{
            //load JDBC/ODBC driver
            Class.forName("sun.jdbc.odbc.JdbcOdbcDriver");
            //connect to MS Access data source mydsn
            con = DriverManager.getConnection(url, "", "");}
             catch( ClassNotFoundException x)
               {System.out.println("Driver Exceptions");}
             catch( SQLException x)
               {System.out.println("SQL Exceptions");}

      //Construct three Text field GUI components
      //t1 is for input query
      t1=new JTextField("Customer ID",20);
      c.add(t1);

      t2=new JTextField("Order",20);
      c.add(t2);

      t3=new JTextField("Phone",20);
      c.add(t3);

      b1 = new JButton("Execute");
      c.add(b1);

      //Registration of Execute button with the action
      //listener so that
      //actionPerformed method will be invoked when
      //the button is clicked

      b1.addActionListener(this);
```

```
    addWindowListener(
           new WindowAdapter(){
              public void windowClosing(WindowEvent e)
             {System.exit(0);}});
    setSize(300,200);
    //enable the frame
    show();}

     public void actionPerformed(ActionEvent e) {

       //JDBC processing
       if (e.getSource() == b1) {
       int numCols;

       //Search for customer information for which
       //CustomerId is given

       String query = "select * from Customers
          where CustomerID like '"  + t1.getText() + "'";

       //Following JDBC code is almost identical to
       //the code of last example

       try{
          Statement stmt = con.createStatement();
          ResultSet rs = stmt.executeQuery(query);
          numCols = rs.getMetaData().getColumnCount();

          while(rs.next()){
             t2.setText(rs.getString(1));
             t3.setText(rs.getString(3));
          }
          rs.close();
          stmt.close();
          con.close();}
           catch(SQLException ex){
             System.out.println("Exceptions");}
    }
}
```

```
        public static void main(String args[])
          {
             new QueryTest();
          }
}
```

Let us run this Java Windows application.

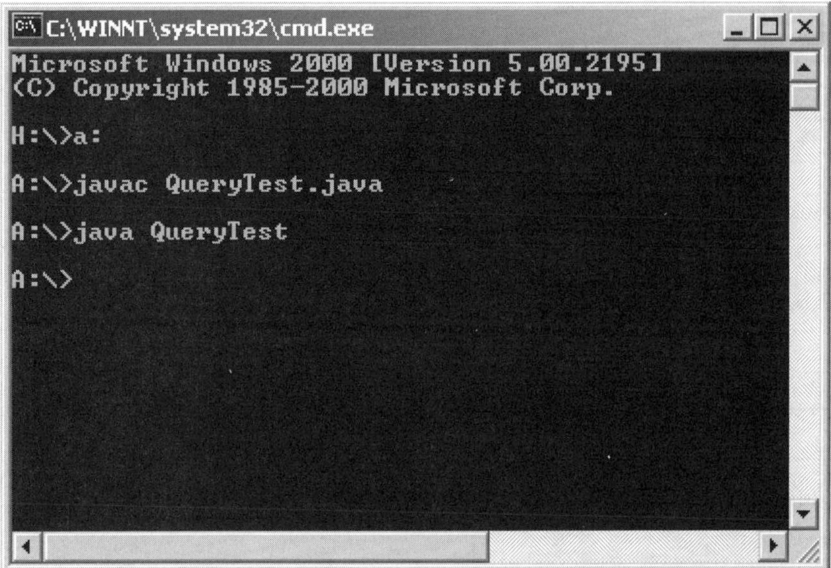

After starting up the `QueryTest.class` class with the Java interpreter you will see the following Java frame.

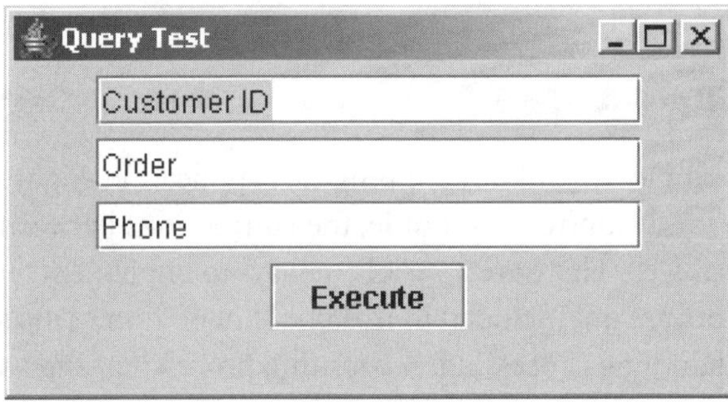

If you request any customer information with a customer ID SLOW you will see

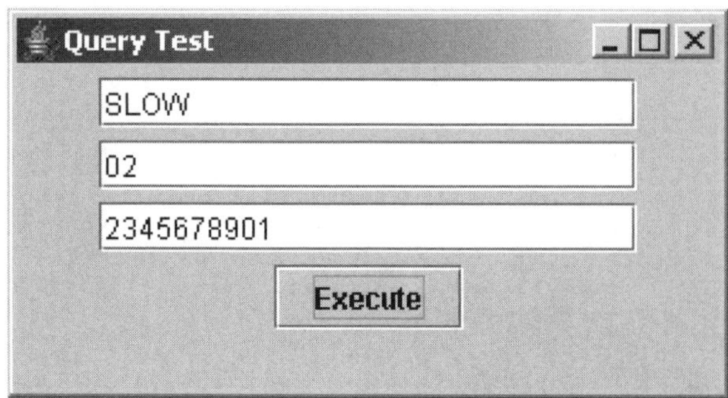

If you ask about QUICK's information, you will see

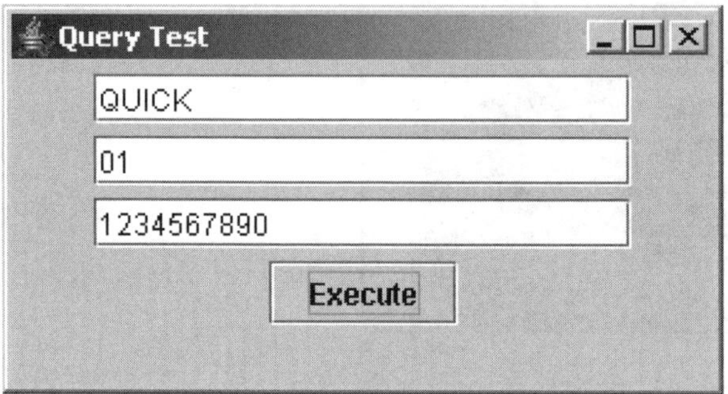

From these two examples you can see that the JDBC technology makes it much easier for a Java client program to process table data in a relational database on a database server.

5.4 A Case Study: Online Shopping Application

This section presents a Java MVC architecture design for an online shopping cart application. Figure 5.10 illustrates the Model module, View module, and Controller module, the connections between the modules, and the back-end database support as well. There are a variety of ways to implement an online store. Many functionalities of an online store are not included in this implementation such as customer information processing, shipping and handling processing, accounting processing, and so on. We have simplified the implementation in order to focus on the MVC design architecture so you will have a better picture of it. We divide the system into three subsystems that will be discussed in

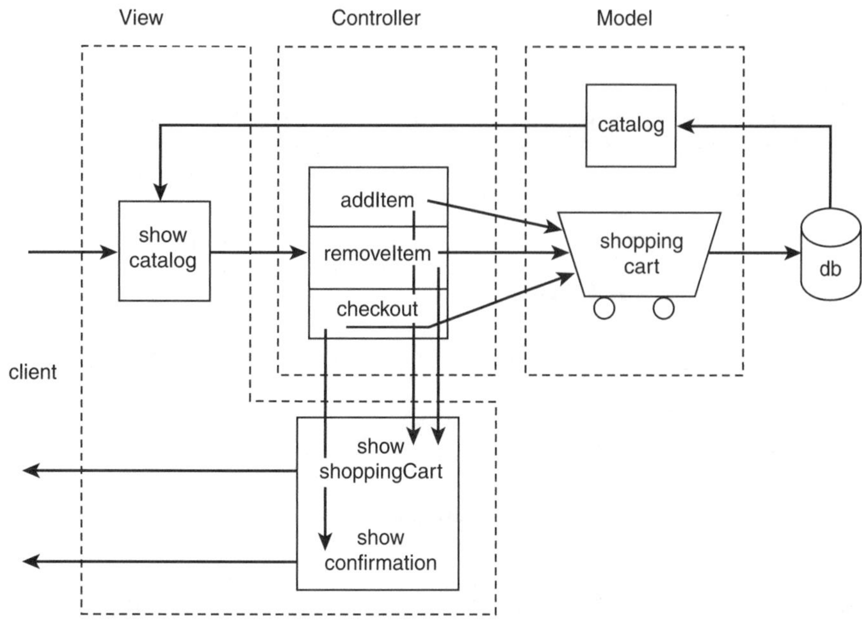

Figure 5.10
DVD Online Store Architecture

the following sections. Figure 5.10 depicts the overall MVC architecture of this DVD online store Web application.

5.4.1 View Module of DVD Online Shopping Cart Application

In this section, we present the presentation logic (View module) that has the following responsibilities:

- enabling client browsing of the DVD catalog
- selecting the items and adding them to the shopping cart
- removing items from the shopping cart
- displaying the shopping cart contents
- checking out

The View module is also responsible for displaying a confirmation message after clients check out or error messages when an error occurs.

First, we look at the front page, ShowProductCatalog.jsp, which displays the DVD catalog. The initial page looks like the one below.

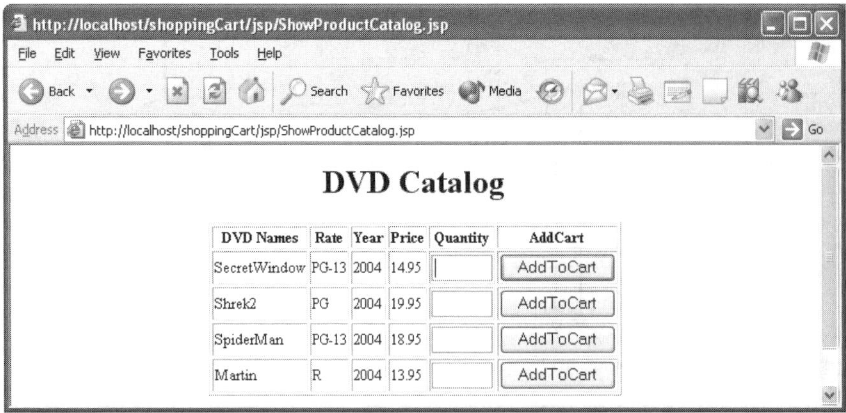

The ShowProductCatalog.jsp is a JSP file that displays the DVD catalog from the database. The ProductDataBean JavaBean is responsible for retrieving the catalog data from the database. The first time clients browse this page, the <jsp:useBean> tag will instantiate the ProductDataBean, which makes a connection to a database to load the catalog data and display them as shown above. This page also includes another DisplayShoppingCart.jsp page as part of itself. If the cart is empty, then nothing is displayed. The details of the JavaBean classes here will be discussed in the Model module section. When the client adds any item to the shopping cart, the parameter data is saved in the implicit request object and the request is sent to the addToShoppingCart.ava Servlet for processing.

```
<%@ page import = "java.util.*" import="cart.*,java.net.*,java.text.*" %>
<jsp:useBean id = "data" scope= "session" class = "cart.ProductDataBean"/>
<html>
<body>

//Call getProductList() of the ProductDataBean to get the DVD product
//catalog and put it on the productList

<%
    List productList = data.getProductList();
    Iterator prodListIterator = productList.iterator();
%>
<p>
<center>
<h1>DVD Catalog</h1>
```

```
<table border="1">
<thread><tr>
        <th>DVD Names</th>
        <th>Rate</th>
        <th>Year</th>
        <th>Price</th>
        <th>Quantity</th>
        <th>AddCart</th>
        </tr></thread>
  <%

//Display all DVD products row by row on the table, add an
//"addCart" button at the end of each row to allow clients
//to select

        while (prodListIterator.hasNext())
        {
          DVD movie = (DVD)prodListIterator.next();
          String movieQuantity = "movieQuantity";
  %>
        <tr>

<form action="/shoppingCart/servlet/addToShoppingCart" method="POST">
   <td><%= movie.getMovie() %></td>
   <td><%= movie.getRating() %></td>
   <td><%= movie.getYear() %></td>
   <td><%= movie.getPrice() %></td>
   <td><input type = text name = <%= movieQuantity %> size ="5" /></td>
   <td>
  <input type="hidden" name= "movieName" value='<%= movie.getMovie() %>'>
  <input type="hidden" name= "movieRate" value='<%= movie.getRating() %>'>
  <input type="hidden" name= "movieYear" value='<%= movie.getYear() %>'>
  <input type="hidden" name= "moviePrice" value='<%= movie.getPrice() %>'>
  <input type="submit" value="AddToCart">    </td>
 </form>
  </tr>
  <%
        }
  %>
 </table>
 <p>
 <hr>
```

```
//Display the current shopping cart by including
//DisplayShoppingCart.jsp

    <jsp:include page="DisplayShoppingCart.jsp" flush="true" />

</center>
</body>
</html>
```

The `DisplayShoppingCart.jsp` is responsible for displaying the contents of the current shopping cart. There is a Remove button at the end of each item row of the displayed shopping cart. This button connects to `RemoveItemServlet.java` in the Controller module. It has a Check Out button for clients to check out. This button connects to `checkoutServlet.java` in the Controller module.

```
<%@ page import="cart.*, java.util.*,java.text.*" %>
<%
    ShoppingCart cart = (ShoppingCart)
    session.getAttribute("ShoppingCart");

//the ShoppingCart is stored as an attribute of implicit
//object shared by other Web components in the shopping
//session

    if (cart == null)
    {
        cart = new ShoppingCart();
        session.setAttribute("ShoppingCart", cart);
    }

    Vector items = cart.getItems();

    if (items.size() != 0)

    {
%>
<%-- Display the heading of the shoppingCart --%>

<h1>Shopping Cart</h1>
<br>
<table border=4>
<tr><th>DVD Names<th>Rate<th>Year<th>Price<th>Quantity<th>Remove
<%
        int numItems = items.size();
        NumberFormat currency = NumberFormat.getCurrencyInstance();

        for (int i=0; i < numItems; i++)
```

```
        {
            DVD item = (DVD) items.elementAt(i);
%>
        <tr>
        <form action="/shoppingCart/servlet/removeItem" method="POST">
           <td><%= item.getMovie() %></td>
           <td><%= item.getRating() %></td>
           <td><%= item.getYear() %></td>
           <td><%= item.getPrice() %></td>
           <td><%= item.getQuantity() %></td>
           <td>
           <input type="hidden" name= "item" value='<%= i %>'>
           <input type="submit" value="Remove">  </td>
          </form>
         </tr>
<%
        }
%>
</table>

<form  action="/shoppingCart/servlet/checkout" method="POST">
<input type="submit" name="Submit" value="Check out">
</form>
<%
}
%>
```

The ShowConfirmation.jsp is responsible for displaying a confirmation message and showing a total amount charged to the client. It then terminates the current session.

```
<%@ page import="cart.*, java.text.*" %>
<html>
<body>
<h1>Order Submitted Successfully!</h1>
<%
    DecimalFormat twoDigits = new DecimalFormat("0.00");
    String totalPrice =
    twoDigits.format(((ShoppingCart)session.getAttribute("ShoppingCart")).
    getTotalPrice());
%>
<h1>The total ammount is $<%=totalPrice %></h1>
<% session.invalidate(); %>
</body>
</html>
```

5.4.2 Controller Module of an Online DVD Shopping Cart Application

Because all Servlet classes are placed in the Controller module and all of them have their URL-patterns, we include the web.xml here for your reference.

```
<?xml version="1.0" encoding="ISO-8859-1"?>
<!DOCTYPE web-app
PUBLIC "-//Sun Microsystems, Inc.//DTD Web Application 2.3//EN"
    "http://java.sun.com/dtd/web-app_2_3.dtd">

<web-app>

  <servlet>
    <servlet-name>addToShoppingCartServlet</servlet-name>
    <servlet-class>cart.AddToShoppingCartServlet</servlet-class>
  </servlet>

  <servlet>
    <servlet-name>removeItemServlet</servlet-name>
    <servlet-class>cart.RemoveItemServlet</servlet-class>
  </servlet>

  <servlet>
    <servlet-name>checkoutServlet</servlet-name>
    <servlet-class>cart.CheckoutServlet</servlet-class>
  </servlet>

  <servlet-mapping>
    <servlet-name>addToShoppingCartServlet</servlet-name>
    <url-pattern>/servlet/addToShoppingCart</url-pattern>
  </servlet-mapping>

  <servlet-mapping>
    <servlet-name>removeItemServlet</servlet-name>
    <url-pattern>/servlet/removeItem</url-pattern>
  </servlet-mapping>

  <servlet-mapping>
    <servlet-name>checkoutServlet</servlet-name>
    <url-pattern>/servlet/checkout</url-pattern>
  </servlet-mapping>

</web-app>
```

The following code, `AddToShoppingCartServlet.java`, is a Servlet that is responsible for adding DVD items to a shopping cart. It uses both the DVD JavaBean and the `ShoppingCart` JavaBean. It retrieves all parameter data for a new DVD item from the front page via `request.object`, instantiates a DVD instance and calls the `addItem(0)` method of the `ShoppingCart` JavaBean to add a new DVD item to the shopping cart, and then transfers control to `ShowProductCatalog.jsp`, which will be in charge of rendering the catalog and the updated shopping cart. This conforms to a typical pattern of an MVC Controller.

```
package cart;

import javax.servlet.*;
import javax.servlet.http.*;
import java.io.*;

public class AddToShoppingCartServlet extends HttpServlet
{
    public void service(HttpServletRequest request,
        HttpServletResponse response)
        throws IOException, ServletException
    {

// Get the DVD from the request
        String movieName = request.getParameter("movieName");
        String movieRate = request.getParameter("movieRate");
        String movieYear = request.getParameter("movieYear");
        String price = request.getParameter("moviePrice");

        int movieQuantity = Integer.parseInt(
            request.getParameter("movieQuantity"));
        double moviePrice = Double.parseDouble(price);

// Create this DVD and add to the cart
       DVD DVDItem = new DVD(movieName, movieRate, movieYear, moviePrice,
                      movieQuantity);
        HttpSession session = request.getSession();

// Get the cart
        ShoppingCart cart = (ShoppingCart) session.
            getAttribute("ShoppingCart");

        if (cart == null)
        {
            cart = new ShoppingCart();
```

```
            session.setAttribute("ShoppingCart", cart);
        }
        cart.addItem(DVDItem);
        String url="/jsp/ShowProductCatalog.jsp";
        ServletContext sc = getServletContext();
        RequestDispatcher rd = sc.getRequestDispatcher(url);
        rd.forward(request, response);
    }
}
```

The following `RemoveItemServlet.java` is a Servlet that is responsible for removing DVD items from a shopping cart. It gets a DVD item to be removed from the front page via the `request` object and calls the `removeItem(0)` method of `ShoppingCart` JavaBean to remove the DVD item from the shopping cart, and then transfers the control to `ShowProductCatalog.jsp`, which will be in charge of rendering the catalog and the updated shopping cart. This also conforms to a typical pattern of a MVC Controller.

```
package cart;

import javax.servlet.*;
import javax.servlet.http.*;
import java.io.*;

public class RemoveItemServlet extends HttpServlet
{
    public void service(HttpServletRequest request,
        HttpServletResponse response)
        throws IOException, ServletException
    {

// Get the index of the item to remove
        int itemIndex = Integer.parseInt(request.getParameter("item"));
        HttpSession session = request.getSession();

// Get the cart
        ShoppingCart cart = (ShoppingCart) session.
            getAttribute("ShoppingCart");
        cart.removeItem(itemIndex);

// Display the cart and allow user to check out or order
// more items

        String url="/jsp/ShowProductCatalog.jsp";
        ServletContext sc = getServletContext();
        RequestDispatcher rd = sc.getRequestDispatcher(url);
        rd.forward(request, response);
    }
}
```

The following `CheckoutServlet.java` is a Servlet that obtains the `ShoppingCart` object and redirects control to the `ShowConfirmation.jsp` JSP page for rendering the confirmation message.

```
package cart;

import javax.servlet.*;
import javax.servlet.http.*;
import java.io.*;
import java.net.*;

public class CheckoutServlet extends HttpServlet
{
    public void service(HttpServletRequest request,
        HttpServletResponse response)
        throws IOException, ServletException
    {
        HttpSession session = request.getSession();
// Get the cart
        ShoppingCart cart = (ShoppingCart) session.
            getAttribute("ShoppingCart");
            try{
                 cart.completeOrder();
             }catch(Exception e){e.printStackTrace();}
           response.sendRedirect(response.encodeRedirectURL(
                     "/shoppingCart/jsp/ShowConfirmation.jsp"));
    }
}
```

5.4.3 Model Module of an Online DVD Shopping Cart Application

There are three JavaBeans in this MVC Model module: `DVD.java`, `ShoppingCart.java`, and `Product-DataBean.java`. All of them are used for presentations of the input or output user interface in this Web application.

The following `DVD.java` JavaBean represents a single DVD item that can be added to or removed from a shopping cart. It has five properties: `m_movie`, `m_rated`, `m_year`, `m_price`, and `quantity`. It also provides access methods to these properties.

```
package cart;
import java.io.*;

public class DVD implements Serializable {
  String m_movie;
```

```
String m_rated;
String m_year;
double m_price;
int quantity;
public DVD() {
  m_movie="";
  m_rated="";
  m_year="";
  m_price=0;
  quantity=0;
}

public DVD(String movieName, String movieRate, String movieYear, double
           moviePrice, int movieQuantity)
  {
   m_movie=movieName;
   m_rated=movieRate;
   m_year=movieYear;
   m_price=moviePrice;
   quantity=movieQuantity;
  }
public void setMovie(String title) {
  m_movie=title; }
public String getMovie() {
  return m_movie; }
public void setRating(String rating) {
  m_rated=rating;}
public String getRating() {
  return m_rated; }
public void setYear(String year) {
  m_year=year;  }
public String getYear() {
  return m_year; }
public void setPrice(double p) {
  m_price=p; }
public double getPrice() {
  return m_price; }
public void setQuantity(int q) {
  quantity=q; }
public int getQuantity() {
  return quantity; }
}
```

The following `shoppingCart.java` is a JavaBean in which all the items are stored in a Java vector (Java collection data structure). It provides all necessary access methods for shopping cart business logic processing such as getItems(), which returns the shopping cart as a vector; addItem(), which adds a new item to the shopping cart and updates the quantity of the item in the cart; removeItem(), which removes an item from the shopping cart and updates the quantity of this item in the cart; completeOrder() method, which saves the shopping cart records in a database for future processing; and getTotalPrice(), which reports the total charges of this purchase to clients when the order is confirmed. A shopping cart is saved in the shoppingCart table in the eshopdb database. All detail implementations of this bean are in the following ShoppingCart.java file.

```
package cart;

import java.util.*;
import java.io.*;
import java.sql.*;

public class ShoppingCart implements java.io.Serializable
{
     private Connection connection;
     private PreparedStatement addRecord, getRecords;
     private Statement statement;
     private double totalPrice;
     static int CARTID =1;

    protected Vector items;

    public ShoppingCart()
    {
        items = new Vector();
    }

    public Vector getItems()
    {
        return (Vector) items.clone();
    }

    public void addItem(DVD newItem)
    {
         Boolean flag = false;
         if(items.size()==0)
         {
              items.addElement(newItem);
              return;
         }
          for (int i=0; i< items.size(); i++)
         {
```

```
            DVD dvd = (DVD) items.elementAt(i);
            if (dvd.getMovie().equals(newItem.getMovie()))
            {
                dvd.setQuantity(dvd.getQuantity()+newItem.getQuantity());
                items.setElementAt(dvd,i);
                flag = true;
                break;
            }
        }
         if(newItem.getQuantity()>0 && (flag == false))
        {
             items.addElement(newItem);
        }
    }

    public void removeItem(int itemIndex)
    {
        items.removeElementAt(itemIndex);
    }

    public void completeOrder()
        throws Exception
    {
            Enumeration e = items.elements();
            connection = ProductDataBean.getConnection();
            statement = connection.createStatement();

            while (e.hasMoreElements())
            {
                DVD item = (DVD) e.nextElement();
                String itemQuantity = "" + item.getQuantity();
                totalPrice = totalPrice + item.getPrice() *
                                        Integer.parseInt(itemQuantity);
                String movieName = item.getMovie();

                String updateString = "INSERT INTO shoppingCart " +
                    " VALUES (" + CARTID  + ", '" +
                   item.getMovie() + "', '" +
                    item.getRating() + "', '" +
                    item.getYear() + "', " +
                    item.getPrice() + ", " +
                    item.getQuantity() + ")";
                statement.executeUpdate(updateString);
            }
            CARTID ++;
```

```
    }
    public double getTotalPrice()
    {
        return this.totalPrice;
    }
}
```

The ProductDataBean.java JavaBean represents the DVD online store catalog that is supported by the products table in the eshopdb database. The first time a client accesses the online DVD store, the catalog is loaded from the database by JDBC calls.

```
package cart;

import java.io.*;
import java.sql.*;
import java.util.*;

public class ProductDataBean implements Serializable
{
     private static Connection connection;
     private PreparedStatement addRecord, getRecords;

    public ProductDataBean()
     {
        try
        {
          Class.forName("sun.jdbc.odbc.JdbcOdbcDriver");
          connection = DriverManager.getConnection("jdbc:odbc:eshopdb");
        }catch(Exception e){e.printStackTrace();}
     }

    public static Connection getConnection()
     {
          return connection;
     }

    public ArrayList getProductList() throws SQLException
     {
     ArrayList productList = new ArrayList();
     Statement statement = connection.createStatement();
ResultSet results = statement.executeQuery("SELECT * FROM products");
          while (results.next())
          {
               DVD movie = new DVD();
                movie.setMovie(results.getString(1));
```

```
                movie.setRating(results.getString(2));
                movie.setYear(results.getString(3));
                movie.setPrice(results.getDouble(4));
                productList.add(movie);
            }
            return productList;
        }
}
```

5.4.4 Back-End Tier of an Online DVD Shopping Cart Application

In this example we use two relational tables, `Products` and `ShoppingCarts`, in an MS Access database to support the `ProductDataBean` catalog and `ShoppingCart` data, respectively. The next two screens show the table schema and data in these two tables. The name of this database is `eshopdb.mdb` and it has a DSN name of `eshopdb`.

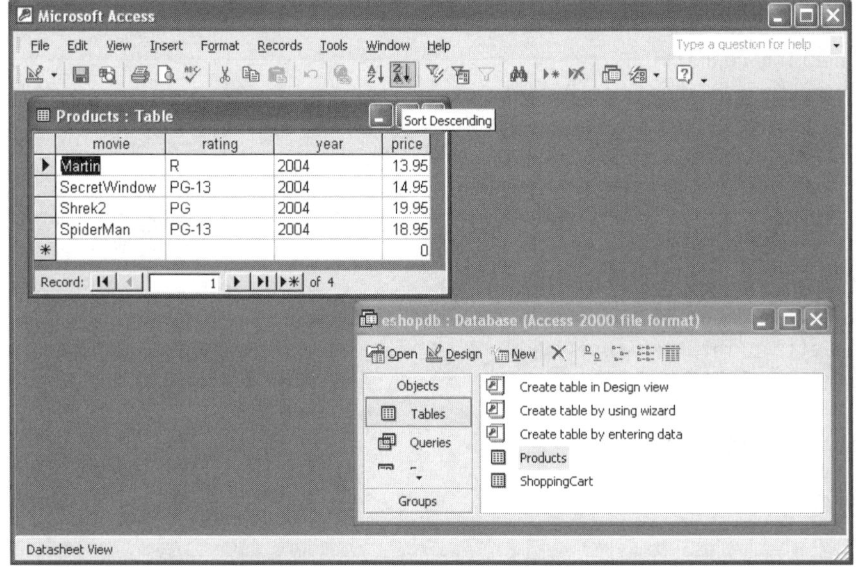

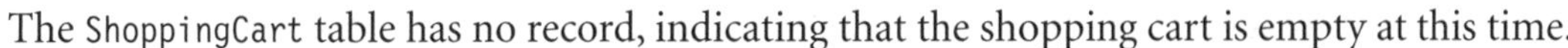

The ShoppingCart table has no record, indicating that the shopping cart is empty at this time.

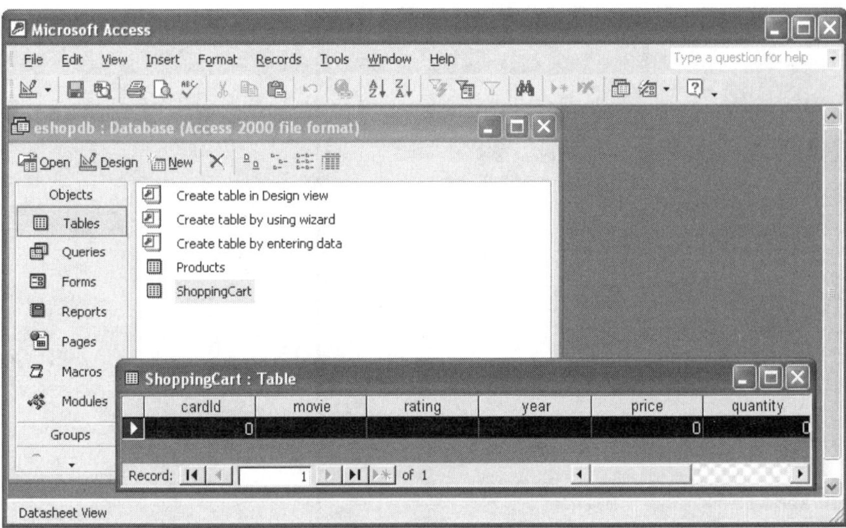

Assume that the ROOT directory of this Web application is the shoppingCart directory under the webapps directory of the Tomcat server. All JSP files are placed in the jsp subdirectory of the shoppingCart directory. All the Servlets are stored in the WEB-INF subdirectory of the shoppingCart directory. We can use the URL http://localhost/shoppingCart/jsp/ShowProductCatalog.jsp to start a purchase from this online DVD store.

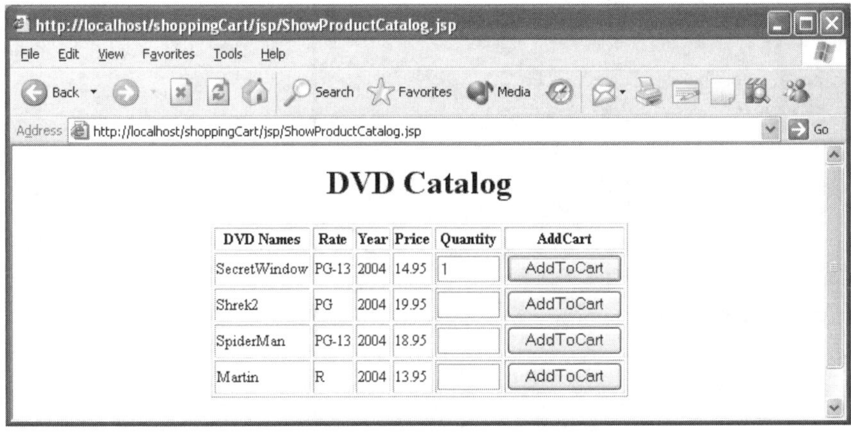

We add one "Secret Window" DVD to the shopping cart and see the change in the shopping cart.

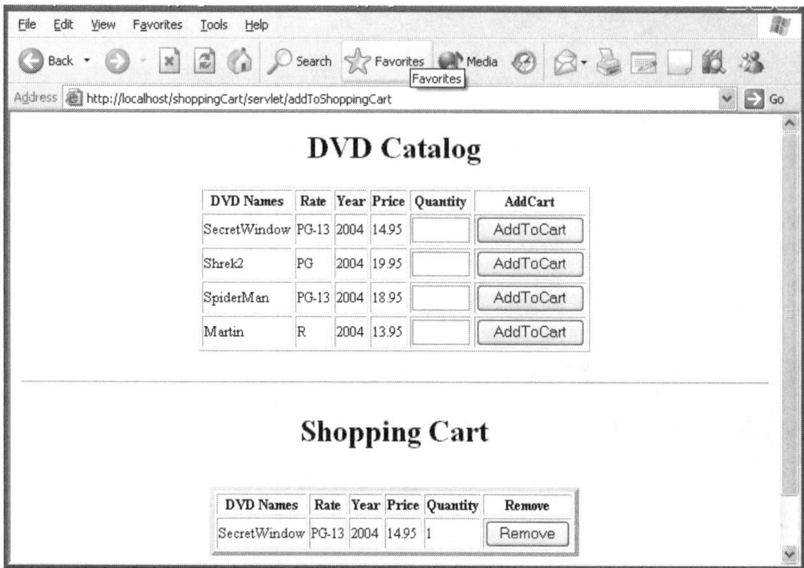

We add two "Spiderman" DVDs to the shopping cart afterward.

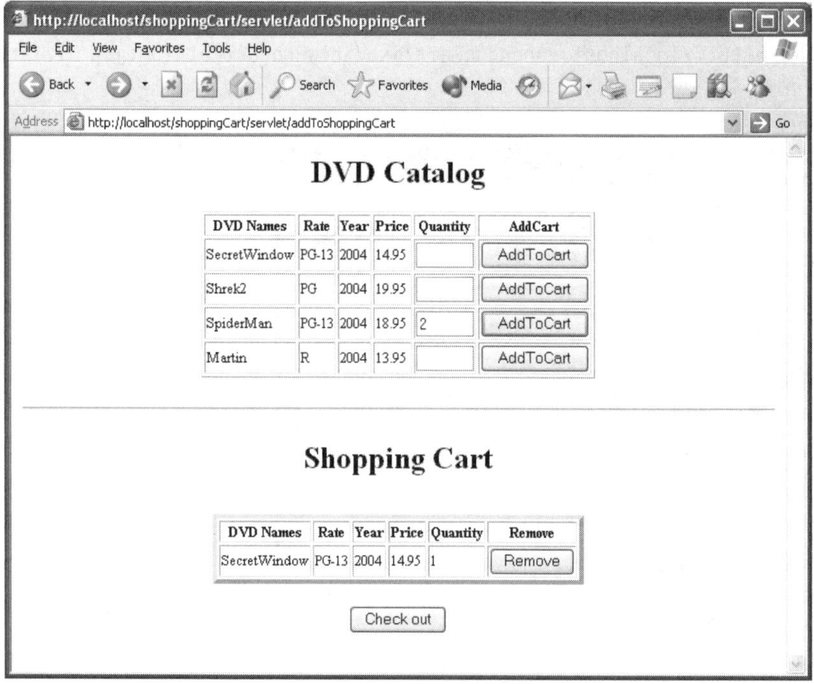

Now the shopping cart has two items.

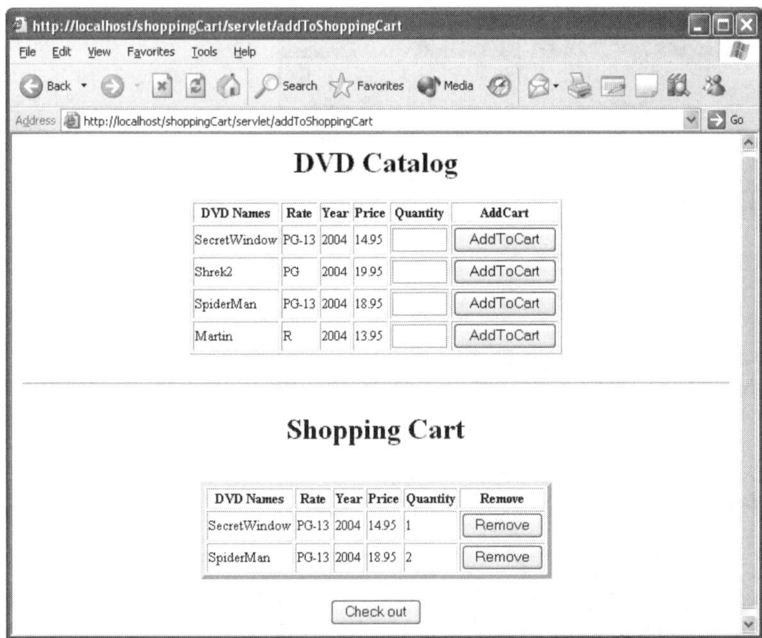

After adding one more DVD named "Martin," there are three items in the cart.

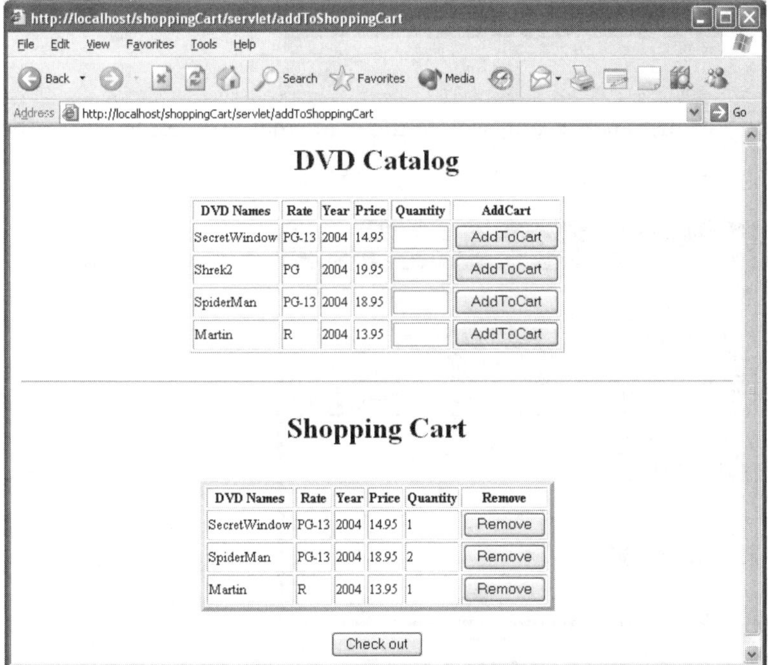

After that we remove the first item from the shopping cart, only two items are left in the cart.

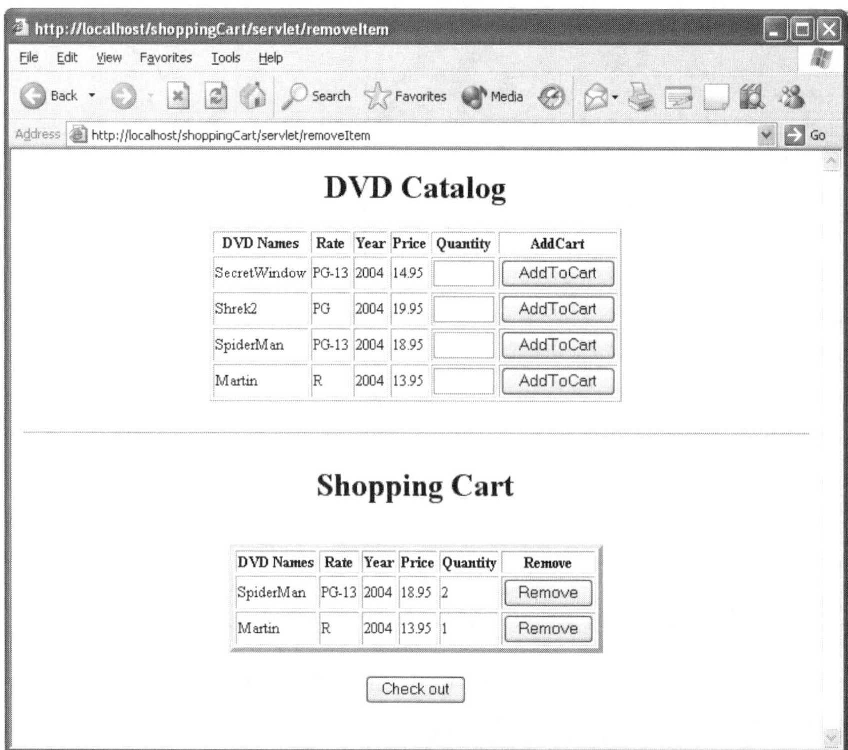

When we click on the Check out button to check out, we see the confirmation message from the online DVD store.

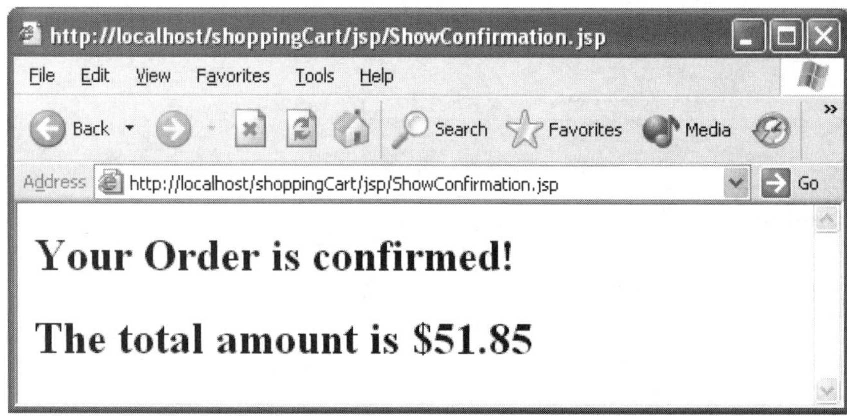

Let us examine the ShoppingCart table in the eshopdb database. The transaction records are kept in the database as follows.

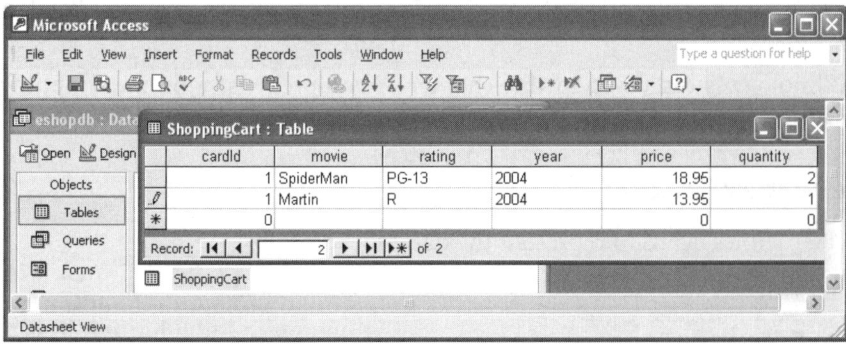

5.5 Summary

This chapter introduced a widely adopted MVC architectural design pattern for Web applications such as e-commerce. The MVC architecture integrates Java Servlets, JSP, JavaBeans, and JDBC technologies in the Controller module, View module, Data Model module, and back-end module. The MVC architecture changes the overall system design such that each module has its own responsibility.

Think of an MVC architecture design in the following workflow. The data is represented by JavaBeans, which is backed up by database tables most of the time. The client requests are handled by Java Servlets that read request parameters and verify and validate the input data. The Servlets then populate the related JavaBean, invoke the business logic code and data access code to obtain query results, and store the results in the JavaBeans. The Servlets store the beans as attributes of the request, session, or Servlet application-context implicit objects. The Servlets finally need to decide which JSP page is appropriate to forward, based on the requests. This is done by the forward method of a RequestDispatcher object. After this point, the control is transferred to the View module from the Controller module. The JSP pages in the View module can access JavaBeans to get the query result data and display the data that the Servlets created.

The MVC architecture can even be applied to a single request if it will result in many outcomes with different pages and several pages have common processing. The MVC architecture works well for most small and moderately complex application systems. Some design frameworks such as Strusts and JavaServer Faces may also help for a more complex system design. The MVC architecture design pattern can also be applied to other systems in addition to Web application systems.

JDBC technology is discussed in this chapter. A comprehensive online shopping cart application is explored as a case study in this chapter.

5.6 Self-Review Questions

1. JSP defines beans to represent the data.

   a. True

   b. False

2. A JavaBean populates itself.

   a. True

   b. False

3. JSP should update the JavaBean.

   a. True

   b. False

4. JSP populates the JavaBean.

   a. True

   b. False

5. JSP forwards requests to Servlets.

   a. True

   b. False

6. Servlets store beans in attributes of scoped implicit objects.

   a. True

   b. False

7. Servlets extract data from beans.

   a. True

   b. False

8. Servlets invoke the business logic methods provided by beans.

a. True

b. False

9. Servlets provide a user interface to get client input parameters.

   a. True

   b. False

10. There are many ways for Servlets and JSPs to share data.

    a. True

    b. False

11. A JDBC query statement may return many rows.

    a. True

    b. False

12. Type-3 and type-4 JDBC drivers are thin drivers.

    a. True

    b. False

13. Type-1 and type-2 JDBC drivers can be used by Java applets.

    a. True

    b. False

14. The JDBC connection is closed automatically after the execution of a JDBC statement.

    a. True

    b. False

15. There are many ways to load a JDBC driver-manager.

    a. True

    b. False

16. A JDBC driver must register with its manager.

    a. True

    b. False

17. The ODBC driver can talk to many DBMS vendor databases.

    a. True

    b. False

18. JSPs, Servlets, and JavaBeans are working on the same Web server.
    a. True
    b. False
19. The `next()` method of the JDBC `ResultSet` class returns a Boolean value.
    a. True
    b. False
20. The `ResultSet` object is a collection-type object.
    a. True
    b. False

5.7 Keys to the Self-Review Questions

1. b 2. b 3. a 4. b 5. b, 6. a 7. b 8. a 9. b 10. a 11. a 12. a 13. b 14. b 15. c 16. a 17. a 18. a 19. a 20. a

5.8 Exercises

1. What is MVC-1 architecture?
2. What is MVC-2 architecture?
3. What is JDBC?
4. What is a JDBC driver?
5. What is a JDBC API?
6. What is the `ResultSet` of JDBC API?
7. What is a JDBC driver-manager?
8. How many different ways are there for a Servlet to create a JavaBean?
9. How many different ways are there for a JSP to share data with a Servlet?
10. How many different ways are there for a JSP to access a JavaBean?
11. Should a JSP update a JavaBean?
12. How many different ways are there to transfer the flow control from one Servlet to a JSP?

5.9 Programming Exercises

1. Modify `simple.java` to access an Oracle database by Oracle's type-2 OCI driver.
2. Modify the MVC type-2 example in Section 5.2.3 to provide a GUI to take the username on a Windows form and send it to the Controller module in the MVC architecture.
3. Based on the revision of programming exercise 2, provide JDBC support to the JavaBean in the Model module in the MVC architecture.
4. Modify `simple.java` to access an Oracle database by Oracle's type-4 thin driver.
5. Modify `queryTest.java` to access an Oracle database by Oracle's type-2 OCI driver.
6. Modify `queryTest.java` to access an Oracle database by Oracle's type-2 OCI driver.
7. Modify the online shopping cart case study to handle shipping processing.
8. Develop an online bookstore Web application by MVC architecture design.

5.10 References

1. Armstrong, E., Ball, J., Bodoff, S., Carson, D. B., Evans, J., Green, D., Haase, K., and Jendrock, E. 2005. *The J2EE 1.4 Tutorial.* Santa Clara, CA: Sun Microsystems, Inc. http://java.sun.com/j2ee/1.4/docs/tutorial/doc/index.html.
2. Brown, Larry, and Hall, Marty. 2004. *Core Servlets and JAVAServer Pages, Vol. 1: Core Technologies.* 2nd ed. Santa Clara, CA: Sun Microsystems, Inc.
3. Wutka, Mark. 2000. *Using Java Server Pages and Servlets,* Special Edition. (Adobe e-book). Indianapolis, IN: Que.

CHAPTER 6

Enterprise JavaBeans (EJB)

Objectives of This Chapter

- Introduce J2EE framework and EJB architecture
- Introduce the concepts and types of EJB
- Discuss the integration of EJB with other Web components
- Demonstrate comprehensive EJB Web applications
- Provide step-by-step tutorials on building, deploying, and using EJB components

6.1 Overview

6.1.1 Overview of the EJB Architecture and J2EE Platform

The new specification of Java EJB 2.1 was released by Sun Microsystems Inc. in 2002. The EJB technology is widely used for large-scale distributed applications where the resources, data, and users are distributed. Such distributed applications usually require system scalability and transaction management for data integrity. An EJB component is a reusable, WORA (Write Once Run Anywhere), portable, scalable, and compiled software component that can be deployed on any EJB server such as the Java 2 Platform Enterprise Edition (J2EE), JBoss, and WebLogic Enterprise environment. The Java EJB technology is part of J2EE, which provides a set of APIs, and other system services. The EJB implementations concentrate on business logic. J2EE is an enterprise reference architecture for Java enterprise applications. J2EE not only supports EJB components, but also supports other Web components such as JSP and Servlets.

The EJB architecture makes Web enterprise application development much easier, because most of the system-level services such as transaction management, security management, and multithreading management are supported by the EJB container instead of the applications themselves.

The EJB architecture also manages the EJB component life cycle from the creation to termination, including activation and deactivation of an EJB component. An EJB component is a server-side component that provides services to remote Web clients or local and remote application clients.

Figure 6.1 shows a sample EJB application in a Web multitier architecture. Web clients access this application via a Web browser in the client tier. The services may be provided by Java Servlets or JSPs

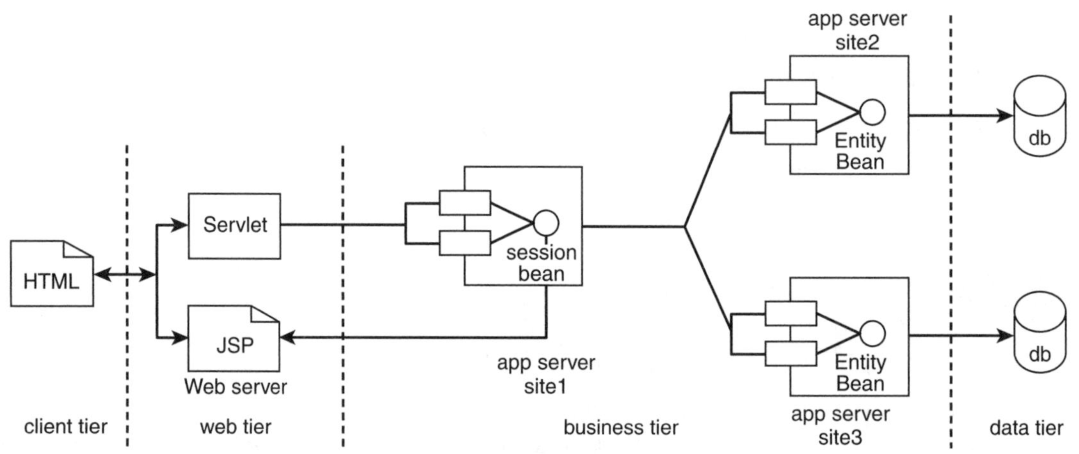

Figure 6.1
J2EE EJB Architecture

on Web servers in the Web tier. The Servlets or JSPs need to access services provided by EJB beans located on remote distributed application servers in the business tier. The business tier is supported by databases in the Enterprise Information System (EIS) data tier. The Web servers, application servers, and data servers may all be in different locations connected by the Internet. The EJB technology is suitable for developments of very large and complex distributed applications such as business-to-business (B2B).

6.1.2 EJB Container

All EJB instances are running within the EJB container. The container is a runtime environment (set of classes generated by deployment) that controls an EJB component instance and provides all necessary management services for its whole lifetime. Below is a list of such services:

- Transaction management: ensuring transaction properties of multiple distributed transaction executions
- Persistence management: ensuring a persistent state of an entity bean that is backed up by database
- Life cycle management: ensuring the EJB component state transitions in its life cycle
- Security management: providing authentication and authorization services, integrity, and encryption management

All access requests to the EJB component and responses from the EJB component must pass through the EJB container. The EJB container is a runtime environment that isolates the EJB component from direct access by its clients. The container will intercept the invocation from clients to ensure the persistence, properties of transaction, and security of client operations on EJB. Figure 6.2 demonstrates that the EJB container supports all services needed by EJB components. An EJB component needs the container to reach outside and to obtain necessary information from its context interface. The EJB container is in charge of generating an EJB home object, which helps to locate, create, and remove the EJB component object. The EJB context interface provided by the EJB container encapsulates relevant information of the container environment and initialization parameters.

6.1.3 EJB Components

An enterprise bean is a distributed server component that resides in an EJB container and is accessed by remote clients over a network via its remote interface or is accessed by other local enterprise beans on the same server via its local interface. The EJB component is a remotely executable component deployed on its server; it is a self-descriptive component specified by its Deployment Descriptor (DD) in XML format.

Each EJB component has a business logic interface that clients can use to run the business logic operations without having to know the detail implementation behind the interface. We call such an

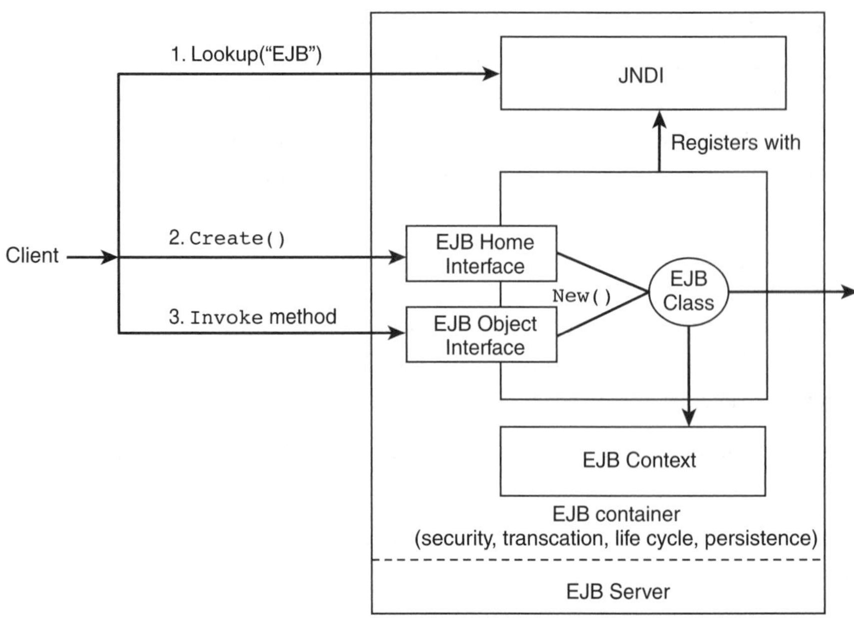

Figure 6.2
The Client Access to EJB on the Server

interface a *Remote* or *Local interface.* An instance of an EJB component is created and managed by its factory-named *Home interface* on the EJB container. Every enterprise bean must have a Home interface and a Remote (local) interface. The EJB component can be configured at deployment time by specifying its deployment descriptor. Figure 6.2 depicts the structure of an EJB component and the process flowchart of an interaction between a client and an EJB component. The EJB classes behind Home and Remote (or Local) interfaces are the implementations of these two interfaces. An EJB component is a black box component. A client of an EJB component knows only what the component does, not how it does it. A client makes a request to an EJB component with its deployed name by looking up a JNDI to obtain an Object Reference (OR) of this EJB component. The client can then create an instance of this EJB component on the server according to the reference. Finally, the client invokes the business methods of this EJB instance. The EJB class may also locate and access other EJB beans at remote sites by using EJB context information. The message-driven bean is an exception; it does not have an interface such as the Home or Remote interfaces that a classic EJB has.

The EJB technology supports the following enterprise bean categories:

1. Session Bean

   a. Stateless session beans that implement various business logics, such as language translation, logon process, tax calculation, and currency conversion

b. Stateless session beans that are wrapped in a Web service

Any existing enterprise bean can be encapsulated in an external Web service by a WSDL document, which describes the Web service endpoint of the bean implementations. Such a special bean does not provide interfaces that a regular EJB component provides.

c. Stateful session beans, which play the same roles as stateless session beans except they keep tracking the states of the conversation during a session. For instance, a shopping cart bean can be a typical stateful session bean.

A session bean does not have a permanent state.

2. Entity Bean

a. Bean-Managed-Persistence (BMP) entity beans, where persistent storage management (JDBC SQL) is coded by bean developers

b. Container-Managed-Persistence (CMP) entity beans, where the persistent storage management is specified by the deployment tool and managed by the container

An entity bean is backed up by a relational database.

3. Message-Driven Beans (MDB)

MDB represents a new EJB component type that works in an asynchronous communication mode just like an event-driven delegation model in Java.

Each EJB bean has two interfaces and one implementation class as shown in Figure 6.2. The EJB interface hierarchy is shown in Figure 6.3. The Remote interface of an EJB component implements the `javax.ejb.EJBObject` interface, which in turn implements the `java.rmi.Remote` interface. The

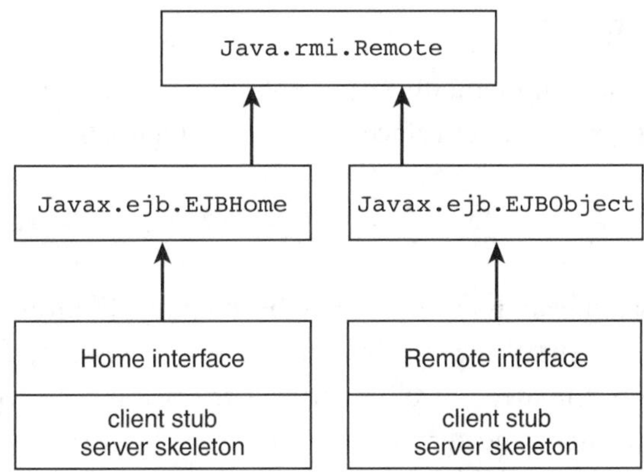

Figure 6.3
EJB Interfaces

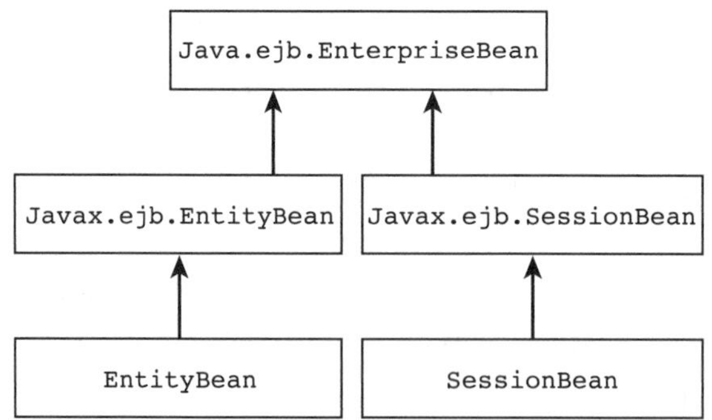

Figure 6.4
EJB Implementation Class Hierarchy

Home interface of an EJB component implements the `javax.ejb.EJBHome` interface, which again implements the `java.rmi.remote` interface.

A Local interface implements a `javax.ejb.EJBLocalObject` interface and a Local Home interface implements a `javax.ejb.EJBLocalHome` interface. The Local interface is used by another EJB component running on the same server in order to reduce the overhead caused by the Remote access. The Remote interface provides the location independence, but it is more expensive because it must provide a stub and a skeleton to support the Remote communications. The Local interface makes invocation much more efficient than the Remote interface. Another important difference between Local and Remote interfaces is that the method invocation in a Local interface uses passing-by-reference and the method invocation in a Remote interface uses passing-by-value, which needs serialization, i.e., marshaling and unmarshaling.

The EJB implementation class implements either a `sessionBean` or an `entityBean` interface, both of which implement an `EnterpriseBean` interface as shown in Figure 6.4.

6.2 Session Beans

As its name implies, a session bean is an interactive bean and its lifetime is during the session with a specific client. It is nonpersistent. When a client terminates the session, the bean is no longer associated with the client and is terminated as well. A server-site session bean represents a particular client. It responds on behalf of a client and terminates when the client session is over. Session beans are often designed for major and complex business logic and flow control in front of entity beans. A session bean may control the dialogues with entity bean business objects. They may also make requests to another session bean or to other Web components such as JSP, Servlet, or HTML pages. There are two session bean types: stateless session beans and stateful session beans.

6.2.1 Stateless Session Beans

The stateless session bean simply defines a set of independent operations that can be performed on behalf of clients. A stateless session bean plays the role of the Controller and performs a procedural operation on behalf of the client during its session.

Life Cycle of a Stateless Session Bean

The life cycle of a stateless session bean is very simple because it does not need to keep any state and it lives only during the session. Its life cycle has only two stages: *not-exist* and *method-ready* for the invocation of business methods. Figure 6.5 illustrates the stages of the life cycle for a stateless session bean. The not-exist stage is where the bean interface and class files are located. The method-ready stage is where the instantiated bean instance is loaded into memory. The EJB container may instantiate session beans when the server starts. The EJB container manages a bean instance pool to reduce the number of component instantiations in order to significantly reduce expenses on the creations and removals of bean instances. There are two types of methods in an enterprise bean: the business methods and the bean life cycle methods. The business methods are called by clients and life cycle methods (callback) methods are called back by the EJB container when the EJB container thinks it is necessary. In Figure 6.5, the EJB callback methods are underlined in the diagram and the others are notated in the boxes.

A client requests a new session bean instance by the `create()` method of bean home interface, and the container calls the class's `newInstance()` method to create a new bean object. The container then calls the `setSessionContext()` method to pass in the context environment object and it calls back the `ejbCreate()` method to initialize the instance. The last two methods are the EJB container callback methods that programmers can define. At this time, this session bean is in its method-ready pool stage and ready to respond to client method invocation. The `ejbCreate()` method is only called once during any stateless session bean life cycle. When the `remove()` method is called, the `ejbRemove()` is then called next; the bean may be pulled out from the method-ready stage and is back to not-exist stage. [1][2][3]

Stateless Session Bean Implementation

In this section we demostrate a simple stateless session bean that performs a temperature conversion from a Fahrenheit temperature to its Celsius temperature. First, two interfaces (Home interface and Remote interface) are specified in `F2CHome.java` and `F2C.java` files, respectively.

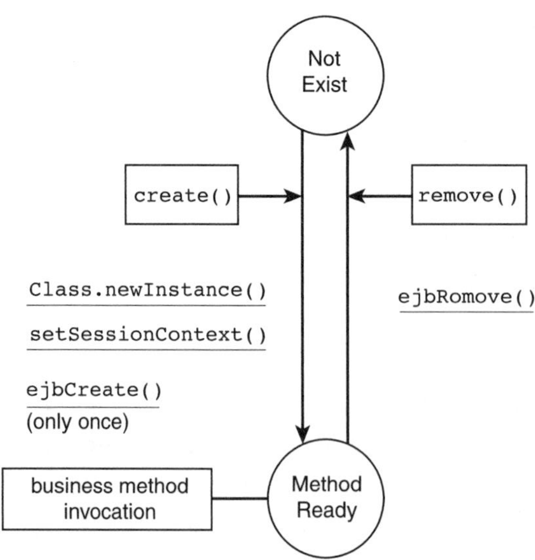

Figure 6.5
Life Cycle of a Stateless Session Bean

```
//F2C.java specifies remote interface for this converter
//session bean. It exposes the business method fToC()

package f2c;

import javax.ejb.EJBObject;
import java.rmi.RemoteException;
import java.math.*;

public interface F2C extends EJBObject {

public double fToC(double f) throws RemoteException;

  }

//The file F2CHome.java specifies the home interface for this EJB

package f2c;
import java.io.Serializable;
import java.rmi.RemoteException;
```

```
import javax.ejb.CreateException;
import javax.ejb.EJBHome;

public interface F2CHome extends EJBHome {

    Converter create() throws RemoteException, CreateException;
}
```

Next we define the implementation of this stateless session bean in the `F2CBean.java` file. The `fToC()` method implementation is specified in this file; the declaration of this method is listed in its remote interface. Notice that this bean class does not have its own state property. It simply takes client inputs, performs the conversion operations, and then returns the results. It specifies the implementations of the EJB interfaces listed above. After it completes its service it will not remember what happened in the past.

```
//The file F2CBean.java specifies the EJB implementation
//class for above interfaces of this EJB component.

package f2c;
import java.rmi.RemoteException;
import javax.ejb.SessionBean;
import javax.ejb.SessionContext;
import java.math.*;

public class F2CBean implements SessionBean {

      public double fToC(double f) {

      double temp=(f-32)*5./9;
      return temp;
   }

// It must have a default constructor; all EJB container
// callback methods are also listed

   public F2CBean() {}
   public void ejbCreate() {}
   public void ejbRemove() {}
   public void ejbActivate() {}
   public void ejbPassivate() {}
   public void setSessionContext(SessionContext sc) {}

}
```

Finally, we develop a Web JSP client for this stateless session bean EJB component in the `index.jsp` file.

```
<%-- Web Client for the EJB: index.jsp --%>

<%@ page import="f2c.TempConv,f2c.TempConvHome,javax.ejb.*,
java.rmi.RemoteException, javax.naming.*,javax.rmi.*,
java.text.DecimalFormat" %>
<%!
   private TempConv conv = null;

   public void jspInit() {
      try {
         InitialContext ic = new InitialContext();
         Object objRef = ic.lookup("java:comp/env/ejb/myBean");
         TempConvHome home = (TempConvHome)PortableRemoteObject.narrow(objRef,
TempConvHome.class);
         conv = home.create();
      } catch (RemoteException ex) {
System.out.println("Couldn't create bean."+
ex.getMessage());
      } catch (CreateException ex) {
System.out.println("Couldn't create bean."+
ex.getMessage());
      } catch (NamingException ex) {
System.out.println("Unable to lookup home: "+ "myBean "+
ex.getMessage());
      }
   }

   public void jspDestroy() {
         conv = null;
   }
%>
<html>
<head>
    <title>Temperature Converter</title>
</head>

<body bgcolor="white" ><center>
<h4><b>Temperature Converter</b></h4>

<p>Enter a temperature in Fahrenheit degree:</p>
<form method="get">
<input type="text" name="degree" size="25">
<br>
<p>
```

```
<input type="submit" name="fToC" value="Fahrenheit to Celsius">

</form>
<%
    DecimalFormat twoDigits = new DecimalFormat ("0.00");
    String degree = request.getParameter("degree");
     if ( degree != null && degree.length() > 0 ) {
          double d = Double.parseDouble(degree);
%>
<%        if  (request.getParameter("fToC") != null ) {
%>
            <p>
<%= degree %> in Fahrenheit degree is equivalent to
<%= twoDigits.format(conv.fToC(d)) %> in Celsius degree.
<%
          }
%>
<%
    }
%>
</center></body>
</html>
```

Web clients of this application locate the home object of this session bean by the Java Naming and Directory Interface (JNDI). The `InitialContext` class is the context for performing JNDI naming operations. The `lookup()` method takes the bean's JNDI name "myBean" (deployed name) as the argument:

```
Context initialContext = new InitialContext();
F2CHome home = (F2CHome)PortableRemoteObject.narrow(initialContext.lookup("
                   java:comp/env/ejb/myBean"),F2CHome.class);
```

The `PortableRemoteObject.narrow()` method must be used in order to access a remote bean object via JNDI lookup. This method converts the RMI-IIOP compatible remote home stub into a Java object. For local clients, the client and EJB bean are in the same server, the return value of the `InitialContext.lookup()` method is not a stub, and it can be directly cast to the local home interface just like the following statement.

```
LocalF2CHome home =
(LocalF2CHome)initialContext.lookup("java:comp/env/ejb/myBean");
```

The detail procedures of the compilation, configuration, and deployment of this session bean and its Web client can be found in Section 6.7, Examples and Lab Practice. The following screen shots illustrate this stateless session bean Web application, which converts 32 Fahrenheit degrees to 0 Celsius degrees. Clients can use any Web browser to browse the `index.jsp` JSP page, which is the default JSP page; it does not even need to be included as the URL. The `index.jsp` gets the input from the client and locates this session EJB; it then gets the required services from the bean and displays the converted temperature on the page. This is a simple Web application of a stateless Java enterprise session bean.

6.2.2 The Stateful Session Bean

Overview

A stateful session bean represents a specific client and holds related data for this client during the session. For example, a shopping cart session bean or a student registration session bean is stateful because the session must keep track of which items or courses have been selected so far. A session bean class may have a Collection type data member pertaining to the client during a session, but it

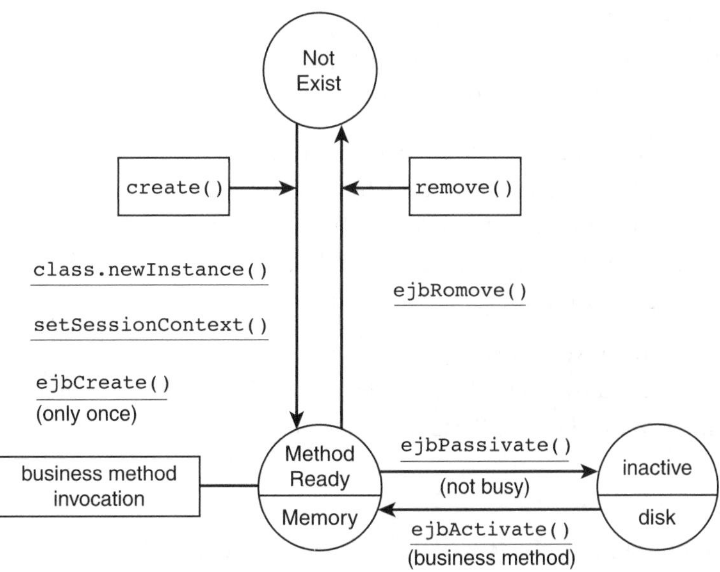

Figure 6.6
Life Cycle of a Stateful Session Bean

does not have any permanent data storage to support. The operations of a stateful EJB are context-dependent. They use and update the state data and are performed on behalf of a client. A stateful session bean is not supposed to be shared by multiple clients, but it keeps its data for a client in many request transactions within the same session.

The Life Cycle of a Stateful Session Bean

The life cycle of a stateful session bean is more complicated than a stateless session bean in that it has an additional inactive pool state. The main flow of the life cycle is as follows (see Figure 6.6).

Clients invoke the bean's home `create()` method in the client application via the stub; the EJB container instantiates an instance, calls the `setSessionContext()` and `ejbCreate()` methods, and moves it into the method-ready stage. The EJB container may instantiate a number of bean instances when the server starts. While in the method-ready stage, the EJB container may passivate the bean by calling `ejbPassivate()` to move it from memory to secondary storage following a least recently used (LRU) rule. If a client invokes a business method of the bean while it is in the passive stage, the EJB container activates the bean, calls the bean's `ejbActivate()` method, and then moves it to the method-ready stage. When a client invokes the `remove()` method, the EJB container calls the bean's `ejbRemove()` method.

All the methods named with `ejbXXX` are invoked by the EJB container. The `ejbCreate()` method, for example, inside the bean class, allows you to perform certain initiation operations, such as database connection, right after the bean is instantiated.

There are three ways for a stateful session bean to move into the method-ready stage. The EJB container allocates and instantiates the instance when the server starts or when clients invoke the `create()` method causing the EJB container to call the `ejbCreate()` and `ejbPostCreate()` methods, or the EJB container invokes the `ejbActivate()` method when it is needed. While a bean is in the method-ready stage, its business methods can be invoked.

There are two ways to move beans away from the method-ready stage. Clients can invoke the `remove()` method, which causes the EJB container to call the `ejbRemove()` method. The second way is for the EJB container to invoke the `ejbPassivate()` method.

Stateful Session Bean Implementation

This is a simple online shopping cart stateful session bean class with its Home interface and Remote interface. The stateful session bean has a `vector` data state, which is a cart holding all the items the customer added during the shopping session. The customer can also remove any items from this cart and review the cart during that session. [3][4][5]

We now discuss the following:

- Home interface (`CartHome`)
- Remote interface (`Cart`)
- Session bean class (`CartBean`)

The Home interface is like an EJB factory that defines the `create()` methods. Clients may invoke it to create a new instance of the bean. For example, clients call this `create()` method:

```
Cart myCart = home.create("Allen");
```

Every `create()` method in the Home interface has its corresponding `ejbCreate()` callback method in the bean class. The signatures of the `ejbCreate()` methods in the `CartBean` class are as follows.

```
public void ejbCreate(String name) throws CreateException
```

The `CartHome.java` is a Home interface file for this stateless session bean. This Home interface extends the `javax.ejb.EJBHome` interface.

```
import java.io.Serializable;
import java.rmi.RemoteException;
import javax.ejb.*;

public interface CartHome extends EJBHome {
   Cart create(String name) throws RemoteException, CreateException;
}
```

The `Cart.java` is a Remote interface file that declares all business methods the `CartBean` implements. This Remote interface extends `javax.ejb.EJBObject` and defines the business methods that a remote client may invoke.

```
import java.util.*;
import javax.ejb.EJBObject;
import java.rmi.RemoteException;

public interface Cart extends EJBObject {

   public void addItem(String item) throws RemoteException;
   public void removeItem(String item) throws RemoteException;
   public Vector getCart() throws RemoteException;
}
```

The `CartBean.java` is a stateful session bean class file that implements all bean interfaces and overrides the container callback methods.

```
import java.util.*;
import javax.ejb.*;

public class CartBean implements SessionBean {

   String name;
   Vector cart;
   SessionContext sessionContext;

//ejbCreate() is called back by EJB container after clients
//invoke create() method. Some initialization is done here. The
//main job here is to create a vector to hold all shopped
//items for this cart.

   public void ejbCreate(String name)
      throws CreateException {

      if (name == null) {
         throw new CreateException("creation failed.");
      }
      else {
         this.name = name;
      }
         cart = new Vector();
   }

//Add a new item to the cart
```

```
   public void addItem(String item) {
      cart.add(item);
   }

//Remove an existing item from the cart

public void removeItem(String item) throws RemoteException {

      boolean result = cart.remove(item);
      if (result == false) {
         throw new RemoteException("Can't find it");
      }
   }

//Return this cart

   public Vector getCart() {
      return cart;
   }

   public CartBean() {}
   public void ejbRemove() {}
   public void ejbActivate() {}
   public void ejbPassivate() {}
   public void setSessionContext(SessionContext sc)
                              {sessionContext=sc ;}
   // sessionContext is useful when this session needs to
   // use other resources in the session context
}
```

The following code shows a simple application of this stateful session bean. A client, "Allen," creates his shopping cart, adds two items, views the cart, and then decides to remove the first item he added. This client application is written in a Java command-line application, but it is very easy to convert it to a Web application as shown for the stateless session example.

```
import java.util.*;
import javax.naming.*;
import javax.rmi.*;

public class Client {
    public static void main(String[] args) {
        try {

 //Locate the bean with a deployed name "myCart"

         Context ic = new InitialContext();
```

```
        CartHome cartHome = (CartHome)PortableRemoteObject.narrow(
        ic.lookup("java:comp/env/ejb/myCart"),CartHome.class);

  //Create a shopping cart for Allen

         Cart myCart = home.create("Allen");

 //Add two items

           myCart.addItem("Item1");
           myCart.addItem("Item2");

//Browse the cart

           Vector v = new Vector();

           v = myCart.getCart();

           Iterator iterator = v.iterator();

           while (iterator.hasNext()) {
               String item = (String) iterator.next();

               System.out.println(item);
           }

//Remove one item from the cart

           myCart.removeItem("Item1");}
           catch (Exception ex) {
           System.err.println("Exception!");
           ex.printStackTrace(); }
    }
}
```

A client locates the Home object of this session bean by the Java Naming and Directory Interface (JNDI). The `InitialContext` class is the context for performing JNDI naming operations. The `lookup()` method takes the bean's JNDI name (deployed name) as the argument:

```
Context initialContext = new InitialContext();
CartHome cartHome = (CartHome)PortableRemoteObject.narrow(initialContext.lookup("
                  java:comp/env/ejb/myCart"),CartHome.class);
```

The `PortableRemoteObject.narrow()` method must be used on the object returned from the JNDI lookup for a remote home object. This method converts the RMI-IIOP compatible remote home stub into a Java object. For local clients, the return value of the `InitialContext.lookup()` method is not a stub and can be directly cast to the local Home interface.

```
CartHome cartHome =
(CartHome)initialContext.lookup("java:comp/env/ejb/myCart");
```

The rest of the code is not difficult to follow. The vector of the Cart holds a conversation state during the client's session. It does not have permanent persistent state stored in the database, although it has a state for the current session.

A session bean can be accessed by any client just like a procedure or function. It does not keep any persistent state for a particular client during the conversation. It simply takes the input from the client and sends the results back to the client. Other examples of session beans would be an online session bean calculator or a logon verification bean.

6.3 Entity Beans

6.3.1 Overview

An entity bean represents a business object by a persistent database table instead of representing a client. Students, teachers, and courses are some examples of entity beans. Each entity bean has an underlying table in the database and each instance of the bean is stored in a row of the table. An entity bean does not correspond to any specific client. It provides shared entities for clients. It is supported by the EJB transaction service via its container. It has a persistent state with a unique primary key identifier that can be used by a client to locate a particular entity bean. Clients look up an existing entity bean by its primary key that is implemented by finding a row in its corresponding data table. A session bean does not have any primary identifier so that it does not have any findXXX() methods. Just like a session bean, an entity bean also has two interfaces and one implementation bean class. There are two types of entity beans: Bean-Managed-Persistence (BMP) entity beans and Container-Managed-Persistence (CMP) entity beans.

6.3.2 Life Cycle of an Entity Bean

Since BMP and CMP beans have very similar life cycles, we will not discuss the life cycle of a CMP or BMP entity bean separately. BMP developers have full control over database access, but for CMP, the EJB container takes care of it. For example, in BMP the insertion of a row into the table for an new instance of BMP is specified in the ejbCreate() method; the removal of a BMP object is done by deleting a row in its table specified in the ejbRemove() method; the synchronization of BMP with its database table is specified in the ejbLoad() and ejbStore() methods; the search for an entity bean is specified in the ejbFindXXX() methods. Clearly, EJB developers must know JDBC very well. For CMP, EJB developers do not need to know the detailed JDBC implementations. Figure 6.7 illustrates the life cycle of an entity bean.

Because an entity bean has its persistent state, clients can share and use an existing entity bean. Each entity bean must associate a primary key so that clients can find the entity bean by its key. The findXXX() methods are used to locate a particular entity bean instance where XXX may be a primary key

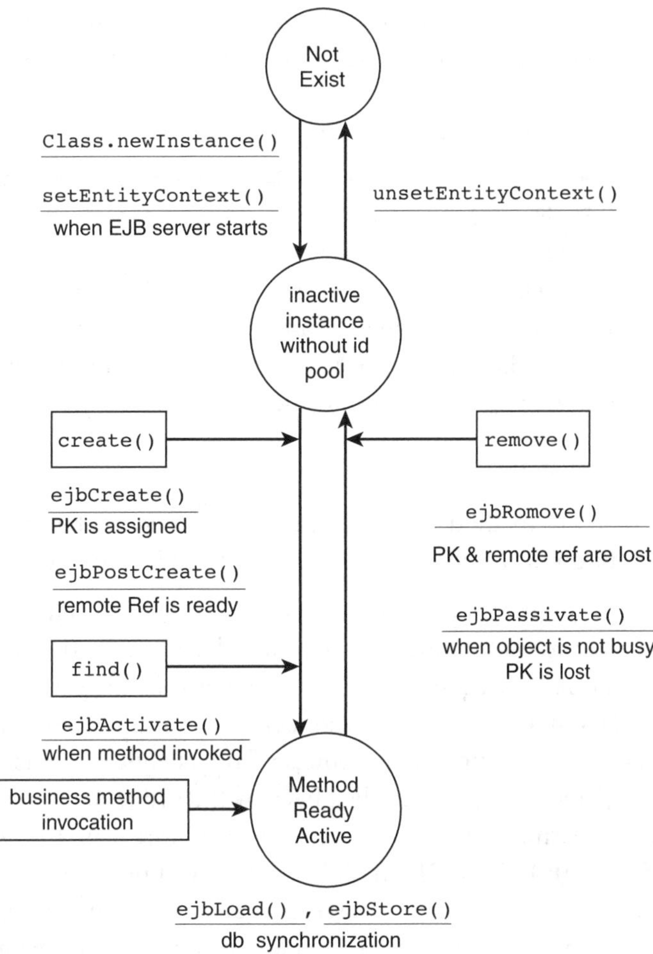

Figure 6.7
Life Cycle of an Entity Bean

or other properties of the bean. In other words, in addition to `create()` and `remove()` methods, clients normally invoke `findXXX()` methods to locate a specific entity bean.

Let us look at the work flows of `create()`, `findXXX()`, and `remove()` operations.[1]

Work Flow of the `create()` Method

Clients invoke the `create()` method of an EJB bean. The container allocates an instance from the pool. The `ejbCreate()` is called back and one new row is inserted into its persistent data table. The container assigns a primary key to this EJB object, which becomes active when the ID is associated. The `ejbPostCreate()` is called back and the context is available for this EJB object to access other EJB resources. Clients receive a reference to this EJB object and can use this object reference to call this EJB's business methods now because the EJB is in its method-ready stage with an assigned key.

Work Flow of the `findByPrimaryKey(ID)` Method

Clients may call this method after looking up the Naming server to obtain a reference to the EJB Home object. Then `ejbFindByPimaryKey()` is called back. The container searches for the row in its corresponding table with this key. The container associates an instance in the pool with this primary key and makes it active. Clients get the reference to this EJB bean and invoke business methods. Then `ejbLoad()` is called back. If the business is a transaction, then `ejbStore()` may be called back and `ejbPassivate()` may also be called back if this bean is no longer busy. The other `findXXX()` method may pull out multiple EJB beans from its persistent data table.

Work Flow of the `remove()` Method

The client calls the `remove()` method when the transaction is over. Then `ejbRemove()` is called back and one row is deleted from its persistent data table; the bean is returned back to the pool state.

Typically, the EJB container pre-allocates some entity beans. When clients make a `create()` request, the `ejbCreate()` and `ejbPostCreate()` methods are called back and an ID is assigned to this instance. When clients make a `findXXX()` request, the EJB container calls the `ejbActivate()` method on this bean and assigns an ID to it. Once an entity bean gets its ID, it is moved to the method-ready stage and is able to respond to method invocation requests from clients. If clients invoke any requests, the `ejbLoad()` or `ejbStore()` methods may be called back by the EJB container to synchronize the entity bean in memory and its permanent image in the secondary storage. In the pooled stage, an instance is not associated with any EJB object ID. With bean-managed persistence, when the EJB container moves an instance from the pooled state to the ready state, it does not automatically set the primary key. Therefore, the `ejbCreate()` or `ejbActivate()` methods must assign a primary key.

6.3.3 BMP Entity Bean

Overview

BMP is a better choice in some application development cases. JDBC-proficient entity bean developers feel more comfortable assuming the responsibility of managing the EJB persistence by themselves in the sense of flexibility or for other reasons. An entity bean with BMP must perform JDBC storing data code to store the bean to its persistent storage and loading data code to load the bean from its persistent storage and insert and delete operation as well.

The life cycle of a BMP entity bean is introduced in Section 6.3.2, Life Cycle of an Entity Bean. When a business method is called by a BMP bean, the `ejbActivate()` method is called first, followed by the `ejbLoad()` method where the developer must load the persistent data to synchronize the bean with its data table. Then the business method is invoked. The `ejbLoad()` method should be specified by

EJB developers. Like the `ejbStore()` method, it must be specified by EJB developers to guarantee the synchronization before a bean moves to its inactive stage.

BMP Entity Bean Implementation

The following is an example of a student BMP entity bean. It stores pairs of student IDs and GPAs. A database table for this bean must be created by the following SQL statement:

```
CREATE TABLE student
   (id         VARCHAR(3) CONSTRAINT pk_student PRIMARY KEY,
    score      Number(1,0)
    );

//The following is the Home interface for this student BMP
//entity bean.

import javax.ejb.*;
import java.util.*;
public interface StudentHome extends EJBHome {
    public Student create(String id, double gpa)
        throws RemoteException, CreateException;
    public Account findByPrimaryKey(String id)
        throws FinderException, RemoteException;
}

//The following code is the Remote interface for this
//student BMP entity bean.

import javax.ejb.EJBObject;
import java.rmi.RemoteException;

public interface Student extends EJBObject {
    public double getScore() throws RemoteException;
}

//The following is the BMP implementation entity bean where
//SQL statements are explicitly included.

import java.sql.*;
import javax.sql.*;
import java.util.*;
import javax.ejb.*;
import javax.naming.*;

public class StudentEJB implements EntityBean {
```

```
    private String id;
    private double score;
    private EntityContext context;
    private Connection con;
    private String dbName = "java:comp/env/jdbc/StudentDB";
    public double getScore() {
       return score;
    }

//The following ejb callback methods are executed by EJB
//container. When a new bean instance is created the method
//ejbCreate() is automatically called by the container to insert a row
//in a corresponding table in the database.

    public String ejbCreate(String id, double gpa)
       throws CreateException {
       try {
          insertRow(id, score);
       } catch (Exception ex) {
           throw new EJBException("ejbCreate: ");
       }

       this.id = id;
       this.score = score;
       return id;
    }

   public String ejbFindByPrimaryKey(String primaryKey)
      throws FinderException {
         try {
         Boolean result = selectByPrimaryKey(primaryKey);
       } catch (Exception ex) {
         throw new EJBException("ejbFindByPrimaryKey: ");
       }
      if (result) {
         return primaryKey;
      }
      else {
         throw new ObjectNotFoundException
            ("Row for id " + primaryKey + " not found.");
      }
   }

   public void ejbRemove() {
      try {
```

```
            deleteRow(id);
         } catch (Exception ex) {
            throw new EJBException("ejbRemove: ");
         }
   }

   public void setEntityContext(EntityContext context) {
      this.context = context;
      try {
         makeConnection();
      } catch (Exception ex) {
          throw new EJBException("Failed to connect to database.");
      }
   }

 public void ejbActivate() {
      id = (String)context.getPrimaryKey();
   }

   public void ejbPassivate() {
      id = null;
   }

   public void ejbLoad() {
      try {
         loadRow();
       } catch (Exception ex) {
          throw new EJBException("ejbLoad: ");
       }
   }

   public void ejbStore() {
      try {
         storeRow();
       } catch (Exception ex) {
          throw new EJBException("ejbLoad: " );
       }
   }

   public void ejbPostCreate(String id, double score) { }

   void makeConnection() throws NamingException, SQLException
     { InitialContext ic = new InitialContext();
      DataSource ds = (DataSource) ic.lookup(dbName);
      con =  ds.getConnection();
   }
```

```
//The following methods are callback methods to invoke SQL
//statements to access database

   void insertRow (String id, double gpa) throws SQLException {

String insertStatement = "insert into student values (?,?)";
          PreparedStatement prepStmt =
                con.prepareStatement(insertStatement);
          prepStmt.setString(1, id);
          prepStmt.setDouble(2, gpa);
          prepStmt.executeUpdate();
          prepStmt.close();
   }

   void deleteRow(String id) throws SQLException {
String deleteStatement = "delete from student where id = ? ";
      PreparedStatement prepStmt=con.prepareStatement(deleteStatement);
      prepStmt.setString(1, id);
      prepStmt.executeUpdate();
      prepStmt.close();
   }

   boolean selectByPrimaryKey(String primaryKey) throws SQLException
   {
      String selectStatement="select id "+"from student where id = ? ";
      PreparedStatement prepStmt =
            con.prepareStatement(selectStatement);
      prepStmt.setString(1, primaryKey);
      ResultSet rs = prepStmt.executeQuery();
      boolean result = rs.next();
      prepStmt.close();
      return result;
   }

   void loadRow() throws SQLException {
      String selectStatement =
            "select score " + "from student where id = ? ";
      PreparedStatement prepStmt =
            con.prepareStatement(selectStatement);
      prepStmt.setString(1, this.id);
      ResultSet rs = prepStmt.executeQuery();
      if (rs.next()) {
         this.score = rs.getDouble(2);
```

```
            prepStmt.close();
         }
         else {
            prepStmt.close();
            throw new NoSuchEntityException(id + " not found.");
         }
      }

      void storeRow() throws SQLException {
         String updateStatement =
               "update student set score =  ? " + "where id = ?";
         PreparedStatement prepStmt =
               con.prepareStatement(updateStatement);
         prepStmt.setDouble(1, score);
         prepStmt.setString(2, id);
         int rowCount = prepStmt.executeUpdate();
         prepStmt.close();
         if (rowCount == 0) {
            throw new EJBException("Store id " + id + " failed.");
         }
      }
}
```

This bean class implements `ejbCreate()` and `ejbFindbyXXX()` for the Home interface, implements the `getScore()` method for the Remote interface and all other `ejb` callback methods in the `java.ejb.EntityBean` interface.[3]

6.3.4 CMP Entity Bean

Overview

For entity bean developers without much JDBC experience, the CMP is a better and easier choice because bean deployers can help take care of persistence management. Generally, CMP is a preferred choice over BMP due to its high performance, database independence, and easy development and deployment.

An entity bean with CMP relies on the EJB container to perform all database operations that are specified in the deployment descriptor. CMP is simpler than BMP in terms of programming coding, but CMP requires the deployment administrator to perform the configuration. For the life cycle of CMP, developers need to do nothing with `ejbLoad()` and `ejbStore()` because the synchronization is managed by the EJB container itself.

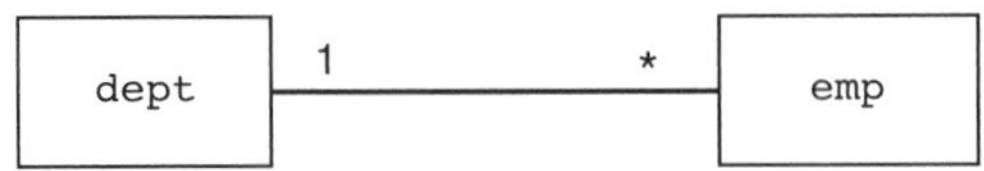

Figure 6.8
The Relationship Between dept and emp CMP Entity Beans

CMP Bean Implementation

This simple CMP bean application demonstrates a company department and employee management with a deparment CMP entity bean named `dept`, an employee CMP entity bean named `emp`, and a CMR one-to-many relationship between the `dept` entity bean and the `emp` entity bean. For any department there may be zero or many employees. (Some departments may be established with no employees.) For each employee there must be one and only one department. Figure 6.8 shows the relationship between these two entity beans.

The `LocalDeptHome.java` specifies the Local Home interface for the `dept` CMP bean. A Local interface is intended to be used by a Local client at the same server.

```
package company;
import java.util.*;
import javax.ejb.*;

public interface LocalDeptHome extends EJBLocalHome {
    public LocalCustomer create (String deptID, String deptLoc )
               throws CreateException;
     public LocalCustomer findByPrimaryKey (deptID)
        throws FinderException;
}
```

The `LocalDept.java` specifies the Local object interface for the `dept` CMP bean. A Local interface is intended to be used by a Local client at the same server.

```
package company;
import java.util.*;
import javax.ejb.*;

public interface LocalDept extends EJBLocalObject {
    public String getDeptID();
    public String getDeptLoc();
    public Vector getEmp();
    public void addEmp (LocalEmp emp);
}
```

The `DeptBean.java` implements two interfaces of this `dept` CMP bean. The `getDeptID()` and `setDeptID()` and `getDeptLoc()` and `setDeptLoc()` imply that this CMP bean has two CMP property fields: `DeptID` and `DeptLoc`. The `getEmp()` and `addEmp()` are used for the CMR relationship field between `dept` and `emp`.

```
package company;
import java.util.*;
import javax.ejb.*;

public abstract class DeptBean implements EntityBean {

    private EntityContext context;

  // cmp fields: pmk and other fields, all abstract methods

    public abstract String geDeptID();
    public abstract void setDeptID(String id);

    public abstract String getDeptLoc();
    public abstract void setDeptLoc(String loc);

  //cmr fields: 1:n relationship from dept to emp, all abstract methods

    public abstract Collection getEmp();
    public abstract void setEmp (Collection emp);

    //business methods

    public Vector getEmp() {
        Vector v = new Vector();
        Iterator i = getEmp().iterator();
        while (i.hasNext()) {
            v.add((LocalEmp)i.next());}
        return v;
    }

    public void addEmp (LocalEmp emp) {
        getEmp().add(emp);
    }

    private String create(String id, String loc)  throws
                CreateException
    {
       setDeptID(id);
```

```
        setDeptLoc(loc);
        return id;
    }

    public String ejbCreate (String id, String loc)  throws
                  CreateException
     {   return create(id, loc); }

    public void ejbPostCreate (String id, String loc)
        throws CreateException { }

    public void setEntityContext(EntityContext ctx) {}
    public void unsetEntityContext() {}
    public void ejbRemove() { }
    public void ejbLoad() { }
    public void ejbStore() { }
    public void ejbPassivate() { }
    public void ejbActivate() { }
}
```

The LocalEmpHome.java specifies the Local Home interface for the emp CMP entity bean.

```
package company;
import javax.ejb.*;

public interface LocalEmpHome extends EJBLocalHome {
    public LocalEmp create (
            String dpetID,
            String empID,
            String name,
            Float salary)  throws CreateException;

    public LocalEmp findByPrimaryKey(String empID)
        throws FinderException;
}
```

The LocalEmp.java specifies the local object interface for this emp CMP entity bean.

```
package company;
import javax.ejb.*;

public interface LocalEmp extends EJBLocalObject{
    public String getEmpID();
    public String getName();
    public float  getSalary();
}
```

The EmpBean.java specifies the bean class implementation for this emp CMP entity bean. It indicates that this bean has three CMP property fields: empID, empName, and Salary.

```
package company;
import java.util.*;

import javax.ejb.*;
import javax.naming.*;

public abstract class EmpBean implements EntityBean {

    private EntityContext context;

//for cmp fields: all abstract access methods

    public abstract String getEmpID();
    public abstract void setEmpID(String id);

    public abstract String getName();
    public abstract void setName(String name);

   public abstract float getSalary();
    public abstract void setSalary(float sal);

public String ejbCreate(String did, String eid, String name, float sal)
         throws CreateException {return create (eid, name, sal); }

    private String create( String id, String name, float sal)
           throws CreateException {
        setEmpID(id);
        setName(name);
        setSalary(sal);
        return id;
    }

//Other EntityBean callback methods. Notice ejbPostCreate()
//must add this new employee by dept.addEmp() to make sure
//each employee has one department to work for.

public void ejbPostCreate(String did,String eid,String name, float sal)
        throws CreateException {
       postCreate(did);}
```

```
    private void postCreate (String did) {
        try {
            Context ic = new InitialContext();
            LocalCustomerHome home = (LocalDeptHome)
            ic.lookup("java:comp/env/ejb/DeptRef");
            LocalDept dept = home.findByPrimaryKey(did);
            dept.addEmp((LocalEmp)context.getEJBLocalObject());
        } catch (Exception ex) {
            context.setRollbackOnly();
            ex.printStackTrace();
        }
    }

    public void setEntityContext(EntityContext ctx) {
        context = ctx;
    }

    public void unsetEntityContext() {
        context = null;
    }

    public void ejbRemove() { }
    public void ejbLoad() { }
    public void ejbStore() { }
    public void ejbPassivate() { }
    public void ejbActivate() { }
}
```

A complete detailed CMP entity bean application example is given in Section 6.7, Examples and Lab Practice. This example shows all detailed CMP development processing including compilation, assembly, deployment, and execution.

6.4 Message-Driven Beans (MDB)

The MDB component is another type of Java server component running on the EJB container. The MDB component works as a listener that listens to a queue supported by the Java Message Server (JMS). Once a client sends a message to the queue, the MDB component will be able to receive the message as long as MDB has registered with it. MDB works in an asynchronous communication mode.

The MDB technology is available in J2EE 1.4 (EJB2.x). The MDB technology can work in two different ways: PTP (point-to-point) and publisher/subscriber. PTP works in one-to-one mode and publisher/subscriber works in a broadcasting (one-to-many) mode. The MDB technology works in an asynchronous fashion in that a notification can be received by an MDB component and its reactions are immediate as long as MDB is active. MDB can also be integrated into any Web application if the necessary asynchronous communication is there.

An MDB component works in the following way:

1. The container registers this MDB component with JMS.
2. The JMS registers all JMS destinations (Topic for broadcasting or Queue for PTP) with Java Naming and Directory Interface (JNDI).
3. The EJB container instantiates this MDB component.
4. Clients look up the destination with the MDB.
5. Clients send a message to the destination.
6. The EJB container selects the corresponding MDB to consume the message.

MDB components work in a producer/consumer asynchronous mode and the message type can be a text message, object message, stream message, or byte message. Messages are pushed and processed in a `MessageListener`'s method called `onMessage()`.

6.5 EJB Web Service Components

Web services are becoming popular due to the ubiquitous and platform-independent features of Web applications. It is important to be able to enable an existing EJB application to run in a Web service environment. EJB2.x can wrap a stateless session bean with a Web service endpoint interface that can be accessed by any Web service client. EJB can also provide Web service via a Servlet front end by JAX-RPC. A stateless session bean usually plays a front-end role in most EJB-distributed applications so that the whole system can be converted to be Web service ready. The details of Web service implementation are discussed in Chapter 8, Web Services. [3]

The following is a simple `hiUser` Web service endpoint interface implemented by a stateless session bean that extends the `Remote` class in an `rmi` package. The `hiUser` Web service endpoint wraps the session bean named `HiUserBean`.

```
//HiUser.java is a Web service endpoint interface for the stateless
//session bean

package hiUser;
import java.rmi.*;

public interface HiUser extends Remote{
    Public String hiUser(String user) throws RemoteException;
}

//HiUserBean.java is a stateless session bean implementation class
```

```
package hiUser;
import java.rmi.RemoteException;
import java.ejb.*;

public class HiUserBean implements SessionBean{
public String hiUser(String user){
   Return "Hi " + user + "!";}}
```

Here HiUserBean may be an existing stateless session bean. In order to provide Web service, we must provide a WSDL file by a command-line wscompile. The steps to create a Web service endpoint are as follows.

1. Create all EJBs.
2. Create a wsdl Web service interface specification file by a wscompile command.
3. Package the wsdl.xml file with all class files.
4. Assemble them into an ejb.ear file.
5. Deploy the .ear file on a J2EE-compliant server.

A Web service can be accessed by any Web service client via HTTP at a designated port. This session bean can also be accessed by a remote client if any additional Remote and Home interfaces are available.

6.6 The Deployment Model of EJB

A developer for CMP entity beans does not need to write any database access code. However, he or she must map the CMP entity bean to a table in the database along with related database operations at deployment time. On the other hand, BMP entity beans let developers have full control of database access for the bean. Of course, CMP is more portable and flexible than BMP, and all details of database operations are specified in its deployment descriptor.

An EJB component is packaged as a .jar file, which is assembled in turn with other Web archive component packages (.war) and J2EE application archive client packages (.jar) in a J2EE enterprise archive application file (.ear). The hierarchical structure of a J2EE application package is shown in Figure 6.9.

After creating the code for the enterprise bean and after its client code is compiled into its class files, the developer needs to pack EJB components, Web components, or clients into Java archive files (.jar) or Web archive files (.war) with their deployment descriptor XML files (DD) and then assemble all of these archive files into an enterprise archive file (.ear) to be deployed on a server. The detailed steps are shown in Section 6.7, Examples and Lab Practice.

A deployment descriptor (DD) is a deployment definition file in XML format. It specifies EJB types, class names for Remote interfaces, Home interfaces, implementation beans, transaction

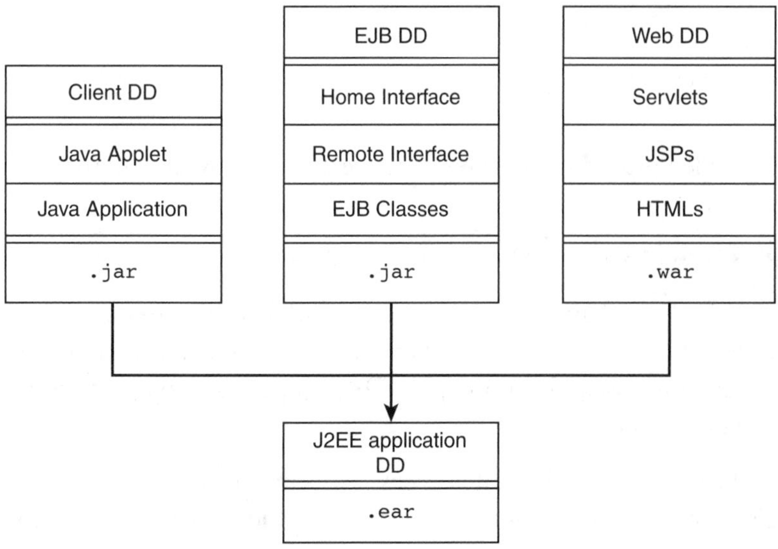

Figure 6.9
J2EE Assembly and Deployment

management specification, access control security, and persistence property of entity beans. DD is created automatically by `deploytool` after the deployment wizard is completed.

The following is a partial content of a DD:

```
<?xml version="1.0">
<ejb-jar>
   <enterprise-beans>
       <entity>
          <ejb-name>studentBean</ejb-name>
          <home>studenthome</home>
          <remote>student</remote>
           <ejb-class>Student</ejb-class>
           <persistence-type>Container</persistence-type>
           <pri-key-class>Integer</pri-key-class>
           ...
           <cmp-field><field-name>id</field-name></cmp-field>
           ...
           <cmp-field><field-name>name</field-name></cmp-field>
      </enterprise-beans>
      <assembly-descriptor>
         <security-role>
         ...
```

```
        </security-role>
        . . .
      </assebly-descriptor>
  </ejb-jar>
```

You will see the detailed procedures of the enterprise bean deployment in the next section.

6.7 Examples and Lab Practice

This section is designed to enhance the understanding of the EJB concepts by three Web application examples. This lab practice section provides step-by-step guidelines demonstrating how to build EJB components, how to assemble and deploy EJB components, and how to build and run Web applications for these components.

Lab 1 describes the steps to build a stateless session bean called `discountCalc` that calculates the conference registration fee according to the category of the attendee and deploys it by the utility tool `deploytool` in J2EE 1.4.x. The session bean is capable of getting the discount rate stored in the database. A Web-based interface will make the application available from the Internet at a single stroke.

Lab 2 shows how to create and deploy a Java CMP entity bean. The entity bean is handled by the EJB container. The session bean created in Lab 1 is modified so that it can access the database through the entity bean.

Lab 3 extends Lab 2 to implement a simple online conference registration system. This application includes a stateful `register` session EJB component and two CMP entity EJB components for `conference` and `attendee`, respectively. Lab 3 shows the connection between the session bean and the entity beans and the association relationship between two entity beans.

6.7.1 Lab Environments

Step 1: Installation and Configuration

First, you need to install, configure, and set up the EJB environments, which can be shared by all labs in this section. All the labs will run on the J2EE platform. Next, you need to create database tables that can be used by all labs.

1. Download the J2EE 1.4 All-In-One bundle from `www.java.sun.com`. (The Windows platform is used in this lab.)

2. Install J2EE 1.4 on your machine and ensure that the `<install_dir>/bin` directory is included in the environment's path.

3. All the source code and configuration files are available on this book's Web site (www. ?). Download the `ejb` folder for Lab 1, Lab 2, and Lab 3 and put it under c:\.

4. Set up the environment for the Java-based `Ant Build` facility.

   The J2EE 1.4 All-In-One bundle includes the `Ant Build` Tool, which is used in this lab for compiling Java source code and other processing. `Ant` has a very simple XML syntax. It is easy to learn and to use. In order to run the `asant` scripts, the directory structure is built as below:

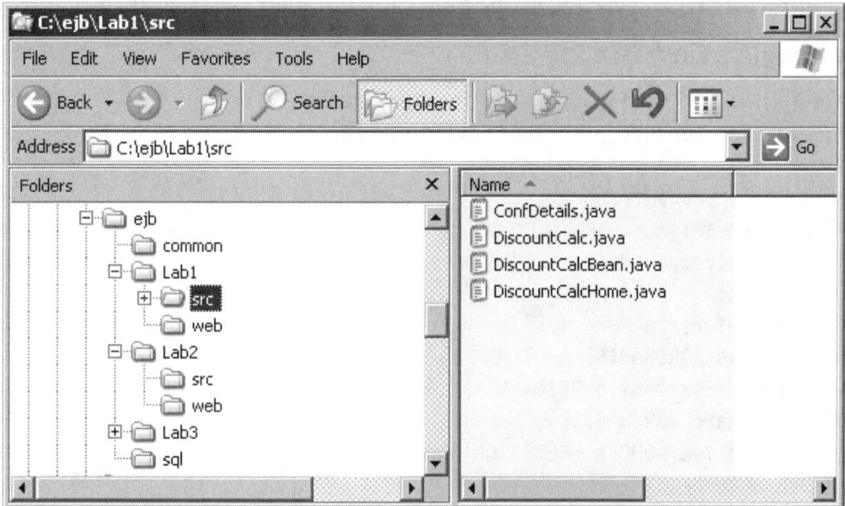

It is not strictly necessary to follow the suggested directory structure, but it is strongly recommended until you are comfortable enough to make your own modifications. There are five subfolders in the `ejb` folder: `common`, `sql`, `lab1`, `lab2`, and `lab3`. Under the `common` folder there are two `Ant` scripts: `build.properties` and `targets.xml`. Verify the variables in the `build.properties` based on the installation. Modify it if necessary. The `sql` folder has a `sql` script `create_table.sql`. In each lab folder there are two subfolders: `src` and `web`, and one configuration file called `build.xml`. All the Java source code is in the `src` directory. JSP or HTML files are in the `web` directory. The configuration file `build.xml` is available in each lab's working directory. By default, `Ant` looks for this file to find the environment setting and commands. When using the `Ant Build` Tool to compile Java source code, a new directory `build` will be automatically created under the lab's directory with all the class files.

5. Start the J2EE application server, `deploytool`, and the `PointBase` database.

   On the Windows Start menu, choose Program | Sun Microsystems | Application Server | Start Default Server to start the J2EE Application Server. To start `deploytool`, choose Programs | Sun Microsystems | Application Server | deploytool from the Windows Start menu. To start `PointBase`, choose Programs | Sun Microsystems | Application Server | Start PointBase from the Start menu.

Step 2: Create the Database

The labs in this section are tested with a `PointBase` database, which provides persistent storage for application data. The `PointBase` is included in the J2EE SDK. An `sql` script file named `create_table.sql` under the `ejb\sql` directory will be used to create tables and populate `conference` data.

1. Prepare the `sql` script, `create_table.sql`.

```
-- create tables for online registration application
-- jdbc:pointbase:server://localhost:9092/sample

DROP TABLE conference;
DROP TABLE attendee;
DROP TABLE register;

CREATE TABLE conference
   (conference_id VARCHAR(8)
       CONSTRAINT pk_confid PRIMARY KEY,
    conference_name VARCHAR(30),
    registration_fee DOUBLE PRECISION);
CREATE TABLE attendee
   (ssn VARCHAR(9)
       CONSTRAINT pk_ssn PRIMARY KEY,
    name VARCHAR(30),
    attendee_type VARCHAR(30));
CREATE TABLE register
   (conference_id VARCHAR(8),
    ssn VARCHAR(9));
INSERT INTO conference
   VALUES ('001', 'Distributed Computing',  150.00);
INSERT INTO conference
   VALUES ('002', 'Component Based Computing',  100.00);
```

```
INSERT INTO conference
   VALUES ('003', 'Grid Computing', 100.00);
COMMIT;
```

2. To create the database tables for this lab, do the following:

   a. Ensure the database `PointBase` is running.

   b. Open a terminal window and go to `c:\ejb\lab1`.

   c. Enter the following command: `>asant create-db`

   The `create-db` is defined in the `Ant` configuration file `targets.xml`.

```
Command Prompt
     [java] 1 row(s) affected

     [java] SQL> INSERT INTO conference
     [java]     VALUES ('002', 'Component Based Computing',  100.00);
     [java] 1 row(s) affected

     [java] SQL> INSERT INTO conference
     [java]     VALUES ('003', 'Grid Computing', 100.00);
     [java] 1 row(s) affected

     [java] SQL> COMMIT;
     [java] OK

BUILD SUCCESSFUL
Total time: 5 seconds
```

3. To view the data in the database, go to `c:\sun\appserver\pointbase\tools\serveroption` and run `startconsole.bat` to start the `PointBase` console; enter the following values in the Connect To Database form:

Driver:	`com.pointbase.jdbc.jdbcUniversalDriver`
URL:	`jdbc:pointbase:sun-appserv-samples`
User:	`PBPUBLIC`
Password:	`PBPUBLIC`

   Then click OK to connect to the database.

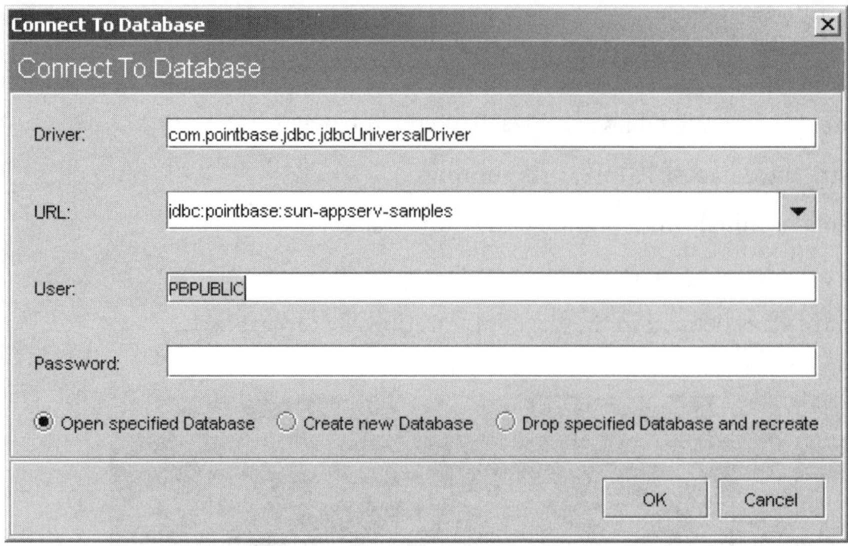

To run an `sql` script, select File | Open to open the script file or directly type the `sql` commands in the Enter SQL Commands box, then click Execute to run the script.

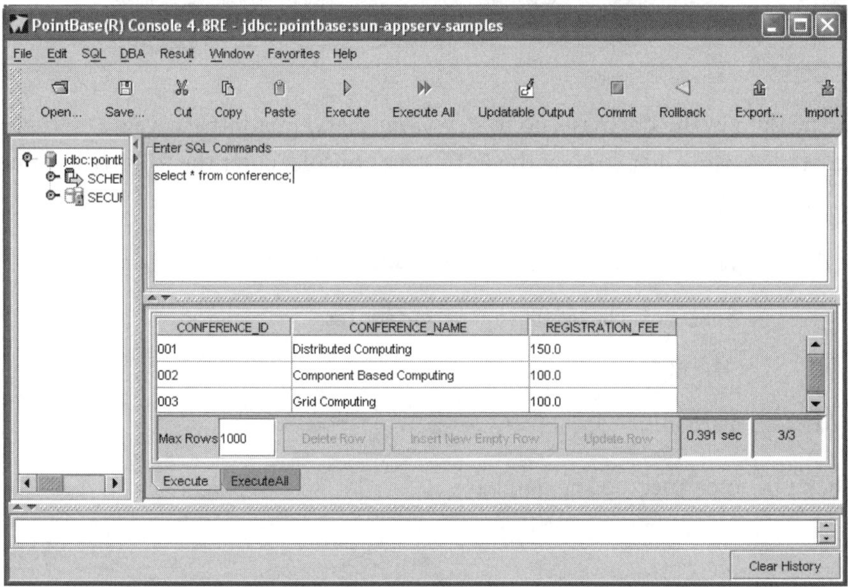

Lab 1: Stateless Session Bean for Registration Fee Calculation

Lab 1 is a Web application of conference registration fee discount calculation. There may be subconferences for attendees to select. The registration fee varies for different subconferences. There is a

20% discount for a membership participant and a 50% discount for a student participant. The conference information and regular registration fees are stored in a database table called `Conference` so that the conference administrator can modify the rates in the database instead of hard code. A stateless session bean `DiscountCalculator` accesses the database table and retrieves the conference information there. A method `getDiscountedFee()` calculates the registration fee based on the attendee's category. The following diagram shows the structure of this Web application.

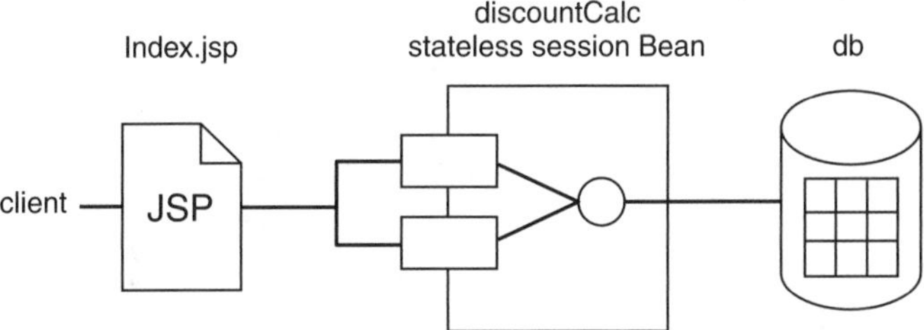

Step 1: Develop the Session Bean

The enterprise bean in this example includes the following code:

- Remote interface: `DiscountCalc.java`
- Home interface: `DiscountCalcHome.java`
- Enterprise bean class: `DiscountCalcBean.java`
- Helper Class: `ConfDetails`

The main purpose of a session bean is to run business tasks for the client. The `DiscountCalc` Remote interface, which extends `javax.ejb.EJBObject`, defines two business methods: `getAllConference()` returns all conferences and their registration fees, and `getDiscountedFee()` returns the discounted registration fee for a specific attendee category. The client invokes business methods on the remote object reference that is retuned by the `create()` method.

```
//DiscountCalc.java is a Remote interface of DiscountCalc
//session bean

package discountCalc;

import java.util.*;
import javax.ejb.EJBObject;
import java.rmi.RemoteException;

public interface DiscountCalc extends EJBObject {

    public ArrayList getAllConferences() throws RemoteException;
```

```
    public double getDiscountedFee (double registFee, String
           attendeeType) throws RemoteException;
}
```

The Home interface `DiscountCalcHome`, which extends the `javax.ejb.EJBHome` interface, has a single method `create()`. The `ejbCreate()` method in the bean that will be called back when this method is invoked.

```
//DiscountCalcHome.java is a Remote home interface of
//DiscountCalc session bean

package discountCalc;

import java.rmi.RemoteException;
import javax.ejb.*;

public interface DiscountCalcHome extends EJBHome {

    DiscountCalc create() throws RemoteException, CreateException;
}
```

The `discountCalcBean` implements the `sessionBean` interface. The `ejbCreate()` method specifies some necessary initialization and configuration for the bean. It performs a JNDI lookup to obtain a data source. The bean contains two business methods. The `getAllConferences()` method provides connection to the database. It uses `sql` code to retrieve data from the conference table and returns an ArrayList of `confDetails` objects. The `getDiscountedFee()` method implements the business logic of registration fee calculation.

```
//DiscountCalcBean.java is the Stateless Session Bean
//implementation

package discountCalc;

import java.util.*;
import javax.ejb.*;
import javax.naming.*;
import java.rmi.RemoteException;
import java.math.*;
import java.sql.*;
import javax.sql.*;

public class DiscountCalcBean implements SessionBean {

    DataSource dataSource;
```

```
public void ejbCreate () {

  InitialContext ic = null;
  try {
       ic = new InitialContext();
       dataSource =
      (DataSource)ic.lookup("java:comp/env/jdbc/PointBase");
  } catch (NamingException ex) {
       System.out.println("Naming Exceptions");
    }
}

public ArrayList getAllConferences()  {
  ArrayList confList = new ArrayList();
  Connection con = null;
  PreparedStatement stmt = null;
  ResultSet rs = null;
  try {
       con = dataSource.getConnection();
       stmt = con.prepareStatement
             ("SELECT * FROM conference ");
       rs =stmt.executeQuery();

       while (rs.next()) {
           ConfDetails confDetail = new ConfDetails(
           rs.getString(1), rs.getString(2), rs.getDouble(3));
           confList.add( confDetail );
       }
       rs.close();
  stmt.close();
  con.close();

  } catch (SQLException ex) {
    System.out.println("SQL Exceptions");
  }
  return confList;
}

public double getDiscountedFee (double registFee, String attendeeType) {
  int discountRate = 0;
  if ( attendeeType.equals ("Member") )  discountRate = 20;
     else if ( attendeeType.equals ("Student") ) discountRate = 50;
     else discountRate = 0;
```

```
        return  (registFee * (1 - (double)discountRate/100 ));
    }

    public DiscountCalcBean() {}
    public void ejbActivate() {}
    public void ejbPassivate() {}
    public void ejbRemove() {}
    public void setSessionContext(SessionContext sc) {}

} // DiscountCalcBean
```

The `DiscoutCalc` session bean has a helper class called `confDetails`. The serializable `confDetails` class contains three variables: `confid`, `confName`, and `registFee`, which correspond to the three columns in the conference table. It is particularly useful to work with the `ArrayList` to store and retrieve data. Helper classes must reside in the `EJB.jar` file that contains the enterprise bean class.

```
//ConfDetails class is a helper class

package discountCalc;

public class ConfDetails implements java.io.Serializable {

    private String confId;
    private String confName;
    private double registFee;

    public ConfDetails (String confId, String confName, double registFee) {
        this.confId = confId;
        this.confName = confName;
        this.registFee = registFee;
    }
    public String getConfId() {
        return confId;
    }
    public String getConfName() {
        return confName;
    }
    public double getRegistFee() {
        return registFee;
    }
  } // conferenceDetails;
```

Step 2: Compiling All Source Code

In the `c:\ejb\lab1` directory, compile the source files at the command prompt. Type `>asant build`.

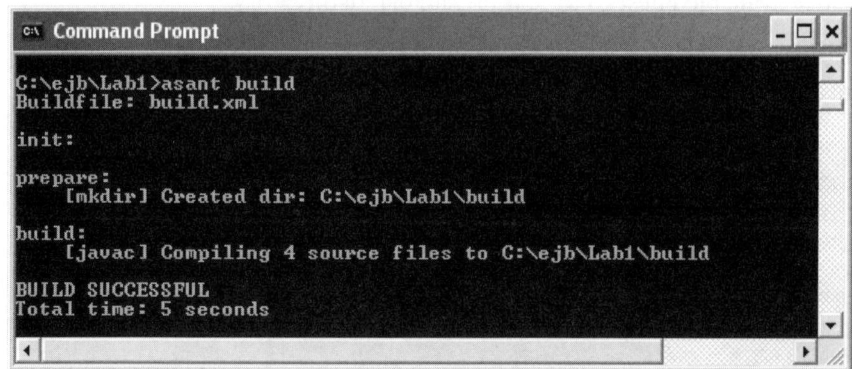
Command Prompt
C:\ejb\Lab1>asant build
Buildfile: build.xml
init:
prepare:
[mkdir] Created dir: C:\ejb\Lab1\build
build:
[javac] Compiling 4 source files to C:\ejb\Lab1\build
BUILD SUCCESSFUL
Total time: 5 seconds

A new directory `build` is created with four class files.

Step 3: Packaging the Session Bean

1. Start the J2EE Application Server, `PointBase` database, and `deploytool`.
2. Create the J2EE application:
   a. In `deploytool`, select File | New | Application.
   b. Click Browse.
   c. In the file chooser, navigate to `c:\ejb\Lab1`.
   d. In the File Name field, enter `DiscountCalcApp1.ear`.
   e. Click New Application and OK.
3. Package the EJB.

   To package an enterprise bean, run the New Enterprise Bean Wizard of the `deploytool` utility, which will create the bean's deployment descriptor, package the deployment descriptor and the bean's classes in an EJB `.jar` file, and insert the EJB `.jar` file into the application's `DiscountCalcApp.ear` file. To start the New Enterprise Bean Wizard, select File | New | Enterprise Bean.

   a. In the EJB JAR General Settings dialog box, select the Create New JAR Module in Application radio button.
   b. In the combo box, select DiscountCalcApp.

c. In the JAR Name field, enter `DiscountCalcJar`.

d. Click Edit Contents.

e. In the tree under Available Files, go to `c:\ejb\lab1\build` directory.

f. Select the `discountCalc` folder from the Available Files tree, and click Add.

g. Click OK and Next.

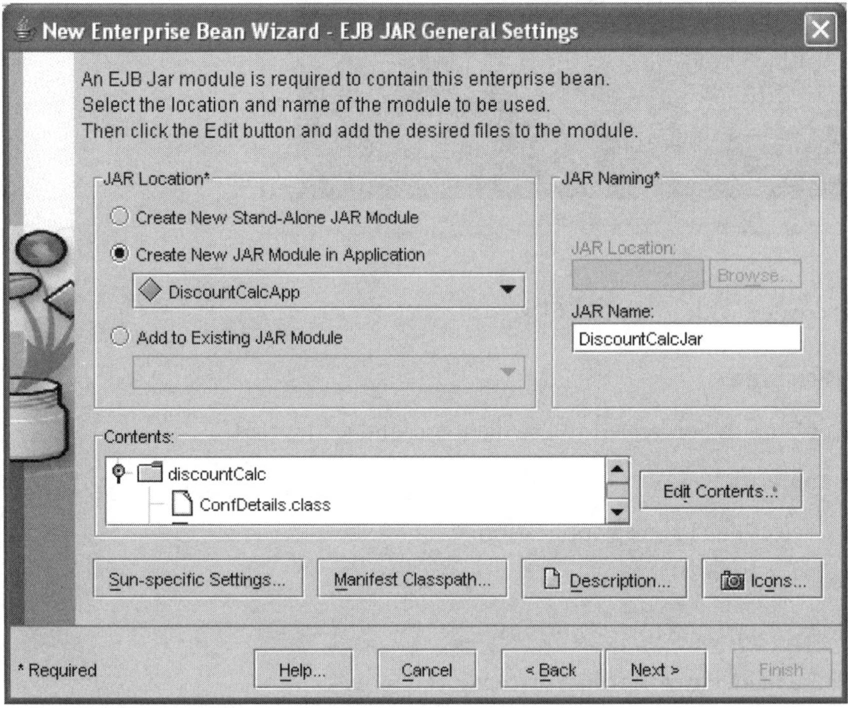

h. In the Bean General Settings dialog box, select discountCalc.DiscountCalcBean in the Enterprise Bean Class combo box. Verify DiscountCalcBean in the Enterprise Bean Name field. Under Bean Type, select the Stateless Session radio button.

i. Select DiscountCalc.DiscountCalcHome in the Remote Home Interface combo box. Select DiscountCalc.DiscountCalc in the Remote Interface combo box. Click Next.

j. In the Expose as Web Service Endpoint dialog box, select the No radio button, and click Next and Finish.

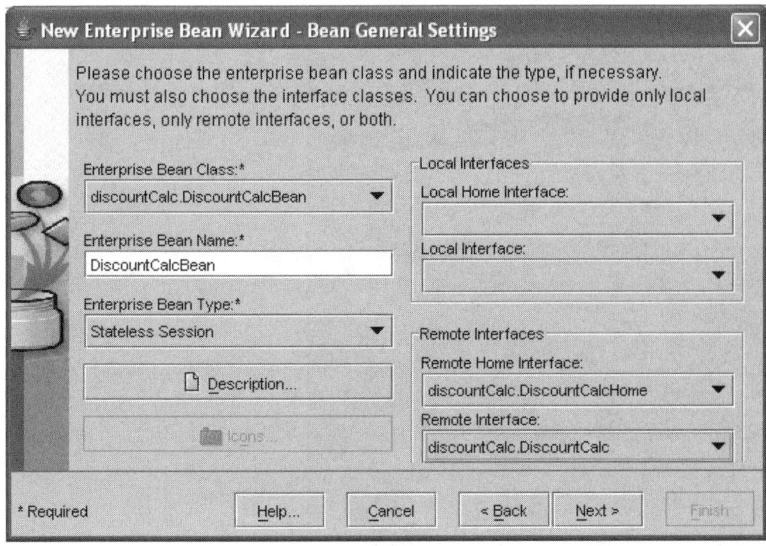

4. Specify the Resource Reference.

   a. In the tree, select DiscountCalcBean.

   b. Click the Resource Ref tab and Add.

   c. Enter `jdbc/PointBase` for Coded Name, select javax.sql.Datasource for Type, Container for Authentication, and Shareable.

   d. In the Sun Specific Settings for jdbc/PointBase box, enter `jdbc/PointBase` for the JNDI name, `pbpublic` for the User Name and Password.

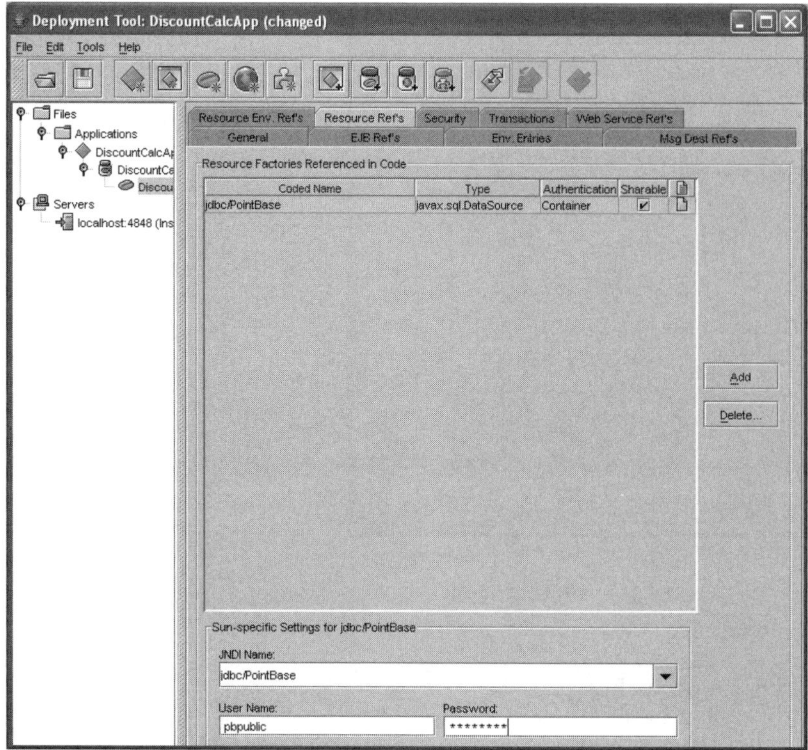

After the packaging process, you can view the deployment descriptor by selecting Tools | Descriptor Viewer.

```
<?xml version='1.0' encoding='UTF-8'?>
<ejb-jar
      version=" 2.1"
      xmlns=" http://java.sun.com/xml/ns/j2ee"
      xmlns:xsi=" http://www.w3.org/2001/XMLSchema-instance"
      xsi:schemaLocation=" http://java.sun.com/xml/ns/j2ee
          http://java.sun.com/xml/ns/j2ee/ejb-jar_2_1.xsd ">
   <display-name> DiscountCalcJar</display-name>
   <enterprise-beans>
      <session>
         <display-name> DiscountCalcBean</display-name>
         <ejb-name> DiscountCalcBean</ejb-name>
         <home> discountCalc.DiscountCalcHome</home>
         <remote> discountCalc.DiscountCalc</remote>
         <ejb-class> discountCalc.DiscountCalcBean</ejb-class>
         <session-type> Stateless</session-type>
         <transaction-type> Bean</transaction-type>
         <resource-ref>
            <res-ref-name> jdbc/PointBase</res-ref-name>
            <res-type> javax.sql.DataSource</res-type>
```

```
            <res-auth> Container</res-auth>
            <res-sharing-scope> Shareable</res-sharing-scope>
         </resource-ref>
         <security-identity>
            <use-caller-identity>
            </use-caller-identity>
         </security-identity>
      </session>
   </enterprise-beans>
</ejb-jar>
```

Step 4: Coding the Web Component

The `index.jsp` is a Web GUI interface for this application. It uses a JSP page and a `JavaBean` component to dynamically construct an HTML page to display conference registration fee lists. By default, it displays the registration fee list for a nonmember attendee. (See the page below.) The Web page takes the user's inquiry and responds with a calculated discounted registration fee list for a specific category request.

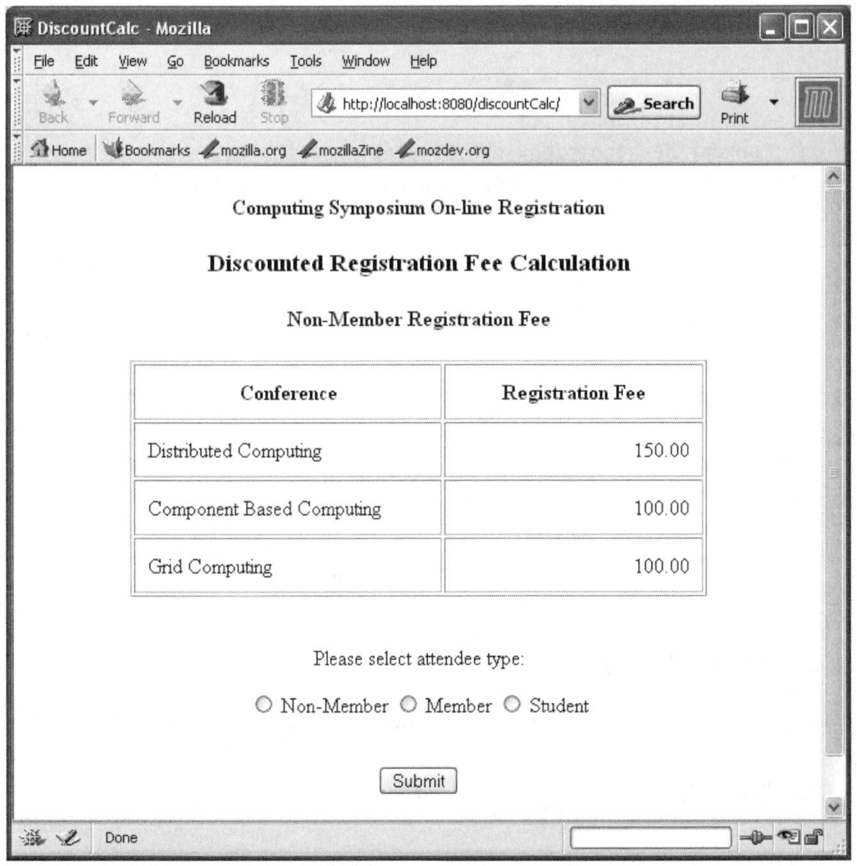

The `index.jsp` source code contains a `jspInit()` method that references the session bean's Home interface by a JNDI lookup and creates a bean instance. Two business methods, `getAllConference()` and `getDiscountedFee()`, which are defined in the `DiscountCalcBean`, are invoked on this page.

```
<%-- Web Client for the EJB: Index.jsp  --%>

<%@page import="javax.naming.*" %>
<%@page import="javax.rmi.PortableRemoteObject"%>
<%@page import="java.rmi.RemoteException"%>
<%@page import="javax.ejb.*"%>
<%@page import="java.util.*"%>
<%@page import="java.text.DecimalFormat"%>
<%@page import="discountCalc.*"%>
<%!
   private DiscountCalc discountCalc = null;
   String attendeeType = null;
   double  registFee = 0.00;
   ConfDetails confDetail;

   public void jspInit() {
      try {
         InitialContext ic = new InitialContext();
         Object objRef = ic.lookup("java:comp/env/ejb/SimpleDiscountCalc");
         DiscountCalcHome home = (DiscountCalcHome)PortableRemoteObject.narrow(objRef,
DiscountCalcHome.class);
         discountCalc = home.create();
      } catch (Exception ex) {
           System.out.println(ex.getMessage());
      }
   }

   public void jspDestroy() {
         discountCalc = null;
   }
%>
<head><center>
  <title>DiscountCalc</title>
  <h4>Computing Symposium On-line Registration </h4>
  <h3>Discounted Registration Fee Calculation</h3>
</center></head>
<%  attendeeType = request.getParameter("selectAttendeeType");
    if (attendeeType == null)
        attendeeType = "Non-Member";
```

```
%>
<body><center>
 <h4><%= attendeeType %> Registration Fee </h4>
  <table border="1" cellpadding="10">
    <tr><th width="220">Conference</th>
        <th width="180">Registration Fee</th>
    </tr>
<%  List confList = discountCalc.getAllConferences();
    Iterator i = confList.iterator();
    while (i.hasNext()) {
    confDetail = (ConfDetails) i.next();
registFee = discountCalc.getDiscountedFee
            (confDetail.getRegistFee(), attendeeType);
    DecimalFormat twoDigits = new DecimalFormat ("0.00");
%>
    <tr><td> <%= confDetail.getConfName() %> </td>
        <td align="right"> <%= twoDigits.format(registFee) %></td>
    </tr>
<%  }
%>
  </table>

  <form method="get" action="index.jsp" >
    <br>
    <p>Please select attendee type: </p>
    <input type="radio" name="selectAttendeeType" value="Non-Member">
    </input> Non-Member
    <input type="radio" name="selectAttendeeType" value="Member">
    </input>Member
    <input type="radio" name="selectAttendeeType" value="Student">
    </input>Student </p>
    <br>
    <input type="submit" name="Submit" value="Submit" /> </p>
    <br>
  </form>
</center></body>
</html>
```

Step 5: Packaging the Web Client

To package a Web client, we first run the New Web Component Wizard that will create a Web application deployment descriptor. Next, we add all component files to a .war file and add the .war file to the application's `DiscountCalcApp1.ear` file. We build the Web component by the New Web Component Wizard, selecting File | New | Web Component. See the following dialog boxes.

1. In the WAR File dialog box select Create New WAR Module in Application.
2. Select DiscountCalcApp in the combo box.
3. Enter `DiscountCalcWar` in the WAR Name field.
4. Click Edit Contents.
5. In the tree under Available Files, go to the `c:\ejb\lab1\web` directory.
6. Select index.jsp and click Add.
7. Click OK and Next.
8. In the Choose Component Type dialog box, select the JSP radio button. Click Next.
9. In the Component General Properties dialog box, select index.jsp in the JSP FileName combo box.
10. Click Finish.

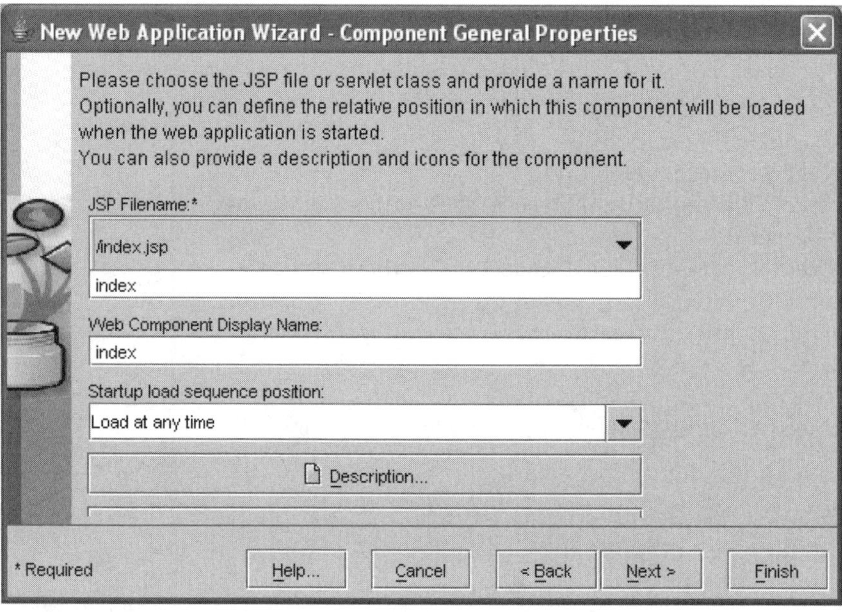

Specifying the Web Client's Enterprise Bean Reference:

1. In the tree, select DiscountCalcWar.

2. Select the EJB Refs tab.
3. Click Add.
4. In the Coded Name field, enter `ejb/SimpleDiscountCalc`.
5. Select Session in the Type field.
6. Select Remote in the Interfaces field.
7. Type `DiscountCalc.DiscountCalcHome` in the Home Interface field, and type `DiscountCalc.DiscountCalc` in the Local/Remote Interface field.
8. Select the JNDI Name radio button for the Target EJB, enter `MyDiscountCalc`, and click OK.

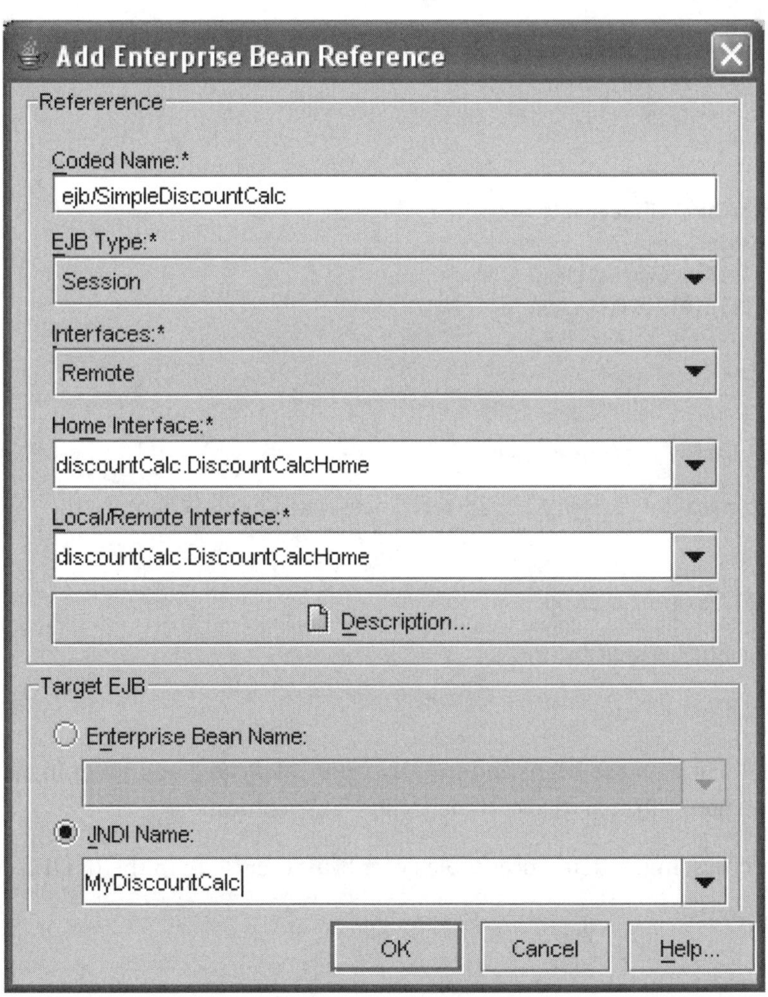

After the packaging process, you can view the following deployment descriptor by selecting Tools | Descriptor Viewer.

```
<?xml version='1.0' encoding='UTF-8'?>
<web-app
      version=" 2.4"
      xmlns=" http://java.sun.com/xml/ns/j2ee"
      xmlns:xsi=" http://www.w3.org/2001/XMLSchema-instance"
      xsi:schemaLocation=" http://java.sun.com/xml/ns/j2ee
_     http://java.sun.com/xml/ns/j2ee/web-app_2_4.xsd "
      >
   <display-name> DiscountCalcWar</display-name>
   <servlet>
      <display-name> index</display-name>
      <servlet-name> index</servlet-name>
      <jsp-file> /index.jsp</jsp-file>
   </servlet>
   <ejb-ref>
      <ejb-ref-name> ejb/SimpleDiscountCalc</ejb-ref-name>
      <ejb-ref-type> Session</ejb-ref-type>
      <home> discountCalc.DiscountCalcHome</home>
      <remote> discountCalc.DiscountCalcHome</remote>
   </ejb-ref>
</web-app>
```

Step 6: Specifying the JNDI Names and Context Root

Follow the steps below to map the enterprise bean references, used by the client, to the JNDI name of the bean.

1. In the tree, select DiscountCalcApp.
2. Click the Sun-Specific Settings button.
3. Choose JNDI Names for View.
4. To specify a JNDI name for the bean, find the DiscountCalcBean component in the Application table, and enter `MyDiscountCalc` in the JNDI Name column.
5. To map the references, in the References table enter `MyDiscountCalc` in the JNDI Name.

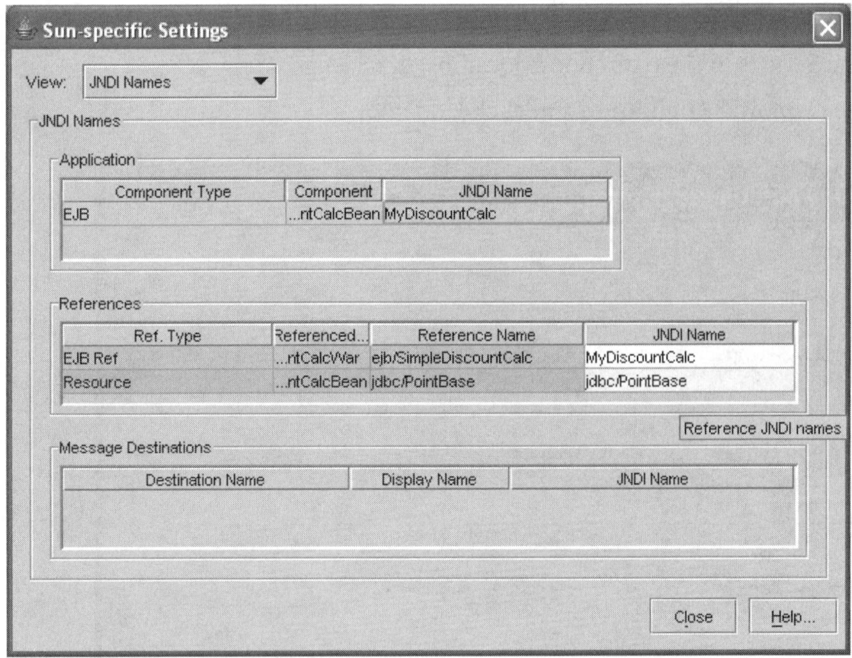

Specifying the Context Root

1. In the tree, select DiscountCalcWar.
2. Click the General tab, enter `discountCalc` in the Context Root field, so discountCalc becomes the context root in the URL.
3. Save the application file.

Step 7: Deploying the J2EE Application

At this time, the J2EE application contains all components; it is ready for deployment.

1. Select the DiscountCalcApp application.
2. Select Tools | Deploy.
3. Click OK.

Note: To undeploy an application, follow these:

1. Under the Servers in the tree, choose localhost:4848.
2. Select the Deployed Application and click Undeploy.

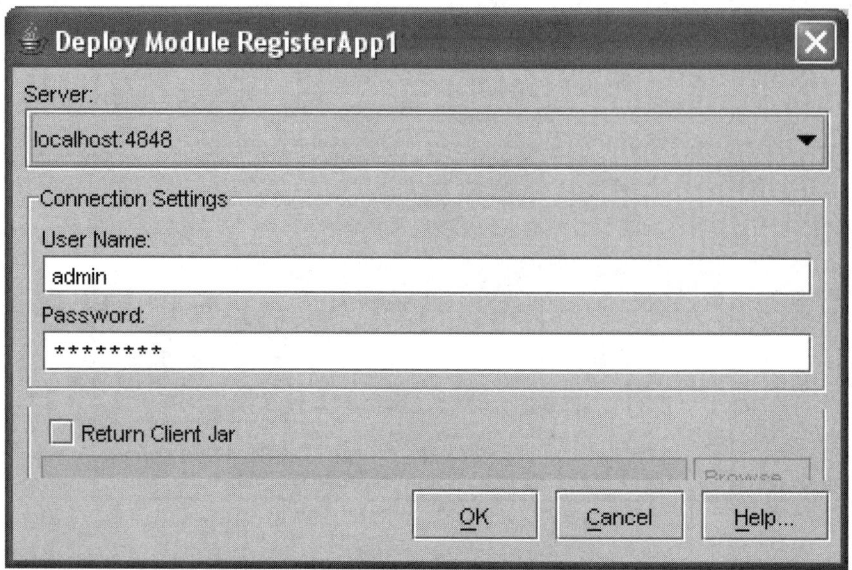

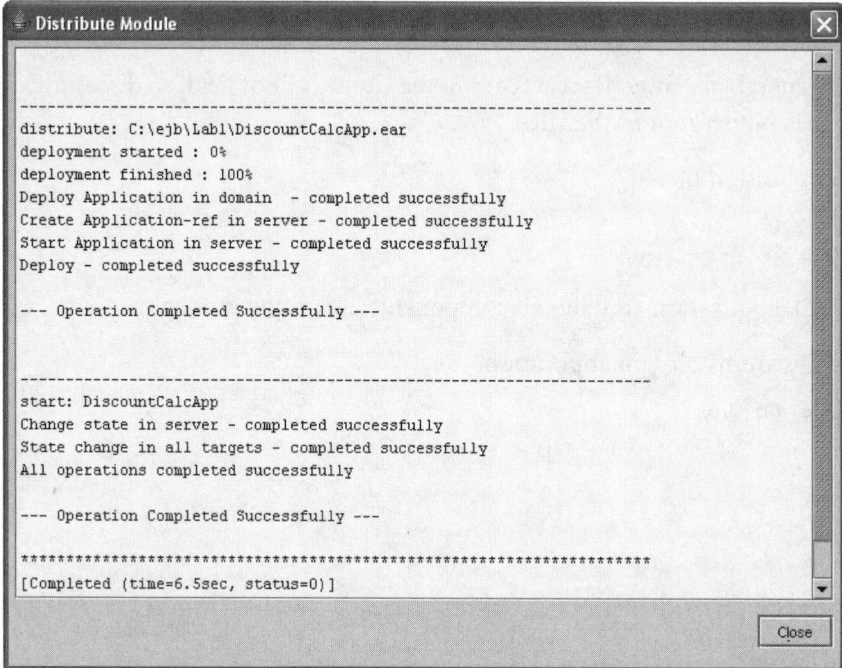

Step 8: Running the J2EE Web Client

To run the Web client, point your browser at the following URL:

```
http://localhost:8080/discountCalc
```

You can replace `localhost` with the name of the host running the J2EE server if your browser is running on a different machine. Selecting Student and clicking the Submit button will display the registration fees for students.

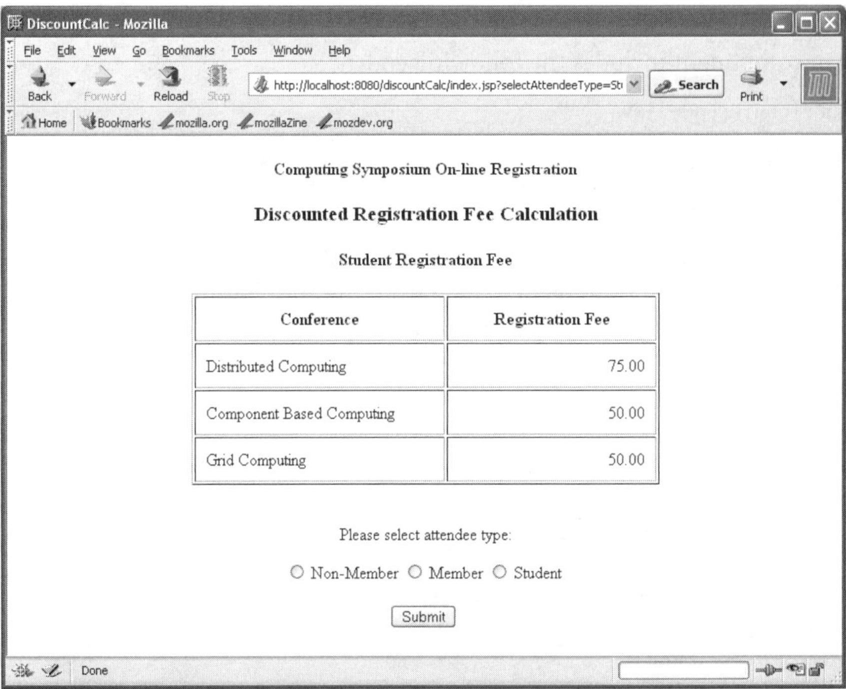

Lab 2: CMP Entity Bean Working with Session Bean for the Discount Calculation

The session bean in Lab 1 uses the JDBC connection to retrieve conference information from the back-end database directly. Lab 2 extends the application in Lab 1 and adds a new entity bean, `ConferenceBean`, to separate the data model from the front-end input processing. The session bean is revised to access the entity bean, and the entity bean is a container-managed persistence mapped to the database table, `Conference`. The EJB container handles data storage and retrieval on behalf of the entity bean. The purpose of this lab is to demonstrate how session beans work together with entity beans and how to divide the responsibilities between session beans and entity beans. In most distributed applications the persistent data are handled by entity beans instead of session beans. The process logic is shown in the following diagram.

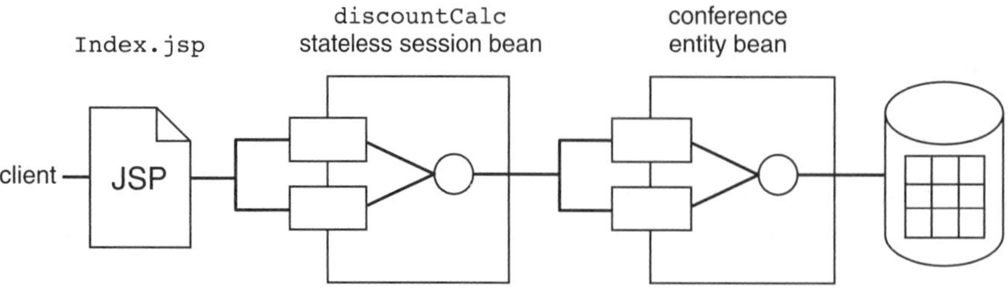

Step 1: Coding the Enterprise Bean

The Conference entity bean component includes the following code:

- Local interface: `LocalConference.java`
- Local Home interface: `LocalConferenceHome.java`
- Entity bean class: `ConferenceBean.java`

The local interface LocalConference defines three `get` access methods for the persistent fields in order for a Local client to invoke the methods to retrieve data from the entity bean. The Local interface must be converted to a Remote interface if the client of the bean is remote.

```
package Data;

import java.util.*;
import javax.ejb.*;

// Local interface of conference CMP entity bean

public interface LocalConference extends EJBLocalObject {
    public String getConferenceId();
    public String getConferenceName();
    public double getRegistrationFee();
}
```

The `LocalConferenceHome.java` defines the Home interface for the bean. The `create()` method in the conference entity bean Home interface takes three parameters: conference ID, conference name, and registration fee. When the session bean instantiates the Home interface and calls its `create()` method, the container creates a conference instance and calls the `ejbCreate()` method. The `conferenceHome.create()` and the `conferenceBean.ejbCreate()` methods must have the same signatures, so that the parameter values can be passed from the Home interface to the entity bean via the entity bean's container. The `findByPrimary()` method, which takes the primary key `conferenceId` as a parameter, is handled by the container. It must be specified in the entity bean Home interface to locate the `Conference` entity bean instance. The `findALL()` method is a customized finder method handled by the container, but a developer must define the `EJB-QL` query at deployment time.

```
package data;

import java.util.*;
import javax.ejb.*;

// Home interface of conference CMP entity bean

public interface LocalConferenceHome extends EJBLocalHome {

  public LocalConference create (String confid, String confname,
          double registfee) throws CreateException;

  public LocalConference findByPrimaryKey (String id)
        throws FinderException;

  public Collection findAll ()
        throws FinderException;
}
```

The `ConferenceBean.java` defines the entity bean implementation. The `ConferenceBean` is a container-managed entity bean. The EJB container handles data persistence and transaction management automatically. EJB developers do not need to write any code to transfer data between the entity bean and the database. The `ConferenceBean` class defines several `get` and `set` access methods for the persistent fields. The set methods are hidden from their bean's clients because they are not defined in the `LocalConference` interface. The EJB container implements all the `get` and `set` abstract methods.

```
import java.util.*;
import javax.ejb.*;
import javax.naming.*;

public abstract class ConferenceBean implements EntityBean {

    private EntityContext context;

// Access methods for persistent fields: conferenceId, conference name,
// registration fee

    public abstract String getConferenceId();
    public abstract void setConferenceId(String confid);

    public abstract String getConferenceName();
    public abstract void setConferenceName(String confname);

    public abstract double getRegistrationFee();
```

```
    public abstract void setRegistrationFee(double registfee);


 // EntityBean container callback methods

    public String ejbCreate (String confid, String confname, double
                             registfee)
        throws CreateException {
        setConferenceId(confid);
        setConferenceName(confname);
        setRegistrationFee(registfee);
        return null;
    }

    public void ejbPostCreate (String confid, String confname, double
                             registfee)
        throws CreateException { }

    public void setEntityContext(EntityContext ctx) {
        context = ctx;
    }

    public void unsetEntityContext() {
        context = null;
    }

    public void ejbRemove() {}
    public void ejbLoad() {}
    public void ejbStore() {}
    public void ejbPassivate() { }
    public void ejbActivate() { }

} // ConferenceBean class
```

Step 2: Modify Session Bean

All detailed code of the SQL database connection and processing is removed from the previous session bean in Lab 1 because the entity bean will provide the logic for accessing the database rather than the session bean itself. The Remote interface, Home interface, and helper class `ConfDetails` are still the same. The modified source code `DiscountCalc.Java` is shown below:

```
//DiscountCalcBean.java

package discountCalc;

import java.util.*;
```

```
import javax.ejb.*;
import javax.naming.*;
import java.rmi.RemoteException;
import java.math.*;
import data.*;

public class DiscountCalcBean implements SessionBean {

   private LocalConferenceHome conferenceHome = null;

   public void ejbCreate () {

      try {
         InitialContext ic = new InitialContext();
         conferenceHome = (LocalConferenceHome)
         ic.lookup("java:comp/env/ejb/SimpleConference");
          }
      catch (NamingException ex) {
           System.out.println("Naming Exceptions");
          }
    }

       public ArrayList getAllConferences() {
        Collection conferences = null;

        try {
            conferences = conferenceHome.findAll();
        } catch (Exception ex) {
            throw new EJBException(ex.getMessage());
        }
        return confDetailList(conferences);
    } // getAllconferences

    private ArrayList confDetailList(Collection conferences) {

        ArrayList detailsList = new ArrayList();
        Iterator i = conferences.iterator();

        while (i.hasNext()) {
            LocalConference conference = (LocalConference) i.next();
            ConfDetails details = new
            ConfDetails(conference.getConferenceId(),
       conference.getConferenceName(),conference.getRegistrationFee());
            detailsList.add(details);
        }
        return detailsList;
   } // confDetailList

     public double getDiscountedFee (double registFee, String attendeeType) {
```

```
      int discountRate = 0;
      if ( attendeeType.equals ("Member") )  discountRate = 20;
         else if ( attendeeType.equals ("Student") ) discountRate = 50;
         else discountRate = 0;
      return  (registFee * (1 - (double)discountRate/100 ));
   }

   public DiscountCalcBean() {}
   public void ejbActivate() {}
   public void ejbPassivate() {}
   public void ejbRemove() {}
   public void setSessionContext(SessionContext sc) {}

} // DiscountCalcBean
```

Step 3: Compiling the Source Files

To compile the source files, open a terminal window, go to `c:\ejb\lab2` directory, and type the following command:

```
> asant build
```

A new directory, `build`, with all the class files will be created under `c:\ejb\lab2`.

Step 4: Create the Database Schema File

To map an entity bean to a database table, a schema file needs to be created.

1. Start the `PointBase` database.
2. Open a terminal window, go to the `c:\ejb\lab2` directory, and type the following command:

   ```
   > asant capture-db-schema
   ```

A database schema file named `register.dbschema` will be created under the `c:\ejb\lab2\build` directory. The `capture-db-schema` is defined in the `targets.xml` file.

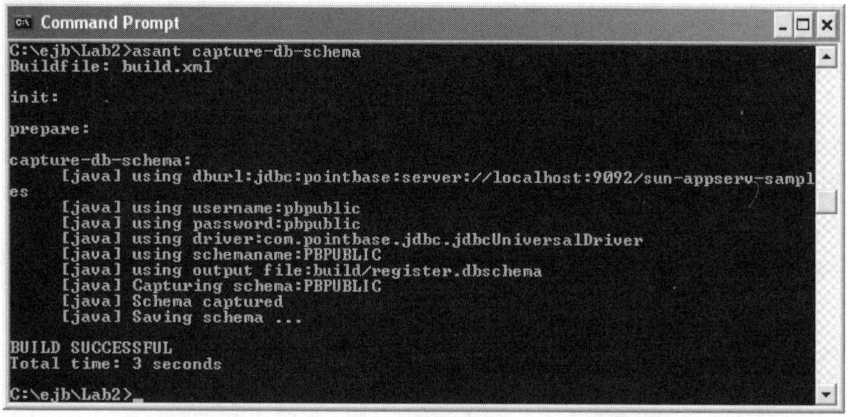

```
Command Prompt
C:\ejb\Lab2>asant capture-db-schema
Buildfile: build.xml

init:

prepare:

capture-db-schema:
     [java] using dburl:jdbc:pointbase:server://localhost:9092/sun-appserv-sampl
es
     [java] using username:pbpublic
     [java] using password:pbpublic
     [java] using driver:com.pointbase.jdbc.jdbcUniversalDriver
     [java] using schemaname:PBPUBLIC
     [java] using output file:build/register.dbschema
     [java] Capturing schema:PBPUBLIC
     [java] Schema captured
     [java] Saving schema ...

BUILD SUCCESSFUL
Total time: 3 seconds

C:\ejb\Lab2>_
```

Step 5: Deployment

1. Start the application server, `PointBase` database, and `deploytool`.
2. Create a new application named `DiscountCalcApp2.ear` under `c:\ejb\lab2`.
3. Create the ConferenceBean entity bean.
   a. Select File | New | Enterprise Bean to start the New Enterprise Bean Wizard.
   b. In the EJB JAR dialog box, select the Create New JAR File in the Application radio button. In the combo box, select DiscountCalcApp2.
   c. In the JAR Name field, enter `DataJar`.
   d. Click Edit Contents.
   e. In the tree under Available Files, locate the `c:\ejb\lab2\build` directory, select Contents under the data folder, and click Add.
   f. Select register.dbschema, click Add, then click OK.
   g. In the EJB JAR General Settings dialog box, select data.ConferenceBean for the Enterprise Bean Class combo box.
   h. Verify that the Enterprise Bean name field is ConferenceBean.
   i. Select the Entity for the Bean Type.
   j. In the Local Home Interface combo box, select data.LocalConferenceHome.
   k. In the Local Interface combo box, select data.LocalConference.
   l. Click Next.

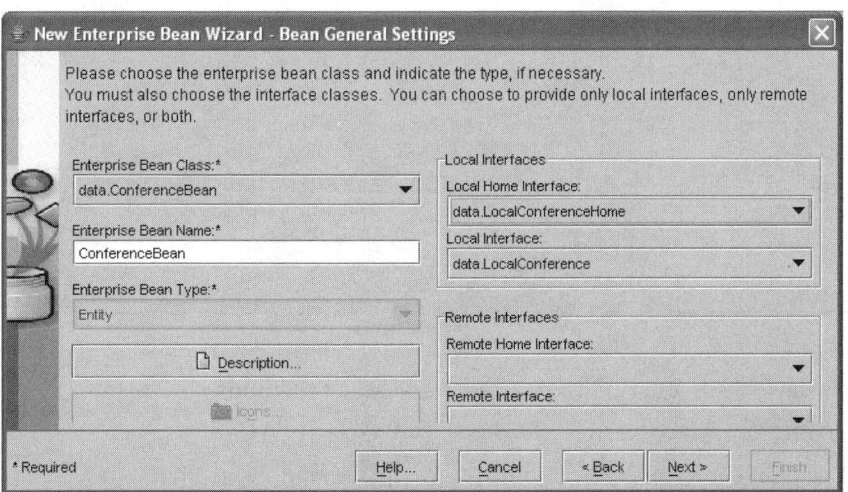

4. Select the Persistent Fields and Abstract SchemaName.

   a. In the Entity Bean Settings dialog box, select the fields that will be saved in the database. In the Fields To Be Persisted list, for the Conference entity bean, select conferenceId, conferenceName and registrationFee.

   b. Choose Select an existing field for the Primary Key Class.

   c. Select conferenceId from the combo box.

   d. In the Abstract Schema Name field, enter Conference. This name will be referenced in the EJB QL queries.

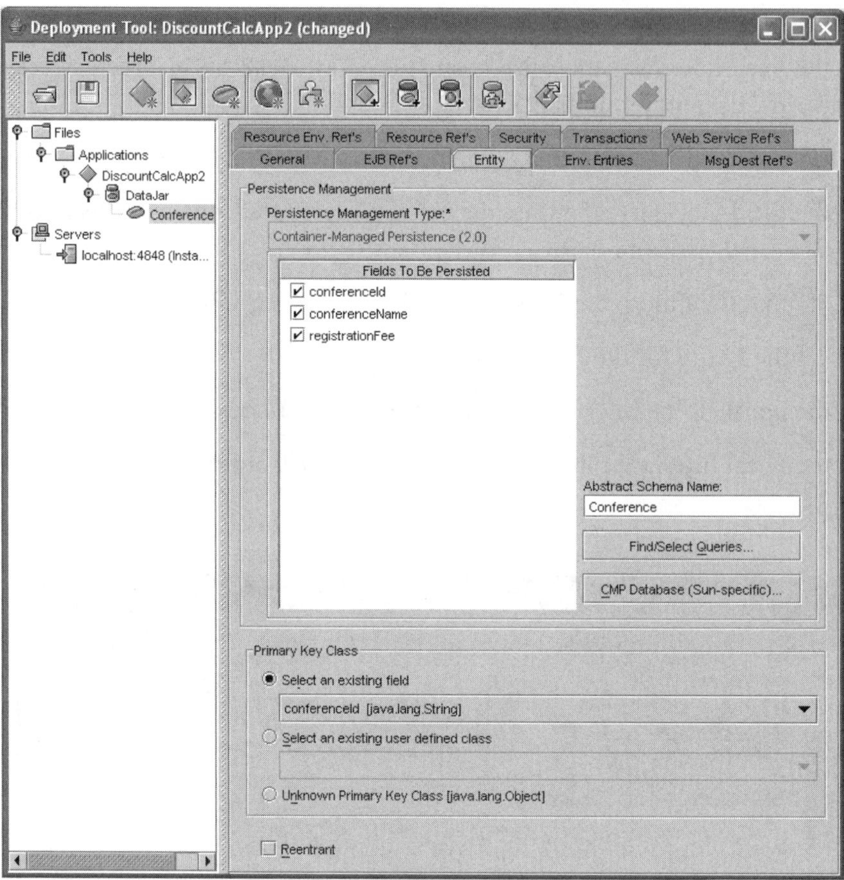

5. Define the EJB-QL queries for the finder and select methods.

a. Click the Finder/Select Queries button to open the Finder/Select Methods for ConferenceBean dialog box.

b. To display a set of finder or select methods, click one of the radio buttons under the Show label.

c. To specify an EJB-QL query, choose the name of the finder or select method from the Method list and then enter the query in the field labeled EJB QL Query. Select findAll and type the following EJB-QL Query for `findAll`:

```
select object(c) from Conference c
```

d. Click OK.

e. Click Next and Finish.

f. Save the application.

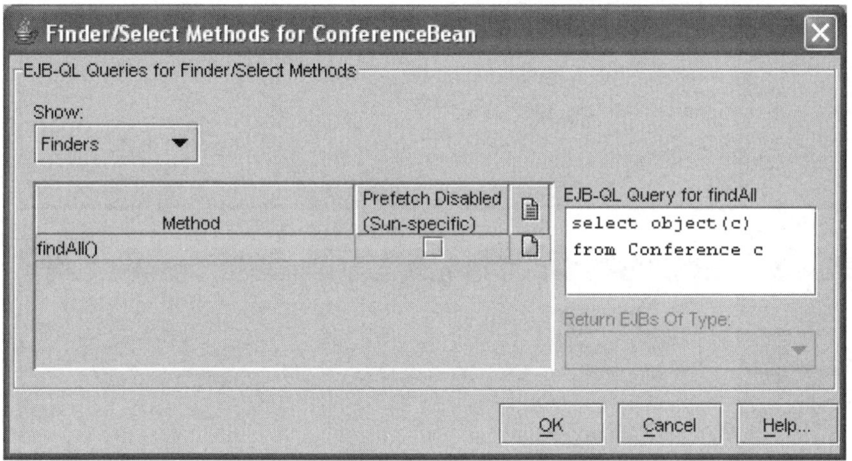

6. Specify the persistent field and database mappings.

   a. In the tree, select ConferenceBean and click the Entity tab.

   b. Click the CMP Database (Sun Specific).

   c. Enter `jdbc/PointBase` in the JNDI Name of the CMP Resource field.

   d. Select ConferenceBean for the Enterprise Bean.

   e. Click Create Database Mapping.

f. Select the Map to Tables in Database Schema File.
g. Choose register.dbschema for the Database Schema Files in Module.
h. Click OK.
i. Verify the field mappings and then click Close.

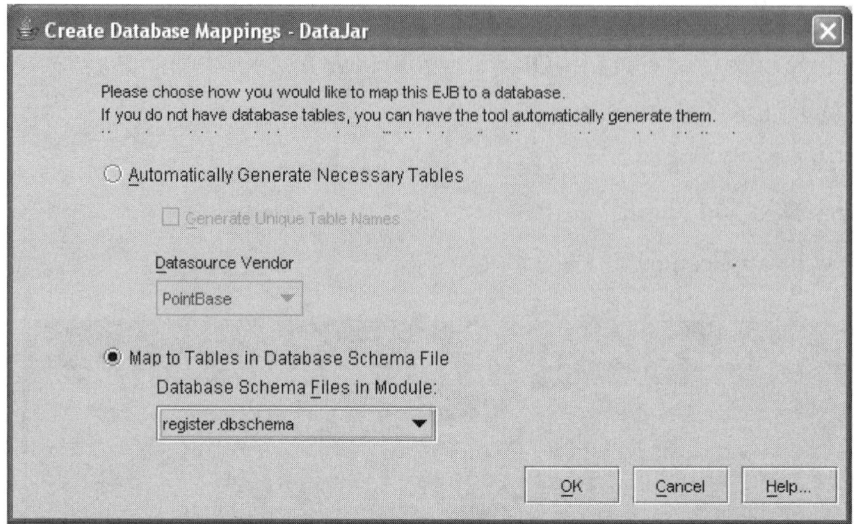

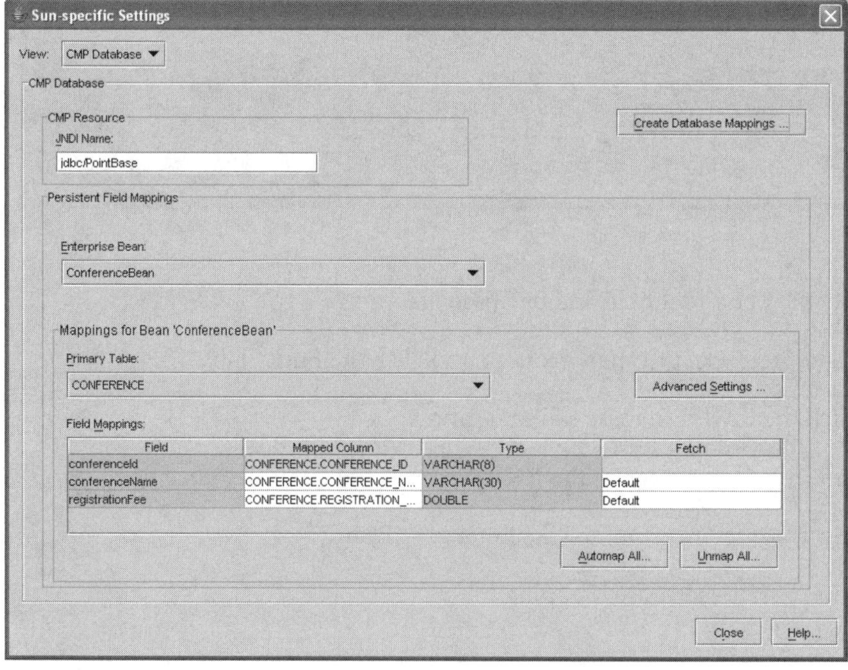

7. Specify Transaction Settings.
   a. Select ConferenceBean in the tree.
   b. Click the Transactions tab.
   c. Select Container-Managed.
   d. Verify the methods and their attributes for Local, LocalHome, and Bean.

   After the packaging process, you can view the deployment descriptor by selecting Tools | Descriptor Viewer.

```
<?xml version='1.0' encoding='UTF-8'?>
<ejb-jar
      version=" 2.1"
      xmlns=" http://java.sun.com/xml/ns/j2ee"
      xmlns:xsi=" http://www.w3.org/2001/XMLSchema-instance"
      xsi:schemaLocation=" http://java.sun.com/xml/ns/j2ee
                  http://java.sun.com/xml/ns/j2ee/ejb-jar_2_1.xsd ">
   <display-name> DataJar</display-name>
   <enterprise-beans>
      <entity>
         <display-name> ConferenceBean</display-name>
         <ejb-name> ConferenceBean</ejb-name>
         <local-home> data.LocalConferenceHome</local-home>
         <local> data.LocalConference</local>
         <ejb-class> data.ConferenceBean</ejb-class>
         <persistence-type> Container</persistence-type>
         <prim-key-class> java.lang.String</prim-key-class>
         <reentrant> false</reentrant>
         <cmp-version> 2.x</cmp-version>
         <abstract-schema-name> Conference</abstract-schema-name>
         <cmp-field>
            <description> no description</description>
            <field-name> registrationFee</field-name>
         </cmp-field>
         <cmp-field>
            <description> no description</description>
            <field-name> conferenceName</field-name>
         </cmp-field>
         <cmp-field>
            <description> no description</description>
            <field-name> conferenceId</field-name>
         </cmp-field>
         <primkey-field> conferenceId</primkey-field>
         <security-identity>
```

```
            <use-caller-identity>
            </use-caller-identity>
         </security-identity>
         <query>
            <query-method>
               <method-name> findAll</method-name>
               <method-params>
               </method-params>
            </query-method>
            <ejb-ql> select object (c)<BR>
                          from Conference c</ejb-ql>
         </query>
      </entity>
   </enterprise-beans>
   <assembly-descriptor>
      <container-transaction>
         <method>
            <ejb-name> ConferenceBean</ejb-name>
            <method-intf> Local</method-intf>
            <method-name> getConferenceId</method-name>
         </method>
         <trans-attribute> Required</trans-attribute>
      </container-transaction>
      <container-transaction>
         <method>
            <ejb-name> ConferenceBean</ejb-name>
            <method-intf> Local</method-intf>
            <method-name> getConferenceName</method-name>
         </method>
         <trans-attribute> Required</trans-attribute>
      </container-transaction>
      <container-transaction>
         <method>
            <ejb-name> ConferenceBean</ejb-name>
            <method-intf> Local</method-intf>
            <method-name> remove</method-name>
         </method>
         <trans-attribute> Required</trans-attribute>
      </container-transaction>
      <container-transaction>
         <method>
            <ejb-name> ConferenceBean</ejb-name>
```

```
            <method-intf> Local</method-intf>
            <method-name> getRegistrationFee</method-name>
         </method>
         <trans-attribute> Required</trans-attribute>
      </container-transaction>
   </assembly-descriptor>
</ejb-jar>
```

8. Package the Session Bean: *DiscountCalcBean*.

   In this application the data transaction is handled by the container. The session bean accesses the database via the entity beans so that the Resource Refs is not required. Follow the steps in Lab 1 to package the session bean with the settings below.

Session Bean Settings

Setting	Value
JAR Name	DiscountCalcJar
Contents	DiscountCalc.class, DiscountCalcHome.class, DiscountCalcBean.class, ConfDetails.class
Enterprise Bean Class	discountCalc.DiscountCalcBean
Enterprise Bean Name	DiscountCalcBean
Bean Type	Stateless
Remote Home Interface	discountCalc.DiscountCalcHome
Remote Interface	discountCalc.DiscountCalc

9. Specify the Session Bean Reference.

   The `DiscountCalcBean` session bean accesses the `ConferenceBean` entity bean. When it invokes the lookup method, the `DiscountCalcBean` refers to the Home of the entity beans:

```
conferenceHome = (LocalConferenceHome.ic.lookup
("java:comp/env/ejb/SimpleConference");
```

   a. In the tree, select `DiscountCalcBean`.

   b. Select the EJB Refs tab and click Add. The settings are as on the next page.

Setting	Value
Coded Name	ejb/SimpleConference
Type	Entity
Interface	Local
Home Interface	data.LocalConferenceHome
Local/Remote Interface	data.LocalConference
Target EJB/Enterprise Bean Name	ejb-jar-ic.jar#ConferenceBean

10. Specify Transaction Settings.
    a. Select DiscountCalcBean in the tree.
    b. Click the Transactions tab.
    c. Select Container-Managed.
    d. Verify methods and their attributes for Remote, RemoteHome, and Bean.
11. Implement the Web component.

    The `index.jsp` file in Lab 1 will be used for this lab. Follow the steps in Lab 1 to package the Web component and specify the JNDI name and context root.
12. Deployment:
    a. Save the application.
    b. Select Tools | Deploy and click OK.

Step 6: Running the Application

You can follow the instruction in step 4 of Lab 1 to run the `DiscountCalcApp` application. The result is exactly the same as in Lab 1.

Lab 3: A J2EE Application with Stateful Session Beans and CMP Entity Beans

Based on Lab 2, Lab 3 implements an online symposium registration application, `RegisterApp`, which consists of a front session bean and two CMPs supported by database tables. It can allow a new attendee to register one or more specific conferences online. The application calculates the discount registration fee according to the attendee's category and reports the conference registration confirmation with total fees for the attendee after a successful registration.

This `RegisterApp` application has four components. The `RegisterWar` component is a J2EE Web application client that accesses the `RegisterBean` session bean through the bean's Remote interface. The `RegisterBean` talks to two entity beans—`AttendeeBean` and `ConferenceBean`—through their Local interfaces because all beans are locally deployed at the same server. The entity beans provide the logic for accessing the database by using container-managed persistence and relationship. The `AttendeeBean` and `ConferenceBean` entity beans have a many-to-many relationship. One conference may have many participants and one participant may join more than one conference. Each CMP bean has a relationship field whose value identifies the related bean instance. The diagram below shows the components and their relationships of the `RegisterApp` application.

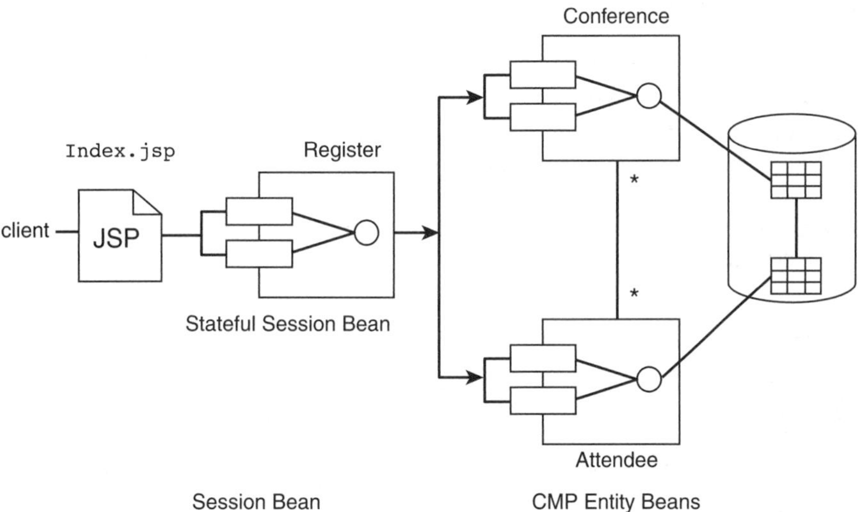

Step 1: Develop EJB Beans

1. Modify the conference entity bean.

   The coding for the conference entity bean component in this lab is similar to the coding in Lab 2. In the `RegisterApp` application, however, a conference has many attendees, so a conference bean instance may be related to many attendee instances. To specify this relationship, the deployment descriptor of `ConferenceBean` defines a relationship field named `Attendees` and a collection that represents the `attendees` of the conference. The ConferenceBean.java needs to be modified to add two abstract access methods for the relationship field.

The code of the access methods for the *attendees* relationship field is as follows.

```
Public abstract Collection getAttendees();
Public abstract void setAttendees (Collection attendees);
```

2. Code the attendee entity bean.

   The attendee entity bean component has the following files:

   a. Local interface: LocalAttendee.java

   b. Local Home interface: LocalAttendeeHome.java

   c. Entity bean class: AttendeeBean.java

   In the attendee entity bean, there are two business methods, addConference() and removeConference(), which invoke the getConference() access method to fetch the collection of the related LocalConference object, and then invoke the add (or remove) method of the collection interface to add (or remove) the member from the collection.

```
//LocalAttendee.java is a Local interface for attendee CMP
//entity bean. It can be a remote interface if its client is remote.

package data;

import java.util.*;
import javax.ejb.*;

public interface LocalAttendee extends EJBLocalObject {

    public String getSsn();
    public String getName();
    public String getAttendeeType();
    public Collection getConferences();

    public void addConference(LocalConference conference);
    public void removeConference(LocalConference conference);
}
// LocalAttendeeHome.java is a Home interface of attendee
//CMP entity bean. It can be defined as a remote Home interface if it
//is accessed by a remote client

package data;

import java.util.*;
```

```
import javax.ejb.*;

public interface LocalAttendeeHome extends EJBLocalHome {

    public LocalAttendee create (String ssn, String name,
                                 String attendeetype)
        throws CreateException;

    public LocalAttendee findByPrimaryKey (String ssn)
        throws FinderException;
}

// AttendeeBean.java CMP entity bean class implementation

package data;

import java.util.*;
import javax.ejb.*;
import javax.naming.*;

public abstract class AttendeeBean implements EntityBean {

    private EntityContext context;

// Access methods for persistent fields, implicit definition of class
// members

    public abstract String getSsn();
    public abstract void setSsn(String ssn);

    public abstract String getName();
    public abstract void setName(String firstname);

    public abstract String getAttendeeType();
    public abstract void setAttendeeType (String attendeeType);

// Access methods for relationship fields, many-to-many
// connection from Attendee to Conference entity bean

    public abstract Collection getConferences();
    public abstract void setConferences(Collection conferences);

// Select methods, Business methods, EntityBean  methods

   public void addConference(LocalConference conference) {
        try {
            Collection conferences = getConferences();
            conferences.add(conference);
```

```
        } catch (Exception ex) {
            throw new EJBException(ex.getMessage());
        }
    }

    public void removeConference(LocalConference conference) {
        try {
            Collection conferences = getConferences();
            conferences.remove(conference);
        } catch (Exception ex) {
            throw new EJBException(ex.getMessage());
        }
    }
    public String ejbCreate (String ssn, String name,
                             String attendeetype )
       throws CreateException {
        setSsn(ssn);
        setName(name);
        setAttendeeType(attendeetype);
        return null;
    }

    public void ejbPostCreate (String ssn, String name,
                             String attendeeType )
        throws CreateException { }

    public void setEntityContext(EntityContext ctx) {
        context = ctx;
    }

    public void unsetEntityContext() {
        context = null;
    }

    public void ejbRemove() {}
    public void ejbLoad() {}
    public void ejbStore() {}
    public void ejbPassivate() { }
    public void ejbActivate() { }

} // AttendeeBean class
```

3. The `Register` entity bean component includes the following files:
    a. Remote interface: `Register.java`
    b. Remote Home interface: `RegisterHome.java`
    c. Entity bean class: `Register.java`

d. Helper class: `ConferenceDetails.java` (same as in Lab 2)

The `Register` session bean is a revised version of the `DiscountCalc` session bean in Lab 2. In the `RegisterApp` application the `register` bean is a stateful session bean, which can access two entity beans and, in turn, access the database. Four new business methods are added to the session bean. The `createAttendee()` invokes `attendeeHome.create()` to create a `LocalAttendee` instance. The `addRegistraion()` and `cancelRegistration()` methods locate the `AttendeeBean` and `ConferenceBean` instances by calling `findByPrimaryKey()`, then invoke the `addConference()` (or `removeConference()`) methods on the instance to update the relationship between the conference and the attendee. Database manipulations are automatically implemented by the container. The `getConfOfAttendee()` method returns the `ArrayList` of `ConfDetails` object for an attendee.

```
//Register.java is a Remote interface of Register session bean

package register;

import java.util.*;
import javax.ejb.EJBObject;
import java.rmi.RemoteException;

public interface Register extends EJBObject {

public void createAttendee(String ssn, String name, String
                           attendeeType)
        throws RemoteException;

    public ConfDetails getConfDetail( String confId)
        throws RemoteException;

    public void addRegistration(String ssn, String conferenceId)
        throws RemoteException;
    public void cancelRegistration(String ssn, String conferenceId)
        throws RemoteException;

    public ArrayList getConfsOfAttendee(String ssn)
        throws RemoteException;
    public ArrayList getAllConferences()
        throws RemoteException;

public double getDiscountedFee (double registFee, String
                                attendeeType)
        throws RemoteException;
  }
```

```
// register

//RegisterHome.java is a Remote Home interface of Register
//session bean

package register;
import java.rmi.RemoteException;
import javax.ejb.*;

public interface RegisterHome extends EJBHome {

    Register create() throws RemoteException, CreateException;
}
//RegisterBean.java

package register;

import java.util.*;
import javax.ejb.*;
import javax.naming.*;
import java.rmi.RemoteException;
import data.*;

public class RegisterBean implements SessionBean {

    private  LocalAttendeeHome attendeeHome = null;
    private  LocalConferenceHome conferenceHome = null;

// attendee business methods

        public void createAttendee(String ssn, String name, String
                                   attendeeType) {
        try {
LocalAttendee attendee = attendeeHome.create(ssn, name,
                                            attendeeType);
            } catch (Exception ex) {
            throw new EJBException(ex.getMessage());
            }
    }

public ConfDetails getConfDetail( String confId)
            throws RemoteException  {
        ConfDetails confDetail;
        LocalConference conference = null;
        try {
```

```
          conference = conferenceHome.findByPrimaryKey(confId);
          confDetail = new ConfDetails(confId,
conference.getConferenceName(), conference.getRegistrationFee());
             } catch ( Exception ex) {
                     throw new EJBException (ex.getMessage());
             }
        return confDetail;
    }

// register for a conference
    public void addRegistration(String ssn, String conferenceId) {
         try {
LocalConference conference =
conferenceHome.findByPrimaryKey(conferenceId);
            LocalAttendee attendee =
                         attendeeHome.findByPrimaryKey(ssn);
            attendee.addConference(conference);

        } catch (Exception ex) {
            throw new EJBException(ex.getMessage());
        }
    }

 // cancel a conference registration

    public void cancelRegistration(String ssn, String conferenceId) {
        try {
            LocalAttendee attendee =
                         attendeeHome.findByPrimaryKey(ssn);
LocalConference conference =
conferenceHome.findByPrimaryKey(conferenceId);
            attendee.removeConference(conference);
        } catch (Exception ex) {
            throw new EJBException(ex.getMessage());
        }
    }

// get registed conference list for an attendee
    public ArrayList getConfsOfAttendee(String ssn) {
        Collection conferences = null;
        try {
LocalAttendee attendee =
attendeeHome.findByPrimaryKey(ssn);
            conferences = attendee.getConferences();
```

```
        } catch (Exception ex) {
            throw new EJBException(ex.getMessage());
        }
        return confDetailList(conferences);
    } // getconfsOfAttendee

     public ArrayList getAllConferences() {
        Collection conferences = null;
        try {
            conferences = conferenceHome.findAll();
        } catch (Exception ex) {
            throw new EJBException(ex.getMessage());
        }
        return confDetailList(conferences);
    } // getAllconferences

        private ArrayList confDetailList(Collection conferences) {

        ArrayList detailsList = new ArrayList();
        Iterator i = conferences.iterator();
        while (i.hasNext()) {
            LocalConference conference = (LocalConference) i.next();
            ConfDetails details = new
                ConfDetails(conference.getConferenceId(),
     conference.getConferenceName(),conference.getRegistrationFee());
            detailsList.add(details);
        }
        return detailsList;
    } // confDetailList

    public double getDiscountedFee (double registFee, String
                                    attendeeType) {
       int discountRate = 0;
       if ( attendeeType.equals ("Member") )  discountRate = 20;
          else if ( attendeeType.equals ("Student") ) discountRate = 50;
               else discountRate = 0;
       return  (registFee * (1 - (double)discountRate/100 ));
    }
    public void ejbCreate() throws CreateException {
         try {
             attendeeHome = lookupAttendee();
             conferenceHome = lookupConference();
             } catch (NamingException ex) {
               throw new CreateException(ex.getMessage());
               }
        }
```

```
    public void ejbActivate() {
       try {
            attendeeHome = lookupAttendee();
            conferenceHome = lookupConference();
           } catch (NamingException ex) {
            throw new EJBException(ex.getMessage());
         }
    }

    public void ejbPassivate() {

        attendeeHome = null;
        conferenceHome = null;
     }

    public RegisterBean() {}
    public void ejbRemove() {}
    public void setSessionContext(SessionContext sc) {}

  // Private methods

    private LocalAttendeeHome lookupAttendee() throws NamingException {
        Context initial = new InitialContext();
        Object objref =
               initial.lookup("java:comp/env/ejb/SimpleAttendee");
        return (LocalAttendeeHome) objref;
    }

private LocalConferenceHome lookupConference()
                            throws NamingException {
        Context initial = new InitialContext();
        Object objref =
               initial.lookup("java:comp/env/ejb/SimpleConference");
        return (LocalConferenceHome) objref;
    }
} // RegisterBean
```

Step 2: Compile the Source Files and Generate the Database Schema File

1. To compile the source files, go to `c:\ejb\lab3` directory and run the `asant build` command; 10 source files will be compiled.
2. Start up the database.
3. Type `asant capture-db-schema` to create the database schema file.

Step 3: Packaging Entity Beans

1. Start up the application server, `deploytool`, and the database.
2. Create a new application, `RegisterApp.ear`, under the `c:\ejb\lab3` directory.
3. Follow the steps in Lab 2 to package the entity bean `ConferenceBean` in the JAR file named `DataJar`.
4. Add the `AttendeeBean` entity bean to the existing JAR file.
   a. Select File | New | Enterprise Bean to start the New Enterprise Bean Wizard.
   b. In the EJB JAR dialog box, select Add to Existing JAR File.
   c. In the Existing JAR File, select DataJar and click Next.
   d. Follow the steps of creating the entity bean of the `ConferenceBean` to complete the AttendeeBean creation with the following settings.

EJB JAR General Settings	
Setting	**Value**
Contents	LocalAttendee.class, LocalAttendeeHome.class, AttendeeBean.class
Enterprise Bean Class	Data.AttendeeBean
Enterprise Bean Name	AttendeeBean
Enterprise Bean Type	Entity
Local Home Interface	Data.LocalAttendeeHome
Local Interface	Data.LocalAttendee

Entity Bean Settings	
Setting	**Value**
Fields To Be Persisted	Name, ssn, attendeeType
Primary Key Class	Select an existing field - ssn
Abstract Schema Name	Attendee
Transactions	Container-managed

5. Define entity relationships.

   After you create `ConferenceBean` and `AttendeeBean`, you can define the relationships that reside in the same EJB JAR file.

a. Select DataJAR in the tree view and then select the Relationships tab.

b. Click the Add button to open (or Edit to modify) the Add Relationship dialog box.

c. Select Many to Many in the combo box.

d. In the Enterprise Bean A area, select ConferenceBean for the Enterprise Bean Name, attendees for the Field Referencing Bean B, and java.util.Collection for the Field Type.

e. In the Enterprise Bean B area, select AttendeeBean for the Enterprise Bean Name, conferences for the Field Referencing Bean A, and java.util.Collection for the Field Type.

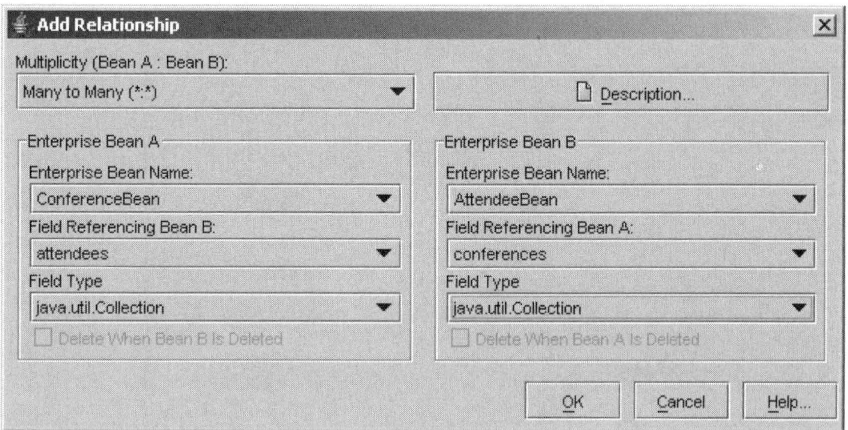

6. Specify the database mapping.

   a. Select DataJar from the tree in `deploytool`.

   b. Select the General tab.

   c. Click the Sun-Specific Settings button.

   d. In the JNDI Name field, enter `jdbc/PointBase`.

   e. Click the Create DataBase Mappings button.

   f. Select Map to Tables in the Database Schema File.

   g. Choose register.dbschema for the Database Schema Files in the Module.

   h. Click OK to go to the Sun-Specific Settings dialog box.

   i. Under Persistent File Mapping, select AttendeeBean for Enterprise Bean and Attendee for Primary table. Verify field mappings for ssn, name, and attendeeType; locate the row of conferences; select <map relationship field> in the Mapped Column; and go to the Map Relationship Field dialog box.

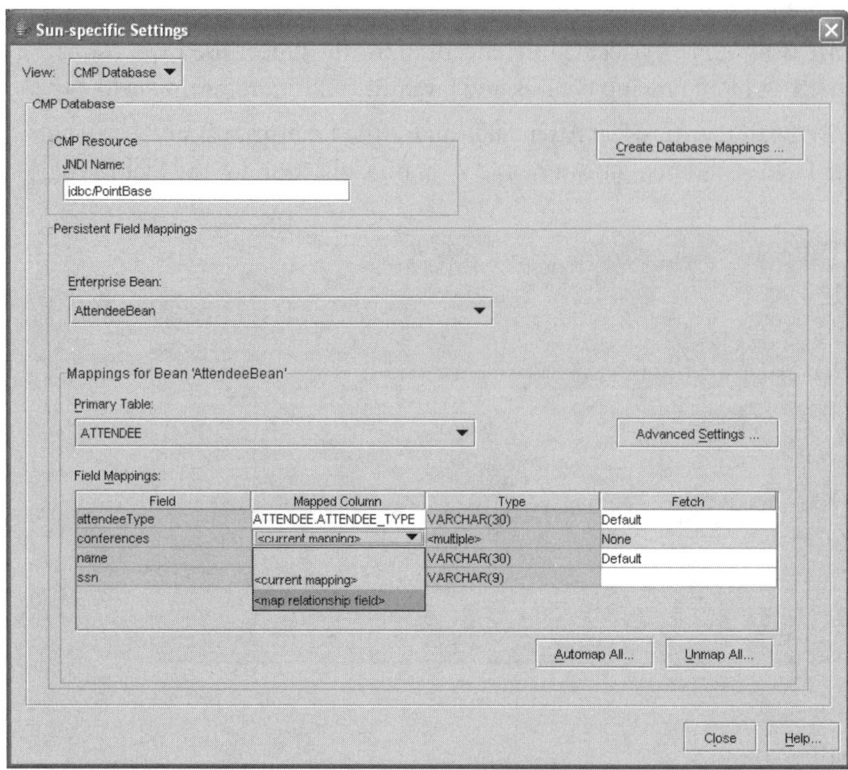

j. On the Initial Setup [1 of 3] page, verify the following settings.

Setting	Value
This Bean	AttendeeBean
This Field	conferences
Primary Table	ATTENDEE
Related Bean	ConferenceBean
Related Field	attendees
Primary Table	CONFERENCE

k. Select the Link Mapped Tables Using a Join Table radio button, and then click Next.

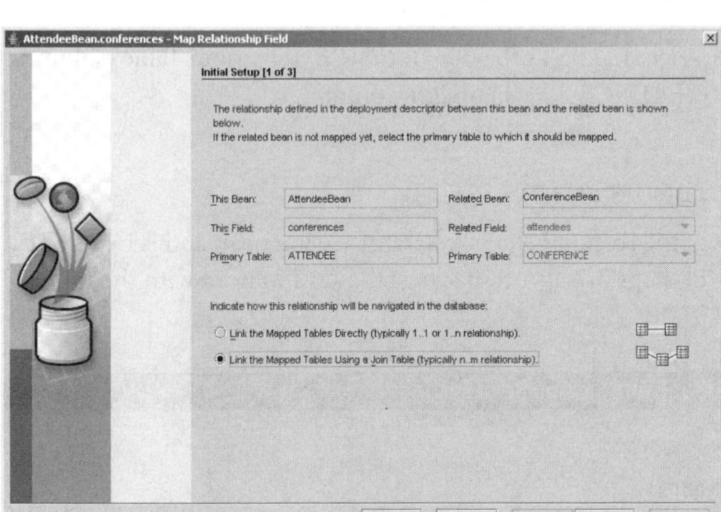

l. On the Map to key: Local to Join [2 of 3] page, verify that This Bean is Attendee and This Field is conferences, and then select REGISTER as Join Table.

m. Under Key Column Pairs, select ATTENDEE.SSN for Local Column, and REGISTER.SSN for the Join Table Column.

n. Click Next.

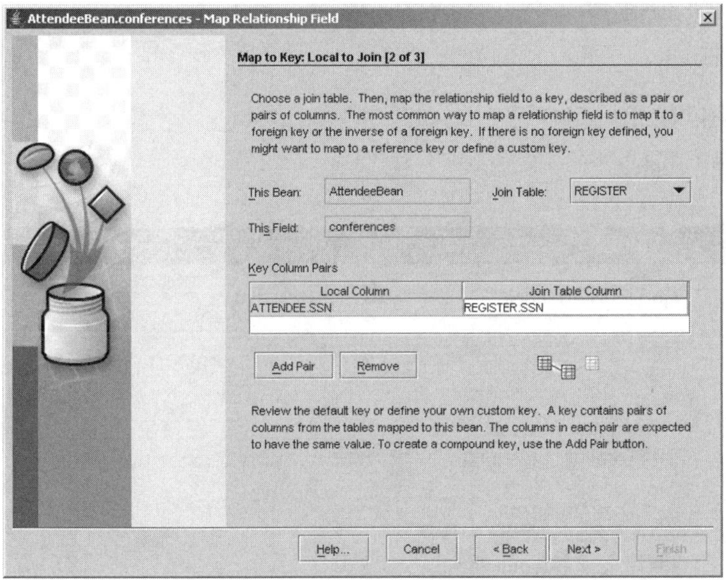

o. On the Map to Key: Join to Foreign [3 of 3] page, verify that Join Table is REGISTER, Related Bean is Conference Bean, and Related Field is attendees.

p. Under Key Column Pairs, select REGISTER.CONFERENCE_ID as Join Table Column and CONFERENCE.CONFERENCE_ID as Foreign Column.

q. Click Finish.

7. Package the Session Bean: RegisterBean.

In the `RegisterApp` application, the session bean is a stateful session bean and is handled by container-managed. Follow the steps in Lab 1 to package the session bean with the following settings.

EJB JAR and Session Bean Settings	
Setting	**Value**
JAR Name	RegisterJar
Contents	Register.class, RegisterHome.class, RegisterBean.class, ConfDetails.class
Enterprise Bean Class	register.RegisterBean
Enterprise Bean Name	RegisterBean
Bean Type	Stateful
Remote Home Interface	register.RegisterHome
Remote Interface	register.Register

8. Specify the Session Bean Reference.

a. In the tree, select RegisterBean.

b. Select the EJB Refs tab and click Add.

Setting	Value
Coded Name	ejb/SimpleAttendee
Type	Entity
Interface	Local
Home Interface	data.LocalAttendeeHome
Local/Remote Interface	data.LocalAttendee
Target EJB/Enterprise Bean Name	ejb-jar-ic.jar#AttendeeBean

c. Add another line for conferenceBean.

9. Specify the Transaction Settings.

   a. Select RegisterBean in the tree.

   b. Click the Transactions tab.

   c. Select Container-Managed.

Step 4: Implement the Web Client

The Web component includes an html file `index.html` and a JSP file `register.jsp`. The `index.html` is a simple html page, which enables users to enter their social security number, name, attendee type, and select the conference they are interested in. When the user submits the form, the page `index.jsp` passes the request to `register.jsp`.

```
<-- index.jsp  -->
<html><center>
<head>
<title>Register</title>
<h4>Computing Symposium On-line Registration</h4>
</head>
<body>
  <form method="get" action="register.jsp">
    <P>Please Enter your SSN, Name and Attendee Type: </P>
  <table width="320">
    <tr><td>SSN:</td>
<td><input type="TEXT" name="ssn"></input></td></tr>
    <tr><td>Name: </td>
<td><input type="TEXT" name="name"></input></td></tr>
    <tr><td> Attendee Type: </td>
<td> <input type="radio" name="attendeeType" value="Non-Member" checked>
             </input> Non-Member</td></tr>
    <tr><td></td>
<td> <input type="radio" name="attendeeType" value="Member">
             </input> Member </td></tr>
    <tr><td></td>
<td><input type="radio" name="attendeeType" value="Student">
            </input> Student </td></tr>
  </table>
  <p> Please select the conference you are interested in, <br>
       and then click Submit to register for the conference. </p>
  <select name="confId" size="1" >
    <option value="001">Distributed Computing</option>
    <option value="002">Component Based Computing</option>
```

```
    <option value="003">Grid Computing</option>
  </select>
  <br><br>
  <input type="submit" name="newAttendee" value="Submit">
  <input type="reset" name="Reset" value="Reset">
</form>
</body>
</center></html>
```

The `register.jsp` uses the method `jspInit()` to look up the session bean Home interface and create its instance. When the `register.jsp` receives a request from `index.html` the Register Web client invokes the `createAttendee()` business method of the `RegisterBean` session bean to create a new attendee. The `register.jsp` page also accepts an input for conference. When the user selects a conference and clicks the Add button, the Web client invokes the `addRegistraion()` method to add a relationship, and the table `register` will be updated. After the database is manipulated the method `getConfsOfAttendee()` returns the registered conference list for the user.

```
<%-- register.jsp    --%>

<%-- page settings --%>
<%@page import="javax.naming.*" %>
<%@page import="javax.rmi.PortableRemoteObject"%>
<%@page import="java.rmi.RemoteException"%>
<%@page import="javax.ejb.*"%>
<%@page import="java.util.*"%>
<%@page import="java.text.DecimalFormat"%>
<%@page import="register.*"%>

<%!
   private Register theRegister = null;
   String ssn = "";
   String name = "";
   String attendeeType = "";
   String confId = null;
   String confName = null;
   ConfDetails confDetail;
   double registFee = 0.00;
   double totalFee = 0.00;
   DecimalFormat twoDigits = new DecimalFormat ("0.00");
   ArrayList confsOfAttendeeList = null;

   public void jspInit() {
      try {
         InitialContext ic = new InitialContext();
```

```
         Object objRef = ic.lookup("java:comp/env/ejb/SimpleRegister");
         RegisterHome home = (RegisterHome)PortableRemoteObject.narrow(objRef,
RegisterHome.class);
         theRegister = home.create();
      } catch (Exception ex) {
            System.out.println(ex.getMessage());
      }
   }

   public void jspDestroy() {
         theRegister = null;
   }
%>
<%  ssn = request.getParameter("ssn");
    name = request.getParameter("name");
    attendeeType = request.getParameter("attendeeType");
    confId = request.getParameter("confId");

   if (ssn.equals ("") || name.equals ("")) {
%>
    <jsp:forward page = "index.html" />
<% } else {
%>
<html><center>
<head>
    <title>Register</title>
    <h4>Computing Symposium On-line Registration </h4>
</head>
<body>
<% if ( request.getParameter("newAttendee") != null) {
       try { theRegister.createAttendee(ssn, name, attendeeType);
       } catch (Exception ex) {
           System.out.println(ex.getMessage());
       }
%>
       <P> <%= name %> , Welcome to Computing Symposium</P>
<% }

   if (confId != null && ssn != null) {
        try {
         if (request.getParameter("Add")!= null ||
             request.getParameter("newAttendee")!= null  )
            theRegister.addRegistration(ssn, confId);
```

```
          if (request.getParameter("Remove")!= null)
             theRegister.cancelRegistration (ssn, confId);
        } catch (Exception ex) {
             System.out.println(ex.getMessage());
        }
    }
    try {ArrayList confsOfAttendeeList =
           theRegister.getConfsOfAttendee(ssn); %>
         <p> You have registered the following conferences </p>
         <table>
         <tr><th width="160">Conference</th>
             <th width="130">Registration Fee</th>
         </tr>
 <%
         Iterator i = confsOfAttendeeList.iterator();
         totalFee = 0.00;
         while (i.hasNext()) {
         confDetail = (ConfDetails)i.next();
         registFee = theRegister.getDiscountedFee
                     (confDetail.getRegistFee(), attendeeType);
         totalFee += theRegister.getDiscountedFee
                      (confDetail.getRegistFee(), attendeeType); %>
         <tr><td> <%= confDetail.getConfName() %> </td>
             <td align="right"> $ <%= twoDigits.format(registFee) %>
         </td></tr>
<%       }
%>
         <tr><td></td>
             <td align="right">_______________</td></tr>
         <tr><td> Total registration fee: </td>
             <td align="right"> $ <%= twoDigits.format(totalFee) %>
         </td></tr>
         </table>
<%
        } catch (Exception ex) {
           System.out.println(ex.getMessage());
        }
%>
   <form method="get" action="register.jsp">
   <P> Please select the conference you are interested in, <br>
        and then click Add  to register for the conference, <br>
        or click Remove to cancel the registration. </P>
   <select name="confId" size="1" >
     <option value="001">Distributed Computing</option>
     <option value="002">Component Based Computing</option>
```

```
    <option value="003">Grid Computing</option>
  </select>
  <br><br>
  <input type="hidden" name="ssn" value= "<%= ssn %>">
  <input type="hidden" name="name" value="<%= name %>">
  <input type="hidden" name="attendeeType" value="<%= attendeeType %>">
  <input type="submit" name ="Add" value="Add">
  <input type="submit" name ="Remove" value="Remove">
</form>
</body>
</center></html>
<% }
%>
```

Step 5: Packing the Web Component

1. Follow the steps in Lab 1 to create the .war file `RegisterWar`. The settings for the Web component are as follows:

Setting	Value
WAR Name	RegisterWar
Contents	Under c:\ejb\lab3\web Index.html, register.jsp
Component Type	JSP
JSP File Name	Register.jsp
Web Component Display Name	register
Startup Load Sequence Position	Load at any time

2. Specify the Web component reference.

Setting	Value
Coded Name	ejb/SimpleRegister
Type	Session
Interface	Remote
Home Interface	register.RegisterHome
Local/Remote Interface	register.Register
TargetEJB/JNDI Name	MyRegister

3. Sun-Specific Settings (see Lab 1):
   a. Use MyRegister for the `JNDI name`.
   b. Use register for the `Context Root`.
4. Deploy.
   a. Save the application.
   b. Click Tools | Deploy.

Step 6: Run the `RegisterApp` Application

To access the online registration application, point your browser to `http://localhost:8080/register`.

1. Fill in a Social Security Number.
2. Fill in a Name.
3. Select Attendee Type.
4. Select the conference.
5. Click the Submit button.

The `index.html` will forward the request to the `register.jsp` after the Submit button is clicked. The following two screens show a sample execution of this Web application.

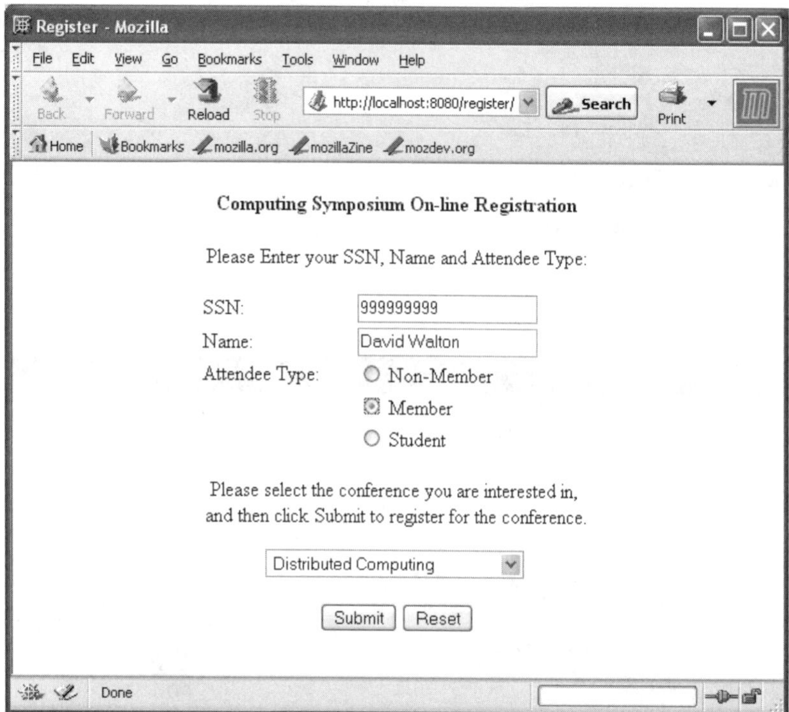

After you select the conference of distributed computing and component-based computing, the total registration fee is listed as $200 at the membership discount rate. You can add more conferences afterward.

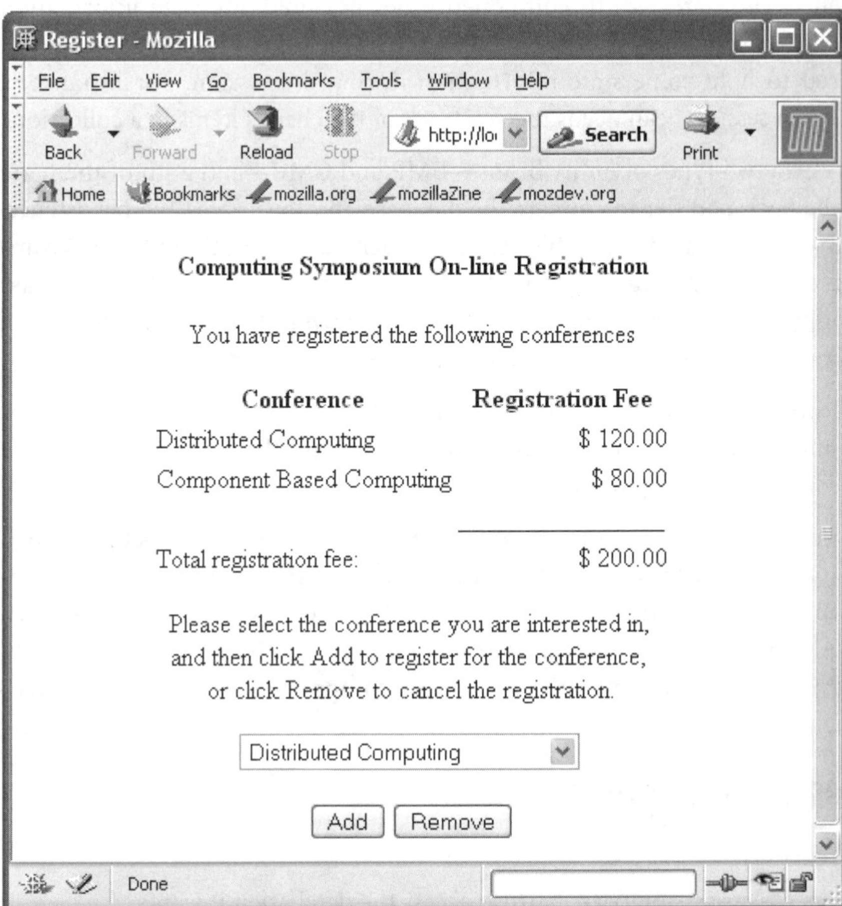

6.8 Summary

Sun Microsystems' EJB2.x provides a complete component infrastructure similar to CORBA 3.0. The EJB technology is widely used for building the Java Web enterprise application in the distributed computing environment. Any EJB component has two interfaces (except MDB) and one bean class implementing the interfaces. The EJB Home (can be Local Home or Remote Home) interface manages the life cycle of an EJB object such as creating or removing an EJB instance, and finding an entity bean instance by primary key.

There are three EJB types: session bean, entity bean, and message-driven bean. A session bean may be stateless or stateful, and both types act on the behaviors of their clients. The stateless EJB component does not hold any state information during its session such as an online calculator. On the other hand, stateful session beans need to hold some state information during the session. For instance, a shopping cart session bean needs to keep track of the client's items in a collection.

There are also two types of entity beans—BMP and CMP—and both of them are used in the back-end tier to connect the database and to support the persistence. Each entity bean has a relation table behind it. Each instance of the entity EJB component is stored in the table as a row. CMP entity beans are free of SQL database programming and the mapping to database implementation is completed by an enterprise application deployer at deployment time.

Any EJB component is hosted by an EJB container, which provides all the necessary services and makes EJB more portable and scalable. An EJB component is packed, assembled, and finally deployed on a server.

EJB components are server-side reusable components. This compares to the JavaBeans components discussed in Chapter 3, which are client-side reusable components. EJB components are widely used in distributed computing applications in a LAN, WAN, Internet, or wireless network environment. The EJB component can work with other components such as CORBA components, Servlets, or JSP Web components.

6.9 Self-Review Questions

(True or False)

1. A stateless session bean can also access the database if it wants.
2. CMP entity beans can be deployed to any J2EE server with any relational database.
3. The primary key is available when the `ejbCreate()` method is called.
4. Every session bean instance has a primary key.
5. An EJB inactive instance is available even before the client creates it explicitly.
6. An EJB bean in its pooled state is not available to respond to any client's invocation.

7. The `ejbCreate()` method of a stateless session bean is called back many times by its container.
8. The `ejbActivate()` method of a stateless session bean is called back by its container.
9. Session beans may have their own states.
10. An EJB Local interface is accessible only locally.
11. The business logic is defined in the Remote interface.
12. The finder method should be defined in session beans.
13. An EJB component can be reached by another EJB component.
14. A session bean acts in front of entity beans in most cases.

6.10 Keys to the Self-Review Questions

1. T 2. T 3. F 4. F 5. T 6. T 7. F 8. F 9. T 10. T 11. T 12. F 13. T 14. T

6.11 Exercises

1. What is the life cycle of a stateless session EJB?
2. What is the life cycle of a stateful session EJB?
3. How does the EJB container work?
4. What is the life cycle of the entity bean?
5. What are the major differences between EJB and JavaBeans?
6. What are the major differences between EJB and MDB?
7. Is EJB architecture a cross-language platform?
8. What is the justification of using EJB?
9. How is an object reference of an EJB obtained?
10. Where will EJB components be deployed?
11. Why do we need Lcal interfaces?
12. Why is a Local Home needed?
13. What is a Local EJB object interface?
14. What is a Remote interface?

15. When is a stub of a remote EJB?
16. What is EJB packaging?
17. What is EJB assembly?
18. What does a `.jar` file usually contain?
19. What does a `.war` file usually contain?
20. What does an `.ear` file usually contain?

6.12 Programming Exercises

A. Session Bean Programming

1. Design a stateful session bean that provides a calculator service. The calculator has the functionality to perform addition, subtraction, multiplication, and division of two real numbers. It can also detect zero divisors in division operations. Use namespaces in this component.
2. Deploy the server component Calculator.
3. Design a Web client of the calculator in the previous exercise.
4. Design an application client of the calculator EJB.
5. Plug this Calculator component into another EJB.

B. Entity Bean Programming

1. Design an online poll survey application using entity beans, session beans, and other Java Web components. The poll checks the user preference on Java and .NET technologies.
2. Develop an online prototype banking system that allows customers to open new accounts, deposit to their accounts, or withdraw from their accounts. Authentication is required.

6.13 References

1. Shin, Sang, and Culter, Jeff. 2004. Java Beans. http://www.javapassion.com/-j2ee/entityBean4. pdf.
2. Sun Microsystems, Inc. *EJB 2.1 Specification Final Release 2.1 FR*. Download available at https://sdiclb.sun.com:443/ECom/EComActionServlet;jsessionid= 2EB8AD1A189D1D5BA85FC7F630224B62.

3. Armstrong, E., Ball, J., Bodoff, S., Carson, D. B., Evans, J., Green, D., Haase, K., and Jendrock, E. 2005. *The J2EE 1.4 Tutorial.* Santa Clara, CA: Sun Microsystems, Inc. http:java.sun.com/j2ee/1.4/docs/tutorials/doc.

4. Sun Microsystems, Inc. 2000. *Java 2 Enterprise Edition Developer's Guide.* http://java.sun.com/j2ee/sdk_1.2.1/techdocs/guides/ejb/html/DevGuideTOC.html.

5. Pawlan, Monica. 1999. *Writing Enterprise Applications with Java 2 SDK, Enterprise Edition.* Sun Microsystems, Inc. http://courses.cs.tamu.edu/cpsc609/-lively/spring98/j2EE.pdf.

CHAPTER 7

SOAP

Objectives of This Chapter

- Describe what SOAP is used for and the concept behind SOAP.
- Identify what the SOAP specification is composed of and where it can be found.
- Describe the SOAP Message Exchange Patterns.
- Describe the structure of the SOAP message and explain all of its parts.
- Describe how data is encoded in a SOAP message.
- Provide a step-by-step example of how to program with SOAP in Java.

7.1 Overview

SOAP[1] is a specification that describes a standard structure for encoding and packaging data and exchanging that data between distributed software applications. SOAP deals exclusively with the content and format of data that is transmitted between remote applications, that is, data sent over the electrical wires that connect computers. It is important to understand the distinction between specifications such as SOAP and application programming interface (API) specifications. API specifications focus on describing abstractions of a software implementation that addresses a specific need in order to ensure the portability of the code. For example, the Java Servlet specification is an API specification that ensures the portability of Java Servlets between Java Servlet containers implemented by different vendors (i.e., Tomcat, Jetty, etc.). In contrast, specifications such as SOAP describe how the data transported between computers must be structured and handled. Java programmers are accustomed to dealing with API specifications, and as a consequence, the Java Community Process (JCP)[2] has developed API specifications for programming with SOAP in Java, which is discussed in a later chapter. However, specifications such as SOAP are important because they provide what APIs do not, which is interoperability between applications written in different programming languages.

The primary use of SOAP is application-to-application (A2A) communication, specifically business-to-business (B2B) and enterprise application integration (EAI). B2B is electronic commerce between businesses (see Figure 7.1), as opposed to electronic commerce between a business and a consumer (B2C). EAI is the use of software called middleware to integrate the applications, databases, and legacy systems that support an organization's critical business processes (see Figure 7.2).

SOAP is typically transported from one computer to another as the payload of some other network protocol. The most common method of transporting SOAP is to embed SOAP in an HTTP[3] (Hypertext Transfer Protocol) request or response, though this is not the only way that SOAP can be transported. HTTP is one of the most widespread network protocols in use today due to the advent of the Internet and the fact that Web browsers and Web servers use HTTP to exchange HTML[4]

---

[1]Early versions of SOAP defined the SOAP name as an acronym for **S**imple **O**bject **A**ccess **P**rotocol. The latest version of SOAP has dropped the spelled-out version, and now SOAP is just a name.

[2]Sponsored by Sun Microsystems, JCP is an open organization of active members and non-member public input that guides the development and approval of specifications for new Java technology. Their Web site is located at `http://www.jcp.org`.

[3]The HTTP specification can be found at `http://www.ietf.org/rfc/rfc2616.txt`. The HTTP specification is maintained by the Internet Engineering Task Force (IETF), a large open international community of network designers, operators, vendors, and researchers concerned with the evolution of Internet architecture and the smooth operation of the Internet. The Web site for IETF is located at `http://www.ietf.org`.

[4]The HTML specification can be found at `http://www.w3.org/TR/html4/`. The World Wide Web Consortium (see footnote 5) is the organization that maintains the HTML specification.

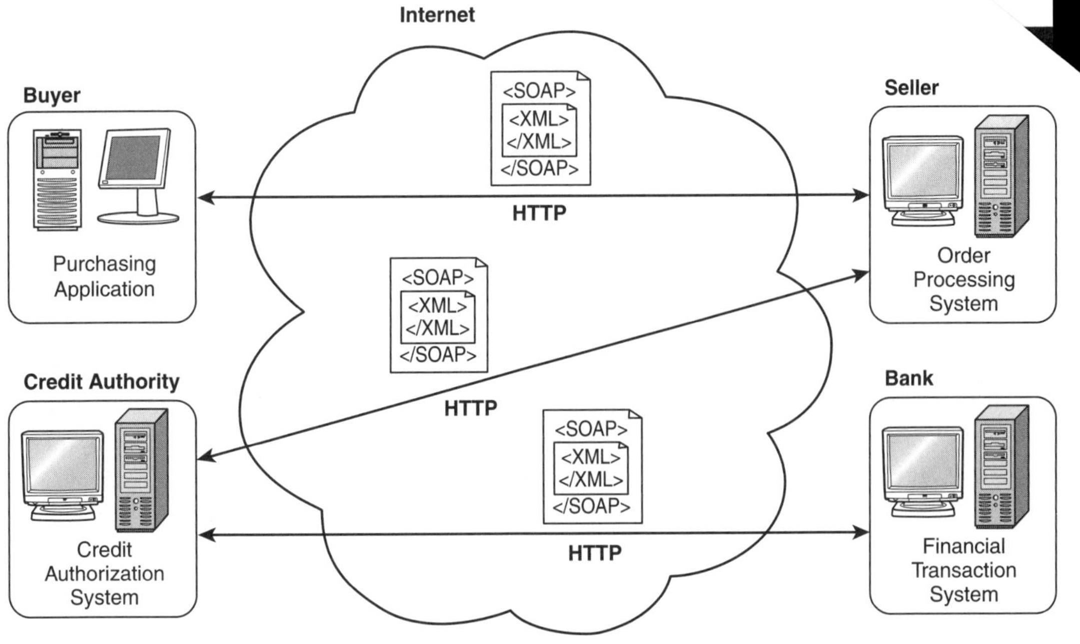

Figure 7.1

B2B Using SOAP over HTTP

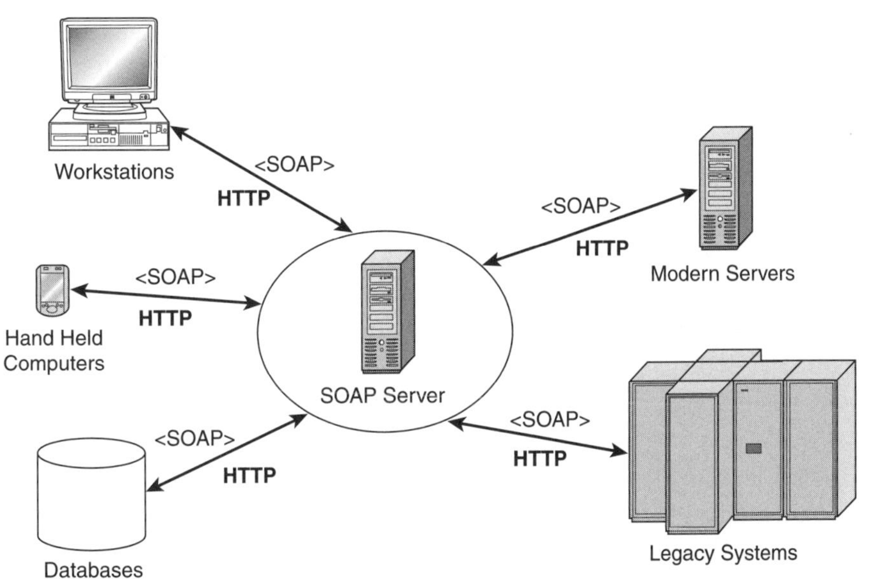

Figure 7.2

EAI Using SOAP over HTTP

…anguage) Web pages. By convention, Web servers use communication port 80 …s. Since companies today use firewalls to block or restrict most network traffic …ffic through port 80, the use of HTTP allows SOAP messages to freely pass through … firewalls. The process of embedding another protocol inside of HTTP in order to pass th…gh a firewall is called *HTTP tunneling.*

SOAP is based on the eXtensible Markup Language (XML), and like XML, is flexible and independent of programming languages, operating systems, and hardware, which makes it truly effective in B2B and EAI. XML by itself is an excellent technology for exchanging data between applications and is widely used for just that purpose. But XML does not provide standards for the networking, addressing, and routing protocols that EAI and B2B systems require. Before SOAP came along, businesses had to either define their own protocols or use a proprietary system provided by a vendor. Since vendors were using different protocols and some businesses were creating their own, interoperability between business applications was very difficult to achieve. Before SOAP, achieving interoperability between XML-based systems usually meant implementing a custom-built solution, which was tedious and expensive.

Attempts have been made before SOAP to develop a standard for cross-platform interoperability. The most popular among these are the Distributed Computing Environment Remote Procedure Call (DCE RPC) and the Common Object Request Broker Architecture Internet Inter-ORB Protocol (CORBA IIOP). DCE RPC is developed and maintained by the Open Group (`http://www.opengroup.org`). CORBA IIOP is developed and maintained by the Object Management Group (`http://www.omg.org`). The major difference between SOAP and these other technologies is that SOAP represents data in a text-based form using XML, whereas CORBA IIOP and DCE RPC transmit data in binary form. Binary data has the benefit of consuming less space than text data, but binary data presents more of an interoperability challenge than text data because binary data can be encoded in many different forms that are not supported by all platforms. CORBA IIOP and DCE RPC have enjoyed some widespread use and acceptance by vendors, however, they have never been embraced by the software industry as a whole. Microsoft application vendors, in particular, have typically used Microsoft's Distributed Component Object Model (DCOM), which is primarily supported only on the Microsoft Windows platform (`http://www.microsoft.com/com`). Sun Microsystems also developed a proprietary distributed communication mechanism for Java called the Java Remote Method Protocol (JRMP), which is used by Java RMI (Remote Method Invocation). Java RMI works very well when you need to communicate between distributed Java applications. If distributed Java applications do not need to communicate with applications written in other languages, then Java RMI is much more expedient and less complicated to implement than SOAP. On the other hand, if cross-platform interoperability is desired, SOAP is a great solution.

SOAP has enjoyed rapid widespread acceptance and is endorsed by most enterprise software vendors and standards organizations such as the World Wide Web Consortium (W3C),[5] the Organization for the Advancement of Structured Information Systems (OASIS),[6] the Web Services Interoperability Organization (WS-I),[7] among others. Due to its platform independence and vendor backing, SOAP has become the de facto communication protocol standard for invoking applications over a network. At the time of this writing, two versions of SOAP are primarily in use, versions 1.1 and 1.2.[8] The SOAP 1.1 specification was released to the public as a W3C Note[9] in May of 2000. Most systems in existence at the time of this writing use SOAP 1.1. The SOAP 1.2 specification was released by the W3C as a Recommendation[10] in June of 2003.

SOAP 1.2 is a significant improvement over SOAP 1.1 and presents several changes in syntax and clarified semantics for SOAP syntax. Many of the complaints about SOAP 1.1 were in regard to the fact that it omits important details. For a specification to provide valuable interoperability, it must spell out all of the details. If it does not, then vendors will implement their own custom solutions for the details (i.e., a nonstandard solution), typically as a means of promoting their product, thereby hindering interoperability between applications. Many interoperability improvements have been made with SOAP 1.2, but it may take some time for vendors to adopt SOAP 1.2 because they are currently focusing on providing SOAP 1.1 solutions.

Fortunately, WS-I develops guidelines, conventions, and best practices for how specifications such as SOAP 1.1 should be implemented as a means of ensuring interoperability. These guidelines are documented in specifications that WS-I calls Profiles. The WS-I Basic Profile 1.0 and 1.1 cover guidelines for using SOAP 1.1. This chapter will describe version 1.2 of the SOAP specification, as well as highlight differences between SOAP 1.1 and 1.2, and aspects of SOAP that are sanctioned by the WS-I Basic Profile (BP). In general, the basic structure of SOAP has not changed from version 1.1 to 1.2 and likely will not change in the near future.

---

[5]W3C is an international consortium of organizations devoted to leading the World Wide Web to its full potential by developing common protocols that promote its evolution and ensure its interoperability. Their Web site is located at `http://www.w3.org`.

[6]OASIS is a not-for-profit, international consortium that drives the development, convergence, and adoption of e-business standards. Their Web site is located at `http://www.oasis-open.org`.

[7]WS-I is an open industry effort chartered to promote Web service interoperability across platforms, applications, and programming languages. Their Web site is located at `http://www.ws-i.org`.

[8]The SOAP 1.1 specification can be found on the Web at `http://www.w3.org/TR/2000/NOTE-SOAP-20000508/`. The SOAP 1.2 specification can be found on the Web at `http://www.w3.org/TR/soap12`.

[9]A *W3C Note* is a dated, public record of an idea, comment, or document, and does not represent the results of a formal standards-setting process by the W3C. Therefore, a Note does not indicate an endorsement by the W3C. The widespread acceptance of SOAP 1.1, however, has made it a de facto standard.

[10]A *W3C Recommendation* is a technical report that is the end result of the W3C's formal standards-setting process.

7.1.1 SOAP Concepts

The specification defines *SOAP* as a decentralized, stateless, one-way message exchange paradigm where XML messages are passed from an initiator, through zero or more intermediate locations, to a final destination. A *SOAP message* is the SOAP XML document instance that is exchanged between *SOAP applications* over a network. The peers exchanging the SOAP message are called *SOAP nodes* (SOAP nodes are also called SOAP applications). Within SOAP messages a SOAP node is identified by a URI (Uniform Resource Identifier). SOAP nodes handle routing and processing of the SOAP message and are categorized into one of the following concepts.

- *SOAP sender* is a SOAP node that generates and transmits a SOAP message.
- *SOAP receiver* is a SOAP node that receives and processes the SOAP message that was generated by a SOAP sender.
- *SOAP intermediary* is a SOAP node that is considered a SOAP receiver as well as a SOAP sender. Zero or more intermediaries can lie between the initial SOAP sender and the ultimate SOAP receiver. These intermediaries can perform preprocessing of the message before it reaches its final destination. Common uses for intermediaries are security, logging, and transactions.

The set of SOAP nodes through which the SOAP message passes, including the initial sender and the ultimate receiver, make up the *SOAP message path*. The *initial SOAP sender* is the SOAP sender that generated the original SOAP message. In other words, the initial SOAP sender is the SOAP node at the beginning of the SOAP message path. A SOAP intermediary cannot be the initial SOAP sender since intermediaries are not at the beginning of the SOAP message path. The *ultimate SOAP receiver* is a SOAP receiver that is the final destination of a SOAP message. Simply put, the ultimate SOAP receiver is the SOAP node at the end of the SOAP message path, and, therefore, also cannot be a SOAP intermediary. Figure 7.3 illustrates a SOAP message path. The initial sender of a SOAP

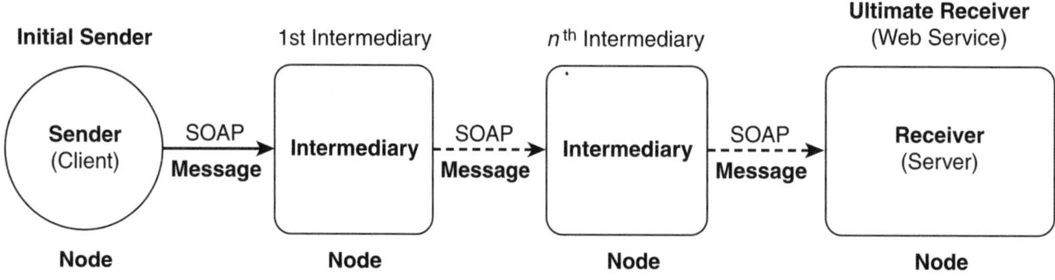

Figure 7.3
SOAP Message Path

message in a SOAP message path is often referred to as the *SOAP client*, and the ultimate receiver of the SOAP message is often referred to as the *SOAP server* or *Web service*.

The terminology used to describe SOAP concepts is different than the traditional terminology that is used to describe client-server type systems (e.g., the words "client" and "server"). The developers of the SOAP specification developed this terminology to avoid associating SOAP with a single specific messaging paradigm such as Remote Procedure Calls (RPC). RPC allows code from one application to invoke code in another remotely located application using a procedural syntax, which is very familiar to software programmers. Traditional protocols, such as CORBA IIOP and DCE RPC are mostly limited to using an RPC-style of messaging. Conversely, SOAP is not limited to any single messaging paradigm and the authors fully expect it to be used with many different types of messaging systems (such as asynchronous, synchronous, one-way) in nontraditional combinations.

7.1.2 The SOAP Specification

The SOAP specification, version 1.2, is essentially composed of the following three documents.

- SOAP Version 1.2 Part 0: Primer

  The Primer is a tutorial of the SOAP specifications, which describes its features through various usage scenarios. The actual SOAP specifications are described in Part 1 and Part 2. The Primer can be found on the Web at `http://www.w3.org/TR/soap12-part0/`.

- SOAP Version 1.2 Part 1: Messaging Framework

  Part 1 defines an overall framework for representing the contents of a SOAP message, as well as identifying which parties involved in the communication must handle what parts of the SOAP message, and whether handling such parts are optional or mandatory. In addition, SOAP Part 1 defines a framework for writing a specification that can be used to bind SOAP to an underlying protocol. Part 1 is on the Web at `http://www.w3.org/TR/soap12-part1/`.

- SOAP Version 1.2 Part 2: Adjuncts

  Part 2 defines a set of specifications that one may use with the SOAP messaging framework. These adjunct specifications include a data model for SOAP, an encoding scheme for the SOAP Data Model that may be used for conveying Remote Procedure Calls (RPC), a convention for describing extensions to the SOAP messaging framework, and a concrete usage of the underlying protocol binding[11] framework (defined in Part 1) to specify a SOAP binding to HTTP. Part 2 is on the Web at `http://www.w3.org/TR/soap12-part2/`.

---

[11]The use of the word *binding* in this context refers to the formal set of rules for carrying a SOAP message within or on top of another protocol for the purpose of communication. For example, *SOAP HTTP binding* is a formal set of rules that applications should follow when transmitting SOAP messages over HTTP. In this case HTTP is referred to as the *underlying protocol.*

Generally speaking, Part 1 is the most important part of the specification, because this is where all of the core concepts for SOAP are defined. Part 1 defines many requirements that *must* be correctly implemented for an application to be conformant with the SOAP specification. These requirements include things such as exactly how a SOAP message must be structured and how a receiving node must process a SOAP message. In addition, Part 1 defines a framework for extending SOAP to add capabilities that are found in richer messaging frameworks.

The SOAP extensibility model is where SOAP really becomes useful to companies. The SOAP messaging framework by itself does not provide details on *how* a SOAP message is going to be transported from one computer to another. Yet how a SOAP message is going to be transported must be defined if companies are to actually use the messaging framework. However, SOAP was designed to be independent of the underlying protocol so that SOAP messages could provide interoperability. How does a company actually use SOAP? This is where the SOAP extensibility model comes in.

The SOAP extensibility model defines the notion of an abstract *feature*, which is an extension of the SOAP messaging framework. A feature specification must include a URI used to name and reference the feature, the processing required by each SOAP node involved in the interaction, the information required by each node, and any data that is transmitted from node to node. Features are typically things such as routing, reliability, security, or transactions, but they can be anything that you might imagine distributed applications using SOAP may need.

Since features are abstract, features do not specify how the SOAP messages are actually transported. To complete this important piece of the puzzle, the SOAP extensibility model provides two mechanisms through which features can be *expressed*—turned into practical reality via the use of some mechanism (such as binding to HTTP). The two mechanisms are the SOAP Processing Model and the SOAP Protocol Binding Framework. The SOAP processing model is used to describe how a SOAP node must behave when processing an individual SOAP message. The SOAP protocol binding framework is used to describe how a SOAP message is transported between two adjacent SOAP nodes along a SOAP message path via an underlying protocol. The specification of the syntax and semantics necessary to realize zero or more features via the SOAP processing model is referred to as a SOAP *module*. On the other hand, the specification of the syntax and semantics for describing how a SOAP message is to be transported using a specific underlying protocol is called a *binding*. Protocol bindings are specified using the rules described in the SOAP protocol binding framework.

Part 2 of the specification builds onto the concepts defined in Part 1 by describing some practical extensions (features) to the basic messaging framework—that applications *may* use. These extensions, in particular the HTTP binding and RPC conventions, provide the puzzle piece that is missing from Part 1, which companies need in order to build real functional interoperable SOAP applications. Applications that claim to be conformant with SOAP are not required to follow the requirements specified in Part 2. However, if an application is going to make use of a technology that is specified in Part 2, such as RPC or HTTP binding, then that application will be more interoperable with other SOAP applications if it adheres to the specifications laid out in Part 2.

Additionally, Part 2 of the specification also defines a convention for describing features and bindings as *properties. Properties* are abstractions that are used to represent any state relevant to a feature or binding. This state includes the SOAP message itself, any information essential to accomplishing a message exchange that is not part of the message itself, and any other information that is necessary for features to work. The SOAP protocol binding framework mandates that a feature or binding describe the state of a SOAP message at each node as well as information (state) known to a SOAP node at any point in time. The states of all the nodes and messages are called *distributed states.* This SOAP convention for describing features and bindings as properties is sufficient for feature and binding specification writers to use when describing the distributed states of their feature or binding and is actually used in the section of Part 2 that defines a SOAP HTTP binding (on the Web at `http://www.w3.org/TR/soap12-part2/#soapinhttp`).

The following is a list of documents that are not part of the SOAP version 1.2 specification, but are related and very useful.

- SOAP Version 1.2 Specification Assertions and Test Collection

  This document lists many of the SOAP version 1.2 conformance requirements found in the SOAP specifications and provides a set of tests, which can be used to help determine whether a specific SOAP implementation is SOAP version 1.2–compliant. These tests do not provide 100% coverage of all SOAP version 1.2 conformance requirements, but they do provide a valuable tool for developers creating SOAP implementations that must comply with SOAP version 1.2 specifications. The creators of the document hope that it will facilitate the creation of interoperable SOAP implementations. If two different SOAP implementations written in different programming languages pass these tests, then the hope is they will be interoperable. This document is located on the Web at `http://www.w3.org/TR/soap12-testcollection/`.

- SOAP Version 1.2 Email Binding

  This document is a W3C Note, which defines an example of a SOAP protocol binding to the standard IETF's Request For Comments (RFC) 2822, Internet Message Format. In other words, this document describes how a SOAP message can be transported as an e-mail message or attachment (using the SOAP protocol binding framework and the SOAP convention for describing features and bindings, discussed above). The SOAP Primer (Part 0) gives an example of a SOAP message carried in a SMTP (Simple Mail Transfer Protocol) message (see `http://www.w3.org/TR/soap12-part0/#SMTP`). SMTP is a protocol that is commonly used to transport e-mail messages. This document serves to prove an important point: the SOAP specification is not limited to being used with HTTP, but is flexible enough to be

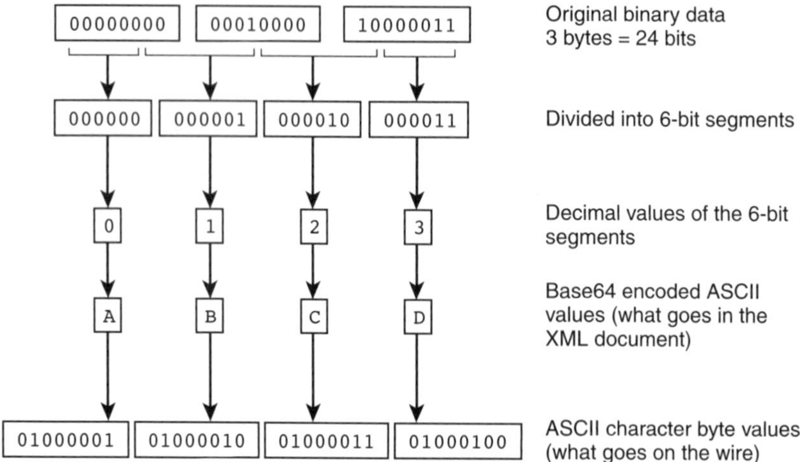

Figure 7.4
Base64 Binary Encoding

used with other protocols as well. This document is located on the Web at `http://www.w3.org/TR/soap12-email`.

- SOAP Message Transmission Optimization Mechanism (MTOM)

  A significant issue with much discussion in the SOAP area is how to transmit binary data (such as a JPEG image or word processor document) along with the XML data that is text. One way to do this is to encode the binary data as text and include the resultant text in the XML. This means that a SOAP sender has to encode the binary data, and the SOAP receiver has to decode the binary data. This type of encoding is supported by XML via the Base64 encoding algorithm, which simply takes a block of 24 bits, divides it into four segments of six bits each, and converts the four segments into their corresponding ASCII characters (see Figure 7.4). The main drawback with this scheme is that the resultant data is increased in size by 33% or more. Another popular method of transmitting binary data with SOAP is to use Multipurpose Internet Mail Extensions (MIME). MIME is used with e-mail for sending attachments. In this scheme, the SOAP message is embedded as a MIME `Multipart/Related` content type and the binary files are embedded as attachments. The SOAP message (XML) refers to the attachments (non-XML) (see Figure 7.5). The MTOM document is a W3C Recommendation that describes an abstract SOAP feature (called Abstract Transmission Optimization Feature) for selectively encoding portions of the message so as to optimize the transmission format of a SOAP message. The MTOM also describes a mechanism (called Inclusion Mechanism) for implementing the Abstract Transmission Optimization Feature in a binding-independent manner. Lastly, the MTOM uses this Inclusion Mechanism for

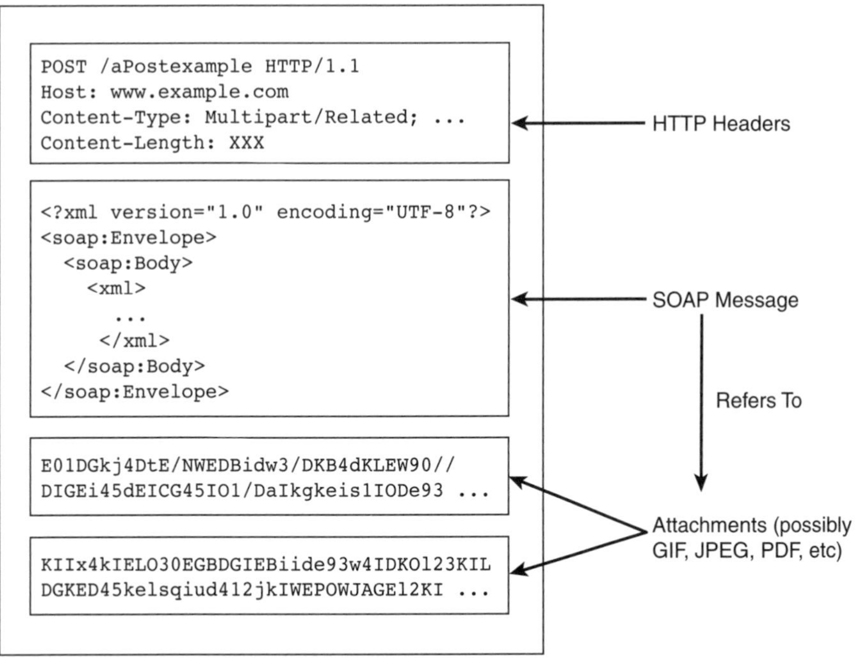

Figure 7.5

Structure of a SOAP Message with Attachments

implementing the Abstract Transmission Optimization Feature for an HTTP binding. The MTOM is located on the Web at `http://www.w3.org/TR/soap12-mtom/`.

The specification for SOAP version 1.1 is defined in a single document, which is located on the Web at `http://www.w3.org/TR/2000/NOTE-SOAP-20000508/`. The differences between SOAP 1.1 and SOAP 1.2 are listed in the SOAP 1.2 Primer, section 6 (located at `http://www.w3.org/TR/soap12-part0/#L4697`). The MOTM document described above was the result of incorporating ideas from earlier documents that described how to use binary attachments with SOAP 1.1 and SOAP 1.2. These documents include SOAP Messages with Attachments (for SOAP 1.1, located at `http://www.w3.org/TR/SOAP-attachments`), Proposed Infoset Addendum to SOAP Messages with Attachments (for SOAP 1.1, located at `http://www.gotdotnet.com/team/jeffsch/paswa/paswa61.html`), and SOAP 1.2 Attachment Feature (located at `http://www.w3.org/TR/soap12-af/`). It is worth noting that since SOAP 1.1 has received widespread use and most applications at the time of this writing use SOAP 1.1, many applications also use SOAP Messages with Attachments (SwA). In fact, J2EE version 1.4 supports SwA and the WS-I Basic Profile 1.1 mandates the use of SwA (with constraints on its use to ensure interoperability). It is likely that a future Profile from WS-I will mandate the use of SOAP 1.2 and MTOM.

It is important to note that the SOAP extensibility model and the fact that SOAP is built using XML provide SOAP with a large amount of flexibility. This flexibility is wonderful because it will most likely allow SOAP to endure the waves of change that sweep over the software development community every five to ten years. On the other hand, this flexibility allows vendors so much freedom they tend to implement language-dependent features, thereby creating systems that cannot interoperate with systems written in a different programming language. The WS-I Basic Profile (mentioned earlier in Section 7.1) reins in some of this open flexibility in order to ensure interoperability.

7.1.3 SOAP Message Exchange Patterns

The SOAP specification only defines a SOAP message as a one-way transmission between SOAP nodes, but in real-world applications SOAP senders and SOAP receivers use various message exchange patterns (MEP) to communicate SOAP messages. A MEP is a template that specifies how many messages are exchanged in a given interaction, where the messages originate, and where the messages end. Which MEP a particular SOAP node implementation can use depends on which MEP the underlying protocol supports. For example, one can infer that a SOAP implementation that uses HTTP as the underlying protocol should support a SOAP message as a request (from SOAP sender to SOAP receiver), as well as a SOAP message as a response (from SOAP receiver back to SOAP sender). This is the same kind of MEP that is used when a Web browser sends a request to a Web server for an HTML Web page, and the Web server responds by sending the requested HTML Web page back to the Web browser embedded in HTTP (see Figure 7.6).

The SOAP specification was designed to be independent of the underlying protocol, which is why the SOAP specification does not describe the full implementation of a MEP and only defines the SOAP message as a one-way transmission. However, the SOAP specification does expect SOAP messages to be combined by applications using specific protocols to implement more complex message interactions. In fact, the SOAP specification does describe two MEPs in an abstract manner (as fea-

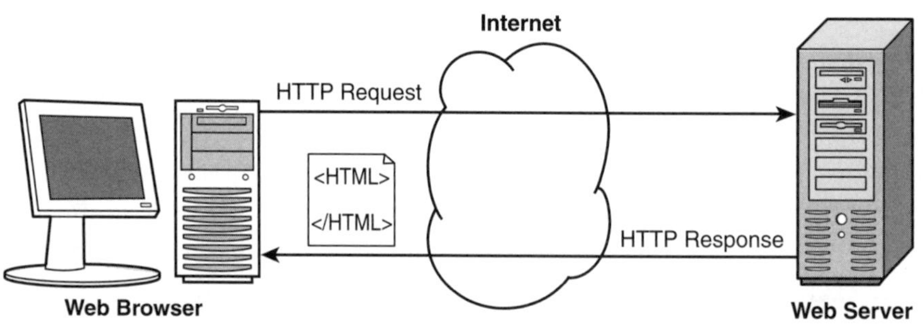

Figure 7.6
HTTP Request-Response Used to Transport HTML

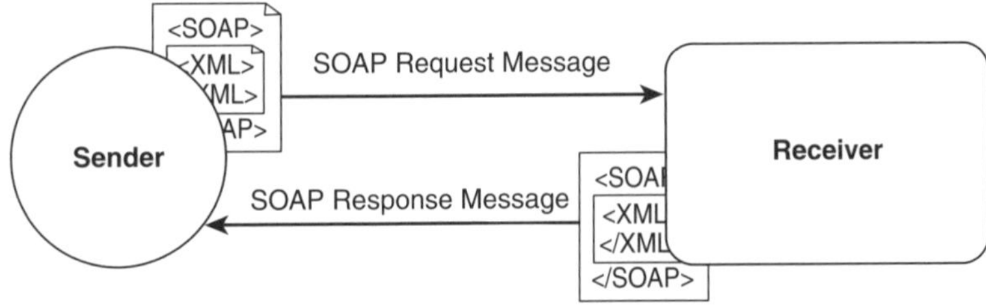

Figure 7.7
Request-Response MEP

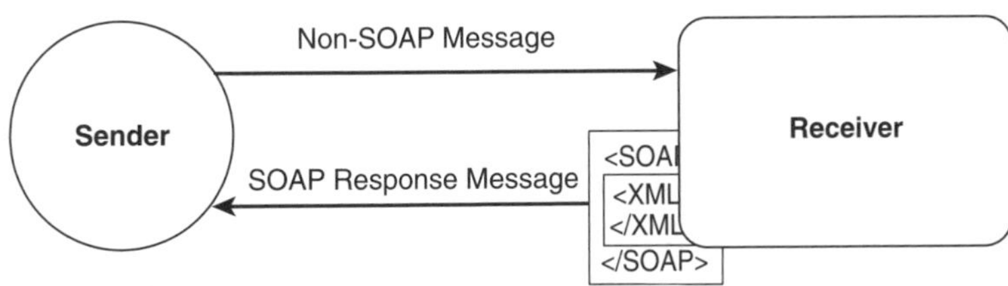

Figure 7.8
SOAP Response MEP

tures), leaving out the implementation details (i.e., the binding to the underlying protocol). These two MEPs are Request-Response (see Figure 7.7) and SOAP Response (see Figure 7.8).

The Request-Response MEP is described as consisting of two SOAP nodes and two SOAP messages. The semantics of the message exchange pattern are as follows. First, the SOAP sender node transmits a SOAP message to the SOAP receiver node. This SOAP message is called the *request.* Then, upon the successful processing of the request message, the SOAP receiver node replies by transmitting a SOAP message back to the SOAP sender node. This SOAP message is called the *response.* It is important to keep in mind that the response message corresponds to the request message, and thus the SOAP sender must be able to associate the response with a specific request.

Several possibilities for failure are present in the Request-Response MEP. For example, the SOAP sender may fail to send the request message, the SOAP receiver may fail to process the SOAP message, or the SOAP receiver may fail to transmit the response message. The Request-Response MEP specifies that if the SOAP receiver fails to process the request message, then the SOAP receiver shall generate a SOAP fault and transmit that fault along with the response message. A *SOAP fault* is a method by which SOAP nodes can transmit a message containing information on an abnormal condition that occurred while processing a SOAP message. SOAP faults are similar to exceptions in Java and are discussed more thoroughly in Section 7.6.

The SOAP Response MEP consists of two SOAP nodes—one non-SOAP message and one SOAP message. The semantics of this message exchange pattern are similar to the Request-Response MEP, except that the request message is *not* a SOAP message. Essentially, the semantics are as follows. First, the SOAP sender node transmits a non-SOAP request message to the SOAP receiver node. The non-SOAP message will most likely be specific to the underlying protocol. Since the request message is not a SOAP message, it does not involve SOAP processing by the SOAP receiver. The SOAP receiver node then transmits a SOAP response message back to the SOAP sender. Finally, the SOAP sender processes the SOAP response.

As mentioned earlier, the most common underlying protocol with which SOAP is used is HTTP. As a consequence, it is no surprise that the two MEPs the SOAP specification describes mimic an HTTP GET and an HTTP POST. The SOAP Response MEP mimics an HTTP GET, and the Request-Response MEP mimics an HTTP POST. An example of an HTTP POST is when a form on a Web site is completed and then submitted. The form data that is entered is typically packaged into a message, which is embedded in HTTP and transmitted by a Web browser to a Web server. The Web server then typically responds by packaging an HTML page into a message, which is embedded in HTTP and transmitted back to the Web browser, which, in turn, displays the page. An example of an HTTP GET is when a link for a Web page is selected. The selected link is transmitted via HTTP by the Web browser to a Web server. The Web server then responds by transmitting the requested HTML page, as a message embedded in HTTP, back to the Web browser (as before in the POST example). The difference between the two is that the GET requires no packaging of a message that is embedded in the initial HTTP request.

Difference between SOAP 1.1 and SOAP 1.2: HTTP GET

SOAP 1.1 only describes how to use SOAP within HTTP POST requests; it does not describe how to use SOAP in correlation with HTTP GET. The HTTP GET was intended basically for retrieving data, which should have no side effects on the system. In other words, every time a GET (retrieve data) is performed, the same response should be received, and this operation should cause no changes anywhere in the system except, possibly, a new display of the response. Since an HTTP GET returns the same response every time (within a time frame), the HTTP GET allows responses to be cached, thereby improving the performance of the system. On the other hand, the HTTP POST was intended for storing or updating data, ordering a product, sending e-mail, and so forth. The intention of the POST was to change the state of the system. Therefore, the HTTP GET and HTTP POST are fundamentally different.

The software development community reacted negatively to the fact that SOAP 1.1 did not specify the use of HTTP GET. Without HTTP GET, simple requests for data such as a stock quote, the current weather, or the current time could not benefit from caching, requiring the unnecessary overhead of processing the initial SOAP request and making use of the HTTP POST in a

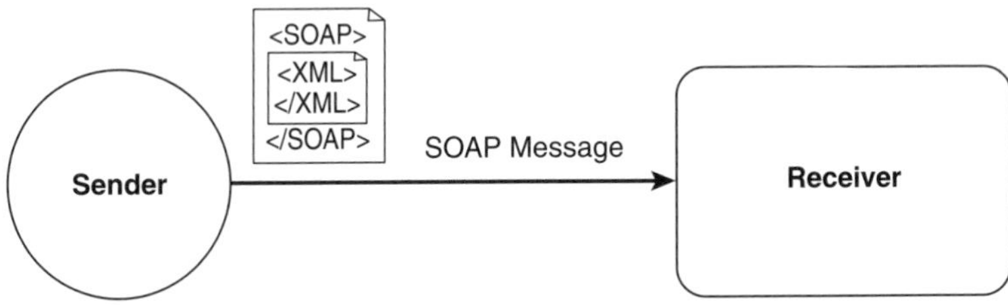

Figure 7.9
One-Way MEP

fundamentally incorrect fashion. Consequently, the SOAP 1.2 specification added the use of SOAP with HTTP GET, and this is why the strange-looking SOAP Response MEP is defined.

Real-world distributed applications make use of several other types of MEPs, beyond the two that are defined in the SOAP specification. The flexibility of the SOAP specification does not prevent developers from defining and using other MEPs and remaining SOAP-compliant. Remember that a SOAP message is fundamentally a one-way transmission. Therefore, a particular SOAP implementation could simply combine several one-way transmissions into a complex interaction and define that interaction as a MEP, which is exactly what the SOAP specification expects to happen. The following is a list of common MEPs in use today.

- One-Way

  This pattern involves the SOAP sender transmitting a SOAP message to the SOAP receiver without a response being returned (see Figure 7.9). Another common name for this pattern is Fire-And-Forget. E-mail messages utilize this pattern. Additionally, this pattern can be used to model asynchronous remote procedure calls.

- Notification

  In this pattern, the SOAP receiver (server) transmits one or more SOAP messages to the SOAP sender (client) without a response being returned to the server (see Figure 7.10). This pattern resembles event notification and is how an asynchronous remote procedure call can receive a response.

- Single Request/Multiple Response

  This pattern is similar to the Request-Response MEP, except the SOAP receiver transmits zero or more SOAP messages back to the SOAP sender in response to the initial SOAP request (see Figure 7.11). Another common name for this pattern is Request/N*Response.

- Solicit-Response

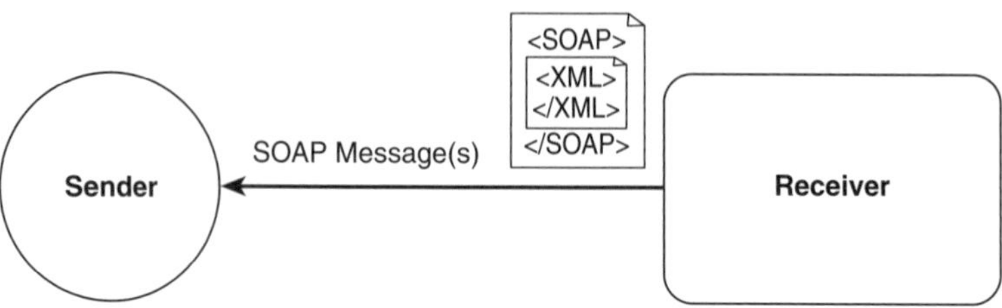

Figure 7.10
Notification MEP

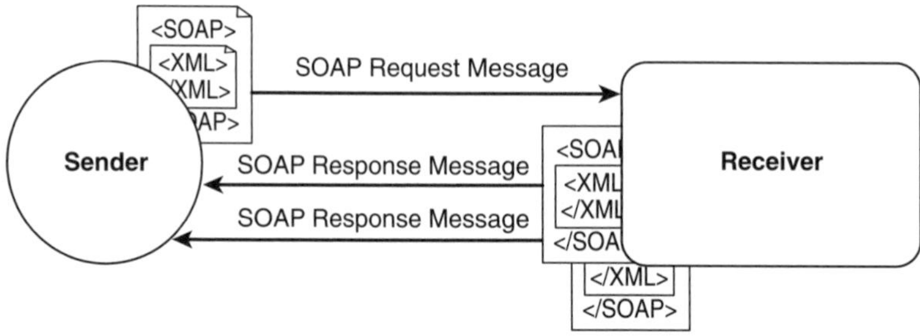

Figure 7.11
Single Request/Multiple Response MEP

In this pattern, the SOAP receiver (server) transmits a SOAP message to the SOAP sender (client), and the SOAP sender sends a response back to the SOAP receiver (see Figure 7.12). This is the exact opposite of the Request-Response MEP.

7.2 SOAP Message Structure

A SOAP message is simply an XML document with its own XML schema, XML namespaces, and processing rules. The XML document that defines a SOAP message is composed of the following four elements.

- `Envelope` (mandatory)

  Every XML document must have a root element. The SOAP `Envelope` element is the root element of the XML document that defines a SOAP message, and because of this, there can

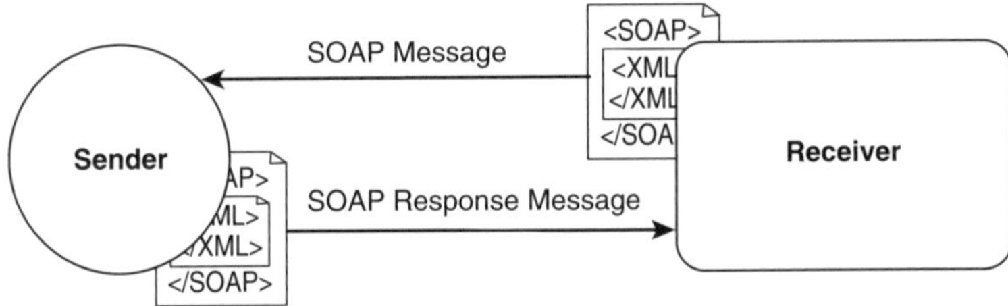

Figure 7.12
Solicit-Response MEP

be only one `Envelope` element. All other SOAP message elements are contained within the `Envelope`. The `Envelope` element serves to package the SOAP message for transport.

- `Header` (optional)

  The SOAP `Header` element is optional in a SOAP message, but if it is used, there can be only one and it must appear as the first child element of the `Envelope`. The `Header` element is an extension mechanism that can be used to pass application-specific information not contained in the message itself. This information can be processed by zero or more intermediaries, which can provide value-added services. Typical uses of the `Header` element include transaction processing, authentication, and logging.

- `Body` (mandatory)

  The actual application data that is being transported between applications is contained in the SOAP `Body` element encoded in XML. The `Envelope` element must contain a `Body` element. If no `Header` element is being used, then the `Body` element must be the first child element of the `Envelope`; otherwise the `Body` element must immediately follow the `Header` element.

- `Fault` (optional)

  The SOAP `Fault` element is used to report errors back to a SOAP sender. A SOAP `Fault` is analogous to an `Exception` in Java and is typically mapped to a subclass of `java.lang.Exception`. If a `Fault` is used, it must be present inside the `Body` element, and it must be the only child element of the SOAP `Body`.

The SOAP `Envelope` concept is often compared to a paper envelope mailed by the postal service. The SOAP `Envelope` is a package for data (a message) that is transported from a sender node to a receiver

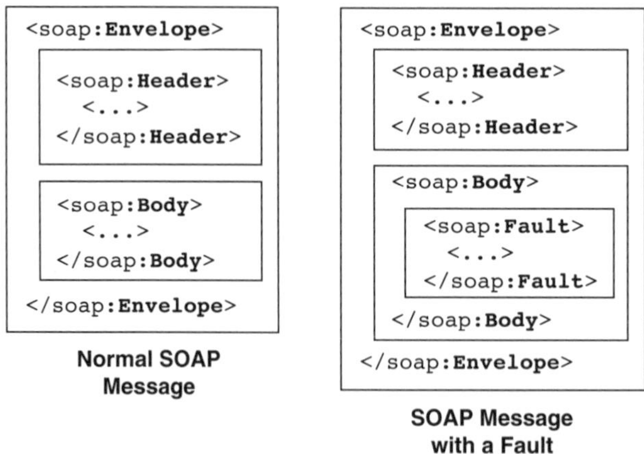

Figure 7.13
The Structure of a SOAP Message With and Without a Fault

node in the same fashion that a physical paper envelope is a package for some information that is transported from a sender person to a receiver person. The SOAP `Header` and SOAP `Body` can be considered the contents of the paper envelope. When SOAP is transported via HTTP, the HTTP headers are analogous to the physical address information on the outside of the paper envelope. The structure of a SOAP message is illustrated in Figure 7.13.

A SOAP message may have an XML declaration, in which case the declaration must mark the version of XML as 1.0 and the encoding must either be absent or marked as UTF-8 or UTF-16. If the encoding is absent, then UTF-8 is assumed. Recall that an XML declaration, if present, must be the first line in an XML document. The XML declaration is not required, and the WS-I Basic Profile recommends that an interoperable SOAP receiver process a SOAP message, whether or not it contains an XML declaration. The following is a valid XML declaration.

```
<?xml version="1.0" encoding="UTF-8"?>
```

The `Body` element and the `Header` element may contain any type of data associated with an application as long as it is encoded in XML. The `Body` element may contain any number of application-specific child elements, or a SOAP `Fault`, but not both. If the `Body` contains an application-specific element, that element can contain any number of child elements. The `Header` element can contain any number of child elements. The child elements in a `Header` element are called *header blocks.* Header blocks typically contain information such as transaction IDs, routing instructions, security credentials, auditing information, debugging information, payment tokens, and so forth. Header blocks are often processed by SOAP intermediaries, which have the option to remove header blocks from or add header blocks to the SOAP `Header`. The `Envelope` element may *not* contain any other child elements than the one mandatory `Body` element and an optional `Header` element. The following listing is an example of a SOAP message, which contains routing and security-related header blocks.

Listing 7.1 SOAP Example with Security and Routing Header Blocks

```
<?xml version="1.0" encoding="UTF-8"?>
<soap:Envelope xmlns:soap="http://www.w3.org/2003/05/soap-envelope"
    xmlns:ds="http://www.w3.org/2000/09/xmldsig#"
    xmlns:wsa="http://schemas.xmlsoap.org/ws/2004/08/addressing"
    xmlns:wsse="http://docs.oasis-open.org/wss/2004/01/oasis-200401-wsswssecurity-secext-1.0.xsd"
    xmlns:wsu="http://docs.oasis-open.org/wss/2004/01/oasis-200401-wsswssecurity-utility-1.0.xsd">
  <soap:Header>
    <wsa:MessageID>uuid:6B29FC40-CA47-1067-B31D-00DD010662DA
    </wsa:MessageID>
    <wsa:ReplyTo><wsa:Address>http://mybusiness/client1</wsa:Address>
    </wsa:ReplyTo>
    <wsa:To>http://yourbusiness/Purchasing</wsa:To>
    <wsa:Action>http://yourbusiness/SubmitPO</wsa:Action>
    <wsse:Security>
      <wsse:BinarySecurityToken ValueType="...#X509v3"
          EncodingType="...#Base64Binary" wsu:Id="X509Token">
        MIIEZzCCA9CgAwIBAgIQEmtJZc0rqrKh5i...
      </wsse:BinarySecurityToken>
      <ds:Signature>
        <ds:SignedInfo>
          <ds:CanonicalizationMethod
              Algorithm="http://www.w3.org/TR/2001/REC-xml-c14n-20010315"/>
          <ds:SignatureMethod
              Algorithm="http://www.w3.org/2000/09/xmldsig#dsa-sha1"/>
          <ds:Reference URI="#Body">
            <ds:Transforms>
              <ds:Transform
                Algorithm="http://www.w3.org/TR/2001/REC-xml-c14n-20010315"/>
            </ds:Transforms>
            <ds:DigestMethod
                Algorithm="http://www.w3.org/2000/09/xmldsig#sha1"/>
            <ds:DigestValue>w1cJdTvtONxK2NTwV+uwu34ahx8=</ds:DigestValue>
          </ds:Reference>
```

```
        </ds:SignedInfo>
        <ds:SignatureValue>
          kxv7mRwjSbCkfQ7Zv9pu/DFqPbALAT4755Tz8AoHAIe74TTZF5c3Vw==
        </ds:SignatureValue>
        <ds:KeyInfo>
          <wsse:SecurityTokenReference><wsse:Reference URI="#X509Token"/>
          </wsse:SecurityTokenReference>
        </ds:KeyInfo>
      </ds:Signature>
    </wsse:Security>
  </soap:Header>
  <soap:Body wsu:Id="Body">
    <po:purchaseOrder xmlns:po="http://yourbusiness/PO">
      <po:customer>...<po:customer>
      <po:creditCardType>...</po:creditCardType>
      <po:creditCardNumber>...</po:creditCardNumber>
      <po:purchaseItems>...</po:purchaseItems>
    </po:purchaseOrder>
  </soap:Body>
</soap:Envelope>
```

Parts of Listing 7.1 have been eliminated for brevity. The SOAP example demonstrates the use of the XML declaration at the top of the message, plus the Envelope, Header, and Body elements. As seen in the example, the Envelope element surrounds all the other elements. The Header element contains multiple child elements, which are header blocks for WS-Addressing[12] (prefixed with wsa) and WS-Security[13] (prefixed with wsse). The Body element contains only one child element, which is application-specific data; in this case it is a purchase order. There will be no involved description of WS-Addressing and WS-Security because that is not the focus of this chapter. As a short description, the wsa-prefixed elements provide the SOAP application with information on where the message should be delivered in a SOAP network, and the wsse-prefixed elements provide a digital signature for the message as a means of ensuring the integrity of the message.

---

[12]The WS-Addressing specification provides a standard way to specify how a SOAP message should route through a network from SOAP node to SOAP node. The specification can be found on the Web at http://www.w3.org/Submission/ws-addressing/.

[13]The WS-Security specification describes enhancements to SOAP messaging to provide message integrity and confidentiality. The specification is on the Web at http://docs.oasis-open.org/wss/2004/01/oasis-200401-wss-soap-message-security-1.0.pdf.

7.2.1 SOAP Namespaces

All SOAP elements must adhere to the SOAP XML Schema, which requires that *local elements* (including their attributes) be fully qualified via the use of prefixes or default namespaces.[14] Additionally, the WS-I BP requires that all local elements within the SOAP `Body` be fully qualified as well. On the other hand, the local elements of header blocks may be qualified or unqualified, although the best practice is to qualify them. The use of XML namespaces eliminates ambiguity among all XML elements and attributes in a SOAP message. Each of the different XML elements in the `Header` and `Body` must be identified by a unique namespace. Because a SOAP message may include several different application-specific XML elements in the `Header` and `Body`, as well as the standard SOAP message elements (`Envelope`, `Header`, `Body`, and `Fault`) and their associated attributes, a particular instance of a SOAP message may contain references to many different namespaces in order to avoid name collisions. For example, the SOAP message in Listing 7.1 references five different namespaces. The namespace in bold in the following snippet identifies the standard SOAP elements.

```
<soap:Envelope xmlns:soap="http://www.w3.org/2003/05/soap-envelope"
    xmlns:ds="http://www.w3.org/2000/09/xmldsig#"
    xmlns:wsa="http://schemas.xmlsoap.org/ws/2004/08/addressing"
    xmlns:wsse="http://docs.oasis-open.org/wss/2004/01/oasis-200401-wsswssecurity-secext-1.0.xsd"
    xmlns:wsu="http://docs.oasis-open.org/wss/2004/01/oasis-200401-wsswssecurity-utility-1.0.xsd">
  ...
</soap:Envelope>
```

The namespaces in bold in the following snippet identify the header blocks.

```
<soap:Envelope xmlns:soap="http://www.w3.org/2003/05/soap-envelope"
    xmlns:ds="http://www.w3.org/2000/09/xmldsig#"
    xmlns:wsa="http://schemas.xmlsoap.org/ws/2004/08/addressing"
    xmlns:wsse="http://docs.oasis-open.org/wss/2004/01/oasis-200401-wsswssecurity-secext-1.0.xsd"
    xmlns:wsu="http://docs.oasis-open.org/wss/2004/01/oasis-200401-wsswssecurity-utility-1.0.xsd">
  ...
</soap:Envelope>
```

The namespace in bold in the following snippet identifies the application-specific XML of the `Body`.

```
<soap:Envelope ...>
  <soap:Body wsu:Id="Body">
    <po:purchaseOrder xmlns:po="http://yourbusiness/PO">
```

---

[14]Global elements and attributes of an XML document must always be qualified, but local elements may not need to be qualified depending on values set for the `elementFormDefault` and `attributeFormDefault`. If either is set to "`qualified`", then the elements and/or attributes (depending on which is set) must be qualified. The SOAP XML Schema specifies `elementFormDefault` as "`qualified`".

```
      ...
    </po:purchaseOrder>
  </soap:Body>
</soap:Envelope>
```

In addition to eliminating ambiguity, XML namespaces in a SOAP message provide versioning and processing control. For example, a particular namespace can be used to identify a specific version of a software module that must be used to process the XML data in a namespace-qualified header block. Each header block in a `Header` element should be qualified with its own namespace so that SOAP applications can identify each individual header block and process it appropriately. The XML namespace of a header block is typically used to not only identify the schema for that header block, but also to identify the processing requirements.

Similar to header blocks, XML namespaces should be used to properly identify the application-specific XML elements in the `Body` element, thereby allowing a SOAP receiver to validate the data against the correct XML schema, process the data with the appropriate software modules, or reject the message if the application does not support the specified namespace. If a SOAP receiver does reject a SOAP message because of lack of support for the namespace, then the SOAP receiver should return a SOAP `Fault` to the SOAP sender. In fact, the WS-I BP mandates that if a SOAP 1.1 node receives a SOAP message with the standard SOAP elements identified by some namespace other than the SOAP 1.1 namespace, then it must generate a fault. Doing so ensures that the communicating SOAP nodes are using the same XML schema and processing rules, that is, they should be able to interoperate.

Difference between SOAP 1.1 and SOAP 1.2: Namespace

The XML namespace for the standard SOAP elements (`Envelope`, `Header`, `Body`, and `Fault`) changed from SOAP 1.1 to SOAP 1.2. This is an example of versioning described above. The namespace for the SOAP 1.1 elements is `http://schemas.xmlsoap.org/soap/envelope`, whereas the namespace for the SOAP 1.2 elements is `http://www.w3.org/2003/05/soap-envelope`.

Labeling each part of a SOAP message (`Envelope`, `Header`, `Body`, `Fault`, header blocks, and XML in the `Body`) with namespaces also provides a flexible way for a SOAP message to change over time. The different namespaces make the SOAP message modular, such that a particular header block can migrate to a new version of the processing logic, while the rest of the SOAP message remains the same. As an alternative, a new version of SOAP can be used, while the processing logic for the application-specific XML in the `Body` element remains the same. In other words, the code that processes the `Envelope` element can be independent of the code that processes the header blocks, which can be independent of the code that processes the application-specific XML in the `Body`.

7.3 The Envelope Element

The SOAP `Envelope` element is the root of the XML document that is a SOAP message, therefore all other SOAP elements are contained within the `Envelope`. The use of the `Envelope` element is mandatory and may contain a single, optional Header element followed by a single, mandatory Body element. The Envelope element may also contain namespace declarations and attributes. If attributes are used in the Envelope, they must be namespace qualified. The Envelope element serves to tie the application-specific data in the Body element together with the header blocks in the Header element. The following code snippet shows how the Envelope element appears in a SOAP message.

```
<soap:Envelope xmlns:soap="http://www.w3.org/2003/05/soap-envelope">
  ...
</soap:Envelope>
```

Difference between SOAP 1.1 and SOAP 1.2: Envelope Subelements (SOAP Trailers)

The SOAP 1.1 specification allows for additional namespace-qualified child elements to appear inside the Envelope element following the Body element. The WS-I BP forbids this practice because the interpretation of these elements defined by the SOAP 1.1 specification is unclear. Additionally, SOAP 1.2 has removed this semantic and mandates that the only direct child elements that the Envelope element may contain are the Header and Body elements.

7.4 The Header Element

The Header element is optional, but if it is present, it must be the immediate child of the Envelope element and precede the Body element. As mentioned earlier, this element must be namespace-qualified. The Header element may contain zero or more optional child elements, which are called *header blocks*. The following listing shows how the Header element, containing a header block, appears in a SOAP message.

Listing 7.2 Transaction Header Element

```
<soap:Envelope xmlns:soap="http://www.w3.org/2003/05/soap-envelope">
  <soap:Header>
    <trns:transactions xmlns:trns="http://transaction.example/version1"
        soap:role="http://www.w3.org/2003/05/soap-envelope/role/next"
        soap:mustUnderstand="1">
      <trns:transaction>
        <trns:id>http://bank/account1/withdraw</trns:id>
        <trns:status>ACTIVE</trns:status>
      </trns:transaction>
    </trns:transactions>
  </soap:Header>
  <soap:Body>
    ...
  </soap:Body>
</soap:Envelope>
```

The designers of SOAP incorporated the `Header` element as a way to include any information in the SOAP message that lies outside the semantics of the `Body`, but may be useful or even necessary to process the message appropriately. The SOAP `Header` is a powerful extension mechanism, which allows the user to add features and define high-level functionality such as security, transactions, and auditing. In effect, the `Header` element provides a standardized framework for implementing arbitrary, user-defined extensibility to a SOAP message. For example, imagine that a bank is using SOAP to transfer funds from one account to another. The bank has many different remote divisions that run different systems exposed as SOAP nodes, which handle different parts of the process involved in transferring money from one account to another. One system may handle the account that is being withdrawn from, and therefore must withdraw the funds from the account but cannot complete the transaction until the depositing account registers a deposit of the same amount. To solve the problem of keeping track of whether all transactions have successfully completed before the data change is committed to distributed databases, the bank could define its own header block that tracks transactions as illustrated by Listing 7.2. In doing so, the bank would have created an application-specific extension to the basic SOAP processing model. This bank could then make an effort to get other banks to agree on the same standard header for tracking transactions, thereby establishing some interoperability with other financial institutions. This type of standardization effort on SOAP header extensions is occurring today as a way to create interoperability among organizations in application-specific areas that require special multifeatured message exchange patterns. When a SOAP feature specification is created that details the constraints, rules, preconditions, and data formats for using one or more SOAP features, the specification is referred to as a *SOAP module.* Header blocks use URIs to identify a specific SOAP module that they are associated with. For example, the `transaction` header block in Listing 7.2 could be associated with a SOAP module identified by the URI `http://transaction.example/version1`.

Using header blocks to add functionality to SOAP messages is referred to as *vertical extensibility.* The header blocks build on top of the message, thereby vertically extending the message (both physically and conceptually). One advantage of header blocks is that the act of adding header blocks to a SOAP message does not alter the original application-specific XML contained in the `Body`. The transaction information in Listing 7.2 could have been added to the XML in the `Body`, but doing so would interfere with the original intent of the message. Also, adding extra data to the `Body` would require the initial sender and ultimate receiver to change in order to know how to process the data. Using the header blocks means that the initial sender and ultimate receiver processing logic does not have to change, but the additional feature of transactions can simply be "tacked on" or upgraded or even removed when necessary.

Other popular protocols also make use of this header concept. Both HTTP and e-mail use extensible user-defined headers. For example, it is very common for Web applications to place cookies in the header of an HTTP message as a way of tracking user sessions. The headers used in SOAP are much more powerful than the headers used in HTTP and e-mail, because, while headers in HTTP and e-mail are simple text, the headers in SOAP are XML, which means far more information can be encoded in a SOAP header. The power and flexibility that the SOAP `Header` extensibility mechanism provides is another reason for SOAP's enormous success.

The SOAP specification defines rules, which describe how a header block is to be processed, as a SOAP message hops from one SOAP node to the next SOAP node along the message path. The word *process* in the specification means to fulfill the contract indicated by a particular piece of a SOAP message (a header block or the application-specific XML in the `Body`). Processing a header block means following whatever rules are defined by the SOAP feature specification identified by the namespace of the header block, and processing the `Body` means performing whatever operation is defined by the Web service (the ultimate SOAP receiver node). The SOAP specification rules describe how to define which node must process a specific header block and what that node must do with the header block once it has been processed. Each SOAP header block may be intercepted and processed by any number of SOAP intermediaries along the message path. When processing a header block, each SOAP intermediary reads, acts on, and removes the specific header block that it has been tagged to process from the SOAP message before sending the message on to the next SOAP node. Additionally, each SOAP node may optionally add a header block to the SOAP `Header` element of the message. The SOAP `role` attribute is used to identify the nodes that must process a specific header block, and the SOAP `mustUnderstand` attribute is used to specify that nodes that attempt to process the header block must know how to process it or otherwise generate an error. The `role` and `mustUnderstand` attributes, both parts of the SOAP namespace (i.e., `http://www.w3.org/2003/05/soap-envelope`), are described in the next two sections.

7.4.1 The `role` Attribute

The purpose of the optional `role` attribute is to identify a function to be performed by a particular node; in other words, it identifies a role that the node must play in the SOAP message path. A `role` attribute is associated with a header block in the `Header` element. The `role` attribute must be assigned a URI as the value, which identifies (either implicitly or explicitly) the particular node (intermediary) that should process the header block. The URI might refer to a specific node (such as an authenticating node) or a whole class of nodes (such as any logger along the message path). When a node receives a SOAP message, it examines the `Header` element to determine which header blocks have specified a `role` that is supported by that node. A node may support multiple roles and therefore use several code modules to process multiple header blocks. For example, the `Header` element of a SOAP message may contain two header blocks, one that is used to authenticate the sender of the SOAP message and another that is used to log information about the message for auditing purposes. This is shown below in Listing 7.3.

Listing 7.3 Authentication and Logging Header Blocks Associated with Roles

```
<soap:Envelope xmlns:soap="http://www.w3.org/2003/05/soap-envelope">
  <soap:Header>
    <sec:authenticate xmlns:sec="http://security.example/version1"
        soap:role="http://security.example/authenticator">
      <sec:username>brighton</sec:username>
      <sec:key>w1cJdTvtONxK2NTwV+uwu34ahx8=</sec:key>
    </sec:authenticate>
    <log:audit xmlns:log="http://auditing.example/version1"
        soap:role="http://auditing.example/logger"/>
  </soap:Header>
  <soap:Body>
    ...
  </soap:Body>
</soap:Envelope>
```

A SOAP node receiving the message in Listing 7.3 may examine the header blocks and find that it supports both of them. The SOAP node can then use the `role` attribute in combination with the XML namespace to select the two appropriate code modules for processing the header blocks. One of these code modules might use the username and key to authenticate the user before allowing the message to pass through this node. The other code module might, for auditing purposes, log the attempt made by the indicated user to pass the specified message through this node. In this case, user authentication and auditing are two roles played by a single SOAP node.

> Difference between SOAP 1.1 and SOAP 1.2: `role` Attribute
>
> SOAP 1.1 specified that the role a node must play in a SOAP message path be identified by the `actor` attribute. Conceptually, an actor refers to a single node, but actually a single node can perform as many different "actors." When the SOAP 1.2 specification was written, the designers realized that since nodes *acted* in many different *roles*, the term actor did not actually reflect what the attribute meant. They changed the name of the attribute from **`actor`** to **`role`**. Thus, a SOAP node can play one or more different roles in a SOAP message path.

SOAP nodes are required to ignore any header blocks with role attributes they do not support. Header blocks can be targeted at any of the intermediary nodes in the SOAP message path or the ultimate receiver node. Therefore, even though a header block passes through a SOAP node without being processed, it may be processed by another SOAP node downstream in the message path.

The SOAP specification requires that a SOAP intermediary node remove its targeted header blocks from the `Header` element before passing the SOAP message along. However, the SOAP specification also states that a SOAP intermediary node can insert new header blocks into the `Header` element before sending the message on to the next node. This allows a SOAP node to reinsert a header block that was removed but is also needed by a downstream node, in addition to any other header blocks that the intermediary node deems necessary. Instead of explicitly removing a targeted header block that will need to be reinserted back into the message for a downstream node, node implementations will often simply make any modifications they need to the header block without actually removing it.

The SOAP 1.2 specification identifies the following three standard values that a `role` attribute can be assigned.

- `http://www.w3.org/2003/05/soap-envelope/role/next`

  This role is used to indicate that the next node in the message path must process this header block. Use this type of role when each node in the message path is needed to process the header block. An example might be a header block that logs a trace of what nodes have processed the SOAP message for debugging or auditing purposes.

- `http://www.w3.org/2003/05/soap-envelope/role/ultimateReceiver`

  This role is used to indicate that the ultimate receiver node should be the only node in the message path that processes the header block. Using an empty value for the `role` attribute ("") or omitting the `role` attribute will also imply that the ultimate receiver of the SOAP message should process the header block. The ultimate receiver of the SOAP message is also the node that processes the application-specific XML in the `Body` element.

- `http://www.w3.org/2003/05/soap-envelope/role/none`

  This role is used to indicate that none of the SOAP nodes along the message path should process this header block. This may leave you wondering, what would I use this role for if my nodes cannot process the header block it is associated with? The specification says that a SOAP node can read the data in the header blocks even if it is not intended to process them. Headers marked for the `none` role can still be used to carry data.

As an example, we can use the `next` role for a `transactions` header block (used earlier) to indicate that each SOAP node must record its transaction data in the header. Listing 7.4 shows this header block before any nodes have processed it.

Listing 7.4 Use of the `next` Value for a `role` Attribute

```
<soap:Envelope xmlns:soap="http://www.w3.org/2003/05/soap-envelope">
  <soap:Header>
    <sec:authenticate xmlns:sec="http://security.example/version1"
        soap:role="http://security.example/authenticator">
```

```
      <sec:username>brighton</sec:username>
      <sec:key>w1cJdTvtONxK2NTwV+uwu34ahx8=</sec:key>
    </sec:authenticate>
    <trns:transactions xmlns:trns="http://transaction.example/version1"
        soap:role="http://www.w3.org/2003/05/soap-envelope/role/next">
    </trns:transactions>
  </soap:Header>
  <soap:Body>
    ...
  </soap:Body>
</soap:Envelope>
```

When a SOAP node processes a header block, it must remove it from the `Header`. In addition, the SOAP node can add header blocks to the `Header` element when subsequent nodes downstream in the message path require them. Listing 7.5 shows Listing 7.4 after a few nodes have processed the header blocks. In this example, the `authenticate` header block from Listing 7.4 has been processed and removed, and two nodes have processed and added their transaction information to the `transactions` header block. One node has processed the SOAP message to make a withdrawal from account1, and another node has processed the SOAP message farther downstream to make a deposit to account2.

Listing 7.5 SOAP Message After Header Blocks Are Processed

```
<soap:Envelope xmlns:soap="http://www.w3.org/2003/05/soap-envelope">
  <soap:Header>
    <trns:transactions xmlns:trns="http://transaction.example/version1"
        soap:role="http://www.w3.org/2003/05/soap-envelope/role/next">
      <trns:transaction>
        <trns:id>http://bank/account1/withdraw</trns:id>
        <trns:status>COMMITTED</trns:status>
      </trns:transaction>
      <trns:transaction>
        <trns:id>http://bank/account2/deposit</trns:id>
        <trns:status>COMMITTED</trns:status>
      </trns:transaction>
    </trns:transactions>
  </soap:Header>
  <soap:Body>
    ...
  </soap:Body>
</soap:Envelope>
```

Difference between SOAP 1.1 and SOAP 1.2: Standard `role` Attribute Values

The SOAP 1.1 specification only describes one standard value for the `actor` attribute (the `role` attribute in SOAP 1.2). That value is the `next` URI (`http://www.w3.org/2003/05/soap-`

envelope/role/next). The standard `ultimateReceiver` and `none` URIs were added with the SOAP 1.2 specification. However, SOAP 1.1 did mention that the absence of a SOAP `actor` attribute indicates that the header block is intended for the ultimate receiver.

The SOAP `Header` attributes, which include `role`, `mustUnderstand`, and `relay` (`mustUnderstand` and `relay` are discussed in Sections 7.4.2 and 7.4.3) must appear in the header block element and should not appear in the header block child elements. Using Listing 7.5 as an example, the `role` attribute should appear in the `transactions` header block, but must not appear in the `transaction` child element of the `transactions` header block.

7.4.2 The `mustUnderstand` Attribute

The optional `mustUnderstand` attribute is used to indicate whether or not the processing of a header block by a targeted node is mandatory. SOAP messages have the possibility of traveling through many SOAP nodes that were unknown by the developer when a SOAP application was designed. Therefore, it may not always be known if nodes can process a header block correctly, but it may be required that the SOAP nodes be able to process the header block for the overall application to function properly. On the other hand, some header blocks might carry data that is nice to know but not critical to the operation of the application. Thus, those header blocks can be safely ignored.

A SOAP node will first look through the SOAP `Header` element for header blocks with `role` attributes that have targeted the SOAP node for processing. If the node does not understand how to process one of the header blocks, then the node will look at the `mustUnderstand` attribute to determine if it can ignore the header block and relay it. A header block can indicate that a SOAP node must know how to process it by setting the value of the `mustUnderstand` attribute to `1`. If the SOAP node does not need to know how to process the header block, then the `mustUnderstand` attribute can be set to `0`. If the `mustUnderstand` attribute is omitted, then its default value is `0`. Explicitly setting values in XML to their default is a bad practice because it increases the size of the data that must be sent across the network and processed while providing no additional value. Thus, if it is not necessary for the targeted node to understand how to process the header block, then the `mustUnderstand` attribute may be omitted.

<u>Difference between SOAP 1.1 and SOAP 1.2: `mustUnderstand` Attribute Values</u>

The SOAP 1.1 specification states that the `mustUnderstand` attribute can only be set to a value of `0` or `1`. The XML schema for SOAP 1.1 and SOAP 1.2 defines the `mustUnderstand` attribute as an XML schema `boolean` type. This means that the `mustUnderstand` attribute can actually take any one of four values—`1`, `true`, `0`, or `false`. Thus, the SOAP 1.2 specification states that the `mustUnderstand` attribute accepts any one of the four values (`1/true`, `0/false`), but that a SOAP sender should use the value `true`. The WS-I BP 1.0, which seeks to ensure interoperability by applying restrictions to SOAP 1.1, states that the `mustUnderstand` attribute should be set only to either `0` or `1`. To avoid confusion and increase the chance of backward compatibility, the author suggests that the reader follow the WS-I BP guidelines and only set the attribute to either `0` or `1`.

Header blocks with a `mustUnderstand` attribute value of `1` are called *mandatory header blocks*. The targeted node of a mandatory header block must recognize the header block by its XML structure and namespaces, and know how to process it in accordance with the specification that describes that SOAP extension. If a targeted SOAP node does not "understand" a mandatory header block, then that node must not forward that message on to the next node. Instead, the targeted SOAP node must discard the message, generate a SOAP `Fault` (faults are discussed in Section 7.6), and, if involved in a request-response exchange, send the `Fault` as a response back to the SOAP sender. When the SOAP node is not involved in a request-response exchange, it is not required to send the SOAP `Fault` back to the sender; instead the WS-I BP recommends that, when practical, the SOAP receiver notify the end user that a SOAP `Fault` has been generated by whatever means deemed appropriate for the circumstance.

If a header block is not mandatory but is targeted at a SOAP node, and that node does not "understand" the header block, then that node is not required to process the header block, but it is still required to remove the header block before passing it on. Additionally, SOAP receivers must not reject a SOAP message if it contains header blocks that are targeted at some other node and that node has not processed (and removed) them. The specification states that the `mustUnderstand` attribute was not intended as a mechanism for detecting that a node upstream in the message path did not perform its intended roles. These rules were established because the SOAP message path was designed to be flexible and dynamic, such that removing or adding intermediary nodes would not require changes to every other node on the message path. If nodes were allowed to reject messages based upon header blocks that other nodes in the message path were supposed to process, then changes to a single node would have to be reflected throughout the entire message path, thereby negating its dynamic nature. An example of the `mustUnderstand` attribute is illustrated below where the `mustUnderstand` attribute for the `transactions` header block is set to true.

Listing 7.6 Use of the `mustUnderstand` Attribute to Make a Header Block Mandatory

```
<soap:Envelope xmlns:soap="http://www.w3.org/2003/05/soap-envelope">
  <soap:Header>
    <trns:transactions xmlns:trns="http://transaction.example/version1"
        soap:role="http://www.w3.org/2003/05/soap-envelope/role/next"
        soap:mustUnderstand="1">
    </trns:transactions>
  </soap:Header>
  <soap:Body>
    ...
  </soap:Body>
</soap:Envelope>
```

7.4.3 The `relay` Attribute

The optional `relay` attribute is new to SOAP 1.2. Earlier we discussed how a SOAP node must remove a header block for which it is targeted regardless of whether it understands the header block or not. But what if we want to pass a header block through any targeted intermediary nodes that do not understand it? Since a SOAP message path is very dynamic, it is possible that a group of SOAP nodes are targeted for a header block, but only a few of the nodes have already been upgraded to know how to process the header. Before SOAP 1.2, the targeted node that didn't understand the header block would have to explicitly know to reinsert the header block back into the `Header` element. This would require the targeted node to have some special knowledge, which serves to introduce bad design and some unusual processing logic.

Like the `mustUnderstand` attribute, the `relay` attribute is an XML schema `boolean` type, which accepts a value of `1`, `true`, `0`, or `false`. The same concepts apply in relation to the attribute value as they do for the `mustUnderstand` attribute. If the attribute is omitted, then a value of `0`, or `false` is assumed. If a value of `0` or `false` is intended, then the SOAP receiver should simply omit it from the message, because the inclusion attribute would use space and add no value. The SOAP 1.2 specification recommends that a SOAP sender use the value `true` instead of 1 (which is the opposite of what the WS-I BP recommends for the `mustUnderstand` attribute value when used with SOAP 1.1).

If a SOAP intermediary node receives a SOAP message that contains a targeted header block with the relay attribute set to `1` or `true`, then the intermediary node must forward the header block to the next node if it does not understand it. Listing 7.7 demonstrates the use of the `relay` attribute to specify that the `audit` header block must be forwarded if the next node in the message path does not understand it. This attribute helps to allow the construction of a dynamic message path where all nodes of the message path do not have to be upgraded at the same time to support a new header block such as audit. Instead, the nodes in the message path can be upgraded one at a time.

Listing 7.7 Use of the `relay` Attribute to Forward a Header Block

```
<soap:Envelope xmlns:soap="http://www.w3.org/2003/05/soap-envelope">
  <soap:Header>
    <log:audit xmlns:log="http://auditing.example/version1"
        soap:role="http://www.w3.org/2003/05/soap-envelope/role/next"
        soap:relay="1"/>
  </soap:Header>
  <soap:Body>
    ...
  </soap:Body>
</soap:Envelope>
```

Table 7.1 Effect of the `role` Attribute and the `relay` Attribute on the Forwarding of a Header Block

Role		Header block	
Short-name	**Assumed**	**Understood & Processed**	**Forwarded**
`next`	Yes	Yes	No, unless reinserted
		No	No, unless `relay=true`
user-defined	Yes	Yes	No, unless reinserted
		No	No, unless `relay=true`
	No	N/A	Yes
`ultimateReceiver`	Yes	Yes	N/A
		No	N/A
`none`	No	N/A	Yes

The `relay` attribute has no effect when the `mustUnderstand` attribute is set to true. This makes sense because the `relay` attribute is for describing what should happen when a node does not have to understand a targeted header block. The SOAP 1.2 specification includes a valuable table (Table 7.1) that summarizes whether or not a header block is forwarded to the next node in a message path based upon the value of the `role` attribute and the `relay` attribute. The column labeled *Assumed* refers to whether or not the intermediary node plays the specified role. The cells with a value of N/A mean that the particular settings do not affect the forwarding nature of the header. For example, when the intermediary node does not assume a user-defined role specified by a header block, then the intermediary node will not attempt to process the header block; therefore, the *Understood & Processed* column is not applicable (N/A).

7.4.4 SOAP Intermediaries

SOAP intermediaries were discussed earlier. Intermediaries are SOAP nodes within the middle of the message path, meaning they are nodes in the message path that are not the initial SOAP sender or the ultimate SOAP receiver (see Figure 7.14). Essentially, intermediaries are applications that can process parts of the SOAP message on its way from the initial SOAP sender to the ultimate SOAP receiver. Intermediaries act as both a SOAP receiver and a SOAP sender. Intermediaries are targeted by URIs that are defined as values of `role` attributes in the header blocks of a SOAP message. Thus, the URI is used to identify a SOAP intermediary either explicitly via the use of custom URIs (for example, `http://myBusinessLogger/logger`) or implicitly via the use of a standard URI (for example, `http://www.w3.org/2003/05/soap-envelope/role/next`).

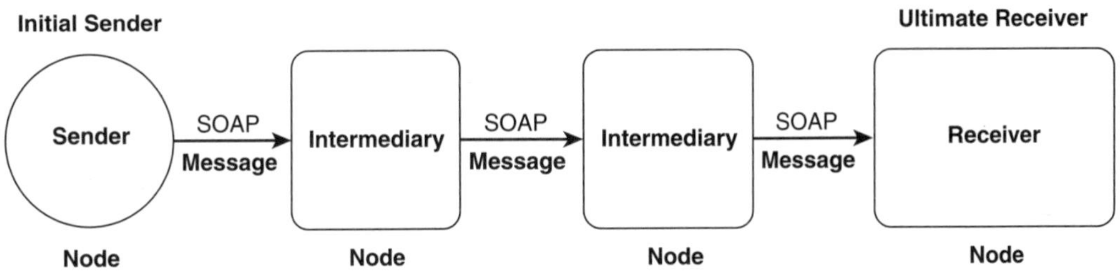

Figure 7.14
Intermediary Nodes in the SOAP Message Path

Earlier we discussed the notion of SOAP header blocks providing a mechanism for *vertical extensibility* to a SOAP message. SOAP intermediaries provide another mechanism for extending SOAP that is referred to as *horizontal extensibility*. Whereas vertical extensibility extends the SOAP message (both conceptually and physically) in a vertical fashion by adding additional information (via header blocks) to the `Header` element, the idea behind horizontal extensibility is targeting different parts of the SOAP message for different recipients (intermediaries). More intermediaries can be added to the message path and extend the message path horizontally.

SOAP intermediaries serve several purposes. The most prominent purpose is as a mechanism for allowing distributed systems to easily scale in response to changes and to provide value-added services along the message path. No distributed architecture will be universally accepted among vendors of distributed systems without addressing scalability. One method for judging the success of a software system is simply to see if it is used often and for how long. Highly successful systems are used often and for a very long period of time. If a system is to withstand the test of time, it must be able to adapt to changes. SOAP intermediaries provide a very simple mechanism for distributed systems to scale (to expand) by adding valuable services along the message path. Valuable services may include systems that address *qualities of service* (QoS) such as security, transactions, routing, and message persistence.

As a simple example, suppose you built a SOAP-based distributed system on a local area network (LAN) but decided not to include any authentication. This decision was made because it was unnecessary at the time to include authentication because no messages were going to travel outside of the LAN, that is, no SOAP messages were going to be exposed to the World Wide Web. Later, your business decided that they wanted to connect this system to another division that is located in another country, and to connect this system using the Internet. Now your business has decided that they need an authentication mechanism. Because you are using SOAP, it is no problem. Simply interject an authenticating node in the appropriate point of the message path and add the appropriate header blocks to the SOAP message.

A SOAP sender may not know of intermediaries in the message path that will process the SOAP message. Intermediaries that the SOAP sender knows nothing about are typically referred to as *transparent intermediaries.* Transparent intermediaries can act as proxies to the ultimate SOAP receiver. The opposite of a transparent intermediary is an *explicit intermediary.* Explicit intermediaries are ones that the SOAP sender knows the SOAP message will pass through and often expects to perform some function that is critical to the application. These categories of SOAP intermediaries are not defined in the SOAP specification, but they provide a nice description of two real types of intermediaries. The SOAP specification specifically describes the following two categories for intermediaries.

- Forwarding Intermediaries

  The header blocks of a SOAP message that is inbound to a SOAP receiver (or the MEP used) may require that an intermediary node forward a SOAP message to another SOAP node on behalf of the initiator of the inbound SOAP message. In other words, the inbound message may have header blocks that tell an intermediary node how to forward the message to another node. *Forwarding intermediaries* are intermediaries that only perform processing that is defined by the contents (in this case the header blocks) of the inbound message and then forward the message to another node in the message path. These intermediaries do not modify the contents of the message in any way that is not defined by the SOAP features that are used in the inbound message. A forwarding intermediary must adhere to the same processing rules for header blocks that have been described above.

- Active Intermediaries

  When an intermediary node modifies the SOAP message in ways that are not described by the contents (header blocks) of the inbound message, then this node is called an *active intermediary.* The results of the processing performed by active intermediaries could have an impact on the interpretation of the SOAP message by downstream nodes. For example, an intermediary node may be used to encrypt an outbound SOAP message from a service to prevent snooping of the contents by Internet hackers. A header of the message may not describe this encryption mechanism, and, therefore, the receiving node must know how to decrypt the message if it expects to use it. The SOAP specification recommends that alterations to the contents of a SOAP message be documented in a manner that allows downstream nodes to detect the changes (typically, by adding a header block).

7.5 The Body Element

The SOAP `Body` element is mandatory, and must be the first child element of the `Envelope` element, unless a `Header` element is present, in which case the `Body` element must follow the `Header` element. The `Body` element can contain either application-specific XML or a `Fault` element, but not both. The application-specific data is the data that we are trying to exchange between the remotely located systems. In essence, the Body element is just a wrapper for the XML document that we want to exchange. The Fault element is used only when an error occurs. Listing 7.8 gives an example of using the Body element to transport application-specific data. No header blocks are used in this example, instead the Body element contains a request for tracking information on a package shipped via the imaginary company kellys-fast-shipping.co.

Listing 7.8 SOAP Message with Parcel Tracking Data in the Body

```
<soap:Envelope xmlns:soap="http://www.w3.org/2003/05/soap-envelope">
  <soap:Body>
    <shp:trackingRequest xmlns:shp="http://kellys-fast-shipping.co">
      <shp:trackingNum>1Z 999 999 99 9999 999 9</shp:trackingNum>
    </shp:trackingRequest>
  </soap:Body>
</soap:Envelope>
```

The SOAP specification provides no specific rules for how application-specific XML in the Body element should be structured or processed because this is determined by the needs of the application. However, the specification does state that the ultimate SOAP receiver must be able to process the data; otherwise it should generate a SOAP Fault.

Of the two SOAP intermediary types discussed in Section 7.4.4, active intermediaries are expected to possibly modify the contents of the SOAP Body element (forwarding intermediaries are not). Therefore, other than stating that forwarding intermediaries should not modify the contents of the Body, the SOAP specification does not explicitly prohibit an intermediary node from modifying the contents of the Body before it reaches the ultimate receiver node. This can present a problem because the ultimate receiver has no way of knowing whether the contents of the Body have been altered somewhere along the message path. The consensus among most SOAP experts is that only the ultimate receiver should process the contents of the Body. Intermediary nodes along the message path may view the Body contents to aid in processing a header block, but should not modify the Body contents. This applies to both application-specific XML data in the Body or a SOAP Fault. The Body contents are intended only for the ultimate receiver, unlike header blocks, which are typically intended for (and processed by) intermediary nodes. The encryption of SOAP messages presents one deviation from this line of thought. For security purposes, SOAP extensions (remember the SOAP features discussed earlier) have been written that present a standard way for a SOAP message to be encrypted so that hackers cannot readily view the contents of the message. A nice way to introduce this line of security into an application is to interject an intermediary node that encrypts the message immediately after the initial SOAP sender. Of course, you also need to interject an intermediary node that decrypts the message before the ultimate receiver.

7.6 SOAP 1.2 Faults

The SOAP specification provides a standard mechanism for handling errors called the `Fault` element. Receivers, either an intermediary node or the ultimate receiver, can generate a SOAP `Fault`. In Java programs, an error condition is handled by throwing a subclass of `java.lang.Exception`, which notifies the calling code of the error. In SOAP a `Fault` element is generated, which is placed inside the `Body` element, and the message with the `Fault` is sent back to the previous SOAP sender in the message path. This essentially notifies the "calling code" of the error. A receiver is required only to send a `Fault` upstream to a sender if the MEP being used is Request/Response. If a one-way MEP is being used, then the receiver must generate a `Fault`, but is not required to attempt to send the `Fault` to the sender. Faults are generated as the result of several conditions, such as the following:

- The namespace for the standard SOAP elements in the message is a different version than the version used by the SOAP receiver (e.g., SOAP 1.1 when expecting SOAP 1.2)
- The SOAP message contains a mandatory header block that the SOAP receiver does not understand (mentioned earlier in Section 7.4.2)
- The SOAP receiver receives a message with invalid data or an invalid structure
- The application-specific XML in the `Body` is not recognized by the SOAP receiver because of the use of unknown namespaces or elements
- The SOAP message may be valid, but the SOAP receiver is not functioning properly or has encountered some other abnormal condition that caused it to generate a fault

When the `Fault` element is used, the `Body` element must contain only the `Fault` as a single child element and no others. The presence of the `Fault` element indicates to a SOAP node that an error has occurred. A SOAP message containing a `Fault` element is called a *fault message.*

Difference between SOAP 1.1 and SOAP 1.2: The `Fault` Element

The `Fault` element underwent a major revision for SOAP version 1.2. The differences between faults in SOAP 1.1 and SOAP 1.2 are so large that this chapter contains two sections on faults. This section covers SOAP 1.2 and Section 7.7 covers SOAP 1.1.

As a means of describing what went wrong, the `Fault` element may contain the following child elements. These elements only apply to SOAP 1.2. The elements for SOAP 1.1 are described in section 7.7.

- `Code` (mandatory)

  The `Code` element is used to classify the SOAP `Fault`.

- `Reason` (mandatory)

  The `Reason` element contains one or more human-readable explanations of the `Fault`.

- Node (optional)

  The Node element can be used to provide information about which SOAP node on the message path generated the Fault.

- Role (optional)

  The Role element can be used to identify the role the node was acting in when it generated the Fault.

- Detail (optional)

  The Detail element is used to carry additional application-specific information (typically machine-readable) about the error, which is related to the fault code.

The following listing illustrates the use of a Fault element. In this example a Fault is returned because a message was sent to kellys-fast-shipping.co (see Listing 7.8) that requested tracking information using a tracking number with an incorrect format.

Listing 7.9 SOAP Fault Element Example

```
<soap:Envelope xmlns:soap="http://www.w3.org/2003/05/soap-envelope"
       xmlns:xml="http://www.w3.org/XML/1998/namespace"
       xmlns:shp="http://kellys-fast-shipping.co">
  <soap:Body>
    <soap:Fault>
      <soap:Code>
        <soap:Value>soap:Sender</soap:Value>
        <soap:Subcode>
          <soap:Value>shp:InvalidTrackingRequest</soap:Value>
        </soap:Subcode>
      </soap:Code>
      <soap:Reason>
        <soap:Text xml:lang="en">
          Incorrect format used for the tracking number
        </soap:Text>
      </soap:Reason>
      <soap:Detail>
        <shp:trackingNumSubmitted>123456781234</shp:trackingNumSubmitted>
        <shp:validTrackingNumFormats>
          <shp:trackingNumFormat>
            1Z ### ### ## #### ### #
          </shp:trackingNumFormat>
          <shp:trackingNumFormat>#### #### ####</shp:trackingNumFormat>
          <shp:trackingNumFormat>T### #### ###</shp:trackingNumFormat>
        </shp:validTrackingNumFormats>
      </soap:Detail>
    </soap:Fault>
```

```
  </soap:Body>
</soap:Envelope>
```

The Code Element

The `Code` element is a mandatory element, which is used to classify faults and to provide a context for the `Detail` element. A SOAP node must understand the information in a `Code` element to be able to interpret the information in the `Detail` element. The `Code` element must contain a single mandatory child element called `Value`, which is restricted to containing one of a set of XML QNames (qualified names) whose local names are described in the following list. The namespace prefix must also be used along with the local name; in this chapter we use **`soap:`**.

- `VersionMismatch`

  This code is to be used when the SOAP receiver is expecting the SOAP message to use a specific SOAP version (e.g., SOAP 1.2) but the standard SOAP elements in the SOAP message are identified by a different SOAP version (e.g., SOAP 1.1). This is part of the mechanism by which SOAP handles versioning of the SOAP protocol.

- `MustUnderstand`

  When the SOAP receiver obtains a message with a header block that it does not understand and the header block is labeled with `mustUnderstand="1"` (see Section 7.4.2), the receiver can return this code to identify the error.

- `DataEncodingUnknown`

  Encoding of the application-specific data in a SOAP message is discussed later in Section 7.8. The data encoding the SOAP message are the rules that the SOAP sender used to encode the application-specific data in XML in order to transfer the data to the receiver in a SOAP message. The SOAP receiver must understand the data encoding used by the SOAP sender to be able to process the message. If the SOAP receiver does not understand the data encoding, it can identify the error to the SOAP sender via the use of the `DataEncodingUnknown` fault code inside a SOAP `Fault`.

- `Sender`

  This code should be used when the SOAP message is erroneous for some reason, such as an invalid structure or invalid data. Typically, this code indicates that something in the message can be corrected and the message resent.

- `Receiver`

  If some abnormal condition occurs on the SOAP receiver side that is not attributable to the SOAP message (such as a database being temporarily down), then the receiver can indicate that with this code.

The Value element must be the first child element of the Code element. The Code element may also contain a single optional Subcode element as the second child element. The Subcode element is used to provide further detail about what caused the Fault to be generated. Just as the Code element requires a single mandatory Value element as its first child, so too does the Subcode element. Additionally, an arbitrary hierarchy of Subcode elements may be specified (that is, the Subcode element of the Code element may have a child element of Subcode and that Subcode may also have a child element of Subcode, and so on, as many levels deep as the application requires). Typically this hierarchy is no more than a few levels deep. A snippet from Listing 7.9 is included below that highlights the use of the Code, Value, and Subcode elements as well as the Sender code.

```
<soap:Envelope xmlns:soap="http://www.w3.org/2003/05/soap-envelope"
       xmlns:shp="http://kellys-fast-shipping.co">
  <soap:Body>
    <soap:Fault>
      <soap:Code>
        <soap:Value>soap:Sender</soap:Value>
        <soap:Subcode>
          <soap:Value>shp:InvalidTrackingRequest</soap:Value>
        </soap:Subcode>
      </soap:Code>
      <soap:Reason>...</soap:Reason>
      <soap:Detail>...</soap:Detail>
    </soap:Fault>
  </soap:Body>
</soap:Envelope>
```

To illustrate the use of another SOAP code, the following listing uses the VersionMismatch code to signify that the SOAP receiver was sent a message compliant with SOAP 1.1 when it was expecting a message compliant with SOAP 1.2.

Listing 7.10 Use of the VersionMismatch Code

```
<soap:Envelope xmlns:soap="http://www.w3.org/2003/05/soap-envelope"
       xmlns:xml="http://www.w3.org/XML/1998/namespace"
       xmlns:shp="http://kellys-fast-shipping.co">
  <soap:Body>
    <soap:Fault>
      <soap:Code>
        <soap:Value>soap:VersionMismatch</soap:Value>
        <soap:Subcode>
          <soap:Value>shp:InvalidTrackingRequest</soap:Value>
        </soap:Subcode>
      </soap:Code>
      <soap:Reason>
```

```
        <soap:Text xml:lang="en">
          Message was not conformant to SOAP 1.2
        </soap:Text>
      </soap:Reason>
      <soap:Detail>
        <shp:soapNs>http://schemas.xmlsoap.org/soap/envelope/
        </shp:soapNs>
      </soap:Detail>
    </soap:Fault>
  </soap:Body>
</soap:Envelope>
```

The Upgrade Header Block

SOAP 1.2 includes a standard mechanism for indicating which versions of SOAP a node supports when that node generates a `Fault` with the `VersionMismatch` code. This mechanism is a standard header block called `Upgrade`. The SOAP specification recommends that a node include an `Upgrade` header block when returning a fault message that is generated because the message requires a version of SOAP that the receiver does not support. The `Upgrade` header block can contain only one or more `SupportedEnvelope` child elements. The `SupportedEnvelope` child element must contain an attribute with the name of `qname` that is used to identify the XML QName (qualified name) of the SOAP namespace that the node supports. The `SupportedEnvelope` child elements should be ordered from the most preferred SOAP version to the least preferred. For example, the following listing shows a fault message that indicates the SOAP receiver prefers SOAP 1.2 but supports SOAP 1.1.

Listing 7.11 Use of the `Upgrade` Header Block

```
<soap:Envelope xmlns:soap="http://www.w3.org/2003/05/soap-envelope"
       xmlns:shp="http://kellys-fast-shipping.co">
  <soap:Body>
    <soap:Header>
      <soap:Upgrade>
        <soap:SupportedEnvelope qname="s12:Envelope"
            xmlns:s12="http://www.w3.org/2003/05/soap-envelope"/>
        <soap:SupportedEnvelope qname="s11:Envelope"
            xmlns:s11="http://schemas.xmlsoap.org/soap/envelope/"/>
      </soap:Upgrade>
    </soap:Header>
    <soap:Fault>
      <soap:Code>
        <soap:Value>soap:VersionMismatch</soap:Value>
        <soap:Subcode>
          <soap:Value>shp:InvalidTrackingRequest</soap:Value>
```

```
        </soap:Subcode>
      </soap:Code>
      <soap:Reason>
        <soap:Text>
          Message was not conformant to SOAP 1.2 or SOAP 1.1
        </soap:Text>
      </soap:Reason>
    </soap:Fault>
  </soap:Body>
</soap:Envelope>
```

The NotUnderstood Header Block

When a SOAP receiver generates a fault message because it does not understand a header block with the mustUnderstand attribute set to true, it can include information in the fault message indicating which header block it does not understand via the NotUnderstood header block. Knowing which header block was not understood is a key piece of information, and the standard NotUnderstood header block provides a convenient means for SOAP receivers to uniformly provide this information. A SOAP sender may be able to use this information to automatically determine how to modify the SOAP message so that it can be resent, or the end user might use this information for debugging a SOAP application.

The NotUnderstood header block must contain an attribute by the name of qname that contains the XML QName (qualified name) of the header that is not understood. The SOAP receiver should include a NotUnderstood header block for each header block in the inbound message it does not understand. The following fault message illustrates the use of the NotUnderstood header block to identify the transactions header block of Listing 7.6 as the header block that is not understood.

Listing 7.12 Use of the NotUnderstood Header Block

```
<soap:Envelope xmlns:soap="http://www.w3.org/2003/05/soap-envelope">
  <soap:Body>
  <soap:Header>
    <soap:NotUnderstood qname="trns:transactions"
        xmlns:trns="http://transaction.example/version1"/>
  </soap:Header>
    <soap:Fault>
      <soap:Code>
        <soap:Value>soap:MustUnderstand</soap:Value>
      </soap:Code>
      <soap:Reason>
        <soap:Text>Header not understood</soap:Text>
      </soap:Reason>
    </soap:Fault>
```

```
  </soap:Body>
</soap:Envelope>
```

7.6.1 The Reason Element

The Reason element, which is mandatory, contains human-readable explanations of the Fault. The Reason element must appear as the second child element of the Fault element (after the Code element) and contain one or more Text child elements, which wrap the text of the human-readable explanations. The SOAP specification recommends that each Text element have a different xml:lang attribute specifying a different language. The xml:lang attribute is part of the XML 1.0 namespace and values for xml:lang are defined by IETF RFC 1766.[15] It is expected that the Text element will be used to display a message to the user and that multiple Text elements will simply be used to display that message in different languages. If this logic is followed when implementing a SOAP application, then multiple Text elements with the same xml:lang attribute will serve only to confuse the software. The xml:lang attribute is not required, and if it is omitted, the assumed language is English (i.e., xml:lang="en"). An example with the Reason element is given below.

Listing 7.13 Use of the Reason Element in a Fault

```
<soap:Envelope xmlns:soap="http://www.w3.org/2003/05/soap-envelope"
       xmlns:xml="http://www.w3.org/XML/1998/namespace"
       xmlns:shp="http://kellys-fast-shipping.co">
  <soap:Body>
    <soap:Fault>
      <soap:Code>
        <soap:Value>soap:MustUnderstand</soap:Value>
      </soap:Code>
      <soap:Reason>
        <soap:Text xml:lang="en">Header not understood</soap:Text>
        <soap:Text xml:lang="es">Encabezamiento no entendió</soap:Text>
      </soap:Reason>
    </soap:Fault>
  </soap:Body>
</soap:Envelope>
```

7.6.2 The Node Element

The Node element, which is sometimes optional, is used to identify what element along the SOAP message path generated the Fault (commonly referred to as the *faulting node*). The Node element is only sometimes optional because the SOAP 1.2 specification states that any node generating a Fault and not

---

[15]The Internet Engineering Task Force (IETF) RFC 1766 is available on the Web at http://www.ietf.org/rfc/rfc1766.txt.

acting as the ultimate receiver must include a Node element to identify itself. The Node element, if used, must appear as the third child element of the Fault (after the Reason element). Node elements accept a single URI as their only value. Remember from the discussions earlier that SOAP nodes are identified by URIs, so this makes perfectly good sense. An example with the Node element is given below.

Listing 7.14 Use of the Node Element in a Fault

```
<soap:Envelope xmlns:soap="http://www.w3.org/2003/05/soap-envelope"
       xmlns:xml="http://www.w3.org/XML/1998/namespace"
       xmlns:shp="http://kellys-fast-shipping.co">
  <soap:Body>
    <soap:Fault>
      <soap:Code>
        <soap:Value>soap:Receiver</soap:Value>
      </soap:Code>
      <soap:Reason>
        <soap:Text xml:lang="en">
          Unable to connect to the database
        </soap:Text>
      </soap:Reason>
      <soap:Node>http://kellys-fast-shipping.co/auditor</soap:Node>
    </soap:Fault>
  </soap:Body>
</soap:Envelope>
```

7.6.3 The Role Element

The optional Role element, if used, must follow the Node element and precede the Detail element. If the Node element is not used, then the Role element must immediately follow the Reason element. The Role element is used to identify the role that the node was processing when it generated the Fault. Recall that the role attribute is specified in a header block to target one or more nodes for processing. Because the Role element is supposed to identify a role, its only required value is a URI. The URI may be one of the standard URIs for roles discussed earlier (see Section 7.4.1), or a custom URI. An example with the Role element is given below.

Listing 7.15 Use of the Role Element in a Fault

```
<soap:Envelope xmlns:soap="http://www.w3.org/2003/05/soap-envelope"
       xmlns:xml="http://www.w3.org/XML/1998/namespace"
       xmlns:shp="http://kellys-fast-shipping.co">
  <soap:Body>
    <soap:Fault>
      <soap:Code>
```

```
      <soap:Value>soap:Receiver</soap:Value>
    </soap:Code>
    <soap:Reason>
      <soap:Text xml:lang="en">
        Unable to connect to the database
      </soap:Text>
    </soap:Reason>
    <soap:Node>http://kellys-fast-shipping.co/auditor</soap:Node>
    <soap:Role>
      http://www.w3.org/2003/05/soap-envelope/role/next
    </soap:Role>
   </soap:Fault>
  </soap:Body>
</soap:Envelope>
```

7.6.4 The `Detail` Element

The `Detail` element is optional and, if used, must appear as the last child element of the `Fault`. The `Detail` element can contain any number of child elements, including none at all. Child elements of the `Detail` element are used to include any application-specific details about the fault condition. Application-specific details that may be included in the `Detail` element include things such as a stack trace to help with debugging an application, the value of elements in the `Body` that caused the `Fault` to be generated, and what those values should be. An example with the `Detail` element is given below.

Listing 7.16 Use of the `Detail` Element in a `Fault`

```
<soap:Envelope xmlns:soap="http://www.w3.org/2003/05/soap-envelope"
       xmlns:xml="http://www.w3.org/XML/1998/namespace"
       xmlns:shp="http://kellys-fast-shipping.co">
  <soap:Body>
    <soap:Fault>
      <soap:Code>
        <soap:Value>soap:Sender</soap:Value>
        <soap:Subcode>
          <soap:Value>shp:InvalidTrackingRequest</soap:Value>
        </soap:Subcode>
      </soap:Code>
      <soap:Reason>
        <soap:Text xml:lang="en">
          Incorrect format used for the tracking number
        </soap:Text>
      </soap:Reason>
      <soap:Detail>
```

```
        <shp:trackingNumSubmitted>123456781234</shp:trackingNumSubmitted>
        <shp:validTrackingNumFormats>
          <shp:trackingNumFormat>
            1Z ### ### ## #### ### #
          </shp:trackingNumFormat>
          <shp:trackingNumFormat>#### #### ####</shp:trackingNumFormat>
          <shp:trackingNumFormat>T### #### ###</shp:trackingNumFormat>
        </shp:validTrackingNumFormats>
      </soap:Detail>
    </soap:Fault>
  </soap:Body>
</soap:Envelope>
```

7.7 SOAP 1.1 Faults

The SOAP 1.2 faults are a great improvement over the SOAP 1.1 faults, but SOAP 1.1 is still widely used. This section shows you how to use faults in SOAP 1.1.

Both SOAP 1.1 and SOAP 1.2 use a `Fault` element to package information about the fault. To some extent, the names of the SOAP 1.1 `Fault` child elements have just been renamed in SOAP 1.2. But the SOAP 1.2 `Fault` child elements are more clearly defined and have been enhanced from SOAP 1.1 to include more elements and provide more valuable information. Table 7.2 maps the SOAP 1.1 `Fault` child elements to the SOAP 1.2 `Fault` child elements.

As seen in Table 7.2, the `Value`, `Subcode`, and `Text` elements of SOAP 1.2 have no corresponding element in SOAP 1.1. You may also notice that the purpose of the SOAP 1.1 `faultactor` element has

Table 7.2 SOAP 1.2 versus SOAP 1.1 Fault `Child` Elements

SOAP 1.2	SOAP 1.1
`Code`	`faultcode`
`Value`	N/A
`Subcode`	N/A
`Reason`	`faultstring`
`Text`	N/A
`Node`	`faultactor`
`Role`	`faultactor`
`Detail`	`detail`

Table 7.3 SOAP 1.2 versus SOAP 1.1 Fault Codes

SOAP 1.2	SOAP 1.1
Sender	Client
Receiver	Server
VersionMismatch	VersionMismatch
MustUnderstand	MustUnderstand
DataEncodingUnknown	N/A

been divided into the Node and Role elements in SOAP 1.2. The following list describes the SOAP 1.1 Fault child elements and highlights the differences between them and SOAP 1.2 faults.

- faultcode (mandatory)

  Like the Code element of SOAP 1.2, this element is mandatory, must be the first child element of the Fault element, and is used to classify faults. Also similar to the Code element is the contents of the faultcode element. The faultcode element must contain an XML QName value, which is the code that the fault is associated with. Recall from Section 7.6.1 that the code value for the Code element is wrapped by the Value element. In SOAP 1.1 the code value is directly inside the faultcode element. Additionally, in SOAP 1.1 the faultcode can technically contain any XML QName whereas in SOAP 1.2 the code can only come from a fixed set of predefined codes. The mapping of SOAP 1.2 predefined fault codes to SOAP 1.1 fault codes is illustrated in Table 7.3.

- As seen in Table 7.3, SOAP 1.1 has no corresponding code for the SOAP 1.2 DataEncodingUnknown code. The Client and Server SOAP 1.1 codes were renamed to avoid unwanted interpretation of how SOAP applications should be implemented. Although SOAP 1.1 allows the use of arbitrary fault codes, the WS-I BP mandates that only the codes listed above or non-standard fault codes that belong to a separate namespace are used. For instance, the WS-Security specification that was mentioned in Section 7.2 defines its own fault codes.

  It should become clear at this point that the faultcode element of SOAP 1.1 does not handle subcodes in the same manner as SOAP 1.2 because the faultcode element has no child elements. The SOAP 1.1 specification states that subcodes can be specified using a dot notation on the faultcode value. For instance, in SOAP 1.1 a code with a subcode might look like the following:

  ```
  <faultcode>Sender.InvalidTrackingRequest</faultcode>
  ```

In SOAP 1.2, however, the same code and subcode looks like the following snippet from Listing 7.16:

```
<soap:Code>
  <soap:Value>soap:Sender</soap:Value>
  <soap:Subcode>
    <soap:Value>shp:InvalidTrackingRequest</soap:Value>
  </soap:Subcode>
</soap:Code>
```

Although the SOAP 1.1 specification allows the use of this dot notation, the WS-I BP mandates that the dot notation not be used because it leads to namespace collisions.

- `faultstring` (mandatory)

  Like the `Reason` element in SOAP 1.2, the `faultstring` element of SOAP 1.1 is mandatory, must appear as the second child element of the `Fault` element, and is used to provide a human-readable description of the fault. Unlike the `Reason` element, the text of the description must appear directly inside the `faultstring` element. Recall that the `Reason` element must contain one or more `Text` child elements, which contain the actual text. The `faultstring` element does not provide a mechanism for including the text in multiple languages such as the `Reason` element does. Use the `xml:lang` attribute to specify the language of the text in the `faultstring` element; however, because only one `faultstring` element can be used, only one language version of the text can be included.

- `faultactor` (optional)

  The `faultactor` element identifies which node generated the fault via a URI. The `faultactor` may contain any URI, but it typically is assigned the URI of the node that generated the fault or the URI of the `actor` attribute if a header block was the cause of the error. Recall that the SOAP 1.1 `actor` attribute was renamed in SOAP 1.2 to `role`.

  As with the `Node` element in SOAP 1.2, this element is mandatory if the node that generated the fault is the ultimate receiver, but is otherwise optional. In SOAP 1.1 the concept of a role is not distinct from the concept of a node as it is in SOAP 1.2. The `faultactor` element is used to identify both the node that generates the fault as well as the role the node is acting in when it generates the fault. This limits the amount of information a SOAP receiver can include in a `Fault` element, so the SOAP 1.2 specification divides the `faultactor` element into two separate elements—the `Node` element and the `Role` element.

- `detail` (optional)

  The `detail` element of SOAP 1.1 is nearly the same as the `Detail` element of SOAP 1.2 (notice the difference in capitalization) in that it is optional, it must appear as the last child element of the Fault element, it can contain any number of application-specific XML elements, and it is used to include application-specific information about the Fault. The major difference between SOAP 1.1 and SOAP 1.2 in regard to this element is that SOAP 1.1 requires the detail element be included if the fault is generated because of an error that occurs while processing the Body element. If the fault is generated because of an error that occurs while processing a header block, then the detail element must not be included; instead application-specific information must be included as header blocks. This restriction was removed in SOAP 1.2 because adding application-specific XML to the message as header blocks presented no benefit over adding that same XML in the Body.

SOAP 1.1 provides no functionality that corresponds to the Upgrade and NotUnderstood header blocks of SOAP 1.2. To illustrate the use of the SOAP 1.1 Fault child elements, the shipment tracking service from previous examples has been re-created below using SOAP 1.1.

Listing 7.17 SOAP 1.1 Fault Elements

```
<soap:Envelope xmlns:soap="http://schemas.xmlsoap.org/soap/envelope"
       xmlns:xml="http://www.w3.org/XML/1998/namespace"
       xmlns:shp="http://kellys-fast-shipping.co">
  <soap:Body>
    <soap:Fault>
      <faultcode>soap:Sender</faultcode>
      <faultstring xml:lang="en">
        Incorrect format used for the tracking number
      </faultstring>
      <faultactor>http://kellys-fast-shipping.co/shipmentTrackingService
      </faultactor>
      <detail>
        <shp:trackingNumSubmitted>123456781234</shp:trackingNumSubmitted>
        <shp:validTrackingNumFormats>
          <shp:trackingNumFormat>
            1Z ### ### ## #### ### #
          </shp:trackingNumFormat>
          <shp:trackingNumFormat>#### #### ####</shp:trackingNumFormat>
          <shp:trackingNumFormat>T### #### ###</shp:trackingNumFormat>
        </shp:validTrackingNumFormats>
      </detail>
    </soap:Fault>
  </soap:Body>
</soap:Envelope>
```

You may have noticed that the SOAP 1.1 elements in Listing 7.17 are not qualified with a namespace (they do not have prefixes such soap: in SOAP 1.2). That is because the WS-I BP mandates that the

`Fault` child elements of SOAP 1.1 be unqualified. On the contrary, all SOAP 1.2 `Fault` child elements must be qualified. The SOAP 1.1 specification also states that you can use your own XML elements as immediate children of the `Fault` element, but the WS-I BP mandates that only the `faultcode`, `faultstring`, `faultactor`, and `detail` elements may be used as immediate children of the `Fault` element.

7.8 Data Encoding

The purpose of SOAP is to transfer data between applications in a platform-independent manner that promotes interoperability between disparate, distributed systems. The previous sections have discussed how that data is packaged for transport and the rules for how the package is processed at each stop, which is much like the way a letter is packaged in a paper postal envelope for transport (including a postal stamp and address) and the postal service has rules for how to process the envelope when it arrives at each postal office. Knowing that two distributed systems support packaging and processing data with SOAP is not enough to get the two systems to interoperate. In addition to defining how the data is packaged and processed, you must also define how the package is transported and how the payload of the package (the data) is formatted so that both parties can understand the data.

We have already touched on the fact that SOAP messages (the package) are typically transported using HTTP. What we have not yet discussed is how the data (the payload of the SOAP message), which traditionally originates from a programming language such as Java, is translated into XML so that it can be packaged into a SOAP envelope. How the data is translated to XML is called *data encoding*. Data encoding involves defining the organization of the data structure, the type of data that can be encoded, and the value of the data. Both communicating parties must know how the data is encoded. The sender must know how to translate the data into XML such that the receiver will know how to translate that XML data back into some form it can use. An analogy with a paper envelope and a letter is the following. A person in the USA has information (data) to send to another person in Spain. What if the person in the USA (sender) transferred the information to paper by writing a letter (data) in the English language and then sent that letter to the person in Spain (receiver), but the receiver knew only Spanish? The receiver person would not know how to translate (decode) the letter. For the sender person and receiver person to communicate, they would both need to use the same language (data encoding).

The Java language provides a mechanism that allows a Java application to encode Java objects into binary data that can be sent across a network and then decoded by the receiving Java application back into Java objects. This mechanism is called *object serialization*. Java RMI uses object serialization to allow a Java application to make method calls on Java objects that are running in a separate virtual machine on a remotely located computer. The drive behind SOAP is to accomplish the same communication that Java RMI provides (and more), but independent of programming language, operating system, etc. SOAP accomplishes platform independence by encoding data in XML, which is simply text data, as opposed to the binary data format that RMI uses.

How the data is encoded in XML (the encoding style) is not restricted by the SOAP specification. Both the sender and receiver just need to know what encoding style is being used and how to translate it. However, Part 2, section 3 of the SOAP 1.2 specification (section 5 in SOAP 1.1) defines a style of encoding that may be used that provides support for RPC (Remote Procedure Call) style messaging. This encoding style is commonly referred to as *SOAP Encoding* or *SOAP Section 5 Encoding* (section 5 is where the encoding style is defined in SOAP 1.1). Most SOAP programming toolkits in use today support SOAP Encoding, but the WS-I BP strictly prohibits its use because it has been a major source of confusion and interoperability problems. Just as specifying the use of SOAP alone does not provide enough information for interoperability, specifying the encoding style as SOAP Encoding does not provide enough information for SOAP nodes to know how to encode and decode the data in a SOAP message. That is because nothing in SOAP Encoding forces the use of a specific typing system for data. SOAP Encoding describes a structure for the data but leaves describing the types of data up to the implementation. The general practice is to use XML Schema data types, but SOAP Encoding does not enforce this. Thus, even if a SOAP receiver specifies the use of SOAP Encoding, a SOAP sender must make an assumption as to the typing scheme used. Nonetheless, SOAP Encoding is part of the specification in use today, so it will be described, albeit somewhat briefly, in this section.

7.8.1 SOAP Data Model

SOAP experts suggest that data in SOAP messages be structured and typed using XML Schema Part 1: Structures[16] and XML Schema Part 2: Datatypes[17] because XML Schema is perceived as having a better type of system and better interoperability than SOAP Encoding. SOAP Encoding was developed largely because, when the SOAP 1.1 specification was written, the XML Schema specification was still in draft form and only supported simple types (such as integers and strings) and not complex types (such as your own Java class). Additionally, the XML Schema structures data in a tree form (see Figure 7.15), which is not nearly as flexible as the object-graph form that SOAP Encoding uses. Often, there is no easy way to map a class in Java to an XML Schema structure such that RPC messaging is readily supported. Therefore, the designers of SOAP created the *SOAP Data Model* and *SOAP Encoding*.

The purpose of the SOAP Data Model is to provide a language-independent abstraction for data types used by common programming languages. The SOAP Data Model represents data as a graph

---

[16]XML Schema Part 1: Structures is found on the Web at `http://www.w3.org/TR/xmlschema-1/`.

[17]XML Schema Part 2: Datatypes is found on the Web at `http://www.w3.org/TR/xmlschema-2/`.

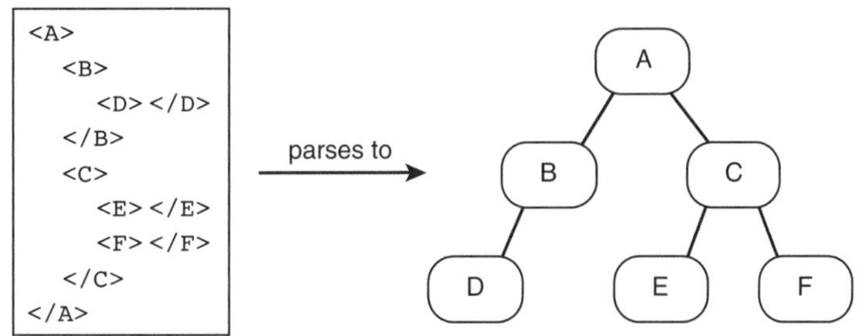

Figure 7.15
Example XML Tree

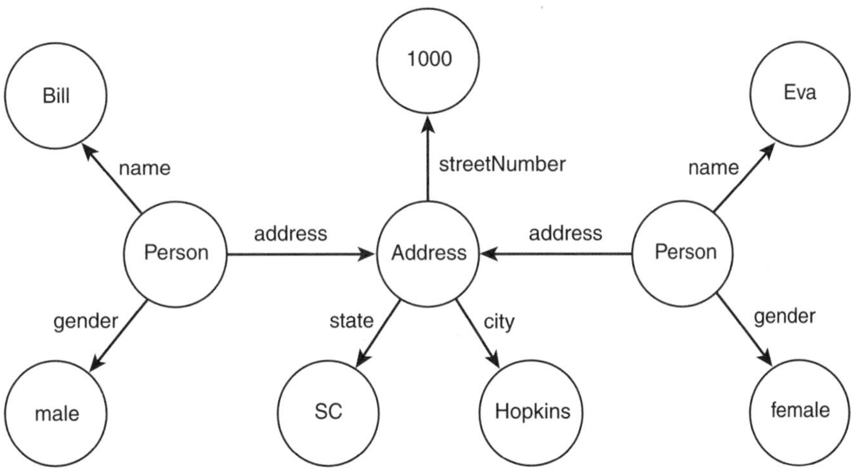

Figure 7.16
Example SOAP Data Model

of *nodes* connected by directional *edges* (see Figure 7.16). The nodes represent a piece of encoded data, which the SOAP specification refers to as *values*, and the edges are referred to as *labels*. A *simple value* is a node with no outgoing edges, in other words, a node with no arrows (edges) pointing from it to another node, only arrows pointing from other nodes to it. A *compound value* is just the opposite; it is a node with outgoing edges. A compound value may reference simple values or other compound values. Values with multiple incoming edges are called multireference values or *multirefs*. Figure 7.16 includes an example of a multireference value in the middle, the Address, which is being referenced by both Person nodes in the figure.

Examples of simple values in Java are `java.lang.String`, `int`, `float`, `long`, `double`, `byte`, and `char`. Compound values in Java are arrays, classes that are defined by the Java Software Development Kit

(SDK), and any classes that the user creates. When the outgoing edges of a compound value have names (as in Figure 7.16), the node is referred to as a *struct* (a `class` in Java or `struct` in C/C++). A compound value with outgoing edges that are not named is called an *array* (like an array in Java or C/C++). A compound value may represent either an array or a struct, but not both. The mechanism that is used to refer to the values within a compound value is called an *accessor*. In the case of a Java class, the fields within the class are accessed via the field names (labels in the SOAP Data Model). With a Java array, the data the array holds are accessed by indicating an ordinal position. With a hash table, the data is accessed using keys to an associative array. An example of the graph in Figure 7.16 coded in Java is shown in the following snippet.

```
class Address {
  int streetNumber;
  String city;
  String state;

  public Address(int streetNumber, String city, String state) {
    this.streetNumber = streetNumber;
    this.city = city;
    this.state = state;
  }
}

class Person {
  string name;
  string gender;
  Address address;

  public Person(String name, String gender, Address address) {
    this.name = name;
    this.gender = gender;
    this.Address = address;
  }
}

Address home = new Address(1000, "Hopkins", "SC");
Person Bill = new Person("Bill", "male", home);
Person Eva = new Person("Eva", "female", home);
```

In the above example, the named accessors (`name`, `gender`, and `address`) are used to get at the values referenced by the `Bill` and `Eva` objects. The values in SOAP are associated with a data type, just as in most programming languages. The simple data types used in SOAP are typically those defined in XML Schema. You will see several examples of simple and complex types represented in XML in Section 7.8.2.

7.8.2 SOAP Encoding

The purpose of SOAP Encoding is to describe a standard convention for taking a SOAP Data Model and writing it out as XML. The resultant XML may be used in a SOAP header block or the SOAP `Body`. XML by itself provides a very flexible means for encoding data. SOAP Encoding defines a narrower set of rules than that provided by XML such that SOAP applications will know how to process data using the SOAP Data Model. Keep in mind that the SOAP Data Model and SOAP Encoding are optional. You can use whatever encoding style you wish to use. The software industry as a whole is trending toward solely using XML Schema to encode the application data used in SOAP messages because of the interoperability problems that SOAP Encoding has presented. However, SOAP Encoding does provide some benefits over XML Schema such as shared references to pieces of data and a common definition of an array, which is a data structure that is found in most programming languages.

The `encodingStyle` Attribute

If you are going to use SOAP Encoding, then it is strongly recommended that you indicate this fact by using the SOAP `encodingStyle` attribute, which is part of the same namespace as the standard SOAP elements (`http://www.w3.org/2003/05/soap-envelope`). The `encodingStyle` attribute is used to specify a URI that identifies the encoding style (rules) you are using to serialize and deserialize data elements. The SOAP 1.2 specification states that the `encodingStyle` attribute can only appear on header blocks or their children, the immediate child of the `Body` element or its children (except the `Fault` element), and the immediate child of a `Fault Detail` element or its children. The `encodingStyle` attribute cannot be used on any other elements. When used, the `encodingStyle` attribute applies encoding rules to the element it appears on and all of its children, unless a child also contains an `encodingStyle` attribute. The SOAP specification indicates no default value for the encoding style; therefore, if the `encodingStyle` attribute is omitted or assigned an empty value (`""`), then no claims and thus no assumptions are to be made of the encoding in use. The values that can be assigned to the `encodingStyle` attribute are:

- `http://www.w3.org/2003/05/soap-encoding`

  This value must be used if you want to indicate that you are using SOAP Encoding.

- `http://www.w3.org/2003/05/soap-envelope/encoding/none`

  This value has the same effect of setting the `encodingStyle` attribute to an empty value (`""`). You may want to use this (or set the encoding style to an empty value) if you have a child element that should not specify an encoding style but its parent element does. In other words, this value and the empty value turn off encoding claims for an element and its descendants.

- You may use a custom value (such as `http://mySpecialEncodingStyle`) that indicates some other encoding style is in use.

Because the WS-I BP strictly prohibits the use of SOAP Encoding and expects all data to be encoded using the XML Schema, it also prohibits the use of the `encodingStyle` attribute.

Difference between SOAP 1.1 and SOAP 1.2: The `encodingStyle` Attribute

The SOAP 1.1 specification states that the `encodingStyle` attribute can appear on any element in the SOAP message. This includes all of the standard SOAP elements, such as `Envelope`, `Header`, `Body`, and `Fault`. The problem with this convention is that, in reality, data encoding does not apply to the standard SOAP elements, just the data they contain. Therefore, SOAP 1.2 has restricted the use of the `encodingStyle` attribute to the data elements (header blocks and application-specific XML in the `Body`). Additionally, the SOAP 1.1 specification defined only one standard value for the `encodingStyle` attribute, which is the value used to signify that SOAP Encoding is being used. That value changed from SOAP 1.1 to SOAP 1.2. The value for SOAP 1.1 is `http://schemas.xmlsoap.org/soap/encoding/`.

The `encodingStyle` attribute can also be assigned multiple URIs, separated by spaces, in order of preference. The first URI is the most preferred encoding style and the last URI is the least preferred. An example SOAP message that uses the sample data model from Figure 7.16 and the `encodingStyle` attribute is given below.

Listing 7.18 Example Usage of the `encodingStyle` Attribute

```
<soap:Envelope xmlns:soap="http://www.w3.org/2003/05/soap-envelope"
    xmlns:myNs="http://myNs">
  <soap:Body>
    <myNs:Person
        soap:encodingStyle="http://www.w3.org/2003/05/soap-encoding">
      <myNs:name>Bill</myNs:name>
      <myNs:gender>male</myNs:gender>
      <myNs:address>
        <myNs:streetNumber>1000</myNs:streetNumber>
        <myNs:city>Hopkins</myNs:city>
        <myNs:state>SC</myNs:state>
      </myNs:address>
    </myNs:Person>
    <myNs:Person
        soap:encodingStyle="http://www.w3.org/2003/05/soap-encoding">
      <myNs:name>Eva</myNs:name>
      <myNs:gender>female</myNs:gender>
      <myNs:address>
        <myNs:streetNumber>1000</myNs:streetNumber>
```

```
        <myNs:city>Hopkins</myNs:city>
        <myNs:state>SC</myNs:state>
      </myNs:address>
    </myNs:Person>
  </soap:Body>
</soap:Envelope>
```

The conversion from the data model of Figure 7.16 to the XML in the Body of Listing 7.18 is quite straightforward. SOAP Encoding states simply that the edges of the graph be encoded as elements in XML. A compound value itself is encoded as an XML element and its outgoing edges are encoded as child elements of that XML element. A simple value is encoded as the text within the XML element that represents its incoming edge. Another way of stating this is that all outgoing edges are encoded as XML elements, which contain either a text value (if the edge terminates at a simple value) or child elements (if the edge terminates at a compound value). So the Person compound values in Figure 7.16 get encoded as the Person XML elements that you see in Listing 7.18. The outgoing edges from the Person compound value are encoded as name, gender, and address elements. Since the nodes at the end of the name and gender edges are simple values, they are encoded as text within the name and gender elements. Because the node at the end of the address edge is a compound value, its outgoing edges are encoded as XML elements. Thus the streetNumber, city, and state edges become XML elements. Because the nodes at the end of the streetNumber, city, and state edges are simple values, they are encoded as text within the streetNumber, city, and state XML elements.

Multi-Reference Values

In Listing 7.18 notice that the address elements in the Person element representing Bill and the Person element representing Eva contain the same data. This is because the address elements are representations of a multi-reference value in the object graph of Figure 7.16. Duplicating data in this fashion is both wasteful, because it unnecessarily consumes space, and inaccurate, because it does not truly represent the object graph. The object graph shows one instance of address while the XML shows two instances. To resolve this problem, the creators of SOAP Encoding decided to allow a single element to be referenced by multiple other elements. This is accomplished by adding an id attribute to the XML element that you wish to reference and a ref attribute to the XML element that points to the referenced element. The ref attribute is assigned the same value as the id attribute. The listing below has restructured Listing 7.18 to use references.

Listing 7.19 Example Multi-Reference Value in SOAP 1.2 Encoding

```
<soap:Envelope xmlns:soap="http://www.w3.org/2003/05/soap-envelope"
    xmlns:myNs="http://myNs">
  <soap:Body>
    <myNs:Person
```

```
      soap:encodingStyle="http://www.w3.org/2003/05/soap-encoding">
    <myNs:name>Bill</myNs:name>
    <myNs:gender>male</myNs:gender>
    <myNs:address id="1">
      <myNs:streetNumber>1000</myNs:streetNumber>
      <myNs:city>Hopkins</myNs:city>
      <myNs:state>SC</myNs:state>
    </myNs:address>
  </myNs:Person>
  <myNs:Person
      soap:encodingStyle="http://www.w3.org/2003/05/soap-encoding">
    <myNs:name>Eva</myNs:name>
    <myNs:gender>female</myNs:gender>
    <myNs:address ref="1"/>
  </myNs:Person>
 </soap:Body>
</soap:Envelope>
```

Notice that the data has been reduced in size because the address is not duplicated, and there is only one instance of address as in the object graph. In this example, only one element has an id attribute. SOAP processors, as a common practice, often add an id attribute to each compound value when it is serialized to XML even though not all of the elements with id attributes are going to be referenced. This practice saves SOAP processors time, because when they encounter a multi-reference value, they can notice that the value it references has already been serialized with an id attribute and use that id instead of having to reserialize the referenced object with an id. This practice causes a few more bytes to be serialized, but it is worth the time it saves in processing.

Difference between SOAP 1.1 and SOAP 1.2: Encoding References

References are encoded differently in SOAP 1.1 than in SOAP 1.2. First of all, the **ref** attribute used in SOAP 1.2 was previously named **href** in SOAP 1.1. The type of the attribute also changed. In SOAP 1.1 the type is an XML Schema anyURI, which means that the value must either be a URI (such as http://example.com/picture.gif) or a value prefixed by # (such as #1 for the reference in Listing 7.19). A value prefixed by # for an anyURI type is used to indicate a reference to another location in that document. This practice is commonly used in HTML documents. In SOAP 1.2 the type is an XML Schema IDREF, which means that it is a reference to an ID somewhere in that document. An IDREF type takes the same value as the ID it is referencing, so it does not require a # prefix.

The application-specific XML elements in a SOAP message are classified as either *independent* or *embedded*. Embedded elements are child elements of other application-specific XML elements. Independent elements have no application-specific XML parent elements, that is, they are immediate children of either the SOAP Body element or the SOAP Header element. SOAP 1.1 Encoding restricts multi-reference values to independent elements. SOAP 1.2 Encoding allows multi-reference values to either be independent or embedded (also called inline). Listing 7.19 uses SOAP 1.2 to show an example of an inline multi-reference value. Below, Listing 7.20 reconstructs Listing 7.19 in SOAP 1.1 using an independent multi-reference value.

Listing 7.20 Example Multi-Reference Value in SOAP 1.1 Encoding

```
<soap:Envelope xmlns:soap="http://schemas.xmlsoap.org/soap/envelope"
    xmlns:myNs="http://myNs">
  <soap:Body>
    <myNs:address id="1"
      soap:encodingStyle="http://schemas.xmlsoap.org/soap/encoding/">
      <myNs:streetNumber>1000</myNs:streetNumber>
      <myNs:city>Hopkins</myNs:city>
      <myNs:state>SC</myNs:state>
    </myNs:address>
    <myNs:Person
      soap:encodingStyle="http://schemas.xmlsoap.org/soap/encoding/">
      <myNs:name>Bill</myNs:name>
      <myNs:gender>male</myNs:gender>
      <myNs:address href="#1"/>
    </myNs:Person>
    <myNs:Person
      soap:encodingStyle="http://schemas.xmlsoap.org/soap/encoding/">
      <myNs:name>Eva</myNs:name>
      <myNs:gender>female</myNs:gender>
      <myNs:address href="#1"/>
    </myNs:Person>
  </soap:Body>
</soap:Envelope>
```

Specifying Data Types

For a SOAP receiver to fully understand the data in a SOAP message, the type of data that each XML element contains must be specified. For example, in Listing 7.19 the `streetNumber` element could be interpreted as several different data types in Java including `java.lang.String`, `int`, or `float`. Interpreting the data type incorrectly could potentially cause the processing of the SOAP message by the SOAP receiver to fail. Suppose for a moment that the `streetNumber` element contained a value of `1000A` and did not indicate its data type. If the SOAP receiver made the assumption that the data type was `int`, it would generate an error when it tried to convert the value of `1000A` to an `int`.

One of the following three ways can be used to specify the data type for an application-specific XML element in a SOAP message.

- The XML element can include the XML Schema attribute called `type` with an assigned value equal to one of the valid type identifiers specified in XML Schema Part 2: Datatypes. These XML Schema datatypes (called built-in datatypes) include such values as `string`, `boolean`, `base64Binary`, `hexBinary`, `float`, `decimal`, `date`, `time`, as well as some types that are derived from those built-in datatypes such as `integer` and `nonNegativeInteger`. (The `nonNegativeInteger` is exactly the way it sounds, an integer type that cannot be assigned negative values.) The `type` attribute is defined in the XML Schema instance namespace, `http://www.w3.org/2001/XMLSchema-instance`. The XML Schema built-in datatypes are defined in the XML Schema namespace, `http://www.w3.org/2001/XMLSchema`. While not required by XML, it is a common convention to use the `xsi` prefix for the XML Schema instance namespace, and the `xsd` prefix for XML Schema namespace. Listing 7.19 has been rewritten below to use the `type` attribute.

Listing 7.21 Specifying Data Types Using the `xsi:type` Attribute

```
<soap:Envelope xmlns:soap="http://www.w3.org/2003/05/soap-envelope"
    xmlns:xsi="http://www.w3.org/2001/XMLSchema-instance"
    xmlns:xsd="http://www.w3.org/2001/XMLSchema"
    xmlns:myNs="http://myNs">
  <soap:Body>
    <myNs:Person
        soap:encodingStyle="http://www.w3.org/2003/05/soap-encoding">
      <myNs:name xsi:type="xsd:string">Bill</myNs:name>
      <myNs:gender xsi:type="xsd:string">male</myNs:gender>
      <myNs:address id="1">
        <myNs:streetNumber xsi:type="xsd:int">1000</myNs:streetNumber>
        <myNs:city xsi:type="xsd:string">Hopkins</myNs:city>
        <myNs:state xsi:type="xsd:string">SC</myNs:state>
      </myNs:address>
    </myNs:Person>
    <myNs:Person
        soap:encodingStyle="http://www.w3.org/2003/05/soap-encoding">
      <myNs:name xsi:type="xsd:string">Eva</myNs:name>
      <myNs:gender xsi:type="xsd:string">female</myNs:gender>
      <myNs:address ref="1"/>
    </myNs:Person>
  </soap:Body>
</soap:Envelope>
```

- An XML element can include the SOAP Encoding `itemType` attribute, which restricts all child elements of that element to the data type specified by the assigned value. The `itemType` attribute is included in the SOAP Encoding namespace, `http://www.w3.org/2003/05/soap-`

encoding, and accepts any XML QName (qualified name). Again, while not required by XML, it is a common convention to use the soapenc prefix for the SOAP Encoding namespace. Arrays in SOAP Encoding are defined using the itemType attribute. An example is given below. In this example the itemType attribute of the numbers array element restricts all of the child number elements to a data type of xsd:int.

Listing 7.22 Specifying Data Types Using the soapenc:itemType Attribute

```
<soap:Envelope xmlns:soap="http://www.w3.org/2003/05/soap-envelope"
    xmlns:soapenc="http://www.w3.org/2003/05/soap-encoding"
    xmlns:xsd="http://www.w3.org/2001/XMLSchema"
    xmlns:myNs="http://myNs">
  <soap:Body>
    <myNs:numbers soapenc:itemType="xsd:int" soapenc:arraySize="3"
      soap:encodingStyle="http://www.w3.org/2003/05/soap-encoding">
      <myNs:number>123456</myNs:number>
      <myNs:number>098765</myNs:number>
      <myNs:number>675849</myNs:number>
    </myNs:numbers>
  </soap:Body>
</soap:Envelope>
```

- The XML element names can be associated with data types defined by an associated XML schema. To use this method, simply create an XML schema document separate from the SOAP message, and then associate the application-specific XML elements of the SOAP message with the namespace for the XML schema. The XML schema defines the application-specific XML elements that are used and their associated data types. The use of an XML schema to define data types in a SOAP message is the method that SOAP experts recommend because, among the three options, XML schema causes less interoperability problems. The following two listings illustrate an example XML schema and the use of that schema in a SOAP message. Listing 7.23 is an XML schema that defines the Person element and the address child element from Listing 7.19. Listing 7.24 references the namespace for this XML schema and uses the Person element within the Body of a SOAP message (Listing 7.24 is just a reprint of Listing 7.19.)

Listing 7.23 Example XML Schema Defining Person and Address Types

```
<?xml version="1.0" encoding="UTF-8"?>
<schema xmlns="http://www.w3.org/2001/XMLSchema"
    xmlns:myNs="http://myNs" targetNamespace="http://myNs">
  <element name="Address" type="myNs:addressType"/>
  <complexType name="addressType">
```

```
    <sequence>
      <element name="streetNumber"  type="int"/>
      <element name="city"          type="string"/>
      <element name="state"         type="string"/>
    </sequence>
  </complexType>

  <element name="Person" type="myNs:personType"/>
  <complexType name="personType">
    <sequence>
      <element name="name" type="string"/>
      <element name="gender" type="string"/>
      <element name="address" type="myNs:addressType"/>
    </sequence>
  </complexType>
</schema>
```

Listing 7.24 Specifying Data Types Using XML Schema

```
<?xml version="1.0" encoding="UTF-8"?>
<soap:Envelope xmlns:soap="http://www.w3.org/2003/05/soap-envelope"
    xmlns:myNs="http://myNs">
  <soap:Body>
    <myNs:Person
        soap:encodingStyle="http://www.w3.org/2003/05/soap-encoding">
      <myNs:name>Bill</myNs:name>
      <myNs:gender>male</myNs:gender>
      <myNs:address id="1">
        <myNs:streetNumber>1000</myNs:streetNumber>
        <myNs:city>Hopkins</myNs:city>
        <myNs:state>SC</myNs:state>
      </myNs:address>
    </myNs:Person>
    <myNs:Person
        soap:encodingStyle="http://www.w3.org/2003/05/soap-encoding">
      <myNs:name>Eva</myNs:name>
      <myNs:gender>female</myNs:gender>
      <myNs:address ref="1"/>
    </myNs:Person>
  </soap:Body>
</soap:Envelope>
```

Simple types are datatypes like the Java primitives (i.e., `boolean`, `int`, `long`, `float`, `double`, etc.). The simple types that can be used in SOAP Encoding are the XML Schema built-in datatypes (described by the first bullet above and illustrated by Listing 7.21), and a set of elements that are based on the XML Schema built-in datatypes but defined in the SOAP Encoding namespace. The XML elements defined in the SOAP Encoding namespace can be used in place of the XML Schema built-in datatypes or used to create an arbitrary element with a specified data type. Both of these uses are illustrated by the listing below, which is a rewrite of Listing 7.22.

Listing 7.25 Use of SOAP Encoding Built-In Datatypes

```
<soap:Envelope xmlns:soap="http://www.w3.org/2003/05/soap-envelope"
    xmlns:soapenc="http://www.w3.org/2003/05/soap-encoding"
    xmlns:myNs="http://myNs">
  <soap:Body>
    <myNs:numbers soapenc:itemType="soapenc:int" soapenc:arraySize="3"
      soap:encodingStyle="http://www.w3.org/2003/05/soap-encoding">
      <soapenc:int>123456</soapenc:int>
      <soapenc:int>098765</soapenc:int>
      <soapenc:int>675849</soapenc:int>
    </myNs:numbers>
  </soap:Body>
</soap:Envelope>
```

SOAP experts recommend that the XML Schema built-in datatypes be used instead of the SOAP Encoding built-in data types because the XML Schema types cause fewer interoperability problems. For further information on the SOAP Encoding built-in data types see the XML Schema for SOAP 1.2 Encoding, `http://www.w3.org/2003/05/soap-encoding`.

If you are wondering how binary data can be encoded, recall from Section 7.1.2 and Figure 7.4 that one option is to use the Base64 encoding algorithm. To specify that data is encoded in Base64, use the XML Schema built-in datatype, such as

```
<myImage xsi:type="xsd:base64Binary">aG93IG5vDyBicmBjb3cNCg==</myImage>
```

or the SOAP Encoding built-in datatype, such as

```
<myImage xsi:type="soapenc:base64">aG93IG5vDyBicmBjb3cNCg==</myImage>
```

As mentioned in Section 7.1.2, the Base64 encoding algorithm unfortunately increases the data size by about one-third, so SOAP implementations often transmit binary data as SOAP attachments (see Figure 7.5), which does not reduce the size of the transmission, but does reduce the size of the data within the SOAP `Envelope`, thus improving the performance of the SOAP processing.

Complex Types

In Section 7.8.1, we mentioned that object graph nodes in the SOAP Data Model can represent a simple value or a compound value, and the compound values are either classified as a struct or an array. A struct has named outgoing edges, and an array has outgoing edges that do not have names. The values that the struct contains are referenced via named accessors, but the values the array contains are referenced via ordinal positions (i.e., an index). This section covers encoding structs and the next section covers encoding arrays.

A struct in SOAP Encoding is used to describe, in XML, the complex types that can be created in common programming languages, such as the `struct` in C/C++ or the `class` in Java. A struct can contain simple values and other compound values. For example, the `Person` struct from the data model in Figure 7.16 contains both simple values, that is, `name` and `gender`, as well as a compound value, the `Address` struct. A Java class representing the `Address` struct was given earlier, and is rewritten below in a simpler form such that all of the fields are public, just to demonstrate the programming data structure that the SOAP Encoding struct was designed to describe.

```
class Address {
  public int streetNumber;
  public String city;
  public String state;
}
```

Although not yet discussed, an example of how a struct is encoded in XML using the rules of SOAP Encoding has already been given in Listing 7.21. In Listing 7.21, the `Address` and `Person` structs of the data model in Figure 7.16 were encoded in an example SOAP message. This example was used to demonstrate how to specify the data types of the simple values that the `Person` and `Address` structs contain using the `xsi:type` attribute. A snippet showing the `Address` struct from Listing 7.21 is given below.

```
<myNs:address id="1">
  <myNs:streetNumber xsi:type="xsd:int">1000</myNs:streetNumber>
  <myNs:city xsi:type="xsd:string">Hopkins</myNs:city>
  <myNs:state xsi:type="xsd:string">SC</myNs:state>
</myNs:address>
```

As you can see, each field of the `Address` Java class receives a corresponding element (an accessor) in the `address` XML element. Notice that the simple values are typed (using `xsi:type`), but the compound value, the struct, is not typed. The `Address` class in the Java code is considered a type, but in this case, the XML element named `address`, which is supposed to represent it, is not typed. This is due to the fact that the struct value is not typed in SOAP Encoding. This weak typing in SOAP Encoding is one of its drawbacks and a reason why SOAP experts suggest that data in a SOAP message be encoded using XML Schema instead of SOAP Encoding. When SOAP 1.1 was written, the XML Schema was in draft form and had not yet defined a mechanism for handling complex types. Since XML Schema had defined simple types by that time, the SOAP specification made use of them as the snippet above illustrates. When it came to complex types, the creators of SOAP had to devise their own data model and encoding to handle them.

Now that the XML Schema is a full W3C Recommendation that covers complex types, XML Schema is the preferred method of encoding data for a SOAP message. An example of using XML Schema to describe complex types for a SOAP message has also already been given in Listing 7.23 and Listing 7.24. Listing 7.23 illustrates an XML schema that was created to describe the types in the data model of Figure 7.16, and Listing 7.24 uses an instance of that schema to describe the data in a SOAP message. The `Address` element from the schema in Listing 7.23 is reprinted below.

```
<element name="Address" type="myNs:addressType"/>
<complexType name="addressType">
  <sequence>
    <element name="streetNumber"  type="int"/>
    <element name="city"          type="string"/>
    <element name="state"         type="string"/>
  </sequence>
</complexType>
```

This schema definition of an address type is used in the SOAP message of Listing 7.24, which is reprinted below.

```
<myNs:address id="1">
  <myNs:streetNumber>1000</myNs:streetNumber>
  <myNs:city>Hopkins</myNs:city>
  <myNs:state>SC</myNs:state>
</myNs:address>
```

The target namespace for the schema, which is prefixed `myNs`, is used to associate the elements in the SOAP message with the schema definition. The schema defines types for both simple values and compound values, such as the address. Thus, in this example, the address has a type in XML just as it does in Java.

Array Types

SOAP 1.2 Encoding defines two attributes that can be used in combination to encode an array in XML—`itemType` and `arraySize`. An example that uses both of these attributes to encode an array was given in Listing 7.22, where the `itemType` attribute was described. The `itemType` attribute is used to specify the data types that the array holds, and the `arraySize` attribute is used to specify the size of the array. Both of these attributes are part of the SOAP Encoding namespace (`http://www.w3.org/-2003/05/soap-encoding`). The following example illustrates the use of these two attributes to encode an array of three people.

Listing 7.26 SOAP Encoded Array of Simple Types

```
<soap:Envelope xmlns:soap="http://www.w3.org/2003/05/soap-envelope"
    xmlns:soapenc="http://www.w3.org/2003/05/soap-encoding"
```

```
    xmlns:xsd="http://www.w3.org/2001/XMLSchema">
  <soap:Body>
    <people soapenc:itemType="xsd:string" soapenc:arraySize="3"
      soap:encodingStyle="http://www.w3.org/2003/05/soap-encoding">
      <person>Richard</person>
      <person>Kelly</person>
      <person>Brighton</person>
    </people>
  </soap:Body>
</soap:Envelope>
```

Notice in Listing 7.26 that the array (the `people` element) and the items the array holds (the `person` elements) are not typed. These elements do not have to be typed in SOAP Encoding. The fact that the `people` element contains the `itemType` and `arraySize` attributes indicates to a SOAP processor that it is an array. The `itemType` attribute indicates to a SOAP processor what types are contained in the child elements of `people`, which in this case are called `person`. The name of the array element and its child elements can be anything you like. The information that is important to the SOAP processor is contained within the `itemType` and `arraySize` attributes. The items of the array are only distinguishable by position, so the element names are irrelevant, but a good practice is to give the elements a name that indicates to the reader what the element is intended to represent. However, the ordering of the elements within the array is important. The first child element of the array element in the encoded XML will become the first element in the array that is created by the SOAP processor in the target programming language. For example, if the SOAP receiver was written in Java and it received the array in Listing 7.26, then `Richard` would be placed in index `0` of the Java array, `Kelly` would be placed in index `1`, and `Brighton` would be placed in index `2`.

As mentioned previously in the specifying Data Types section, the `itemType` attribute accepts any XML QName (qualified name). Therefore, an array can take any type that can be specified by XML. For instance, Listing 7.26 can be rewritten to use the `personType` of the XML schema in Listing 7.23 as illustrated below.

Listing 7.27 SOAP Encoded Array of Compound Types

```
<soap:Envelope xmlns:soap="http://www.w3.org/2003/05/soap-envelope"
    xmlns:soapenc="http://www.w3.org/2003/05/soap-encoding"
    xmlns:xsd="http://www.w3.org/2001/XMLSchema"
    xmlns:myNs="http://myNs">
  <soap:Body>
    <family soapenc:itemType="myNs:personType" soapenc:arraySize="3"
      soap:encodingStyle="http://www.w3.org/2003/05/soap-encoding">
      <member>
        <myNs:Person>
          <myNs:name>Richard</myNs:name>
          <myNs:gender>male</myNs:gender>
```

```
        <myNs:address id="1">
          <myNs:streetNumber>1000</myNs:streetNumber>
          <myNs:city>Acworth</myNs:city>
          <myNs:state>GA</myNs:state>
        </myNs:address>
      </myNs:Person>
    </member>
    <member>
      <myNs:Person>
        <myNs:name>Kelly</myNs:name>
        <myNs:gender>female</myNs:gender>
        <myNs:address ref="1"/>
      </myNs:Person>
    </member>
    <member>
      <myNs:Person>
        <myNs:name>Brighton</myNs:name>
        <myNs:gender>male</myNs:gender>
        <myNs:address ref="1"/>
      </myNs:Person>
    </member>
  </family>
 </soap:Body>
</soap:Envelope>
```

The SOAP Encoded array will also accept any types that are derived from the type specified by the `itemType` attribute. This allows languages that support polymorphism, such as Java, to encode arrays similar to the following, which illustrate the fact that the `byte`, `short`, and `int` types of XML Schema are derived from the `integer` type.

```
<numbers soapenc:itemType="xsd:integer" soapenc:arraySize="3"
    soap:encodingStyle="http://www.w3.org/2003/05/soap-encoding">
  <number xsi:type="byte">127</number>
  <number xsi:type="short">32767</number>
  <number xsi:type="int">2147483647</number>
</numbers>
```

In addition to the fixed, one-dimension array examples given so far, the `arraySize` attribute can also be used to specify unbounded arrays and multidimensional arrays. The `arraySize` attribute used in the listings above contained a value of `"3"`, that is, the array is constrained to three elements. If the `arraySize` attribute was given a value of `"*"`, then the array becomes unbounded, meaning the size is unspecified. For instance, the following code snippet illustrates a one-dimensional, unbounded array.

```
<numbers soapenc:itemType="xsd:int" soapenc:arraySize="*"
```

```
    soap:encodingStyle="http://www.w3.org/2003/05/soap-encoding">
  <number>1</number>
  <number>2</number>
  <number>3</number>
</numbers>
```

The default value for the arraySize attribute is "*", meaning if the arraySize attribute is omitted, then the array will be unbounded and one-dimensional. Thus the previous snippet could be rewritten as:

```
<numbers soapenc:itemType="xsd:int"
    soap:encodingStyle="http://www.w3.org/2003/05/soap-encoding">
  <number>1</number>
  <number>2</number>
  <number>3</number>
</numbers>
```

Multidimensional arrays can be specified by listing each dimension of the array in the arraySize attribute, separated by spaces. The special value of "*" can be used in a multidimensional array to make the first dimension of the array unbounded, but cannot be used on any other dimension of the array. In other words, the value "* 3 3" is acceptable, but the value "3 * 3" is not. A code snippet of a two-dimensional array is given below. The first dimension of the array is a fixed size of 2 and the second dimension is a fixed size of 3. The contents of a multidimensional array are encoded in XML in the order they appear in the array. This means the first dimension is encoded first including each of its elements in order, then the second dimension, and so on.

```
<values soapenc:itemType="xsd:string" soapenc:arraySize="2 3"
    soap:encodingStyle="http://www.w3.org/2003/05/soap-encoding">
  <value>row 1, column 1</value>
  <value>row 1, column 2</value>
  <value>row 1, column 3</value>
  <value>row 2, column 1</value>
  <value>row 2, column 2</value>
  <value>row 2, column 3</value>
</values>
```

Difference between SOAP 1.1 and SOAP 1.2: Encoding Arrays

The methods for serializing an array using SOAP Encoding changed fairly significantly from SOAP 1.1 to SOAP 1.2. First of all, the type of the array and the size of the array are specified by two separate attributes in SOAP 1.2, but SOAP 1.1 uses only one attribute, the arrayType attribute. In SOAP 1.1 the SOAP processor must parse the value of the arrayType attribute to obtain the two separate values, type and size. As an example, Listing 7.26 has been rewritten below to use

SOAP 1.1 Encoding. The value before the brackets specifies the type, and the value within the brackets specifies the size.

Listing 7.28 SOAP 1.1 Encoding of an Array with Simple Types

```
<soap:Envelope xmlns:soap="http://schemas.xmlsoap.org/soap/envelope"
    xmlns:soapenc="http://schemas.xmlsoap.org/soap/encoding/"
    xmlns:xsd="http://www.w3.org/2001/XMLSchema">
  <soap:Body>
    <people soapenc:arrayType="xsd:string[3]"
      soap:encodingStyle="http://schemas.xmlsoap.org/soap/encoding/">
      <person>Richard</person>
      <person>Kelly</person>
      <person>Brighton</person>
    </people>
  </soap:Body>
</soap:Envelope>
```

Unbounded arrays in SOAP 1.1 are specified using empty brackets, such as `soapenc:arrayType="xsd:string[]"`. Multidimensional arrays are specified by inserting a comma-delimited list of numbers between the brackets, such as `soapenc:arrayType="xsd:string[2,3]"`. Each dimension in a SOAP 1.1 multidimensional array can be specified as unbounded by simply omitting the numbers, for example, `soapenc:arrayType="xsd:string[,]"`. You may also see examples such as `int[][3]` or `int[,][3]`. The first example specifies an array of 3 members where each member is of type `int[]` (`int` array). The second example specifies an array of 3 members where each member is of type `int[,]` (unbounded two-dimensional `int` array).

SOAP 1.1 also defines an `Array` XML element (that SOAP 1.2 removed), which can be used to encode an array in XML. In addition, SOAP 1.1 Encoding defines elements for the XML Schema simple types, such that Listing 7.28 can be rewritten as the following.

Listing 7.29 SOAP 1.1 Encoding of an Array with Simple Types Using the `Array` Element

```
<soap:Envelope xmlns:soap="http://schemas.xmlsoap.org/soap/envelope"
    xmlns:soapenc="http://schemas.xmlsoap.org/soap/encoding/"
    xmlns:xsd="http://www.w3.org/2001/XMLSchema">
  <soap:Body>
    <soapenc:Array soapenc:arrayType="xsd:string[3]"
      soap:encodingStyle="http://schemas.xmlsoap.org/soap/encoding/">
      <soapenc:string>Richard</soapenc:string>
      <soapenc:string>Kelly</soapenc:string>
      <soapenc:string>Brighton</soapenc:string>
    </soapenc:Array>
  </soap:Body>
</soap:Envelope>
```

Because the `Array` XML element accepts members of any type, heterogeneous arrays in SOAP 1.1 can be specified using `xsd:ur-type`. These arrays can contain multiple unrelated types as the following code snippet demonstrates.

```
<values soapenc:arrayType="xsd:ur-type[3]"
    soap:encodingStyle="http://schemas.xmlsoap.org/soap/encoding/">
  <value xsi:type="int">2147483647</value>
  <value xsi:type="float">125.25</value>
  <value xsi:type="string">Paid with cash</value>
</values>
```

Additionally, SOAP 1.2 removed the support that SOAP 1.1 had for *partially transmitted arrays* and *sparse arrays*. Sometimes an array does not have values for all of its indicated ordinal positions. One instance of this is where the array is only partially filled but the populated positions are contiguous. For instance, there may be an array of size 3 where the second and third positions are occupied but the first position is empty. In this case, the values at the second and third positions are contiguous. Normally it would be necessary to specify that the first position is `null` as follows.

```
<numbers soapenc:arrayType="xsd:int[3]"
    soap:encodingStyle="http://schemas.xmlsoap.org/soap/encoding/">
  <number xsi:null="1"/>
  <number>2</number>
  <number>3</number>
</numbers>
```

However, SOAP 1.1 allows the transmission of this array as a partial array by omitting the first position and including an `offset` attribute, as follows. Doing so reduces the size of the document that must be transmitted.

```
<numbers soapenc:arrayType="xsd:int[3]" soapenc:offset="[1]"
    soap:encodingStyle="http://schemas.xmlsoap.org/soap/encoding/">
  <number>2</number>
  <number>3</number>
</numbers>
```

If the array is missing values and the values in the array are not contiguous, then SOAP 1.1 allows a sparse array to be specified by using the `position` attribute on all elements of the array. The `position` attribute indicates the ordinal position in the array for that element. For instance, if an array has a size of 3 where the first and third positions are populated but the second position is empty, this array may be specified as follows.

```
<numbers soapenc:arrayType="xsd:int[3]" soapenc:offset="[1]"
    soap:encodingStyle="http://schemas.xmlsoap.org/soap/encoding/">
  <number soapenc:position="0">1</number>
  <number soapenc:position="2">3</number>
</numbers>
```

SOAP 1.2 removed the support for these arrays because they weren't being used much and they created interoperability problems.

As has been mentioned several times in this section, SOAP experts believe that the future use of SOAP Encoding is dim and developers should instead use XML Schema wherever possible. Thus the following example is given to demonstrate how an array in XML can be encoded using XML Schema and SOAP.

Listing 7.30 Use of the `maxOccurs` Attribute in an XML Schema to Identify an Array

```
<?xml version="1.0" encoding="UTF-8"?>
<schema xmlns="http://www.w3.org/2001/XMLSchema"
    xmlns:myNs="http://myNs" targetNamespace="http://myNs">
  <element name="member" type="myNs:FamilyMember"/>
  <complexType name="FamilyMember">
    <sequence>
      <element name="firstName" type="string"/>
      <element name="gender" type="string"/>
    </sequence>
  </complexType>

  <element name="family" type="myNs:Family"/>
  <complexType name="Family">
    <sequence>
      <element name="surname" type="string"/>
      <element name="members" type="myNs:FamilyMember"
               maxOccurs="unbounded"/>
    </sequence>
  </complexType>
</schema>
```

Listing 7.31 Use of an XML Schema in a SOAP Message to Specify an Array

```
<?xml version="1.0" encoding="UTF-8"?>
<soap:Envelope xmlns:soap="http://www.w3.org/2003/05/soap-envelope"
    xmlns:myNs="http://myNs">
  <soap:Body>
    <myNs:family>
      <myNs:surname>Allen</myNs:surname>
      <myNs:members>
        <myNs:member>
          <myNs:firstName>Richard</myNs:firstName>
          <myNs:gender>male</myNs:gender>
        </myNs:member>
```

```
        <myNs:member>
          <myNs:firstName>Kelly</myNs:firstName>
          <myNs:gender>female</myNs:gender>
        </myNs:member>
        <myNs:member>
          <myNs:firstName>Brighton</myNs:firstName>
          <myNs:gender>male</myNs:gender>
        </myNs:member>
      </myNs:members>
    </myNs:family>
  </soap:Body>
</soap:Envelope>
```

XML Schema does not explicitly define an array type such as SOAP Encoding. However, most SOAP processors will treat an XML schema element with a `maxOccurs` attribute assigned to a value of `unbounded` as an array. Therefore, the `members` element in Listing 7.31 could be translated to a `members` field in a Java class with a type of `FamilyMember[]` as the code snippet below illustrates.

```
class Family {
  public String surname;
  public FamilyMember[] members;
}
```

The `FamilyMember` class would be defined as a Java class containing fields `firstName` and `gender` of type `java.lang.String` just as the complex type defined in Listing 7.30. Note that complex types in XML Schema are analogous to compound types in SOAP Encoding.

7.9 Message Styles and Encoding Styles

Because SOAP was designed to be independent of underlying platforms and programming languages, it leaves some implementation decisions up to the developer of the SOAP application. For instance, SOAP does not mandate any specifics about the data or structure of the data that must go into the SOAP `Body` element, except, of course, when a SOAP `Fault` is being transmitted. Even when transmitting a SOAP `Fault`, the developer can put whatever wanted into the `Detail` element of the `Fault`. This freedom not only makes the SOAP specification independent of any particular implementation details, it also provides a very important level of flexibility. Distributed systems can be very complex and developers often need that flexibility when trying to integrate disparate systems.

The choices made when implementing a SOAP-based system directly affect the interoperability of that system. If interoperability is not important, then there are other distributed architectures that Java developers can use, which are easier to implement than SOAP and allow use of many features of Java that are lost when using SOAP. Keep in mind that when data is represented in XML, the developers will not be able to match exactly what was present in the object-oriented world of Java. That being said, if the developer must integrate two very different environments, such as Java on Linux and .NET on Windows, then a SOAP-based implementation could be best. As long as smart decisions are made when deciding on the structure and encoding of the data put in the `Body`, there should be a fairly smooth integration.

Two of the decisions that greatly affect interoperability as well as ease of implementation and performance are message style and encoding style. The choices of message style are as follows.

- RPC

  Recall that RPC is an acronym for Remote Procedure Call. An RPC-style message is designed to model the semantics of procedure calls made in programming languages such as Java where method calls are used to exchange parameters and return values (synchronous style of communication). Programmers are familiar with this semantic so the creators of SOAP defined an optional structure for defining an RPC-style request and response SOAP message. In the SOAP-defined RPC model, the RPC-style request message contains a single application-specific child element in the `Body`, which specifies the method name and a list of input parameters (called *in* parameters) for the procedure call. The RPC response message also contains a single child element in the `Body`, which can be either a `Fault` (exceptional condition) or an application-specific element containing the response and any other parameters (called *out* parameters). Because SOAP is independent of programming language and some languages support multiple return parameters from a procedure call, SOAP RPC provides a structure for handling multiple out parameters.

- Document

  This message style means that no SOAP formatting rules (such as SOAP RPC) are being applied to the data in the `Body`. The SOAP `Body` simply contains one or more XML elements that hold some arbitrary data the sender and receiver have agreed upon.

The message styles above can be combined with an encoding style that describes how the data in the `Body` is serialized and deserialized. SOAP does not mandate any specific encoding style so the user is free to choose anything. The developer can even create and use his or her own encoding style if desired. Two popular encoding styles in use today are the following.

- SOAP Encoding

  This is an optional set of serialization rules that is defined by the SOAP specification. SOAP Encoding was described in Section 7.8. Typically SOAP Encoding is used with the RPC message style.

- Literal

  Literal encoding simply means that the payload of a SOAP message is defined completely by a schema. The language typically used to express the schema is XML Schema, but not always. The XML Schema does not always provide the capability that is needed, so other schema languages are sometimes used in place of or in concert with XML Schema. Examples include RELAX NG[18] and Schematron.[19]

Each message style can be combined with each encoding style to form four different message formats—RPC/Encoded, RPC/Literal, Document/Encoded, and Document/Literal. Examples of the four formats are given in the following sections.

7.9.1 SOAP RPC Representation

Before the four different message formats are discussed, we present information about the SOAP RPC Representation used by two of the formats. The SOAP RPC Representation is an optional convention for structuring SOAP request and response messages to facilitate conveniently mapping those messages to procedure or method calls commonly used by programming languages such as Java. This convention was partially covered by the RPC discussion in the previous section. This section will describe it in a little more detail.

The SOAP RPC Representation depends on the SOAP Data Model (discussed in Section 7.8.1) for representing the data being exchanged, but does not require SOAP Encoding, and does not require a specific underlying transport protocol. However, the protocol used needs to support the request-response MEP (as HTTP does) if synchronous communication is needed, which is typically what remote procedure calls use. The following is required to represent RPC in SOAP.

- The URI of the target SOAP node
- The procedure or method name to call
- The parameters to pass to the remote procedure or method
- Values for properties that are required by any features being used
- Any header data that is needed

The only mandatory items listed above are the URI of the target node, the method name, and the parameters. The particular implementation may not be using any additional features and may not require that header data be passed along. How the target URI is specified is left up to the underlying protocol binding, so there is no specific location where it must be included in the message. If HTTP

---

[18]RELAX NG (Regular Language Description for XML, Next Generation) can be found at `http://www.relaxng.org`.

[19]Schematron is on the Web at `http://www.schematron.com`.

is being used, then the requested URI becomes the URI of the target SOAP node (i.e., the URL that is typed into the Web browser when navigating to an Internet site can be a target URI).

The SOAP RPC Representation requires that the `Body` contain only a single immediate child element, which is a struct (sometimes called the *operation struct*) that is used to identify the operation to be invoked. (Do not confuse the struct mentioned here with the `struct` in C/C++. Although they are similar in concept, the SOAP Data Model defines this struct.) The name of the struct (an XML element) must be the same as the name of the method being called, although some toolkits do allow a different name in the SOAP message to be mapped to the actual method name. The operation struct must contain a child element (called *accessors*) for each of the in or in/out parameters, where the name of the child element represents the name of the parameter. The child elements can be simple or compound values, thus they can be structs themselves. An example RPC request message is given below.

Listing 7.32 SOAP RPC Request Message

```
<soap:Envelope xmlns:soap="http://www.w3.org/2003/05/soap-envelope"
    xmlns:tem="http://soap-weather.co/Temp">
  <soap:Body>
    <tem:getTemperature>
      <tem:zipCode>30332</tem:zipCode>
      <tem:scale>Fahrenheit</tem:scale>
    </tem:getTemperature>
  </soap:Body>
</soap:Envelope>
```

The example in Listing 7.32 could represent a request from a weather Web service for the current temperature in Fahrenheit at the postal code 30332. Notice that the `getTemperature` element is the only child element of the `Body`. Also notice that the `getTemperature` element resembles a method or procedure name and its child elements resemble parameters.

The `Body` of the SOAP RPC response message must either contain a single `Fault` element (discussed in Section 7.6), or a single child element modeled as a struct. If the response contains a single struct, then the struct must contain accessors (child elements) for all out and in/out parameters of the method call, as well as the return value. An example response to the request in Listing 7.32 is given below.

Listing 7.33 SOAP RPC Response Message

```
<soap:Envelope xmlns:soap="http://www.w3.org/2003/05/soap-envelope"
    xmlns:rpc="http://www.w3.org/2003/05/soap-rpc"
    xmlns:tem="http://soap-weather.co/Temp">
  <soap:Body>
```

```
    <tem:getTemperatureResponse>
      <rpc:result>80</rpc:result>
      <tem:zipCode>30332</tem:zipCode>
      <tem:scale>Fahrenheit</tem:scale>
    </tem:getTemperatureResponse>
  </soap:Body>
</soap:Envelope>
```

Notice that the name of the response struct in Listing 7.33 is the same name as the request struct (the operation name) with the word "Response" appended. This is not required but is a common convention. The name of the response struct is irrelevant to SOAP processors. Notice also that the response struct in Listing 7.33 contains three accessors (child elements). Although Java only supports returning a single value from a method call, some languages allow multiple values to be returned as out or in/out parameters, and as a result, SOAP allows for this possibility in its RPC Representation. In Java, all parameters (except primitives) are passed by reference to a method, so any parameter can act as an in/out parameter. Java does not provide a mechanism for specifying out parameters that aren't also in parameters. In SOAP, all parameters are passed by value, so do not expect to pass a parameter to SOAP RPC and have that parameter changed by the call as in Java. Since SOAP does not specify how a particular programming language such as Java is to obtain the in/out and out parameters, SOAP Java toolkits provide their own methods for handling these parameters.

Conceptually, a procedure only has one result, so SOAP mandates that an accessor of the response struct called `result` specify the result of the remote procedure call. In Listing 7.33 the temperature value, 80, is contained by the `result` element. The `result` element is defined by the SOAP RPC namespace, `http://www.w3.org/2003/05/soap-rpc`.

Difference between SOAP 1.1 and SOAP 1.2: SOAP RPC Response

The `result` element was the outcome of lessons learned by SOAP 1.1, which does not have a `result` element. In SOAP 1.1 determining which element in the response struct is the result of the remote procedure call and which elements are out parameters can be confusing and error-prone. The best way to handle this in SOAP 1.1 is to use a schema to define the response struct and all of its accessors. The schema will identify which element is the response struct in the result of the procedure call.

The actual remote interface for the method invoked by the RPC request message of Listing 7.32 could possibly look something like the following in Java.

```
public interface WeatherService extends java.rmi.Remote {
  // Get the current temperature.
  public int getTemperature(String zipCode, String scale)
    throws java.rmi.RemoteException;
}
```

7.9.2 RPC/Encoded

The RPC/Encoded message format is the easiest for the developer, because when using this format, the SOAP processor does most of the work. The developer simply makes a call to a method that is implemented as a remote procedure. In an actual system, the client code is really calling a proxy stub that is a surrogate for the real procedure. The proxy stub has the same interface as the remote procedure, but instead of implementing the procedure's functionality, it handles preparing and transporting the data for the RPC across the network. The proxy stub performs a process typically called *marshalling* where it takes the method parameters and encodes them into a SOAP message using the rules defined by SOAP Encoding. The proxy stub then serializes the SOAP message across the network to the SOAP receiver using some underlying transport protocol (typically HTTP or SMTP). The SOAP receiver reverses the marshalling process by translating the application-specific XML of the SOAP request message back into objects that represent the procedure call parameters. The parameters are passed to the correct procedure and the procedure returns a result. The result is then marshalled by the SOAP receiver and serialized back to the SOAP sender, which translates the application-specific XML of the SOAP response message into objects that represent the result of the procedure call. This process gives the business logic the illusion that it is calling a local method.

The RPC/Encoded message format creates a tightly coupled interobject-style communication. Developers have often used this format in the past to expose existing systems via SOAP. SOAP toolkits make it fairly simple to take an existing interface and generate the necessary code to expose that interface as a SOAP-based Web service using the RPC/Encoded format. However, RPC/Encoded has had its share of interoperability problems, so the WS-I BP strictly forbids its use and the SOAP community has begun using other alternative message formats. An example RPC/Encoded SOAP request and SOAP response message is given below.

Listing 7.34 RPC/Encoded SOAP Request Message

```
<soap:Envelope xmlns:soap="http://www.w3.org/2003/05/soap-envelope"
    xmlns:xsi="http://www.w3.org/2001/XMLSchema-instance"
    xmlns:xsd="http://www.w3.org/2001/XMLSchema"
    xmlns:mon="http://computer-monitors.co/Pricing">
  <soap:Body>
    <mon:getMonitorPrice
        soap:encodingStyle="http://www.w3.org/2003/05/soap-encoding">
      <mon:productId xsi:type="xsd:string">VP912b</mon:productId>
      <mon:currency xsi:type="xsd:string">USD<mon:currency>
    </mon:getMonitorPrice>
  </soap:Body>
</soap:Envelope>
```

Listing 7.35 RPC/Encoded SOAP Response Message

```
<soap:Envelope xmlns:soap="http://www.w3.org/2003/05/soap-envelope"
    xmlns:rpc="http://www.w3.org/2003/05/soap-rpc"
    xmlns:xsi="http://www.w3.org/2001/XMLSchema-instance"
    xmlns:xsd="http://www.w3.org/2001/XMLSchema"
    xmlns:mon="http://comp-monitors.co/Pricing">
  <soap:Body>
    <mon:getMonitorPriceResponse
        soap:encodingStyle="http://www.w3.org/2003/05/soap-encoding">
      <rpc:result xsi:type="xsd:float">700.00</rpc:result>
    </mon:getMonitorPriceResponse>
  </soap:Body>
</soap:Envelope>
```

In this example, the request message is calling the operation `getMonitorPrice` and passing a `productId` parameter to indicate for what computer monitor to return a price and a `currency` parameter to indicate what currency the pricing value should reflect. The response struct contains a single accessor, which is the result of the remote procedure call, a price of $700.00.

7.9.3 RPC/Literal

The RPC/Literal message format is similar to RPC/Encoded except the application-specific data is not marshalled to and from XML using the rules of SOAP Encoding. The SOAP sender and SOAP receiver do not agree on the set of rules for serializing the data (SOAP Encoding), instead they agree on the exact format of the data (a schema). The data format is typically specified using XML Schema so that the SOAP processor can automatically marshall the data to and from XML. The use of XML Schema is not required. The word *literal* just means that the SOAP message is not encoded using SOAP Encoding. How the SOAP sender and receiver interpret the data needs to agree. Most SOAP toolkits will automatically handle marshalling data specified by an XML schema.

Even though the data is not encoded using SOAP Encoding, the RPC still indicates that the data is structured according to the rules of SOAP RPC, which makes it possible for a SOAP processor to automatically marshall the parameters and the result of the procedure call. Thus, the major difference between RPC/Encoded and RPC/Literal is the fact that in RPC/Literal the developer must create a schema to represent the format and types of the parameters and result, whereas in RPC/Encoding the SOAP Encoding can be used to specify that. SOAP experts prefer RPC/Literal to RPC/Encoded because of the interoperability problems that have been encountered when using SOAP Encoding and because Literal encoding leaves more power of choice in the developer's hands. The developer can describe the data in any number of ways using a schema, thereby providing more opportunities for inventing ways to get two disparate systems to communicate. An example RPC/Literal request and response message is given below in Listing 7.37 and Listing 7.38, respectively. These examples assume that the namespace for the application-specific data of the body points to the XML schema defined in Listing 7.36, which describes the format and types of the parameters and result.

Listing 7.36 XML Schema for RPC-Style Monitor Pricing Service

```
<?xml version="1.0" encoding="UTF-8"?>
<schema xmlns="http://www.w3.org/2001/XMLSchema"
    xmlns:mon="http://computer-monitors.co/RpcPricing"
    targetNamespace="http://computer-monitors.co/RpcPricing">
  <element name="productId"  type="string"/>
  <element name="currency"   type="string"/>
  <element name="price"      type="float"/>
</schema>
```

Listing 7.37 RPC/Literal SOAP Request Message

```
<?xml version="1.0" encoding="UTF-8"?>
<soap:Envelope xmlns:soap="http://www.w3.org/2003/05/soap-envelope"
    xmlns:ns1="http://computer-monitors.co/"
    xmlns:mon="http://computer-monitors.co/RpcPricing">
  <soap:Body>
    <ns1:getMonitorPrice>
      <mon:productId>VP912b</mon:productId>
      <mon:currency>USD</mon:currency>
    </ns1:getMonitorPrice>
  </soap:Body>
</soap:Envelope>
```

Listing 7.38 RPC/Literal SOAP Response Message

```
<?xml version="1.0" encoding="UTF-8"?>
<soap:Envelope xmlns:soap="http://www.w3.org/2003/05/soap-envelope"
    xmlns:rpc="http://www.w3.org/2003/05/soap-rpc"
    xmlns:ns1="http://computer-monitors.co/">
  <soap:Body>
    <ns1:getMonitorPriceResponse>
      <rpc:result>700.00</rpc:result>
    </ns1:getMonitorPriceResponse>
  </soap:Body>
</soap:Envelope>
```

Notice that the XML schema in Listing 7.36 does not include types for the `getMonitorPrice` and `get-MonitorResponse` elements, thus these elements are using a different namespace in the SOAP message. The schema could have included these types, but it is not necessary because the structure of SOAP RPC indicates what these elements represent. You can see from the listings above that the RPC/Literal message format requires a little more effort on the part of the developer because the developer needs to create a schema. However, the WS-I BP sanctions the use of RPC/Literal, whereas it strictly forbids the use of RPC/Encoded.

7.9.4 Document/Encoded

The Document/Encoded format is not very well understood, rarely used, and is strictly prohibited by the WS-I BP. Do not use the Document/Encoded format; it is practically obsolete. Nevertheless, to be comprehensive an example is provided below. Document/Encoded applies SOAP Encoding but not SOAP RPC. This means that the data is marshalled according to the rules of SOAP Encoding, but the data is not structured according to the rules of SOAP RPC. So the SOAP processor cannot make any assumptions about the data as it can do with the example in Listing 7.37. Listing 7.37 does not use SOAP Encoding, but the SOAP processor can assume that the name of the immediate child element of the `Body`, `getMonitorPrice` in this case, is the name of the operation to invoke because Listing 7.37 is using SOAP RPC.

Listing 7.39 Document/Encoded SOAP Request Message

```
<soap:Envelope xmlns:soap="http://www.w3.org/2003/05/soap-envelope"
    xmlns:xsi="http://www.w3.org/2001/XMLSchema-instance"
    xmlns:xsd="http://www.w3.org/2001/XMLSchema"
    xmlns:mon="http://computer-monitors.co/Pricing">
  <soap:Body>
    <mon:getMonitorPrice
        soap:encodingStyle="http://www.w3.org/2003/05/soap-encoding"/>
    <mon:productId xsi:type="xsd:string"
        soap:encodingStyle="http://www.w3.org/2003/05/soap-encoding">
      VP191B
    </mon:productId>
    <mon:currency xsi:type="xsd:string"
        soap:encodingStyle="http://www.w3.org/2003/05/soap-encoding">
      USD
    <mon:currency>
  </soap:Body>
</soap:Envelope>
```

Listing 7.40 Document/Encoded SOAP Response Message

```
<soap:Envelope xmlns:soap="http://www.w3.org/2003/05/soap-envelope"
    xmlns:xsi="http://www.w3.org/2001/XMLSchema-instance"
```

```
    xmlns:xsd="http://www.w3.org/2001/XMLSchema"
    xmlns:mon="http://comp-monitors.co/Pricing">
  <soap:Body>
    <mon:getMonitorPriceResponse
        soap:encodingStyle="http://www.w3.org/2003/05/soap-encoding"/>
    <mon:price xsi:type="xsd:float"
        soap:encodingStyle="http://www.w3.org/2003/05/soap-encoding">
      635.49
    </mon:price>
  </soap:Body>
</soap:Envelope>
```

Listing 7.39 and Listing 7.40 intentionally do not have a single child element in the `Body` so that they are distinguished from the RPC/Encoded example of Listing 7.34 and Listing 7.35. Document-style messages are not restricted to having a single immediate child element of the `Body` as RPC style messages are. Even though the RPC/Encoded and Document/Encoded examples are very similar, the difference is the inherent structure of the data. The SOAP receiver cannot look at the Document/Encoded message and immediately assume that the `getMonitorPrice` element indicates a method to be invoked as it does in the RPC/Encoded message. With that same train of thought, the SOAP sender cannot look at the Document/Encoded message and immediately assume that the `price` element is the result of a method invocation as it can be in the RPC/Encoded message, where this element is identified as the `result`.

7.9.5 Document/Literal

The Document/Literal message format is quickly becoming the most popular format among the SOAP community. Although it requires the most effort from the developer, it provides the least amount of coupling and therefore the greatest amount of scalability. In addition, the WS-I BP sanctions the Document/Literal format because it has been found to create the fewest interoperability problems. It also provides the highest level of performance because it requires the least amount of processing from the SOAP processor. In general, a significant part of the processing can be shifted from the SOAP processor to the developer's application, which then can be fine-tuned for performance.

When using a Document/Literal message format, the application-specific data need not be structured according to SOAP RPC conventions. The developer can use any structure that suits the application. The `Body` can contain zero or more XML elements, although it is very common for the `Body` to only contain one well-formed XML element that represents an XML document fragment. SOAP Encoding is not used to marshall the data. Instead the data is completely described by some schema, typically written in XML Schema. As with RPC/Literal, XML Schema is not required, though, so any schema language can be used. One advantage of using XML Schema is that many SOAP toolkits already support it.

The parsing of the XML in the Document/Literal message format is not implicitly handled by the SOAP processor as it can be in RPC/Literal, so this is where the developer is left with more work but, ame time, more control. Even though the SOAP processor may not know implicitly how to dle the data, as in SOAP RPC, several APIs exist for processing XML that make the developer's job of parsing the XML into objects or some other form quite easy. The RPC/Literal example has been rewritten in Document/Literal form below.

Listing 7.41 XML Schema for Document-Style Monitor Pricing Service

```
<?xml version="1.0" encoding="UTF-8"?>
<schema xmlns="http://www.w3.org/2001/XMLSchema"
    xmlns:mon="http://computer-monitors.co/Pricing"
    targetNamespace="http://computer-monitors.co/Pricing">
  <element name="getMonitorPrice" type="mon:GetMonitorPrice"/>
  <complexType name="GetMonitorPrice">
    <sequence>
      <element name="productId"  type="string"/>
      <element name="currency"   type="string"/>
    </sequence>
  </complexType>

  <element name="getMonitorPriceResponse"
          type="mon:GetMonitorPriceResponse"/>
  <complexType name="GetMonitorPriceResponse">
    <sequence>
      <element name="price" type="float"/>
    </sequence>
  </complexType>
</schema>
```

Listing 7.42 Document/Literal SOAP Request Message

```
<?xml version="1.0" encoding="UTF-8"?>
<soap:Envelope xmlns:soap="http://www.w3.org/2003/05/soap-envelope"
    xmlns:mon="http://computer-monitors.co/Pricing">
  <soap:Body>
    <mon:getMonitorPrice>
      <mon:productId>VP191B</mon:productId>
      <mon:currency>USD</mon:currency>
    </mon:getMonitorPrice>
  </soap:Body>
</soap:Envelope>
```

Listing 7.43 Document/Literal SOAP Response Message

```
<?xml version="1.0" encoding="UTF-8"?>
```

```
<soap:Envelope xmlns:soap="http://www.w3.org/2003/05/soap-envelope"
    xmlns:mon="http://comp-monitors.co/Pricing">
  <soap:Body>
    <mon:getMonitorPriceResponse>
      <mon:price>635.49</mon:price>
    </mon:getMonitorPriceResponse>
  </soap:Body>
</soap:Envelope>
```

The difference between the RPC/Literal example and this Document/Literal example is fairly subtle and may be hard to recognize at first. In this Document/Literal example, the `getMonitorPrice` and `getMonitorPriceResponse` elements are defined in the XML schema of Listing 7.41, whereas they are not defined in the XML schema of Listing 7.36. They are not defined in the RPC/Literal example because the SOAP processor can make an assumption as to their purpose. The benefit of these elements being defined by the schema in the Document/Literal example is that the entire application-specific data in the `Body` can now be validated against its XML schema. If the data does not pass validation, then a `Fault` can be returned to the SOAP sender. This could not be done with the RPC/Literal example.

Document/Literal is a natural fit when the data being transmitted is already an XML document. An example might be a shipping notice in response to a purchase order. The shipping notice is more like a receipt than data that must be processed by an application, so it often makes perfect sense to send it as a complete XML document.

At this point you may be wondering which message format you should use. It really depends on what makes sense for your application. You must balance how quickly you need to get the application up and running against how much interoperability means to your application. In the past, the SOAP toolkits have made it much easier to get an application running with SOAP if the RPC/Encoded format is used, but with the APIs available today, Document/Literal is not that much more difficult. We already know that Document/Encoded is nearly obsolete, so using that format is not a wise decision. We also know that the WS-I BP only sanctions the use of RPC/Literal and Document/Literal. It appears as if the future of SOAP Encoding is bleak. Another decision factor you may use is the knowledge that RPC/Encoding message formats tend to process slower than Document/Literal. The performance of RPC/Literal is in the middle, between RPC/Encoding on the slow end and Document/Literal on the fast end. The RPC/Encoding format requires less effort from the developer but more effort from the SOAP processor. At the other end of the spectrum, the Document/Literal format requires more effort from the developer and less effort from the SOAP processor.

Notice that while there is a method for specifying the encoding style via the `encodingStyle` attribute (the absence thereof indicates "literal" encoding), there is no direct way of specifying the message style in SOAP. However, there are two different means by which this information is typically communicated. The first is via some proprietary means that most SOAP toolkits provide; we show an example in Section 7.10. The preferred method is to use the standard Web Services Description Language (WSDL). Since WSDL is discussed in the next chapter it will not be covered here. For now, just keep in mind that a standard does exist to describe what styles the SOAP receiver intends to use to communicate, and that standard is WSDL.

7.10 Examples and Practice Labs

SOAP is simply a document defining platform-independent standards that can be used to transmit data between distributed applications. As such, SOAP does not provide a programming model or any programming language–specific bindings for an implementation. The programming language used and the implementation of SOAP in that programming language is left up to the application developer. Therefore, to develop a SOAP application, you have to start by either developing your own SOAP processor that conforms to the SOAP specification, or obtaining one of the many SOAP toolkits provided by vendors. Most organizations do not want to spend the time writing their own SOAP processor when they need to spend that time writing the business logic of their application, so they typically choose to obtain one from a vendor. That is what we do for this example.

SOAP and Java are a special combination for developing distributed applications. Java provides a highly scalable and portable programming language for writing the business logic for applications, and SOAP gives Java a means to communicate with other applications, including applications written in different programming languages. With your application written in Java, you can expect that you will not have to modify the code to endure a change in platform—for example, porting from Windows to Linux.

Several SOAP implementations in Java exist, including one from Sun Microsystems called the Java Web Services Developer Pack (JWSDP), located at `http://java.sun.com/webservices/jwsdp/index.jsp`. For the example in this chapter we choose to use the Apache Software Foundation's (`http://www.apache.org`) open-source SOAP implementation called Axis (`http://ws.apache.org/axis`). The benefit of using an open-source implementation is that you, as the student, can spend your free time pouring over the source code to see how Axis works internally if you like. Additionally, if you were so inclined, you could fix any bugs you found in the software along the way. Axis was originally written in Java, but the project now also provides an implementation in C++. Since the subject of this book is Java, we use the Java implementation. Axis has a predecessor called Apache SOAP (`http://ws.apache.org/soap`), which also has a predecessor, the IBM SOAP4J implementation.

7.10.1 Downloading and Installing Apache Axis

To begin with the examples, you first need to obtain a copy of Axis and the programs that Axis depends on. As you might expect, since Axis is written in Java, you first need to have the Java Development Kit (JDK) installed on your computer. We use HTTP to transport the SOAP messages in the examples, so you will also need a Web server that supports HTTP. Axis includes both a stand-alone server and a server that plugs into a Java Servlet engine. Usually Axis is plugged into a Java Servlet engine, so this is what we do with the help of the Apache Tomcat Servlet engine (`http://jakarta.apache.org/tomcat/`). Axis also needs the JavaBeans Activation Framework (`http://java.sun.com/products/javabeans/-glasgow/jaf.html`) and an XML parser to process SOAP messages. The JDK comes with the Java API for XML Processing (JAXP), which is simply an interface that needs an actual XML parser to work. The JDK does include a default XML parser, but for the examples we use the Apache Xerces parser (`http://xml.apache.org/xerces2-j/`). Finally, we use Apache Ant to help build and run our examples (`http://ant.apache.org/`). To set up these applications and your development environment, perform the following steps.

1. Download and install the latest version of the Java 2 Platform, Standard Edition Development Kit (JDK) from `http://java.sun.com/downloads/index.html`. The JDK is distributed as a Microsoft Windows installer executable or a shell script for Unix-based computers such as Linux. Just run the executable or shell script and follow the installation instructions. Accept all the defaults if you like. Once installed, to make the development easier, set an environment variable called `JAVA_HOME` that points to the installation directory of the JDK. You should also add the bin directory of your JDK installation directory to your `Path` environment variable.

2. Download and install the latest binary version of Ant from `http://ant.apache.org/`. Apache provides both a binary distribution and a source distribution. The source download requires compiling. If you do not want to try to compile Ant, then just download the binary distribution. Ant is distributed as a compressed archive file in ZIP form (`.zip`) or a TAR form that has been compressed by GZIP (`.tar.gz`). GZIP is a common compression format used on Unix-based platforms and the utility for both Windows and Unix-based platforms can be found at `http://www.gzip.org`. TAR is a common archive format used on Unix-based platforms. A free utility for handling TAR files on Windows is 7-zip, which can be found at `http://www.7-zip.org/`. If you are using a Unix-based platform, you probably already have utilities for handling GZIP and TAR. If you are using Windows, you may or may not already have a utility for handling ZIP files. Apache typically provides these two formats (`.zip` and `.tar.gz`) for all of its distributions. Once you have downloaded Ant, all you need to do to install Ant is unzip (Windows) or untar (Unix) the archive file into a directory on your hard drive. You then need to set an `ANT_HOME` environment variable that points to the installation directory of Ant, and you need to add the `ANT_HOME/bin` directory to your `Path` environment variable. Note that the forward slash (/) is used in directories described in this chapter, which is a Unix-based platform convention. If you are using Windows, then you must replace the forward slashes with backslashes (\).

3. Download and install the latest binary version of Tomcat from `http://jakarta.apache-.org/tomcat/`. As with Ant, Tomcat is distributed in both binary and source distribution.

Download the binary distribution. Tomcat can be downloaded as either a Microsoft Windows installer-executable or a compressed archive file (`.zip` for Windows or `.tar.gz` for Unix-based platforms). For the purposes of this installation it is assumed that you downloaded the compressed archive file. To install Tomcat on your computer, all you need do is unzip (Windows) or untar (Unix) the archive file into a directory on your hard drive. Once Tomcat is installed you need to set an environment variable called `TOMCAT_HOME` that points to the installation directory of Tomcat. To ensure that Tomcat is installed and working correctly, bring up a command prompt and start Tomcat by executing the following command in Windows:

```
C:> %TOMCAT_HOME%\bin\startup.bat
```

Or the following command on Unix-based systems:

```
% $TOMCAT_HOME/bin startup.sh
```

Now, open a Web browser and enter the URL, `http://localhost:8080/`. You should see a page similar to the following.

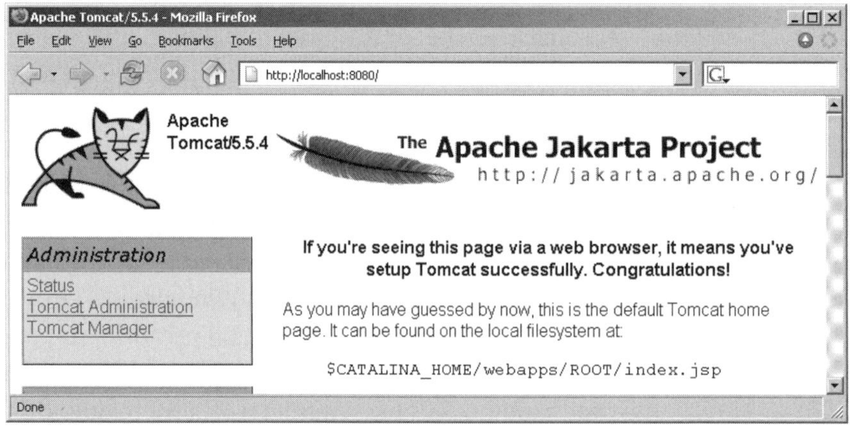

If you do not see a page similar to the one above, then something is wrong. You can either try uninstalling what you have installed up to this point and start over, or try reading through the Tomcat documentation for the version you are trying to run. The Tomcat documentation can be found on the Tomcat Web site.

4. Download and install the latest version of Axis from `http://ws.apache.org/axis/`. As with Tomcat, Axis is distributed in binary or source form. The binary distribution includes “bin” in

the filename, and the source distribution includes "src" in the filename. Download the binary version. Axis comes as either a `.zip` for Windows or a `.tar.gz` for Unix-based systems. Unzip (Windows) or untar (Unix) the archive file into a directory on your hard drive. Set an environment variable called `AXIS_HOME` that points to the installation directory of Axis.

5. Axis requires the JavaBeans Activation Framework (JAF), which can be downloaded from `http://java.sun.com/products/javabeans/glasgow/jaf.html`. JAF comes as a `.zip` archive file. Download the latest version of JAF and unzip the archive into a directory on your hard drive. Inside the directory you will find a file named `activation.jar`. Copy the `activation.jar` file to the `AXIS_HOME/webapps/axis/WEB-INF/lib` directory.

6. Axis also requires an XML parser. We use Apache Xerces, which can be downloaded from `http://xml.apache.org/xerces2-j/`. Again, as with all Apache projects, Xerces is distributed in binary and source form. Download the latest version of the Xerces binary distribution and unzip (Windows) or untar (Unix) the archive file into a directory on your hard drive. Inside the directory you will find two files named `xercesImpl.jar` and `xml-apis.jar`. Copy both of these files to the `AXIS_HOME/webapps/axis/WEB-INF/lib` directory.

7. Now we test Axis to make sure it has everything it needs. Copy the `axis` directory from the `AXIS_HOME/webapps` directory to the `TOMCAT_HOME/webapps` directory. If Tomcat is running, then it will load the Axis SOAP server automatically. If Tomcat is not running, then start it. Test whether Axis is running by opening a Web browser and entering the URL, `http://localhost:8080/axis`. You should see a welcome page for Axis, which may be similar to the following.

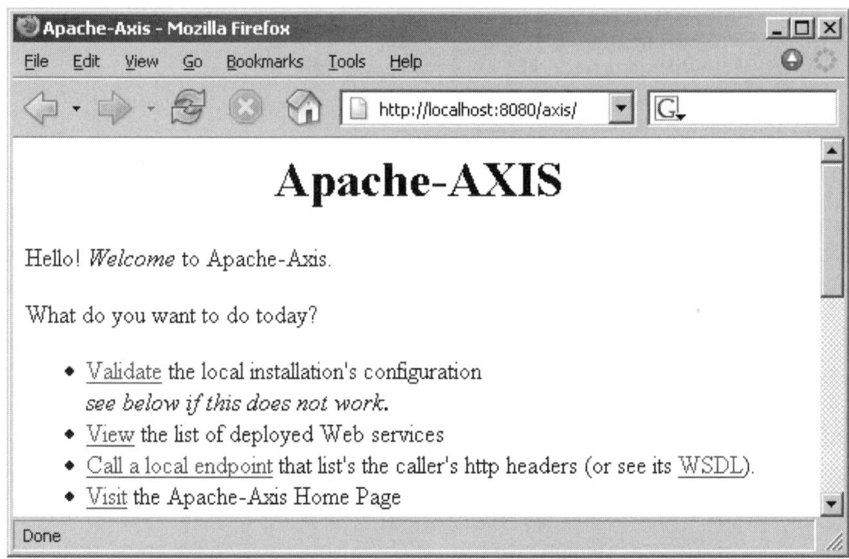

If you do not see a welcome page for Axis, then something is wrong. As with Tomcat, you can either try uninstalling what you have installed up to this point and start over, or try reading through the Axis documentation that comes with the Axis distribution. The Axis documentation for your distribution can be located at `AXIS_HOME/docs/index.html`.

8. Validate the configuration of Axis by opening a Web browser and entering the URL, `http://localhost:8080/axis/happyaxis.jsp`. This will cause Axis to check for libraries that it requires and display the results of its findings. The page displayed is called the "Axis Happiness Page" and should look similar to the following.

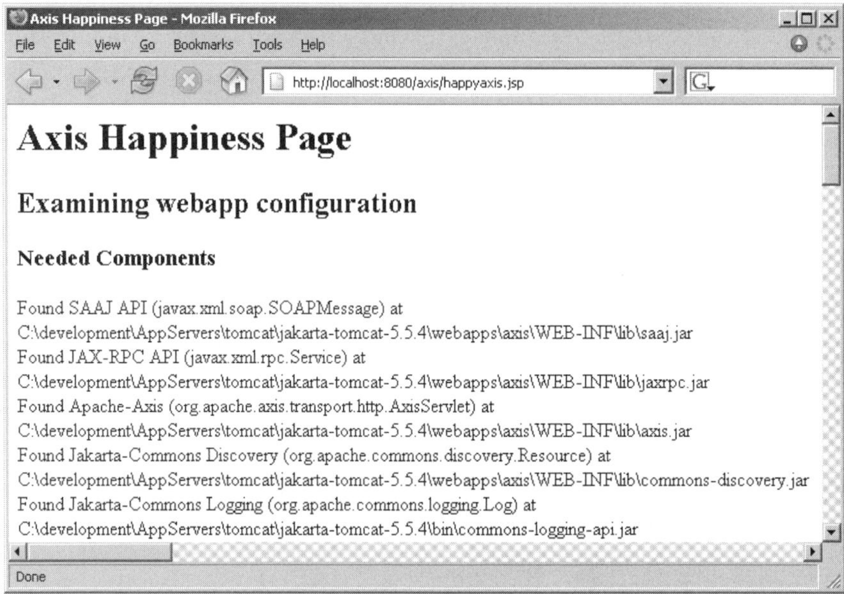

The word *Error* should not appear on this page. If it does, then Axis is not configured correctly, most likely because it is missing one or more libraries. Do not worry if the word *Warning* appears on this page. This probably just means that some optional libraries are missing. The Axis Happiness Page will display a list of Needed Components and another list below that of Optional Components. Needed components must be found for Axis to work properly. Optional components are required for extra functionality such as handling SOAP attachments. If you get an error, then read what it says, determine if a library is missing and obtain the library, or read the Axis documentation for further help. If you want to install the optional libraries, then feel free to gather them and drop them into the `AXIS_HOME/webapps/axis/WEB-INF/lib` directory. Of course, the `axis` directory will then need to be recopied to the Tomcat `webapps` directory and Tomcat will have to be restarted.

9. Finally, you can view the Web services that come with Axis and should already be running by opening a Web browser and entering the URL, `http://localhost:8080/axis/servlet/-AxisServlet`. You should see a page similar to the following.

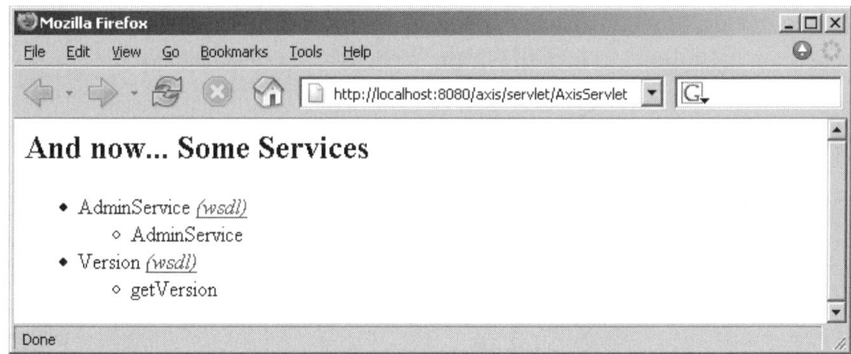

Tomcat can be stopped by executing the following command in Windows:

```
C:> %TOMCAT_HOME%\bin\shutdown.bat
```

or the following command on Unix-based systems:

```
% $TOMCAT_HOME/bin shutdown.sh
```

Now that you have Axis installed as a Web application within Tomcat, Axis will start up and shut down along with Tomcat. Next we demonstrate the use of the TCP Monitor that comes with Axis to view SOAP messages as they are transmitted to and from Axis.

7.10.2 Lab 1: Using the Axis TCP Monitor

Apache Axis is distributed with two utilities for viewing SOAP messages on the wire—TCP Monitor and SOAP Monitor. TCP Monitor is a Java Swing application and SOAP Monitor is a Java Applet. This lab demonstrates the use of the TCP Monitor with a simple RPC/Encoded example.

First we create and deploy a SOAP receiver to Axis. Axis supports two different ways for deploying a SOAP receiver. The simplest way is to create a Java class that is to be the SOAP receiver, then copy that class to the `TOMCAT_HOME/webapps/axis` directory and rename the extension from `.java` to `.jws`. Axis will detect the file and automatically deploy it. JWS files are quick and easy, but they provide no opportunity for customization. The better way to deploy a SOAP receiver to Axis is to use a Web Service Deployment Descriptor (WSDD). The WSDD is an XML file with format and elements proprietary to Axis. It allows several different options for customizing the deployment to be specified. This is the approach we use. Because Axis is not the focus of this chapter, we do not cover the details of WSDD. To learn more about WSDD, see the Axis user guide on the Axis Web site at `http://-ws.apache.org/axis/java/user-guide.html`.

The examples in this chapter are defined in a package called `javawebbook`. Therefore, to start, you should create a directory on your hard drive called `javawebbook`, which is where we will put the source code. Now, create the following Java file in the directory `javawebbook/simple`.

Listing 7.44 A Simple SOAP Receiver Than Echos the Request

```
package javawebbook.simple;

public class SimpleEchoService {
  public String echoString(String inString) {
    return inString;
  }
}
```

The Listing 7.44 is our SOAP receiver. It simply receives a string and then sends that string back to the SOAP sender. This example uses an RPC/Encoded-style message. As mentioned before, RPC/Encoded is the simplest way to create a SOAP service because SOAP toolkits such as Axis do most of the work. Now that you have created the Java class that will be the SOAP receiver, you need to create a WSDD for deploying that SOAP receiver to Axis. In the same directory as `SimpleEchoSer-vice.java`, create the following file and call it `deploy.wsdd`.

Listing 7.45 The WSDD for the Simple SOAP Receiver

```
<deployment name="SimpleEchoService"
    xmlns="http://xml.apache.org/axis/wsdd/"
    xmlns:java="http://xml.apache.org/axis/wsdd/providers/java">
  <service name="SimpleEchoService" provider="java:RPC">
    <parameter name="className"
        value="javawebbook.simple.SimpleEchoService" />
    <parameter name="allowedMethods" value="*" />
    <namespace>http://javawebbook/Simple</namespace>
  </service>
</deployment>
```

This WSDD tells Axis what class we want to deploy, what methods of that class clients are allowed to access, what message style is to be used, what the namespace is for elements of the SOAP `Body`, and by what name the SOAP receiver should be identified. Before we can use this deployment descriptor, we need to compile `SimpleEchoService.java` and then copy the .class file to Axis. To be able to compile and run the examples in this chapter, you first need to set a CLASSPATH environment variable that includes every JAR file found in the AXIS_HOME/webapps/axis/WEB-INF/lib directory. If you followed the setup described in Section 7.10.1, then the lib directory should include the libraries distributed with Axis as well as the JavaBeans Activation Framework and Xerces. Once you have created the CLASSPATH environment variable, ensure that Tomcat and Axis are running, then open a new command prompt and navigate to the directory that is one level above the javawebbook directory. From that directory, enter the following command to compile SimpleEchoService.java.

```
java –cp %CLASSPATH%;. javawebbook\simple\SimpleEchoService.java
```

On a Unix-based platform enter:

```
java –cp $CLASSPATH:. javawebbook/simple/SimpleEchoService.java
```

The –cp option used with the java command is necessary so that the CLASSPATH you defined, as well as the current directory (.), are included in the classpath that Java will search. Now copy the javawebbook directory to TOMCAT_HOME/webapps/axis/WEB-INF/classes. This makes SimpleEchoService.class available to the Java Virtual Machine that is running Axis so that it can load the class when you ask Axis to deploy it. To deploy the SOAP receiver, enter the following command:

```
java org.apache.axis.client.AdminClient javawebbook\simple\deploy.wsdd
```

On a Unix-based platform enter:

```
java org.apache.axis.client.AdminClient javawebbook/simple/deploy.wsdd
```

After you enter the command, you should receive output similar to the following:

```
Processing file javawebbook/simple/deploy.wsdd
<Admin>Done processing</Admin>
```

This lets you know that the example has been deployed to Axis. If you receive a message that some required classes are missing and attachment-support is disabled, do not worry. That is not an error; it is just a warning. If you want to stop the warning from displaying, you can add the Optional Components listed on the Axis Happiness Page mentioned above. If you receive a ClassNotFoundException, then you most likely do not have your CLASSPATH environment variable set correctly.

Now that you have the Axis example deployed, create a client to test it. Create the following Java file in the directory javawebbook/simple.

Listing 7.46 A Client for the `SimpleEchoService` SOAP Receiver

```
package javawebbook.simple;

import java.rmi.RemoteException;

import javax.xml.namespace.QName;
import javax.xml.rpc.Call;
import javax.xml.rpc.ParameterMode;
import javax.xml.rpc.Service;
import javax.xml.rpc.ServiceException;
import javax.xml.rpc.ServiceFactory;
import javax.xml.rpc.encoding.XMLType;

public class Client {
  public static void main(String[] args)
    throws ServiceException, RemoteException {

    Service service = ServiceFactory.newInstance().createService(null);

    // Create and configure the remote procedure call.
    Call call = service.createCall();
    call.setTargetEndpointAddress("http://localhost:" + args[0]
      + "/axis/services/SimpleEchoService");
    call.setProperty(Call.SOAPACTION_USE_PROPERTY, Boolean.TRUE);
    call.setProperty(Call.SOAPACTION_URI_PROPERTY, "echoString");
    call.setProperty(Call.ENCODINGSTYLE_URI_PROPERTY,
      "http://schemas.xmlsoap.org/soap/encoding");
    call.setOperationName(
      new QName("http://javawebbook/Simple", "echoString"));
    call.addParameter("inString", XMLType.XSD_STRING,
      ParameterMode.IN);
    call.setReturnType(XMLType.XSD_STRING);

    // Invoke the remote procedure call.
    String returnValue = (String)
      call.invoke(new Object[] { args[1] });
    System.out.println("Sent "" + args[1] + "", received ""
     + returnValue + """);
  }
}
```

The Listing 7.46 defines a Java class with a single method that accepts two arguments. The first is the port where the SOAP sender should send a SOAP message. The second is a string that should be sent to the `SimpleEchoService`. This client assumes that Tomcat is running on your local machine (`local-host`). If it is not, then you can change the word `localhost` in the `setTargetEnpointAddress` method call to the name or IP address of the server running Tomcat.

`Client.java` uses a Java API called the Java API for XML-Based RPC (JAX-RPC). JAX-RPC is not discussed until the next chapter. For now, just know that the code in `Client.java` identifies a method of a SOAP receiver that it would like to invoke via RPC, and then it invokes it. To invoke the method, JAX-RPC creates a SOAP request message using the structure required by SOAP RPC (discussed in Section 7.9.1) and sends that message to the SOAP receiver. The SOAP receiver will process the message and then send a response back. In this example, we tell JAX-RPC to encode the message using SOAP Encoding by setting the `encodingStyle` attribute to a URI of `http://schemas.xmlsoap.org/soap/encoding`. Compile `Client.java` by entering the following command:

```
java –cp %CLASSPATH%;. javawebbook\simple\Client.java
```

On a Unix-based platform enter:

```
java –cp $CLASSPATH:. javawebbook/simple/Client.java
```

If you receive a `ClassNotFoundException`, you most likely do not have your `CLASSPATH` environment variable set correctly. Remember that your `CLASSPATH` must include all of the JARs from the `AXIS_HOME/webapps/axis/WEB-INF/lib` directory. Now test the client using the following command:

```
java –cp %CLASSPATH%;. javawebbook.simple.Client 8080 "Hello!"
```

The first argument given to `Client.java` in this example is 8080. If your Tomcat server is listening on a different port, then just change 8080 to the correct port. After you have entered the command you should receive output similar to the following:

```
Sent 'Hello!', received 'Hello!'
```

In this example, the SOAP receiver (called `SimpleEchoService`) simply returns the string that you sent to it. The SOAP sender in this example is the class `Client`. Just as before, you may receive a warning message that you can ignore if you like. If you find the need to undeploy the service, you can use a WSDD such as the following:

Listing 7.47 WSDD for Undeploying the `SimpleEchoService` SOAP Receiver

```
<undeployment name="SimpleEchoService"
    xmlns="http://xml.apache.org/axis/wsdd/">
  <service name="SimpleEchoService"/>
</undeployment>
```

This WSDD tells Axis the name of the service that you want to undeploy and is used the same way as a deployment WSDD. If you save this WSDD to a file named `undeploy.wsdd`, you can execute the following command to use it:

```
java org.apache.axis.client.AdminClient javawebbook\simple\undeploy.wsdd
```

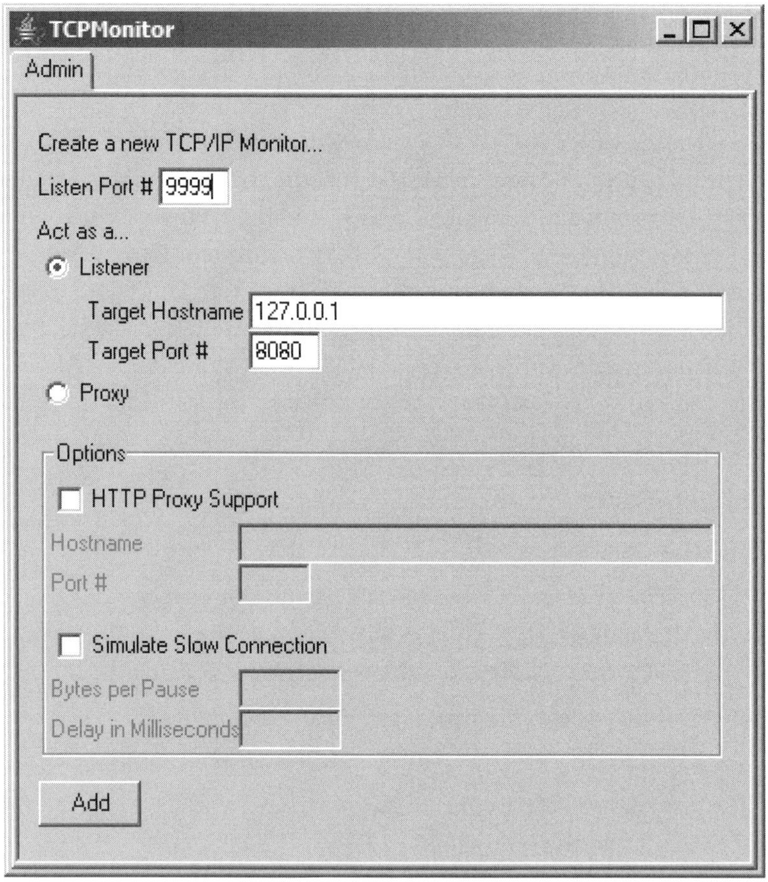

Figure 7.17
Axis TCP Monitor Configuration

Now that we have the SOAP example working, let us demonstrate the TCP Monitor so you can see the actual SOAP messages that are transmitted. The Axis TCP Monitor is located in the `org.apache.axis.utils` package, which is included in the JARs provided by the distribution (the ones that you added to your `CLASSPATH`). To start the TCP Monitor, enter the following command:

```
java org.apache.axis.utils.tcpmon
```

This command will bring up a Java GUI that looks similar to the one shown in Figure 7.17. Be patient, it may take a little while to start the program.

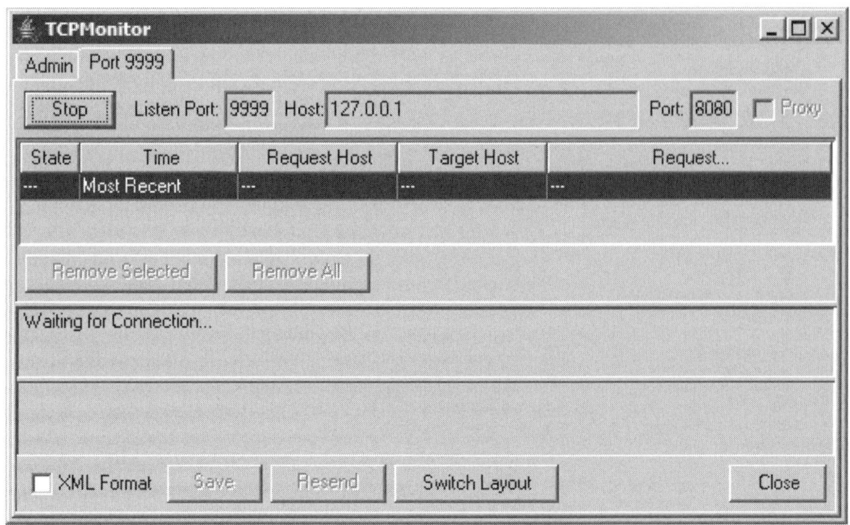

Figure 7.18
TCP Monitor With a TCP/IP Monitor Added

From this window you need to enter a local port that the TCP Monitor will monitor for incoming connections (Listen Port # in the figure) as well as the host name and port where the SOAP messages are targeted (Target Hostname and Target Port # in the figure). Your SOAP sender will need to send its SOAP messages to the Listen Port # and the TCP Monitor will forward those messages to the Target Hostname and Target Port #. That is how the TCP Monitor is able to display your SOAP messages, because you are sending them. That is also why the client for `SimpleEchoService` takes a port number. In the figure, we entered 9999 for the Listen Port #, so you do the same. Then click the Add button. This will create another tab next to the Admin tab called Port 9999. Click on that tab and you should see something similar to what is shown in Figure 7.18.

You can add more of these TCP/IP monitors if you like, but they must all listen on different ports. When a TCP/IP monitor receives a message, it displays it in the box where you see Waiting for Connection... in Figure 7.18. The response message is displayed in the box immediately below. Each time a TCP/IP monitor receives a message it caches it and adds it to the list where you see Most Recent in Figure 7.18. You can view old messages by clicking on a row in the table. You can also edit and resend any of these old cached messages. This is a great way for you to experiment with sending and receiving SOAP messages. As an example, let us capture the messages sent to `SimpleEchoService`. With a TCP/IP monitor listening to port 9999, enter the following command into your command prompt:

```
java –cp %CLASSPATH%;. javawebbook.simple.Client 9999 "Hello Again!"
```

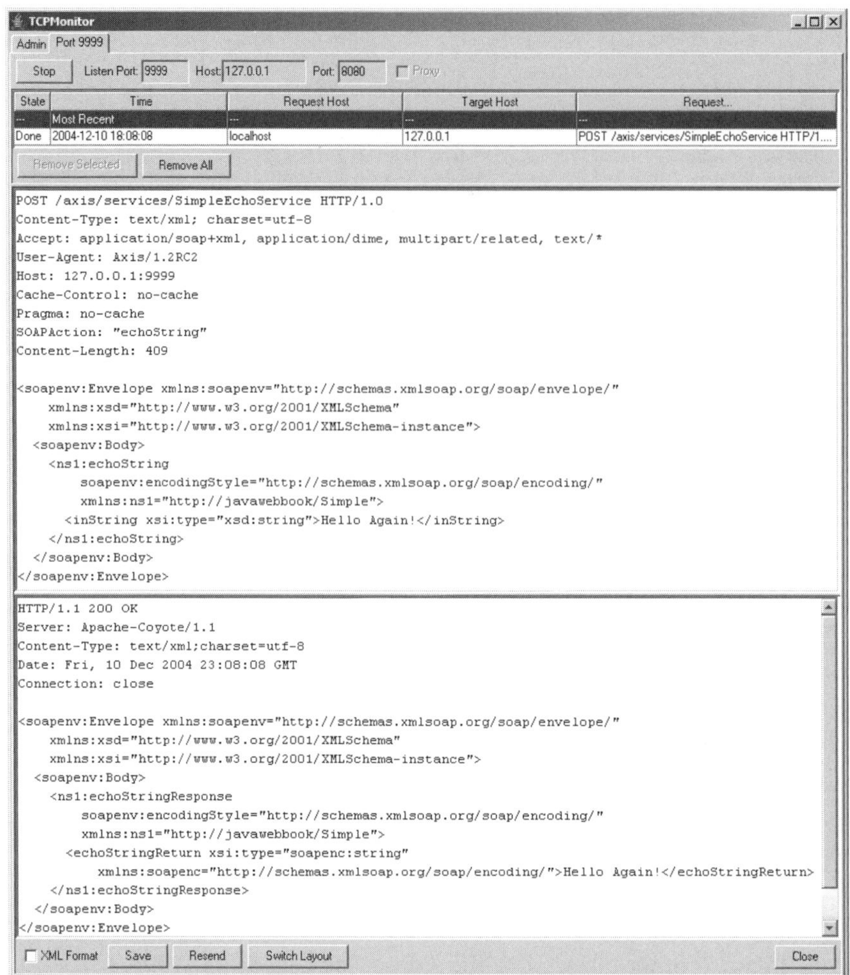

Figure 7.19

TCP Monitor Capturing RPC/Encoded SOAP Messages

After you have entered the command, you should receive output similar to the following:

```
Sent 'Hello Again!', received 'Hello Again!'
```

When you look at the TCP Monitor, you should see the SOAP request message (top) and the SOAP response message (bottom) as in Figure 7.19, but without the nice formatting. Notice the new entry in the table above the SOAP messages.

The TCP Monitor captures the payload of the TCP transport protocol. Because we are using HTTP as the underlying protocol for sending and receiving SOAP messages, the messages shown in Figure

7.19 above also include HTTP headers. You can see from the HTTP headers that the request message is sent as an HTTP POST. Also note that the HTTP Content-Type used for SOAP messages is the MIME type `text/xml`. This is a requirement defined by the SOAP specification.

Seen in the SOAP request message is that the immediate child of the `Body` element has the name of the method being invoked as required by SOAP RPC. Also the XML element containing the string that is being sent to `SimpleEchoService` has the same name as the parameter of the method being invoked. The immediate child of the `Body` element of the SOAP response message has the same name as the method that was invoked plus a suffix of Response, which is a common convention. Also notice that the request and response messages both use the `encodingStyle` attribute with a value identifying SOAP Encoding. Recall that SOAP Encoding requires the use of the `encodingStyle` attribute.

Notice that this example uses SOAP version 1.1. At the time of this writing, JAX-RPC only supports SOAP 1.1, although there are plans to support SOAP 1.2 in the next major release of JAX-RPC. This is discussed more in the next chapter.

7.10.3 Lab 2: RPC/Literal Example

The last lab gave an example of using an RPC/Encoded message style. This lab will give an example of using an RPC/Literal message style. Before we begin the example, you first need to learn a little about how to tell Axis what message style you want to use. One way of doing this is through the `provider`, `style`, and `use` attributes of the Web Service Deployment Descriptor (WSDD). The other way is via the use of the Web Services Description Language (WSDL), which will not be discussed until the next chapter.

The word *style* in the context of SOAP has multiple meanings—message-encoding style and programming style. We have discussed the message-encoding styles in Section 7.9, which are RPC/Encoded, RPC/Literal, Document/Encoded, and Document/Literal. There are two types of programming styles used—remote procedure call and what is commonly referred to as messaging. This is a common source of confusion because the word *style* is overloaded and the acronym *RPC* is used in the message style *and* the programming style. The difference between RPC and messaging-programming styles basically is how you handle the data that is transmitted. In RPC, you mimic a procedure or method call and expect the SOAP processor to handle converting your method call into a SOAP request message that it sends to the SOAP receiver. Additionally, you expect the SOAP processor to convert the SOAP response message back into the procedure call semantics that you are using. Therefore, your code does not look much different than a normal Java method call to another object. This is the programming style that was used in Lab 1. On the other hand, in messaging, you expect to manually build the XML that is the SOAP request message and parse the XML that is the SOAP response message yourself. Of course, the Java community provides APIs that make this processing fairly easy, including the Java API for XML Messaging (JAXM), which is built on the lower-level API called SOAP with Attachments API for Java (SAAJ).

Axis determines what programming style you want to use by reading the `style` attribute of the WSDD. The `style` attribute accepts one of the following four values.

- `rpc`—Tells Axis to use the SOAP RPC conventions and SOAP Encoding
- `document`—Tells Axis to use the RPC programming style but not to use SOAP Encoding

  Axis will still marshall Java to XML and back again so that you work with Java objects instead of XML. If you use this style, then Axis assumes that the immediate child of the `Body` element of the SOAP request message is a Java Bean, which is passed as a single parameter to the method that is being invoked. In other words, the method that you are invoking must accept only a single parameter, which is a Java Bean. This will become clearer after this lab and the next.
- `wrapped`—Is the same as `document` except for the part about the immediate child of the `Body` element representing a Java Bean

  Whereas with `document`, the method being invoked can only accept a single parameter, this style assumes that the immediate child of the `Body` element of the SOAP request message is just a wrapper for the list of parameters that must be passed to the method being invoked. This style is similar to `rpc`, except that SOAP Encoding is not being used.
- `message`—Tells Axis that the XML in the SOAP `Body` should not be marshalled to/from Java objects, but should simply be passed directly to the application

  If you want to work directly with XML, this is the style to use. This style puts the least amount of burden on the SOAP processor by shifting a part of the processing burden to the application.

The `use` attribute in the WSDD accepts a value of `encoded` or `literal`. These values correspond to the meaning of those words when used in the terms RPC/Encoded and RPC/Literal. If `encoded` is specified, then SOAP Encoding is used; if `literal` is specified, then an XML schema is used. Therefore, setting `style="rpc"` and `use="encoded"` in the WSDD tells Axis that you want to use an RPC programming style and an RPC/Encoded-message style.

The provider attribute accepts either a value of `java:RPC` or `java:MSG`. You can set `provider="java:RPC"` and omit the `style` and `use` attributes to achieve the same effect as setting `style="rpc"` and `use="encoded"`. If you set `provider=java:MSG`, then you achieve the same effect as setting `style="message"` and `use="literal"`. You must specify either the `provider` attribute or the `style` attribute, but `use` is optional. If `use` is not specified, then a default value is used based upon what you specify for `provider` or `style`. You can specify `provider` and `style` together with corresponding values and not generate an error.

In this example we imagine that we have a company that sells computer monitors. We want to give this company a SOAP interface that other companies can use to order the monitors. A real life application of this sort would most likely be quite complex and involved to write. Since we do not have time for that, we make it very simple and leave out most of the details. It will still provide enough detail for you to understand how Java SOAP toolkits can be used to exchange an RPC/Literal message.

Basically, we want to create SOAP request and response messages similar to the ones you saw in Section 7.9.3 where we discussed the RPC/Literal encoding style. Since we start with the assumption that we have a warehouse of monitors to sell, then we first need some monitor data to reference. Normally this data would be stored in a database, but to make this example as simple as possible, we store the data statically in a class called `Monitors`. In the directory `javawebbook`, create the following file and call it `Monitors.java`.

Listing 7.48 A Class to Hold Monitor Data

```
package javawebbook;

import java.util.Collections;
import java.util.HashMap;
import java.util.Map;

public class Monitors {
  public static Map data = null;

  static {
    Map map = new HashMap();
    // Store monitor product IDs and prices
    map.put("VP912b", new Float(700.00f));
    map.put("ENFL768", new Float(899.00f));
    map.put("DU1905fp", new Float(629.00f));
    map.put("SS193P", new Float(779.00f));
    map.put("PB190P5EB", new Float(749.00f));
    map.put("LGEFL1930B", new Float(580.00f));
    data = Collections.synchronizedMap(map);
  }
}
```

Listing 7.48 creates a `java.util.Map` in which it stores monitor product IDs and corresponding prices. Because we are making this example as simple as possible, we are not storing any more information than this. You can just make the assumption that these monitors are all well-made 19-inch LCD displays and the prices are given in US dollars. Because we are selling and therefore dealing with money, we create a class to convert the monitor prices from US dollars to a few other currencies. To accomplish this, create the following file in the `javawebbook` directory and call it `CurrencyExchange.java`.

Listing 7.49 A Class to Handle Currency Exchange

```
package javawebbook;

public class CurrencyExchange {
```

```
  public static float convertPrice(float usPrice, String currency)
    throws IllegalArgumentException{

    float convertedPrice = 0.0f;

    if (currency.equals("EUR")) { // Euro
      convertedPrice = (float) (usPrice * 1.32);
    }
    else if (currency.equals("GBP")) { // British Pound
      convertedPrice = (float) (usPrice * 1.91);
    }
    else if (currency.equals("CAD")) { // Canadian Dollar
      convertedPrice = (float) (usPrice * 0.81);
    }
    else if (currency.equals("AUD")) { // Australian Dollar
      convertedPrice = (float) (usPrice * 0.75);
    }
    else if (currency.equals("USD")) { // US Dollar
      convertedPrice = usPrice;
    }
    else {
      throw new IllegalArgumentException(
        "Unsupported currency: " + currency);
    }

    return convertedPrice;
  }
}
```

Now that we have some helper classes in place, we create a SOAP receiver. We use the RPC programming style, so the Java class looks identical to any other Java class that we call directly from a standalone Java application. Because we want to generate SOAP messages similar to the ones given in Section 7.9.3, we create a service that accepts a product ID and a currency and returns the price of the monitor associated with the specified product ID in the specified currency. We have done that for you in the listing below. Create this file in the `javawebbook/rpc` directory and name it `RpcPriceService.java`. This class simply looks up the price for the monitor and returns the price converted to the currency that was requested.

Listing 7.50 Monitor RPC Price Service

```
package javawebbook.rpc;

import javawebbook.CurrencyExchange;
```

```
import javawebbook.Monitors;

public class RpcPriceService {
  public float getMonitorPrice(String productId, String currency)
    throws IllegalArgumentException {

    Float usPrice = (Float) Monitors.data.get(productId);

    if (usPrice == null) {
      throw new IllegalArgumentException("Unknown product ID: " + productId);
    }

    return CurrencyExchange.convertPrice(usPrice.floatValue(), currency);
  }
}
```

We want to deploy this service to Axis, so we need a Web Service Deployment Descriptor (WSDD). Because we want the messages exchanged to be in the style RPC/Literal, then we need to set `style="rpc"` and `use="literal"`. The WSDD we use is given below. Create this file in the `javawebbook/rpc` directory and call it `deploy.wsdd`.

Listing 7.51 WSDD for Deploying Monitor RPC Price Service

```
<deployment name="RpcPriceService"
            xmlns="http://xml.apache.org/axis/wsdd/"
            xmlns:java="http://xml.apache.org/axis/wsdd/providers/java">
  <service name="RpcPriceService" style="rpc" use="literal">
    <parameter name="className" value="javawebbook.rpc.RpcPriceService"/>
    <parameter name="allowedMethods" value="*" />
    <namespace>http://computer-monitors.co/RpcPricing</namespace>
  </service>
</deployment>
```

Before we deploy the service, we need to compile it and its helper classes. To deploy the helper classes, enter the following command into your command prompt. Remember from Lab 1 that you need your `CLASSPATH` environment variable to be set to include all of the libraries from the `AXIS_HOME/webapps/axis/WEB-INF/lib` directory.

```
javac -cp %CLASSPATH%;. javawebbook\CurrencyExchange.java javawebbook\Monitors.java
```

On a Unix-based platform, enter:

```
javac -cp $CLASSPATH:. javawebbook/CurrencyExchange.java javawebbook/Monitors.java
```

To compile the service enter the following command:

```
javac -cp %CLASSPATH%;. javawebbook\rpc\RpcPriceService.java
```

On a Unix-based platform, enter:

```
javac -cp $CLASSPATH:. javawebbook/rpc/RpcPriceService.java
```

Copy the `javawebbook` directory to the `TOMCAT_HOME/webapps/axis/WEB-INF/classes` directory. Then make sure that Tomcat is running with Axis deployed and execute the following command to deploy the service to Axis:

```
java org.apache.axis.client.AdminClient javawebbook\rpc\deploy.wsdd
```

On a Unix-based platform, enter:

```
java org.apache.axis.client.AdminClient javawebbook/rpc/deploy.wsdd
```

We now create a client to call our price service. This time we demonstrate the use of SOAP 1.2 messages. Because JAX-RPC only supports SOAP 1.1 as of this writing, we need to manually create our SOAP request message. Fortunately, this also gives you a good opportunity to really get your hands dirty with SOAP. Our client uses a Java API called SAAJ (mentioned earlier) that, like JAX-RPC, is not discussed until the next chapter. However, we only use SAAJ to call our SOAP receiver and send it a message that we wrote by hand. The hand-written message will be read in from a file. The code for the client is given below. It simply uses SAAJ to read the SOAP message from an XML file into memory as a SAAJ object called `SOAPMessage` uses SAAJ to send the message to the URL specified as a command-line argument, then uses Xerces to pretty print the response message to `System.out`. Create this file in the `javawebbook` directory and call it `SoapSender.java`.

Listing 7.52 A Generic SOAP Client for Sending Manually Created SOAP Messages

```
package javawebbook;

import java.io.ByteArrayInputStream;
import java.io.ByteArrayOutputStream;
import java.io.FileInputStream;
import java.io.IOException;
import java.net.URL;

import javax.xml.parsers.DocumentBuilder;
import javax.xml.parsers.DocumentBuilderFactory;
import javax.xml.parsers.FactoryConfigurationError;
import javax.xml.parsers.ParserConfigurationException;
import javax.xml.soap.MessageFactory;
import javax.xml.soap.MimeHeaders;
import javax.xml.soap.SOAPConnection;
import javax.xml.soap.SOAPConnectionFactory;
import javax.xml.soap.SOAPException;
```

```
import javax.xml.soap.SOAPMessage;

import org.apache.xml.serialize.OutputFormat;
import org.apache.xml.serialize.XMLSerializer;
import org.w3c.dom.Document;
import org.xml.sax.SAXException;

/**
 * Reads a SOAP request message from a file, sends it to a SOAP receiver,
 * and receives and outputs the SOAP response message to System.out.
 */
public class SoapSender {
  /**
   * The main method expects two arguments. The first is the location
   * of the SOAP request message file. The second is the URL of the
   * SOAP receiver to send the message to.
   */
  public static void main(String[] args) throws SOAPException, ParserConfigurationException,
    FactoryConfigurationError, SAXException, IOException {

    if (args.length < 2) {
      System.err.println(
        "Usage: SoapSender <soap-file> <soap-receiver-url>");
      System.exit(1);
    }

    MessageFactory messageFactory = MessageFactory.newInstance();

    // Create the appropriate mime type header.
    MimeHeaders mimeHeaders = new MimeHeaders();
    mimeHeaders.addHeader("Content-Type", "text/xml; charset=UTF-8");

    // Build a SOAP message in memory from a SOAP message in a file.
    FileInputStream fileIS = new FileInputStream(args[0]);
    SOAPMessage requestMessage =
      messageFactory.createMessage(mimeHeaders, fileIS);

    // Send the SOAP message to the SOAP receiver and get the response.
    SOAPConnectionFactory connectionFactory =
      SOAPConnectionFactory.newInstance();
    SOAPConnection connection = connectionFactory.createConnection();
    URL url = new URL(args[1]);
    SOAPMessage responseMessage = connection.call(requestMessage, url);
    fileIS.close();
```

```
    // Use Xerces to pretty print the SOAP response message to System.out.
    ByteArrayOutputStream out = new ByteArrayOutputStream();
    responseMessage.writeTo(out);
    ByteArrayInputStream in = new ByteArrayInputStream(out.toByteArray());
    out.close();
    DocumentBuilder builder =
      DocumentBuilderFactory.newInstance().newDocumentBuilder();
    Document doc = builder.parse(in);
    in.close();
    OutputFormat formatter = new OutputFormat();
    formatter.setLineWidth(80);
    formatter.setIndenting(true);
    formatter.setIndent(2);
    XMLSerializer serializer = new XMLSerializer(System.out, formatter);
    serializer.serialize(doc);
  }
}
```

Compile the client using the following command:

```
javac -cp %CLASSPATH%;. javawebbook\SoapSender.java
```

The SOAP request message we use is the exact same as the one in Listing 7.37. Write Listing 7.37 to a file called `priceRequest.xml` and put in the directory `javawebbook/rpc`. Make sure that the TCP Monitor is running with a listener listening to port 9999 (discussed in Lab 1) and then enter the following command into your command prompt.

```
java -cp %CLASSPATH%;. javawebbook.SoapSender "javawebbook\rpc\priceRequest.xml"
"http://localhost:9999/axis/services/RpcPriceService"
```

The previous command should be typed on one line. It is only on multiple lines in this book because there is not enough space to put it on one line. When the command executes, you should receive output similar to the following.

Listing 7.53 RPC/Literal Response Message

```
<?xml version="1.0" encoding="UTF-8"?>
<soapenv:Envelope
  xmlns:soapenv="http://www.w3.org/2003/05/soap-envelope"
  xmlns:xsd="http://www.w3.org/2001/XMLSchema"
  xmlns:xsi="http://www.w3.org/2001/XMLSchema-instance">
  <soapenv:Body>
    <getMonitorPriceResponse xmlns="http://computer-monitors.co/">
      <ns2:result xmlns:ns1="http://computer-monitors.co/"
```

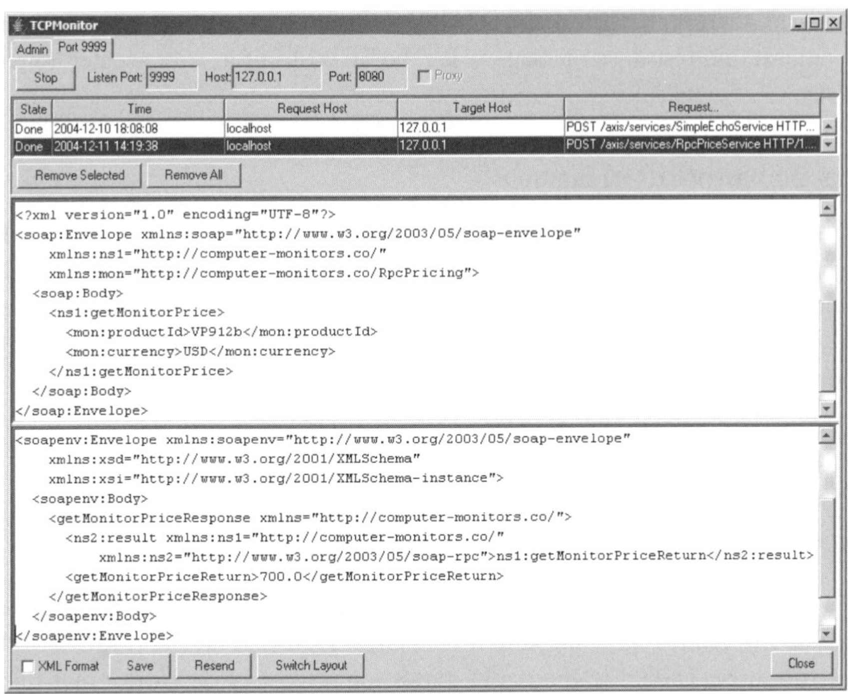

Figure 7.20

TCP Monitor Capturing RPC/Literal SOAP Messages

```
        xmlns:ns2="http://www.w3.org/2003/05/soap-rpc">
      ns1:getMonitorPriceReturn
    </ns2:result>
    <getMonitorPriceReturn>700.0</getMonitorPriceReturn>
  </getMonitorPriceResponse>
 </soapenv:Body>
</soapenv:Envelope>
```

Additionally, in your TCP Monitor listener window you should see something similar to the window shown in Figure 7.20, which has been resized to eliminate the HTTP header from the view for brevity.

Let us summarize what we have done here. We created some business logic for a SOAP service and deployed it to Axis as an RPC/Literal style SOAP receiver. We then created a client that reads in an XML file that is a SOAP request message, sends that message to the specified URL (in this case it was our SOAP receiver), then pretty prints the SOAP response message to `System.out`. We captured the actual SOAP request and response messages with the TCP Monitor. Next we demonstrate a Document/Literal example.

7.10.4 Lab 3: Document/Literal Example

This lab covers an example of using the `wrapped` style in Axis to handle Document/Literal messages. This example is a price service just as in Lab 2. The service will look the same as the `RpcPriceService` of Lab 2, so copy `RpcPriceService.java` to the `javawebbook/document` directory and rename the file to `PriceService.java` and the Java class to `PriceService`. Then compile the new class using the following command:

```
javac -cp %CLASSPATH%;. javawebbook\document\PriceService.java
```

On a Unix-based platform, enter:

```
javac -cp $CLASSPATH:. javawebbook/document/PriceService.java
```

Copy the `javawebbook` directory to `TOMCAT_HOME/webapps/axis/WEB-INF/classes`. Next create the WSDD by typing the following listing into a file called `deployPS.wsdd` and save it to the `javawebbook/document` directory. The PS in the name stands for price service. Notice that this WSDD sets `style="wrapped"` and `use="literal"`.

Listing 7.54 WSDD for Deploying Wrapped Monitor RPC Price Service

```
<deployment name="PriceService"
            xmlns="http://xml.apache.org/axis/wsdd/"
            xmlns:java="http://xml.apache.org/axis/wsdd/providers/java">
  <service name="PriceService" style="wrapped" use="literal">
    <parameter name="className" value="javawebbook.document.PriceService"/>
    <parameter name="allowedMethods" value="*" />
    <namespace>http://computer-monitors.co/Pricing</namespace>
  </service>
</deployment>
```

Then make sure that Tomcat is running with Axis deployed and execute the following command to deploy the service to Axis:

```
java org.apache.axis.client.AdminClient javawebbook\document\deployPS.wsdd
```

On a Unix-based platform, enter:

```
java org.apache.axis.client.AdminClient javawebbook/rpc/deployPS.wsdd
```

We wrote the client `SoapSender.java` in Lab 2 so that it accepts a URL identifying the SOAP receiver to call; therefore, you do not have to create another client for this lab. You do need to create a SOAP request message. Type the following listing into a file called `priceRequest.xml` and save it to the `javawebbook/document` directory.

Listing 7.55 Document/Literal SOAP Request Message for Invoking Wrapped PRC Price Service

```
<?xml version="1.0" encoding="UTF-8"?>
<soap:Envelope xmlns:soap="http://www.w3.org/2003/05/soap-envelope"
    xmlns:mon="http://computer-monitors.co/Pricing">
  <soap:Body>
    <mon:getMonitorPrice>
      <mon:productId>DU1905fp</mon:productId>
      <mon:currency>AUD</mon:currency>
    </mon:getMonitorPrice>
  </soap:Body>
</soap:Envelope>
```

Make sure that the TCP Monitor is running with a listener listening to port 9999 (discussed in Lab 1) and then enter the following command into your command prompt.

```
java -cp %CLASSPATH%;. javawebbook.SoapSender "javawebbook\document\priceRequest.xml"
"http://localhost:9999/axis/services/PriceService"
```

The previous command should be typed on one line. When the command executes, you should receive output similar to the following.

Listing 7.56 (Wrapped) Document/Literal SOAP Response Message

```
<?xml version="1.0" encoding="UTF-8"?>
<soapenv:Envelope
  xmlns:soapenv="http://www.w3.org/2003/05/soap-envelope"
  xmlns:xsd="http://www.w3.org/2001/XMLSchema"
  xmlns:xsi="http://www.w3.org/2001/XMLSchema-instance">
  <soapenv:Body>
    <getMonitorPriceResponse xmlns="http://computer-monitors.co/Pricing">
      <getMonitorPriceReturn>471.75</getMonitorPriceReturn>
    </getMonitorPriceResponse>
  </soapenv:Body>
</soapenv:Envelope>
```

Additionally, in your TCP Monitor listener window, you should see something similar to that shown in Figure 7.21. For brevity, the window in the following figure has been resized to eliminate the HTTP header from the view.

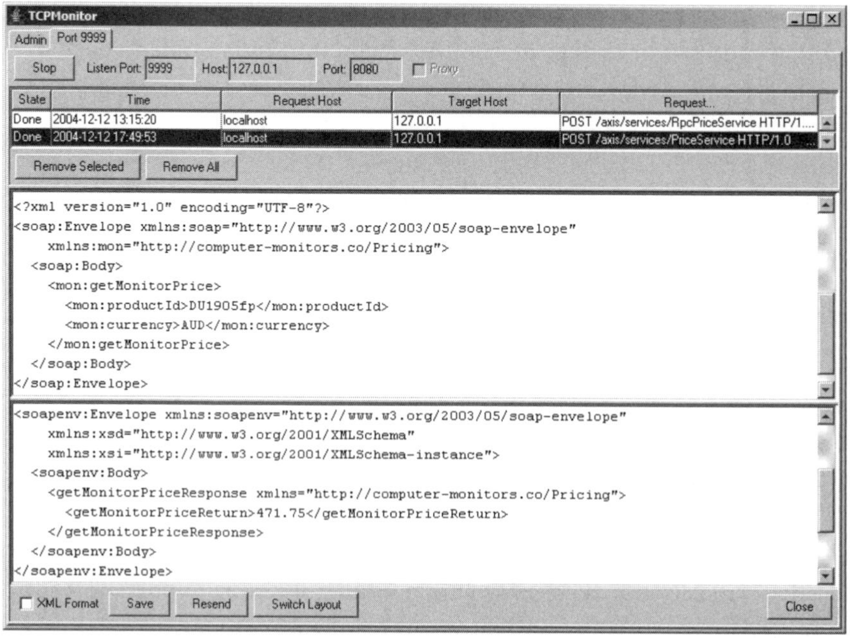

TCPMonitor

Admin | Port 9999

Stop | Listen Port: 9999 | Host: 127.0.0.1 | Port: 8080 | Proxy

State	Time	Request Host	Target Host	Request...
Done	2004-12-12 13:15:20	localhost	127.0.0.1	POST /axis/services/RpcPriceService HTTP/1....
Done	2004-12-12 17:49:53	localhost	127.0.0.1	POST /axis/services/PriceService HTTP/1.0 ...

Remove Selected | Remove All

```
<?xml version="1.0" encoding="UTF-8"?>
<soap:Envelope xmlns:soap="http://www.w3.org/2003/05/soap-envelope"
    xmlns:mon="http://computer-monitors.co/Pricing">
  <soap:Body>
    <mon:getMonitorPrice>
      <mon:productId>DU1905fp</mon:productId>
      <mon:currency>AUD</mon:currency>
    </mon:getMonitorPrice>
  </soap:Body>
</soap:Envelope>
```

```
<soapenv:Envelope xmlns:soapenv="http://www.w3.org/2003/05/soap-envelope"
    xmlns:xsd="http://www.w3.org/2001/XMLSchema"
    xmlns:xsi="http://www.w3.org/2001/XMLSchema-instance">
  <soapenv:Body>
    <getMonitorPriceResponse xmlns="http://computer-monitors.co/Pricing">
      <getMonitorPriceReturn>471.75</getMonitorPriceReturn>
    </getMonitorPriceResponse>
  </soapenv:Body>
</soapenv:Envelope>
```

XML Format | Save | Resend | Switch Layout | Close

Figure 7.21

TCP Monitor Capturing (Wrapped) Document/Literal SOAP Message

7.11 Summary

One of the biggest challenges that computing professionals face today is getting distributed, disparate systems to communicate via the Internet. Companies want to link their applications with services provided by other organizations and they realize that the Internet provides a cheap communications channel with which they can make that happen. Additionally, organizations would like to link their legacy systems to their newer systems via their corporate intranets. Programming environments for handling such communications needs have been around for years. The major problems with the solutions of the past have been a lack of widespread and limited interoperability. With the multitude of services that companies all over the world are making available via the Internet, the vision of the future is that applications can be rapidly created, possibly somewhat automatically, by simply linking some business logic to various Web-based distributed systems. To make this happen, the method of communication has to be standardized, widely accepted, and provide a basis for true interoperability among nearly any programming language and platform. That is why SOAP was created.

SOAP is a lightweight protocol for exchanging XML-based messages between peers in a decentralized, distributed environment (such as the Internet). SOAP messages provide structure and typing for business data as well as a system for processing that data such that it can be exchanged with disparate systems in a manner that is independent of any programming language, operating system, hardware, or transport protocol.

Fundamentally, SOAP is a stateless, one-way message exchange framework. However, applications typically combine the one-way messages to create more complex message exchange patterns such as request-response and request-multiple response. Because SOAP is designed to be platform-independent, it does not make use of advanced facilities provided by specific platforms that have been incorporated into other messaging frameworks. However, SOAP provides an extension framework by which applications can incorporate advanced features into their applications. SOAP has enjoyed rapid, widespread acceptance by nearly all of the major software vendors and organizations, most likely due to its platform-independence, support for true interoperability, and extensibility.

A SOAP message is transmitted from an initial SOAP sender node, through zero or more SOAP intermediary nodes, to the ultimate SOAP receiver node, forming what is called the SOAP message path. Each SOAP node is a SOAP processor that is compliant with the SOAP specification. The SOAP intermediary nodes provide SOAP with a mechanism for horizontal extensibility whereby application-specific processing can be interjected along the SOAP message path. The SOAP specification defines how each SOAP node is to handle the SOAP message including exceptional conditions in which a SOAP node may generate an error called a fault. Under normal circumstances, a SOAP sender transmits a SOAP request message to a SOAP receiver, which processes the message and may or may not reply with a SOAP response message, depending on the message exchange pattern being used. If the SOAP receiver encounters an error while processing the SOAP request message, it must generate a fault. If the message exchange pattern being used is a request-response type, then the SOAP receiver is required to transmit the fault in a SOAP message back to the SOAP sender.

The SOAP message is fairly simple in design, consisting only of four major XML elements: the SOAP `Envelope`, `Header`, `Body`, and `Fault`. The `Envelope` element is the root of the XML document that is a SOAP message and houses the `Header`, `Body`, and `Fault` elements. The `Header` element is the key to SOAP's extensibility, providing a mechanism by which systems can add application-specific processing to the normal SOAP processing defined by the SOAP specification. The `Header` element can contain one or more application-specific XML elements, which are called header blocks. SOAP intermediary nodes are allowed to process header blocks, but are not supposed to process data in the `Body` element. The `Body` element can contain one or more XML elements that contain the application-specific data being transmitted from the initial SOAP sender to the ultimate SOAP receiver. The data in the `Body` is intended for processing by the ultimate SOAP receiver, but possibly may not reach the ultimate SOAP receiver because a SOAP intermediary node may generate a `Fault`. A SOAP fault is analogous to an exception in Java. If a SOAP message contains a `Fault` element, it must appear as the only immediate child element of the SOAP `Body` element. The SOAP `Fault` element is designed to contain information about the error that occurred so the SOAP receiver can take some action, and, if possible, modify and resend the SOAP message.

How the application-specific data of the SOAP message is formatted and typed is up to the developer. The SOAP specification provides an optional method for encoding objects from a programming language to the XML that is transmitted over the wire, called SOAP Encoding. The SOAP specification also provides an optional convention for structuring the application-specific data of a SOAP message such that it can easily be processed as a remote procedure call, which is called the SOAP RPC Representation. Popular alternatives to these methods are encoding application-specific data using the XML Schema, which is referred to as literal encoding, and leaving the knowledge of how the application-specific XML is to be processed up to the application, which is referred to as document-style messaging. Combined, these two encoding styles and message styles form four message formats known as RPC/Encoded, RPC/Literal, Document/Encoded, and Document/Literal. Document/Encoded is rarely, if ever used, and the WS-I BP strictly prohibits both RPC/Encoded and Document/Encoded. RPC/Encoded has been used quite frequently in the past, so it is bound to be seen somewhere. RPC/Literal and Document/Literal are very similar. In fact, the application-specific XML used in an instance of an RPC/Literal message, when converted to Document/Literal, turns out to be a subset of the application-specific XML used in the Document/Literal message. The Literal formats require less processing by the SOAP processor, and as such have better performance. The software industry as a whole appears to be trending toward using Document/Literal because it provides the least amount of coupling, the greatest scalability, and the best performance. However, it may not always be the best solution for the application. The RPC styles can be used to get an application up and running in a shorter amount of time. Ultimately, the choice is up to the developer.

There is much more to SOAP and surrounding technologies than this chapter could cover. Whole books have been written on the subject. The next chapter will cover some technologies that work in concert with SOAP and Java APIs that have been written to make the job easier when programming applications that communicate via SOAP. Areas that provide some interesting and practical reading outside the scope of this book of which you might be interested in Googling are routing (WS-Addressing), security (WS-Security), and transactions (WS-Coordination, WS-AutomicTransaction, WS-BusinessActivity).

7.12 Self-Review Questions

1. What is the underlying transport protocol that SOAP must use?

   a. HTTP

   b. TCP/IP

   c. SMTP

   d. None (SOAP is independent of the underlying transport protocol.)

2. What programming language must SOAP use?

   a. Java

   b. C++

   c. Perl

   d. None (SOAP is independent of programming languages.)

3. SOAP is fundamentally what kind of message exchange paradigm?

   a. Request-response

   b. One-way

   c. Request-multiple response

   d. Solicit-response

4. What organization maintains SOAP?

   a. JCP

   b. WS-I

   c. W3C

   d. OASIS

5. SOAP can be used to transport binary data.

   a. True

   b. False

6. What MEP is most commonly used with SOAP?
   a. Solicit-response
   b. Notification
   c. Request-response
   d. One-way
7. For which SOAP node is the SOAP `Body` targeted for processing?
   a. Intermediary node
   b. Initial sender node
   c. Ultimate receiver node
   d. None of the above
8. What part of the SOAP message is an intermediary node limited to processing?
   a. Envelope.
   b. Header.
   c. Body.
   d. An intermediary node can only view the SOAP message, not process it.
9. What is another name used for the ultimate SOAP receiver node?
   a. SOAP server
   b. SOAP application
   c. Web service
   d. All of the above
10. What is the name for the set of nodes through which the SOAP message passes?
    a. Data model
    b. Message path
    c. SOAP application
    d. Transport path
11. How many intermediary nodes can a SOAP message pass through?
    a. 1
    b. 2

c. 3

d. Any number

12. Which HTTP method was the SOAP response MEP designed for?

a. POST

b. PUT

c. GET

d. DELETE

13. How many header blocks can appear in a SOAP message?

a. 2

b. 4

c. 5

d. Any number

14. How many immediate child elements can appear in the `Body` when using SOAP RPC?

a. 1

b. 2

c. 3

d. Any number

15. What message style provides the least amount of coupling?

a. RPC/Encoded

b. RPC/Literal

c. Document/Encoded

d. Document/Literal

16. What message style is the easiest for the developer to use?

a. RPC/Encoded

b. RPC/Literal

c. Document/Encoded

d. Document/Literal

17. What message style(s) typically infer the use of XML Schema?

    a. RPC/Encoded

    b. RPC/Literal

    c. Document/Encoded

    d. Document/Literal

18. What message style causes the fewest interoperability problems?

    a. RPC/Encoded

    b. RPC/Literal

    c. Document/Encoded

    d. Document/Literal

19. Which SOAP element is analogous to a Java exception?

    a. Envelope

    b. Header

    c. Body

    d. Fault

20. Which attribute is used to target a header block for processing by a specific intermediary node?

    a. `role`

    b. `relay`

    c. `mustUnderstand`

    d. None of the above

21. What namespace is used to identify the main elements of a SOAP 1.2 message?

    a. `http://schemas.xmlsoap.org/soap/envelope`

    b. `http://www.w3.org/2003/05/soap-envelope/role/next`

    c. `http://www.w3.org/2003/05/soap-envelope`

    d. `http://www.w3.org/2003/05/soap-rpc`

22. When using SOAP RPC conventions, what is the element used to identify the return value of the remote procedure call?

    a. `returnValue`

    b. `response`

    c. `result`

    d. `out`

23. Which element can appear alongside a `Fault` element in the SOAP `Body`?

    a. A `Detail` element

    b. Another `Fault` element

    c. Any application-specific XML

    d. None (The `Fault` element, if present, must be the only element in the `Body`.)

7.13 Keys to the Self-Review Questions

1. b 2. d 3. d 4. b 5. c 6. a 7. c 8. c 9. b 10. d 11. b 12. d 13. c 14. d 15. a 16. d 17. a 18. b, d 19. d 20. d 21. a 22. c 23. c 24. d

7.14 Exercises

1. Define SOAP, describe who maintains the specification, and what purpose it serves in the software industry.
2. Why does SOAP succeed with interoperability while other attempts have failed?
3. What is the difference between a protocol such as SOAP and an application programming interface?
4. How can SOAP be used to freely pass through firewalls?
5. On what language is SOAP based? Explain how the use of that language provides SOAP with a basis for platform-independence.
6. If you had two distributed systems that were both written in Java and you wanted to get them communicating, what protocol would you use and why?
7. What does interoperability mean in the context of SOAP?

8. What is the WS-I BP, and what is its purpose? List three restrictions that the WS-I BP places on SOAP usage.
9. What are XML namespaces used for in a SOAP message?
10. Describe the SOAP message path and each of its components. Be sure to use SOAP terminology.
11. List and describe each of the four major elements that are used to compose a SOAP message. Which SOAP element is analogous to what Java class and why?
12. Which SOAP node is the SOAP `Body` intended for? Which nodes can read the contents of the SOAP `Body`? Which SOAP nodes should not process the SOAP `Body` and why?
13. What underlying transport protocol is SOAP typically bound to and why?
14. Describe two different methods for transporting binary data with a SOAP message.
15. What is a message exchange pattern? List and describe the two message exchange patterns defined in the SOAP specification.
16. Describe the SOAP extensibility mechanism and how it can be used to interject application-specific processing into the SOAP message path.
17. Describe some reasons why you would use SOAP header blocks. By what SOAP nodes are header blocks intended to be processed? What is the `role` attribute used for? What is the `relay` attribute used for?
18. Write out a SOAP 1.1–compliant message containing a SOAP `Fault`. Do the same for a SOAP 1.2–compliant message.
19. List 10 differences between SOAP 1.1 and SOAP 1.2.
20. Define data encoding.
21. List and describe the two SOAP message styles and the two popular SOAP encoding styles. Which message format is the easiest to use? Which message format provides the least amount of coupling?
22. Describe the different methods for indicating the data types in a SOAP message. Which method do SOAP experts prefer?
23. What benefits does SOAP Encoding have over XML Schema? What benefits does XML Schema have over SOAP Encoding?

24. Create a SOAP object graph using the rules defined by the SOAP Data Model. Translate that object graph to XML using the rules of SOAP Encoding.

25. Create an XML schema and use that schema in a SOAP message to define the application-specific data in the SOAP `Body`.

7.15 Programming Exercises

1. Develop, deploy on Axis, and test a SOAP application that uses the RPC/Literal message style to return the calculation identified by the SOAP request message. For instance, if the request message includes the numbers '3' and '4' and a '+' sign, then the SOAP application should return '7'.

2. Rewrite Programming Exercise #1 to use a Document/Literal message style.

3. Rewrite Programming Exercise #1 to use an RPC/Encoded message style.

4. Redeploy one of the services developed in Programming Exercises #1, #2, or #3 to explicitly throw an exception. View the `Fault` element that was generated by Axis when you test it.

5. Develop, deploy, and test a Web service that corresponds to Lab 3, which allows a company to order a monitor. The Web service must be deployed with a WSDD that specifies `style="document"` and `use="literal"`. This kind of example would typically accept a Java Bean that represents a purchase order. You will probably need to read the Axis documentation for this exercise.

6. Apache Axis supports header blocks in a SOAP message via message handlers. Do some research and create a SOAP implementation that uses SOAP headers.

7.16 References

Basic Profile Version 1.0, Final Material. April 16, 2004. http://www.ws-i.org/Profiles/BasicProfile-1.0.html.

Basic Profile Version 1.1, Final Material. August 24, 2004. http://www.ws-i.org/Profiles/BasicProfile-1.1.html.

Englander, Robert. 2002. *Java and SOAP*. Sebastopol, CA: O'Reilly & Associates, Inc.

Graham, Steve, Doug Davis, Simeon Simeonov, Glen Daniels, Peter Brittenham, Yuichi Nakamura, Paul Fremantle, Dieter Koenig, and Claudia Zentner. 2004. *Building Web Services with Java: Making Sense of XML, SOAP, WSDL, and UDDI*. 2nd ed. Indianapolis: Sams Publishing.

Monson-Haefel, Richard. 2004. *J2EE Web Services*. Boston: Addison-Wesley.

Nagappan, Ramesh, Robert Skoczylas, and Rima Patel Sriganesh. 2003. *Developing Java Web Services, Architecting and Developing Secure Web Services Using Java*. Indianapolis: Wiley Publishing Inc.

Singh, Inderjeet, Sean Brydon, Greg Murray, Vijay Ramachandran, Thierry Violleau, and Beth Stearns. 2004. *Designing Web Services with the J2EE 1.4 Platform: JAX-RPC, SOAP, and XML Technologies*. Boston: Addison-Wesley.

W3C Note. *Simple Object Access Protocol (SOAP) 1.1*. May 8, 2000. http:///www.w3.org/TR/SOAP.

W3C Note. *SOAP Messages with Attachments*. December 11, 2000. http://www.w3.org/TR/SOAP-attachments.

W3C Note. *SOAP Version 1.2 Email Binding*. July 3 2002. http://www.w3.org/TR/soap12-email.

W3C Recommendation. *Extensible Markup Language (XML) 1.0* (Third Edition). February 4, 2004. http://www.w3.org/TR/REC-xml.

W3C Recommendation. *Namespaces in XML*. 1999. http://www.w3.org/TR/REC-xml-names.

W3C Recommendation. *SOAP Version 1.2 Part 0: Primer*. June 24, 2003. http://www.w3.org/TR/soap12-part0/.

W3C Recommendation. *SOAP Version 1.2 Part 1: Messaging Framework*. June 24, 2003. http://www.w3.org/TR/soap12-part1/.

W3C Recommendation. *SOAP Version 1.2 Part 2: Adjuncts*. June 24, 2003. http://www.w3.org/TR/soap12-part2/.

W3C Recommendation. *XML Schema Part 0: Primer Second Edition.* October 28, 2004. http://www.w3.org/TR/xmlschema-0/.

W3C Recommendation. *XML Schema Part 1: Structures Second Edition.* October 28, 2004. http://www.w3.org/TR/xmlschema-1/.

W3C Recommendation. *XML Schema Part 2: Datatypes Second Edition.* October 28, 2004. http://www.w3.org/TR/xmlschema-2/.

Additional Resources

Various articles from IBM developerWorks. http://www-130.ibm.com/developerworks/webservices/.

Various articles from Microsoft Developer Network (MSDN) Library. http://msdn.microsoft.com/library/.

CHAPTER 8

Web Services

Objectives of This Chapter

- Describe the Web services approach to the service-oriented architecture concept
- Describe the WSDL specification and how it is used to define Web services
- Describe the Java APIs for programming Web services and give examples of their use
- Discuss how to expose plain Java objects and EJBs as Web services and deploy Web services in J2EE
- Describe the UDDI specification and how is used as a Web service discovery mechanism
- Describe the Java API that can be used to interact with a UDDI registry and give examples of its use
- Provide detailed step-by-step examples of how to program Web services in Java

8.1 Overview

The term *Web services* is used to categorize software applications that are exposed over a network via the use of XML standards and Internet protocols in such a manner that they are highly interoperable with other disparate distributed applications. Web services are based on an architectural style called *service-oriented architecture (SOA)*. The concept behind SOA is that different functional units of a business process are exposed via software as services to be consumed over a network. By the term *service* we mean a unit of work done by a *service provider* to achieve desired results for a *service consumer* (also commonly referred to as *service requester*). Examples of services in the banking industry might be loan processing, withdrawals, deposits, transfers, processing charges to credit cards. Think of the service provider as the server in a client–server relationship where the service consumer is the client.

Some of the primary goals of SOA are *interoperability* and *loose coupling* among interacting software applications, a *separation of concerns*, and *reusability* of services. Most of the design effort in an SOA is focused on creating service interfaces that serve as contracts for how the services are to be invoked and to respond. A well-defined service interface provides a clear separation from any hardware, operating systems, programming languages, or protocols that may compose the service implementation. This separation of interface from implementation is intended to allow service consumer applications the ability to interoperate with service provider applications regardless of whether their underlying implementations are compatible. In an SOA, applications are integrated via the service interface, not the service implementation. As a result, the applications are loosely coupled. The benefit of loosely coupled applications lies in their ability to survive evolutionary changes in their structure and implementation. Tightly coupled systems are based on interfaces that are tightly interrelated in function and form, thus making them brittle to any form of change that may be required.

Earlier approaches to designing distributed systems typically focused on specific implementation environments, which often resulted in systems that were tied to the features and idiosyncrasies of that particular technology, such as CORBA, DCOM, or J2EE. As a result, these systems were not flexible or scalable enough to handle the rapidly changing requirements demanded by the businesses that use them. In contrast, SOA focuses on integrating independent business services, regardless of the technology used to implement the services. This way of thinking allows businesses to better align their services with business needs rather than the technology in which their systems are implemented.

In an SOA, large business processes are broken down into generic, loosely coupled, functional units in which each unit performs a different task. Each functional unit is then exposed as a separate service, which achieves a separation of concerns. Each service handles a specific concern (task). These services can then be orchestrated together to form any number of different business processes. If a

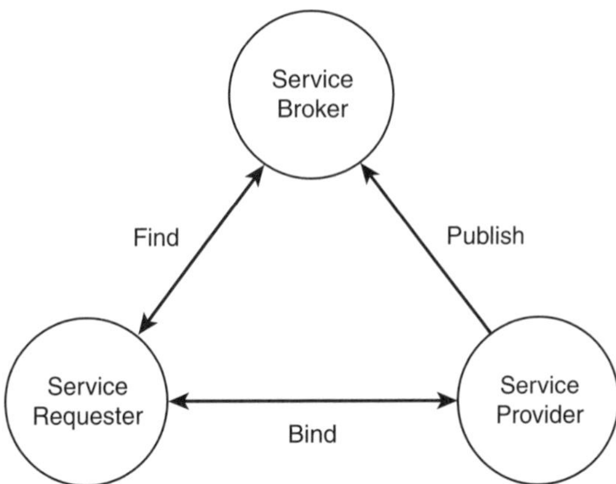

Figure 8.1

Roles and Operations in a Service-Oriented Architecture

company finds that it is more cost-effective to use a service provided by a different company than maintain their own, they can quickly swap out that service. Since integration is tied to interfaces and not the implementation, changing a service provider is not hindered by incompatibilities in underlying platforms. If later the company finds that another service provider has better prices, then the system can easily be repositioned to use that provider. The system can also be designed to dynamically choose among different service providers (if they have the same service interface) based on price or even some other policy such as performance or reliability. In addition, when it comes time to build another system to accomplish some other business process, existing services can readily be reused. In essence, in SOA individual software units, called services, become the building blocks to develop complete applications.

Service-oriented architectures can be conceptualized as containing three roles and three operations, which are depicted in Figure 8.1. The roles are service provider, service broker, and service requester. The operations are publish, find, and bind. The three operations define the relationships between the three roles. The three roles typically communicate by sending request messages and processing any response messages.

- Service Provider

  The service provider develops the service interface and implementation and deploys the service so that it is available to be invoked over a network. The service provider also creates a service description and publishes that service description with one or more service brokers. (This is the publish operation.) The service description describes everything that a service requester must know to invoke the service made available by the service provider.

This information typically includes the format for the request message, the format for the response message (if any), and where to send the request message.

- Service Broker

  The service broker is also commonly called the service registry. The broker accepts requests from service providers to publish information about the services they want to make available. The information published includes the type of the service, a description of the service, and the location where the service can be invoked. The service requester can then query the service broker to find a particular service. (This is the find operation.) An analogy to the service broker is a phone book. A company publishes information on a particular service they are providing in a phone book. In turn, people look in the phone book to find companies providing that same service. People find the company that published their service and use the contact information to request the service from that company. Once a service requester has the service description of the service provider, it no longer needs the service broker.

- Service Requester

  The service requester uses the service broker to find services that match some set of criteria. The service requester can then use the service description to connect to the service and invoke it. (This is the bind operation.) The act of finding a service is also called service discovery.

SOA is an approach to building software systems in which a set of loosely coupled services is developed such that they can be dynamically composed to form an application. The key to making this work is the service description and the interface it describes. The service interface provides a mechanism for decoupling different software functional units (services). The service description provides a mechanism that can be used to dynamically compose the resulting services. The service description is published to the service registry by the service provider, then retrieved by the service requester via the find operation, and then used to dynamically bind to the service to form a business process.

A Web service is one approach to implementing a service-oriented architecture that uses XML-based data representations and communications protocols to achieve platform independence and thus interoperability. Web services are considered the next evolutionary step in distributed computing beyond technologies such as CORBA, DCOM, and J2EE. Web services are usually discussed in relation to their use over the Internet, or the World Wide Web. However, Web services, despite the name, can and are deployed on all types of networks including local area networks (typically corporate intranets).

The focus of Web services has been to ease the difficulty of enterprise application integration, particularly between organizations, which is commonly referred to as business-to-business (B2B) communication. The goal of Web services is to allow business systems to be built quickly by combining Web services built internal to an organization with those of business partners. Some of these services can be developed from scratch and others can be constructed by simply wrapping existing systems with a lightweight Web service interface. Web services promise to give businesses a better return on investment than past software projects, a faster time to project completion, and an ability to more quickly respond to changing business requirements.

The full complement of Web service technologies available today is so large that it cannot be covered in one book, much less a single chapter. Additionally, the field of Web services is changing so rapidly that many technologies will soon be phased out of use as the industry converges. Consequently, this chapter will only concentrate on discussing the four core Web service technologies—XML, SOAP, Web Services Description Language (WSDL), and Universal Description, Discovery, and Integration (UDDI). These four technologies have unprecedented industry backing and are the foundation for many other Web service technologies. These core technologies are also the basis for Web services in J2EE version 1.4.

- XML

  XML (eXtensible Markup Language) is the basis for SOAP, WSDL, and UDDI. Depending on the definition of Web services, XML is really the foundation for all Web service technologies. Representing data in XML is one of the primary keys to Web service interoperability. XML is a language for defining other languages, which is defined by a specification and is independent of operating systems and programming languages. XML defines rules for creating XML markup languages, which in turn define a set of tags that are used to organize and describe text. Thus, an XML document is simply a text file that can be read by human and machine alike. Because XML was covered in detail in an earlier chapter of this book, it will not be described further in this chapter. You need to understand XML to understand how Web services work; if you have not learned XML, I suggest you do so before continuing on with this chapter.

- SOAP

  Web services basically involve the exchange of XML documents or data that is organized into an XML format. SOAP is a specification that defines a standard routing and packaging format for transmitting XML data between applications on a network. Because SOAP was designed to be independent of the underlying platform, it can be used by just about any application regardless of the programming language that it is written in or the operating system that it runs on. Web services interact by transmitting SOAP request messages and processing SOAP response messages, which are typically conveyed using HTTP. A SOAP message is simply an XML document; however, it is specifically designed to contain other XML documents as well as information related to routing, processing, security, transactions, and other qualities of service. As with XML, SOAP was covered in an earlier chapter of this book and will not be described further in this chapter.

- WSDL

  WSDL (commonly pronounced "whiz dul") is the technology that is used to write the service description. Recall that the service description is used to describe everything that a service requester must know to invoke a Web service. In essence, WSDL allows an organization to describe the types of XML documents and SOAP messages that must be used to interact with their Web services. A WSDL service description is just an XML document that is conformant to the WSDL schema definition. WSDL will be discussed further later in this chapter.

- UDDI

  UDDI is a technology that enables service discovery. Before the members of an organization can use a Web service, they must first discover the Web service description. UDDI defines a standard set of operations that can be invoked via SOAP messages, which are used to publish and find Web service descriptions. In other words, UDDI is one approach to creating a service registry (service broker in Figure 8.1). A UDDI registry stores information on businesses and their Web services including detailed information on how to bind to the Web services. UDDI also provides support for categorizing Web services and indicating that specific Web services adhere to certain technical specifications. UDDI will be discussed further later in this chapter.

These four Web services technologies are used together to provide Web services applications with a universal mechanism for structuring data and defining data types (XML), exchanging data between applications over a network (SOAP), defining application interfaces (WSDL), and publishing and finding information on existing Web services (UDDI). XML is used to format data into a document such that all interacting applications know how to process it, and SOAP is used to package the XML document in order that it can be transported between applications. WSDL is used to describe the manner in which XML and SOAP messages must be used to invoke an organization's Web services and UDDI allows organizations to publish information about their Web services, including where the WSDL documents are located, so that other businesses can find and use them. The interaction that makes use of these four technologies is illustrated below.

Figure 8.2 illustrates the interaction that occurs between service provider, service broker, and service requester. In step 1 a service provider publishes its Web service information to a UDDI registry (or multiple registries). The information published would include a link to the location of its WSDL service description and may include a description of the service, the name of the company providing the service, a category for the service, and links to any industry specifications to which it adheres. In step 2 a service requester searches the UDDI registry and finds the published Web service. In step 3 the service requester uses the information found on the Web service to locate and download a copy

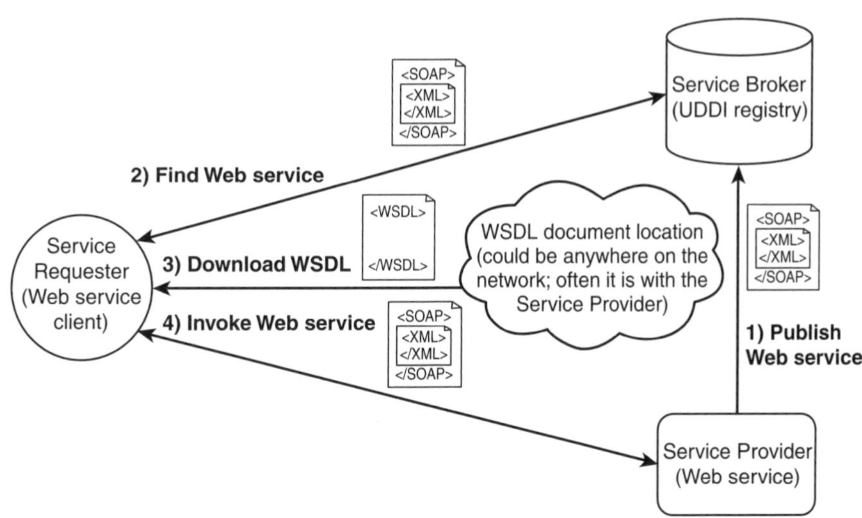

Figure 8.2
Web Services Interaction

of the WSDL service description. In step 4 the service requester uses information provided by the WSDL service description to bind to the Web service (generate network proxy code) and invoke it.

Since Web services technologies are based on XML, the interaction illustrated in Figure 8.2 is accomplished through the exchange of XML documents. The publish and find operations of the UDDI registry are invoked using SOAP messages, and the Web service is invoked using the exchange of SOAP messages. SOAP messages and WSDL documents are both instances of XML documents, and the data SOAP messages contain is also XML. XML is great for helping to achieve interoperability but tedious to write manually. Writing and exchanging XML documents as a way of invoking operations is also much different than the traditional procedure call programming that developers are accustomed to writing. Consequently, the Java Community Process (JCP) has developed Java APIs that do the XML processing work for you, allowing developers to create and use Web services applications through traditional Java programming without having to write any XML. These APIs include the Java API for XML Processing (JAXP), the Java API for XML-based RPC (JAX-RPC), the SOAP with Attachments API for Java (SAAJ), and the Java API for XML Registries (JAXR). JAXP is used to create, parse, and transform XML documents. JAX-RPC can be used to communicate with Web services by generating and transmitting SOAP request messages or create Web service components from Java servlets and EJBs that will correctly process incoming SOAP request messages and generate and transmit SOAP response messages. SAAJ is a low-level API that allows the user to create, transmit, and process SOAP messages and SOAP messages with attachments. Under the covers,

JAX-RPC actually uses SAAJ for SOAP message processing. JAXR provides an API that simplifies the process of publishing to and searching UDDI registries. Application servers that are compliant with J2EE version 1.4 must provide an implementation for all these APIs. The detailed requirements for the support of Web services by application servers that are compliant with J2EE version 1.4 can be found in the J2EE 1.4 specification (`http://jcp.org/en/jsr/detail?id=151`), the Implementing Enterprise Web Services specification (`http://jcp.org/en/jsr/detail?id=109`), and the maintenance revision of the Implementing Enterprise Web Services specification (`http://jcp.org/en/jsr-/detail?id=921`). In this chapter we cover JAX-RPC, SAAJ, and UDDI.

The last chapter discussed the role that the Web Services Interoperability Organization (WS-I) has taken in establishing a standard for using SOAP that helps to ensure interoperability. The SOAP specification is somewhat ambiguous such that SOAP application and toolkit vendors are left to interpret aspects of the specification as they see fit. This creates a problem because vendors are bound to interpret the ambiguities in different ways, thereby creating incompatibilities in Web services applications. However, one of the primary goals of Web services is interoperability. Therefore, the WS-I was established and has since defined restrictions on the use of SOAP to help ensure interoperability among Web services applications. These restrictions are documented in the WS-I Basic Profile (`http://www.ws-i.org/deliverables/workinggroup.aspx?wg=basicprofile`). The WS-I Basic Profile (BP) contains restrictions on the use of the three other Web services technologies as well. Ambiguities exist in the XML, WSDL, and UDDI specifications that could also be left to interpretation, thereby hindering interoperability. J2EE version 1.4 mandates that compliant application servers support applications that conform to the WS-I BP. The restrictions that the WS-I BP mandates are highlighted throughout the rest of this chapter.

8.2 Web Services Description Language (WSDL)

In order to invoke a Web service, there are several pieces of information that must be known in advance: what message exchange protocol the Web service is using (such as SOAP), how the messages to be exchanged are structured (such as what data the Web service expects in a request, and what, if any, data the Web service will send back in a response), what transport protocol is employed by the Web service (such as HTTP or SMTP), and the network address of the Web service. Essentially, what is needed is the service description.

A service description is a concept and as such can be implemented in any number of ways. One way to provide a service description might be to simply write out a textual description in natural language (such as English) and post it on a public Web site for businesses to read. The problem with this approach is that natural language is far too ambiguous and open to interpretation. Since we need to describe an interface to software, the description must be precise so that it will not be misinterpreted. Another drawback to the natural language approach is that it would not produce a description that is readily machine-readable. Since one of the goals behind Web services is to produce applications that can dynamically bind to other remote applications, we need a description that can be easily processed by software. Therefore, we need a standard format to follow when creating our service descriptions so that the resultant descriptions are precise, any business can understand them, and software tools can process them. That is why the Web Services Description Language (WSDL) was created.

WSDL was designed as an IDL (interface definition language) for Web services that is independent of any specific protocol, programming language, or operating system. Even though this chapter discusses how to use WSDL to describe SOAP-based Web services, WSDL is not specific to SOAP. Additionally, WSDL was designed to be modular so that its artifacts can be used to describe more than one Web service. Unfortunately, the design goals of WSDL have made resultant WSDL documents fairly complex and somewhat difficult to understand at first sight. However, the complexity of WSDL is offset by the fact that many tools available today will automatically create and process WSDL documents for the user. Most toolkits, such as Apache Axis used in the last chapter, will generate a WSDL document from a predefined Java interface as well as do the opposite—generate a Java interface (and network stubs) from a predefined WSDL document.

The WSDL specification was the result of combined efforts from IBM, Microsoft, and many other companies. Originally, Microsoft developed the Service Definition Language (SDL) that later evolved into the SOAP Contract Language (SCL), and on a separate front IBM developed the Network Accessible Service Specification Language (NASSL). The two companies decided that having competing specifications would hinder the adoption of Web services; they came together and compromised on a new specification, WSDL. Version 1.1 of WSDL was submitted to the W3C as a W3C Note in March of 2001 and is currently available at `http://www.w3.org/TR/wsdl`. W3C is now working on a standard version of WSDL, which will eventually be a W3C Recommendation. WSDL version 2.0 is currently in draft form available at `http://www.w3.org/TR/wsdl20`. The concentration of this section is on WSDL 1.1 because WSDL 2.0 is still in draft form, the current version of J2EE (version 1.4) only supports WSDL 1.1, and the current version of the WS-I BP mandates the use of WSDL 1.1.

8.2.1 WSDL Document Structure

A WSDL service description is composed of two major sections—a service interface definition and a service implementation definition. The service interface definition defines the service at an abstract level by describing the messages it sends and receives. It answers the question about what the Web service does in terms of the operations it provides and the data it requires as well as the data (if any) with which it responds. Essentially, it describes the operation signatures of a Web service similar to the way a Java `interface` describes the method signatures of an object. The Java `interface` defines methods (operations in Web services lingo) plus a parameter list (data) and a return value (data) for each method.

The service implementation definition defines the concrete implementation of the Web service interface by describing the wire and transport protocols in use (e.g., SOAP and HTTP) and the network address (i.e., a URL). It answers the questions about how a service is accessed and where a service is located. The separation of interface and implementation within a WSDL document allows multiple Web service implementations to be described that reuse the same interface within the same document. This can reduce the size of the document and consequently the time required to process it. You will understand this more clearly when you see an example later in this section.

A WSDL service description is simply an XML document with its own XML schema, XML namespaces, and processing rules. A WSDL document is composed of the following key XML elements, listed in their recommended order of appearance. The WSDL specification does not mandate this order; however, the WS-I BP does.

- `definitions` (mandatory)

  The `definitions` element is the root element of the XML document that defines a WSDL service description. As the root element, there can be only one `definitions` element in a WSDL document and it contains all the other WSDL elements.

- `documentation` (optional)

  The `documentation` element may be used to describe aspects of the WSDL document to human readers. It is optional and may be used within any other WSDL element, meaning it can appear multiple times throughout the document. If it appears as an immediate child element of the `definitions` element, then it must be the first child.

- `import` (optional)

  The `import` element can be used to make available in the current WSDL document the definitions from other WSDL documents. This allows one to modularize the WSDL documents. For example, the user might want to leave a set of interface definitions in one document and import them into a series of other WSDL documents containing implementation definitions. The `import` element is optional, may be used multiple times in a single WSDL document, and all uses must appear immediately after the `documentation` element. If no `documentation` element is used, the `import` element must be the first child of the `definitions` element.

- `types` (optional)

  The `types` element is used to define all the data types used by other elements throughout the WSDL document. WSDL does not mandate the use of any specific typing system, but the default typing system is XML Schema. The specification states that all WSDL-compliant processors must support the use of XML Schema. The `types` element is optional, only one `types` element can appear in the document, and, if it is used, it must appear immediately after the `import` element.

- `message` (optional)

  The `message` element is used to describe the data transmitted between the service provider and the service requester, which represents a set of operation parameters and return values. Each `message` element represents the payload of a one-way message, either a request message or a response message. One or more `message` elements are referenced by `operation` elements to form service operation signatures. The `message` element is optional, may be used multiple times, and all uses must follow the `types` element and precede the `portType` element.

- `portType` (optional)

  The `portType` element defines a Web service's abstract interface definition (similar to a Java `interface`). It contains various `operation` elements that abstractly define the operations (methods) supported by a Web service. The `portType` element is optional, may be used multiple times, and all uses must follow the `message` element and precede the `binding` element. Although the `portType` element can be used multiple times in a single WSDL document, it typically only appears once to describe a single Web service.

- `operation` (optional)

  The `operation` element is analogous to a Java method declaration. It defines an operation that may be invoked on a Web service, including the name of the operation and the list of input parameters and output values. The `operation` element references one or more `message` elements to describe the parameter list. The `operation` element is optional, can be used multiple times, and all uses must appear as child elements of either the `portType` or `binding` elements. In other words, unlike all of the elements described thus far, the `operation` element is not an immediate child of the `definitions` element.

- `binding` (optional)

  The `binding` element is used to associate `operation` elements of a `portType` with a data format (such as XML Schema) and a protocol (such as SOAP over HTTP). Conceptually, the binding element is a concrete implementation of the abstract service interface (the portType). In essence, it describes the "language" that the Web service is using for communication and, as such, how clients must format and transmit messages to have them successfully invoke an operation. The binding element is optional, can be used multiple times, and all uses must follow the portType element and precede the service element.

- service (optional)

  The service element aggregates one or more bindings and assigns a network address to each binding. In other words, it defines the network address for the Web service. The service element is optional, can be used multiple times (to represent multiple services), and all uses must follow the binding element.

- port (optional)

  The port element is used as the immediate child of the service element to accomplish the actual association between a binding element and a network address. The port element can be used multiple times within a single service element.

The portType element (contains operation elements that reference message elements) is used to define the abstract service interface (i.e., what the Web service does). The binding element (references operation elements) and the service element (references binding elements) are used to define the concrete service implementation. The binding element describes how the Web service is accessed and the service element describes where the Web service is located. All of the elements listed above belong to the WSDL 1.1 namespace http://schemas.xmlsoap.org/wsdl/, which is commonly prefixed with wsdl:. The WSDL 1.1 namespace is also the Internet address for the WSDL 1.1 schema. Figure 8.3 illustrates the concepts and organization of a WSDL document.

Figure 8.3 illustrates that the binding is a concrete implementation of the portType, which is an abstract interface for the Web service. The service aggregates multiple port elements, each assigning a network address to a binding; the result is referred to as a concrete Web service endpoint. Essentially, the service element defines the capability of a Web service to be invoked over multiple bindings (i.e., protocols).

The sections of the document in Figure 8.3 labeled <-- *extensibility element* --> are placeholders that would be replaced in a real document by XML elements that define specific binding information for a particular protocol (such as SOAP) or a data format. Use of this extensibility is optional, but is often used when binding a protocol such as SOAP to the implementation of the Web service. If extensibility elements are used, they must have their own XML namespace different from that of WSDL. Extensibility elements may define that the use of a particular technology is mandatory by adding the attribute wsdl:required="true" to the extensibility element. Extensibility elements are

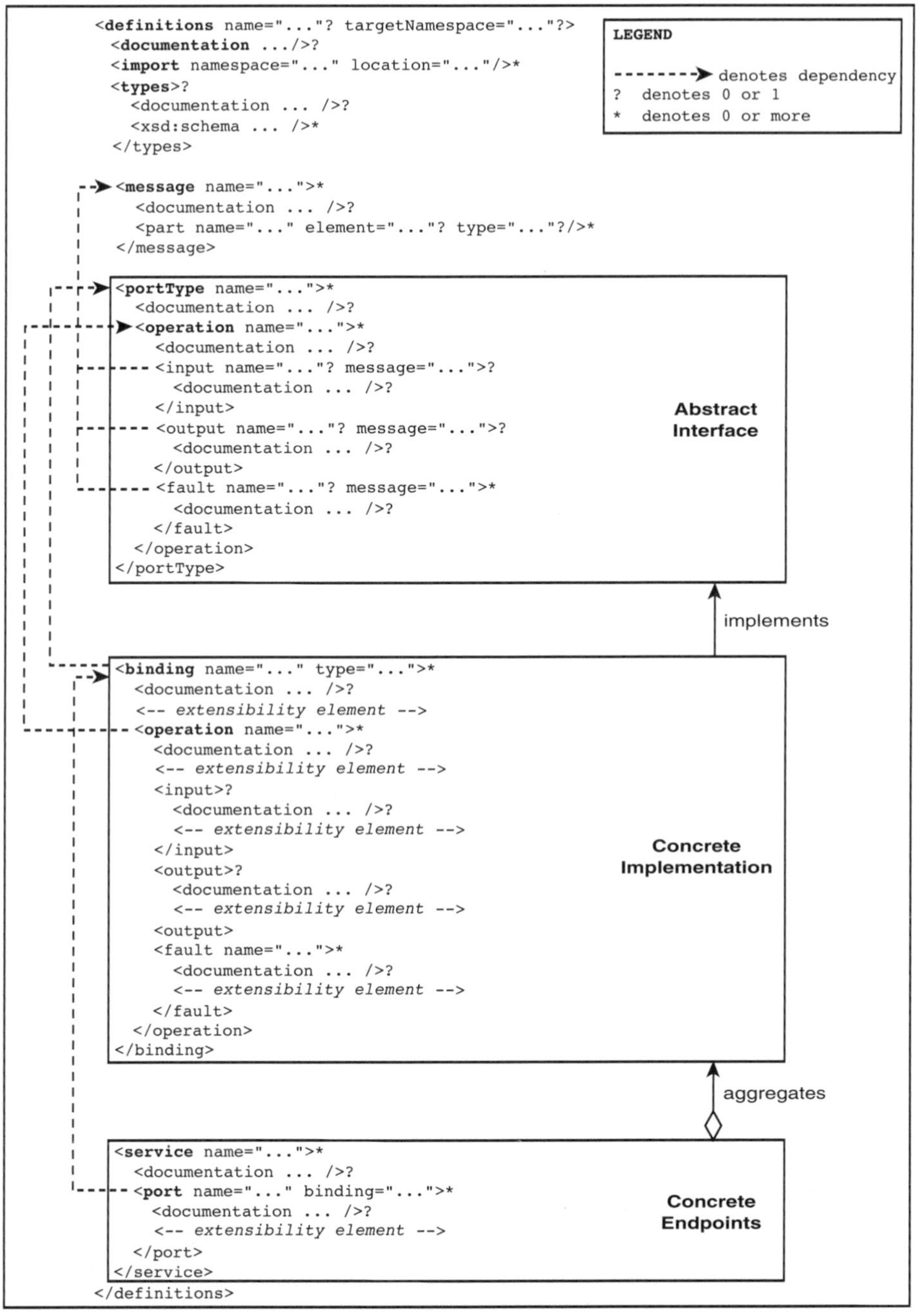

```
<definitions name="..."? targetNamespace="..."?>
  <documentation .../>?
  <import namespace="..." location="..."/>*
  <types>?
    <documentation ... />?
    <xsd:schema ... />*
  </types>

  <message name="...">*
    <documentation ... />?
    <part name="..." element="..."? type="..."?/>*
  </message>

  <portType name="...">*
    <documentation ... />?
    <operation name="...">*
      <documentation ... />?
      <input name="..."? message="...">?
        <documentation ... />?
      </input>
      <output name="..."? message="...">?
        <documentation ... />?
      </output>
      <fault name="..."? message="...">*
        <documentation ... />?
      </fault>
    </operation>
  </portType>

  <binding name="..." type="...">*
    <documentation ... />?
    <-- extensibility element -->
    <operation name="...">*
      <documentation ... />?
      <-- extensibility element -->
      <input>?
        <documentation ... />?
        <-- extensibility element -->
      </input>
      <output>?
        <documentation ... />?
        <-- extensibility element -->
      <output>
      <fault name="...">*
        <documentation ... />?
        <-- extensibility element -->
      </fault>
    </operation>
  </binding>

  <service name="...">*
    <documentation ... />?
    <port name="..." binding="...">*
      <documentation ... />?
      <-- extensibility element -->
    </port>
  </service>
</definitions>
```


Figure 8.3

WSDL 1.1 Document Components

very useful because they allow new network and message protocols to be used in a service description without having to revise the WSDL specification. The following is an example of a WSDL document that contains SOAP extensibility elements.

Listing 8.1 WSDL Document for a Monitor Pricing Service

```
<?xml version="1.0" encoding="UTF-8"?>
<definitions name="MonitorPricingWS"
    targetNamespace="http://monitors.co/ws/Pricing"
    xmlns:mon="http://monitors.co/ws/Pricing"
    xmlns:montypes="http://monitors.co/ns/pricing/types"
    xmlns:soapbind="http://schemas.xmlsoap.org/wsdl/soap/"
    xmlns:xsd="http://www.w3.org/2001/XMLSchema"
    xmlns="http://schemas.xmlsoap.org/wsdl/">

  <types>
    <xsd:schema targetNamespace="http://monitors.co/ns/pricing/types">
      <xsd:element name="MonitorPriceRequest">
        <xsd:complexType>
          <xsd:sequence>
            <xsd:element name="productId" type="xsd:string"/>
            <xsd:element name="currency" type="xsd:string"/>
          </xsd:sequence>
        </xsd:complexType>
      </xsd:element>

      <xsd:element name="price" type="xsd:float"/>

      <xsd:element name="InvalidArgumentFaultDetail">
        <xsd:complexType>
          <xsd:sequence>
            <xsd:element name="invalidValue" type="xsd:string"/>
            <xsd:element name="message" type="xsd:string"/>
          </xsd:sequence>
        </xsd:complexType>
      </xsd:element>
    </xsd:schema>
  </types>

  <message name="GetMonitorPriceRequest">
    <part name="priceRequest" element="montypes:MonitorPriceRequest"/>
  </message>
  <message name="GetMonitorPriceResponse">
    <part name="price" element="montypes:price"/>
  </message>
```

```
  <message name="InvalidArgumentFault">
    <part name="errorMessage" element="montypes:InvalidArgumentFaultDetail"/>
  </message>

  <portType name="MonitorPricingPortType">
    <operation name="getMonitorPrice">
      <input message="mon:GetMonitorPriceRequest"/>
      <output message="mon:GetMonitorPriceResponse"/>
      <fault name="InvalidArgumentFault" message="mon:InvalidArgumentFault"/>
    </operation>
  </portType>

  <binding name="MonitorPricingSOAPBinding"
           type="mon:MonitorPricingPortType">
    <soapbind:binding style="document"
        transport="http://schemas.xmlsoap.org/soap/http"/>
    <operation name="getMonitorPrice">
      <soapbind:operation
          soapAction="http://monitors.co/ws/Pricing/GetMonitorPrice"/>
      <input><soapbind:body use="literal"/></input>
      <output><soapbind:body use="literal"/></output>
      <fault name="InvalidArgumentFault">
        <soapbind:fault name="InvalidArgumentFault" use="literal"/>
      </fault>
    </operation>
  </binding>

  <service name="MonitorPricingService">
    <port name="MonitorPricingPort" binding="mon:MonitorPricingSOAPBinding">
      <soapbind:address location="http://monitors.co/ws/Pricing"/>
    </port>
  </service>
</definitions>
```

The elements in Listing 8.1 with a prefix of `soapbind:` are extensibility elements. They are used to define SOAP-specific details of the Web service. The `soapbind:binding` element of Listing 8.1 defines the messaging style of the Web service operations as document and the network protocol used to transport SOAP messages as HTTP. The `soapbind:body` element defines the encoding for the input and output messages as literal and the `soapbind:fault` element defines the encoding for the fault message as literal. All of the SOAP-specific binding elements are discussed in more detail later.

Listing 8.1 included an XML declaration as the first line of the document. The XML declaration states the version of XML and the character encoding used to create the WSDL document. The WS-I BP mandates that WSDL 1.1–compliant documents use XML version 1.0 and either UTF-8 or UTF-16 encoding. If the encoding attribute is omitted, then UTF-8 encoding is assumed.

8.2.2 The definitions Element

The definitions element is the root of the WSDL document and, as such, all other WSDL XML elements are contained within definitions. The concept behind the name of this element is that the WSDL document is a container for a set of service definitions. In practice a single WSDL document is typically used to define a single Web service, not multiple services.

Several XML namespace declarations are usually defined in the definitions element including the namespace of the WSDL XML schema, which, for WSDL 1.1, is http://schemas.xmlsoap.org/wsdl/. The definitions element also contains a targetNamespace attribute. This attribute is used to define the default namespace for all elements of the WSDL document. Identifying the targetNamespace as the WSDL XML schema prevents having to prefix all the WSDL elements in order to form proper QNames (qualified names). All elements that are not in the WSDL XML schema must be prefixed.

The message, portType, and binding elements of the WSDL document are commonly referred to as the WSDL definitions. The name attribute of these elements is used to label them. These labels automatically assume the namespace defined by the targetNamespace of the definitions element. Other elements in the WSDL document refer to the definitions elements using their prefixed labels. For example, in Listing 8.1 the portType's operation element uses the prefixed label mon:GetMonitorPriceRequest to reference the message element with the name attribute value of GetMonitorPriceRequest.

The name attribute of the definitions element is used to give a name to the entire WSDL document. The name attribute is optional and in practice is not very important because it only serves as documentation. It is commonly given a value equal to the name of the Web service described by the WSDL document.

The definitions element is mandatory and may contain zero or more documentation elements, zero or more import elements, one optional types element, zero or more message elements, zero or more portType elements, zero or more binding elements, and zero or more service elements. Since a single WSDL document is typically used to describe a single Web service, WSDL documents usually contain single portType, binding, and service elements. The following code snippet shows how the definitions element may appear in a WSDL document.

```
<definitions name="MonitorPricingWS"
    targetNamespace="http://monitors.co/ws/Pricing"
    xmlns:mon="http://monitors.co/ws/Pricing"
    xmlns:montypes="http://monitors.co/ns/pricing/types"
    xmlns:soapbind="http://schemas.xmlsoap.org/wsdl/soap/"
    xmlns:xsd="http://www.w3.org/2001/XMLSchema"
    xmlns="http://schemas.xmlsoap.org/wsdl/">
  ...
</definitions>
```

This example defines namespaces for WSDL, XML Schema (prefix xsd), the SOAP-WSDL binding (prefix soapbind), custom data types (prefix montypes), and a target namespace for the WSDL definitions (prefix mon). These prefixes and the default namespace (identified by xmlns="...") are used to identify the namespace for every element in the WSDL document.

8.2.3 The documentation Element

The only purpose of the documentation element is to provide human-readable information about the Web service. Any WSDL element (except the documentation element) can contain a documentation element. The WSDL 1.1 specification and the XML Schema are inconsistent as to where documentation elements can be placed inside of other WSDL elements. Consequently, the WS-I Basic Profile mandates that a documentation element, if present, be the first child element of its parent element.

WS-I Conformance Claims

A common use of the documentation element is to claim that a WSDL document conforms to the WS-I Basic Profile. A WS-I Claim element can be placed inside the documentation element of the binding, portType, operation (as a child of the portType, but not of binding), or message elements to indicate conformance. The conformance claim applies to the WSDL element to which it is attached as well as all elements recursively referenced by it. Therefore, the most common place to put a conformance claim is in the documentation element of the port element because it will then apply to all other elements associated with the port (i.e., binding, portType, operation, and message). A WS-I conformance claim attached to the WSDL port element of Listing 8.1 would look similar to the following.

Listing 8.2 Use of the documentation Element in a WSDL WS-I Conformance Claim

```
<definitions name="MonitorPricingWS"
    targetNamespace="http://monitors.co/ws/Pricing"
    ...
    xmlns:wsi="http://ws-i.org/schemas/conformanceClaim"
    xmlns="http://schemas.xmlsoap.org/wsdl/">
  ...
  <service name="MonitorPricingService">
    <port name="MonitorPricingPort" binding="mon:MonitorPricingSOAPBinding">
      <documentation>
        <wsi:Claim conformsTo="http://ws-i.org/profiles/basic/1.0"/>
      </documentation>
      <soapbind:address location="http://monitors.co/ws/Pricing"/>
    </port>
  </service>
</definitions>
```

The conformsTo attribute of the WS-I Claim element may contain the URI http://ws-i.org/profiles/basic/1.1 if you wish to claim conformance with version 1.1 of the WS-I Basic Profile.

8.2.4 The import Element

The import element is used to import WSDL definitions from other WSDL documents. It works the same as the import element of XML Schema by binding a network location to an XML namespace, but do not confuse the use of the two. The WS-I BP mandates that the WSDL import element only be used to import WSDL documents, and the XML Schema import element only be used to import schema definitions. Additionally, the WS-I BP mandates that the namespace attribute of the WSDL import element cannot contain a relative URI, the location attribute cannot be empty, and the import element must precede all other WSDL elements except the documentation element. A code snippet of the WSDL import element is given below. "URI" is a placeholder for a real URI.

```
<import namespace="URI" location="URI"/>
```

A typical use of the WSDL import element is to split a WSDL document into service interface definition and service implementation definition (well, almost). The "service interface definition" WSDL document usually contains the types, message, portType, and binding elements and the "service implementation definition" WSDL document contains the service and port elements. The binding element is really a part of the implementation, but this particular split is popular because it allows the "service interface definition" WSDL document to be published on a public Web site where multiple organizations that wish to implement the Web service can download it. These organizations can simply define a "service implementation definition" WSDL document for their Web service and have it import the publicly available "service interface definition." Therefore, industry-standard Web service interfaces can be defined and published, and then implemented by compatible Web services provided by various organizations. When industry Web services are defined and implemented in this manner, a service requester can easily choose between multiple Web services based on price, performance, or other qualities of service.

If we were to remove the service element from Listing 8.1, then it would become a "service interface definition." Below is an example of how a service implementation definition might appear if the service interface definition were at the URI http://monitors.co/ws/itf/pricing.wsdl.

Listing 8.3 Use of the import Element in a WSDL Service Implementation Definition

```
<definitions name="PricingService"
    targetNamespace="http://monitors.co/PricingService"
    xmlns:mon="http://monitors.co/ws/Pricing"
    xmlns:soapbind="http://schemas.xmlsoap.org/wsdl/soap/"
    xmlns="http://schemas.xmlsoap.org/wsdl/">
```

```
  <import namespace="http://monitors.co/ws/Pricing"
          location="http://monitors.co/ws/itf/pricing.wsdl"/>

  <service name="MonitorPricingService">
    <port name="PricingPort" binding="mon:MonitorPricingSOAPBinding">
      <soapbind:address location="http://monitors.co/PricingService"/>
    </port>
  </service>
</definitions>
```

In Listing 8.3 the types and WSDL definitions come from the WSDL document of Listing 8.1 minus the `service` element. Listing 8.3 defines a Web service that uses the interface and bindings of Listing 8.1 and is located at the network address `http://monitors.co/PricingService`. Notice the prefix `mon:` is assigned to the namespace associated with the imported WSDL document of Listing 8.1 via a namespace declaration in the `definitions` element. That prefix is used to reference the `binding` element of Listing 8.1 from the `port` element of Listing 8.3 (i.e., `mon:MonitorPricingSOAPBinding`). Separating the interface from the implementation is a nice way to reuse the interface with multiple Web service implementations.

8.2.5 The types Element

A WSDL document can have, at most, a single `types` element. The `types` element defines data types used in the WSDL document. These data types are used within the `message` elements to define the payloads of the messages transmitted to and from the Web service. The default type system of WSDL is XML Schema, and therefore all XML Schema built-in types (such as `xsd:string`, `xsd:float`, etc.) are immediately available. However you will often need to define your own custom complex and simple types. The following code snippet was taken from Listing 8.1 where the `types` element was used to define both complex types and a simple type.

Listing 8.4 Use of the types Element

```
<definitions name="MonitorPricingWS"
    targetNamespace="http://monitors.co/ws/Pricing"
    xmlns:mon="http://monitors.co/ws/Pricing"
    xmlns:montypes="http://monitors.co/ns/pricing/types"
    xmlns:soapbind="http://schemas.xmlsoap.org/wsdl/soap/"
    xmlns:xsd="http://www.w3.org/2001/XMLSchema"
    xmlns="http://schemas.xmlsoap.org/wsdl/">

  <types>
    <xsd:schema targetNamespace="http://monitors.co/ns/pricing/types">
      <xsd:element name="MonitorPriceRequest">
        <xsd:complexType>
```

```
          <xsd:sequence>
            <xsd:element name="productId" type="xsd:string"/>
            <xsd:element name="currency" type="xsd:string"/>
          </xsd:sequence>
        </xsd:complexType>
      </xsd:element>

      <xsd:element name="price" type="xsd:float"/>

      <xsd:element name="InvalidArgumentFaultDetail">
        <xsd:complexType>
          <xsd:sequence>
            <xsd:element name="invalidValue" type="xsd:string"/>
            <xsd:element name="message" type="xsd:string"/>
          </xsd:sequence>
        </xsd:complexType>
      </xsd:element>
    </xsd:schema>
  </types>

  <message name="GetMonitorPriceRequest">
    <part name="priceRequest" element="montypes:MonitorPriceRequest"/>
  </message>
  <message name="GetMonitorPriceResponse">
    <part name="price" element="montypes:price"/>
  </message>
  <message name="InvalidArgumentFault">
    <part name="errorMessage" element="montypes:InvalidArgumentFaultDetail"/>
  </message>
  ...
</definitions>
```

In Listing 8.4 a complete XML schema is nested inside the types element and associated with a namespace via the use of the targetNamespace attribute. This same namespace is given a prefix in the namespace declaration of the definitions element. The prefix is then used to reference the defined types in the parts of the message elements.

The value of the targetNamespace attribute of the xsd:schema element cannot be empty and must be valid as mandated by the WS-I BP. The only exception to this rule is if the schema is only used to import other schemas. In that case the import statement assigns a namespace as illustrated in the following code snippet.

```
<types>
  <xsd:schema>
```

```
    <xsd:import namespace="http://monitors.co/ns/pricing/types"
        schemaLocation="http://monitors.co/schema/pricing/types.xsd"/>
  </xsd:schema>
</types>
```

Remember that the XML Schema `import` element is different from the WSDL `import` element. Use of the XML Schema `import` element within the WSDL `types` element allows you to define the data types of your application separate from WSDL. Some of the benefits of independently defining your XML schemas are that developers can divide the workload and the data types can be reused in other WSDL documents or other parts of the application (or even other applications) that require XML processing.

It is worth noting here that both SOAP and WSDL define methods for indicating array types that have been prohibited by the WS-I BP. SOAP encoding defines the `Array` data type and the `arrayType` attribute, and WSDL defines its own `arrayType` attribute. Because these elements have been interpreted in various ways, they have caused interoperability problems. The preferred method for defining array types is to use XML Schema. To define an array using XML Schema, all that needs to be done is to create a complex type with a `maxOccurs` attribute value greater than 0. Additionally, the WS-I BP also prohibits labeling your array types with the naming convention "ArrayOfXXX."

8.2.6 The `message` Element

The `message` element is used to describe the logical abstract payload of a message transmitted to or from a Web service. It can describe incoming messages, outgoing messages, SOAP header blocks, and SOAP fault `Detail` elements. A WSDL document may contain zero or more `message` elements, all of which must have names that are unique within the WSDL document (because other WSDL elements reference them by name). In turn, each `message` element may contain zero or more `part` elements that describe each part of the message.

A `message` element can be modeled to represent either a document-style message or an RPC-style message. In a document-style message the `part` elements represent XML document fragments. Even though WSDL is independent of messaging protocols, SOAP is typically used as the messaging protocol. Therefore, a single `part` element in a document-style message essentially describes the entire content of the SOAP `Body` element in a SOAP message. The WS-I BP mandates that, if a document-style `message` contains more than one `part` element, only one of those `part` elements can be bound to the `Body` of a SOAP message. The other `part` elements, if any, can be bound as SOAP header blocks. This will become clearer when we cover the `binding` element where we give examples of SOAP messages that are formed according to their descriptions in the WSDL document.

Listing 8.1 uses document-style messaging. The `message` elements from Listing 8.1 are repeated in the listing below (some parts of the WSDL document were removed for brevity). The `GetMonitorPriceRequest` message is the message that is transmitted from a client to the Web service in order to invoke it. These messages are commonly referred to as input messages or request messages. The

GetMonitorPriceResponse message is the message that is transmitted from the Web service back to the client. These messages are commonly referred to as output messages or response messages. The name of the message can be anything you like. A common naming convention is to append "Request" to the end of the Web service name for input messages and "Response" to the end of your Web service name for output messages. Although we have given names to these messages that give you a hint as to the direction of the message, the only true way of determining whether a message is input or output is by examining how it is used in the operation element. The message element describes one-way messages independent of direction. This allows a single message definition to be used as both an input and output message. The operation element is discussed later.

Listing 8.5 Description of a Document-Style Web Service with the message Element

```
<definitions name="MonitorPricingWS" ...>
  <types>
    <xsd:schema targetNamespace="http://monitors.co/ns/pricing/types">
      <xsd:element name="MonitorPriceRequest">
        <xsd:complexType>
          <xsd:sequence>
            <xsd:element name="productId" type="xsd:string"/>
            <xsd:element name="currency" type="xsd:string"/>
          </xsd:sequence>
        </xsd:complexType>
      </xsd:element>
      <xsd:element name="price" type="xsd:float"/>
      <xsd:element name="InvalidArgumentFaultDetail">
        <xsd:complexType>
          <xsd:sequence>
            <xsd:element name="invalidValue" type="xsd:string"/>
            <xsd:element name="message" type="xsd:string"/>
          </xsd:sequence>
        </xsd:complexType>
      </xsd:element>
    </xsd:schema>
  </types>

  <message name="GetMonitorPriceRequest">
    <part name="priceRequest" element="montypes:MonitorPriceRequest"/>
  </message>
  <message name="GetMonitorPriceResponse">
    <part name="price" element="montypes:price"/>
  </message>
  <message name="InvalidArgumentFault">
    <part name="errorMessage" element="montypes:InvalidArgumentFaultDetail"/>
```

```
  </message>
  ...
</definitions>
```

Notice that each part in Listing 8.5 refers to an XML element from the types definition. The content of both the request and response messages is completely defined by XML Schema. Also notice that the last message describes a SOAP fault. SOAP faults are defined in WSDL the same as input and output messages. However, the WS-I BP mandates that message definitions for SOAP faults use Document/Literal encoding regardless of whether the input and output messages are using document style or RPC style. Therefore the part element describing a SOAP fault must always refer to an XML element defined in the types definition. The part element of a SOAP fault definition describes the contents of the SOAP Detail element. Recall from the last chapter that the SOAP Detail element is a child element of the SOAP Fault element used to carry any additional application-specific information about the error.

When a message element is modeled as an RPC-style message its part elements represent input or output parameters of a procedure call. Although Java limits methods to a single return value, several other programming languages such as C++, C#, and Perl allow procedures to declare a return value as well as multiple output parameters. Consequently, to support programming language independence, Web services that return multiple values may be defined. The Java Web service APIs provide facilities for handling this, which are discussed later in the sections on SAAJ and JAX-RPC. To illustrate RPC-style message elements, Listing 8.5 has been rewritten in the listing below.

Listing 8.6 Description of an RPC-Style Web Service with the message Element

```
<definitions name="MonitorPricingWS" ...>
  <types>
    <xsd:schema targetNamespace="http://monitors.co/ns/pricing/types">
      <xsd:element name="InvalidArgumentFaultDetail">
        <xsd:complexType>
          <xsd:sequence>
            <xsd:element name="invalidValue" type="xsd:string"/>
            <xsd:element name="message" type="xsd:string"/>
          </xsd:sequence>
        </xsd:complexType>
      </xsd:element>
    </xsd:schema>
  </types>

  <message name="GetMonitorPriceRequest">
    <part name="productId" type="xsd:string"/>
    <part name="currency" type="xsd:string"/>
  </message>
```

```
  <message name="GetMonitorPriceResponse">
    <part name="price" type="xsd:float"/>
  </message>
  <message name="InvalidArgumentFault">
    <part name="errorMessage" element="montypes:InvalidArgumentFaultDetail"/>
  </message>
  ...
</definitions>
```

Notice that the SOAP fault definition of Listing 8.6 was not changed from Listing 8.5 because, as described above, SOAP fault definitions in WSDL must always use Document/Literal encoding. However, the `part` elements of the input and output messages no longer refer to XML elements in the `types` definition. The input `message` element contains two `part` elements, one for each parameter that is passed to the Web service. The output `message` element contains a single `part` that is the result of the Web service operation. This output message could have contained several parts if we had more information to return to the client. Additionally, the `part` elements for the input and output messages of Listing 8.6 could have referred to XML types defined by the `types` elements as illustrated by the following listing.

Listing 8.7 Alternative Description of an RPC-Style Web Service with the `message` Element

```
<definitions name="MonitorPricingWS" ...>
  <types>
    <xsd:schema targetNamespace="http://monitors.co/ns/pricing/types">
      <xsd:complexType name="parameters">
        <xsd:sequence>
          <xsd:element name="productId" type="xsd:string"/>
          <xsd:element name="currency" type="xsd:string"/>
        </xsd:sequence>
      </xsd:complexType>
      <xsd:simpleType name="price">
        <xsd:restriction base="xsd:float">
          <xsd:fractionDigits value="2"/>
        </xsd:restriction>
      </xsd:simpleType>
      <xsd:element name="InvalidArgumentFaultDetail">
        <xsd:complexType>
          <xsd:sequence>
            <xsd:element name="invalidValue" type="xsd:string"/>
            <xsd:element name="message" type="xsd:string"/>
          </xsd:sequence>
        </xsd:complexType>
      </xsd:element>
```

```
    </xsd:schema>
  </types>

  <message name="GetMonitorPriceRequest">
    <part name="parameters" type="montypes:parameters"/>
  </message>
  <message name="GetMonitorPriceResponse">
    <part name="price" type="montypes:price"/>
  </message>
  <message name="InvalidArgumentFault">
    <part name="errorMessage" element="montypes:InvalidArgumentFaultDetail"/>
  </message>
  ...
</definitions>
```

Notice that some of the `part` elements use an attribute of `type` and others use an attribute of `element`. The `type` attribute is used to refer to an XML Schema type (`xsd:simpleType` or `xsd:complexType`) and the `element` attribute is used to refer to an XML Schema element (`xsd:element`), both of which are declared (or imported) by the `types` definition. A part element may use either `type` or `element` but not both. If you use the `element` attribute, then you are specifying that the payload of the message be exactly the XML element that you referenced. If you use the `type` attribute, then all you are specifying is what the data type of the element must be. The element that is actually used is determined by the `binding` element. You will see examples of this later when we cover the `binding` element. In the end, which attribute you use, `type` or `element`, is really determined by what messaging style you choose. The WS-I BP mandates that `part` elements use the `type` attribute for RPC-style messaging and the `element` attribute for document-style messaging. This makes sense because document-style messages are meant to carry XML document fragments (XML elements) and RPC-style messages are meant to carry parameters for a procedure (defined as specific data types).

8.2.7 The `portType` Element

The `portType` element is used to define the abstract interface of a Web service. A `portType` is similar in concept to a Java interface. A Java interface defines a collection of method signatures under an identifying abstract type, and a `portType` element defines a collection of `operation` elements under an identifying name. The identifying name is defined by the `name` attribute of the `portType`, which is its only attribute. The interface that the `portType` defines is implemented by the `binding` and `service` elements. The `binding` element references the `portType` element by its name to specify the protocols and encoding of the Web service implementation. The `service` element references the `binding` element by name to define the network address where the Web service implementation can be invoked.

A WSDL document may contain zero or more portType definitions. However, WSDL documents typically contain only a single portType, limiting the description to a single Web service, which is a best practice that promotes reuse of the description. A single portType element may contain one or more operation elements that declare the "methods" of the Web service. The portType from Listing 8.1 is repeated below in the following code snippet.

```
<portType name="MonitorPricingPortType">
  <operation name="getMonitorPrice">
    <input message="mon:GetMonitorPriceRequest"/>
    <output message="mon:GetMonitorPriceResponse"/>
    <fault name="InvalidArgumentFault" message="mon:InvalidArgumentFault"/>
  </operation>
</portType>
```

A common naming convention for portTypes is to append "PortType" to the end of your Web service name, but the name can be anything you like. The portType above defines a single Web service operation—getMonitorPrice. The details of the portType element are in the operation elements, which are described next.

8.2.8 The operation Element

The operation element is analogous to a Java method signature. It can contain zero or one input element, zero or one output element, and zero or more fault elements. The input element declares the message payload that is transmitted from the client to the Web service, and the output element declares the message payload that is transmitted from the Web service to the client. The fault elements declare the payloads of fault messages that may be transmitted from the Web service to the client in the event of an error. Each input, output, and fault element must contain a message attribute, the value of which is a QName (qualified name) for one of the message elements defined earlier in the WSDL document. For example, in the following listing, the input, output, and fault elements reference the name of the message elements by qualifying their names with a prefix of mon:. The WSDL definitions fall under the targetNamespace of the WSDL document, which is assigned the mon prefix in the definitions element. See Figure 8.3 for a visual illustration of how the input, output, and fault elements reference the message elements.

```
<definitions name="MonitorPricingWS"
    targetNamespace="http://monitors.co/ws/Pricing"
    xmlns:mon="http://monitors.co/ws/Pricing"
    xmlns:montypes="http://monitors.co/ns/pricing/types"
    xmlns:soapbind="http://schemas.xmlsoap.org/wsdl/soap/"
    xmlns:xsd="http://www.w3.org/2001/XMLSchema"
    xmlns="http://schemas.xmlsoap.org/wsdl/">
  <types>
    ...
```

```
  </types>

  <message name="GetMonitorPriceRequest">
    <part name="priceRequest" element="montypes:MonitorPriceRequest"/>
  </message>
  <message name="GetMonitorPriceResponse">
    <part name="price" element="montypes:price"/>
  </message>
  <message name="InvalidArgumentFault">
    <part name="errorMessage" element="montypes:InvalidArgumentFaultDetail"/>
  </message>

  <portType name="MonitorPricingPortType">
    <operation name="getMonitorPrice">
      <input message="mon:GetMonitorPriceRequest"/>
      <output message="mon:GetMonitorPriceResponse"/>
      <fault name="InvalidArgumentFault" message="mon:InvalidArgumentFault"/>
    </operation>
  </portType>
  ...
</definitions>
```

The fault element is required to have a name attribute. The input and output elements may contain an optional name attribute. If the name is omitted on a one-way or notification message, then it defaults to the name of the operation element. If the name is omitted on a request-response or solicit-response message, then the name defaults to the operation name with "Request-Response" or "Solicit-Response" appended.

Recall from the last chapter that one-way, notification, request-response, and solicit-response are four different message exchange patterns (MEPs). At this point you may be wondering how the MEP is defined. It is quite simple in WSDL. When the operation element contains only an input element, then the MEP is one-way. Recall that a one-way MEP is when the client sends a message to the Web service but does not expect a reply. No output or fault elements can be declared in a one-way MEP. An example of a one-way MEP is given below.

```
<portType name="MonitorPurchaseOrderPortType">
  <operation name="submitPurchaseOrder">
    <input name="order" message="mon:SubmitPurchaseOrderMessage"/>
  </operation>
</portType>
```

To define a request-response MEP, the operation element must contain a single input and a single output element, and the input element must precede the output element. By listing the input element first, you are declaring that the communication between the client and the Web service is initiated by the client. In addition, by listing an `output` element after the `input` element you are declaring that the Web service is expected to reply to the initial request message from the client by returning a response message. In a request-response MEP, you are also allowed to list zero or more `fault` elements after the `output` element. The `fault` elements are errors that may be returned to the client in the event of an error. An example request-response MEP is given below.

```
<portType name="MonitorPricingPortType">
  <operation name="getMonitorPrice">
    <input message="mon:GetMonitorPriceRequest"/>
    <output message="mon:GetMonitorPriceResponse"/>
    <fault name="InvalidArgumentFault" message="mon:InvalidArgumentFault"/>
  </operation>
</portType>
```

A notification MEP is declared by including only a single `output` element within the `operation`. As with the one-way MEP, no `fault` elements can be used. The concept behind the notification MEP is that a client may register to receive some events from the Web service. The Web service will then push messages to the client without expecting a reply message. WSDL does not specify how the Web service is to find out where it should send the message, so implementations must devise their own method. Typically, this MEP is initiated by previous registration with the Web service by the client in which the client gives the Web service the network address where it should send the messages. Because the details of the WSDL notification MEP are vague, it is rarely used and is not supported by J2EE version 1.4. An example notification MEP is given below.

```
<portType name="SomePortType">
  <operation name="notification">
    <output message="tns:OrderReadyNotification"/>
  </operation>
</portType>
```

A solicit-response MEP is declared by including in the `operation` a single `output` element followed by a single `input` element followed by one or more optional `fault` elements. The solicit-response MEP is similar to the notification MEP except that the Web service expects a reply from the client. In other words, the Web service will push a message to the client and the client must send a reply back to the Web service. The fault messages in solicit-response travel in the opposite direction as those in request-response. The Web service will push a fault to the client for an error or exceptional condition. The solicit-response MEP has the same problems as the notification MEP and is not supported by J2EE version 1.4. An example solicit-response MEP is shown below.

```
<portType name="SomePortType">
  <operation name="solicitResponse">
    <output message="tns:PushMessage"/>
    <input message="tns:ReplyToPushedMessage"/>
    <fault name="someFault" message="tns:PushFaultMessage"/>
```

```
  </operation>
</portType>
```

In addition to a name attribute, operation elements may also contain an optional parameterOrder attribute. The parameterOrder attribute is used to enforce a proper order of parameters in an RPC-style message. Since an RPC-style message is intended to represent a procedure call, the parameters passed to the procedure must be in the correct order or the procedure invocation will fail. The default order of the parameters is the order in which they appear in the message element, which is usually intentional by the developer; consequently the parameterOrder attribute is rarely necessary.

If the parameterOrder attribute is used, it must include all of the operation's input parts and only output parts that are not the return value of the procedure call. If an output message contains only a single part, then that part is assumed to be the return value. If an output part is listed in the parameterOrder attribute, then it is treated as an OUT parameter. If both an input and output message contain a part with the same name, then that part is assumed to be the same parameter and is treated as an INOUT parameter. An example use of the parameterOrder attribute is given below. Parts of the WSDL document were removed from this code snippet for brevity.

```
<message name="GetMonitorPriceRequest">
  <part name="productId" type="xsd:string"/>
  <part name="currency" type="xsd:string"/>
</message>
<message name="GetMonitorPriceResponse">
  <part name="price" type="xsd:float"/>
</message>
<portType name="MonitorPricingPortType">
  <operation name="getMonitorPrice" parameterOrder="productId currency">
    <input message="mon:GetMonitorPriceRequest"/>
    <output message="mon:GetMonitorPriceResponse"/>
  </operation>
</portType>
```

The parameterOrder attribute has caused interoperability problems because of its various interpretations, so the WS-I BP mandates that it be used only to identify the return value of a procedure call. A procedure call may have only a single return value but may have multiple OUT or INOUT parameters. The WS-I BP mandates that the order of the parameters transmitted in a message follow the order of the part elements in the input and output message definitions (the default order). Because the return value cannot be listed in the parameterOrder attribute, the single part element that is omitted from the list is identified as the return value. For example, in the code snippet above, the only parts listed by the parameterOrder attribute are those of the input message (productId and currency), which are in the same order as they appear in the message element. The only part omitted from the list is the one from the output message (price). Therefore we know that price is the return value.

8.2.9 The binding Element

The individual WSDL elements discussed up to this point are all used to describe the service interface definition. The service implementation definition is described by the `binding` and `service` elements. The `binding` element defines the format for the messages in a protocol-specific manner. It maps an abstract `portType` to a concrete implementation that uses specific messaging styles (RPC or document), protocols (such as SOAP and HTTP), and encoding styles (such as literal or SOAP encoding). A single WSDL document may contain multiple `bindings` for each `portType`. For example, you may want to bind a single `portType` to both a SOAP-over-HTTP implementation and a SOAP-over-SMTP implementation. The binding from Listing 8.1 is repeated below as an example. Parts of the WSDL document were omitted in this example for brevity.

Listing 8.8 Use of the binding Element

```
<definitions name="MonitorPricingWS"
    targetNamespace="http://monitors.co/ws/Pricing"
    xmlns:mon="http://monitors.co/ws/Pricing"
    xmlns:montypes="http://monitors.co/ns/pricing/types"
    xmlns:soapbind="http://schemas.xmlsoap.org/wsdl/soap/"
    xmlns:xsd="http://www.w3.org/2001/XMLSchema"
    xmlns="http://schemas.xmlsoap.org/wsdl/">
  ...
  <portType name="MonitorPricingPortType">
    <operation name="getMonitorPrice">
      <input message="mon:GetMonitorPriceRequest"/>
      <output message="mon:GetMonitorPriceResponse"/>
      <fault name="InvalidArgumentFault" message="mon:InvalidArgumentFault"/>
    </operation>
  </portType>

  <binding name="MonitorPricingSOAPBinding"
           type="mon:MonitorPricingPortType">
    <soapbind:binding style="document"
        transport="http://schemas.xmlsoap.org/soap/http"/>
    <operation name="getMonitorPrice">
      <soapbind:operation
          soapAction="http://monitors.co/ws/Pricing/GetMonitorPrice"/>
      <input><soapbind:body use="literal"/></input>
      <output><soapbind:body use="literal"/></output>
      <fault name="InvalidArgumentFault">
        <soapbind:fault name="InvalidArgumentFault" use="literal"/>
      </fault>
    </operation>
```

```
  </binding>
  ...
</definitions>
```

The name of the binding can be anything as long as it is unique among all other bindings. The binding element may contain one or more operation elements. Each operation element may optionally contain a single input and output element, and one or more fault elements. The operation elements within a binding reference to the operations are defined by the associated portType. The type attribute of the binding element is used to link the binding to its associated portType. The value of the type attribute must be the QName of a portType defined in the WSDL document or imported from another WSDL document. In Listing 8.8 this value is mon:MonitorPricingPortType. Recall that the WSDL definitions (message, portType, binding) fall under the targetNamespace of the WSDL document, which in Listing 8.8 is assigned the prefix mon:. See Figure 8.3 for a visual illustration of how all these elements relate.

Note that the operation, input, output, and fault elements are used differently inside the binding element than inside the portType element. Inside the portType, these elements are used to describe the operation signature and the payload of the input and output messages. Inside the binding, these elements are simply used to reference their counterparts in the portType so they can be assigned specific protocols, message styles, and encoding styles.

The protocols used in the binding are declared with WSDL extensibility elements. WSDL provides standard binding extensions for SOAP-over-HTTP, HTTP-GET/POST, and SOAP-with-MIME (Multipurpose Internet Mail Extensions) attachments. Listing 8.8 uses the most popular binding, which is SOAP-over-HTTP. These extensibility elements are prefixed in Listing 8.8 by soapbind:. They are included in the namespace for SOAP-WSDL binding (http://schemas.xmlsoap.org/-wsdl/soap/), which is separate from the WSDL namespace (http://schemas.xmlsoap.org/wsdl/) that encompasses all of the WSDL elements (definitions, types, message, binding, etc.).

SOAP Binding

The SOAP-WSDL extensibility elements include soapbind:binding, soapbind:operation, soapbind:body, soapbind:fault, soapbind:header, and soapbind:headerfault. These elements allow us to define the SOAP-specific details of the Web service. The following list briefly describes each element.

- soapbind:binding

  This element is used to describe the default message style (RPC or document) of the operations in the WSDL binding and the underlying network protocol (such as HTTP) that will be used to transport the messages. The style attribute of soapbind:binding identifies the message style with a value of either "rpc" or "document" and the transport attribute identifies the network protocol with a URI. An example use of the soapbind:binding element is given below. The transport attribute in this example indicates the use of HTTP via the URI http://schemas.xmlsoap.org/soap/http.

```
<binding ...>
  <soapbind:binding style="document"
      transport="http://schemas.xmlsoap.org/soap/http"/>
  <operation ...>...</operation>
</binding>
```

The message style defined by the soapbind:binding element can be overridden by any operation element in the WSDL binding, but this practice is discouraged because it causes interoperability problems. The WS-I BP requires the soapbind:binding element to be used within the WSDL binding element and the style and transport attributes to be present with valid non-null values. The WS-I BP also restricts the values for style to "rpc" and "document," and the value for transport to "http://schemas.xmlsoap.org/soap/http." This means that only HTTP can be used as the underlying transport protocol if you wish to be compliant with the WS-I BP, but this does not prevent you from using HTTPS. If you wish to use HTTPS, it can be specified by the port element, which will be discussed later.

- soapbind:operation

  This element is used to specify a message style for the operation that overrides the default style in the soapbind:binding element and to specify a value for the SOAPAction HTTP header field. An example use of the soapbind:operation element is given below.

```
<binding ...>
  ...
  <operation ...>
    <soapbind:operation style="rpc"
        soapAction="http://monitors.co/ws/Pricing/GetMonitorPrice"/>
    ...
  </operation>
</binding>
```

  The style attribute of the soapbind:operation element specifies the message style and the soapAction attribute specifies the SOAPAction. It is considered bad practice to override the message style defined by the soapbind:binding element, so the style attribute is often omitted from soapbind:operation. Omitting the style attribute means that the operation should use the message style defined by soapbind:binding. The WS-I BP mandates that each soapbind:operation in a binding have the same message style as indicated by soapbind:binding.

The SOAP 1.1 `SOAPAction` HTTP header field is used to identify the payload of an HTTP message as SOAP so that processors do not need to parse the payload just to determine what type it is (expensive action) and to convey the intent of the message with a URI. In SOAP 1.1, this header field was helpful because the media type of the message was `text/xml`, which was too generic because it only says that the contents of the message are XML. This header field was removed from SOAP in version 1.2 and replaced with a more descriptive media type, `application/soap+xml`, which includes an `action` parameter for carrying the `SOAPAction` URI. An example of an HTTP message that includes the `SOAPAction` header is given below.

```
POST /ws/Pricing HTTP/1.1
Host: monitors.co
Content-Type: text/xml; charset="utf-8"
Content-Length: 298
SOAPAction="http://monitors.co/ws/Pricing/GetMonitorPrice"

<?xml version="1.0" encoding="UTF-8"?>
<soap:Envelope>
  ...
</soap:Envelope>
```

For SOAP 1.2, the previous message would look like the following (except the `Content-Type` header would actually all appear on a single line).

```
POST /ws/Pricing HTTP/1.1
Host: monitors.co
Content-Type: application/soap+xml; charset="utf-8";
    action="http://monitors.co/ws/Pricing/GetMonitorPrice"
Content-Length: 298

<?xml version="1.0" encoding="UTF-8"?>
<soap:Envelope>
  ...
</soap:Envelope>
```

The `soapAction` attribute of the `soapbind:operation` element is optional, meaning it can be omitted. It can also be assigned an empty value (`""`), which is the same as omitting it. Whether or not the `soapAction` attribute is used, the WS-I BP mandates that a `SOAPAction` header appear in the HTTP message. If the `soapAction` attribute is omitted or assigned an empty value, then the `SOAPAction` header must be assigned an empty string. When the `SOAPAction` header is assigned an empty string, then the intent of the message is considered to be the URI of the request.

- soapbind:body

  This element is used to describe how the message part elements will be formatted in the SOAP Body element. It defines the encoding style of the message payload, the namespace for the elements of the message payload, and which part elements are going to appear in the message. The soapbind:body element has four attributes: use, encodingStyle, namespace, and part. The use attribute can be assigned a value of "literal" or "encoded". If "encoded" is used, then the encoding style must be specified by the encodingStyle attribute. For example, an input message that uses SOAP 1.1 encoding would look like the following.

```
<binding ...>
  ...
  <operation ...>
  ...
    <input>
      <soapbind:body use="encoded"
          encodingStyle="http://schemas.xmlsoap.org/soap/encoding/"
          namespace="http://someNamespace"/>
    </input>
  </operation>
</binding>
```

  The WS-I BP prohibits the use of "encoded" and consequently the encodingStyle attribute. To be WS-I BP compliant, all messages must use literal encoding, which means that an XML schema defines how the data is encoded. The WS-I BP also mandates that the namespace attribute be assigned a valid URI for RPC-style messages and that it be omitted for document-style messages. In document-style messages the namespace comes from the XML schema. The following code snippet from Listing 8.1 illustrates a WS-I BP–compliant binding for a document-style message.

```
<binding ...>
  <soapbind:binding style="document"
      transport="http://schemas.xmlsoap.org/soap/http"/>
  <operation name="getMonitorPrice">
    <soapbind:operation
        soapAction="http://monitors.co/ws/Pricing/GetMonitorPrice"/>
    <input><soapbind:body use="literal"/></input>
    <output><soapbind:body use="literal"/></output>
    ...
  </operation>
</binding>
```

The `part` attribute can be used to specify what `part` elements are used in the message. You need only to use this attribute if you are not using all of the `message`'s `part` elements, which typically is not the case.

- `soapbind:fault`

  The `soapbind:fault` element serves a similar purpose to the `soapbind:body` element except it applies to faults instead of input and output messages. It has the same attributes as `soapbind:body`, including one addition—a `name` attribute. The `name` attribute, which references a specific fault defined in the associated `portType`, is mandatory according to the WS-I BP. A `soapbind:fault` element is defined for each `fault` element of an `operation`. The restrictions that the WS-I BP places on indicating encoding for `soapbind:body` also apply to `soapbind:fault`. In other words, to be WS-I BP–compliant, all `soapbind:fault` elements must either specify the `use` as `"literal"` or omit the `use` attribute. If the `use` attribute is omitted, it is assumed that the value is `"literal"`. An example of the `soapbind:fault` element is given below.

```
<portType name="MonitorPricingPortType">
  <operation name="getMonitorPrice">
    ...
    <fault name="InvalidArgumentFault"
           message="mon:InvalidArgumentFault"/>
  </operation>
</portType>

<binding name="MonitorPricingSOAPBinding"
         type="mon:MonitorPricingPortType">
  ...
  <operation name="getMonitorPrice">
    <soapbind:operation
        soapAction="http://monitors.co/ws/Pricing/GetMonitorPrice"/>
    ...
    <fault name="InvalidArgumentFault">
      <soapbind:fault name="InvalidArgumentFault" use="literal"/>
    </fault>
  </operation>
</binding>
```

- `soapbind:header`

  This element is used to describe SOAP header blocks for input or output messages. Each `input` and `output` element can have one or more `soapbind:header` elements, which makes sense, because a single SOAP message can have multiple header blocks. The `soapbind:header` element has five attributes: `message`, `part`, `use`, `encoding`, and `namespace`. The `message` attribute must specify the QName of a `message` element defined earlier in the WSDL document.

The part attribute must specify the name of a single part of the referenced message element. In other words, the header block defined by soapbind:header can consist only of a single part (unlike soapbind:body, which can reference multiple parts). The use and encoding attributes are used to indicate the encoding just as with the soapbind:body element. However the WS-I BP restricts the use attribute to a value of "literal" as with soapbind:body. The WS-I BP also mandates that the part referenced by soapbind:header be defined as an XML Schema element, not an XML Schema type. Therefore the part must use the element attribute, not the type attribute. The namespace attribute is used to indicate the namespace for the elements that make up the header block. But if you follow the recommendations of the WS-I BP, you cannot use the namespace attribute because the namespace should be derived from the XML Schema. An example use of the soapbind:header is given below.

```
<definitions name="MonitorPricingWS" ...>
  <types>
    <xsd:schema targetNamespace="http://monitors.co/ns/pricing/types">
      <xsd:element name="Transaction">
        <xsd:complexType>
          <xsd:sequence>
            <xsd:element name="id" type="xsd:string"/>
            <xsd:element name="status" type="xsd:string"/>
          </xsd:sequence>
        </xsd:complexType>
      </xsd:element>
      ...
    </xsd:schema>
  </types>

  <message name="Headers">
    <part name="transaction" element="montypes:Transaction"/>
  </message>
  ...

  <portType name="MonitorPricingPortType">
    ...
  </portType>

  <binding name="MonitorPricingSOAPBinding"
           type="mon:MonitorPricingPortType">
    ...
    <operation name="getMonitorPrice">
      ...
      <input>
        <soapbind:header message="mon:Headers" part="transaction"
                         use="literal"/>
```

```
      <soapbind:body use="literal"/>
    </input>
    ...
  </operation>
</binding>
...
</definitions>
```

- soapbind:headerfault

  The soapbind:headerfault element is used to describe a fault that is specific to a header block. SOAP requires that faults associated with header blocks be placed in the SOAP Header, and consequently, WSDL requires soapbind:headerfault elements to be nested within their associated soapbind:header elements. The use and WS-I BP rules for soapbind:headerfault elements are the same as soapbind:header elements. An example is given below.

```
<soapbind:header message="mon:Headers" part="transaction"
                 use="literal">
  <soapbind:headerfault message="mon:HeaderFaults"
                        part="InvalidStatusFaultDetail"
                        use="literal"/>
</soapbind:header>
```

8.2.10 The service Element

The service element is quite simple; it contains a set of port elements that assign a network address to a binding. A WSDL document may contain multiple service elements, but usually only one is used. The service element must have a name attribute and the value must be unique among all service elements in the WSDL document. One or more port elements can appear in a single service element and all should be related to the same Web service. Multiple port elements within a service can assign different network addresses to the same binding, which can be useful for supporting failover or load balancing. As an example, the service element from Listing 8.1 is repeated in the code snippet below.

```
<service name="MonitorPricingService">
  <port name="MonitorPricingPort" binding="mon:MonitorPricingSOAPBinding">
    <soapbind:address location="http://monitors.co/ws/Pricing"/>
  </port>
</service>
```

The binding attribute of the port element must specify the QName of a binding defined earlier in the WSDL document. The soapbind:address element must have a location attribute with a valid URI that is the network address where a client will send messages to invoke the Web service. The WSDL specification allows any kind of network address (HTTP, SMTP, FTP, etc.) to be specified, but the WS-I BP restricts them to HTTP and HTTPS. Additionally, the WS-I BP does not allow more than one port element within the same WSDL document to use the same network address.

8.3 SOAP with Attachments API for Java (SAAJ)

Although XML provides a nice platform-independent foundation for Web services, it can be very tedious to manually write and process. Fortunately, the Java community has remedied this by supplying several APIs that make the developer's job much easier. The first Web service–related API that we discuss is SOAP with Attachments API for Java, version 1.2, or SAAJ, commonly pronounced like the meat-seasoning herb, sage. SAAJ provides the ability to produce and consume SOAP messages from Java that are compliant with SOAP version 1.1 (`http://www.w3.org/TR/2000/NOTE-SOAP-20000508/`) and the WS-I Basic Profile version 1.0, or the SOAP Messages with Attachments specification (`http://www.w3.org/TR/SOAP-attachments`).

Sun Microsystems maintains a Web site for SAAJ at `http://java.sun.com/xml/saaj` where you can find the JavaDocs, specifications, and related downloads. SAAJ is also included with the Java Web Services Developer Pack (`http://java.sun.com/webservices/downloads/webservicespack.html`) and J2EE version 1.4 (`http://java.sun.com/j2ee/1.4/download.html`). Although SAAJ is included with J2EE, you can use it independently of J2EE as we did in the labs at the end of the last chapter. However, like many of the Java APIs, SAAJ is a hollow API, meaning it is not complete and cannot be used without a vendor implementation. Fortunately, Sun Microsystems provides an implementation with the Java Web Services Developer Pack and the reference implementation of J2EE. Other J2EE vendors are free to provide their own.

You can use SAAJ to process SOAP messages both with and without attachments. The concept of associating MIME attachments with a SOAP message in order to facilitate the transmission of binary data is controversial in the SOAP community. However, it is widely used and has become somewhat of a de facto standard. SAAJ includes classes and interfaces that correspond to the SOAP `Envelope`, `Body`, `Header`, and `Fault` elements, as well as MIME attachments. Figure 8.4 illustrates the relationship between interfaces and classes of the SAAJ API and the SOAP elements.

The SAAJ API is completely contained within the `javax.xml.soap` Java package. A SAAJ `SOAPMessage` instance contains a mandatory `SOAPPart` object and optionally one or more `AttachmentPart` objects. `AttachmentPart` objects are only necessary when you are working with a SOAP message with an attachment. All new instances of a `SOAPMessage`, by default, contain a `SOAPPart` that contains a `SOAPEnvelope`, which in turn contains an empty `SOAPHeader` and `SOAPBody`. Since SOAP messages are not required to have headers, you are allowed to delete the `SOAPHeader` object when you do not need it. The `SOAPFault` object is not automatically included in a new `SOAPMessage` instance, but can be added to the `SOAPBody` when required.

The SAAJ API essentially models an XML document in Java (except for the `AttachmentPart`, which may contain any type of data—XML, binary, or other). Many of the SAAJ interfaces and classes represent XML elements in a SOAP message. XML elements in SAAJ are referred to as nodes. Conse-

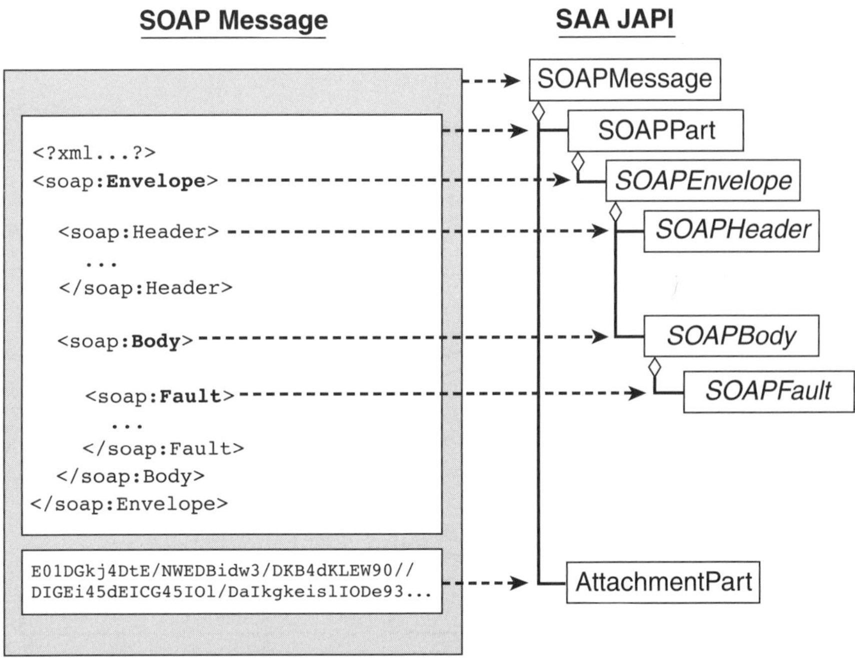

Figure 8.4
SOAP Message and SAAJ Types

quently the SAAJ API includes the interface `Node`, which is the base interface for all SAAJ interfaces and classes that represent SOAP XML elements. SAAJ's `javax.xml.soap.Node` interface extends the `org.w3c.dom.Node` interface from the Java API for the Document Object Model (DOM) version 2. Basing SAAJ on the Java DOM API makes it very flexible. You can use DOM parsers to process parts of a SAAJ SOAP message, import DOM `Nodes` from some arbitrary XML document into a SAAJ SOAP message, or pull SAAJ `Nodes` from a SAAJ SOAP message and include them in a separate arbitrary XML document. Figure 8.5 illustrates the hierarchy of the SAAJ API including how it relates to the Java DOM API.

SAAJ implements the Abstract Factory[1] design pattern, creating nearly every instance of a SAAJ type by calling a factory method. Notice that all the types in Figure 8.5 are either interfaces or abstract classes, so you cannot simply make a call to a type's constructor when you want a new instance. For example, to create a SAAJ `SOAPMessage` you must first ask the `MessageFactory` class to create an

---

[1]Erich Gamma, Richard Helm, Ralph Johnson, and John Vlissides, *Design Patterns: Elements of Reusable Object-Oriented Software.* Boston: Addison-Wesley, 1995, p. 87.

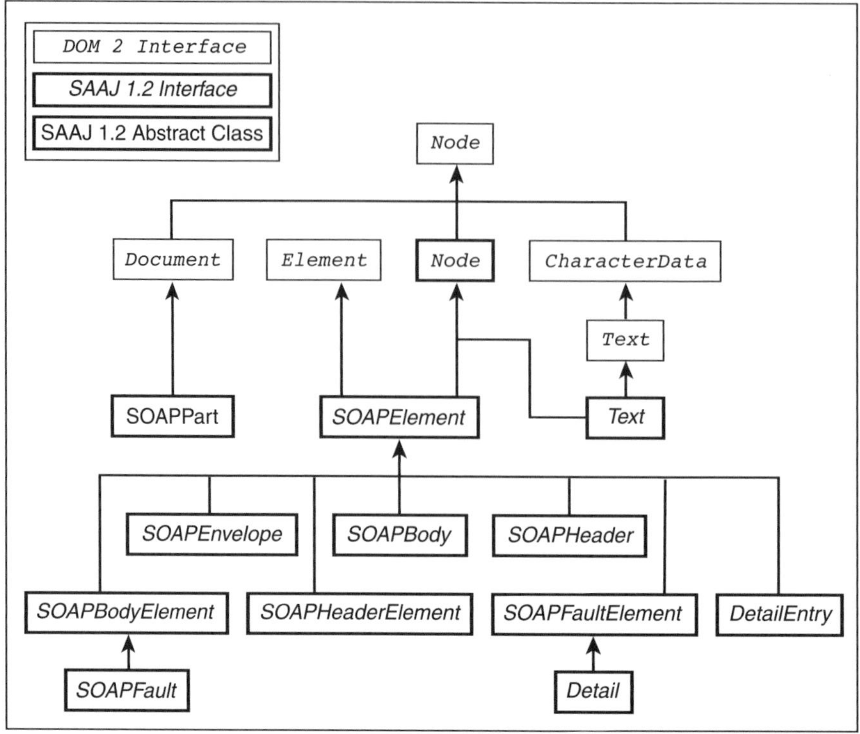

Figure 8.5
SAAJ 1.2 and DOM 2 Inheritance

instance of itself and then use the resultant `MessageFactory` instance to create an instance of `SOAPMessage`. The following code snippet illustrates these steps.

```
javax.xml.soap.MessageFactory msgFactory =
    javax.xml.soap.MessageFactory.newInstance();
javax.xml.soap.SOAPMessage message = msgFactory.createMessage();
```

Once you have a reference to an instance of `SOAPMessage`, you can get a reference to its associated `SOAPPart`, and the `SOAPPart`'s associated `SOAPEnvelope`, and the `SOAPEnvelope`'s associated `SOAPHeader` and `SOAPBody`, and the `SOAPBody`'s associated `SOAPFault` by making calls as in the following code snippet.

```
javax.xml.soap.SOAPPart soapPart = message.getSOAPPart();
javax.xml.soap.SOAPEnvelope soapEnv = soapPart.getEnvelope();
javax.xml.soap.SOAPHeader soapHeader = soapEnv.getHeader();
javax.xml.soap.SOAPBody soapBody = soapEnv.getBody();
javax.xml.soap.SOAPFault soapFault = soapBody.getFault();
```

You can also delete and add SOAP elements as the following code snippet illustrates. If an element already exists, then you will get a SOAPException when you try to add it. By default, a SOAPEnvelope is created with an empty SOAPHeader and SOAPBody, but no SOAPFault.

```
// Delete header (exists initially).
soapEnv.getHeader().detachNode();
// Add header back.
soapEnv.addHeader();

// Delete body (exists initially).
soapEnv.getBody().detachNode();
// Add body back.
soapEnv.addBody();

// Add fault (does not initially exist).
soapBody.addFault();
// Delete fault.
soapBody.getFault().detachNode();
```

You can also add an arbitrary XML document to the SOAPBody as in the following code snippet.

```
javax.xml.parsers.DocumentBuilderFactory docBuilderFactory =
    javax.xml.parsers.DocumentBuilderFactory.newInstance();
javax.xml.parsers.DocumentBuilder docBuilder =
    docBuilderFactory.newDocumentBuilder();
org.w3c.dom.Document doc = docBuilder.parse("C:\soapMsgBody.xml");
soapBody.addDocument(doc);
```

Or you can set the entire SOAP message as in the following code snippet.

```
java.io.File soapMsg = java.io.File("C:\completeSoapMsg.xml");
javax.xml.transform.stream.StreamSource soapMsgSource =
    javax.xml.transform.stream.StreamSource(soapMsg);
soapPart.setContent(soapMsgSource);
```

To send and receive SOAP messages with SAAJ you use the abstract SOAPConnection class. To get a concrete instance of SOAPConnection, you ask SOAPConnectionFactory, which must first create an instance of itself. This mirrors the factory logic used to get a SOAPMessage. For example, the following code snippet creates an instance of SOAPMessage from a file that contains a complete SOAP request message, then sends that message to a Web service and receives a response message; just as we did in the labs of the last chapter.

```
// Create the appropriate mime type header.
javax.xml.soap.MimeHeaders mimeHeaders = new javax.xml.soap.MimeHeaders();
```

```
mimeHeaders.addHeader("Content-Type", "text/xml; charset=UTF-8");

// Build a SOAP message in memory from a SOAP message in a file.
FileInputStream fileIS = new FileInputStream("C:\soapReqMsg.xml");
MessageFactory messageFactory = MessageFactory.newInstance();
SOAPMessage requestMessage =
    messageFactory.createMessage(mimeHeaders, fileIS);

// Send the SOAP message to the SOAP receiver and get the response.
java.net.URL url = new java.net.URL("http://someWebService.com");
SOAPConnectionFactory connectionFactory =
    SOAPConnectionFactory.newInstance();
SOAPConnection connection = connectionFactory.createConnection();
SOAPMessage responseMessage = connection.call(requestMessage, url);
```

SAAJ is a small API that makes creating, manipulating, sending, and receiving SOAP messages relatively easy. To learn more about SAAJ, read the specification and peruse the JavaDocs, which can be downloaded from `http://java.sun.com/xml/downloads/saaj.html`.

8.4 Java API for XML-Based RPC (JAX-RPC)

SAAJ is a low-level API, in that you use it to work directly with the messaging protocol—SOAP. Although SAAJ is great for creating and manipulating the XML for SOAP messages, Java developers are accustomed to working at a higher level with objects and procedure call semantics. Consequently, the Java community provides the Java API for XML-Based RPC (JAX-RPC). JAX-RPC hides the details involved in forming the XML for SOAP messages and exchanging those messages with a Web service. It allows Java developers to simply make method calls to invoke Web services as if they were simply making a remote procedure call. JAX-RPC handles marshalling method parameters from Java types to XML, forming a SOAP message to package the parameters for transmission, sending the resultant SOAP request message to the Web service you wish to invoke, receiving the Web service's response message, and unmarshalling the XML from the SOAP response message into Java types. Thus JAX-RPC handles most of the tedious work for you, making it quite easy for you to invoke a Web service from your Java code, or even expose your Java applications as a Web service.

Under the covers, JAX-RPC version 1.1 uses SAAJ version 1.2 to process SOAP messages. Therefore JAX-RPC 1.1 supports SOAP 1.1 and SOAP Messages with Attachments, as well as the WS-I Basic Profile 1.0. With JAX-RPC you can use one-way and request-response message exchange patterns; RPC/Literal, RPC/Encoded, and Document/Literal message styles; and HTTP as the underlying transport protocol. JAX-RPC also provides a standard mapping from WSDL service definitions to Java interfaces and from XML data types to Java data types. JAX-RPC is a hollow API like SAAJ and, therefore, requires a vendor implementation. The standard WSDL-XML to Java mapping provided by JAX-RPC has allowed vendors to create extremely useful tools that allow you to automatically generate Java code from a WSDL document, or go the other direction and automatically create a WSDL document from your Java code. In all, JAX-RPC is about saving you development time when you want to work with Web services in Java.

The Web site for JAX-RPC is `http://java.sun.com/xml/jaxrpc/index.jsp`, where you can find JavaDocs, specifications, and other related downloads. JAX-RPC is included with the Java Web Services Developer Pack (`http://java.sun.com/webservices/downloads/webservicespack.html`) and J2EE version 1.4 (`http://java.sun.com/j2ee/1.4/download.html`). JAX-RPC is really the standard programming model in J2EE for Web service clients and endpoints. JAX-RPC provides J2EE with a simple object-oriented programming environment for interoperating with other non-Java applications using standard Web services technologies.

JAX-RPC consists of a client-side programming model and a server-side programming model. The client-side programming model provides the ability to communicate with remote Web services by making method calls to a local object serving as a proxy. The server-side programming model allows you to expose Java objects or Enterprise JavaBeans as Web services. We first discuss the server-side programming model.

8.4.1 JAX-RPC Server-Side Programming

One of the great things about JAX-RPC is how easily it allows you to expose the Java application as a Web service. You can either expose an existing application as a Web service or create a JAX-RPC-based Web service from scratch. The functionality provided by the JAX-RPC server-side programming model allows you to create Web services that are fully interoperable with clients implemented in other languages because it is based on the standard Web service technologies and the WS-I BP.

When creating a Web service using JAX-RPC you have two options for your implementation: servlet-based service endpoint or EJB-based service endpoint. Web services implemented by JAX-RPC are referred to as *JAX-RPC service endpoints.* JAX-RPC service endpoints can be implemented as either stateless EJBs or plain Java objects that, when deployed, are backed by a Java Servlet and execute in a Java Servlet container. For the rest of this chapter, Servlet-based service endpoints will be referred to as *Servlet endpoints* and EJB-based service endpoints will be referred to as *EJB endpoints.* The easier of the two to develop is the Servlet service endpoint, which we discuss next.

Servlet Endpoint

The Servlet endpoint is easy to develop because all it requires is a plain Java object that implements an interface that extends `java.rmi.Remote`. The interface is called the JAX-RPC *service endpoint interface (SEI)* and the plain Java object that implements it is referred to as the *service implementation.* Recall the service interface definition and the service implementation definition from WSDL. The

WSDL service interface definition, which is defined by the `wsdl:portType`, corresponds directly to the JAX-RPC service endpoint interface. You will see later how exactly the two are mapped by JAX-RPC. The following two listings show a simple RPC-style Servlet-based service endpoint interface and implementation for the monitor pricing service.

Listing 8.9 JAX-RPC Service Endpoint Interface

```
public interface MonitorPricingSEI extends java.rmi.Remote {
  public float getMonitorPrice(String productId, String currency)
    throws java.rmi.RemoteException;
}
```

Listing 8.10 Implementation of Service Endpoint Interface

```
public class MonitorPricing_Impl implements MonitorPricingSEI {
  public float getMonitorPrice(String productId, String currency) {
    // To keep this simple, assume the currency is USD and
    // the price of the specified monitor is the following:
    return 700.00f;
  }
}
```

The SEI is required to extend the `java.rmi.Remote` interface and each of its declared methods must throw the `java.rmi.RemoteException`. The SEI defines the Web service operations that will be publicly available once the Servlet endpoint is deployed. Of course, you are free to add other methods to the service implementation that do not appear in the service interface.

Once the classes for the SEI and its implementation are defined, you will need to deploy them to a Java Servlet container (such as Tomcat) to run it. On deployment, the Servlet container will create a special JAX-RPC Java Servlet to handle the requests for the service endpoint. The JAX-RPC Servlet will respond to HTTP-based SOAP requests, parse incoming SOAP request messages, marshal the XML data to the appropriate Java types, and invoke the correct method on the service endpoint, passing it the resultant Java types as parameters. When the method invocation is complete, the JAX-RPC Servlet will unmarshal the Java return type (result from the method call) to XML, formulate a SOAP response message to include the resultant XML data, and transmit that SOAP response message back to the client via HTTP. If the service endpoint throws an exception, then the JAX-RPC Servlet will unmarshal the Java exception type into a SOAP `Fault` and transmit the fault message back to the client.

A Servlet endpoint has access to the same resources as a normal Java Servlet, which includes JDBC `DataSources`, EJBs, environment variables, and other Web services, plus the `ServletContext` and the

HttpSession. Servlet endpoints can use the Java Naming and Directory Interface (JNDI) Environment Naming Context (ENC) to look up resources that have been configured dynamically at runtime or statically via deployment descriptors, and Servlet endpoints can implement the javax.xml.rpc.server.ServiceLifecycle interface to access the underlying ServletContext.

The following two listings illustrate the use of JNDI ENC to access a javax.sql.DataSource that was configured with a deployment descriptor. DataSources are commonly configured to provide pooled JDBC connections to a database. Listing 8.11 shows the relevant parts of a web.xml deployment descriptor that names the Servlet endpoint and a DataSource for JNDI. Listing 8.12 shows the code for the Servlet endpoint, which looks up the DataSource via JNDI and uses it to retrieve the monitor price from the database.

Listing 8.11 Abbreviated Servlet Endpoint Deployment Descriptor (web.xml)

```
<web-app version="2.4" xmlns="http://java.sun.com/xml/ns/j2ee"
         xmlns:xsi="http://www.w3.org/2001/XMLSchema-instance"
         xsi:schemaLocation="http://java.sun.com/xml/ns/j2ee
             http://java.sun.com/xml/ns/j2ee/web-app_2_4.xsd">
  ...
  <servlet>
    <servlet-name>MonitorPricingSE</servlet-name>
    <servlet-class>MonitorPricing_Impl</servlet-class>
  </servlet>
  <resource-ref>
    <res-ref-name>jdbc/MonitorDatasource</res-ref-name>
    <res-type>javax.sql.DataSource</res-type>
    <res-auth>Container</res-auth>
  </resource-ref>
  ...
</web-app>
```

Listing 8.12 Using JNDI ENC From Servlet Endpoint to Get a DataSource

```
public class MonitorPricing_Impl implements MonitorPricingSEI {
  public float getMonitorPrice(String productId, String currency) {
    java.sql.Connection connection = null;
    java.sql.Statement statement = null;

    try {
     javax.naming.InitialContext jndiEnc = new javax.naming.InitialContext();
      javax.sql.DataSource dataSource = (javax.sql.DataSource)
```

```
          jndiEnc.lookup("java:comp/env/jdbc/MonitorDataSource");
        connection = dataSource.getConnection();
        statement = connection.createStatement();
        // Execute some query to get the product from the database.
        java.sql.ResultSet resultSet = statement.executeQuery("...");

        if (resultSet.next()) {
          return resultSet.getFloat("price");
        }

        return -1;
      }catch (java.sql.SQLException e) {
        throw new RuntimeException("Query failed", e);
      }catch (javax.naming.NamingException e) {
        throw new RuntimeException("JNDI lookup failed", e);
      }finally {
        try {
          statement.close();
        }catch (Exception e) { // Just cleaning up. }
        try {
          connection.close();
        }catch (Exception e) { // Just cleaning up. }
      }
    }
}
```

javax.xml.rpc.server.ServiceLifecycle The `ServiceLifecycle` interface can be implemented by a Servlet endpoint to gain access to the JAX-RPC Servlet's context and to perform initialization when the Servlet endpoint is created plus cleanup when the Servlet endpoint is destroyed. The `ServiceLifecycle` interface declares only two methods: `init()` and `destroy()`. The `init()` method is called by the Servlet container just after the Servlet endpoint is instantiated and before it handles any requests. The `destroy()` method is called by the Servlet container just before the Servlet endpoint is removed from service. You can count on the `init()` method being called only once in a Servlet endpoint's life cycle. Listing 8.13 illustrates use of the `init()` method to lookup a `DataSource` instead of having to look it up for every request.

Listing 8.13 Implementing the `ServiceLifecycle` Interface to Obtain a `DataSource`

```
import javax.naming.InitialContext;
import javax.sql.DataSource;
import javax.xml.rpc.ServiceException;
```

```
import javax.xml.rpc.server.ServiceLifecycle;

public class MonitorPricing_Impl implements MonitorPricingSEI,
  ServiceLifecycle {

  private DataSource dataSource = null;

  // Called at the beginning of a Servlet endpoint's life cycle
  public void init(Object context) throws ServiceException {
    try {
      InitialContext jndiEnc = new InitialContext();
      dataSource = (DataSource)
        jndiEnc.lookup("java:comp/env/jdbc/MonitorDataSource");
    }catch (javax.naming.NamingException e) {
      throw new ServiceException("JNDI lookup failed", e);
    }
  }

  // Called at the end of a Servlet endpoint's life cycle
  public void destroy() {
    // Perform some cleanup.
  }

  public float getMonitorPrice(String productId, String currency) {
    java.sql.Connection connection = null;
    java.sql.Statement statement = null;

    try {
      connection = dataSource.getConnection();
      statement = connection.createStatement();
      // Execute some query to get the product from the database.
      java.sql.ResultSet resultSet = statement.executeQuery("...");

      if (resultSet.next()) {
        return resultSet.getFloat("price");
      }

      return -1;
    }catch (java.sql.SQLException e) {
      throw new RuntimeException("Query failed", e);
    }finally {
      try {
        statement.close();
      }catch (Exception e) { // Just cleaning up. }
```

```
      try {
        connection.close();
      }catch (Exception e) { // Just cleaning up. }
    }
  }
}
```

Next we discuss how you may use the `Object` that is passed into the `init()` method of the `ServiceLifecycle` interface.

javax.xml.rpc.server.ServletEndpointContext The parameter to the `init()` method of the `ServiceLifecycle` interface is an `Object` because the `ServiceLifecycle` interface was intended to be generic enough to be used outside of a J2EE Servlet container (such as a standalone Axis server). However, inside a J2EE Servlet container you can expect the `Object` passed to `init()` to be of type `ServletEndpointContext`, which is given in the following listing.

Listing 8.14 The `javax.xml.rpc.server.ServletEndpointContext` Interface

```
package javax.xml.rpc.server;
public interface ServletEndpointContext {
  public java.security.Principal getUserPrincipal();
  public boolean isUserInRole(String role);
  public javax.servlet.http.HttpSession getHttpSession()
    throws javax.xml.rpc.JAXRPCException;
  public javax.servlet.ServletContext getServletContext();
  public javax.xml.rpc.handler.MessageContext getMessageContext();
}
```

The Servlet endpoint only receives a reference to the `ServletEndpointContext` one time (during the call to `init()`), but the values returned from the methods of the `ServletEndpointContext` will change for each request made to the Servlet endpoint. The `getUserPrincipal()` method returns the identity of the client that made the request, which will be `null` unless the Servlet endpoint was configured to use container-managed security. The `isUserInRole()` method, which also depends on container-managed security, will tell you if the client belongs to a specific configured role. The `getHttpSession()` method will return the `HttpSession` object that is being used to track the client's session. If session tracking is not being used, then `getHttpSession()` will return `null`. The `getServletContext()` method will return the `ServletContext` object associated with the JAX-RPC Servlet backing the service endpoint. This is the same `ServletContext` object that is associated with any normal Servlet. The `ServletContext` object can be used to access initialization parameters, files, container information, logging, and the `RequestDispatcher` for forwarding requests to other Servlets. All the previous methods discussed give the Servlet endpoint access to the typical J2EE information that you should be familiar with by now. However, the `getMessageContext()` method is specific to JAX-RPC Web services.

The MessageContext object returned from getMessageContext() encapsulates the actual SOAP message as well as other information that may be transferred between the Servlet endpoint and message handlers. Message handlers are objects that implement the javax.xml.rpc.handler.Handler interface. They are managed by the J2EE container and are configured via deployment descriptors to pre- and postprocess the SOAP messages. Messages handlers are typically used to process SOAP header blocks to perform Quality of Service related functionality, that is, logging and security.

When using JAX-RPC to process SOAP (which is currently the only messaging protocol supported by JAX-RPC) the MessageContext returned by getMessageContext() will always be of type javax.xml.rpc.handler.soap.SOAPMessageContext. SOAPMessageContext provides the getMessage() method that returns an instance of SOAPMessage from the SAAJ API. Recall from the discussion on SAAJ that SOAPMessage is the Java object representation of a SOAP message. You can use the SOAPMessage object returned from getMessage() to investigate all parts of the SOAP request message. The following listing demonstrates how you may use the ServletEndpointContext to get access to the HttpSession, the client's Principal, and the SOAP message.

Listing 8.15 Use of the ServletEndpointContext

```
import java.security.Principal;
import javax.servlet.ServletContext;
import javax.servlet.http.HttpSession;
import javax.xml.rpc.ServiceException;
import javax.xml.rpc.handler.soap.SOAPMessageContext;
import javax.xml.rpc.server.ServiceLifecycle;
import javax.xml.rpc.server.ServletEndpointContext;

public class MonitorPricing_Impl implements MonitorPricingSEI,
  ServiceLifecycle {

  private ServletEndpointContext endpointContext = null;
  ...
  public void init(Object context) throws ServiceException {
    // Maintain a reference to the ServletEndpointContext.
    endpointContext = (ServletEndpointContext) context;
    ...
  }

  public void destroy() {
    // Perform some cleanup.
  }
```

```
  public float getMonitorPrice(String productId, String currency) {
    HttpSession session = endpointContext.getHttpSession();
    Principal principal = endpointContext.getUserPrincipal();

    // The SOAPMessageContext will be different for every request.
    SOAPMessageContext soapMsgCntxt = (SOAPMessageContext)
      endpointContext.getMessageContext();
    javax.xml.soap.SOAPMessage soapMessage = soapMsgCntxt.getMessage();
    javax.xml.soap.SOAPPart soapPart = message.getSOAPPart();
    javax.xml.soap.SOAPEnvelope soapEnv = soapPart.getEnvelope();
    javax.xml.soap.SOAPHeader soapHeader = soapEnv.getHeader();
    javax.xml.soap.SOAPBody soapBody = soapEnv.getBody();
    javax.xml.soap.SOAPFault soapFault = soapBody.getFault();
    ...
  }
}
```

As you can see, creating a Servlet endpoint is quite easy. Arguably, the most difficult part in creating Servlet endpoints is creating the deployment descriptors to deploy them to the J2EE server. The deployment process is discussed later. For now we talk about how you can expose an EJB as a Web service.

EJB Endpoint

In addition to creating a Servlet endpoint, you have the option to either create an EJB and expose it as a Web service or expose an existing EJB as a Web service. Although Servlet endpoints are simpler than EJB endpoints, you may wish to use EJB endpoints in order to take advantage of EJB's automatic handling of transaction management, persistence, security, and resources. Since EJBs can be deployed as both Web service endpoints and traditional EJBs, a single EJB can be deployed to handle remote, local, and Web service clients simultaneously. Thus you can expose an existing EJB as a Web service without disrupting its usefulness to other non-SOAP clients.

The only restriction to exposing EJBs as Web services is that only stateless session EJBs can be deployed as Web service endpoints. This makes sense when you realize that the underlying messaging protocol, SOAP, is a stateless protocol. Of course, the stateless session bean can act as a façade and make calls to stateful session beans or entity beans. To expose a stateless session bean as a Web service you simply need to define a service endpoint interface (as we did with the Servlet endpoint), have the stateless session bean implement all the methods of the interface, and then deploy it. You do not have to define the typical remote interface that extends `javax.ejb.EJBObject` or the local interface that extends `javax.ejb.EJBLocal` or the EJB home interface. In addition, the stateless session EJB does not have to implement the service endpoint interface itself; it only has to implement the methods that are declared in the interface. One rule to keep in mind when you are implementing the methods of the service endpoint interface in your stateless session bean is the following: The methods of the stateless session bean cannot throw the java.rmi.RemoteException, even though all methods of the service endpoint interface are required to do so. This does not mean that you cannot define your own exceptions and have them thrown from both the interface and the bean. Throwing exceptions other than RemoteException is perfectly valid. For an example, we could use Listing 8.9 as our service endpoint interface and implement the stateless session EJB as follows.

Listing 8.16 The Stateless Session Bean for an EJB Endpoint

```
import javax.ejb.SessionBean;
import javax.ejb.SessionContext;

public class MonitorPricingBean implements SessionBean, MonitorPricingSEI {
  public void setSessionContext(SessionContext context) {}
  public void ejbCreate() {}

  public float getMonitorPrice(String productId, String currency) {
    // To keep this simple, assume the currency is USD and
    // the price of the specified monitor is the following:
    return 700.00f;
  }

  public void ejbRemove() {}
  public void ejbActivate() {}
  public void ejbPassivate() {}
}
```

Notice that the getMonitorPrice() method of Listing 8.16 does not throw the RemoteException declared by Listing 8.9. In this case we decided to implement the service endpoint interface, but we are not required to, as was just stated. Also notice that the stateless session bean implements the typical lifecycle methods that are declared by the SessionBean interface.

Similar to Servlet endpoints, EJB endpoints can get a reference to the javax.xml.rpc.handler.MessageContext. EJB endpoints get a reference to MessageContext by calling the getMessageContext() method of the javax.ejb.SessionContext. As with Servlet endpoints, the MessageContext for EJB endpoints is different for each request (different SOAP message). The following listing demonstrates how you may access the SOAP request message in an EJB.

Listing 8.17 Accessing the SOAPMessage in an EJB Endpoint

```
import javax.ejb.SessionBean;
import javax.ejb.SessionContext;
import javax.xml.rpc.handler.soap.SOAPMessageContext;
```

```
public class MonitorPricingBean implements SessionBean, MonitorPricingSEI {
  private SessionContext sessionContext = null;

  public void setSessionContext(SessionContext context) {
    // Must maintain a reference to SessionContext.
    sessionContext = context;
  }

  public void ejbCreate() {}

  public float getMonitorPrice(String productId, String currency) {
    // The SOAPMessageContext will be different for every request.
    SOAPMessageContext soapMsgCntxt = (SOAPMessageContext)
      sessionContext.getMessageContext();
    javax.xml.soap.SOAPMessage soapMessage = soapMsgCntxt.getMessage();
    javax.xml.soap.SOAPPart soapPart = message.getSOAPPart();
    javax.xml.soap.SOAPEnvelope soapEnv = soapPart.getEnvelope();
    javax.xml.soap.SOAPHeader soapHeader = soapEnv.getHeader();
    javax.xml.soap.SOAPBody soapBody = soapEnv.getBody();
    javax.xml.soap.SOAPFault soapFault = soapBody.getFault();
    ...
  }

  public void ejbRemove() {}
  public void ejbActivate() {}
  public void ejbPassivate() {}
}
```

Now that we have covered how to create a JAX-RPC-based Web service, we talk about how to create a JAX-RPC-based client to call a Web service.

8.4.2 JAX-RPC Client-Side Programming

The JAX-RPC client-side API is designed to be independent of the remote Web service implementation. This means you can use JAX-RPC to invoke a Web service that is implemented on any platform (i.e., .NET, Perl, etc.) as long as that Web service exchanges SOAP messages. JAX-RPC is also not dependent on J2EE. You can use it in any Java application. The following briefly describes the interfaces and classes of the core JAX-RPC client-side API.

Interfaces

- `javax.xml.rpc.Stub`

  Stubs in JAX-RPC act as proxies to the actual Web service. The `Stub` interface is the common base interface for all concrete stub implementations. It defines generic methods for getting and setting configuration properties on the stub. Typically these properties are information such as the address of the Web service endpoint, authentication credentials, and whether or not to participate in a session with the endpoint. The following code snippet illustrates getting and using a `Stub`.

```
Stub stub = (Stub) new MonitorPricingService_Impl().getMonitorPricingPort();
stub._setProperty(Stub.ENDPOINT_ADDRESS_PROPERTY,
                  "http://monitors.co/ws/Pricing");
```

- `javax.xml.rpc.Service`

  `Service` is a factory for creating dynamic proxies for the target Web service endpoint, instances of `Call` that can be used to dynamically invoke a Web service endpoint, and instances of the `Stub` interface described above. A `Service` instance is obtained via the `ServiceFactory` class, which is described below. The following code snippet illustrates getting and using a `Service`.

```
String namespace = "http://monitors.co/ws/Pricing";
QName port = new QName(namespace, "MonitorPricingPort");
QName operation = new QName(namespace, "getMonitorPrice");
Service service = serviceFactory.createService(
  new QName(namespace, "MonitorPricingService"));
Call call = service.createCall(port, operation);
```

  OR

```
URL wsdl = new URL("http://monitors.co/ws/Pricing?WSDL");
Service service = serviceFactory.createService(wsdl,
  new QName(namespace, "MonitorPricingService"));
MonitorPricingSEI dynamicProxy = (MonitorPricingSEI) service.getPort(
  new QName(namespace, "MonitorPricingPort"),
  MonitorPricingSEI.class);
```

- `javax.xml.rpc.Call`

  Instances of the `Call` interface are manufactured by `ServiceFactory` (described below) and are used to dynamically invoke a Web service endpoint. The `Call` interface defines methods for getting and setting the configuration information (from WSDL) that JAX-RPC needs to know in order to invoke a specific Web service endpoint, including the Web service network address, the port type, the operation, and associated parameters. The following code snippet illustrates getting and using a `Call`.

```
String namespace = "http://monitors.co/ws/Pricing";
Service service = serviceFactory.createService(
```

```
  new QName(namespace, "MonitorPricingService"));
Call call = service.createCall(
  new QName(namespace, "MonitorPricingPort"));
call.setTargetEndpointAddress("http://monitors.co/ws/Pricing");
call.setOperationName(new QName(namespace, "getMonitorPrice"));
```

Classes

- `javax.xml.rpc.ServiceFactory`

  The `ServiceFactory` class provides methods for creating and loading `Service` implementations. `ServiceFactory` is an implementation of the Abstract Factory design pattern. To use `ServiceFactory` you must first have it create an instance of itself. The following code snippet illustrates getting and using an instance of `ServiceFactory`.

```
ServiceFactory serviceFactory = ServiceFactory.newInstance();
Service service = serviceFactory.createService(
  new QName(namespace, "MonitorPricingService"));
```

- `javax.xml.rpc.ParameterMode`

  The `ParameterMode` class simply provides a Java type-safe enumeration of parameter modes. It contains three static fields, one for each parameter mode—IN, OUT, and INOUT. When configuring an instance of `Call`, use `ParameterMode` to specify whether parameters are to be of mode IN, INOUT, or OUT. The following code snippet illustrates using `ParameterMode`.

```
Call call = service.createCall(
  new QName(namespace, "MonitorPricingPort"));
call.setOperationName(new QName(namespace, "getMonitorPrice"));
call.addParameter("productId",
  new QName("http://www.w3.org/2001/XMLSchema", "string"),
  ParameterMode.IN);
```

- `javax.xml.rpc.NameConstants`

  The `NameConstants` class simply contains static fields that are common namespace prefixes and URIs used when programming with JAX-RPC. For example, we can use `NameConstants` in place of the XML schema namespace string that we gave in the `ParameterMode` example above, as follows.

```
call.addParameter("productId",
  new QName(NameConstants.NSURI_SCHEMA_XSD, "string"),
  ParameterMode.IN);
```

Exceptions

- `javax.xml.rpc.JAXRPCException`

  Basically, this exception is thrown from the methods defined by the `Stub` and `Call` interfaces when you do something wrong.

- `javax.xml.rpc.ServiceException`

  This exception is thrown from the methods of the `ServiceFactory` class and `Service` interface for such problems as a `Service` instance cannot be created, a `Call` cannot be created, or a WSDL document cannot be loaded.

The JAX-RPC client-side API supports three options for creating your Web service client: generated stub, dynamic proxy, and Dynamic Invocation Interface (DII). Essentially, the three choices vary when you provide the information to JAX-RPC on the Web service that you wish to invoke. The following sections describe these three client implementations.

Generated Stub Client

When you use generated stubs, you provide JAX-RPC with all of the information about the Web service (a WSDL document) at compilation time. JAX-RPC uses this information to generate Java remote interfaces and stubs that implement the operations defined in the WSDL document. You use the resultant interfaces and classes in your code when you develop your client application. The following demonstrates how a generated stub client might look.

Listing 8.18 A Client That Uses Generated Stubs

```
import javax.xml.rpc.ServiceFactory;

public class StaticStubClient {
  public static void main(String[] args) throws Exception {
    String productId = args[0];
    String currency = "USD";

    // Load the service.
    MonitorPricingService service = (MonitorPricingService)
      ServiceFactory.newInstance().loadService(MonitorPricingService.class);
    // Get the stub.
    MonitorPricingPortType stub = service.getMonitorPricingPort();
```

```
// Alternative method for obtaining the stub.
//  stub = new MonitorPricingService_Impl().getMonitorPricingPort();

    // Invoke the service.
    float price = stub.getMonitorPrice(productId, currency);
    System.out.println("monitor=" + productId + " , price=$" + price);
  }
}
```

In Listing 8.18 a vendor's JAX-RPC compiler was used to generate the classes `MonitorPricingService`, `MonitorPricingPortType`, and `MonitorPricingService_Impl` from the Web service's WSDL document. Examples of how to use a vendor's JAX-RPC compiler tool are given later. Because these classes were generated from the WSDL document, they contain all the information that JAX-RPC requires to call a Web service (such as the network address). You can also use the `_setProperty` method of the `Stub` interface to tell JAX-RPC about the Web service that you want to invoke.

If you were to access the service from a J2EE component, you most likely would have the service configured with JNDI using deployment descriptors. An example of a Servlet using JNDI to look up the generated stub for a Web service is given below.

Listing 8.19 A Servlet Web Service Client That Uses Generated Stubs

```
import javax.servlet.*;
import javax.servlet.http.*;

public class StaticStubServlet extends HttpServlet {
  protected void doGet(HttpServletRequest req, HttpServletResponse resp)
    throws ServletException, java.io.IOException {

    try {
      String productId = req.getParamter("productId");
      String currency = "USD";

      javax.naming.InitialContext jndiEnc = new javax.naming.InitialContext();
      MonitorPricingService service = (MonitorPricingService)
        jndiEnc.lookup("java:comp/env/service/MonitorPricingService");
      MonitorPricingPortType stub = service.getMonitorPricingPort();

      float price = stub.getMonitorPrice(productId, currency);
      resp.getWriter().write("<html><body>monitor="
        + productId + " , price=$" + price + "</body></html>");
    }catch (javax.naming.NamingException e) {
      throw new ServletException(e);
```

```
    }catch (javax.xml.rpc.NamingException e) {
      throw new ServletException(e);
    }
  }
}
```

Dynamic Proxy Client

A dynamic proxy client implementation does not require a stub class to be generated statically at compilation time. Instead, the stub is generated dynamically at runtime using the dynamic proxy APIs provided by Java reflection (`java.lang.reflect.Proxy` class and `java.lang.reflect.InvocationHandler` interface). A dynamic proxy client will make a call to the `getPort` method of an implementation of the `javax.xml.rpc.Service` interface to get a reference to the dynamic proxy. Although with a dynamic proxy implementation you do not need a generated stub, you do need a remote interface to the Web service operation you wish to invoke. You will likely get this interface by using a tool to generate it from the Web service's WSDL document. The following demonstrates how a dynamic proxy client might look.

Listing 8.20 A Dynamic Proxy Client

```
import javax.xml.namespace.QName;
import javax.xml.rpc.Service;
import javax.xml.rpc.ServiceFactory;

public class DynamicProxyClient {
  public static void main(String[] args) throws Exception {
    String productId = args[0];
    String currency = "USD";

    String wsdlURL = "http://monitors.co/ws/Pricing?WSDL";
    String namespaceURI = "http://monitors.co/ws/Pricing";
    // From WSDL line: <service name="MonitorPricingService">
    String serviceName = "MonitorPricingService";
    // From WSDL line: <port name="MonitorPricingPort" ...>
    String portName = "MonitorPricingPort";

    // Create a service from the information in the WSDL.
    Service service = ServiceFactory.newInstance().createService(
      new java.net.URL(wsdlURL),
      new QName(namespaceURI, serviceName));

    // Get the proxy.
    MonitorPricingSEI proxy = service.getPort(
      new QName(namespaceURI, portName), MonitorPricingSEI.class);

    // Invoke the service.
```

```
    float price = proxy.getMonitorPrice(productId, currency);
    System.out.println("monitor=" + productId + " , price=$" + price);
  }
}
```

This time we supply the location of the WSDL and which service defined in the WSDL that we want to call. Then, to obtain a concrete implementation of the service endpoint interface, we supply the name of the port that is defined in the WSDL and the service endpoint interface class. The service endpoint interface class could be generated by a vendor's tool or you could code it. If you code the service endpoint interface yourself, you must make sure that it conforms to the JAX-RPC rules for mapping WSDL to Java (discussed later).

Dynamic Invocation Interface (DII) Client

DII is the most dynamic of the three client implementations. It allows you to provide all of the information for invoking the Web service dynamically at runtime; you do not need a generated stub or remote interface. This is the model you will use if you wish to discover and invoke Web services at runtime instead of knowing about them ahead of time (dynamic discovery and invocation). DII clients are more complicated to code but have the benefit of more flexibility than generated stubs and dynamic proxies. The following demonstrates how a DII client might look.

Listing 8.21 A Dynamic Invocation Interface (DII) Client

```
import javax.xml.namespace.QName;
import javax.xml.rpc.Call;
import javax.xml.rpc.ParameterMode;
import javax.xml.rpc.Service;
import javax.xml.rpc.ServiceFactory;
import javax.xml.rpc.encoding.XMLType;

public class DynamicProxyClient {
  public static void main(String[] args) throws Exception {
    String productId = args[0];
    String currency = "USD";

    String wsdlURL = "http://monitors.co/ws/Pricing?WSDL";
    String namespaceURI = "http://monitors.co/ws/Pricing";
    // From WSDL line: <service name="MonitorPricingService">
    String serviceName = "MonitorPricingService";
    // From WSDL line: <port name="MonitorPricingPort" ...>
    String portName = "MonitorPricingPort";
    // From WSDL line: <operation name="getMonitorPrice">
    String operationName = "getMonitorPrice";
```

```
    // From WSDL line: <soapbind:address location="..."/>
    String endpointAddress = "http://monitors.co/ws/Pricing";

    Service service = ServiceFactory.newInstance().createService(
      new QName(namespaceURI, serviceName));

    Call call = service.createCall();
    call.setTargetEndpointAddress(endpointAddress);
    call.setPortTypeName(new QName(namespaceURI, portName));

    // Set the value of the SOAPAction HTTP header field.
    call.setProperty(Call.SOAPACTION_USE_PROPERTY, new Boolean(true));
    call.setProperty(Call.SOAPACTION_URI_PROPERTY, "");
    // Operation style is either "rpc" or "document"
    call.setProperty(Call.OPERATION_STYLE_PROPERTY, "rpc");
    // Encoding used (for example, SOAP Encoding),
    // empty string means literal.
    call.setProperty(Call.ENCODINGSTYLE_URI_PROPERTY, "");

    // Set the name of the operation to be invoked.
    call.setOperationName(new QName(namespaceURI, operationName));
    // Set the name and types of parameters.
    call.addParameter("productId", XMLType.XSD_STRING, ParameterMode.IN);
    call.addParameter("currency", XMLType.XSD_STRING, ParameterMode.IN);
    // Set the type of the return value.
    call.setReturnType(XMLType.XSD_FLOAT);

    // Invoke the service.
    Float price = (Float) call.invoke(new String[]{productId, currency});
    System.out.println("monitor=" + productId
      + " , price=$" + price.floatValue());
  }
}
```

If the Web service you want to invoke utilizes a one-way or asynchronous message exchange pattern (you will not be expecting a return value), you can invoke it using `call.invokeOneWay(parameters)`. Also, it can be useful to know that an instance of the `Call` interface can be reused for multiple calls. For example, if a specific Web service implemented two methods that you wanted to invoke, after invoking the first one you could execute `call.removeAllParameters()` to clear the parameters used for the first method, execute `call.setOperationName()` to set the name of the second method, set the parameters and return type for the second method, and invoke it. This saves you the effort of having to create a new instance of `Call` and set all of the properties that are common between the two Web service operations.

8.4.3 Mapping Java to WSDL and XML

JAX-RPC provides standards for how the definitions in WSDL are mapped to Java interfaces as well as how XML data types map to data types in Java. The JAX-RPC runtime environment hides these complexities by automatically transforming the XML representation of a procedure call and associated parameters (the SOAP message) into a Java method call with Java data type parameters. This process is called *deserialization.* Additionally, JAX-RPC hides the complexities of transforming a Java method call with Java data type parameters (or a single return value Java object) to its XML representation such that it can be transmitted as a SOAP message. This process is call *serialization.* JAX-RPC handles this serialization/deserialization process at both the client and the service endpoint. Even though this process is handled automatically it is important for you to understand a little about how this process happens and what data types are supported because JAX-RPC does not support all Java data types and what you name things in the WSDL document affects what the resulting Java types and methods are named.

WSDL to Java

How WSDL maps to Java is fairly straightforward. We have already discussed how the WSDL `portType` definition is analogous to a Java interface where the `operation` elements are the Java methods, the `parts` of the `input` element are the method parameters, and the `output` element represents the return value and/or OUT or INOUT parameters. Thus, the WSDL `portType` (along with associated `message`, `part`, and `types`) defines the JAX-RPC service endpoint interface. The `name` attributes of the `portType`, `operation`, and `part` elements are, by default, used as the names of the Java interface, methods, and parameters, respectively. JAX-RPC handles this mapping for one-way and request/response message exchange patterns, but does not handle solicit/response or notification.

The package names for Java types cannot be directly derived from the WSDL so they are handled by a JAX-RPC mapping file, which is a file that explicitly maps the definitions in WSDL to their Java representations. The mapping file associates Java package names with XML namespaces defined in the WSDL. JAX-RPC mapping files can be coded by hand but are typically generated by JAX-RPC compilation tools provided by your vendor. JAX-RPC mapping files also allow you to give different names for your Java types than the names defined in the WSDL. You will see examples of JAX-RPC mapping files in the labs at the end of this chapter. This section will give you an idea of how a Java interface would be derived from a WSDL service definition, but actually performing this step requires a tool from the JAX-RPC vendor. Real examples are left for the labs.

The following two listings show the relevant elements from a WSDL document and how the generated JAX-RPC service endpoint interface would look. Notice how the names used in the Java interface correspond to the names defined in the WSDL.

Listing 8.22 Request/Response WSDL portType Definition

```
<types>
  <xsd:schema targetNamespace="...">
    <xsd:element name="MyFault" type="tns:MyFaultType" />
    <xsd:complexType name="MyFaultType">
      <xsd:sequence>
        <xsd:element name="message" type="xsd:string"/>
      </xsd:sequence>
    </xsd:complexType>
  </xsd:schema>
</types>
<message name="TheRequest">
  <part name="param1" type="xsd:string"/>
  <part name="param2" type="xsd:string"/>
</message>
<message name="TheResponse">
  <part name="return1" type="xsd:float"/>
</message>
<message name="MyFault">
  <part name="errorMessage" element="tns:MyFault"/>
</message>
<portType name="MySEI">
  <operation name="getOperation">
    <input message="tns:TheRequest"/>
    <output message="tns:TheResponse"/>
    <fault name="MyFault" message="tns:MyFault"/>
  </operation>
</portType>
```

In Listing 8.22, the `xsd:` prefix is associated with the XML Schema namespace, `http://www.w3.org/2001/XMLSchema`. The `tns:` prefix is associated with whatever the target namespace (tns) of the WSDL may be. Recall that the WSDL `portType` and `message` elements are considered the WSDL service interface definition. The `binding` and `service` elements are considered the WSDL service implementation definition so they are omitted in this listing.

Listing 8.23 JAX-RPC Service Endpoint Interface Generated from the WSDL in Listing 8.22

```
public interface MySEI extends java.rmi.Remote {
  public float getOperation(String param1, String param2)
    throws java.rmi.RemoteException, MyFaultType;
}
```

The name of the JAX-RPC service endpoint interface (SEI) in Listing 8.23 is taken from the name attribute of the portType element. The name of the method in the SEI is taken from the name attribute of the operation element. The names of the parameters are taken from the name attributes of the part elements of the input message. The name of the fault is taken from the name attribute of the complexType element in the types element. JAX-RPC will generate a Java class for the fault that matches its complexType. This is covered more when we talk about how XML maps to Java.

The following listings demonstrate how multiple operations are mapped.

Listing 8.24 WSDL portType with Multiple Operations

```
<message name="Request1">
  <part name="param1" type="xsd:string"/>
</message>
<message name="Request2">
  <part name="param2" type="xsd:string"/>
</message>
<message name="TheResponse">
  <part name="return1" type="xsd:int"/>
</message>
<portType name="MySEI">
  <operation name="getOperation1">
    <input message="tns:Request1"/>
    <output message="tns:TheResponse"/>
  </operation>
  <operation name="getOperation2">
    <input message="tns:Request2"/>
    <output message="tns:TheResponse"/>
  </operation>
</portType>
```

Listing 8.25 JAX-RPC Service Endpoint Interface Generated from the WSDL in Listing 8.24

```
public interface MySEI extends java.rmi.Remote {
  public int getOperation1(String param1)
    throws java.rmi.RemoteException;
  public int getOperation2(String param2)
    throws java.rmi.RemoteException;
}
```

In this example getOperation1 and getOperation2 use different input messages but the same output message to show that operations can share message elements. The name mapping from WSDL to the

JAX-RPC SEI works the same as it does for a `portType` with a single operation. We can also define an operation that uses one-way messaging (no return value) as in the following listings.

Listing 8.26 WSDL `portType` That Specifies One-Way Messaging

```
<message name="Request">
  <part name="param1" type="xsd:boolean"/>
</message>
<portType name="MySEI">
  <operation name="setOperation">
    <input message="tns:Request"/>
  </operation>
</portType>
```

Listing 8.27 JAX-RPC Service Endpoint Interface Generated from the WSDL in Listing 8.26

```
public interface MySEI extends java.rmi.Remote {
  public int setOperation(boolean param1)
    throws java.rmi.RemoteException;
}
```

If the WSDL operation specifies multiple OUT parameters, JAX-RPC has to do something special because Java does not natively support OUT or INOUT parameters. To handle this situation JAX-RPC uses various types that implement the `javax.xml.rpc.holders.Holder` interface for the OUT and INOUT parameters. These holders act as wrappers for the OUT and INOUT parameters at run-time, which allows JAX-RPC to set the value of the OUT and INOUT parameters before the procedure call returns. The `javax.xml.rpc.holders` package contains many types of holders to support the various data types that JAX-RPC allows you to use. The following listings demonstrate a case where JAX-RPC would use holders.

Listing 8.28 WSDL `portType` with Multiple Output Parameters

```
<message name="TheRequest">
  <part name="param1" type="xsd:string"/>
</message>
<message name="TheResponse">
  <part name="param2" type="xsd:int"/>
  <part name="param3" type="xsd:datetime"/>
</message>
<portType name="MySEI">
  <operation name="getOperation">
    <input message="tns:TheRequest"/>
```

```
    <output message="tns:TheResponse"/>
  </operation>
</portType>
```

Listing 8.29 JAX-RPC Service Endpoint Interface Generated from the WSDL in Listing 8.28

```
public interface MySEI extends java.rmi.Remote {
  public void getOperation(String param1,
                           javax.xml.rpc.holders.IntHolder param2,
                           javax.xml.rpc.holders.CalendarHolder param3)
    throws java.rmi.RemoteException;
}
```

Listing 8.30 Invoking the JAX-RPC Service Endpoint Defined by Listing 8.29

```
String param1 = "Test";
IntHolder param2= new IntHolder(5);
CalendarHolder param3 = new CalendarHolder();

MySEI stub = new MyService_Impl().getMyPort();
stub.getOperation(param1, param2, param3);

System.out.println("Returned int: " + param2.value);
System.out.println("Returned date: " + param3.value);
```

Since the WSDL in Listing 8.28 defines multiple output parameters, JAX-RPC generates a SEI that uses holders. The parameter `param1` in Listing 8.29 is an IN parameter and `param2` and `param3` are either OUT or INOUT parameters. Listing 8.30 illustrates how you would invoke the method defined by the SEI and access the values returned by the holders. Notice that Listing 8.29 has no return value. The `parameterOrder` attribute of the WSDL `operation` element can be used to help distinguish between INOUT and OUT parameters and a return value. For example, the following listings modify those above to signify a return value. The return value is the one omitted from the `parameterOrder` attribute list.

Listing 8.31 WSDL `portType` with `parameterOrder` Attribute

```
<message name="TheRequest">
  <part name="param1" type="xsd:string"/>
</message>
<message name="TheResponse">
  <part name="param2" type="xsd:int"/>
  <part name="param3" type="xsd:datetime"/>
</message>
<portType name="MySEI">
```

```
  <operation name="getOperation" parameterOrder="param1 param2">
    <input message="tns:TheRequest"/>
    <output message="tns:TheResponse"/>
  </operation>
</portType>
```

Listing 8.32 JAX-RPC Service Endpoint Interface Generated from the WSDL in Listing 8.31

```
public interface MySEI extends java.rmi.Remote {
  public java.util.Calendar getOperation(String param1,
      javax.xml.rpc.holders.IntHolder param2)
    throws java.rmi.RemoteException;
}
```

JAX-RPC compiler tools will generate both the JAX-RPC service endpoint interface that corresponds to the WSDL `portType` definition and a service interface that corresponds to the WSDL `service` definition. Because one is called the service endpoint interface and the other is called the service interface they can be easily confused, but they are not the same. The `ServiceFactory` class is used to return an implementation of the generated service interface, and in turn that implementation is used to return an implementation of the generated JAX-RPC service endpoint interface. You may not realize it, but you have already seen examples of this. The following listings demonstrate the service interface that would be generated from the WSDL and how that service interface is used to get the generated JAX-RPC service endpoint interface for invoking the Web service.

Listing 8.33 WSDL `service` Definition

```
<message name="TheRequest">
  <part name="param1" type="xsd:string"/>
  <part name="param2" type="xsd:string"/>
</message>
<message name="TheResponse">
  <part name="return1" type="xsd:float"/>
</message>
<portType name="MySEI">
  <operation name="getOperation">
    <input message="tns:TheRequest"/>
    <output message="tns:TheResponse"/>
  </operation>
</portType>
<binding name="MyBinding" type="tns:MySEI">
  ...
</binding>
<service name="MyService">
```

```
  <port name="MyPort" binding="tns:MyBinding">
    <soapbind:address location="..."/>
  </port>
</service>
```

Listing 8.34 Service Interface Generated from the WSDL in Listing 8.33

```
public interface MyService extends javax.xml.rpc.Service {
  public MySEI getMyPort()
    throws javax.xml.rpc.ServiceException;
  ...
}
```

Listing 8.35 Using the Service Interface Defined by Listing 8.34

```
String param1 = "testParam1";
String param2 = "testParam2";

MyService service =
  ServiceFactory.newInstance().loadService(MyService.class);
MySEI stub = service.getMyPort();
float result = stub.getOperation(param1, param2);

System.out.println("Result=" + result);
```

The `name` attribute of the WSDL `service` element becomes the name of the service interface (Listing 8.34). The `name` attribute of the WSDL `port` element becomes the `get` method of the `Service` for getting an implementation of the generated JAX-RPC service endpoint interface. The name of the generated JAX-RPC service endpoint interface is taken from the `name` attribute of the WSDL `portType` element.

XML to Java

The JAX-RPC specification defines how XML data types are mapped to Java data types. The JAX-RPC compiler and runtime environment will automatically translate from XML data types in the WSDL or SOAP message to Java data types as well as translate from Java data types in a method call to their appropriate XML representation. The following table lists the mapping between the built-in XML Schema simple types and Java data types.

The types in Table 8.1 that are prefixed with `xsd:` are XML Schema types and the types prefixed with `soapenc:` are defined by SOAP Encoding. JAX-RPC maps all simple SOAP Encoding types to the Java wrapper associated with the Java primitive. For instance, `soapenc:int` is mapped to

Table 8.1 JAX-RPC Supported Java Types and Their Mapping to XML Types

XML Schema Built-In Simple Type (SOAP Encoded Simple Type)	JAX-RPC Supported Java Type
`xsd:string (soapenc:string)`	`java.lang.String`
`xsd:integer`	`java.math.BigInteger`
`xsd:int (soapenc:int)`	`int (java.lang.Integer)`
`xsd:long (soapenc:long)`	`long (java.lang.Long)`
`xsd:short (soapenc:short)`	`short (java.lang.Short)`
`xsd:decimal (soapenc:decimal)`	`java.math.BigDecimal`
`xsd:float (soapenc:float)`	`float (java.lang.Float)`
`xsd:double (soapenc:double)`	`double (java.lang.Double)`
`xsd:boolean (soapenc:boolean)`	`boolean (java.lang.Boolean)`
`xsd:byte (soapenc:byte)`	`byte (java.lang.Byte)`
`xsd:unsignedInt`	`long (java.lang.Long)`
`xsd:unsignedShort`	`int (java.lang.Integer)`
`xsd:unsignedByte`	`short (java.lang.Short)`
`xsd:QName`	`javax.xml.namespace.QName`
`xsd:dateTime`	`java.util.Calendar` `java.util.Date` (only when Java-to-XML)
`xsd:date`	`java.util.Calendar`
`xsd:time`	`java.util.Calendar`
`xsd:anyURI`	`java.net.URI` (J2SE 1.4 or later) `java.lang.String` (pre J2SE 1.4)
`xsd:base64Binary (soapenc:base64)`	`byte[]`
`xsd:hexBinary`	`byte[]`
`xsd:anySimpleType`	`java.lang.String`

java.lang.Integer instead of the Java primitive int. The SOAP Encoding types are mapped this way because they are all defined as nillable (in terms of Java this essentially means that the type can be assigned null). The following cases exist where the JAX-RPC specification states that built-in simple XML types must be mapped to Java wrappers instead of Java primitives:

1. The element is declared with nillable attribute set to true.
2. The element is declared with the minOccurs attribute set to 0 and the maxOccurs attribute set to 1 or absent.
3. The element is declared with the use attribute set to optional or absent and neither the default nor the fixed attributes are declared.

For example, the following type1, type2, and type3 declarations would all be mapped to java.lang.Integer; the Java wrapper for int Java primitive.

```
<xsd:element name="type1" type="xsd:int" nillable="true"/>
<xsd:element name="type2" type="xsd:int" minOccurs="0"/>
<xsd:element name="description">
  <xsd:complexType>
    <xsd:sequence>
      <xsd:attribute name="type3" type="xsd:int" use="optional"/>
    </xsd:sequence>
  </xsd:complexType>
</xsd:element>
```

The xsd:anyURI XML type is mapped to java.net.URI when you are using J2SE version 1.4 or later and java.lang.String if you are using an earlier version of J2SE. Also, JAX-RPC will serialize (Java-to-XML) java.util.Date as xsd:dateTime, but will always deserialize (XML-to-Java) xsd:dateTime as java.util.Calendar. Therefore, just working with java.util.Calendar in your Web services is recommended.

JAX-RPC also supports mapping XML Schema complexType values to JavaBeans where each element of the complexType is a bean property that has corresponding getters and setters. Of course each element of the complexType must also be a type that JAX-RPC supports. For example, the following two listings show a complexType and the resulting JavaBean.

Listing 8.36 XML complexType Definition

```
<xsd:element name="MonitorPriceRequest">
  <xsd:complexType>
    <xsd:sequence>
      <xsd:element name="productId" type="xsd:string"/>
      <xsd:element name="currency" type="xsd:string"/>
```

```
    </xsd:sequence>
  </xsd:complexType>
</xsd:element>
```

Listing 8.37 JAX-RPC-Generated JavaBean from `complexType` of Listing 8.36

```
public class MonitorPriceRequest {
  private String productId;
  private String currency;

  public MonitorPriceRequest(){}

  public String getProductId(){return productId;}
  public void setProductId(String productId){this.productId = productId;}
  public String getCurrency(){return currency;}
  public void setCurrency(String currency){this.currency = currency;}
}
```

The mapping of WSDL faults to Java types can become pretty involved, but generally the XML type that defines the fault is translated to a Java class that extends `java.lang.Exception`. The parts of the fault become fields of the resulting exception class with corresponding get methods and a constructor that accepts each field so that they can be initially set. A `message` element defining a fault in WSDL can only contain a single `part` element. If the type of that `part` is a simple XML type, that type becomes a field in the resulting exception class. If the type is a `complexType`, the elements of the `complexType` become fields of the resulting exception class. The name of the resulting exception class is taken from the `name` attribute of the `complexType` if one is used, or the `name` attribute of the `message` definition otherwise. The following listings give an example of a fault declaration and the resulting exception class.

Listing 8.38 WSDL Fault Definition

```
<types>
  <xsd:schema targetNamespace="...">
    ...
    <xsd:element name="InvalidArgumentFault"
                 type="InvalidArgumentException"/>
    <xsd:complexType name="InvalidArgumentException">
      <xsd:sequence>
        <xsd:element name="invalidValue" type="xsd:string"/>
        <xsd:element name="message" type="xsd:string"/>
      </xsd:sequence>
    </xsd:complexType>
  </xsd:schema>
```

```
</types>
...
<message name="InvalidArgumentFault">
  <part name="fault" element="tns:InvalidArgumentFault"/>
</message>
<portType name="MonitorPricingPortType">
  <operation name="getMonitorPrice">
    ...
    <fault name="InvalidArgumentFault" message="tns:InvalidArgumentFault"/>
  </operation>
</portType>
```

Listing 8.39 JAX-RPC-Generated Exception from Fault of Listing 8.38

```
public class InvalidArgumentException extends java.lang.Exception {
  private String invalidValue;
  private String message;

  public InvalidArgumentException() { // Default constructor required }

  public InvalidArgumentException(String invalidValue, String message) {
    this.invalidValue = invalidValue;
    this.message = message;
  }

  public String getInvalidValue() { return invalidValue; }
  public String getMessage() { return message; }
}
```

JAX-RPC also supports single and multidimensional arrays as long as the array type is supported. For example, the following method for declaring an array in XML,

```
<xsd:element name="numbers" type="xsd:int" maxOccurs="unbounded"/>
```

is mapped to the following Java array:

```
int[] numbers;
```

Note that the previous discussion applies to both Document/Literal and RPC/Literal message styles. However, if the Document/Literal message style is used and an unsupported XML schema type is used, JAX-RPC will use the SAAJ `SOAPElement` for the parameter. For example, the generated JAX-RPC service endpoint interface for a definition that uses an unsupported type might look like the following.

```
public interface MySEI extends java.rmi.Remote {
  public void submitOperation(javax.xml.soap.SOAPElement element)
    throws java.rmi.RemoteException;
}
```

8.4.4 Deploying JAX-RPC Service Endpoints

After you develop a J2EE-based JAX-RPC service endpoint (Servlet endpoint or EJB endpoint) you have to deploy it to a J2EE server to get it running. Unfortunately, deployment can be complicated, partially because it is vendor-dependent. Most of the process is described by the Java specifications and those parts are vendor-neutral. However, to deploy service endpoints, your vendor implementation will likely require you to use its deployment tools and/or create additional vendor-specific deployment descriptors. This section discusses the vendor-neutral parts of deployment and the labs give an example of deploying on a specific vendor's implementation.

Deploying service endpoints on a J2EE server requires the same deployment descriptors you have used before and more. So for Servlet endpoints you will need to create the typical `web.xml` deployment descriptor, and for EJB endpoints you will need to create the typical `ejb-jar.xml` deployment descriptor. Additionally, you will need to create a `webservices.xml` deployment descriptor (referred to as the Web services deployment descriptor) for both the Servlet endpoints and the EJB endpoints, and you will need to include the WSDL file and the JAX-RPC mapping file that is generated by the JAX-RPC compiler. Actually, vendors will often generate the WSDL and JAX-RPC mapping files for you when you deploy, so you do not have to explicitly generate them. JAX-RPC implementations allow you to start either with a WSDL document and generate your Java code and JAX-RPC mapping file or with your Java code and generate a WSDL document and JAX-RPC mapping file. Starting with Java is more comfortable for most Java developers because they are accustomed to working in Java. However, starting from WSDL is considered a better practice because this forces you to think through your problem in the context of SOAP and XML, which tends to generate code that is more interoperable.

The `webservices.xml` deployment descriptor is placed in the `WEB-INF` directory of the WAR file for a Servlet endpoint and the `META-INF` directory of the EJB JAR file for an EJB endpoint. The WSDL and JAX-RPC mapping files are typically placed in the `WEB-INF/wsdl` directory of the WAR file for a Servlet endpoint and the `META-INF/wsdl` directory of the EJB JAR for an EJB endpoint. A single `webservices.xml` file can be used for every Servlet endpoint in a single WAR file that shares the same WSDL file, and a separate single `webservices.xml` file can be used for every EJB endpoint in a single EJB JAR file that shares the same WSDL file. The `webservices.xml` file is used to identify the following:

1. The name of the Web service
2. The location of the WSDL and JAX-RPC mapping files for the service
3. The EJBs or "servlets" identified in the ejb-jar.xml or web.xml, respectively, that are JAX-RPC service endpoints
4. The WSDL port associated with each service endpoint
5. The JAX-RPC service endpoint interface and implementation classes

The following is an example webservices.xml deployment descriptor for a Servlet endpoint.

Listing 8.40 Example webservices.xml for a Servlet Endpoint

```
<?xml version="1.0" encoding="UTF-8"?>
<webservices version="1.1"
             xmlns="http://java.sun.com/xml/ns/j2ee"
             xmlns:xsi="http://www.w3.org/2001/XMLSchema-instance"
             xmlns:tns="http://my-fake-company.com"
             xsi:schemaLocation="http://java.sun.com/xml/ns/j2ee
    http://www.ibm.com/webservices/xsd/j2ee_web_services_1_1.xsd">
  <webservice-description>
    <webservice-description-name>MyService</webservice-description-name>
    <wsdl-file>WEB-INF/wsdl/MyService.wsdl</wsdl-file>
    <jaxrpc-mapping-file>WEB-INF/wsdl/MyService_mapping.xml
    </jaxrpc-mapping-file>
    <port-component>
      <port-component-name>MyServletEndpoint</port-component-name>
      <wsdl-port>tns:MyPort</wsdl-port>
      <service-endpoint-interface>javawebbook.MySEI
      </service-endpoint-interface>
      <service-impl-bean>
        <servlet-link>MyServletEndpoint</servlet-link>
      </service-impl-bean>
    </port-component>
  </webservice-description>
</webservices>
```

The only differences between a Web services deployment descriptor for a Servlet endpoint and one for an EJB endpoint is that the servlet-link element becomes an ejb-link element and the WSDL is located in the META-INF directory because EJB JAR files do not have a WEB-INF directory. The following listing gives an example of a Web services deployment descriptor for an EJB endpoint.

Listing 8.41 Example `webservices.xml` for an EJB Endpoint

```
<?xml version="1.0" encoding="UTF-8"?>
<webservices version="1.1"
             xmlns="http://java.sun.com/xml/ns/j2ee"
             xmlns:xsi="http://www.w3.org/2001/XMLSchema-instance"
             xmlns:tns="http://my-fake-company.com"
             xsi:schemaLocation="http://java.sun.com/xml/ns/j2ee
    http://www.ibm.com/webservices/xsd/j2ee_web_services_1_1.xsd">
  <webservice-description>
    <webservice-description-name>MyService</webservice-description-name>
    <wsdl-file>META-INF/wsdl/MyService.wsdl</wsdl-file>
    <jaxrpc-mapping-file>META-INF/wsdl/MyService_mapping.xml
    </jaxrpc-mapping-file>
    <port-component>
      <port-component-name>MyEJBEndpoint</port-component-name>
      <wsdl-port>tns:MyPort</wsdl-port>
      <service-endpoint-interface>javawebbook.MySEI
      </service-endpoint-interface>
      <service-impl-bean>
        <ejb-link>MyBean</ejb-link>
      </service-impl-bean>
    </port-component>
  </webservice-description>
</webservices>
```

The `webservices.xml` file serves to bind together several elements of a JAX-RPC service endpoint including the WSDL file, the JAX-RPC mapping file, the WSDL `port` definition, the service endpoint interface, and the service endpoint implementation. The `webservice-description` element describes a collection of endpoints that all share the same WSDL file. Therefore, for each WSDL file in a deployment JAR, you must have a corresponding `webservices.xml` file.

The `webservice-description-name` element is mandatory and simply identifies the collection of endpoints with a unique name. The `wsdl-file` element identifies the location of the WSDL within the deployment JAR. The `jaxrpc-mapping-file` element identifies the location of the JAX-RPC mapping file within the deployment JAR. The `wsdl-file` element and `jaxrpc-mapping-file` element are not mandatory, but if one is present, the other must also be present. It is rare that you would not need to specify these.

The Web services deployment descriptor may contain one or more `port-component` elements. The `port-component` element identifies a single service endpoint. The `port-component-name` element identifies a particular JAX-RPC service endpoint with a unique name. The `wsdl-port` element provides the qualified name of the WSDL port that corresponds to the endpoint. The service-endpoint-interface element identifies the fully qualified name of the JAX-RPC service endpoint interface class. The service-impl-bean element identifies the service implementation class. It provides a link between its associated port-component and the Servlet or EJB identified in the web.xml or ejb-jar.xml, respectively. For Servlet endpoints, the servlet-link element of the webservices.xml file must contain the same name as the servlet-name element in the web.xml. For example, the following code snippet from a web.xml file would correspond with the Web services deployment descriptor of Listing 8.40.

```
<servlet>
  <servlet-name>MyServletEndpoint</servlet-name>
  <servlet-class>javawebbook.MyServletEndpoint</servlet-class>
</servlet>
<servlet-mapping>
  <servlet-name>MyServletEndpoint</servlet-name>
  <url-pattern>/MyService/MyServletEndpoint</url-pattern>
</servlet-mapping>
```

For EJB endpoints, the ejb-link element of the webservices.xml file must contain the same name as the ejb-name element in the ejb-jar.xml. For example, the following code snippet from an ejb-jar.xml file would correspond to the Web services deployment descriptor of Listing 8.41.

```
<session>
  <ejb-name>MyBean</ejb-name>
  <service-endpoint>javawebbook.MySEI</service-endpoint>
  <ejb-class>javawebbook.MyBean</ejb-class>
  <session-type>Stateless</session-type>
  ...
</session>
```

Additionally, the webservices.xml file can contain one or more handler elements after the service-impl-bean element. These elements are used to identify message handlers that pre- and postprocess SOAP messages for the JAX-RPC service endpoint. Message handlers are typically used to process SOAP headers. Message handlers and the handler element are not covered in this book. If you are interested in learning about message handlers in JAX-RPC, it is suggested that you read one of the resources listed at the end of this chapter.

The entire configuration that can normally be specified in the web.xml and ejb-jar.xml deployment descriptors still applies when you are deploying JAX-RPC service endpoints. In fact, there are only a couple of differences between these deployment descriptors when they are used to deploy traditional J2EE components and when they are used to deploy JAX-RPC service endpoints. These differences include the service-endpoint element of the ejb-jar.xml deployment descriptor and the service-ref element that can be used in both the ejb-jar.xml and web.xml deployment descriptors.

The service-endpoint element must be included as a child element of the session element in the ejb-jar.xml file when the associated EJB is a JAX-RPC service endpoint. The service-endpoint element is placed after the ejb-name element and before the ejb-class element. It must contain the fully qualified name of the JAX-RPC service endpoint interface class. An example use of the service-endpoint element was included in the code snippet above.

The service-ref element is used to declare that a J2EE component references a JAX-RPC service endpoint so that the endpoint can be looked up in JNDI ENC. The service-ref element can appear in a web.xml file as in the following listing.

Listing 8.42 The service-ref Element in a web.xml File

```
<?xml version="1.0" encoding="UTF-8"?>
<web-app version="2.4"
         xmlns="http://java.sun.com/xml/ns/j2ee"
         xmlns:xsi="http://www.w3.org/2001/XMLSchema-instance"
         xmlns:tns="http://my-fake-company.com"
         xsi:schemaLocation="http://java.sun.com/xml/ns/j2ee
             http://java.sun.com/xml/ns/j2ee/web-app_2_4.xsd">
  <servlet>
    <servlet-name>MyServlet</servlet-name>
    <servlet-class>javawebbook.MyServlet</servlet-class>
  </servlet>
  ...
  <service-ref>
    <service-ref-name>service/MyService</service-ref-name>
    <service-interface>javawebbook.MyService</service-interface>
    <wsdl-file>WEB-INF/wsdl/MyService.wsdl</wsdl-file>
    <jaxrpc-mapping-file>WEB-INF/wsdl/MyService_mapping.xml
    </jaxrpc-mapping-file>
    <service-qname>tns:MyService</service-qname>
  </service-ref>
  ...
</web-app>
```

The service-ref element can also appear in an ejb-jar.xml file as in the following listing.

Listing 8.43 The service-ref Element in an ejb-jar.xml File

```
<?xml version="1.0" encoding="UTF-8"?>
<ejb-jar version="2.1"
         xmlns="http://java.sun.com/xml/ns/j2ee"
         xmlns:xsi="http://www.w3.org/2001/XMLSchema-instance"
         xmlns:tns="http://my-fake-company.com"
```

```
        xsi:schemaLocation="http://java.sun.com/xml/ns/j2ee
            http://java.sun.com/xml/ns/j2ee/ejb-jar_2_1.xsd">
  <enterprise-beans>
    <session>
      <ejb-name>MyEJB</ejb-name>
      ...
      <service-ref>
        <service-ref-name>service/MyService</service-ref-name>
        <service-interface>javawebbook.MyService</service-interface>
        <wsdl-file>META-INF/wsdl/MyService.wsdl</wsdl-file>
        <jaxrpc-mapping-file>META-INF/wsdl/MyService_mapping.xml
        </jaxrpc-mapping-file>
        <service-qname>tns:MyService</service-qname>
      </service-ref>
      ...
    </session>
  </enterprise-beans>
</ejb-jar>
```

The `service-ref-name` of the `service-ref` declares the JNDI ENC lookup name that a J2EE component will use to obtain a reference to an implementation of the JAX-RPC service interface. For example, the following listing demonstrates how a J2EE component would look up the service identified by the `service-ref` element in Listing 8.42 and Listing 8.43.

Listing 8.44 JNDI Lookup of Service Defined by `service-ref`

```
InitialContext jndiContext = new InitialContext();
MyService service = (MyService)
    jndiContext.lookup("java:comp/env/service/MyService");
MySEI stub = service.getMyPort();
float result = stub.getOperation("testParam1", "testParam2");
```

The `service-interface` element defines the fully qualified name of the JAX-RPC service interface class. This is not the same thing as the JAX-RPC service endpoint interface class. The `wsdl-file` element identifies the location of the WSDL file. The `jaxrpc-mapping-file` element identifies the location of the JAX-RPC mapping file. And the `service-qname` identifies the qualified name of the WSDL `service` definition.

8.5 Universal Description, Discovery, and Integration (UDDI)

UDDI is a specification for a registry service that enables the discovery of business profiles and the services they provide. Implementations of the UDDI specification are called *UDDI registries*.

Essentially a UDDI registry is like an electronic phone book for businesses that provide Web services. A UDDI registry catalogs organizations and their Web services so that prospective customers and/or partners can easily find their information.

A UDDI registry is accessed with SOAP messages, so a UDDI registry is really just a Web service. The UDDI specification includes WSDL descriptions of the UDDI Web service, which you can use to formulate SOAP messages for publishing information to a UDDI registry or searching a UDDI registry for organizations or specific kinds of Web services. Up to this point, we have discussed XML, SOAP, and WSDL. XML is the underlying technology for all Web service technologies that enables platform independence. SOAP is the message exchange standard for Web services. WSDL provides a standard for describing a Web service so that you know how to interact with it. UDDI is the last piece of the Web services puzzle that enables the publication and discovery of Web service descriptions. Of course, UDDI is just one implementation of a service broker, but it is the most widely used today.

The first version of UDDI was developed jointly by IBM, Microsoft, and Ariba and published in September 2000. Later, they formed UDDI.org and invited other companies to participate. In 2002, UDDI.org turned over management of the UDDI specifications to the Organization for the Advancement of Structured Information Standards (OASIS). The official Web site for UDDI is `http://www.uddi.org`. Currently, three versions of UDDI have been published—1.0, 2.0, and 3.0. Since UDDI version 2.0 is the only one supported by J2EE version 1.4 and sanctioned by the WS-I BP versions 1.0 and 1.1, that is what we cover in this chapter.

Two primary types of UDDI registries are used, *public* and *private*. A private UDDI registry is operated by a single organization or a group of collaborating organizations. They are typically located on large corporate intranets with security controls to protect the integrity of the registry data and to prevent access from unauthorized users. Both public and private UDDI registries often have more than one site hosting a UDDI registry. Each of these sites is referred to as a *node*. Nodes typically collaborate to replicate the same information. If you publish information with one of the nodes, you can expect it to be shared with the other nodes, which allows organizations to perform searches on any one of the nodes and find the same information.

Public UDDI registries are freely available for anyone to publish and query over the Internet. There is a massive public UDDI registry called the UDDI Business Registry (UBR) that is jointly hosted by IBM, Microsoft, SAP, and NTT. Each of these companies has their own operator nodes that replicate their data with the others. You can search the registry from any of the sites, but you can only modify registry data from the same operator node through which you originally published. These registries are free for the public to search and provide graphical HTML-based interfaces for you to use. You can even publish for free once you have registered and received a user ID and password. The concept of public registries hasn't really taken off like the developers of UDDI.org had hoped, mostly because organizations have security concerns. As a result, most UDDI registries are private. The Web sites for the four UBR nodes are listed at `http://www.uddi.org/find.html`.

8.5.1 UDDI Data Structures

The UDDI specification defines five data structures, which are XML elements that are used to manage the information in a registry. When you query a UDDI registry, these data structures are what you receive, packaged in a SOAP message. You also submit these data structures, within a SOAP message, to a UDDI registry when you wish to publish information to the registry. The five data structures are listed and briefly described below.

- **`businessEntity`** encapsulates a business's general information such as its name, address, and contact information. The `businessEntity` XML element may contain one or more `businessService` elements.
- **`businessService`** describes a service provided by the business. This service does not have to be a WSDL-based Web service. UDDI was designed to categorize any type of service provided by an organization. A single `businessService` structure can be used by multiple `businessEntity` structures. The `businessService` XML element may contain one or more `bindingTemplate` elements.
- **`bindingTemplate`** provides the technical description of a service, including the service's URL, and how to bind to the Web service, which is encapsulated by `tModel` elements. A `bindingTemplate` structure may contain references to one or more `tModel` structures.
- **`tModel`** is used to define the technical specification for a service. For WSDL-based Web services, the `tModel` structure provides a link to a Web site where the WSDL document can be downloaded. Note that UDDI registries do not actually contain WSDL documents; they

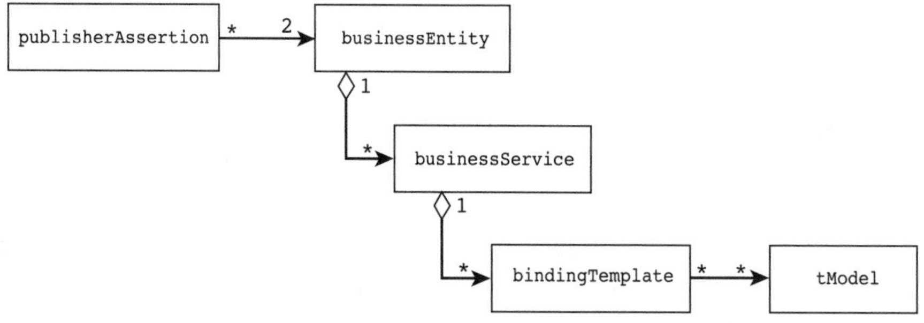

Figure 8.6

Primary UDDI Data Structures

only provide links to them. The tModel structure is also used to describe the categorization systems that identify a business, such as US federal tax ID numbers. Therefore, a tModel structure represents a specific kind of technology, such as SOAP or WSDL, so that you can determine how to invoke a particular Web service, or it represents a type of categorization system so that businesses can be classified, which makes it easier to search for them.

- **publisherAssertion** represents a relationship between two business entities.

Figure 8.6 illustrates the relationship between these five primary data structures.

Four out of five of the primary data structures (businessEntity, businessService, bindingTemplate, and tModel) are identified and referenced by a 128-bit hexadecimal-encoded number called the Universally Unique Identifier (UUID). The UDDI registry generates each UUID when the data structure is added to the registry. It is globally unique so there are no duplicates, not even in other registries. The UDDI attributes and elements that store the UUID are all named xxxKey, where "xxx" is something descriptive of what the key is referencing. Examples are businessKey, serviceKey, bindingKey, and tModelKey. The tModelKey attribute of the tModel element takes a different form than all other keys. It prefixes the UUID with the value "uuid:" so that the key is made a valid URI. The following three listings give examples of the XML for the five primary UDDI data structures for an imaginary lumber company. The UUIDs in bold are the keys that are used to associate the three listings (businessEntity, tModel, and publisherAssertion).

Listing 8.45 UDDI businessEntity, businessService, and bindingTemplate

```
<businessEntity businessKey="BA744ED0-3AAF-11D5-80DC-002035229C64"
                xmlns="urn:uddi-org:api_v2">
  <discoveryURLs>
    <discoveryURL useType="businessEntity">
      http://www.ibm.com/services/uddi/uddiget?businessKey=
      BA744ED0-3AAF-11D5-80DC-002035229C64
    </discoveryURL>
  </discoveryURLs>
  <name>LumberCompany</name>
  <description xml:lang="en">Lumber wholesalers</description>
  <contacts>
    <contact useType="Sales Information">
      <personName>Richard Allen</personName>
      <phone useType="Main Office">1.555.555.5555</phone>
      <email useType="Sales Information">ra@lumbercompany.com</email>
      <address useType="Main Office" sortCode="30332">
        <addressLine>1 Peachtree Street</addressLine>
        <addressLine>Atlanta, GA 30332</addressLine>
```

```
      <addressLine>USA</addressLine>
    </address>
  </contact>
</contacts>
<businessServices>
  <businessService serviceKey="D5921160-3E16-11D5-98BF-002035229C64"
                   businessKey="BA744ED0-3AAF-11D5-80DC-002035229C64">
    <name>Purchase Order Submission</name>
    <description xml:lang="en">Purchase order service</description>
    <bindingTemplates>
      <bindingTemplate bindingKey="D594A970-3E16-11D5-98BF-002035229C64"
                       serviceKey="D5921160-3E16-11D5-98BF-002035229C64">
        <description xml:lang="en">SOAP based service.</description>
        <accessPoint URLType="http">
          http://lumbercompany.com/services/PO
        </accessPoint>
        <tModelInstanceDetails>
          <tModelInstanceInfo
            tModelKey="uuid:0E727DB0-3E14-11D5-98BF-002035229C64">
            <description>
              Reference to tModel service interface definition
            </description>
          </tModelInstanceInfo>
        </tModelInstanceDetails>
      </bindingTemplate>
    </bindingTemplates>
  </businessService>
</businessServices>
<identifierBag>
  <!— D-U-N-S Number Identifier System —>
  <keyedReference keyName="D-U-N-S"
                  keyValue="55-555-5555"
      tModelKey="uuid:8609C81E-EE1F-4D5A-B202-3EB13AD01823"/>
</identifierBag>
<categoryBag>
  <!— North American Industry Classification System (NAICS) 1997 —>
  <keyedReference keyName="Lumber wholesales"
                  keyValue="421310"
      tModelKey="uuid:C0B9FE13-179F-413D-8A5B-5004DB8E5BB2"/>
  <!— Universal Standard Products and Services Classification (UNSPSC)
       version 6.3 —>
  <keyedReference keyName="Framing lumber"
                  keyValue="30.10.36.03"
```

```
        tModelKey="uuid:CD153256-086A-4236-B336-6BDCBDCC6634"/>
    <!— ISO 3166 Geography Taxonomy —>
    <keyedReference keyName="Georgia, USA"
                    keyValue="US-GA"
        tModelKey="uuid:4E49A8D6-D5A2-4FC2-93A0-0411D8D19E88"/>
  </categoryBag>
</businessEntity>
```

Notice that Listing 8.45 defines a purchase order service for the lumber company. The `businessEntity` contains contact and classification information on the business. It contains the URL where the purchase order Web service can be invoked (`accessPoint` element), which must be the same as the address defined by the `port` element of the WSDL `service` definition. The `businessEntity` also contains a reference to the `tModel` that is defined in the following listing. This `tModel` identifies the URL where the WSDL document can be obtained.

Listing 8.46 UDDI `tModel`

```
<tModel tModelKey="uuid:0E727DB0-3E14-11D5-98BF-002035229C64">
  <name>Purchase order service</name>
  <description xml:lang="en">
    Service interface definition for purchase order service.
  </descrition>
  <overviewDoc>
    <description xml:lang="en">
      Reference to the WSDL document for the purchase order service.
    </description>
    <overviewURL>
      http://lumbercompany.com/services/PurchaseOrder.wsdl
      #xmlns(wsdl=http://schemas.xmlsoap.org/wsdl/)
      xpointer(/wsdl:definitions/wsdl:portType{[@]name="SoapRpcLitBinding"]
    </overviewURL>
  </overviewDoc>
  <identifierBag>
    <keyedReference keyName="D-U-N-S"
                    keyValue="55-555-5555"
        tModelKey="uuid:8609C81E-EE1F-4D5A-B202-3EB13AD01823"/>
  </identifierBag>
  <categoryBag>
    <keyedReference keyName="uddi-org:types"
                    keyValue="soapSpec"
        tModelKey="uuid:C1ACF26D-9672-4404-9D70-39B756E62AB4"/>
    <keyedReference keyName="uddi-org:types"
```

```
                  keyValue="wsdlSpec"
        tModelKey="uuid:C1ACF26D-9672-4404-9D70-39B756E62AB4"/>
    <keyedReference keyName="Lumber wholesales"
                  keyValue="421310"
        tModelKey="uuid:C0B9FE13-179F-413D-8A5B-5004DB8E5BB2"/>
    <keyedReference keyName="Framing lumber"
                  keyValue="30.10.36.03"
        tModelKey="uuid:CD153256-086A-4236-B336-6BDCBDCC6634"/>
  <categoryBag>
</tModel>
```

The `tModel` of Listing 8.46 identifies the network location of the purchase order service WSDL document (`overviewURL` element). The `overviewURL` must identify the WSDL `binding` that corresponds to the Web service. The `overviewURL` uses XPointer to identify the WSDL `binding` in the WSDL document. XPointer (`http://www.w3.org/TR/xptr/`) is beyond the scope of this book; just realize that the content inside the `overviewURL` element of Listing 8.46 identifies the WSDL `binding` with the name of "`SoapRpcLitBinding`." To modify the content for your own use, replace the URL to the WSDL document with your URL and the name of the `binding` with your `binding` element's name (the italicized text of Listing 8.46). The `tModel` also references UDDI's standard `tModel` for indicating the use of WSDL (`keyValue="wsdlSpec"`) and SOAP (`keyValue="soapSpec"`). Since this `tModel` (`uddi-org:types`) is standard it has a standard `tModelKey`, `uuid:C1ACF26D-9672-4404-9D70-39B756E62AB4`. The WS-I BP mandates that all `tModels` that are used to identify a WSDL document must reference the `uddi-org:types` `tModel` with a `keyValue` of "`wsdlSpec`," as in Listing 8.46.

An organization that finds this lumber company in the UDDI registry will be able to download the WSDL document and create a client that can invoke the purchase order service. The following `publisherAssertion` defines a relationship to a subsidiary business of the lumber company defined in Listing 8.45. Notice that the `fromKey` element contains the `businessKey` from Listing 8.45.

Listing 8.47 UDDI `publisherAssertion`

```
<publisherAssertion>
  <!— References a businessKey from one organization. —>
  <fromKey>BA744ED0-3AAF-11D5-80DC-002035229C64</fromKey>
  <!— References a businessKey from another organization. —>
  <toKey>RT453243-182W-6290-A345-8IFC8ICC63EF</toKey>
  <!— Defines the relationship between the organizations. —>
  <keyedReference keyName="subsidiary"
                  keyValue="parent-child"
      tModelKey="uuid:1DB53246-183B-6276-A325-8IFCBDCC66UV"/>
</publisherAssertion>
```

8.5.2 Categorization and Identification

One of the main purposes of a UDDI registry is to categorize business profiles and the services they offer. Without categorization, it would be difficult to find a particular type of business or service. You would have to query the UDDI registry and then review all the results to find what you needed. Imagine if phone books did not categorize the businesses in the yellow pages or order the white pages in alphabetical order. Such a phone book would be almost useless because of the time it would take to find what you needed.

The words *categorization* and *classification* are sometimes used interchangeably when discussing UDDI. However, the best way to view categorization is as the process of creating categories, whereas classification can be viewed as the process of distributing items into categories. The UDDI specification requires implementations to support three industry-standard classification systems (also called taxonomies). The systems are described below:

- **North American Industry Classification System (NAICS)**

  This is the most elaborate and comprehensive industry classification scheme. It classifies business by industry across Canada, Mexico, and the United States (members of the North American Free Trade Agreement). There are currently two versions, NAICS 1997 and NAICS 2002. UDDI version 2.0 registries are only required to support NAICS 1997. The Web site for NAICS is `http://www.census.gov/epcd/www/naics.html`.

- **Universal Standard Products and Services Classification (UNSPSC)**

  This was the first industry classification scheme defined for electronic businesses. It is an open source standard that was created by the United Nations and is maintained by volunteer organizations. The Web site for UNSPSC is `http://www.unspsc.org`. You can browse the categories at `http://eccma.org/unspsc`.

- **ISO 3166**

  The scheme categorizes businesses by country and region (city, state, province, etc.), in other words, by geography. The International Organization for Standardization (ISO) first developed this scheme in 1974. Further information can be found at `http://www.iso.org/-iso/en/prods-services/iso3166ma/index.html`.

UDDI also provides support for specifying identification information. The UDDI specification requires UDDI registries to support several identification systems, including two common industry standards, the D-U-N-S Number Identification System (`http://www.dnb.com`) and the Thomas Register Supplier Identifier Code System (`http://www.thomasnet.com`). Dun & Bradstreet, a company that keeps track of the credit histories of many companies, created D-U-N-S, which has become a de facto identification system. Thomas Register is an online registry for products produced by companies in the United States and Canada. UDDI provides the following two XML elements for specifying identification and categorization information.

- **identifierBag** is an optional element that may contain one or more references (keyedReference element) to identifiers that are part of an identification scheme such as D-U-N-S or Thomas Register.
- **categoryBag** is an optional element that may contain one or more references (keyedReference element) to categories that are part of a categorization system such as NAICS or UNSPSC.

Example uses of the identifierBag and categoryBag elements were given in Listing 8.45. UDDI provides standard tModels for the previously mentioned categorization and identification systems. These tModels are summarized in Table 8.2.

Table 8.2 UDDI Standard tModels for Categorization and Identification

Name	tModel Name	tModel Key
NAICS	ntis-gov:naics:1997	uuid:C0B9FE13-179F-413D-8A5B-5004DB8E5BB2
UNSPSC	unspsc-org:unspsc	uuid:CD153256-086A-4236-B336-6BDCBDCC6634
ISO 3166	uddi-org:iso-ch:3166-1999	uuid:4E49A8D6-D5A2-4FC2-93A0-0411D8D19E88
D-U-N-S	dnb-com:D-U-N-S	uuid:8609C81E-EE1F-4D5A-B202-3EB13AD01823
Thomas Register	thomasregister-com:supplierID	uuid:B1B1BAF5-2329-43E6-AE13-BA8E97195039

8.5.3 UDDI Inquiry API

The UDDI inquiry API is used to query a UDDI registry for information about a business. It provides a standard method for clients to search the contents of the registry for specific businesses, types of businesses, or services. You manually perform a similar function when you look through a phone book for a business that offers a specific type of service, such as automobile repair. The UDDI inquiry API defines a set of SOAP-based Document/Literal-style Web service operations with associated XML elements. The XML elements are transmitted to the UDDI Web service in the body of a SOAP request message. In response, the UDDI Web service transmits a SOAP response message with some combination of the previously discussed data structure elements (businessEntity, businessService, etc.) in the body. The UDDI inquiry API is divided into *find operations* and *get operations*. The find operations are for searching the registry, and the get operations are used when you already know the UUID for the data structure you want returned. The following list briefly describes the XML elements that are passed to the UDDI Web service in order to invoke a find operation.

- **find_business** finds matching businessEntity entries. Given a set of criteria (categories specified with a categoryBag element, identifiers specified with an identifierBag element, tModels, or discoverURLs), the find_business operation will return a list of businessInfo XML elements. The businessInfo elements will contain information from the businessEntity, in particular the businessKey.
- **find_relatedBusiness** finds matching publisherAssertion entries. Given a specified businessKey, this operation will return a list of relatedBusinessInfo elements for businesses that have a visible relationship with the specified organization. The relatedBusinessInfo elements will contain information from the businessEntity, in particular the businessKey. Relationships are only visible when both parties have submitted a publisherAssertion. If only one party has submitted a publisherAssertion, claiming a relationship with another organization, that relationship is not visible to queries until the second party also submits the publisherAssertion.
- **find_service** finds matching businessService entries. Given a set of criteria that may include categories and tModel keys, this operation will return a list of businessServiceInfo elements. The businessServiceInfo elements will contain information from the businessService, in particular the serviceKey and the businessKey.
- **find_binding** finds matching bindingTemplate entries. Given a set of tModel keys, this operation will return a list of tModelInstanceInfo elements. The tModelInstanceInfo elements will contain information from the bindingTemplate, in particular the tModelKey.
- **find_tModel** finds match tModel entries. Given a set of tModel names, identifiers, or categories, this operation will return a list of tModelInfo elements. The tModelInfo elements will contain information from the tModel, in particular the tModelKey.

Note that the find operations will only return a subset of the fully published information. To get the fully published information you have to turn around and perform a get operation with the found UUID (key). The following list briefly describes the XML elements that are passed to the UDDI Web service in order to invoke a get operation.

- **get_businessDetail** gets businessEntity entries. Given one or more businessKeys, this operation will return one or more businessEntity data structures.
- **get_businessDetailExt** gets businessEntityExt entries. Given one or more businessKeys, this operation will return one or more businessEntityExt data structures.
- **get_serviceDetail** gets businessService entries. Given one or more serviceKeys, this operation will return one or more businessService data structures.

- **get_bindingDetail** gets bindingTemplate entries. Given one or more bindingKeys, this operation will return one or more bindingTemplate data structures.
- **get_tModelDetail** gets tModel entries. Given one or more tModelKeys, this operation will return one or more tModel data structures.

The following two listings give example SOAP messages for the find and get operations, respectively.

Listing 8.48 Example find_business Operation SOAP Message

```
<?xml version="1.0" encoding="UTF-8"?>
<Envelope xmlns="http://schemas.xmlsoap.org/soap/envelope/">
  <Body>
    <find_business generic="2.0" xmlns="urn:uddi-org:api_v2">
      <findQualifiers>
        <findQualifier>combineCategoryBags<findQualifier>
      </findQualifiers>
      <categoryBag>
        <!– ISO 3166 –>
        <keyedReference keyName="Georgia, USA"
                        keyValue="US-GA"
            tModelKey="uuid:4E49A8D6-D5A2-4FC2-93A0-0411D8D19E88"/>
        <!– NAICS –>
        <keyedReference keyName="Lumber wholesales"
                        keyValue="421310"
            tModelKey="uuid:C0B9FE13-179F-413D-8A5B-5004DB8E5BB2"/>
      </categoryBag>
    </find_business>
  </Body>
</Envelope>
```

Listing 8.48 includes an element we have not yet discussed, findQualifiers. This element allows you to specify one or more findQualifier elements that are used to modify the default matching behavior for a find operation as well as the default sort order for the returned results. The find qualifier combineCategoryBags used in Listing 8.48 tells the find operation to match the specified categoryBag elements with categoryBag entries found at all levels in the businessEntity, inside the businessEntity element as well as inside the businessService element. The other find qualifiers are exactNameMatch, caseSensitiveMatch, sortByNameAsc, sortByNameDesc, sortByDateAsc, sortByDateDesc, orLikeKeys, orAllKeys, andAllKeys, and serviceSubset.

Listing 8.49 Example get_businessDetail Operation SOAP Message

```
<?xml version="1.0" encoding="UTF-8"?>
<Envelope xmlns="http://schemas.xmlsoap.org/soap/envelope/">
```

```
  <Body>
    <get_businessDetail generic="2.0" xmlns="urn:uddi-org:api_v2">
      <businessKey>BA744ED0-3AAF-11D5-80DC-002035229C64
      </businessKey>
    </get_businessDetail>
  </Body>
</Envelope>
```

8.5.3 UDDI Publication API

The UDDI publication API is used to add, update, or delete `businessEntity`, `businessService`, `bindingTemplate`, `tModel`, and `publisherAssertion` entries in a UDDI registry. Unlike the inquiry API, the publication API requires the use of HTTPS (HTTP with Secure Sockets Layer, version 3.0) and authentication. Before you can perform publication operations, you must first execute the `get_authToken` operation, passing it a user ID and password. The `get_authToken` operation will return an authorization token that must be passed back to the UDDI registry with each successive publication operation call that is part of that session. The XML element for the `get_authToken` operation looks like the following.

Listing 8.50 Example `get_authToken` Operation Call

```
<get_authToken generic="2.0" xmlns="urn:uddi-org:api_v2"
               userID="userid" cred="password"/>
```

Authorization tokens typically expire after some period of inactivity. The UDDI publication API also provides an operation for logging out of a session called `discard_authToken`, which simply contains an element called `authInfo` that contains the authorization token. The `authInfo` element (and the authorization token) is also included with all other operation invocations. The rest of the UDDI publication API operations are divided into *save operations*, *delete operations*, and *get operations*. The save operations are for adding or updating the primary data structures. The delete operations are for removing primary data structures from the registry. The get operations are for viewing `publisherAssertions` and a summary of registered information. The following list briefly describes all of the operations.

- **`save_business`**

  Given one or more `businessEntity` elements, this operation will add or update one or more `businessEntity` data structures in the registry.

- **`save_service`**

  Given one or more `businessService` elements, this operation will add or update one or more `businessService` data structures in the registry.

- **save_binding**

  Given one or more bindingTemplate elements, this operation will add or update one or more bindingTemplate data structures in the registry.

- **save_tModel**

  Given one or more tModel elements, this operation will add or update one or more tModel data structures in the registry.

- **add_publisherAssertions**

  Given one or more publisherAssertion elements, this operation will add one or more publisherAssertion data structures in the registry.

- **set_publisherAssertions**

  Given one or more publisherAssertion elements, this operation will update one or more publisherAssertion data structures in the registry.

- **delete_business**

  Given one or more businessKeys, this operation will delete one or more businessEntity data structures from the registry. This operation will also delete businessServices, bindingTemplates, and publisherAssertions that are explicitly owned by the specified businessEntity, but will not remove referenced tModels.

- **delete_service**

  Given one or more serviceKeys, this operation will delete one or more businessService data structures from the registry. This operation will also delete bindingTemplates that are explicitly owned by the specified businessServices, but will not remove referenced tModels.

- **delete_binding**

  Given one or more bindingKeys, this operation will delete one or more businessTemplate data structures from the registry, but will not remove referenced tModels.

- **delete_tModel**

  Given one or more tModelKeys, this operation will remove one or more tModel data structures from view. This operation will not actually delete a tModel, but will make it invisible to all future find operations; however, it can still be retrieved with a get operation. To permanently remove a tModel from a registry you will have to ask the hosting site.

- **delete_publisherAssertions**

  Given one or more publisherAssertions, this operation will delete them from the registry.

- **`get_assertionStatusReport`**

  This operation will return the status of all `publisherAssertions` that you have made or that have been made with `businessEntitys` that you control. You give the operation a `completionStatus` of either `status:complete`, `status:toKey_incomplete`, or `status:fromKey_incomplete`. Incomplete `publisherAssertions` are those where one of the parties (`toKey` or `fromKey`) has not asserted the relationship.

- **`get_publisherAssertions`**

  This operation returns all `publisherAssertion` entries that you have added to the registry whether they are complete or incomplete. You do not need to submit any information except your authorization token for this operation.

- **`get_registeredInfo`**

  This operation returns a list of `businessInfo` and `tModelInfo` elements for all `businessEntity` and `tModel` data structures that you have added to the registry. You do not need to submit any information except your authorization token for this operation.

As an example, the following listing demonstrates what a `save_business` operation SOAP message might look like.

Listing 8.51 Example `save_business` Operation SOAP Message

```
<?xml version="1.0" encoding="UTF-8"?>
<Envelope xmlns="http://schemas.xmlsoap.org/soap/envelope/">
  <Body>
    <save_business generic="2.0" xmlns="urn:uddi-org:api_v2">
      <authInfo>[authorization key goes here]</authInfo>
      <businessEntity businessKey="BA744ED0-3AAF-11D5-80DC-002035229C64">
        ...
      </businessEntity>
    </save_business>
  </Body>
</Envelope>
```

In all, the UDDI APIs are quite large and we have only touched on them here. For further information, read the UDDI specifications, which can be found at `http://www.uddi.org`. Fortunately you will not have to write the SOAP messages to query or publish to a UDDI registry. The Java API for XML Registries (JAXR) handles that for you.

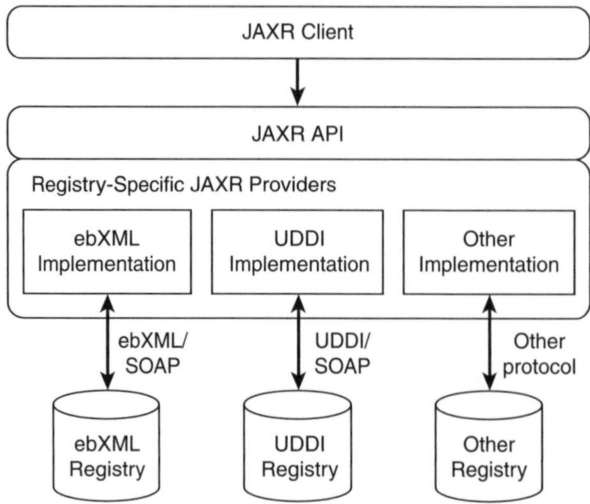

Figure 8.7
JAXR Architecture

8.6 Java API for XML Registries (JAXR)

JAXR (`http://java.sun.com/xml/jaxr`) is an API for accessing various kinds of XML-based registries. It provides a level of abstraction that reduces the complexities involved in communicating with XML-based registries. There can be quite a bit of work involved in forming SOAP messages for UDDI save operations that contain large XML documents such as the `businessEntity`, and then processing these XML documents when they return from UDDI find or get operations. JAXR handles the XML processing for you, allowing the Java developer to work specifically with Java objects.

JAXR standardizes the method by which Java developers communicate with XML registries in a similar fashion to the way JDBC standardizes the method by which Java developers communicate with relational databases. JAXR defines a pluggable architecture where JAXR clients use a generic API that is backed by JAXR providers, which implement the generic API for specific XML registries. Vendors develop an implementation of the JAXR API for their specific registry that you can plug in to use, and you can swap from one implementation to another without changing your code.

The current release of the JAXR specification defines a mapping between the JAXR API and two different XML registries, ebXML and UDDI. The ebXML registry is part of a much larger initiative called "electronic business using eXtensible Markup Language" (`http://www.ebxml.org`), the goal of which is to standardize XML-based communication among organizations to facilitate electronic business over the Internet. An ebXML registry has a much broader capability than a UDDI registry and JAXR is really more in line with ebXML than UDDI. JAXR was designed to encompass the capabilities of a broad range of XML registries so that developers would not be restricted to a limited set of common functionality. The ebXML registry encompasses the capabilities of the UDDI registry and more. The JAXR specification defines two capability profiles for two different levels of functionality: level 0 and level 1. The level 0 capability profile includes a set of Java interfaces that encompass the functionality provided by a UDDI registry. The level 1 capability profile includes a set of Java interfaces that encompass the functionality provided by an ebXML registry. Therefore, the level 1 capability profile provides support for all of the functionality defined by the level 0 capability profile, as well as additional advanced features. Since we are focusing on UDDI, we cover the level 0 capability profile only.

The JAXR packages can be logically divided into the Information Model API (`javax.xml.registry.infomodel`) and the Life Cycle and Query Management API (`javax.xml.registry`). The JAXR Information Model API is largely based on the data structures of ebXML, but includes extensions to support the UDDI data structures. The Life Cycle and Query Management API supports the capability of the UDDI Publication and Inquiry APIs. The primary interfaces of the Life Cycle and Query Management API for the level 0 capability profile are `BusinessLifeCycleManager` and `BusinessQueryManager`. Those for the level 1 capability profile are `LifeCycleManager` and `DeclaritiveQueryManager`. The `BusinessQueryManager` supports the UDDI find and get operations and the `BusinessLifeCycleManager` supports the UDDI save and delete operations. The interfaces of the JAXR Information Model API correspond to the UDDI data structures although their names are different. Table 8.3 lists the primary UDDI data structures and their corresponding JAXR interfaces. The cardinality among these JAXR objects is the same as the cardinality among the UDDI data structures (see Figure 8.6).

Table 8.3 UDDI Data Structures and Corresponding JAXR Interfaces

UDDI Data Structure	JAXR Interface
`businessEntity`	`Organization`
`businessService`	`Service`
`bindingTemplate`	`ServiceBinding`
`tModel`	`Concept`
`publisherAssertion`	`Association`

Some of the other UDDI data structures that we have discussed are represented by the JAXR interfaces that are listed and briefly described below.

- **`SpecificationLink`** is used to associate a `Concept` object (`tModel`) with a `ServiceBinding` object (`bindingTemplate`). In other words, you use this object to associate a WSDL document (really a `tModel` that references your WSDL document) with the service you have registered in UDDI.

- **`Classification`** is used to classify a UDDI data structure. `Classification` represents a UDDI `keyedReference` in a UDDI `categoryBag` (i.e., a reference to a UDDI `tModel` for a specific classification scheme). `Classification` objects refer to `ClassificationScheme` objects.
- **`ClassificationScheme`** represents the UDDI `tModel` for a specific identification or classification scheme (D-U-N-S, NAICS, UNSPSC, etc.).
- **`ExternalIdentifier`** is used to identify a UDDI data structure (typically just `Organization` objects). `ExternalIdentifier` represents a UDDI `keyedReference` in a UDDI `identifierBag` (i.e., a reference to a UDDI `tModel` for a specific identification scheme). `ExternalIdentifier` objects refer to `ClassificationScheme` objects.
- **`ExternalLink`** represents the UDDI `discoveryURL` of a UDDI `businessEntity`. Essentially, the `ExternalLink` is meant to represent a link to information that is managed outside of the registry.

All of the UDDI save and delete operations implemented by the `BusinessLifeCycleManager`, and many of the UDDI find and get operations implemented by the `BusinessQueryManager` return the `BulkResponse` interface. The `BulkResponse` interface is designed to contain a Java `Collection` of the objects returned from an operation. The types returned from an operation depend on which operation was performed. For example, the `BusinessQueryManager.findOrganizations()` method returns a collection of `Organization` objects, while the `BusinessQueryManager.findConcepts()` method returns a collection of `Concept` objects.

The `BulkResponse` interface also serves as an error reporting mechanism. You can call `BulkResponse.getStatus()` to determine if the operation is successful (`JAXRResponse.STATUS_SUCCESS`) or failed (`JAXRResponse.STATUS_FAILURE`). When a method returns a `BulkResponse` interface, that method will return all SOAP faults in the `BulkResponse`. These exceptions can be accessed by calling `BulkResponse.getExceptions()`. However, if the JAXR runtime generates an internal error, the method will throw a `JAXRException`. Methods in JAXR that do not return a `BulkResponse` will throw an exception whether the error was generated by a SOAP fault or the JAXR runtime.

In order to interact with a UDDI registry using JAXR, you must first create a connection to the registry. If you are going to perform any UDDI publication operations you will also need to authenticate to the registry. Use the `javax.xml.registry.ConnectionFactory` class to obtain a `javax.xml.registry.Connection` and call `setCredentials()` on the connection to authenticate. The `ConnectionFactory` is an abstract factory that works the same as the other implementations of the Abstract Factory design pattern that you have seen in this chapter. Have it create an instance of itself and then use that instance to create connections. The following listing illustrates getting a connection to a UDDI registry and authenticating.

Listing 8.52 Connecting and Authenticating to a UDDI Registry

```
import java.net.PasswordAuthentication;
import java.util.*;
import javax.xml.registry.Connection;
import javax.xml.registry.ConnectionFactory;
import javax.xml.registry.JAXRException;

public class JAXRConnectionExample {
  public static void main(String[] args) throws JAXRException {
    String username = args[0];
    String password = args[1];

    // Create an instance of ConnectionFactory.
    ConnectionFactory factory = ConnectionFactory.newInstance();

    Properties props = new Properties();
    // The URL for sending UDDI publication operation request messages.
    props.setProperty("javax.xml.registry.lifeCycleManagerURL",
                      "https://uddi.ibm.com/testregistry/publishapi");
    // The URL for sending UDDI inquiry operation request messages.
    props.setProperty("javax.xml.registry.queryManagerURL",
                      "http://uddi.ibm.com/testregistry/inquiryapi");
    // The method of authentication to be used.
    props.setProperty("javax.xml.registry.security.authenticationMethod",
                      "UDDI_GET_AUTHTOKEN");
    // Set necessary properties on the ConnectionFactory.
    factory.setProperties(props);

    // Connect to the UDDI registry.
    Connection connection = factory.createConnection();

    // Authenticate to the UDDI Web service endpoint for publication.
    PasswordAuthentication credential =
      new PasswordAuthentication(username, password.toCharArray());
    Set credentials = new HashSet();
    credentials.add(credential);
    connection.setCredentials(credentials);

    System.out.println("Connection successful");
    connection.close();
  }
}
```

The JAXR ConnectionFactory requires properties to be set so that it knows what UDDI registry to make a connection with and how you expect to authenticate with the registry. In Listing 8.52 we are connecting to IBM's UBR test registry. Each of the four UBR operators provides test registries where you can run tests against a live UDDI registry. Each UDDI registry publishes a URL for its inquiry Web service and a separate URL for its publication Web service. In Listing 8.52 we set both of the URL properties ("javax.xml.registry.lifeCycleManagerURL" and "javax.xml.registry.queryManagerURL"), but you only have to set the URL for the UDDI API that you are going to use. For example, if you only want to query the UDDI registry, then you would only need to set the inquiry URL and you would not have to authenticate (authentication is only required for the publication API).

Listing 8.52 is a non-J2EE JAXR client. If you are connecting to a UDDI registry from a J2EE component, such as a Servlet or EJB, you are likely to use JNDI ENC to look up the JAXR ConnectionFactory. Exactly how a ConnectionFactory is configured depends on your J2EE vendor (see their documentation), but the following listings illustrate how the configured ConnectionFactory can be listed as a resource in your deployment descriptor and looked up from your J2EE component. Once configured in this fashion, your J2EE container will handle authenticating with the registry every time you get a Connection.

Listing 8.53 Listing a UDDI Registry as a Resource in web.xml

```
<web-app>
  ...
  <resource-ref>
    <res-ref-name>jaxr/SomeUDDIRegistry</res-ref-name>
    <res-type>javax.xml.registry.ConnectionFactory</res-type>
    <res-auth>Container</res-auth>
  </resource-ref>
  ...
</web-app>
```

Listing 8.54 Using JNDI ENC to Look Up a ConnectionFactory

```
InitialContext jndiContext = new InitialContext();
ConnectionFactory factory = (ConnectionFactory)
    jndiContext.lookup("java:comp/env/jaxr/SomeUDDIRegistry");
Connection connection = factory.createConnection();
```

After you have an instance of javax.xml.registry.Connection, use it to get an instance of javax.xml.registry.RegistryService, which represents the UDDI registry. Then use the RegistryService to get an instance of the BusinessLifeCycleManager and the BusinessQueryManager. Once you have an instance of the BusinessLifeCycleManager and the BusinessQueryManager, you can use them to perform UDDI publication and inquiry operations, respectively. The following listing demonstrates the use of these interfaces by adding an `Organization` to a registry with a UDDI save operation, then retrieving the `Organization` with a UDDI get operation, then finding the `Organization` with a UDDI find operation, and finally deleting the `Organization` with a UDDI delete operation.

Listing 8.55 JAXR Example of UDDI Save, Get, Find, and Delete Operations

```
import java.util.*;
import javax.xml.registry.*;
import javax.xml.registry.infomodel.*;

public class JAXRExample throws JAXRException {
  // Assume that getConnection() calls the code in Listing 8.52.
  Connection connection = getConnection(args[0], args[1]);

  // Use Connection to get an instance of RegistryService.
  RegistryService registry = connection.getRegistryService();
  // Use RegistryService to get an instance of BusinessLifeCycleManager.
  BusinessLifeCycleManager lifeCycleManager =
    registry.getBusinessLifeCycleManager();

  // Create an Organization and give it a name.
  String orgName = args[3];
  Organization org = lifeCycleManager.createOrganization(orgName);

  // Add the Organization to the registry by
  // performing a UDDI save operation.
  Set organizations = new HashSet();
  organizations.add(org);
  BulkResponse response =
    lifeCycleManager.saveOrganizations(organizations);

  // Handle any errors.
  handleErrors(response);

  Collection keys = response.getCollection();
  Key newOrgKey = null;
  Iterator iter = keys.iterator();

  if (iter.hasNext()) {
    // Retrieve the UUID of the new businessEntity (Organization).
    newOrgKey = (Key) iter.next();
    System.out.println("save operation successful. Organization UUID="
      + newOrgKey.getId());
```

```
}else {
  System.err.println("No UUID returned from save operation!");
  System.exit(1);
}

// Use RegistryService to get an instance of BusinessQueryManager.
BusinessQueryManager queryManager = registry.getBusinessQueryManager();

// Perform UDDI get operation to retrieve the Organization.
Organization newOrg = queryManager.getRegistryObject(newOrgKey.getId(),
  LifeCycleManager.ORGANIZATION);

if (newOrg == null) {
  System.err.println("get operation failed with new UUID!");
  System.exit(1);
}

// Sorts find results by name ascending. This is actually the default.
Collection qualifiers = new ArrayList();
qualifiers.add(FindQualifier.SORT_BY_NAME_ASC);

// Matches all Organizations with the same name as ours.
String pattern = orgName;
Collection patterns = new ArrayList();
patterns.add(pattern);

// Perform UDDI find operation to retrieve our Organization.
BulkResponse response2 = queryManager.findOrganizations(qualifiers,
  patterns, null, null, null, null);

handleErrors(response2);

Collection orgs = response2.getCollection();
Iterator iterator = orgs.iterator();

if (iterator.hasNext()) {
  // Retrieve the Organization. Of course, several organizations
  // could have been returned if there were other organizations
  // with our name.
  Organization myOrg = (Organization) iterator.next();
  // All strings are encapsulated with InternationalString.
  InternationalString name = org.getName();
```

```
      System.out.println("Find successful. Organization name="
        + name.getValue());
    }else {
      System.err.println("No organization found!");
      System.exit(1);
    }

    // Use the Key Collection returned from save operation to delete.
    lifeCycleManager.deleteOrganizations(keys);
  }

  // Simple method to handle errors returned in a BulkResponse
  public static void handleErrors(BulkResponse response)
    throws JAXRException {

    if (response.getStatus() != JAXRResponse.STATUS_SUCCESS) {
      System.err.println("Failed to save organization!");

      for (Iterator it = response.getExceptions().iterator(); it.next();) {
        ((Exception) it.next()).printStackTrace();
      }

      System.exit(1);
    }
  }
```

Most methods of BusinessLifeCycleManager and BusinessQueryManager use Java Collections to either perform operations on multiple data structures at one time, return multiple results from a single operation, or specify multiple search criteria. Most of the find methods in the BusinessQueryManager interface require Collections in their parameter list. In particular, the findOrganizations() method accepts six different Collections: find qualifiers, name patterns, Classifications, technical specifications (Concepts), ExternalIdentifiers, and ExternalLinks. If the find you are performing does not need a particular Collection, then you can pass the method null for that parameter. The JAXR FindQualifier interface represents the UDDI findQualifier and contains constants that correspond to each of the UDDI find qualifier types. The name patterns passed to the find operation may contain wildcards (i.e., %) that comply with the SQL-92 LIKE specification.

UUID values in JAXR are encapsulated by an instance of the Key interface. Simply call getId() to get a String representation of the UUID. All strings in JAXR are wrapped by InternationalString so as to provide internationalization support. InternationalString associates any string (name, description, etc.) with a Locale so you can determine how it should be displayed to the user (in English, Spanish, Chinese, etc.).

A more comprehensive example of using the JAXR API is given in the labs.

8.7 Examples and Practice Labs

The technologies discussed in this chapter are all specifications, such as SOAP. To do any real development with these technologies, you need a vendor implementation. The J2EE version 1.4 specification requires compliant vendor implementations to include support for all of the technologies that we have discussed in this book, namely: Java Servlets 2.4, JavaServer Pages 2.0, Enterprise Java Beans 2.1, SAAJ 1.2, JAX-RPC 1.1, JAXR 1.0, and consequently SOAP 1.1, WSDL 1.1, and UDDI 2.0. Several open-source or free-to-use implementations of J2EE version 1.4 are available on the Internet, including the Sun Java System Application Server Platform Edition (`http://www.sun.com/software/products/appsrvr_pe/index.xml`), JBoss (`http://www.jboss.org`), JOnAS (`http://jonas. objectweb.org`), and Apache Geronimo (`http://geronimo.apache.org`). A comprehensive list of J2EE application servers, including information on what J2EE APIs they support and how much they cost, can be browsed at `http://www.theserverside.com/reviews/matrix.tss`.

Of course, you can develop Web services in Java without a J2EE application server. The most popular open-source tool for that is Apache Axis (`http://ws.apache.org/axis`). Actually, many J2EE 1.4 application servers use Axis internally to provide Web services support. The first lab in this chapter will use Apache Tomcat (`http://jakarta.apache.org/tomcat/`), Apache Axis, and some of the Java classes that were developed in the labs from the last chapter. If you did not work through the labs of the last chapter, you should do that now. The following labs will assume that you are familiar with the labs from the last chapter and that you have already set up Tomcat, Axis, and your CLASSPATH environment variable.

8.7.1 Lab 1: Java-to-WSDL Example

Before we begin this lab, you should first undeploy and remove classes from Axis that were associated with the labs of the last chapter, just to prevent any conflicts. You will need to create an undeploy Web Service Deployment Descriptor (WSDD) for each of the examples in the last chapter. Then you will need to execute each WSDD against your running Tomcat/Axis instance. Lab 1 from the last chapter discussed how this is done. Essentially, you create a WSDD with the `undeployment` element that names the service you want to undeploy, and then you execute the undeployment from the command line using `org.apache.axis.client.AdminClient`. Once you have undeployed the services, shut down Tomcat/Axis and delete the `javawebbook` directory from the `TOMCAT_HOME/webapps/axis/WEB-INF/classes` directory. Recall from the last chapter that `TOMCAT_HOME` is an environment variable you set that defines the location of your Tomcat installation.

This lab shows how to use Apache Axis to generate a WSDL file from a Java interface for a service (the JAX-RPC service endpoint interface), then deploy that service to Axis, then generate a stub for the service using the WSDL document, and use that stub in a JAX-RPC client to invoke the service. We will deploy the Web service developed in the RPC/Literal lab of the last chapter, which included the following classes: `javawebbook.Monitors`, `javawebbook.CurrencyExchange`, and `javawebbook.rpc.RpcPriceService`. If none of these classes seem familiar, you should probably go back and reread lab 2 of the last chapter.

The first thing we want to do is create our JAX-RPC service endpoint interface (SEI), which is simply a Java interface for our Web service. Recall that a SEI must extend `java.rmi.Remote` and all of its methods must throw `java.rmi.RemoteException`. All we need to do is take the method from `RpcPriceService`, put it in a Java interface that extends `Remote`, and make it throw a `RemoteException`. The resultant interface is given in the listing below.

Listing 8.56 JAX-RPC Service Endpoint Interface for Monitor Pricing Service

```
package javawebbook.rpc;

import java.rmi.Remote;
import java.rmi.RemoteException;

public interface RpcPriceServiceSEI extends Remote {
  public float getMonitorPrice(String productId, String currency)
    throws IllegalArgumentException, RemoteException;
}
```

Create a file from the listing above called `RpcPriceServiceSEI.java` and place it in the `javawebbook/rpc` directory alongside `RpcPriceService.java`. Next, modify `RpcPriceService` to implement `RpcPriceServiceSEI` as illustrated with bold text in the following listing.

Listing 8.57 Monitor Pricing Service Implementation

```
package javawebbook.rpc;

import javawebbook.CurrencyExchange;
import javawebbook.Monitors;

public class RpcPriceService implements RpcPriceServiceSEI {
  public float getMonitorPrice(String productId, String currency)
    throws IllegalArgumentException {

    Float usPrice = (Float) Monitors.data.get(productId);
```

```
    if (usPrice == null) {
      throw new IllegalArgumentException("Unknown product ID: " + productId);
    }

    return CurrencyExchange.convertPrice(usPrice.floatValue(), currency);
  }
}
```

At this point you should have four Java files: `javawebbook/Monitors.java`, `javawebbook/CurrencyExchange.java`, `javawebbook/rpc/RpcPriceService.java`, and `javawebbook/rpc/RpcPriceServiceSEI.java`. These files are your monitor pricing service implementation. To compile these classes, open a command prompt and navigate to the directory *above* the `javawebbook` directory, ensure your CLASSPATH environment variable is set as directed in the labs of the last chapter, and enter the following command.

```
javac -classpath %CLASSPATH%;. javawebbook\CurrencyExchange.java javawebbook\Monitors.java
javawebbook\rpc\RpcPriceService.java javawebbook\rpc\RpcPriceServiceSEI.java
```

Or on a Unix-based operating system change `%CLASSPATH%` to `$CLASSPATH`, "`;`" to "`:`", and "`\`" to "`/`":

```
javac -classpath $CLASSPATH:. javawebbook/CurrencyExchange.java javawebbook/Monitors.java
javawebbook/rpc/RpcPriceService.java javawebbook/rpc/RpcPriceServiceSEI.java
```

Note that the previous commands must be entered on a single line. In fact, all the commands in the labs of this chapter must be entered on a single line. Now that we have the JAX-RPC service endpoint interface, we can generate the WSDL document using the Axis `Java2WSDL` tool. From the same directory that you just entered the `javac` commands above, enter the following `java` command.

```
java -classpath %CLASSPATH%;. org.apache.axis.wsdl.Java2WSDL
-output monitorservice.wsdl
-location "http://localhost:8080/axis/services/RpcPriceService"
-namespace "http://computer-monitors.co/RpcPriceService"
-PkgtoNS "javawebbook.rpc"="http://computermonitors.co/RpcPriceService"
-bindingName RpcPriceServiceSoapBinding
-serviceElementName RpcPriceService
-servicePortName RpcPriceServicePort
-style RPC -use LITERAL javawebbook.rpc.RpcPriceServiceSEI
```

The command above executes the Axis `Java2WSDL` class, passing it the following options:

- `-output`: The name of the WSDL file to generate
- `-location`: The URL where clients will send requests to the Web service
- `-namespace`: The XML namespace to use as the target namespace for the WSDL document
- `-PkgtoNS`: The namespace to associate with the service class Java package

- –bindingName: The name to give the WSDL binding element (optional)
- –serviceElementName: The name to give the WSDL service element (optional)
- –servicePortName: The name to give the WSDL port element (optional)
- –style: The message style
- –use: The encoding style

The command is ended with the fully qualified name of the Java interface that represents the JAX-RPC service endpoint interface, which in our case is javawebbook.rpc.RpcPriceServiceSEI. We specified the names of the WSDL binding, service, and port elements because we did not like the default names that were assigned by Axis. Also, we know the URL for our Web service simply because all Web services deployed to Axis are exposed with the URL http://<host>/axis/services/<service-name>, where <host> is the name of the computer running Axis and <service-name> is the name of your deployed Web service. The exception to this rule is when Web services are deployed via Axis Java Web Service (JWS) files, which are not discussed in this book.

After you execute the command above you should have a file called monitorservice.wsdl that looks similar to the following listing. If the previous command failed for you, verify that you entered it properly and that all of the Axis JAR files are in your CLASSPATH environment variable as discussed in the labs of the last chapter. If you still have problems, try reading the reference documentation for Java2WSDL at http://ws.apache.org/axis/java/reference.html#Java2WSDLReference.

Listing 8.58 RpcPriceService WSDL Document

```
<?xml version="1.0" encoding="UTF-8"?>
<wsdl:definitions
    targetNamespace="http://computermonitors.co/RpcPriceService"
    xmlns:apachesoap="http://xml.apache.org/xml-soap"
    xmlns:impl="http://computermonitors.co/RpcPriceService"
    xmlns:intf="http://computermonitors.co/RpcPriceService"
    xmlns:wsdl="http://schemas.xmlsoap.org/wsdl/"
    xmlns:wsdlsoap="http://schemas.xmlsoap.org/wsdl/soap/"
    xmlns:xsd="http://www.w3.org/2001/XMLSchema">

  <wsdl:message name="getMonitorPriceRequest">
    <wsdl:part name="in0" type="xsd:string"/>
    <wsdl:part name="in1" type="xsd:string"/>
  </wsdl:message>
  <wsdl:message name="getMonitorPriceResponse">
    <wsdl:part name="getMonitorPriceReturn" type="xsd:float"/>
```

```
  </wsdl:message>

  <wsdl:portType name="RpcPriceServiceSEI">
    <wsdl:operation name="getMonitorPrice" parameterOrder="in0 in1">
      <wsdl:input message="impl:getMonitorPriceRequest"
                  name="getMonitorPriceRequest"/>
      <wsdl:output message="impl:getMonitorPriceResponse"
                   name="getMonitorPriceResponse"/>
    </wsdl:operation>
  </wsdl:portType>

  <wsdl:binding name="RpcPriceServiceSoapBinding"
                type="impl:RpcPriceServiceSEI">
    <wsdlsoap:binding style="rpc"
        transport="http://schemas.xmlsoap.org/soap/http"/>
    <wsdl:operation name="getMonitorPrice">
      <wsdlsoap:operation soapAction=""/>
      <wsdl:input name="getMonitorPriceRequest">
        <wsdlsoap:body
            namespace="http://computermonitors.co/RpcPriceService"
            use="literal"/>
      </wsdl:input>
      <wsdl:output name="getMonitorPriceResponse">
        <wsdlsoap:body
            namespace="http://computermonitors.co/RpcPriceService"
            use="literal"/>
      </wsdl:output>
    </wsdl:operation>
  </wsdl:binding>

  <wsdl:service name="RpcPriceService">
    <wsdl:port binding="impl:RpcPriceServiceSoapBinding"
               name="RpcPriceServicePort">
      <wsdlsoap:address
        location="http://localhost:8080/axis/services/RpcPriceService"/>
    </wsdl:port>
  </wsdl:service>
</wsdl:definitions>
```

Now we need to create an Axis WSDD to tell Axis about the Web service that we want to deploy. The WSDD is given in the listing below. Create this file in the directory above the `javawebbook` directory (i.e., alongside `monitorservice.wsdl`) and call it `deploy.wsdd`.

Listing 8.59 WSDD for RpcPriceService

```
<deployment name="RpcPriceService"
    xmlns="http://xml.apache.org/axis/wsdd/"
    xmlns:java="http://xml.apache.org/axis/wsdd/providers/java">
  <service name="RpcPriceService" style="rpc" use="literal">
    <parameter name="className"
               value="javawebbook.rpc.RpcPriceService"/>
    <wsdlFile>/monitorservice.wsdl</wsdlFile>
  </service>
</deployment>
```

Next, copy the `javawebbook` directory and the `monitorservice.wsdl` file to the `TOMCAT_HOME/webapps/axis/WEB-INF/classes` directory. Then, start Tomcat (with Axis deployed) and execute the following command to deploy our Web service:

```
java org.apache.axis.client.AdminClient deploy.wsdd
```

After you run the command above, you should get output on the command line similar to the following:

```
Processing file deploy.wsdd
<Admin>Done processing</Admin>
```

To ensure the Web service has been deployed, enter the following URL in your Web browser: `http://localhost:8080/axis/services`. You should see a listing of the Web services that are deployed on your instance of Axis, and RpcPriceService should appear in the list, as shown in Figure 8.8. If you click on the wsdl link next to the RpcPriceService listing you should get the WSDL document of Listing 8.58.

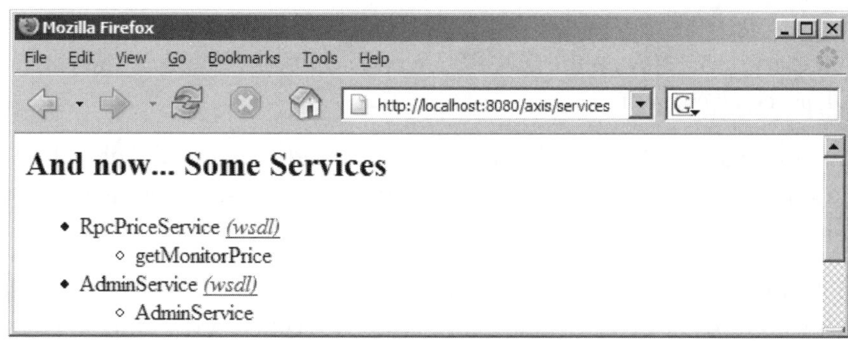

Figure 8.8
Axis Listing Deployed Web Services

If you do not receive a listing of Web services, then Tomcat may not be running or you may not have Axis deployed. You may want to reread the section in the last chapter that discussed how to set up and run both Tomcat and Axis. On the other hand, if you receive a listing of Web services but RpcPriceService is not included in the list, then your deployment probably failed. Make sure that you have copied all of the RpcPriceService-related classes and the WSDL file to the `TOMCAT_HOME/webapps/axis/WEB-INF/classes` directory, and ensure that your WSDD matches the one given above.

Now that we have RpcPriceService deployed, let us create a JAX-RPC client to invoke it. We will use the Axis `WSDLtoJava` class to generate a JAX-RPC stub for our Web service, and then we will write a JAX-RPC client that uses the stub to send a SOAP message to the Web service. To simulate the fact that Web services and their clients are usually separate organizations, we will develop our client in a separate directory from `javawebbook` called `javawebbook-client`. Create the `javawebbook-client` directory, navigate to it from your command prompt, and enter the following command:

```
java –cp %CLASSPATH% org.apache.axis.wsdl.WSDL2Java
–NStoPkg "http://computermonitors.co/RpcPriceService"="javawebbook.rpc"
http://localhost:8080/axis/services/RpcPriceService?wsdl
```

The `–NStoPkg` option tells `WSDL2Java` to put the generated Java classes in the `javawebbook.rpc` package. Therefore, once you have executed the command above, you should have a `javawebbook/rpc` directory below the `javawebbook-client` directory. Within the `javawebbook/rpc` directory, you should have the following four files.

- `RpcPriceService.java` extends the `javax.xml.rpc.Service` interface and corresponds to the WSDL `service` element.
- `RpcPriceServiceLocator.java` is the implementation of `RpcPriceService`. It is used to get the implementation of the JAX-RPC service endpoint interface (`javax.xml.rpc.Stub`) for invoking the Web service.
- `RpcPriceServiceSEI.java` is the JAX-RPC service endpoint interface and corresponds to the WSDL `portType` element.
- `RpcPriceServiceSoapBindingStub.java` is the JAX-RPC generated stub, which implements `javax.xml.rpc.Stub` and also implements `RpcPriceServiceSEI` and acts as a proxy to the actual Web service.

When you look at the files generated by Axis, you will see that they extend Axis classes instead of directly implementing the JAX-RPC interfaces (`javax.xml.rpc.Service` and `javax.xml.rpc.Stub`). These Axis classes implement the JAX-RPC interfaces, so the generated classes implement the JAX-RPC interfaces indirectly. To use the generated classes, create the following listing in the file `javawebbook/rpc/client/Client.java`.

Listing 8.60 JAX-RPC-Generated Stub Client for RpcPriceService

```
package javawebbook.rpc.client;

import java.rmi.RemoteException;
import javawebbook.rpc.RpcPriceService;
import javawebbook.rpc.RpcPriceServiceSEI;
import javax.xml.rpc.ServiceException;
import javax.xml.rpc.ServiceFactory;

public class StaticStubClient {
  public static void main(String[] args)
    throws ServiceException, RemoteException {

    RpcPriceService service = (RpcPriceService)
      ServiceFactory.newInstance().loadService(RpcPriceService.class);
    RpcPriceServiceSEI stub = service.getRpcPriceServicePort();
    float price = stub.getMonitorPrice(args[0], args[1]);
    System.out.println("Price for monitor: " + args[0] + " is $" + price);
  }
}
```

Now compile the generated classes and the client by entering the following command from the `javawebbook-client` directory.

```
javac -classpath %CLASSPATH%;. javawebbook\rpc\RpcPriceService.java
javawebbook\rpc\RpcPriceServiceLocator.java javawebbook\rpc\RpcPriceServiceSEI.java
javawebbook\rpc\RpcPriceServiceSoapBindingStub.java
javawebbook\rpc\client\StaticStubClient.java
```

Finally, run a test by entering the following command.

```
java –cp %CLASSPATH;. Javawebbook.rpc.client.StaticStubClient VP912b USD
```

After the command executes, you should get the following output on the command line.

```
Price for monitor: VP912b is $700.0
```

If you would like to see the SOAP messages transmitted between the client and the Web service, you can set up the Axis TCP Monitor as described in the labs of the last chapter. You will need to modify `RpcPriceServiceLocator.java` so that it sends the SOAP messages to the TCP Monitor instead of directly to the Web service. `RpcPriceServiceLocator.java` contains a line where the URL of the Web service is assigned to a private instance variable (`"http://localhost:8080/axis/services/RpcPriceService"`). Change this line to use the port to which your TCP Monitor is listening, which in my case is 9999 (`"http://localhost:`**`9999`**`/axis/services/RpcPriceService"`). Then recompile `RpcPriceServiceLocator.java`, start the TCP Monitor (if not already running),

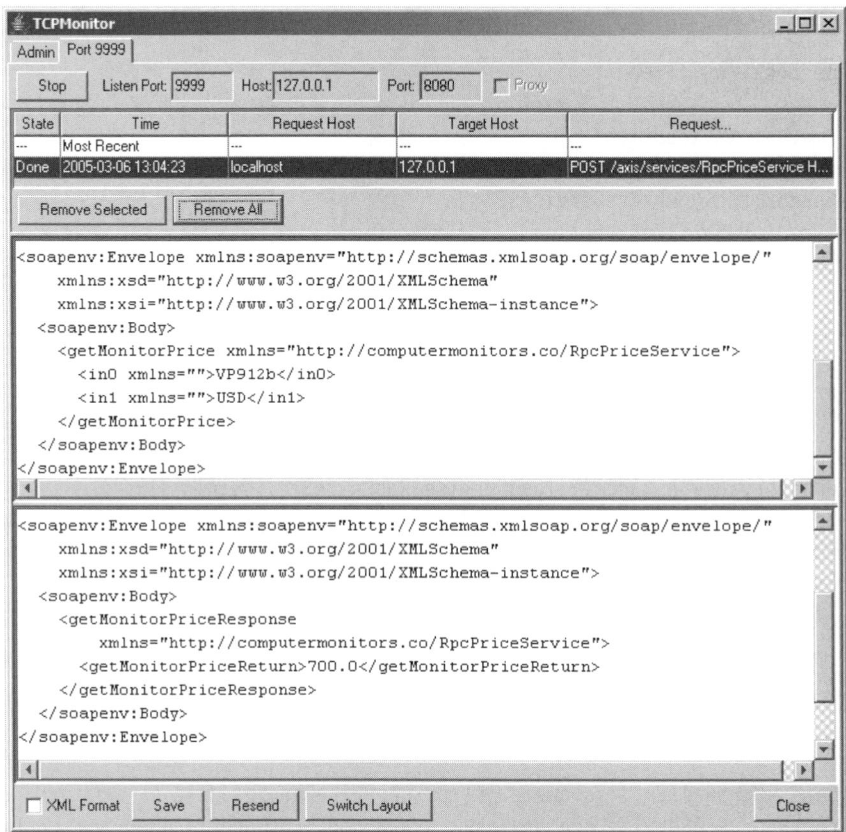

Figure 8.9
TCP Monitor Showing SOAP Messages

and re-execute the client (the command above). You should see output on the TCP Monitor that looks similar to Figure 8.9. For brevity the TCP Monitor window in the figure was resized to eliminate the HTTP headers from the view.

8.7.2 Lab 2: J2EE Example

This lab attempts to provide an example of how developing Web services in Java might be approached in a real-life workplace. However, we will not take all of the steps that a professional organization might. For instance, we will not go through a formal design process, because that would take too long and the focus of this book is not how to formally design a Java-based Web application, but rather how to implement one. Instead, we will create a WSDL document from scratch, publish that WSDL in a UDDI registry, create both types of JAX-RPC service endpoints (Servlet-based and EJB-based) that implement the Web service defined in the WSDL document, publish information on the two Web services in a UDDI registry, and develop various clients to test the Web services. Thus, this lab is fairly involved and could take a while to complete, but does cover several important Web service implementation details.

Installing Sun Java System Application Server Platform Edition 8

Before we begin, there are a few things you will need to download and install. Since this is a J2EE example, the first thing you need is a J2EE application server (Servlet container and EJB container). There are some good open-source J2EE servers available, such as JBoss and JOnAS, but for this lab we chose to use the Sun Java System Application Server Platform Edition 8. While the Platform Edition of the Sun Java System Application Server is not open source, it is free for development, deployment, and distribution. The Sun Java System Application Server Platform Edition 8 (abbreviated as J2EE RI from now on) is Sun's reference implementation of the J2EE 1.4 specifications. We chose the J2EE RI over the open-source options because Sun provides quite a bit of documentation that you can refer to in case you have trouble. The documentation on JBoss and JOnAS is pretty good, but it is not as extensive as the documentation that Sun provides for the J2EE RI. For instance, all of the examples in the well-known J2EE tutorial (`http://java.sun.com/j2ee/1.4/docs/tutorial/doc/`) are written for the J2EE RI. Perform the following steps to download and install the J2EE RI.

1. Download the J2EE RI from `http://java.sun.com/j2ee/1.4/download.html`. You can download the J2EE RI by itself or as one large bundle that also includes the J2SE, J2EE 1.4 examples, and the J2EE API documentation. If you already have the J2SE installed on your computer, you can download the J2EE 1.4 examples and the J2EE API documentation separately if you like. The only thing required for this lab is the J2EE RI, which requires J2SE version 1.4.2 or later to be installed on your computer. If you have performed the previous labs in this book, J2SE should already be installed on your computer. If not, download the latest version of the J2SE from `http://java.sun.com/j2se/downloads/index.html`.

2. Run the J2EE RI executable that you downloaded and follow the directions for installation. Be sure to make the Admin password something you remember, leave the ports as the defaults unless they interfere with something else on your computer, and check the option to add the J2EE RI bin directory to your PATH environment variable. Checking the option to add the bin directory to the PATH environment variable will make it easier for you to manipulate the server from the command line. If you need to know more information about the installation process, read Sun's installation guide at

`http://docs.sun.com/app/docs/doc/819-0080`. This guide provides detailed instructions for installing on Unix/Linux and Windows.

3. When you are done installing the J2EE RI, you should get a link to the quick start guide. This guide is installed on your computer in the location <install_dir>/docs/QuickStart.html (<install_dir> is the directory where you installed the J2EE RI). You should now follow the instructions in the quick start guide to start the server and verify your installation. You can start the server from the command line with the following command:

   ```
   asadmin start-domain domain1
   ```

   If you installed the J2EE RI on the Microsoft Windows operating system, you can start the server from the Start menu with Programs > Sun Microsystems > Application Server PE > Start Admin Server. If you chose to leave the ports as their defaults, then, after starting the server, you should should see the server welcome page when you point your Web browser to the URL `http://localhost:8080`. If you chose a different port for the HTTP server, change 8080 to the port you specified.

4. Finally, create an environment variable called J2EE_RI_HOME that points to the directory where you installed the J2EE RI (<install_dir> in the last step). This environment variable will be used when deploying to the server.

   A listing of additional documentation for the J2EE RI can be found at `http://developers.sun.com/prodtech/appserver/reference/docs/`.

Installing Apache Ant

The other software you need to download is Apache Ant version 1.6 or later (`http://ant.apache.org`). Ant is an open-source Java-based build tool that simplifies building Java projects. You write XML files that describe how your project(s) should be built and the XML build file is platform-independent because Ant is written in Java. Executing javac from the command line to build a large project can be very cumbersome and nearly impossible when projects become large. If you have used Make to build other projects, possibly C or C++ projects, Ant will seem quite familiar to you. For this lab, you really do not have to know Ant, you just need to know how to run the build files that you are instructed to create. That part is very simple and how it is done is discussed later. For now, perform the following instructions to download and install Ant.

1. Download the latest binary distribution of Ant from `http://ant.apache.org/bindownload.cgi`.

2. Unzip or untar (depending on platform) the distribution into the directory where you want Ant installed.

3. Set an ANT_HOME environment variable that points to the root of your Ant installation directory. Also add the bin directory of the installation to your PATH environment variable. If you have any problems, you can read Ant's installation documentation at `http://ant.apache.org/manual/index.html`.

4. Verify that you have installed Ant correctly by opening a new command prompt and entering the following command:

   ```
   ant -help
   ```

   You should receive a description of how the `ant` command must be executed and a list of its options. If not, you may not have added the bin directory of the Ant installation to your PATH environment variable.

Lab Premise

We will base this example around a make-believe real-world scenario in which two different lumber companies want to provide a purchase order Web service that their customers can use to order lumber online. One of the dreams behind Web services is that client applications might one day be able to dynamically look up various Web services and select one or more to invoke based on qualities of service such as price, performance, etc. For example, an online company that builds custom computer systems might be able to dynamically look up the best price on a particular part (such as a motherboard) from various distributors when a customer places an order and then dynamically order that part from the cheapest supplier. This whole process could happen automatically without the company needing to have a predefined partnership with the distributor. This is not how business interactions between companies typically happen in the real world. Usually businesses negotiate predefined relationships before any automated transactions take place, but this is our make-believe example so we will pursue the dream. For automation of this nature to work, you will most likely need to have an industry-wide standard for how transactions in that industry occur. The first thing we must do in this example is create a standard Web service interface description that the two lumber companies will implement.

Creating the WSDL and Domain Model

Our Web service interface will consist of two operations, one to obtain a catalog of the lumber that a company is selling online, and the other to place an order for some lumber from the catalog. The following table summarizes the operations that we will create. We will use the operations defined in the table to construct the WSDL document. The Operation column lists the names of WSDL `operation` elements. The Message Type column defines whether the messages of the `operation` are `input`, `output`, or `fault` elements. The Message column lists the name of the WSDL `message` elements used in the operations. The Part column lists the WSDL `part` element of the `message` that is used in the `operation`. The Type column lists the data types that are referenced by the `part` elements. In other words, the Type column lists the data that is actually transmitted with the SOAP messages.

Table 8.4 Lumber Web Service Operations

operation	Message Type	message	part	Data Type
getCatalog	input	getCatalogRequest		
	output	getCatalogResponse	productCatalog	ProductCatalog
placeOrder	input	placeOrderRequest	purchaseOrder	PurchaseOrder
	output	placeOrderResponse	shippingNotice	ShippingNotice
	fault	InvalidPurchaseOrderFault	InvalidPurchaseOrder	InvalidPurchaseOrder

One can easily look at Table 8.4 and visualize how our Web service interface definition can be written in WSDL, however, there is some significant information missing—a description of our data types. None of the data types listed in Table 8.4 are XML Schema built-in types and we will need to define them ourselves. The following listings define XML schemas for all of our types. The first listing is `ProductCatalog.xsd`, which defines the `ProductCatalog` type along with an associated `Product` type.

Listing 8.61 lab2/schemas/war/ProductCatalog.xsd

```
<?xml version="1.0" encoding="UTF-8"?>
<schema xmlns="http://www.w3.org/2001/XMLSchema"
  xmlns:tns="http://lumber.org/ws/standards/schemas/ProductCatalog.xsd"
  xmlns:misc="http://lumber.org/ws/standards/schemas/Types.xsd"
  targetNamespace="http://lumber.org/ws/standards/schemas/ProductCatalog.xsd"
  elementFormDefault="qualified">

  <import namespace="http://lumber.org/ws/standards/schemas/Types.xsd"
          schemaLocation="Types.xsd" />

  <annotation>
    <documentation xml:lang="en">
      Definition of ProductCatalog type.
    </documentation>
  </annotation>
```

```
  <complexType name="ProductCatalog">
    <sequence>
      <element name="effectiveStartDate" type="dateTime" />
      <element name="effectiveEndDate" type="dateTime" />
      <element name="products" type="tns:Product" maxOccurs="unbounded" />
    </sequence>
  </complexType>

  <complexType name="Product">
    <sequence>
      <element name="productNumber" type="misc:ProductNumber" />
      <element name="name" type="string" />
      <element name="description" type="string" />
      <element name="price" type="misc:Price" />
    </sequence>
  </complexType>
</schema>
```

ProductCatalog.xsd imports Types.xsd, which defines some miscellaneous types including the ProductNumber and Price types that are referenced by ProductCatalog.

Listing 8.62 lab2/schemas/war/Types.xsd

```
<?xml version="1.0" encoding="UTF-8"?>
<schema xmlns="http://www.w3.org/2001/XMLSchema"
    xmlns:tns="http://lumber.org/ws/standards/schemas/Types.xsd"
    targetNamespace="http://lumber.org/ws/standards/schemas/Types.xsd"
    elementFormDefault="qualified">
  <annotation>
    <documentation xml:lang="en">
      Definition of various reusable types.
    </documentation>
  </annotation>

  <simpleType name="Phone">
    <restriction base="string">
      <pattern value="(?(\d{3})\)[-| ]?(\d{3})[-| ]?(\d{4})"/>
    </restriction>
  </simpleType>

  <simpleType name="Email">
    <restriction base="string">
      <pattern value="(.+)@(.+)"/>
    </restriction>
```

```
  </simpleType>

  <simpleType name="Price">
    <restriction base="float">
      <pattern value="[0-9]+\.[0-9]{2}"/>
    </restriction>
  </simpleType>

  <simpleType name="ProductNumber">
    <restriction base="int">
      <minInclusive value="1" />
      <maxInclusive value="999999" />
    </restriction>
  </simpleType>
</schema>
```

The next listing is `PurchaseOrder.xsd`, which defines the `PurchaseOrder` type along with the associated `LineItem` type and the `ShippingNotice` and `InvalidPurchaseOrder` types.

Listing 8.63 lab2/schemas/war/PurchaseOrder.xsd

```
<?xml version="1.0" encoding="UTF-8"?>
<schema xmlns="http://www.w3.org/2001/XMLSchema"
  xmlns:tns="http://lumber.org/ws/standards/schemas/PurchaseOrder.xsd"
  xmlns:cust="http://lumber.org/ws/standards/schemas/Customer.xsd"
  xmlns:addr="http://lumber.org/ws/standards/schemas/Address.xsd"
  xmlns:misc="http://lumber.org/ws/standards/schemas/Types.xsd"
  targetNamespace="http://lumber.org/ws/standards/schemas/PurchaseOrder.xsd"
  elementFormDefault="qualified">

  <import namespace="http://lumber.org/ws/standards/schemas/Customer.xsd"
          schemaLocation="Customer.xsd" />
  <import namespace="http://lumber.org/ws/standards/schemas/Address.xsd"
          schemaLocation="Address.xsd" />
  <import namespace="http://lumber.org/ws/standards/schemas/Types.xsd"
          schemaLocation="Types.xsd" />

  <annotation>
    <documentation xml:lang="en">
      Definition of PurchaseOrder type.
    </documentation>
  </annotation>

  <complexType name="PurchaseOrder">
    <sequence>
```

```
      <element name="customer" type="cust:Customer" />
      <element name="shippingAddress" type="addr:USAddress" />
      <element name="lineItems" type="tns:LineItem" nillable="false"
               maxOccurs="unbounded" />
      <element name="total" type="misc:Price" />
    </sequence>
    <attribute name="orderDate" type="date" />
  </complexType>

  <complexType name="LineItem">
    <sequence>
      <element name="productNumber" type="misc:ProductNumber" />
      <element name="price" type="misc:Price" />
    </sequence>
    <attribute name="quantity" type="unsignedShort" />
  </complexType>

  <complexType name="ShippingNotice">
    <sequence>
      <element name="purchaseOrder" type="tns:PurchaseOrder" />
      <element name="shipDate" type="date" />
    </sequence>
    <attribute name="orderNumber" type="string" />
  </complexType>

  <element name="InvalidPurchaseOrder"
           type="tns:InvalidPurchaseOrderFault"/>
  <complexType name="InvalidPurchaseOrderFault">
    <sequence>
      <element name="reason" type="string"/>
      <element name="message" type="string" nillable="true"
               minOccurs="0" />
    </sequence>
  </complexType>
</schema>
```

PurchaseOrder.xsd imports Customer.xsd, Address.xsd, and Types.xsd. Types.xsd defines the Price and ProductNumber types that are referenced by PurchaseOrder and LineItem. Customer.xsd, listed next, defines the Customer type that is referenced by PurchaseOrder.

Listing 8.64 lab2/schemas/war/Customer.xsd

```
<?xml version="1.0" encoding="UTF-8"?>
<schema xmlns="http://www.w3.org/2001/XMLSchema"
    xmlns:tns="http://lumber.org/ws/standards/schemas/Customer.xsd"
```

```
    xmlns:addr="http://lumber.org/ws/standards/schemas/Address.xsd"
    xmlns:misc="http://lumber.org/ws/standards/schemas/Types.xsd"
    targetNamespace="http://lumber.org/ws/standards/schemas/Customer.xsd"
    elementFormDefault="qualified">
  <import namespace="http://lumber.org/ws/standards/schemas/Address.xsd"
        schemaLocation="Address.xsd" />
  <import namespace="http://lumber.org/ws/standards/schemas/Types.xsd"
        schemaLocation="Types.xsd" />

  <annotation>
    <documentation xml:lang="en">
      Definition of Customer type.
    </documentation>
  </annotation>

  <complexType name="Customer">
    <sequence>
      <element name="firstName" type="string" minOccurs="0"
               nillable="true" />
      <element name="lastName" type="string" minOccurs="0"
               nillable="true" />
      <element name="company" type="string" />
      <element name="phoneNumber" type="misc:Phone" />
      <element name="emailAddress" type="misc:Email" minOccurs="0"
               nillable="true" />
      <element name="billingAddress" type="addr:Address" />
    </sequence>
  </complexType>
</schema>
```

Finally, `Address.xsd` defines the `USAddress` type that is referenced by the `PurchaseOrder` and `Customer` types, as well as the `Address` type, which the `USAddress` type extends.

Listing 8.65 lab2/schemas/war/Address.xsd

```
<?xml version="1.0" encoding="UTF-8"?>
<schema xmlns="http://www.w3.org/2001/XMLSchema"
    xmlns:tns="http://lumber.org/ws/standards/schemas/Address.xsd"
    targetNamespace="http://lumber.org/ws/standards/schemas/Address.xsd"
    elementFormDefault="qualified">
  <annotation>
    <documentation xml:lang="en">
      Definition of address types.
    </documentation>
  </annotation>
```

```
  <complexType name="Address">
    <sequence>
      <element name="street" type="string"/>
      <element name="city" type="string"/>
    </sequence>
  </complexType>

  <complexType name="USAddress">
    <complexContent>
      <extension base="tns:Address">
        <sequence>
          <element name="state" type="string"/>
          <element name="zip" type="tns:USPostalCode"/>
        </sequence>
      </extension>
    </complexContent>
  </complexType>

  <simpleType name="USPostalCode">
    <restriction base="string">
      <pattern value="[0-9]{5}(-[0-9]{4})?"/>
    </restriction>
  </simpleType>
</schema>
```

It is good practice to define different types in their own XML Schema files so that they can be reused in other schemas. For example, the types defined in `Types.xsd` are imported into `ProductCatalog.xsd`, `PurchaseOrder.xsd`, and `Customer.xsd`. Before we go further, transfer the previous XML schemas to files and put the files in the directory `lab2/schemas/war`. The names of the files should be the exact names given in the listing headings, i.e., `ProductCatalog.xsd`, `PurchaseOrder.xsd`, etc. We will eventually deploy these files in a WAR to the J2EE RI so that they can be accessed via a URL.

As a whole, the data types defined in the XML schemas listed above are commonly referred to as a domain model. These data types form the model for our problem domain. Now that we have the data types defined we can write an industry-standard WSDL document for the lumber purchase order Web service. The WSDL listing is given below.

Listing 8.66 lab2/schemas/war/LumberWholesaler.wsdl

```
<?xml version="1.0" encoding="UTF-8"?>
<definitions xmlns="http://schemas.xmlsoap.org/wsdl/"
  xmlns:xsd="http://www.w3.org/2001/XMLSchema"
  xmlns:soapbind="http://schemas.xmlsoap.org/wsdl/soap/"
  xmlns:tns="http://lumber.org/ws/standards/wsdl/LumberWholesaler.wsdl"
```

```
xmlns:pc="http://lumber.org/ws/standards/schemas/ProductCatalog.xsd"
xmlns:po="http://lumber.org/ws/standards/schemas/PurchaseOrder.xsd"
xmlns:wsi="http://ws-i.org/schemas/conformanceClaim/"
targetNamespace="http://lumber.org/ws/standards/wsdl/LumberWholesaler.wsdl"
name="LumberWholesalerService">

<types>
  <xsd:schema>
    <xsd:import
      namespace="http://lumber.org/ws/standards/schemas/ProductCatalog.xsd"
      schemaLocation="ProductCatalog.xsd"/>
    <xsd:import
      namespace="http://lumber.org/ws/standards/schemas/PurchaseOrder.xsd"
      schemaLocation="PurchaseOrder.xsd"/>
  </xsd:schema>
</types>

<message name="getCatalogRequest" />
<message name="getCatalogResponse">
  <part name="productCatalog" type="pc:ProductCatalog" />
</message>
<message name="placeOrderRequest">
  <part name="purchaseOrder" type="po:PurchaseOrder" />
</message>
<message name="placeOrderResponse">
  <part name="shippingNotice" type="po:ShippingNotice" />
</message>
<message name="InvalidPurchaseOrderFault">
  <part name="InvalidPurchaseOrder" element="po:InvalidPurchaseOrder"/>
</message>

<portType name="PurchaseOrderPortType">
  <operation name="getCatalog">
    <documentation>Returns a product catalog</documentation>
    <input message="tns:getCatalogRequest" />
    <output name="productCatalog" message="tns:getCatalogResponse"/>
  </operation>
  <operation name="placeOrder">
    <documentation>
      Accepts an order for quantities of multiple products
    </documentation>
    <input name="purchaseOrder" message="tns:placeOrderRequest"/>
    <output name="shippingNotice" message="tns:placeOrderResponse"/>
    <fault name="InvalidPurchaseOrderFault"
```

```
          message="tns:InvalidPurchaseOrderFault"/>
    </operation>
  </portType>

  <binding name="SoapRpcLitBinding" type="tns:PurchaseOrderPortType">
    <documentation>
      <wsi:Claim conformsTo="http://ws-i.org/profiles/basic1.0/"/>
    </documentation>
    <soapbind:binding style="rpc"
        transport="http://schemas.xmlsoap.org/soap/http"/>
    <operation name="getCatalog">
      <soapbind:operation soapAction="" style="rpc"/>
      <input>
        <soapbind:body use="literal"
  namespace="http://lumber.org/ws/standards/wsdl/LumberWholesaler.wsdl"/>
      </input>
      <output>
        <soapbind:body use="literal"
  namespace="http://lumber.org/ws/standards/wsdl/LumberWholesaler.wsdl"/>
      </output>
    </operation>
    <operation name="placeOrder">
      <soapbind:operation soapAction="" style="rpc"/>
      <input>
        <soapbind:body use="literal"
  namespace="http://lumber.org/ws/standards/wsdl/LumberWholesaler.wsdl"/>
      </input>
      <output>
        <soapbind:body use="literal"
  namespace="http://lumber.org/ws/standards/wsdl/LumberWholesaler.wsdl"/>
      </output>
      <fault name="InvalidPurchaseOrderFault">
        <soapbind:fault name="InvalidPurchaseOrderFault" use="literal"/>
      </fault>
    </operation>
  </binding>
</definitions>
```

`LumberWholesaler.wsdl` does not contain a WSDL `service` element because it is only meant to be an industry-standard interface definition. The two lumber companies that implement the interface will define WSDL documents that import `LumberWholesaler.wsdl` and define their own `service` elements. `Create LumberWholesaler.wsdl` in the directory `lab2/schemas/war`. At this point, you should have six files in the `lab2/schemas/war` directory—`Address.xsd`, `Customer.xsd`, `LumberWholesaler.wsdl`, `ProductCatalog.xsd`, `PurchaseOrder.xsd`, and `Types.xsd`.

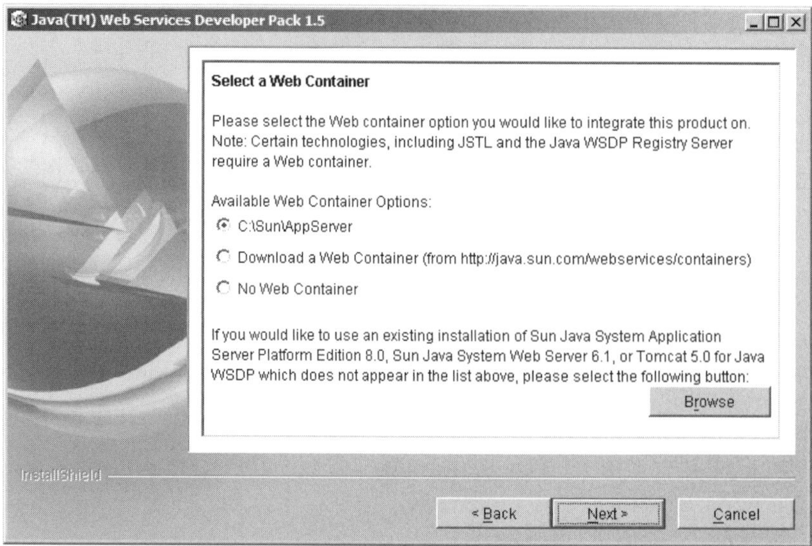

Figure 8.10

Choosing to Integrate the JWSDP with the J2EE RI

Installing and Configuring the UDDI Registry

Next we set up a UDDI registry and create a helper class that we can use for publishing information to the registry. We use the UDDI implementation that is delivered with the Java Web Services Developer Pack (JWSDP). We use the J2EE RI to establish a connection pool for the UDDI registry, and we look up the `javax.xml.registry.ConnectionFactory` created by the pool via the JNDI ENC.

To obtain the UDDI registry implementation, you must download the JWSDP from `http://java.sun.com/webservices/downloads/webservicespack.html`. The JWSDP is Sun's reference implementation for the entire suite of Web services–related Java APIs. You can use it to build and test Java-based Web services applications, but you cannot use it to build and test J2EE-based Web services such as we are doing in this lab. For that, you need a J2EE server. The JWSDP does not include a server, so you must deploy it with your application to a Web server, such as Tomcat or the J2EE RI. Since J2EE 1.4–compliant servers, such as the J2EE RI, are required to provide support for the Java Web services APIs, you do not need the JWSDP when deploying to a J2EE 1.4 server. However, J2EE 1.4 servers are not required to provide an implementation of UDDI (a registry server). They are only required to provide an implementation of JAXR so that you can access a UDDI registry. The only thing we need from the JWSDP is the UDDI registry.

Download the JWSDP, run the installation script (`.exe` for Windows, `.sh` for Unix/Linux), and follow the instructions. When you are asked if you want to integrate the JWSDP with a Web container, choose your installation of the J2EE RI (see Figure 8.10). This will automatically put the files

`RegistryServer.war` and `Xindice.war` in <j2ee-install-dir>/AppServer/domains/domain1/autodeploy directory (where <j2ee-install-dir> is the directory of your installation of the J2EE RI). These WAR files are the implementation of UDDI, called the JWSDP Registry Server. Note that the JWSDP installs several other things on your computer. If you only want to install the JWSDP Registry Server, then choose the custom installation (instead of the typical installation) and deselect all items except the Registry Server.

To verify that you have the JWSDP Registry Server installed correctly, start the J2EE RI server (follow the instructions in the last step of the section titled "Installing Sun Java System Application Server Platform," Edition 8), and access the Admin Console with a Web browser at the URL `http://localhost:4848/asadmin` (assuming you kept the default ports when you installed the J2EE RI; otherwise, the port will be whatever you set it to be). The Admin Console is a tool for configuring the application server. The name and password used to log into the Admin Console are the same that you gave when you installed the J2EE RI. Once you are logged into the Admin Console, expand the Applications node on the left, and then expand the Web Applications node. You should see RegistryServer and Xindice as in Figure 8.11.

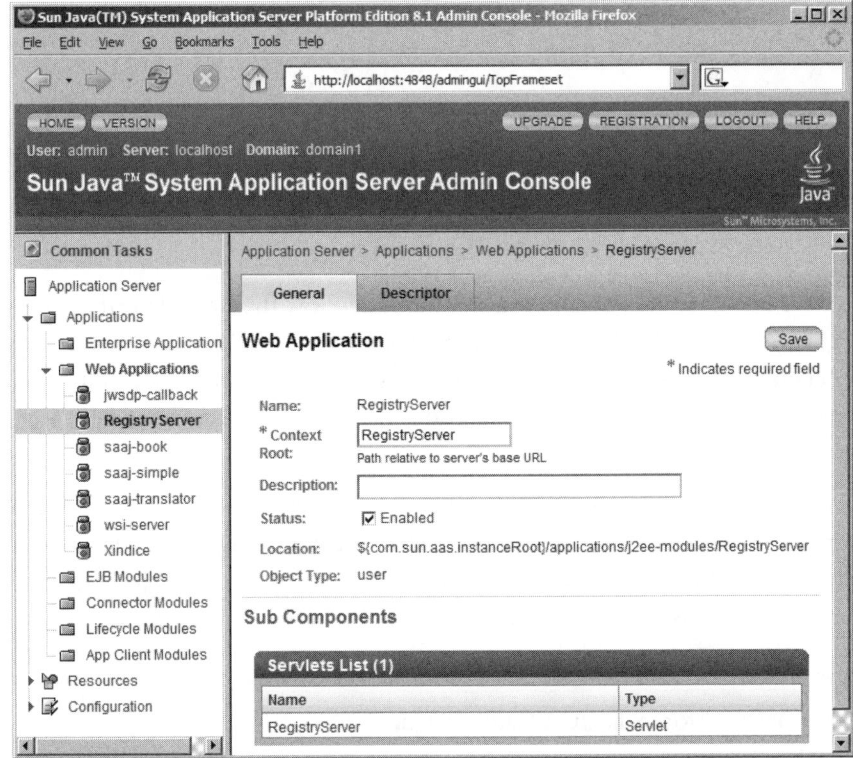

Figure 8.11

J2EE RI Admin Console Showing JWSDP Registry Server

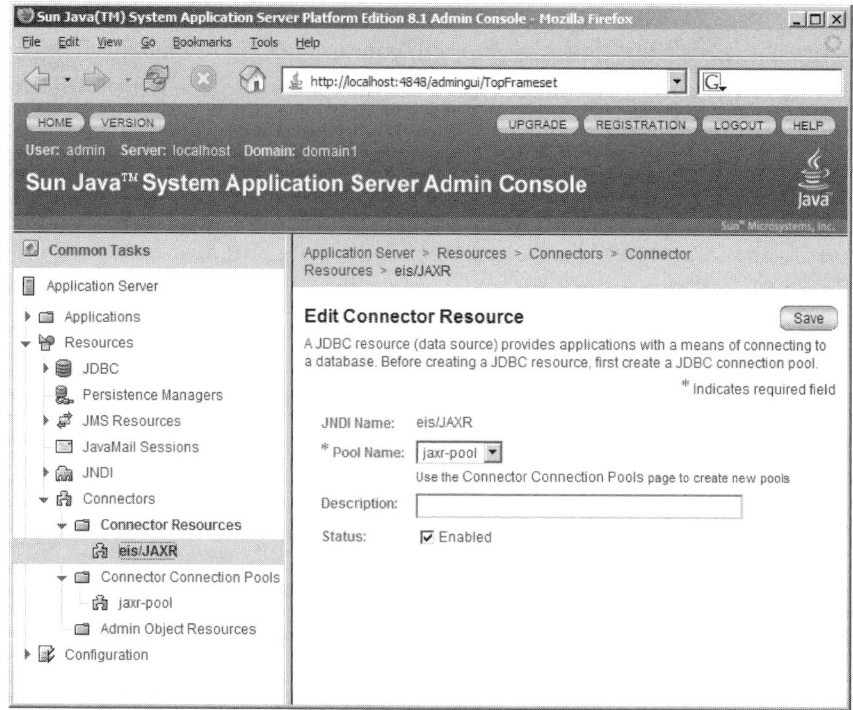

Figure 8.12

Connection Pool and Connector Resource for JWSDP Registry Server

Now that you have installed the JWSDP Registry Server, follow the steps described in the J2EE tutorial at `http://java.sun.com/j2ee/1.4/docs/tutorial/doc/JAXR5.html#wp156475`. These steps describe how to create a connection pool for the UDDI registry and how to create a JNDI resource for looking up the `ConnectionFactory`. Figure 8.12 illustrates how the Connectors node in the Admin Console should look when you are done.

Once you have created the UDDI registry, create the following Java file in the directory `lab2/common/src/common/util`. We use this common helper class for obtaining connections to the UDDI registry and publishing to the UDDI registry. We pass instances of `java.util.ResourceBundle` to the publish methods of this class. The instances of `ResourceBundle` will be created from properties files that contain the information to publish.

Listing 8.67 lab2/common/src/common/util/JAXRHelper.java

```
package common.util;

import java.net.PasswordAuthentication;
```

```
import java.util.*;
import javax.naming.*;
import javax.xml.registry.*;

public class JAXRHelper {
  private static Logger logger =
    Logger.getLogger(JAXRHelper.class.getName());

  /** Creates a connection to the registry. */
  public static Connection makeRegistryConnection(
      String registryJndiName, String lifeCycleManagerURL,
      String queryManagerURL, String userName, String password)
    throws JAXRException {

    Connection connection = null;
    Properties props = new Properties();
    props.setProperty("javax.xml.registry.lifeCycleManagerURL",
                      lifeCycleManagerURL);
    props.setProperty("javax.xml.registry.queryManagerURL",
                      queryManagerURL);

    logger.fine("Attempting to make a connection to the registry.");
    logger.fine("javax.xml.registry.lifeCycleManagerURL = "
      + lifeCycleManagerURL);
    logger.fine("javax.xml.registry.queryManagerURL = "
      + queryManagerURL);

    try {
      // Look up the connection factory via JNDI.
      Context jndiEnc = new InitialContext();
      ConnectionFactory factory = (ConnectionFactory)
        jndiEnc.lookup("java:comp/env/" + registryJndiName);
      // Configure the connection factory.
      factory.setProperties(props);
      // Connect to the registry.
      connection = factory.createConnection();
    }catch (NamingException e) {
      throw new JAXRException("Failed to lookup the registry via JNDI.", e);
    }catch (JAXRException e) {
      throw new JAXRException("Failed to connect to the registry.", e);
    }

    logger.info("Created a connection to the registry.");

    // Log in to the registry.
```

```
    PasswordAuthentication passwordCredential =
      new PasswordAuthentication(userName, password.toCharArray());
    Set credentials = new HashSet();
    credentials.add(passwordCredential);
    connection.setCredentials(credentials);
    logger.fine("Authenticated with the registry.");
    return connection;
  }

  /**
   * Uses information in the specified ResourceBundle
   * to get a connection to the registry.
   */
  public static Connection getConnection(ResourceBundle connectionProperties)
    throws JAXRException {
    Connection connection = makeRegistryConnection(
      connectionProperties.getString(
        "javax.xml.registry.ConnectionFactory.jndiName"),
      connectionProperties.getString(
        "javax.xml.registry.lifeCycleManagerURL"),
      connectionProperties.getString(
        "javax.xml.registry.queryManagerURL"),
      connectionProperties.getString("registry.username"),
      connectionProperties.getString("registry.password"));
    return connection;
  }

  /**
   * Creates an organization, its classification, and its
   * services, and saves it to the registry.
   */
  public static String executePublish(ResourceBundle connectionProperties,
                                      ResourceBundle publishProperties)
    throws JAXRException {
    String key = null;
    Connection connection = getConnection(connectionProperties);

    try {
      key = executePublish(connection, publishProperties);
    }finally {
      try {
        connection.close();
      }catch (Throwable e) {
        // Eat this one.
      }
```

```
    }

    return key;
  }

  /**
   * Creates an organization, its classification, and its services,
   * and saves it to the registry.
   */
  public static String executePublish(Connection connection,
                                      ResourceBundle publishProperties)
    throws JAXRException {
    RegistryService registry = connection.getRegistryService();
    BusinessLifeCycleManager lifeCycleMngr =
      registry.getBusinessLifeCycleManager();
    BusinessQueryManager queryMngr =
      registry.getBusinessQueryManager();
    logger.fine("Got RegistryService, BusinessLifeCycleManager, "
      + "and BusinessQueryManager.");

    // Create the organization.
    Organization org = createOrg(lifeCycleMngr, queryMngr,
      publishProperties);

    // Save the organization in the registry.
    Collection orgs = new ArrayList();
    orgs.add(org);
    BulkResponse response = lifeCycleMngr.saveOrganizations(orgs);

    String id = null;
    if (response.getStatus() == JAXRResponse.STATUS_SUCCESS) {
      logger.info("Organization published to registry.");

      // Retrieve key if successful.
      Collection keys = response.getCollection();
      Iterator keyIter = keys.iterator();

      if (keyIter.hasNext()) {
        Key orgKey = (Key) keyIter.next();
        id = orgKey.getId();
        logger.info("Organization key is " + id);
      }
    }else {
      logExceptions(response);
      throw new JAXRException(
```

```
        "Error publishing organizations. Registry exception occured. "
        + "See log output for details.");
    }
    return id;
  }

  /**
   * Removes the organization with the specified key value.
   * @param key the Key of the organization
   */
  public static void executeRemove(ResourceBundle connectionProperties,
                                   String key)
    throws JAXRException {
    Connection connection = getConnection(connectionProperties);

    try {
      executeRemove(connection, key);
    }finally {
      try {
        connection.close();
      }catch (Throwable e) {
        // Eat this one.
      }
    }
  }

  /**
   * Removes the organization with the specified key value.
   * @param key the Key of the organization
   */
  public static void executeRemove(Connection connection, String key)
    throws JAXRException {
    RegistryService registry = connection.getRegistryService();
    BusinessLifeCycleManager lifeCycleMngr =
      registry.getBusinessLifeCycleManager();

    Key infomodelKey = lifeCycleMngr.createKey(key);
    String id = infomodelKey.getId();
    logger.info("Deleting organization with key " + id);

    Collection keys = new ArrayList();
    keys.add(infomodelKey);

    BulkResponse response = lifeCycleMngr.deleteOrganizations(keys);
    if (response.getStatus() == JAXRResponse.STATUS_SUCCESS) {
```

```
      logger.info("Organization deleted from registry.");
      Collection retKeys = response.getCollection();
      Iterator keyIter = retKeys.iterator();
      Key orgKey = null;

      if (keyIter.hasNext()) {
        orgKey = (Key) keyIter.next();
        id = orgKey.getId();
        logger.fine("Organization key was " + id);
      }
    }else {
      logger.severe("Error deleting organization from registry.");
      logExceptions(response);
    }
  }

  public static void publishWsdlConcept(ResourceBundle connectionProperties,
                                        ResourceBundle publishProperties)
    throws JAXRException {
    Connection connection = getConnection(connectionProperties);

    try {
      RegistryService registry = connection.getRegistryService();
      BusinessLifeCycleManager lifeCycleMngr =
        registry.getBusinessLifeCycleManager();
      BusinessQueryManager queryMngr =
        registry.getBusinessQueryManager();
      logger.fine("Got RegistryService, BusinessLifeCycleManager, and "
        + "BusinessQueryManager.");

      Concept wsdlConcept = createWsdlConcept(lifeCycleMngr,
        queryMngr, publishProperties);
      Set conceptSet = new HashSet();
      conceptSet.add(wsdlConcept);
      BulkResponse response = lifeCycleMngr.saveConcepts(conceptSet);

      if (response.getStatus() != JAXRResponse.STATUS_SUCCESS) {
        logExceptions(response);
        throw new JAXRException(
          "Error publishing WSDL concept. Registry exception occured. "
          + "See log output for details.");
      }
    }finally {
      try {
        connection.close();
```

```
    }catch (Throwable e) {
      // Eat this one.
    }
  }
}

private static Organization createOrg(
    BusinessLifeCycleManager lifeCycleMngr,
    BusinessQueryManager queryMngr,
    ResourceBundle publishProperties)
  throws JAXRException {
  String orgName = publishProperties.getString("org.name");
  String orgDescr = publishProperties.getString("org.description");

  // Create organization and set the description.
  Organization org = lifeCycleMngr.createOrganization(orgName);
  InternationalString iOrgDescr =
    lifeCycleMngr.createInternationalString(orgDescr);
  org.setDescription(iOrgDescr);
  logger.fine(orgName);

  // Create the organization's primary contact.
  User primaryContact = createPrimaryContact(lifeCycleMngr,
    publishProperties);
  org.setPrimaryContact(primaryContact);

  // Create the organization's classifications.
  Collection classifications = createClassifications(lifeCycleMngr,
    queryMngr, publishProperties);
  org.addClassifications(classifications);

  // Create a D-U-N-S identifier for the organization.
  ExternalIdentifier dunsNumber = createDunsNumber(lifeCycleMngr,
    queryMngr, publishProperties);
  org.addExternalIdentifier(dunsNumber);

  // Create a Thomas Register identifier for the organization.
  ExternalIdentifier trNumber =
    createThomasRegisterNumber(lifeCycleMngr, queryMngr,
      publishProperties);
  org.addExternalIdentifier(trNumber);

  // Create the organization's services.
  Collection services = createServices(lifeCycleMngr, queryMngr,
    publishProperties);
```

```
  org.addServices(services);

  return org;
}

private static User createPrimaryContact(
    BusinessLifeCycleManager lifeCycleMngr,
    ResourceBundle publishProperties)
  throws JAXRException {
  String contactName = publishProperties.getString("person.name");
  String contactDescr = publishProperties.getString("contact.description");
  String contactPhone = publishProperties.getString("phone.number");
  String emailAddress = publishProperties.getString("email.address");
  String streetNumber = publishProperties.getString("address.number");
  String street = publishProperties.getString("address.street");
  String city = publishProperties.getString("address.city");
  String state = publishProperties.getString("address.state");
  String postalCode = publishProperties.getString("address.postalCode");
  String country = publishProperties.getString("address.country");
  String addressType = publishProperties.getString("address.type");

  // Create the primary contact.
  User primaryContact = lifeCycleMngr.createUser();

  // Create a person name.
  PersonName primaryContactName =
    lifeCycleMngr.createPersonName(contactName);
  primaryContact.setPersonName(primaryContactName);

  // Create a description.
  InternationalString descr =
    lifeCycleMngr.createInternationalString(contactDescr);
  primaryContact.setDescription(descr);

  // Create a telephone number.
  TelephoneNumber phone = lifeCycleMngr.createTelephoneNumber();
  phone.setNumber(contactPhone);
  phone.setType("Voice");
  Collection phones = new ArrayList();
  phones.add(phone);
  primaryContact.setTelephoneNumbers(phones);

  // Create an email address.
  EmailAddress email = lifeCycleMngr.createEmailAddress(emailAddress);
  Collection emails = new ArrayList();
```

```
    emails.add(email);
    primaryContact.setEmailAddresses(emails);

    // Create a postal address.
    PostalAddress address = lifeCycleMngr.createPostalAddress(
      streetNumber, street, city, state, country, postalCode,
      addressType);
//    PostalAddress address = createPostalAddressUsingSlot(lifeCycleMngr,
//      publishProperties);
    Collection addresses = new HashSet();
    addresses.add(address);
    primaryContact.setPostalAddresses(addresses);

    return primaryContact;
  }

  /** Alternative method for creating an address. */
  private static PostalAddress createPostalAddressUsingSlot(
      LifeCycleManager lifeCycleMngr,
      ResourceBundle publishProperties)
    throws InvalidRequestException, UnsupportedCapabilityException,
           JAXRException {
    String streetNumber = publishProperties.getString("address.number");
    String street = publishProperties.getString("address.street");
    String city = publishProperties.getString("address.city");
    String state = publishProperties.getString("address.state");
    String postalCode = publishProperties.getString("address.postalCode");
    String country = publishProperties.getString("address.country");

    Slot addressLines = (Slot)
      lifeCycleMngr.createObject(LifeCycleManager.SLOT);
    addressLines.setName("addressLines");

    Collection addressValues = new ArrayList();
    addressValues.add(streetNumber + " " + street);
    addressValues.add(city + ", " + state + " " + postalCode);
    addressValues.add(country);

    addressLines.setValues(addressValues);
    addressLines.setSlotType(null);

    PostalAddress address = (PostalAddress)
      lifeCycleMngr.createObject(LifeCycleManager.POSTAL_ADDRESS);

    address.addSlot(addressLines);
```

```
  return address;
}

private static Collection createClassifications(
    BusinessLifeCycleManager lifeCycleMngr,
    BusinessQueryManager queryMngr,
    ResourceBundle publishProperties)
  throws JAXRException {
  String naicsName = publishProperties.getString("naics.1997.name");
  String naicsValue = publishProperties.getString("naics.1997.value");
  String unspscName = publishProperties.getString("unspsc.name");
  String unspscValue = publishProperties.getString("unspsc.value");
  String iso3166Name = publishProperties.getString("iso3166.name");
  String iso3166Value = publishProperties.getString("iso3166.value");

  // Create a classification object for the NAICS 1997 scheme.
  ClassificationScheme naicsScheme =
    queryMngr.findClassificationSchemeByName(null, "ntis-gov:naics:1997");
  Classification naicsClass =
    lifeCycleMngr.createClassification(naicsScheme, naicsName, naicsValue);

  // Create a classification object for the UNSPSC scheme.
  Collection findQualifiers = new HashSet();
  findQualifiers.add(FindQualifier.EXACT_NAME_MATCH);
  Collection namePatterns = new HashSet();
  namePatterns.add("unspsc-org:unspsc");
  BulkResponse response = queryMngr.findClassificationSchemes(
    findQualifiers, namePatterns, null, null);

  if (response.getStatus() != JAXRResponse.STATUS_SUCCESS) {
    logExceptions(response);
    throw new JAXRException("Failed to find unspsc-org:unspsc "
      + "classification schemes.");
  }

  ClassificationScheme unspscScheme = (ClassificationScheme)
    response.getCollection().iterator().next();
  Classification unspscClass = lifeCycleMngr.createClassification(
    unspscScheme, unspscName, unspscValue);

  // Create a classification object for the ISO 3166 scheme.
  ClassificationScheme iso3166Scheme =
    queryMngr.findClassificationSchemeByName(null,
      "uddi-org:iso-ch:3166:1999");
  Classification iso3166Class = lifeCycleMngr.createClassification(
```

```
      iso3166Scheme, iso3166Name, iso3166Value);

    // Add the Classifications to the Organization.
    Collection classifications = new ArrayList();
    classifications.add(naicsClass);
    classifications.add(unspscClass);
    classifications.add(iso3166Class);
    return classifications;
  }

  private static ExternalIdentifier createDunsNumber(
      BusinessLifeCycleManager lifeCycleMngr,
      BusinessQueryManager queryMngr,
      ResourceBundle publishProperties)
    throws JAXRException {
    String orgName = publishProperties.getString("org.name");
    String duns = publishProperties.getString("duns");

    // Create a D-U-N-S identifier (D-U-N-S Number Identifier System).
    ClassificationScheme dunsScheme =
      queryMngr.findClassificationSchemeByName(null, "dnb-com:D-U-N-S");
    ExternalIdentifier dunsNumber =
      lifeCycleMngr.createExternalIdentifier(dunsScheme, orgName, duns);
    return dunsNumber;
  }

  private static ExternalIdentifier
    createThomasRegisterNumber(BusinessLifeCycleManager lifeCycleMngr,
                               BusinessQueryManager queryMngr,
                               ResourceBundle publishProperties)
    throws JAXRException {
    String orgName = publishProperties.getString("org.name");
    String thomasRegister = publishProperties.getString("thomasRegister");

    // Create a Thomas Register identifier
    // (Thomas Register Supplier Identifier Code System).
    ClassificationScheme trScheme =
      queryMngr.findClassificationSchemeByName(null,
        "thomasregister-com:supplierID");
    ExternalIdentifier trNumber = lifeCycleMngr.createExternalIdentifier(
      trScheme, orgName, thomasRegister);
    return trNumber;
  }

  private static Collection createServices(
```

```
  BusinessLifeCycleManager lifeCycleMngr,
  BusinessQueryManager queryMngr,
  ResourceBundle publishProperties)
throws JAXRException {
String serviceName = publishProperties.getString("service.name");
String serviceDescr = publishProperties.getString("service.description");
String serviceBinding = publishProperties.getString("service.binding");
String endpointURL = publishProperties.getString("endpointURL");
String conceptName =
  publishProperties.getString("lumber.org.concept.name");

// Create the service.
Service service = lifeCycleMngr.createService(serviceName);
InternationalString iServiceDescr =
  lifeCycleMngr.createInternationalString(serviceDescr);
service.setDescription(iServiceDescr);

// Create the service binding.
ServiceBinding binding = lifeCycleMngr.createServiceBinding();
InternationalString iBindingDescr =
  lifeCycleMngr.createInternationalString(serviceBinding);
binding.setDescription(iBindingDescr);
binding.setValidateURI(false);
binding.setAccessURI(endpointURL);

// Find the lumber.org WSDL concept.
Collection namePatterns = new HashSet();
namePatterns.add(conceptName);
BulkResponse response = queryMngr.findConcepts(null, namePatterns,
  null, null, null);
Concept wsdlConcept = null;

if (response.getStatus() == JAXRResponse.STATUS_SUCCESS) {
  Iterator iter = response.getCollection().iterator();
  if (iter.hasNext()) {
    wsdlConcept = (Concept) iter.next();
  }
}else {
  logExceptions(response);
  throw new JAXRException("Failed to find the lumber.org WSDL concept.");
}

// Create a SpecificationLink to the lumber.org WSDL concept.
SpecificationLink specLink = lifeCycleMngr.createSpecificationLink();
specLink.setSpecificationObject(wsdlConcept);
```

```
    binding.addSpecificationLink(specLink);

    // Add service bindings to service.
    Collection serviceBindings = new ArrayList();
    serviceBindings.add(binding);
    service.addServiceBindings(serviceBindings);

    // Add service to collection of services.
    Collection services = new ArrayList();
    services.add(service);
    return services;
  }

  private static Concept createWsdlConcept(
      BusinessLifeCycleManager lifeCycleMngr,
      BusinessQueryManager queryMngr,
      ResourceBundle publishProperties)
    throws JAXRException {
    Concept wsdlConcept = lifeCycleMngr.createConcept(null, "", "");

    InternationalString conceptName =
      lifeCycleMngr.createInternationalString(
        publishProperties.getString("lumberWholesaler.concept.name"));
    wsdlConcept.setName(conceptName);

    ExternalLink overviewDoc = lifeCycleMngr.createExternalLink(
      publishProperties.getString("lumberWholesaler.wsdl.location") +
      "#xmlns(wsdl=http://schemas.xmlsoap.org/wsdl/) " +
      "xpointer(/wsdl:definitions/wsdl:portType[" +
      "@name=\"" + publishProperties.getString(
        "lumberWholesaler.wsdl.binding") + "\"])",
      "The WSDL binding for this web service");
    overviewDoc.setValidateURI(false);
    wsdlConcept.addExternalLink(overviewDoc);

    ClassificationScheme uddi_types =
      queryMngr.findClassificationSchemeByName(null, "uddi-org:types");

    if (uddi_types == null) {
      throw new JAXRException("uddi-org:types classification not found.");
    }

    Classification wsdlSpec_Class =
      lifeCycleMngr.createClassification(uddi_types, "WSDL Document",
        "wsdlSpec");
```

```
        wsdlConcept.addClassification(wsdlSpec_Class);

        return wsdlConcept;
    }

    private static void logExceptions(BulkResponse response)
        throws JAXRException {
        logger.severe("Exceptions from bulk response:");

        for (Iterator iter = response.getExceptions().iterator();
             iter.hasNext();) {
            Exception ex = (Exception) iter.next();
            ex.printStackTrace();
        }

        logger.severe("----------");
    }
}
```

Deploying the XML Schemas and the Industry-Standard WSDL

Now we need to deploy the XML schemas of our domain model and the industry-standard WSDL that were created in the section title "Creating the WSDL and Domain Model," and publish the WSDL document to the UDDI registry. We need to deploy these items to our server because we will need to reference their URLs when we create the JAX-RPC service endpoints for the two lumber companies. We are going to imagine that the XML schemas and the industry-standard WSDL are being deployed to a standards organization that we will call lumber.org. That way the lumber companies can reference them when they go to create their own implementations of the Web service interface. This is how a project like this might happen in the real world. A standards organization would maintain the industry-standard documents and participating organizations would refer to the documents posted on the standards organization's Web site and a UDDI WSDL `Concept` that is published in a common UDDI registry.

We deploy these documents to the server in a WAR file with a `javax.servlet.ServletContextListener` for handling publishing the WSDL `Concept` to the UDDI registry when the documents are deployed. After deployment the XML schemas and the WSDL document will be available as static Web content, like HTML pages. We create two properties files that contain information for connecting to the registry and the data to be published. Create the following two listings in the directory `lab2/schemas/src/lumber/org`. The first listing contains connection-specific information and the second listing contains WSDL `Concept` information.

Listing 8.68 lab2/schemas/src/lumber/org/RegistryConnection.properties

```
# JNDI name for the registry connection factory
```

```
javax.xml.registry.ConnectionFactory.jndiName = eis/JAXR

javax.xml.registry.queryManagerURL = http://localhost:8080/RegistryServer/
javax.xml.registry.lifeCycleManagerURL =
  http://localhost:8080/RegistryServer/

registry.username = testuser
registry.password = testuser
```

Listing 8.69 lab2/schemas/src/lumber/org/Registry.properties

```
lumberWholesaler.concept.name=lumber.org:LumberWholesaler
lumberWholesaler.wsdl.location=
  http://localhost:8080/schemas/LumberWholesaler.wsdl
lumberWholesaler.wsdl.binding=SoapRpcLitBinding
```

Note that each line in the two listings above must be entered on a single line. A few lines have been wrapped to fit them on the page. Now create the following listing in the directory `lab2/schemas/-src/lumber/org`. This is our `ServletContextListener` that will read in the properties files listed above and then make a call to `JAXRHelper` to publish the WSDL `Concept`. The location of the properties files will be defined as initialization parameters in the `web.xml` of the WAR, which is listed next.

Listing 8.70 lab2/schemas/src/lumber/org/ContextListener.java

```
package lumber.org;

import java.util.ResourceBundle;
import java.util.logging.Level;
import java.util.logging.Logger;
import javax.servlet.ServletContext;
import javax.servlet.ServletContextEvent;
import javax.servlet.ServletContextListener;
import javax.xml.registry.JAXRException;
import common.util.JAXRHelper;

public class ContextListener implements ServletContextListener {
  private static Logger logger =
    Logger.getLogger(ContextListener.class.getName());
  private ServletContext context = null;
  private ResourceBundle registryBundle = null;
  private ResourceBundle registryConnectionBundle;

  public void contextInitialized(ServletContextEvent event) {
    this.context = event.getServletContext();
```

```
    String registryConnectionProperties =
      context.getInitParameter("registryConnectionProperties");
    logger.info("registryConnectionProperties = "
      + registryConnectionProperties);
    registryConnectionBundle =
      ResourceBundle.getBundle(registryConnectionProperties);

    String registryProperties =
      context.getInitParameter("registryProperties");
    logger.info("registryProperties = " + registryProperties);
    registryBundle = ResourceBundle.getBundle(registryProperties);

    try {
      JAXRHelper.publishWsdlConcept(registryConnectionBundle,
        registryBundle);
    }catch (JAXRException e) {
      String message = "Failed to publish the WSDL concept.";
      logger.log(Level.SEVERE, message, e);
      throw new RuntimeException(message, e);
    }

    logger.fine("WSDL concept published successfully.");
  }

  public void contextDestroyed(ServletContextEvent event) {
    // Nothing to do.
  }
}
```

The last items to create for the WAR are the deployment descriptors. We need both the standard J2EE deployment descriptor `web.xml` and a deployment descriptor that is specific to the J2EE RI called `sun-web.xml`. The `web.xml` deployment descriptor defines the location of our deployment descriptors as `context-param` elements, `ContextListener` as a `listener` element, and the `resource-ref` for the UDDI registry. The `sun-web.xml` deployment descriptor identifies the context root for this WAR (in other words, the root of the access URL) and the name and password for making connections to the UDDI registry. You can read additional information about the `sun-web.xml` deployment descriptor at `http://docs.sun.com/source/819-0079/dgdesc.html#wp129693`. Create the following two listings in the directory `lab2/schemas/war/WEB-INF`.

Listing 8.71 lab2/schemas/war/WEB-INF/web.xml

```
<?xml version="1.0" encoding="UTF-8"?>
<web-app xmlns="http://java.sun.com/xml/ns/j2ee" version="2.4"
         xmlns:xsi="http://www.w3.org/2001/XMLSchema-instance"
```

```
        xsi:schemaLocation="http://java.sun.com/xml/ns/j2ee
          http://java.sun.com/xml/ns/j2ee/web-app_2_4.xsd">
  <display-name>schemas</display-name>
  <context-param>
    <param-name>registryConnectionProperties</param-name>
    <param-value>lumber.org.RegistryConnection</param-value>
  </context-param>
  <context-param>
    <param-name>registryProperties</param-name>
    <param-value>lumber.org.Registry</param-value>
  </context-param>
  <listener>
    <listener-class>lumber.org.ContextListener</listener-class>
  </listener>
  <welcome-file-list>
    <welcome-file>index.html</welcome-file>
  </welcome-file-list>
  <resource-ref>
    <res-ref-name>eis/JAXR</res-ref-name>
    <res-type>javax.xml.registry.ConnectionFactory</res-type>
    <res-auth>Container</res-auth>
    <res-sharing-scope>Shareable</res-sharing-scope>
  </resource-ref>
</web-app>
```

Listing 8.72 lab2/schemas/war/WEB-INF/sun-web.xml

```
<?xml version="1.0" encoding="UTF-8"?>
<!DOCTYPE sun-web-app PUBLIC
  "-//Sun Microsystems, Inc.//DTD Application Server 8.0 Servlet 2.4//EN"
  "http://www.sun.com/software/appserver/dtds/sun-web-app_2_4-0.dtd">
<sun-web-app>
  <context-root>/schemas</context-root>
  <resource-ref>
    <res-ref-name>eis/JAXR</res-ref-name>
    <jndi-name>eis/JAXR</jndi-name>
    <default-resource-principal>
      <name>j2ee</name>
      <password>j2ee</password>
    </default-resource-principal>
  </resource-ref>
</sun-web-app>
```

Now we use Ant for the first time. You are going to create a common Ant build file that will contain some common compilation and deployment tasks. You will then create a specific Ant build file for creating and deploying the schemas WAR. Start by creating the following listing in the directory `lab2/common`. This is the common Ant build file.

Listing 8.73 lab2/common/common-build.xml

```
<!- Common targets for build files ->
<project name="common-build" default="clean" basedir=".">
  <property environment="env" />
  <property name="j2ee.ri.home" value="${env.J2EE_RI_HOME}"/>
  <property name="wscompile.dir" value="${j2ee.ri.home}/bin"/>
  <property name="autodeploy.dir"
            value="${j2ee.ri.home}/domains/domain1/autodeploy"/>
  <property name="compile.debug" value="true"/>
  <property name="compile.deprecation" value="true"/>
  <property name="compile.optimize" value="false"/>
  <property name="src.dir" value="src"/>
  <property name="lib.dir" value="lib"/>
  <property name="build.dir" value="build"/>
  <property name="dist.dir" value="dist"/>

  <path id="j2ee.classpath">
    <fileset dir="${j2ee.ri.home}/lib">
      <include name="*.jar"/>
    </fileset>
  </path>

  <target name="set-wscompile">
    <condition property="wscompile" value="${wscompile.dir}/wscompile.bat">
      <os family="windows"/>
    </condition>
    <condition property="wscompile" value="${wscompile.dir}/wscompile">
      <not>
        <os family="windows"/>
      </not>
    </condition>
  </target>

  <target name="run-wscompile" depends="set-wscompile"
          description="Runs wscompile">
    <echo message="Running wscompile:"/>
    <echo message="  ${wscompile} ${param1}"/>
    <exec executable="${wscompile}">
      <arg line="${param1}"/>
    </exec>
```

```
  </target>

  <target name="undeploy">
    <delete file="${autodeploy.dir}/${deploy.file}"/>
  </target>

  <target name="deploy" depends="undeploy">
    <copy file="${deploy.file}" todir="${autodeploy.dir}"/>
  </target>

  <target name="clean">
    <delete dir="${build.dir}" />
    <delete dir="${assemble.dir}" />
    <delete dir="${dist.dir}" />
  </target>
</project>
```

Next create the following listing in the directory `lab2/schemas`. This is the Ant build file for creating and deploying the schemas WAR.

Listing 8.74 lab2/schemas/build.xml

```
<!- Builds and deploys schemas.war ->
<project name="schemas" default="all" basedir=".">
  <property name="common.dir" value="../common"/>
  <property name="common.build.file"
            value="${common.dir}/common-build.xml"/>
  <property name="context.path" value="schemas"/>
  <property name="dist.dir" value="dist"/>
  <property name="deploy.file" value="${dist.dir}/${context.path}.war"/>
  <!- Import targets from common build file. ->
  <import file="${common.build.file}"/>

  <!- PREPARE ->
  <target name="prepare"
          description="Creates the build and dist directories">
    <mkdir dir="${build.dir}" />
    <mkdir dir="${dist.dir}" />
  </target>

  <!- COMPILE ->
  <target name="compile" depends="prepare"
          description="Compiles the source code.">
    <!- Compile ContextListener.java ->
```

```
    <javac srcdir="${src.dir}:${common.dir}/src/common/util"
           includes="lumber/org/**,JAXRHelper.java"
           destdir="${build.dir}"
           debug="${compile.debug}"
           deprecation="${compile.deprecation}"
           optimize="${compile.optimize}">
      <classpath refid="j2ee.classpath"/>
    </javac>

    <!- Copy all resources. ->
    <copy todir="${build.dir}"
          preservelastmodified="true" includeEmptyDirs="false">
      <fileset dir="${src.dir}" excludes="**/*.java"/>
    </copy>
  </target>

  <!- DIST ->
  <target name="create-war" depends="prepare,compile"
          description="Builds the WAR file">
    <delete file="${deploy.file}" />
    <war destfile="${deploy.file}" webxml="war/WEB-INF/web.xml">
      <fileset dir="war" excludes="**/web.xml"/>
      <classes dir="${build.dir}"/>
    </war>
  </target>

  <!- ALL ->
  <target name="all" depends="clean,create-war,deploy"
          description="Builds the war and deploys it to the server." />
</project>
```

At this point, you should have all of the files necessary for deploying the XML schemas and the WSDL file. These files are listed below for your reference.

- lab2/common/common-build.xml
- lab2/common/src/common/util/JAXRHelper.java
- lab2/schemas/build.xml
- lab2/schemas/src/lumber/org/ContextListener.java
- lab2/schemas/src/lumber/org/Registry.properties
- lab2/schemas/src/lumber/org/RegistryConnection.properties
- lab2/schemas/war/Address.xsd

- `lab2/schemas/war/Customer.xsd`
- `lab2/schemas/war/LumberWholesaler.wsdl`
- `lab2/schemas/war/ProductCatalog.xsd`
- `lab2/schemas/war/PurchaseOrder.xsd`
- `lab2/schemas/war/Types.xsd`
- `lab2/schemas/war/WEB-INF/sun-web.xml`
- `lab2/schemas/war/WEB-INF/web.xml`

To build and deploy the schemas WAR all you have to do is make sure your server is running, then open a command prompt, navigate to the schemas directory where `build.xml` is located, and enter the following command:

```
ant
```

This will execute the `target` element in the `build.xml` file with the name `all`. The `all` target will compile and deploy the WSDL and schemas to the application server. These must be on the application server before continuing to the next step. You can verify that the deployment was successful by opening a browser and navigating to the URL `http://localhost:8080/schemas/LumberWholesaler.wsdl`. You should see the industry-standard WSDL file as in Figure 8.13.

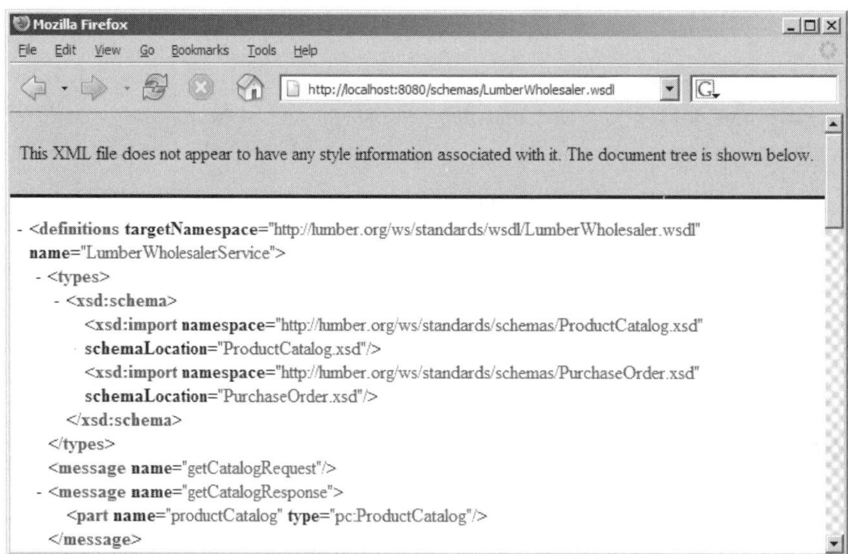

Figure 8.13
Verifying That the Schemas WAR Deployed Successfully

WSDL-to-Java: Generating Classes for LumberCo1

Now that you have a WSDL document describing the industry-standard lumber Web service interface, you can import it into other WSDL documents to describe the Web service implementations for the lumber companies. You can then use those resulting WSDL documents and the tools provided by the J2EE RI to generate the JAX-RPC service endpoint interface, supporting stubs and ties, and Java Beans for the referenced data types that we defined in XML Schema. We then use the generated Java classes to write the JAX-RPC service endpoints (implementations of the Web service interface). Starting with a predefined WSDL document and using it to generate your Web service implementation, either automatically with a tool or manually, is referred to as *top-down* development. Starting with an implementation and using it to generate your WSDL document (as we did in Lab 1), is referred to as *bottom-up* development. When developing Web services, top-down development tends to produce applications that are more interoperable because you start by thinking in terms of the XML that is exchanged, as opposed to thinking in terms of the data types in Java, which may not be supported by an interoperable XML representation.

We start with the implementation of a JAX-RPC Servlet endpoint for the first lumber company. The following listing is the WSDL document that defines the Web service implementation for lumber company 1 (lumberco1). Notice that it imports the industry-standard WSDL from a URL provided by the WAR that you previously deployed. The imported WSDL document is the service *interface* definition and this WSDL document is the service *implementation* definition. The service interface definition contains the `types`, `message`, `portType`, and `binding` definitions, while the service implementation definition contains the `service` definition. Create this listing in the directory `lab2/jaxrpc/lumberco1/war/WEB-INF/wsdl`.

Listing 8.75 lab2/jaxrpc/lumberco1/war/WEB-INF/wsdl/LumberCo1Wholesaler.wsdl

```
<?xml version="1.0" encoding="UTF-8"?>
<definitions xmlns="http://schemas.xmlsoap.org/wsdl/"
  xmlns:soap="http://schemas.xmlsoap.org/wsdl/soap/"
  xmlns:lr="http://lumber.org/ws/standards/wsdl/LumberWholesaler.wsdl"
  xmlns:tns="http://lumber.org/ws/standards/wsdl/LumberWholesaler.wsdl"
 targetNamespace="http://lumber.org/ws/standards/wsdl/LumberWholesaler.wsdl">

  <import
    namespace="http://lumber.org/ws/standards/wsdl/LumberWholesaler.wsdl"
    location="http://localhost:8080/schemas/LumberWholesaler.wsdl"/>
  <service name="LumberSupplierService">
    <port name="LumberPurchaseOrderPort" binding="lr:SoapRpcLitBinding">
      <soap:address
  location="http://localhost:8080/lumberco1/LumberSupplierService/PO"/>
```

```
    </port>
  </service>
</definitions>
```

The tool provided by the J2EE RI for generating Java from WSDL (or vice versa) is called `wscompile` and is located in the `bin` directory of the J2EE RI installation. It provides functionality similar to the WSDL2Java and Java2WSDL tools provided by Axis. Reference documentation for `wscompile` can be found at `http://docs.sun.com/app/docs/doc/819-0082?q=wscompile`.

To run `wscompile`, you must supply it an XML-based configuration file. The root XML element of the configuration file is `configuration`, which may contain a `service`, `wsdl`, or `modelfile` element. We do not discuss the `modelfile` element. If you want to learn about the `modelfile` element, read the reference documentation.

The `service` element is used when you want to generate a WSDL document from a preexisting Java interface for the Web service (bottom-up development). The `wsdl` element is used when you want to generate Java code from a preexisting WSDL document (top-down development). The configuration file that we use to generate the code for lumberco1 is listed below. The `wsdl` element points the WSDL document that we just created in Listing 8.75 and assigns a target Java package for types defined in the WSDL. The `namespaceMapping` elements provide additional mappings from XML namespaces used in the WSDL to the Java packages where we want the generated code to be placed. We place the XML Schema types in the `common` package because we know that we can use these same classes for the second lumber company (a shortcut). Create the following listing in the directory `lab2/jaxrpc/jse/lumberco1`.

Listing 8.76 lab2/jaxrpc/jse/lumberco1/config-wsdlToJava.xml

```
<?xml version="1.0" encoding="UTF-8"?>
<configuration xmlns="http://java.sun.com/xml/ns/jax-rpc/ri/config">
  <wsdl location="./war/WEB-INF/wsdl/LumberCo1Wholesaler.wsdl"
        packageName="lc1.ws.jse">
    <namespaceMappingRegistry>
      <namespaceMapping
  namespace="http://lumber.org/ws/standards/wsdl/LumberWholesaler.wsdl"
  packageName="lc1.ws.jse"/>
      <namespaceMapping
  namespace="http://lumber.org/ws/standards/schemas/ProductCatalog.xsd"
  packageName="common.domain.catalog"/>
      <namespaceMapping
  namespace="http://lumber.org/ws/standards/schemas/PurchaseOrder.xsd"
  packageName="common.domain.order"/>
      <namespaceMapping
```

```
  namespace="http://lumber.org/ws/standards/schemas/Customer.xsd"
  packageName="common.domain.customer"/>
      <namespaceMapping
  namespace="http://lumber.org/ws/standards/schemas/Address.xsd"
  packageName="common.domain.address"/>
      <namespaceMapping
  namespace="http://lumber.org/ws/standards/schemas/Types.xsd"
  packageName="common.domain.types"/>
    </namespaceMappingRegistry>
  </wsdl>
</configuration>
```

When running `wscompile`, supply it a number of options (listed in the reference documentation) and the configuration file. You can do this from the command line (`wscompile` should now be in your PATH), or you can have Ant do it for you, which is what we will do. The following listing is an Ant build file that we will use to run `wscompile` to compile the Web service implementation once we have it coded and deploy the code as a WAR to the server. Create this file in the directory `lab2/jaxrpc/jse/lumberco1`.

Listing 8.77 lab2/jaxrpc/jse/lumberco1/build.xml

```
<!- Builds and deploys the LumberCo1 JAX-RPC servlet endpoint ->
<project name="LumberCo1Wholesaler" default="create-war" basedir=".">
  <property name="common.dir" value="../../../common"/>
  <property name="common.build.file"
            value="${common.dir}/common-build.xml"/>

  <import file="${common.build.file}" />

  <property name="assemble.dir" value="assemble"/>
  <property name="assemble.war.dir" value="${assemble.dir}/war"/>
  <property name="context.path" value="lumberco1"/>
  <property name="dist.dir" value="dist"/>
  <property name="deploy.file" value="${dist.dir}/${context.path}.war"/>
  <property name="config.wsdlToJava.file" value="config-wsdlToJava.xml"/>
  <property name="mapping.file" value="${context.path}_mapping.xml"/>
  <property name="build.sei.src" value="${build.dir}/sei/src" />
  <property name="build.sei.classes" value="${build.dir}/sei/classes" />
  <property name="build.server.classes"
            value="${build.dir}/server/classes" />

  <!- CLASSPATHS  ->
  <path id="compile.classpath">
```

```
    <path refid="j2ee.classpath"/>
    <pathelement location="${build.sei.classes}"/>
    <pathelement location="${build.server.classes}"/>
  </path>

  <!- PREPARE ->
  <target name="prepare" description="Creates the build directories.">
    <mkdir dir="${build.sei.src}" />
    <mkdir dir="${build.sei.classes}" />
    <mkdir dir="${build.server.classes}" />
  </target>

  <!- WSCOMPILE ->
  <!- NOTE: This target requires the lumber.org schemas to be deployed. ->
  <target name="generate-sei" depends="prepare"
    description="Runs wscompile to generate the SEI from the WSDL file.">
    <antcall target="run-wscompile">
      <param name="param1"
             value="-import -f:wsi -keep -d ${build.sei.classes} -s ${build.sei.src} -nd
${build.dir} -mapping ${build.dir}/${mapping.file} ${config.wsdlToJava.file}"/>
    </antcall>
    <delete file="${common.build.basedir}/${dist.dir}/${domain.jar}" />
    <!- JAR the generated common classes and
         put them under the common directory. ->
    <jar jarfile="${common.build.basedir}/${dist.dir}/${domain.jar}">
      <fileset dir="${build.sei.classes}" includes="common/**/*.class" />
    </jar>
  </target>

  <!- COMPILE ->
  <target name="compile-service"
          depends="prepare,generate-sei"
          description="Compiles the server-side source code.">
    <javac srcdir="${src.dir}:${common.dir}/src"
           includes="lc1/**,common/**"
           destdir="${build.server.classes}"
           debug="${compile.debug}"
           deprecation="${compile.deprecation}"
           optimize="${compile.optimize}">
      <classpath refid="compile.classpath"/>
    </javac>
  </target>

  <!- DIST ->
  <target name="create-war" depends="generate-sei,compile-service"
```

```
          description="Builds the WAR file for the server.">
    <mkdir dir="${assemble.war.dir}" />
    <copy todir="${assemble.war.dir}" preservelastmodified="true">
      <fileset dir="war"/>
    </copy>
    <copy todir="${assemble.war.dir}/WEB-INF/classes"
          preservelastmodified="true">
      <fileset dir="${build.server.classes}" />
    </copy>

    <!- Copy associated resources. ->
    <copy todir="${assemble.war.dir}/WEB-INF/classes"
          preservelastmodified="true"
          includeEmptyDirs="false">
      <fileset dir="${src.dir}" excludes="**/*.java"/>
    </copy>

    <!- Copy generated files. ->
    <copy file="${build.dir}/${context.path}_mapping.xml"
          todir="${assemble.war.dir}/WEB-INF/wsdl"
          preservelastmodified="true" />
    <copy todir="${assemble.war.dir}/WEB-INF/classes"
          preservelastmodified="true">
      <fileset dir="${build.sei.classes}" />
    </copy>

    <mkdir dir="${dist.dir}" />
    <delete file="${deploy.file}" />
    <jar destfile="${deploy.file}" basedir="${assemble.war.dir}" />
  </target>
</project>
```

Note that the line in bold text from Listing 8.77 must be written on a single line. This is the line that executes `wscompile`, passing it options and the config file in Listing 8.76. Now have this Ant build file call `wscompile` to generate the JAX-RPC service endpoint interface and supporting classes. Open a command prompt and navigate to the `lab2/jaxrpc/jse/lumbercol` directory where you just created `build.xml`, then execute the following command:

```
ant generate-sei
```

When this command completes you should have several classes under the `lab2/jaxrpc/jse/lumbercol/build/sei/src` directory. You should see two primary Java packages—`common.domain` and `lcl.ws.jse`. The `common.domain` package contains the Java Beans that were generated from the types we defined in XML Schema. The `lcl.ws.jse` contains the generated JAX-RPC service endpoint interface and associated stub classes. Within the `lcl.ws.jse` package you should see a

`LumberSupplierService` class, which corresponds to the WSDL `service` element in the `LumberCo1Wholesaler.wsdl` file. The `lc1.ws.jse` package should also contain a `PurchaseOrderPortType` class, which corresponds to the WSDL `portType` element in the `LumberWholesaler.wsdl` file.

In addition to the Java classes, `wscompile` should have also generated a JAX-RPC mapping file in directory `lab2/jaxrpc/jse/lumberco1/build`. The `lumberco1_mapping.xml` file tells JAX-RPC how to map the definitions and types in the WSDL document to Java. Although not discussed in this chapter, you can use the JAX-RPC mapping file to change the names of the Java parameters and types that are generated.

At this point you should have the following generated files.

- `lab2/jaxrpc/jse/lumberco1/build/lumberco1_mapping.xml`
- `lab2/jaxrpc/jse/lumberco1/build/sei/src/common/domain/address/Address.java`
- `lab2/jaxrpc/jse/lumberco1/build/sei/src/common/domain/address/USAddress.java`
- `lab2/jaxrpc/jse/lumberco1/build/sei/src/common/domain/catalog/Product.java`
- `lab2/jaxrpc/jse/lumberco1/build/sei/src/common/domain/catalog/ProductCatalog.java`
- `lab2/jaxrpc/jse/lumberco1/build/sei/src/common/domain/customer/Customer.java`
- `lab2/jaxrpc/jse/lumberco1/build/sei/src/common/domain/order/InvalidPurchaseOrderFault.java`
- `lab2/jaxrpc/jse/lumberco1/build/sei/src/common/domain/order/LineItem.java`
- `lab2/jaxrpc/jse/lumberco1/build/sei/src/common/domain/order/PurchaseOrder.java`
- `lab2/jaxrpc/jse/lumberco1/build/sei/src/common/domain/order/ShippingNotice.java`
- `lab2/jaxrpc/jse/lumberco1/build/sei/src/lc1/ws/jse/LumberSupplierService.java`
- `lab2/jaxrpc/jse/lumberco1/build/sei/src/lc1/ws/jse/PurchaseOrderPortType_getCatalog_RequestStuct.java`
- `lab2/jaxrpc/jse/lumberco1/build/sei/src/lc1/ws/jse/PurchaseOrderPortType_getCatalog_ResponseStuct.java`
- `lab2/jaxrpc/jse/lumberco1/build/sei/src/lc1/ws/jse/PurchaseOrderPortType_Impl.java`
- `lab2/jaxrpc/jse/lumberco1/build/sei/src/lc1/ws/jse/PurchaseOrderPortType_placeOrder_RequestStuct.java`

- `lab2/jaxrpc/jse/lumberco1/build/sei/src/lc1/ws/jse/PurchaseOrderPortType_placeOrder_ResponseStuct.java`
- `lab2/jaxrpc/jse/lumberco1/build/sei/src/lc1/ws/jse/PurchaseOrderPortType.java`

Coding the JAX-RPC Service Endpoint for LumberCo1

Now that we have the JAX-RPC service endpoint interface, we need to create an implementation of it for the first lumber company (lumberco1). This implementation will be a Servlet-based endpoint. Before we begin coding the implementation, we define some data that describes the supply of lumber that lumberco1 has to sell. This information would normally be stored in a database, but since this example is already fairly complex we bypass database integration, and instead use a properties file to store the data. Create the following properties file in the directory `lab2/jaxrpc/jse/lumberco1/src/lc1/ws/jse`.

Listing 8.78 lab2/jaxrpc/jse/lumberco1/src/lc1/ws/jse/Prices.properties

```
# Item;Name;Description;Price

1=201595;2X12X16;.25 TOP CHOICE TREATED;26.79
2=46905;2X4X8;TOP CHOICE SOUTHERN YELLOW PINE;2.97
3=76854;2X4X10;TOP CHOICE TREATED;5.39
4=77671;2X4X12;TOP CHOICE TREATED;5.97
5=79670;2X4X16;TOP CHOICE TREATED;7.97
6=30906;2X6X8;TOP CHOICE TREATED;5.79
7=84304;2X6X10;TOP CHOICE TREATED;6.97
8=84981;2X6X12;TOP CHOICE TREATED;7.97
9=90297;2X6X16;TOP CHOICE TREATED;11.49
10=91658;2X8X8;TOP CHOICE TREATED;8.69
11=92334;2X8X10;TOP CHOICE TREATED;10.97
12=92781;2X8X12;TOP CHOICE TREATED;11.97
13=201519;2X8X16;TOP CHOICE TREATED;17.97
14=201521;2X10X8;TOP CHOICE TREATED;8.59
15=201523;2X10X10;TOP CHOICE TREATED;12.49
16=201524;2X10X12;TOP CHOICE TREATED;16.79
17=201525;2X10X16;TOP CHOICE TREATED;16.79
18=201578;2X12X12;TOP CHOICE TREATED;21.97
19=21210;5/4X6X8;STANDARD TREATED;4.97
20=21565;5/4X6X10;STANDARD TREATED;4.97
21=21712;5/4X6X12;STANDARD TREATED;5.97
22=86573;5/4X6X16;STANDARD TREATED;6.97
23=201676;5/4X6X8;TOP CHOICE SEVEREWEATHER TREATED;6.97
```

```
23=201688;5/4X6X10;TOP CHOICE SEVEREWEATHER TREATED;9.29
25=201691;5/4X6X12;TOP CHOICE SEVERE WEAHTER TREATED;10.89
26=201704;5/4X6X16;TOP CHOICE SEVEREWEATHER TREATED;14.97
27=121;4X4X6;#2 .40 TREATED;5.97
28=201596;4X4X8;.40 TOP CHOICE TREATED;6.97
29=1467;4X4X10;#2 .40 TREATED;10.97
30=1763;4X4X12;#2 .40 TREATED;13.97
31=2690;4X4X16;#2 .40 TREATED;16.97
32=6118;4X6X8;#2 .40 TREATED;11.97
33=9438;4X6X12;#2 .40 TREATED;19.97
34=2827;6X6X8;#2 .40 TREATED;20.97
35=3557;6X6X10;#2 TREATED;25.97
36=5635;6X6X12;#2 .40 TREATED;32.97
37=201710;1X4X6;TOP CHOICE TREATED APPEARANCE BOARD;1.88
38=201711;1X4X8;TOP CHOICE TREATED APPEARANCE BOARD;2.49
39=201714;1X4X10;TOP CHOICE TREATED APPEARANCE BOARD;2.86
40=201715;1X4X12;TOP CHOICE TREATED APPEARANCE BOARD;3.69
41=201719;1X6X6;TOP CHOICE TREATED APPEARANCE GRADE;2.92
42=201722;1X6X8;TOP CHOICE TREATED APPEARANCE BOARD;4.29
43=201723;1X6X10;TOP CHOICE TREATED APPEARANCE BOARD;4.97
44=201725;1X6X12;TOP CHOICE TREATED APPEARANCE BOARD;6.49
45=201999;1X2X8;#1 TREATED FURRING;1.57
46=204231;2X2X8;#1 TREATED FURRING STRIP;2.39
```

`Prices.properties` contains key-value pairs where the key is simply an identifying number and the value is a semicolon-delimited list that contains the product number, product name, product description, and price. Now we need a Java class to help load this file into Java objects for us. To simplify your work some, we will also use this helper class for the second lumber company (lumberco2). Create the following Java class in the directory `lab2/common/src/common/util`.

Listing 8.79 lab2/common/src/common/util/ProductLoader.java

```
package common.util;

import java.util.ArrayList;
import java.util.Enumeration;
import java.util.ResourceBundle;
import java.util.logging.Logger;
import common.domain.catalog.Product;

public final class ProductLoader {
  private static Logger logger =
    Logger.getLogger(ProductLoader.class.getName());

  public static final Product[] loadProducts(ResourceBundle priceBundle) {
```

```
    Enumeration bundleKeys = priceBundle.getKeys();
    String key = null;
    String value = null;
    String[] values = null;
    Product product = null;
    ArrayList products = new ArrayList();

    while (bundleKeys.hasMoreElements()) {
      key = (String) bundleKeys.nextElement();
      value = priceBundle.getString(key);
      values = value.split(";");

      if (values.length == 4) {
        product = new Product();
        product.setProductNumber(Integer.valueOf(values[0]).intValue());
        product.setName(values[1]);
        product.setDescription(values[2]);
        product.setPrice(Float.valueOf(values[3]).floatValue());
        products.add(product);
      }else {
        String message = "Invalid data in price properties file. Value = "
          + value;
        logger.severe(message);
        throw new RuntimeException(message);
      }
    }

    return (Product[]) products.toArray(new Product[]{});
  }
}
```

ProductLoader.java takes a ResourceBundle that is in the format of Listing 8.78 and parses the values into common.domain.catalog.Product objects. The Product type is one that we defined in XML Schema and was generated as a Java Bean by wscompile. Now we code the implementation of the JAX-RPC service endpoint interface. Create the following Java class in the directory lab2/jaxrpc/jse/lumberco1/-src/ws/jse.

Listing 8.80 lab2/jaxrpc/jse/lumberco1/src/ws/jse/LumberPurchaseOrderJSE.java

```
package lc1.ws.jse;

import java.rmi.RemoteException;
import java.util.Calendar;
import java.util.ResourceBundle;
import java.util.logging.Logger;
import javax.xml.rpc.ServiceException;
import javax.xml.rpc.server.ServiceLifecycle;
```

```
import javax.xml.rpc.server.ServletEndpointContext;
import common.domain.catalog.Product;
import common.domain.catalog.ProductCatalog;
import common.domain.order.InvalidPurchaseOrderFault;
import common.domain.order.PurchaseOrder;
import common.domain.order.ShippingNotice;
import common.util.ProductLoader;

public class LumberPurchaseOrderJSE implements PurchaseOrderPortType,
  ServiceLifecycle {
  private static Logger logger =
    Logger.getLogger(LumberPurchaseOrderJSE.class.getName());
  private ServletEndpointContext context = null;

  public void init(Object context) throws ServiceException {
    this.context = (ServletEndpointContext) context;
  }

  public void destroy() {
    // Nothing to do.
  }

  public ProductCatalog getCatalog() throws RemoteException {
    logger.fine("Prices requested from lumbercol.");
    ProductCatalog catalog = loadCatalog();
    logger.fine("Returning " + catalog.getProducts().length
      + " prices from lumbercol.");
    return catalog;
  }

  public ShippingNotice placeOrder(PurchaseOrder purchaseOrder)
    throws InvalidPurchaseOrderFault, RemoteException {
    Calendar tomorrow = Calendar.getInstance();
    tomorrow.add(Calendar.DAY_OF_YEAR, 1);
    // TODO: create better order number.
    ShippingNotice notice = new ShippingNotice();
    notice.setOrderNumber("1");
    notice.setPurchaseOrder(purchaseOrder);
    notice.setShipDate(tomorrow);

    StringBuffer out = new StringBuffer();
    out.append("\nOrder placed to lumbercol:\n").append(
      purchaseOrder.toString());
    logger.fine(out.toString());
```

```
        return notice;
    }

    private ProductCatalog loadCatalog() {
        Calendar startDate = Calendar.getInstance();
        Calendar endDate = Calendar.getInstance();
        endDate.add(Calendar.DAY_OF_YEAR, 30);

        ResourceBundle priceBundle = (ResourceBundle)
            this.context.getServletContext().getAttribute("priceBundle");
        Product[] products = ProductLoader.loadProducts(priceBundle);
        ProductCatalog catalog = new ProductCatalog();
        catalog.setEffectiveStartDate(startDate);
        catalog.setEffectiveEndDate(endDate);
        catalog.setProducts(products);
        return catalog;
    }
}
```

`LumberPurchaseOrderJSE.java` implements the Web service operations `getCatalog` and `placeOrder`. The `getCatalog` method of `LumberPurchaseOrderJSE` generates and returns the `ProductCatalog` type. The `placeOrder` method accepts a `PurchaseOrder` type and generates and returns a `ShippingNotice` type. To keep the implementation simple, the `placeOrder` method does not really process the order. It just logs the fact that an order was placed and then returns a `ShippingNotice`. The logs generated by these classes can be viewed through the Admin Console. The home page of the Admin Console provides a link to search the logs. You can perform a basic search or an advanced search. Since the log ouput from the J2EE RI is quite lengthy you will probably want to perform an advanced search where you specify a "Custom Logger." The Java classes in this lab are using the logging provided by the `java.util` package. The names specified for logger at the beginning of each class are simply the fully qualified name of that class. So the value you would place in the Custom Logger field of the advanced search is simply the fully qualified name of one of Java classes that you created from this lab. For example, Figure 8.14 shows putting `common.util.JAXRHelper` and `lumber.org.ContextListener` into the Custom Logger field to search for entries in the log made by these classes.

If you ran the search now, the results from the search might look like Figure 8.15.

By this point you should have the JAX-RPC Servlet endpoint for lumberco1 coded. We want to deploy this Web service to the server, but we also want this service to be published in the UDDI registry. We use `JAXRHelper` to accomplish the publishing when the context for this Web service is loaded in the server. That means we need to create a `javax.servlet.ServletContextListener` as we did for the schemas WAR. To save some time, we use this same `ServletContextListener` in the lumberco2 implementation and we will put this class in the common directory. Create the following listing in the directory `lab2/common/src/common/j2ee`.

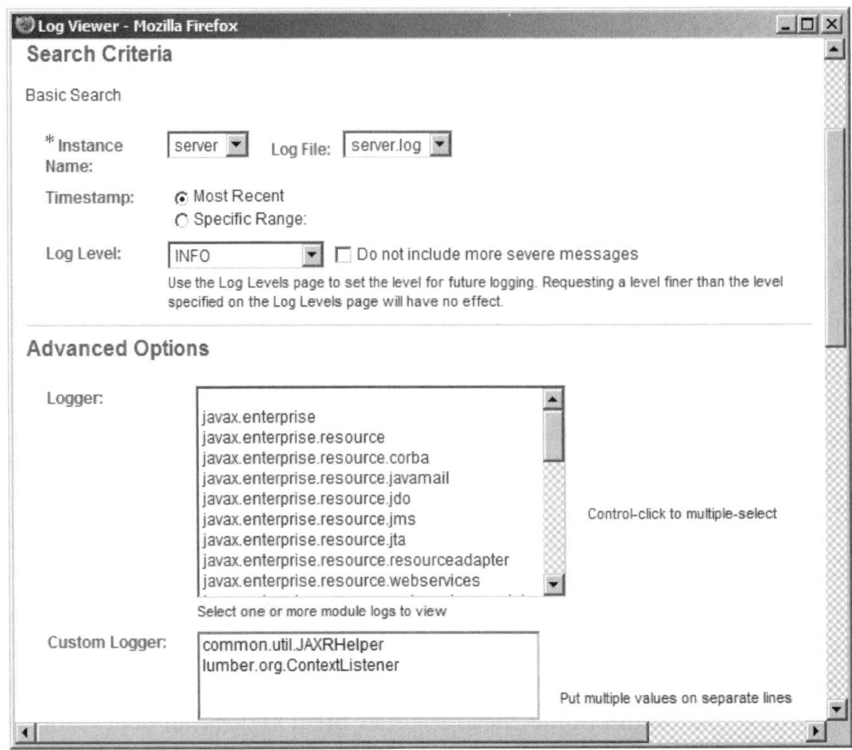

Figure 8.14

J2EE RI Log Viewer Advanced Search

Listing 8.81 lab2/common/src/common/j2ee/ContextListener.java

```
package common.j2ee;

import java.io.FileReader;
import java.io.FileWriter;
import java.io.IOException;
import java.util.ResourceBundle;
import java.util.logging.Level;
import java.util.logging.Logger;
import javax.servlet.ServletContext;
import javax.servlet.ServletContextEvent;
import javax.servlet.ServletContextListener;
import javax.xml.registry.JAXRException;
import common.util.JAXRHelper;

public final class ContextListener implements ServletContextListener {
```

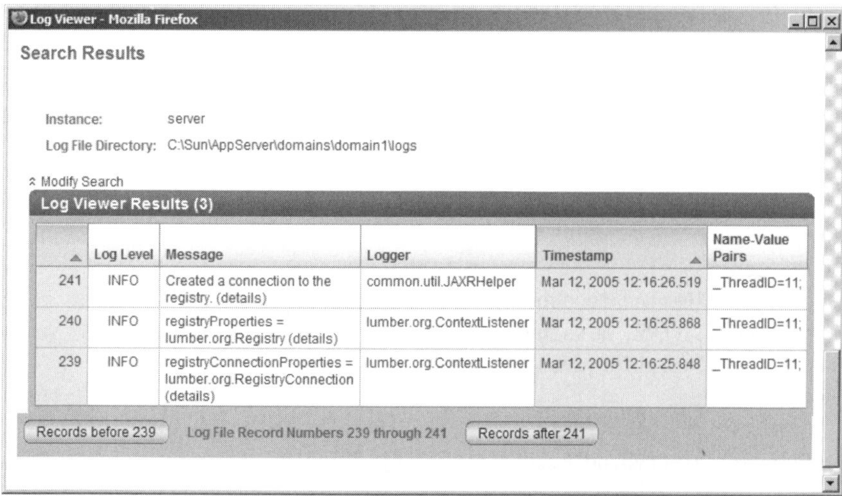

Figure 8.15
J2EE RI Log Viewer Search Results

```
private static Logger logger =
  Logger.getLogger(ContextListener.class.getName());
private ServletContext context = null;
private ResourceBundle registryBundle = null;
private ResourceBundle registryConnectionBundle;

public void contextInitialized(ServletContextEvent event) {
  this.context = event.getServletContext();
  logger.info("Initializing the context...");
  String priceProperties = context.getInitParameter("priceProperties");

  if (priceProperties != null) {
    logger.info("priceProperties = " + priceProperties);
    this.context.setAttribute("priceBundle",
      ResourceBundle.getBundle(priceProperties));
  }

  String registryConnectionProperties =
    context.getInitParameter("registryConnectionProperties");
  logger.info("registryConnectionProperties = "
    + registryConnectionProperties);
  registryConnectionBundle =
    ResourceBundle.getBundle(registryConnectionProperties);

  String registryProperties =
```

```
      context.getInitParameter("registryProperties");
    logger.info("registryProperties = " + registryProperties);
    registryBundle = ResourceBundle.getBundle(registryProperties);

    String key = null;
    try {
      key = JAXRHelper.executePublish(registryConnectionBundle,
        registryBundle);
    }catch (JAXRException e) {
      String message = "Failed to publish lumbercol to registry.";
      logger.log(Level.SEVERE, message, e);
      throw new RuntimeException(message, e);
    }

    String keyFile = registryBundle.getString("key.file");
    try {
      FileWriter out = new FileWriter(keyFile);
      out.write(key);
      out.flush();
      out.close();
    }catch (IOException ex) {
      String message = "Error writing registry key.";
      logger.log(Level.SEVERE, message, ex);
      throw new RuntimeException(message, ex);
    }

    logger.info("Context initialized.");
  }

  public void contextDestroyed(ServletContextEvent event) {
    String keyFile = registryBundle.getString("key.file");
    String key = null;

    try {
      FileReader in = new FileReader(keyFile);
      char[] buf = new char[512];
      while (in.read(buf, 0, 512) >= 0) {
      }
      in.close();
      key = new String(buf).trim();
    }catch (IOException e) {
      String message = "Error reading registry key.";
      logger.log(Level.SEVERE, message, e);
      throw new RuntimeException(message, e);
    }
```

```
    logger.info("Context " + context.getServletContextName()
      + " being destroyed.");

    try {
      JAXRHelper.executeRemove(registryConnectionBundle, key);
    }catch (JAXRException e) {
      String message = "Error removing lumbercol from registry.";
      logger.log(Level.SEVERE, message, e);
      throw new RuntimeException(message, e);
    }
  }
}
```

`ContextListener.java` loads the properties file with the product list and stores it as an attribute of `ServletContext` so that it can be accessed later by `LumberPurchaseOrderJSE`. Then `ContextListener` loads the properties file containing the UDDI information and calls `JAXRHelper` to publish it. Now we need to create a properties file to give to `JAXRHelper`. Create the following file in the directory `lab2/jaxrpc/jse/lumbercol/src/lc1/ws/jse`.

Listing 8.82 lab2/jaxrpc/jse/lumberco1/src/lc1/ws/jse/Registry.properties

```
endpointURL = http://localhost:8080/lumbercol/LumberSupplierService/PO

# A file for storing the Key generated when we store
# this Organization in the UDDI registry.
key.file=lumbercol_orgkey.txt

# General information on the Organization.
org.name=LumberCol
org.description=A supplier of lumber.
person.name=Richard Allen
contact.description=Technical Support
phone.number=(800) 555-1212
email.address=rich.allen@lumbercol.com
address.number=101
address.street=Lumber Lane
address.city=Atlanta
address.state=GA
address.postalCode=30332
address.country=USA
address.type=TechSupport

# Classification information for this Organization.
naics.1997.name=Lumber, plywood, millwork, and wood panel wholesalers
naics.1997.value=421310
```

```
naics.2002.name=Lumber, Plywood, Millwork, and Wood Panel Wholesalers
naics.2002.value=423310
unspsc.name=Framing lumber
unspsc.value=30.10.36.03
iso3166.name=Georgia, USA
iso3166.value=US-GA

# Identification information for this Organization.
duns=55-555-5555
thomasRegister=555555555

# The Service binding.
service.name=LumberSupplierService
service.description=This service provides LumberCo1's current lumber supply, lumber prices,
and lumber sales.
service.binding=The binding to the lumber.org SoapRpcLitBinding.

# The name of the WSDL concept implemented by this Service.
lumber.org.concept.name=lumber.org:LumberWholesaler
```

Registry.properties contains information about lumberco1 and its Web service. We also need to provide information on how to connect to the UDDI registry. Copy `lab2/schemas/src/lumber/org/RegistryConnection.properties` (Listing 8.68) to the directory `lab2/jaxrpc/jse/lumberco1/src/lc1/ws/jse`.

In this section you should have created the following files.

- `lab2/common/src/common/j2ee/ContextListener.java`
- `lab2/common/src/common/util/ProductLoader.java`
- `lab2/jaxrpc/jse/lumberco1/src/lc1/ws/jse/Prices.properties`
- `lab2/jaxrpc/jse/lumberco1/src/lc1/ws/jse/Registry.properties`
- `lab2/jaxrpc/jse/lumberco1/src/ws/jse/LumberPurchaseOrderJSE.java`

Deploying the Web Service for LumberCo1

To deploy the Web service for lumberco1, we need to create three deployment descriptors—`web.xml`, `webservices.xml`, and `sun-web.xml`. The purpose of these deployment descriptors has been discussed by this point, so let us jump into coding them. Create the following three listings in the directory `lab2/jaxrpc/jse/lumberco1/war/WEB-INF`.

Listing 8.83 lab2/jaxrpc/jse/lumberco1/war/WEB-INF/web.xml

```
<?xml version="1.0" encoding="UTF-8"?>
<web-app xmlns="http://java.sun.com/xml/ns/j2ee" version="2.4"
```

```
        xmlns:xsi="http://www.w3.org/2001/XMLSchema-instance"
        xsi:schemaLocation="http://java.sun.com/xml/ns/j2ee
            http://java.sun.com/xml/ns/j2ee/web-app_2_4.xsd">
  <display-name>lumberco1</display-name>
  <context-param>
    <param-name>priceProperties</param-name>
    <param-value>lc1.ws.jse.Prices</param-value>
  </context-param>
  <context-param>
    <param-name>registryConnectionProperties</param-name>
    <param-value>lc1.ws.jse.RegistryConnection</param-value>
  </context-param>
  <context-param>
    <param-name>registryProperties</param-name>
    <param-value>lc1.ws.jse.Registry</param-value>
  </context-param>
  <listener>
    <listener-class>common.j2ee.ContextListener</listener-class>
  </listener>
  <servlet>
    <display-name>LumberPurchaseOrderJSE</display-name>
    <servlet-name>LumberPurchaseOrderJSE</servlet-name>
    <servlet-class>lc1.ws.jse.LumberPurchaseOrderJSE</servlet-class>
  </servlet>
  <servlet-mapping>
    <servlet-name>LumberPurchaseOrderJSE</servlet-name>
    <url-pattern>/LumberSupplierService/PO</url-pattern>
  </servlet-mapping>
  <resource-ref>
    <res-ref-name>eis/JAXR</res-ref-name>
    <res-type>javax.xml.registry.ConnectionFactory</res-type>
    <res-auth>Container</res-auth>
    <res-sharing-scope>Shareable</res-sharing-scope>
  </resource-ref>
</web-app>
```

Listing 8.84 lab2/jaxrpc/jse/lumberco1/war/WEB-INF/webservices.xml

```
<?xml version="1.0" encoding="UTF-8"?>
<webservices version="1.1"
  xmlns="http://java.sun.com/xml/ns/j2ee"
  xmlns:xsi="http://www.w3.org/2001/XMLSchema-instance"
  xmlns:lc1="http://lumber.org/ws/standards/wsdl/LumberWholesaler.wsdl"
  xsi:schemaLocation="http://java.sun.com/xml/ns/j2ee
```

```
  http://www.ibm.com/webservices/xsd/j2ee_web_services_1_1.xsd">
  <webservice-description>
    <webservice-description-name>LumberSupplierService
    </webservice-description-name>
    <wsdl-file>WEB-INF/wsdl/LumberCo1Wholesaler.wsdl</wsdl-file>
    <jaxrpc-mapping-file>WEB-INF/wsdl/lumberco1_mapping.xml
    </jaxrpc-mapping-file>
    <port-component>
      <port-component-name>LumberPurchaseOrderJSE</port-component-name>
      <wsdl-port>lc1:LumberPurchaseOrderPort</wsdl-port>
      <service-endpoint-interface>lc1.ws.jse.PurchaseOrderPortType
      </service-endpoint-interface>
      <service-impl-bean>
        <servlet-link>LumberPurchaseOrderJSE</servlet-link>
      </service-impl-bean>
    </port-component>
  </webservice-description>
</webservices>
```

Listing 8.85 lab2/jaxrpc/jse/lumberco1/war/WEB-INF/sun-web.xml

```
<?xml version="1.0" encoding="UTF-8"?>
<!DOCTYPE sun-web-app PUBLIC
  "-//Sun Microsystems, Inc.//DTD Application Server 8.0 Servlet 2.4//EN"
  "http://www.sun.com/software/appserver/dtds/sun-web-app_2_4-0.dtd">
<sun-web-app>
  <context-root>/lumberco1</context-root>
  <resource-ref>
    <res-ref-name>eis/JAXR</res-ref-name>
    <jndi-name>eis/JAXR</jndi-name>
    <default-resource-principal>
      <name>j2ee</name>
      <password>j2ee</password>
    </default-resource-principal>
  </resource-ref>
</sun-web-app>
```

The `web.xml` file defines the location of the four properties files—the `ServletContextListener` class, the JAX-RPC Servlet endpoint class, the URL pattern for the Web service, and the JAXR resource. The `webservices.xml` file identifies the location of the WSDL and JAX-RPC mapping files and identifies the JAX-RPC service endpoint. The `sun-web.xml` file the URL for the context root and information for the JAXR resource reference.

Just as with the schemas WAR, we use Ant to build and deploy this WAR file. You should have already coded the Ant build file from Listing 8.77. To compile and deploy the lumberco1 WAR, make

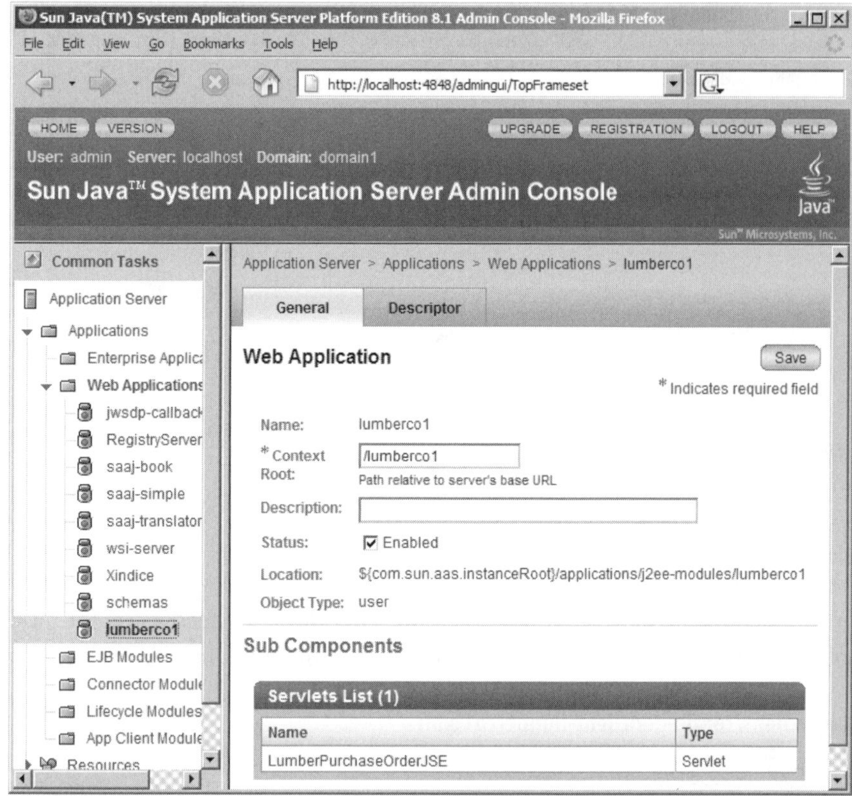

Figure 8.16

Admin Console Showing Deployed lumberco1

sure the server is running open a command prompt, navigate to the directory `lab2/jaxrpc/jse/lumberco1` where `build.xml` is located, and enter the following commands:

```
ant
```

and then the command:

```
ant deploy
```

The first command will compile the code and create the WAR file. The second command will deploy the WAR file to the server. Once you have executed the commands, to verify that the Web service was deployed, open the Admin Console and expand the Applications and Web Applications nodes. You should see lumberco1 in the list of Web applications, similar to Figure 8.16.

You can also read the logged statements from the lumberco1 classes by performing an advanced search in the Log Viewer with `common.util.JAXRHelper` and `common.j2ee.ContextListener` as entries in the Custom Logger field. The results should look something similar to the screenshot in Figure 8.17.

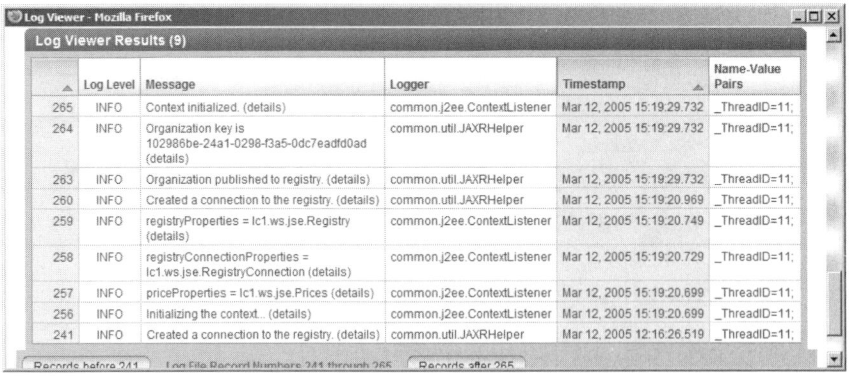

Log Viewer - Mozilla Firefox

Log Viewer Results (9)

	Log Level	Message	Logger	Timestamp	Name-Value Pairs
265	INFO	Context initialized. (details)	common.j2ee.ContextListener	Mar 12, 2005 15:19:29.732	_ThreadID=11;
264	INFO	Organization key is 102986be-24a1-0298-f3a5-0dc7eadfd0ad (details)	common.util.JAXRHelper	Mar 12, 2005 15:19:29.732	_ThreadID=11;
263	INFO	Organization published to registry. (details)	common.util.JAXRHelper	Mar 12, 2005 15:19:29.732	_ThreadID=11;
260	INFO	Created a connection to the registry. (details)	common.util.JAXRHelper	Mar 12, 2005 15:19:20.969	_ThreadID=11;
259	INFO	registryProperties = lc1.ws.jse.Registry (details)	common.j2ee.ContextListener	Mar 12, 2005 15:19:20.749	_ThreadID=11;
258	INFO	registryConnectionProperties = lc1.ws.jse.RegistryConnection (details)	common.j2ee.ContextListener	Mar 12, 2005 15:19:20.729	_ThreadID=11;
257	INFO	priceProperties = lc1.ws.jse.Prices (details)	common.j2ee.ContextListener	Mar 12, 2005 15:19:20.699	_ThreadID=11;
256	INFO	Initializing the context... (details)	common.j2ee.ContextListener	Mar 12, 2005 15:19:20.699	_ThreadID=11;
241	INFO	Created a connection to the registry. (details)	common.util.JAXRHelper	Mar 12, 2005 12:16:26.519	_ThreadID=11;

Figure 8.17

Log Statements from lumberco1

Testing the Lumberco1 Web Service

Now we create a generated stub client to test the deployed lumberco1 Web service. The first thing we need to do is run `wscompile` to generate the static stub. Therefore, we need a configuration file to pass to `wscompile`. Create the following configuration file in the directory `lab2/client`.

Listing 8.86 lab2/client/config-genclient-lumberco1.xml

```
<?xml version="1.0" encoding="UTF-8"?>
<configuration xmlns="http://java.sun.com/xml/ns/jax-rpc/ri/config">
  <wsdl
  location="http://localhost:8080/lumberco1/LumberSupplierService/PO?WSDL"
  packageName="lc1.ws.jse">
    <namespaceMappingRegistry>
      <namespaceMapping
  namespace="http://lumber.org/ws/standards/wsdl/LumberWholesaler.wsdl"
  packageName="lc1.ws.jse"/>
      <namespaceMapping
  namespace="http://lumber.org/ws/standards/schemas/ProductCatalog.xsd"
  packageName="common.domain.catalog"/>
      <namespaceMapping
  namespace="http://lumber.org/ws/standards/schemas/PurchaseOrder.xsd"
  packageName="common.domain.order"/>
      <namespaceMapping
  namespace="http://lumber.org/ws/standards/schemas/Customer.xsd"
  packageName="common.domain.customer"/>
      <namespaceMapping
  namespace="http://lumber.org/ws/standards/schemas/Address.xsd"
  packageName="common.domain.address"/>
```

```
      <namespaceMapping
  namespace="http://lumber.org/ws/standards/schemas/Types.xsd"
  packageName="common.domain.types"/>
    </namespaceMappingRegistry>
  </wsdl>
</configuration>
```

Notice that this configuration file uses a `wsdl` element that gives the location of the WSDL for the deployed lumberco1 Web service. When you deploy a Web service to the J2EE RI, the location of the WSDL file is, by default, the URL of the Web service endpoint appended with "`?WSDL`". This configuration file also gives the appropriate mappings from the XML namespaces to Java packages. To execute wscompile we will again use Ant. The build file for building and running the client is listed below. This build file also includes code for building and running the client for lumberco2 and a UDDI test that we will not discuss until later. Create the following listing in the directory `lab2/client`.

Listing 8.87 lab2/client/build.xml

```
<project name="LumberCoClient" default="build-lc1-client" basedir=".">
  <property name="common.dir" value="../common"/>
  <property name="common.build.file"
            value="${common.dir}/common-build.xml"/>

  <import file="${common.build.file}"/>

  <property name="config.lc1.genclient.file"
            value="config-genclient-lumberco1.xml"/>
  <property name="client.lc1.jar" value="lc1-client.jar"/>
  <property name="client.lc1.class.stub"
            value="lc1.client.Lc1StaticStubTest"/>
  <property name="build.lc1.client.src"
            value="${build.dir}/lc1/client/src" />
  <property name="build.lc1.client.classes"
            value="${build.dir}/lc1/client/classes" />

  <property name="config.lc2.genclient.file"
            value="config-genclient-lumberco2.xml"/>
  <property name="client.lc2.jar" value="lc2-client.jar"/>
  <property name="client.lc2.class.stub"
            value="lc2.client.Lc2StaticStubTest"/>
  <property name="build.lc2.client.src"
            value="${build.dir}/lc2/client/src" />
  <property name="build.lc2.client.classes"
```

```
          value="${build.dir}/lc2/client/classes" />

<property name="client.generic.jar" value="generic-client.jar"/>
<property name="client.generic.class.uddi"
          value="generic.client.UDDITest"/>
<property name="build.generic.client.classes"
          value="${build.dir}/generic/client/classes" />

<!- CLASSPATHS ->
<path id="compile.classpath">
  <path refid="j2ee.classpath"/>
  <pathelement location="${build.lc1.client.classes}"/>
</path>
<path id="run.classpath">
  <fileset dir="${j2ee.ri.home}/lib">
    <include name="*.jar"/>
  </fileset>
  <fileset dir="${j2ee.ri.home}/lib/endorsed">
    <include name="*.jar"/>
  </fileset>
</path>

<!- PREPARE ->
<target name="prepare" description="Creates the build directories.">
  <mkdir dir="${build.lc1.client.src}" />
  <mkdir dir="${build.lc1.client.classes}" />
  <mkdir dir="${build.lc2.client.src}" />
  <mkdir dir="${build.lc2.client.classes}" />
  <mkdir dir="${build.generic.client.classes}" />
</target>

<!- WSCOMPILE ->
<target name="generate-lc1-stubs" depends="prepare"
        description="Runs wscompile to generate the client stub classes.">
  <antcall target="run-wscompile">
    <param name="param1"
           value="-gen:client -f:rpcliteral,wsi -keep -d ${build.lc1.client.classes} -s
${build.lc1.client.src} ${config.lc1.genclient.file}"/>
  </antcall>
</target>

<target name="generate-lc2-stubs" depends="prepare"
        description="Runs wscompile to generate the client stub classes.">
  <antcall target="run-wscompile">
    <param name="param1"
           value="-gen:client -f:rpcliteral,wsi -keep -d ${build.lc2.client.classes} -s
${build.lc2.client.src} ${config.lc2.genclient.file}"/>
```

```
  </antcall>
</target>

<!- COMPILE ->
<target name="compile-lc1-client" depends="prepare,generate-lc1-stubs"
        description="Compiles the client-side source code.">
  <javac srcdir="${src.dir}"
         destdir="${build.lc1.client.classes}"
         debug="${compile.debug}"
         deprecation="${compile.deprecation}"
         optimize="${compile.optimize}">
    <include name="lc1/**"/>
    <classpath refid="compile.classpath"/>
  </javac>
</target>

<target name="compile-lc2-client" depends="prepare,generate-lc2-stubs"
        description="Compiles the client-side source code.">
  <javac srcdir="${src.dir}"
         destdir="${build.lc2.client.classes}"
         debug="${compile.debug}"
         deprecation="${compile.deprecation}"
         optimize="${compile.optimize}">
    <include name="lc2/**"/>
    <classpath refid="compile.classpath"/>
  </javac>
</target>

<target name="compile-generic-client" depends="prepare"
        description="Compiles the client-side source code.">
  <javac srcdir="${src.dir}"
         destdir="${build.generic.client.classes}"
         debug="${compile.debug}"
         deprecation="${compile.deprecation}"
         optimize="${compile.optimize}">
    <include name="generic/**"/>
    <classpath refid="compile.classpath"/>
  </javac>

  <!- Copy all resources. ->
  <copy todir="${build.generic.client.classes}"
        preservelastmodified="true" includeEmptyDirs="false">
    <fileset dir="${src.dir}" includes="generic/**/*"
             excludes="**/*.java"/>
  </copy>
</target>

<!- DIST ->
<target name="package-lc1-client" depends="compile-lc1-client"
```

```
    description="Builds the JAR file that contains the client.">
  <mkdir dir="${dist.dir}"/>
  <delete file="${dist.dir}/${client.lc1.jar}" />
  <jar jarfile="${dist.dir}/${client.lc1.jar}"
       basedir="${build.lc1.client.classes}"/>
</target>

<target name="package-lc2-client" depends="compile-lc2-client"
    description="Builds the JAR file that contains the client.">
  <mkdir dir="${dist.dir}"/>
  <delete file="${dist.dir}/${client.lc2.jar}" />
  <jar jarfile="${dist.dir}/${client.lc2.jar}"
       basedir="${build.lc2.client.classes}"/>
</target>

<target name="package-generic-client" depends="compile-generic-client"
    description="Builds the JAR file that contains the client.">
  <mkdir dir="${dist.dir}"/>
  <delete file="${dist.dir}/${client.generic.jar}" />
  <jar jarfile="${dist.dir}/${client.generic.jar}"
       basedir="${build.generic.client.classes}"/>
</target>

<!- BUILD ->
<target name="build-lc1-client"
     depends="generate-lc1-stubs,package-lc1-client"
     description="Executes the targets needed to build the client files.">
</target>

<target name="build-lc2-client"
     depends="generate-lc2-stubs,package-lc2-client"
     description="Executes the targets needed to build the client files.">
</target>

<target name="build-generic-client"
     depends="package-generic-client"
     description="Executes the targets needed to build the client files.">
</target>

<!- RUN ->
<target name="test-lc1-client-stub"
        description="Runs a test JAX-RPC client.">
  <java fork="on" classpath="${dist.dir}/${client.lc1.jar}"
        classname="${client.lc1.class.stub}">
    <classpath refid="run.classpath" />
  </java>
```

```
  </target>

  <target name="test-lc2-client-stub"
          description="Runs a test JAX-RPC client.">
    <java fork="on" classpath="${dist.dir}/${client.lc2.jar}"
          classname="${client.lc2.class.stub}">
      <classpath refid="run.classpath" />
    </java>
  </target>

  <target name="test-generic-client-uddi"
          description="Runs a test JAX-RPC client.">
    <java fork="on" classpath="${dist.dir}/${client.generic.jar}"
          classname="${client.generic.class.uddi}">
      <classpath refid="run.classpath" />
    </java>
  </target>
</project>
```

As with the previous `build.xml`, the lines in bold text in the listing above must be entered on a single line. Now generate the stub code by making sure the server is running and the lumbercol service is deployed, opening a command prompt, navigating to the `lab2/client` directory where `build.xml` is located, and entering the following command:

```
ant generate-lc1-stubs
```

This command will generate Java files in the `lab2/client/build/lc1/client/src` directory and their compiled classes in the directory `lab2/client/build/lc1/client/classes` directory. The generated classes will include the JAX-RPC service endpoint interface with the associated implementation classes, as well as the types we defined in XML Schema and classes to handle their serialization to XML. It creates quite a few classes. The JAX-RPC compiler is a very useful tool.

Now we can create a client that uses the generated classes to invoke the lumbercol Web service. Create the following listing in the directory `lab2/client/src/lc1/client`.

Listing 8.88 lab2/client/src/lc1/client/Lc1StaticStubTest.java

```
package lc1.client;

import java.text.SimpleDateFormat;
import java.util.*;
import javax.xml.rpc.ServiceException;
import javax.xml.rpc.ServiceFactory;
import lc1.ws.jse.LumberSupplierService;
import lc1.ws.jse.PurchaseOrderPortType;
import common.domain.address.USAddress;
```

```
import common.domain.catalog.Product;
import common.domain.catalog.ProductCatalog;
import common.domain.customer.Customer;
import common.domain.order.LineItem;
import common.domain.order.PurchaseOrder;
import common.domain.order.ShippingNotice;

public class Lc1StaticStubTest {
  public static void main(String[] args) {
    LumberSupplierService service = null;
    PurchaseOrderPortType stub = null;

    try {
      service = (LumberSupplierService)
        ServiceFactory.newInstance().loadService(
          LumberSupplierService.class);
      stub = service.getLumberPurchaseOrderPort();
    }catch (ServiceException e) {
      System.err.println("Failed to get the service and the stub.");
      e.printStackTrace();
      return;
    }

    List purchaseItems = getItemsToOrder(stub);
    placeOrder(stub, purchaseItems);
  }

  /** Gets the ProductCatalog and returns the first two items to order. */
  public static List getItemsToOrder(PurchaseOrderPortType stub) {
    System.out.println("Attempting to get the catalog from lumberco1...");
    List purchaseItems = new ArrayList();

    try {
      ProductCatalog catalog = null;
      catalog = stub.getCatalog();
      System.out.println("lumberco1 prices:\n");

      if (catalog.getProducts().length > 0) {
        Product[] products = catalog.getProducts();

        for (int i = 0; i < products.length; i++) {
          System.out.println("itemNumber = "
            + products[i].getProductNumber());
          System.out.println("name = " + products[i].getName());
          System.out.println("description = "
            + products[i].getDescription());
          System.out.println("price = $" + products[i].getPrice());
```

```
        System.out.println();

        if (i < 2) { // Just order the first two items.
          purchaseItems.add(products[i]);
        }
      }
    }
  }catch (Exception e) {
    System.err.println("Error getting catalog from lumbercol");
    e.printStackTrace();
  }

  return purchaseItems;
}

/** Submits a PurchaseOrder. */
public static void placeOrder(PurchaseOrderPortType stub,
  List purchaseItems) {
  System.out.println("Attempting to place an order with lumbercol");

  try {
    if (purchaseItems.isEmpty()) {
      System.out.println("No items in catalog to order.");
      return;
    }

    USAddress address = new USAddress();
    address.setStreet("555 Peach Lane");
    address.setCity("Atlanta");
    address.setState("GA");
    address.setZip("30332");

    Customer customer = new Customer();
    customer.setFirstName("Kelly");
    customer.setLastName("Allen");
    customer.setCompany("LumberRetailer");
    customer.setPhoneNumber("555-555-5555");
    customer.setEmailAddress("kelly.allen@lumberretailer.com");
    customer.setBillingAddress(address);

    List lineItems = new ArrayList();
    int quantity = 100;
    float total = 0.0f;

    for (Iterator iter = purchaseItems.iterator(); iter.hasNext();) {
      Product product = (Product) iter.next();
```

```
        LineItem item = new LineItem();
        item.setQuantity(quantity);
        item.setProductNumber(product.getProductNumber());
        item.setPrice(product.getPrice());
        lineItems.add(item);
        total += (product.getPrice() * quantity);
      }

      PurchaseOrder purchaseOrder = new PurchaseOrder();
      purchaseOrder.setOrderDate(Calendar.getInstance());
      purchaseOrder.setCustomer(customer);
      purchaseOrder.setShippingAddress(address);
      purchaseOrder.setLineItems((LineItem[])
        lineItems.toArray(new LineItem[]{}));
      purchaseOrder.setTotal(total);

      ShippingNotice shippingNotice = stub.placeOrder(purchaseOrder);
      SimpleDateFormat dateFormat = new SimpleDateFormat("MM/dd/yyyy");
      System.out.println("Order placed successfully.");
      System.out.println("orderNumber = " + shippingNotice.getOrderNumber());
      System.out.println("shipDate = "
        + dateFormat.format(shippingNotice.getShipDate().getTime()));
      System.out.println("total = $" + total);
    }catch (Exception e) {
      System.err.println("Error placing order with lumbercol");
      e.printStackTrace();
    }
  }
}
```

The `build.xml` is already set up to compile and test `Lc1StaticStubTest.java`, so make sure the server is running and the lumbercol Web service is deployed, then open a command prompt, navigate to the `lab2/client` directory where `build.xml` is located, and enter the following command:

```
ant package-lc1-client
```

This command will compile the source code for the client and then JAR the client up so that it is easy to reference when we run the test. To run the test, enter the following command:

```
ant test-lc1-client-stub
```

This command will execute `Lc1StaticStubTest`. You should see output on the command line similar to that shown in Figure 8.18 and Figure 8.19.

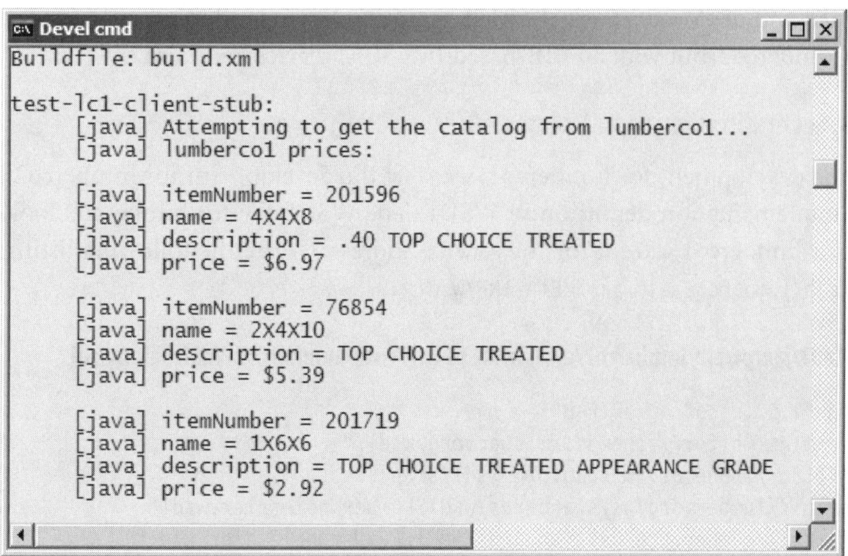

```
Devel cmd
Buildfile: build.xml

test-lc1-client-stub:
     [java] Attempting to get the catalog from lumberco1...
     [java] lumberco1 prices:

     [java] itemNumber = 201596
     [java] name = 4X4X8
     [java] description = .40 TOP CHOICE TREATED
     [java] price = $6.97

     [java] itemNumber = 76854
     [java] name = 2X4X10
     [java] description = TOP CHOICE TREATED
     [java] price = $5.39

     [java] itemNumber = 201719
     [java] name = 1X6X6
     [java] description = TOP CHOICE TREATED APPEARANCE GRADE
     [java] price = $2.92
```

Figure 8.18

Output from the lumberco1 Test

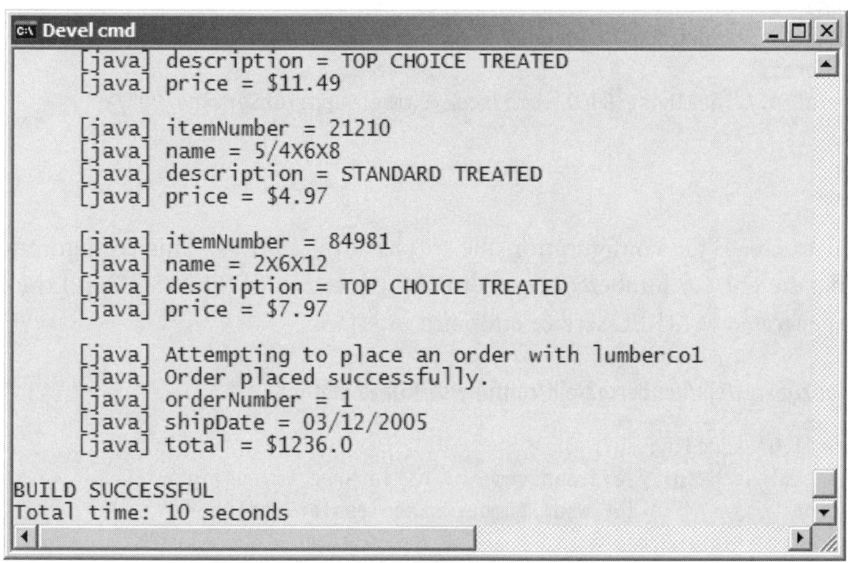

```
Devel cmd
     [java] description = TOP CHOICE TREATED
     [java] price = $11.49

     [java] itemNumber = 21210
     [java] name = 5/4X6X8
     [java] description = STANDARD TREATED
     [java] price = $4.97

     [java] itemNumber = 84981
     [java] name = 2X6X12
     [java] description = TOP CHOICE TREATED
     [java] price = $7.97

     [java] Attempting to place an order with lumberco1
     [java] Order placed successfully.
     [java] orderNumber = 1
     [java] shipDate = 03/12/2005
     [java] total = $1236.0

BUILD SUCCESSFUL
Total time: 10 seconds
```

Figure 8.19

Output from the lumberco1 Test, Continued

We have created and deployed a Servlet-based JAX-RPC service endpoint and tested it. Next we do the same for lumberco2, but with an EJB-based JAX-RPC service endpoint.

WSDL-to-Java: Generating Classes for LumberCo2

Just as with the development for lumberco1, we start the development for lumberco2 by creating a Web service implementation definition in WSDL. The WSDL file for lumberco2 looks almost just like the one for lumberco1, except for the service address. Create the following listing in directory `lab2/jaxrpc/ejb/lumberco2/ejb/jar/META-INF/wsdl`.

Listing 8.89 lab2/jaxrpc/ejb/lumberco2/ejb/jar/META-INF/wsdl/LumberCo2Wholesaler.wsdl

```
<?xml version="1.0" encoding="UTF-8"?>
<definitions xmlns="http://schemas.xmlsoap.org/wsdl/"
 xmlns:soap="http://schemas.xmlsoap.org/wsdl/soap/"
 xmlns:lr="http://lumber.org/ws/standards/wsdl/LumberWholesaler.wsdl"
 xmlns:tns="http://lumber.org/ws/standards/wsdl/LumberWholesaler.wsdl"
 targetNamespace="http://lumber.org/ws/standards/wsdl/LumberWholesaler.wsdl">

  <import
    namespace="http://lumber.org/ws/standards/wsdl/LumberWholesaler.wsdl"
    location="http://localhost:8080/schemas/LumberWholesaler.wsdl"/>

  <service name="LumberSupplierService">
    <port name="LumberPurchaseOrderPort" binding="lr:SoapRpcLitBinding">
      <soap:address
    location="http://localhost:8080/lumberco2/LumberSupplierService/PO"/>
    </port>
  </service>
</definitions>
```

Next we need to create the configuration file to pass to `wscompile`. This configuration file looks almost just like the one for lumberco1, except for the location of the WSDL and the Java package name for the generated JAX-RPC service endpoint interface.

Listing 8.90 lab2/jaxrpc/ejb/lumberco2/ejb/config-wsdlToJava.xml

```
<?xml version="1.0" encoding="UTF-8"?>
<configuration xmlns="http://java.sun.com/xml/ns/jax-rpc/ri/config">
  <wsdl location="./jar/META-INF/wsdl/LumberCo2Wholesaler.wsdl"
        packageName="lc2.ws.ejb">
    <namespaceMappingRegistry>
      <namespaceMapping
```

```
  namespace="http://lumber.org/ws/standards/wsdl/LumberWholesaler.wsdl"
  packageName="lc2.ws.ejb"/>
      <namespaceMapping
  namespace="http://lumber.org/ws/standards/schemas/ProductCatalog.xsd"
  packageName="common.domain.catalog"/>
      <namespaceMapping
  namespace="http://lumber.org/ws/standards/schemas/PurchaseOrder.xsd"
  packageName="common.domain.order"/>
      <namespaceMapping
  namespace="http://lumber.org/ws/standards/schemas/Customer.xsd"
  packageName="common.domain.customer"/>
      <namespaceMapping
  namespace="http://lumber.org/ws/standards/schemas/Address.xsd"
  packageName="common.domain.address"/>
      <namespaceMapping
  namespace="http://lumber.org/ws/standards/schemas/Types.xsd"
  packageName="common.domain.types"/>
    </namespaceMappingRegistry>
  </wsdl>
</configuration>
```

Next we create the Ant build file that we will use to generate classes from the WSDL. This build file is very similar to the one for lumberco1. Create the following listing in directory lab2/jaxrpc/ejb/-lumberco2/ejb.

Listing 8.91 lab2/jaxrpc/ejb/lumberco2/ejb/build.xml

```
<!- Builds the EJB-JAR for LumberCo2 ->
<project name="LumberCo2WholesalerEJB" default="create-ejb-jar" basedir=".">
  <property name="common.dir" value="../../../../common"/>
  <property name="common.build.file" value="${common.dir}/common-build.xml"/>

  <import file="${common.build.file}" />

  <property name="assemble.dir" value="assemble"/>
  <property name="assemble.jar.dir" value="${assemble.dir}/jar"/>
  <property name="context.path" value="lumberco2"/>
  <property name="jar.file" value="${context.path}-ejb.jar"/>
  <property name="config.wsdlToJava.file" value="config-wsdlToJava.xml"/>
  <property name="mapping.file" value="${context.path}_mapping.xml"/>
  <property name="build.sei.src" value="${build.dir}/sei/src" />
  <property name="build.sei.classes" value="${build.dir}/sei/classes" />
  <property name="build.server.classes"
          value="${build.dir}/server/classes" />
```

```
  <!- For generating WSDL from pre-existing Java code.
       Not used in this example.
  <property name="config.interface.file" value="config-javaToWsdl.xml"/>
  <property name="wsdl.file" value="LumberSupplierService.wsdl"/> ->

  <!- CLASSPATHS ->
  <path id="compile.classpath">
    <path refid="j2ee.classpath"/>
    <pathelement location="${build.sei.classes}"/>
    <pathelement location="${build.server.classes}"/>
  </path>

  <!- PREPARE ->
  <target name="prepare" description="Creates the build directories.">
    <mkdir dir="${build.sei.src}" />
    <mkdir dir="${build.sei.classes}" />
    <mkdir dir="${build.server.classes}" />
  </target>

  <!- WSCOMPILE ->
  <!- NOTE: This target requires the lumber.org schemas to be deployed. ->
  <target name="generate-sei" depends="prepare"
    description="Runs wscompile to generate the SEI from the WSDL file.">
    <antcall target="run-wscompile">
      <param name="param1"
             value="-import -f:wsi -keep -d ${build.sei.classes} -s ${build.sei.src} -nd
${build.dir} -mapping ${build.dir}/${mapping.file} ${config.wsdlToJava.file}"/>
    </antcall>
  </target>

  <!- For generating WSDL from preexisting Java code.
       Not ran for this example.
  <target name="generate-wsdl" depends="compile"
          description="Runs wscompile to generate the WSDL file">
    <antcall target="run-wscompile">
      <param name="param1"
             value="-define -f:rpcliteral,wsi -keep -d ${build.sei.classes} -s
${build.sei.src} -nd ${build.dir} -mapping ${build.dir}/${mapping.file} -cp
${build.server.classes};${common.dir}/${dist.dir}/${common.jar};${common.dir}/${dist.dir}/${
domain.jar} ${config.interface.file}"/>
    </antcall>
  </target> ->

  <!- COMPILE ->
```

```
  <target name="compile-service" depends="prepare,generate-sei"
          description="Compiles the server-side source code.">
    <javac srcdir="${src.dir}:${common.dir}/src"
           includes="lc2/**,common/util/ProductLoader.java"
           destdir="${build.server.classes}"
           debug="${compile.debug}"
           deprecation="${compile.deprecation}"
           optimize="${compile.optimize}">
      <classpath refid="compile.classpath"/>
    </javac>
  </target>

  <!- DIST ->
  <target name="create-ejb-jar" depends="generate-sei,compile-service"
          description="Builds the EJB JAR file for the JAX-RPC supplier">
    <mkdir dir="${assemble.jar.dir}" />
    <copy todir="${assemble.jar.dir}" preservelastmodified="true">
      <fileset dir="jar"/>
    </copy>
    <copy todir="${assemble.jar.dir}" preservelastmodified="true">
      <fileset dir="${build.server.classes}"/>
    </copy>

    <!- Copy associated resources. ->
    <copy todir="${assemble.jar.dir}" preservelastmodified="true"
          includeEmptyDirs="false">
      <fileset dir="${src.dir}" excludes="**/*.java"/>
    </copy>

    <!- Copy generated files. ->
    <copy file="${build.dir}/${mapping.file}"
          todir="${assemble.jar.dir}/META-INF/wsdl"
          preservelastmodified="true" />
    <copy todir="${assemble.jar.dir}" preservelastmodified="true">
      <fileset dir="${build.sei.classes}"/>
    </copy>

    <!- Create the JAR. ->
    <delete file="${dist.dir}/${jar.file}" />
    <mkdir dir="${dist.dir}" />
    <jar jarfile="${dist.dir}/${jar.file}" basedir="${assemble.jar.dir}"/>
  </target>
</project>
```

To generate the JAX-RPC service endpoint interface from the WSDL, make sure the server is running and the schemas WAR is deployed, open a command prompt, navigate to the `lab2/jaxrpc/ejb/lumberco2/ejb` directory where `build.xml` is located, and enter the following command:

```
ant generate-sei
```

After this command completes you should have several Java files in the directory `lab2/jaxrpc/ejb/lumberco2/ejb/build/sei/src` and their corresponding compiled classes in the directory `lab2/jaxrpc/ejb/lumberco2/ejb/build/sei/classes`. You should also have a `lumberco2_mapping.xml` file in the directory `lab2/jaxrpc/ejb/lumberco2/ejb/build`. The Java classes and the JAX-RPC mapping file should be nearly identical to the ones generated for lumberco1 in the section titled "WSDL-to-Java: Generating Classes for Lumberco1."

Coding the JAX-RPC Service Endpoint for LumberCo2

This implementation is an EJB-based JAX-RPC service endpoint, but, to save time, it will function just as the endpoint developed for lumberco1. This is an exercise in deploying an EJB endpoint because actually creating it is very simple. We start our development the same as we did for lumberco1. We need to create data that represents the lumber that lumberco2 will be selling online. To save time, just copy `lab2/jaxrpc/jse/lumberco1/src/lc1/ws/jse/Prices.properties` to the directory `lab2/jaxrpc/-ejb/lumberco2/ejb/src/lc2/ws/ejb` and change some of the prices. We will use the `ProductLoader` class from Listing 8.79 to load the properties file into `Product` objects just as we did for lumberco1.

Now we code the EJB implementation. Create the following listing in the directory `lab2/jaxrpc/ejb/lumberco2/ejb/src/lc2/ws/ejb`.

Listing 8.92 lab2/jaxrpc/ejb/lumberco2/ejb/src/lc2/ws/ejb/LumberPurchaseOrderBean.java

```
package lc2.ws.ejb;

import java.rmi.RemoteException;
import java.util.Calendar;
import java.util.ResourceBundle;
import java.util.logging.Logger;
import javax.ejb.EJBException;
import javax.ejb.SessionBean;
import javax.ejb.SessionContext;
import javax.naming.Context;
import javax.naming.InitialContext;
import javax.naming.NamingException;
import common.domain.catalog.Product;
import common.domain.catalog.ProductCatalog;
import common.domain.order.InvalidPurchaseOrderFault;
```

```
import common.domain.order.PurchaseOrder;
import common.domain.order.ShippingNotice;
import common.util.ProductLoader;

public class LumberPurchaseOrderBean implements SessionBean {
  private static Logger logger =
    Logger.getLogger(LumberPurchaseOrderBean.class.getName());
  private SessionContext ejbContext = null;
  private Context jndiContext = null;
  private String priceProperties = null;
  private ResourceBundle priceBundle = null;

  public ProductCatalog getCatalog() {
    logger.fine("Prices requested from lumberco2.");
    ProductCatalog catalog = loadCatalog();
    logger.fine("Returning " + catalog.getProducts().length
      + " prices from lumberco2.");
    return catalog;
  }

  public ShippingNotice placeOrder(PurchaseOrder purchaseOrder)
    throws InvalidPurchaseOrderFault, RemoteException {
    Calendar tomorrow = Calendar.getInstance();
    tomorrow.add(Calendar.DAY_OF_YEAR, 1);
    // TODO: create better order number.
    ShippingNotice notice = new ShippingNotice();
    notice.setOrderNumber("1");
    notice.setPurchaseOrder(purchaseOrder);
    notice.setShipDate(tomorrow);

    StringBuffer out = new StringBuffer();
    out.append("\nOrder placed to lumberco1:\n").append(
      purchaseOrder.toString());
    logger.fine(out.toString());

    return notice;
  }

  private ProductCatalog loadCatalog() {
    Calendar startDate = Calendar.getInstance();
    Calendar endDate = Calendar.getInstance();
    endDate.add(Calendar.DAY_OF_YEAR, 30);

    Product[] products = ProductLoader.loadProducts(priceBundle);
```

```
    ProductCatalog catalog = new ProductCatalog();
    catalog.setEffectiveStartDate(startDate);
    catalog.setEffectiveEndDate(endDate);
    catalog.setProducts(products);

    return catalog;
  }

  public void ejbCreate() {
    System.out.println("Initializing the context...");

    try {
      priceProperties = (String)
        jndiContext.lookup("java:comp/env/priceProperties");
      System.out.println("priceProperties = " + priceProperties);
    }catch (NamingException e) {
      String message = "Failed to lookup registry properties in JNDI.";
      System.err.println(message);
      e.printStackTrace();
      throw new EJBException(message, e);
    }

    priceBundle = ResourceBundle.getBundle(priceProperties);
  }

  public void ejbRemove() {}
  public void ejbActivate() {}
  public void ejbPassivate() {}

  public void setSessionContext(SessionContext cntx) {
    this.ejbContext = cntx;

    try {
      jndiContext = new InitialContext();
    }catch (NamingException ne) {
      throw new EJBException(ne);
    }
  }
}
```

LumberPurchaseOrderBean looks nearly identical to LumberPurchaseOrderJSE, except it extends javax.ejb.SessionBean and implements the necessary methods, which, except for a few, do nothing at all. Also, LumberPurchaseOrderBean uses JNDI to look up the location of Prices.properties.

We also use `ContextListener` from Listing 8.81 to publish information on the lumberco2 Web service to the UDDI registry on context startup, which means we will be deploying a WAR file in addition to the EJB-JAR for the endpoint. We need the same properties files for connecting to the registry and publishing information. Copy `RegistryConnection.properties` and `Registry.properties` from `lab2/jaxrpc-/jse/lumberco1/src/lc1/ws/jse` to `lab2/jaxrpc/ejb/lumberco2/war/WEB-INF/classes`. Then change the lines in `lab2/jaxrpc/ejb/lumberco2/war/WEB-INF/classes/Registry.properties` as shown in bold text in the following listing. Note that the last line in bold text should appear on a single line.

Listing 8.93 lab2/jaxrpc/ejb/lumberco2/war/WEB-INF/classes/Registry.properties

```
endpointURL = http://localhost:8080/lumberco2/LumberSupplierService/PO

# A file for storing the Key generated when we store
# this Organization in the UDDI registry.
key.file=lumberco2_orgkey.txt

# General information on the Organization.
org.name=LumberCo2
org.description=A supplier of lumber.
person.name=Kelly Allen
contact.description=Technical Support
phone.number=(800) 555-1111
email.address=kelly.allen@lumberco2.com
address.number=102
address.street=Lumber Drive
address.city=Jacksonville
address.state=FL
address.postalCode=32259
address.country=USA
address.type=TechSupport

# Classification information for this Organization.
naics.1997.name=Lumber, plywood, millwork, and wood panel wholesalers
naics.1997.value=421310
naics.2002.name=Lumber, Plywood, Millwork, and Wood Panel Wholesalers
naics.2002.value=423310
unspsc.name=Framing lumber
unspsc.value=30.10.36.03
iso3166.name=Florida, USA
iso3166.value=US-FL
```

```
# Identification information for this Organization.
duns=99-999-9999
thomasRegister=999999999

# The Service binding.
service.name=LumberSupplierService
service.description=This service provides LumberCo2's current lumber supply, lumber prices,
and lumber sales.
service.binding=The binding to the lumber.org SoapRpcLitBinding.

# The name of the WSDL concept implemented by this Service.
lumber.org.concept.name=lumber.org:LumberWholesaler
```

Deploying the Web Service for LumberCo2

We deploy the Web service for lumberco2 within an EAR. Inside the EAR is a WAR and an EJB JAR. The EJB JAR contains the `LumberPurchaseOrderBean`, `JAXRHelper`, and the classes generated by `wscompile` (the JAX-RPC compiler). We already have an Ant `build.xml` file for creating the EJB JAR. We still need an Ant `build.xml` for generating the WAR and another for generating the EAR. We also need deployment descriptors for the EJB JAR, the WAR, and the EAR. We start by creating the deployment descriptors for the EJB JAR. Create the following three listings in directory `lab2/jaxrpc/ejb/lumberco2/ejb/jar/META-INF`. The first listing is the `ejb-jar.xml` deployment descriptor that is required by J2EE when deploying EJBs. The second listing is the `webservices.xml` deployment descriptor that is required when deploying Web services to a J2EE container. The third listing is a deployment descriptor that is required by the J2EE RI—`sun-ejb-jar.xml`.

Listing 8.94 lab2/jaxrpc/ejb/lumberco2/ejb/jar/META-INF/ejb-jar.xml

```
<?xml version="1.0"?>
<ejb-jar version="2.1"
         xmlns="http://java.sun.com/xml/ns/j2ee"
         xmlns:xsi="http://www.w3.org/2001/XMLSchema-instance"
         xsi:schemaLocation="http://java.sun.com/xml/ns/j2ee
             http://java.sun.com/xml/ns/j2ee/ejb-jar_2_1.xsd">
  <enterprise-beans>
    <session>
      <description>
        The EJB lumber purchase order service for LumberCo2
      </description>
      <ejb-name>LumberPurchaseOrderEJB</ejb-name>
      <service-endpoint>lc2.ws.ejb.PurchaseOrderPortType</service-endpoint>
      <ejb-class>lc2.ws.ejb.LumberPurchaseOrderBean</ejb-class>
      <session-type>Stateless</session-type>
```

```
        <transaction-type>Container</transaction-type>
        <env-entry>
            <env-entry-name>priceProperties</env-entry-name>
            <env-entry-type>java.lang.String</env-entry-type>
            <env-entry-value>lc2.ws.ejb.Prices</env-entry-value>
        </env-entry>
        <resource-ref>
          <res-ref-name>eis/JAXR</res-ref-name>
          <res-type>javax.xml.registry.ConnectionFactory</res-type>
          <res-auth>Container</res-auth>
        </resource-ref>
      </session>
  </enterprise-beans>
  <assembly-descriptor>
    <method-permission>
      <unchecked/>
      <method>
        <ejb-name>LumberPurchaseOrderEJB</ejb-name>
        <method-name>*</method-name>
      </method>
    </method-permission>
  </assembly-descriptor>
</ejb-jar>
```

The `ejb-jar.xml` deployment descriptor identifies the type of EJB we are deploying (Stateless session), the EJB Java class (`lc2.ws.ejb.LumberPurchaseOrderBean`), the JAX-RPC service endpoint interface Java class (`lc2.we.ejb.PurchaseOrderPortType`), the location of `Price.properties`, the JAXR ConnectionFactory resource, and the security settings for the methods of the EJB (anyone can access all of the EJB methods).

Listing 8.95 lab2/jaxrpc/ejb/lumberco2/ejb/jar/META-INF/webservices.xml

```
<?xml version="1.0" encoding="UTF-8"?>
<webservices version="1.1"
    xmlns="http://java.sun.com/xml/ns/j2ee"
    xmlns:xsi="http://www.w3.org/2001/XMLSchema-instance"
    xmlns:lc2="http://lumber.org/ws/standards/wsdl/LumberWholesaler.wsdl"
    xsi:schemaLocation="http://java.sun.com/xml/ns/j2ee
        http://www.ibm.com/webservices/xsd/j2ee_web_services_1_1.xsd">
  <webservice-description>
    <webservice-description-name>LumberSupplierService
    </webservice-description-name>
    <wsdl-file>META-INF/wsdl/LumberCo2Wholesaler.wsdl</wsdl-file>
    <jaxrpc-mapping-file>META-INF/wsdl/lumberco2_mapping.xml
    </jaxrpc-mapping-file>
```

```
    <port-component>
      <port-component-name>LumberPurchaseOrderEJB</port-component-name>
      <wsdl-port>lc2:LumberPurchaseOrderPort</wsdl-port>
      <service-endpoint-interface>lc2.ws.ejb.PurchaseOrderPortType
      </service-endpoint-interface>
      <service-impl-bean>
        <ejb-link>LumberPurchaseOrderEJB</ejb-link>
      </service-impl-bean>
    </port-component>
  </webservice-description>
</webservices>
```

The webservices.xml deployment descriptor identifies the location of the WSDL and JAX-RPC mapping files, the WSDL port that the EJB implements (wsdl-port), the JAX-RPC service endpoint interface class (lc2.we.ejb.PurchaseOrderPortType), and the EJB in ejb-jar.xml that is being deployed as a Web service (ejb-link).

Listing 8.96 lab2/jaxrpc/ejb/lumberco2/ejb/jar/META-INF/sun-ejb-jar.xml

```
<?xml version="1.0" encoding="UTF-8"?>
<!DOCTYPE sun-ejb-jar PUBLIC
  '-//Sun Microsystems, Inc.//DTD Application Server 8.0 EJB 2.1//EN'
  'http://www.sun.com/software/appserver/dtds/sun-ejb-jar_2_1-0.dtd'>

<sun-ejb-jar>
  <enterprise-beans>
    <name>LumberCo2EJB</name>
    <ejb>
      <ejb-name>LumberPurchaseOrderEJB</ejb-name>
      <jndi-name>LumberPurchaseOrderEJB</jndi-name>
      <resource-ref>
        <res-ref-name>eis/JAXR</res-ref-name>
        <jndi-name>eis/JAXR</jndi-name>
          <default-resource-principal>
            <name>j2ee</name>
            <password>j2ee</password>
          </default-resource-principal>
      </resource-ref>

      <bean-pool>
        <steady-pool-size>1</steady-pool-size>
        <resize-quantity>10</resize-quantity>
        <max-pool-size>100</max-pool-size>
        <pool-idle-timeout-in-seconds>600</pool-idle-timeout-in-seconds>
      </bean-pool>
```

```
      <webservice-endpoint>
        <port-component-name>LumberPurchaseOrderEJB</port-component-name>
        <endpoint-address-uri>lumberco2/LumberSupplierService/PO
        </endpoint-address-uri>
      </webservice-endpoint>
    </ejb>
  </enterprise-beans>
</sun-ejb-jar>
```

The `sun-ejb-jar.xml` deployment descriptor identifies the name and password to the UDDI registry for creating the connection pool resource, information on the number of instances of the EJB to keep in a bean pool, and the URL at which the deployed Web service should be made available.

Now we move on to the WAR file. First, we create an Ant `build.xml` file to create the WAR. Create the following listing in the directory `lab2/jaxrpc/ejb/lumberco2/war`. This build file compiles `common.j2ee.ContextListener.java` and includes it in the WAR along with `RegistryConnection.properties` and `Registry.properties`. We create a `web.xml` deployment descriptor next that identifies `ContextListener` to be loaded on context startup. When `ContextListener` loads, it will connect to the UDDI registry and publish the information in `Registry.properties`.

Listing 8.97 lab2/jaxrpc/ejb/lumberco2/war/build.xml

```
<!- Builds the WAR for LumberCo2 ->
<project name="LumberCo2WholesalerWAR" default="create-war" basedir=".">
  <property name="common.dir" value="../../../../common"/>
  <property name="common.build.file" value="${common.dir}/common-build.xml"/>
  <property name="assemble.dir" value="assemble"/>
  <property name="assemble.war.dir" value="${assemble.dir}/war"/>
  <property name="context.path" value="lumberco2"/>
  <property name="war.file" value="${context.path}.war"/>

  <import file="${common.build.file}" />

  <!- PREPARE ->
  <target name="prepare" description="Creates the build directories.">
    <mkdir dir="${build.dir}/classes" />
  </target>

  <!- COMPILE ->
  <target name="compile" depends="prepare"
          description="Compiles the source code.">
    <javac srcdir="${common.dir}/src"
           includes="common/j2ee/ContextListener.java"
           destdir="${build.dir}/classes"
```

```
           debug="${compile.debug}"
           deprecation="${compile.deprecation}"
           optimize="${compile.optimize}">
      <classpath refid="j2ee.classpath"/>
    </javac>
  </target>

  <!- DIST ->
  <target name="create-war" depends="compile"
          description="Builds the WAR file for the JAX-RPC supplier">
    <mkdir dir="${assemble.war.dir}/WEB-INF/classes"/>
    <copy todir="${assemble.war.dir}/WEB-INF/classes"
          preservelastmodified="true">
      <fileset dir="${build.dir}/classes" />
    </copy>
    <copy todir="${assemble.war.dir}/WEB-INF" preservelastmodified="true">
      <fileset dir="./WEB-INF"/>
    </copy>
    <delete file="${dist.dir}/${war.file}" />
    <mkdir dir="${dist.dir}"/>
    <jar jarfile="${dist.dir}/${war.file}" basedir="${assemble.war.dir}"/>
  </target>
</project>
```

Next we create the deployment descriptors for the WAR. We need both `web.xml` and `sun-web.xml` deployment descriptors. Create the following two listings in the directory `lab2/jaxrpc/ejb/lumberco2/war/WEB-INF`.

Listing 8.98 lab2/jaxrpc/ejb/lumberco2/war/WEB-INF/web.xml

```
<?xml version="1.0" encoding="UTF-8"?>
<web-app xmlns="http://java.sun.com/xml/ns/j2ee" version="2.4"
         xmlns:xsi="http://www.w3.org/2001/XMLSchema-instance"
         xsi:schemaLocation="http://java.sun.com/xml/ns/j2ee
             http://java.sun.com/xml/ns/j2ee/web-app_2_4.xsd">
  <display-name>lumberco2</display-name>
  <context-param>
    <param-name>registryConnectionProperties</param-name>
    <param-value>RegistryConnection</param-value>
  </context-param>
  <context-param>
    <param-name>registryProperties</param-name>
    <param-value>Registry</param-value>
  </context-param>
  <listener>
```

```
    <listener-class>common.j2ee.ContextListener</listener-class>
  </listener>
  <resource-ref>
    <res-ref-name>eis/JAXR</res-ref-name>
    <res-type>javax.xml.registry.ConnectionFactory</res-type>
    <res-auth>Container</res-auth>
    <res-sharing-scope>Shareable</res-sharing-scope>
  </resource-ref>
</web-app>
```

The web.xml deployment descriptor identifies the names of the properties files, the ServletContextListener, and the JAXR resource.

Listing 8.99 lab2/jaxrpc/ejb/lumberco2/war/WEB-INF/sun-web.xml

```
<?xml version="1.0" encoding="UTF-8"?>
<!DOCTYPE sun-web-app PUBLIC
  "-//Sun Microsystems, Inc.//DTD Application Server 8.0 Servlet 2.4//EN"
  "http://www.sun.com/software/appserver/dtds/sun-web-app_2_4-0.dtd">

<sun-web-app>
  <context-root>/lumberco2</context-root>
  <resource-ref>
    <res-ref-name>eis/JAXR</res-ref-name>
    <jndi-name>eis/JAXR</jndi-name>
    <default-resource-principal>
      <name>j2ee</name>
      <password>j2ee</password>
    </default-resource-principal>
  </resource-ref>
</sun-web-app>
```

The sun-web.xml deployment descriptor identifies the context root and the name and password for creating connections to the UDDI registry.

Now we can move on to the EAR. We need a build.xml to create the EAR and an application.xml deployment descriptor. We start with the build.xml file. Create the following listing in directory lab2/jaxrpc/ejb/lumberco2.

Listing 8.100 lab2/jaxrpc/ejb/lumberco2/build.xml

```
<!- Builds and deploys the EAR for LumberCo2 ->
<project name="LumberCo2WholesalerEAR" default="create-ear" basedir=".">
  <property name="common.dir" value="../../../common"/>
  <property name="common.build.file" value="${common.dir}/common-build.xml"/>
```

```
  <import file="${common.build.file}" />

  <property name="assemble.dir" value="assemble"/>
  <property name="assemble.ear.dir" value="${assemble.dir}/ear"/>
  <property name="context.path" value="lumberco2"/>
  <property name="deploy.file" value="${dist.dir}/${context.path}.ear"/>

  <!- COMPILE ->
  <target name="build-war" description="Compiles the code for WAR">
    <ant dir="war" target="create-war" inheritall="false"/>
  </target>
  <target name="build-ejb" description="Compiles the code for EJB">
    <ant dir="ejb" target="create-ejb-jar" inheritall="false"/>
  </target>

  <!- DIST ->
  <target name="create-ear" depends="build-ejb,build-war"
          description="Builds the EAR file for the JAX-RPC application">
    <mkdir dir="${assemble.ear.dir}"/>
    <copy todir="${assemble.ear.dir}" preservelastmodified="true">
      <fileset dir="ear"/>
    </copy>
    <copy todir="${assemble.ear.dir}" preservelastmodified="true">
      <fileset dir="ejb/${dist.dir}" includes="*.jar" />
      <fileset dir="war/${dist.dir}" includes="*.war" />
    </copy>
    <delete file="${deploy.file}" />
    <mkdir dir="${dist.dir}"/>
    <jar destfile="${deploy.file}" basedir="${assemble.ear.dir}"/>
  </target>

  <target name="clean" depends="common-build.clean">
    <ant dir="ejb" target="clean" inheritall="false"/>
    <ant dir="war" target="clean" inheritall="false"/>
  </target>
</project>
```

Next create the following listing in directory `lab2/jaxrpc/ejb/lumberco2/ear/META-INF`.

Listing 8.101 lab2/jaxrpc/ejb/lumberco2/ear/META-INF/application.xml

```
<?xml version="1.0" encoding="UTF-8"?>
<application xmlns="http://java.sun.com/xml/ns/j2ee"
```

```
            xmlns:xsi="http://www.w3.org/2001/XMLSchema-instance"
            xsi:schemaLocation="http://java.sun.com/xml/ns/j2ee
                http://java.sun.com/xml/ns/j2ee/application_1_4.xsd"
            version="1.4">
  <display-name>LumberCo2</display-name>
  <module>
    <web>
      <web-uri>lumberco2.war</web-uri>
      <context-root>lumberco2</context-root>
    </web>
  </module>
  <module>
    <ejb>lumberco2-ejb.jar</ejb>
  </module>
</application>
```

The `application.xml` deployment descriptor simply identifies the J2EE modules that the EAR contains. At this point, you should have created the following files for lumberco2. A significant amount of them are generated by the JAX-RPC compiler.

- `lab2/jaxrpc/ejb/lumberco2/build.xml`
- `lab2/jaxrpc/ejb/lumberco2/ear/META-INF/application.xml`
- `lab2/jaxrpc/ejb/lumberco2/war/build.xml`
- `lab2/jaxrpc/ejb/lumberco2/war/WEB-INF/web.xml`
- `lab2/jaxrpc/ejb/lumberco2/war/WEB-INF/sun-web.xml`
- `lab2/jaxrpc/ejb/lumberco2/war/WEB-INF/classes/RegistryConnection.properties`
- `lab2/jaxrpc/ejb/lumberco2/war/WEB-INF/classes/Registry.properties`
- `lab2/jaxrpc/ejb/lumberco2/ejb/build.xml`
- `lab2/jaxrpc/ejb/lumberco2/ejb/config-wsdlToJava.xml`
- `lab2/jaxrpc/ejb/lumberco2/ejb/jar/META-INF/wsdl/LumberCo2Wholesaler.wsdl`
- `lab2/jaxrpc/ejb/lumberco2/ejb/jar/META-INF/ejb-jar.xml`
- `lab2/jaxrpc/ejb/lumberco2/ejb/jar/META-INF/webservices.xml`
- `lab2/jaxrpc/ejb/lumberco2/ejb/jar/META-INF/sun-ejb-jar.xml`
- `lab2/jaxrpc/ejb/lumberco2/ejb/build/lumberco2_mapping.xml`
- `lab2/jaxrpc/ejb/lumberco2/ejb/build/sei/src/common/domain/address/Address.java`
- `lab2/jaxrpc/ejb/lumberco2/ejb/build/sei/src/common/domain/address/USAddress.java`
- `lab2/jaxrpc/ejb/lumberco2/ejb/build/sei/src/common/domain/catalog/Product.java`

- lab2/jaxrpc/ejb/lumberco2/ejb/build/sei/src/common/domain/catalog/-ProductCatalog.java
- lab2/jaxrpc/ejb/lumberco2/ejb/build/sei/src/common/domain/customer/Customer.java
- lab2/jaxrpc/ejb/lumberco2/ejb/build/sei/src/common/domain/order/InvalidPurchase-OrderFault.java
- lab2/jaxrpc/ejb/lumberco2/ejb/build/sei/src/common/domain/order/LineItem.java
- lab2/jaxrpc/ejb/lumberco2/ejb/build/sei/src/common/domain/order/PurchaseOrder.java
- lab2/jaxrpc/ejb/lumberco2/ejb/build/sei/src/common/domain/order/ShippingNotice.java
- lab2/jaxrpc/ejb/lumberco2/ejb/build/sei/src/lc2/ws/jse/LumberSupplierService.java
- lab2/jaxrpc/ejb/lumberco2/ejb/build/sei/src/lc2/ws/jse/PurchaseOrderPortType_getCat-alog_RequestStuct.java
- lab2/jaxrpc/ejb/lumberco2/ejb/build/sei/src/lc2/ws/jse/PurchaseOrderPortType_getCat-alog_ResponseStuct.java
- lab2/jaxrpc/ejb/lumberco2/ejb/build/sei/src/lc2/ws/jse/Purchase-OrderPortType_Impl.java
- lab2/jaxrpc/ejb/lumberco2/ejb/build/sei/src/lc2/ws/jse/PurchaseOrderPortType_place-Order_RequestStuct.java
- lab2/jaxrpc/ejb/lumberco2/ejb/build/sei/src/lc2/ws/jse/PurchaseOrderPortType_place-Order_ResponseStuct.java
- lab2/jaxrpc/ejb/lumberco2/ejb/build/sei/src/lc2/ws/jse/PurchaseOrderPortType.java
- lab2/jaxrpc/ejb/lumberco2/ejb/src/lc2/ws/ejb/LumberPurchaseOrderBean.java
- lab2/jaxrpc/ejb/lumberco2/ejb/src/lc2/ws/ejb/Prices.properties

To build the EAR, make sure the server is running, the UDDI registry server is deployed, and the schemas WAR is deployed. Open a command prompt and navigate to the directory lab2/jaxrpc/ejb/lumberco2 where the EAR build.xml is located. Enter the following command:

```
ant create-ear
```

Once this command is complete, you should have a lumberco2.ear file in the directory lab2/jaxrpc/ejb/lumberco2/dist. To deploy this EAR, enter the following command:

```
ant deploy
```

If you open the Admin Console for the J2EE RI server, you should see something like Figure 8.20.

You should also be able to open a Web browser and enter the URL http://localhost:8080/lumberco2/LumberSupplierService/PO?WSDL to view the WSDL for the lumberco2 Web service, as in Figure 8.21.

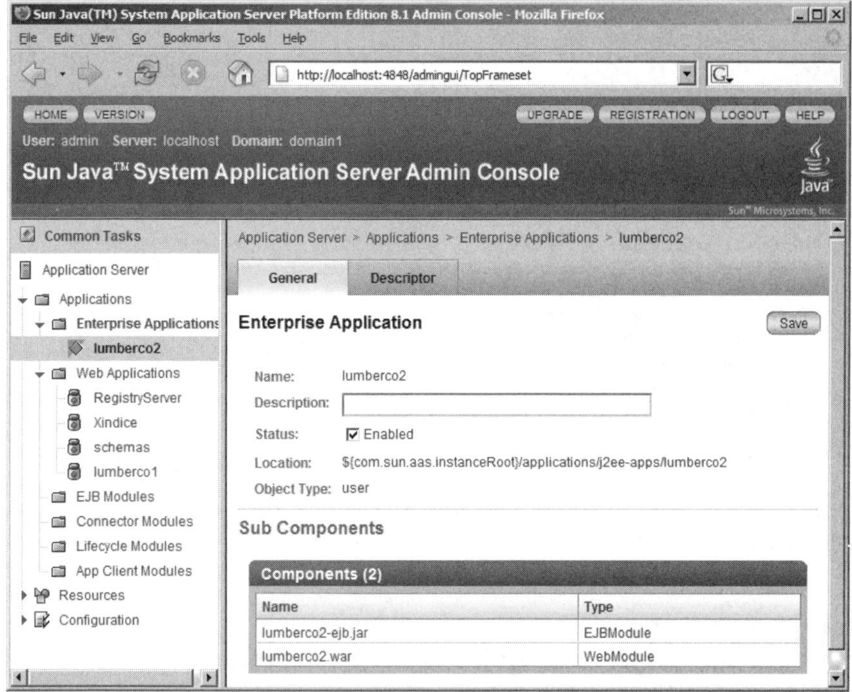

Figure 8.20
Admin Console Showing the LumberCo2 Web Service Deployed

Testing the LumberCo2 Web Service

Now we create a generated stub client to test the deployed lumberco2 Web service. The first thing we need to do is run `wscompile` to generate the static stub. Therefore, we need a configuration file to pass to `wscompile`. Create the following configuration file in the directory `lab2/client`. This configuration file looks nearly identical to the one for lumberco1 (Listing 8.86) except the WSDL location is different and the package name associated with the WSDL namespace is different.

Listing 8.102 lab2/client/config-genclient-lumberco2.xml

```
<?xml version="1.0" encoding="UTF-8"?>
<configuration xmlns="http://java.sun.com/xml/ns/jax-rpc/ri/config">
  <wsdl
  location="http://localhost:8080/lumberco2/LumberSupplierService/PO?WSDL"
  packageName="lc2.ws.ejb">
    <namespaceMappingRegistry>
```

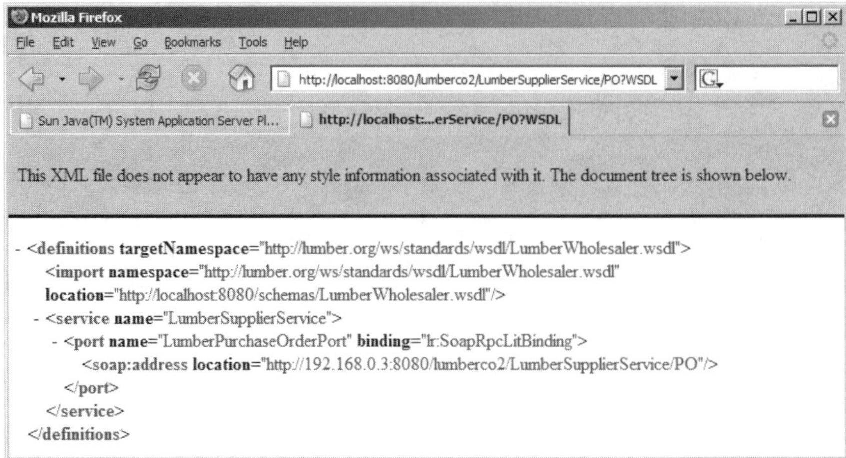

Figure 8.21
Accessing the WSDL for LumberCo2

```
      <namespaceMapping
  namespace="http://lumber.org/ws/standards/wsdl/LumberWholesaler.wsdl"
  packageName="lc2.ws.ejb"/>
      <namespaceMapping
  namespace="http://lumber.org/ws/standards/schemas/ProductCatalog.xsd"
  packageName="common.domain.catalog"/>
      <namespaceMapping
  namespace="http://lumber.org/ws/standards/schemas/PurchaseOrder.xsd"
  packageName="common.domain.order"/>
      <namespaceMapping
  namespace="http://lumber.org/ws/standards/schemas/Customer.xsd"
  packageName="common.domain.customer"/>
      <namespaceMapping
  namespace="http://lumber.org/ws/standards/schemas/Address.xsd"
  packageName="common.domain.address"/>
      <namespaceMapping
  namespace="http://lumber.org/ws/standards/schemas/Types.xsd"
  packageName="common.domain.types"/>
    </namespaceMappingRegistry>
  </wsdl>
</configuration>
```

Notice that this configuration file uses a `wsdl` element that gives the location of the WSDL for the deployed lumberco2 Web service. This configuration file also gives the appropriate mappings from the XML namespaces to Java packages. To execute `wscompile` we again use Ant. The build file for building and running the client has already been created (Listing 8.87).

Generate the stub code by making sure the server is running and the lumberco2 service is deployed, opening a command prompt, navigating to the `lab2/client` directory where `build.xml` is located, and entering the following command:

```
ant generate-lc2-stubs
```

This command will generate Java files in the `lab2/client/build/lc2/client/src` directory and their compiled classes in the directory `lab2/client/build/lc2/client/classes` directory. The generated classes will include the JAX-RPC service endpoint interface with the associated implementation classes, as well as the types we defined in XML Schema and classes to handle their serialization to XML.

Now we can create a client that uses the generated classes to invoke the lumberco2 Web service. Create the following listing in the directory `lab2/client/src/lc2/client`. This listing is nearly identical to Listing 8.88.

Listing 8.103 lab2/client/src/lc2/client/Lc2StaticStubTest.java

```
package lc2.client;

import java.text.SimpleDateFormat;
import java.util.*;
import javax.xml.rpc.ServiceException;
import javax.xml.rpc.ServiceFactory;
import lc1.ws.jse.LumberSupplierService;
import lc1.ws.jse.PurchaseOrderPortType;
import common.domain.address.USAddress;
import common.domain.catalog.Product;
import common.domain.catalog.ProductCatalog;
import common.domain.customer.Customer;
import common.domain.order.LineItem;
import common.domain.order.PurchaseOrder;
import common.domain.order.ShippingNotice;

public class Lc2StaticStubTest {
  public static void main(String[] args) {
    LumberSupplierService service = null;
    PurchaseOrderPortType stub = null;

    try {
      service = (LumberSupplierService)
        ServiceFactory.newInstance().loadService(
          LumberSupplierService.class);
      stub = service.getLumberPurchaseOrderPort();
    }catch (ServiceException e) {
      System.err.println("Failed to get the service and the stub.");
      e.printStackTrace();
      return;
```

```
    }

    List purchaseItems = getItemsToOrder(stub);
    placeOrder(stub, purchaseItems);
  }

  /** Gets the ProductCatalog and returns the first two items to order. */
  public static List getItemsToOrder(PurchaseOrderPortType stub) {
    System.out.println("Attempting to get the catalog from lumberco2...");
    List purchaseItems = new ArrayList();

    try {
      ProductCatalog catalog = null;
      catalog = stub.getCatalog();
      System.out.println("lumberco2 prices:\n");

      if (catalog.getProducts().length > 0) {
        Product[] products = catalog.getProducts();

        for (int i = 0; i < products.length; i++) {
          System.out.println("itemNumber = "
            + products[i].getProductNumber());
          System.out.println("name = " + products[i].getName());
          System.out.println("description = "
            + products[i].getDescription());
          System.out.println("price = $" + products[i].getPrice());
          System.out.println();

          if (i < 2) { // Just order the first two items.
            purchaseItems.add(products[i]);
          }
        }
      }
    }catch (Exception e) {
      System.err.println("Error getting catalog from lumberco2");
      e.printStackTrace();
    }

    return purchaseItems;
  }

  /** Submits a PurchaseOrder. */
  public static void placeOrder(PurchaseOrderPortType stub,
    List purchaseItems) {
    System.out.println("Attempting to place an order with lumberco2");
```

```
try {
  if (purchaseItems.isEmpty()) {
    System.out.println("No items in catalog to order.");
    return;
  }

  USAddress address = new USAddress();
  address.setStreet("111 Peach Lane");
  address.setCity("Atlanta");
  address.setState("GA");
  address.setZip("30332");

  Customer customer = new Customer();
  customer.setFirstName("Brighton");
  customer.setLastName("Allen");
  customer.setCompany("LumberRetailer");
  customer.setPhoneNumber("555-555-5555");
  customer.setEmailAddress("brighton.allen@lumberretailer.com");
  customer.setBillingAddress(address);

  List lineItems = new ArrayList();
  int quantity = 100;
  float total = 0.0f;

  for (Iterator iter = purchaseItems.iterator(); iter.hasNext();) {
    Product product = (Product) iter.next();
    LineItem item = new LineItem();
    item.setQuantity(quantity);
    item.setProductNumber(product.getProductNumber());
    item.setPrice(product.getPrice());
    lineItems.add(item);
    total += (product.getPrice() * quantity);
  }

  PurchaseOrder purchaseOrder = new PurchaseOrder();
  purchaseOrder.setOrderDate(Calendar.getInstance());
  purchaseOrder.setCustomer(customer);
  purchaseOrder.setShippingAddress(address);
  purchaseOrder.setLineItems((LineItem[])
    lineItems.toArray(new LineItem[]{}));
  purchaseOrder.setTotal(total);

  ShippingNotice shippingNotice = stub.placeOrder(purchaseOrder);
  SimpleDateFormat dateFormat = new SimpleDateFormat("MM/dd/yyyy");
  System.out.println("Order placed successfully.");
```

```
      System.out.println("orderNumber = " + shippingNotice.getOrderNumber());
      System.out.println("shipDate = "
        + dateFormat.format(shippingNotice.getShipDate().getTime()));
      System.out.println("total = $" + total);
    }catch (Exception e) {
      System.err.println("Error placing order with lumberco2");
      e.printStackTrace();
    }
  }
}
```

The `build.xml` is already set up to compile and test `Lc2StaticStubTest.java`, so make sure the server is running and the lumberco2 Web service is deployed, open a command prompt, navigate to the `lab2/client` directory where `build.xml` is located, and enter the following command:

```
ant package-lc2-client
```

This command will compile the source code for the client and then JAR the client up so that it is easy to reference when we run the test. To run the test, enter the following command:

```
ant test-lc2-client-stub
```

This command will execute `Lc2StaticStubTest`. You should see output on the command line similar to that shown in Figure 8.22 and Figure 8.23.

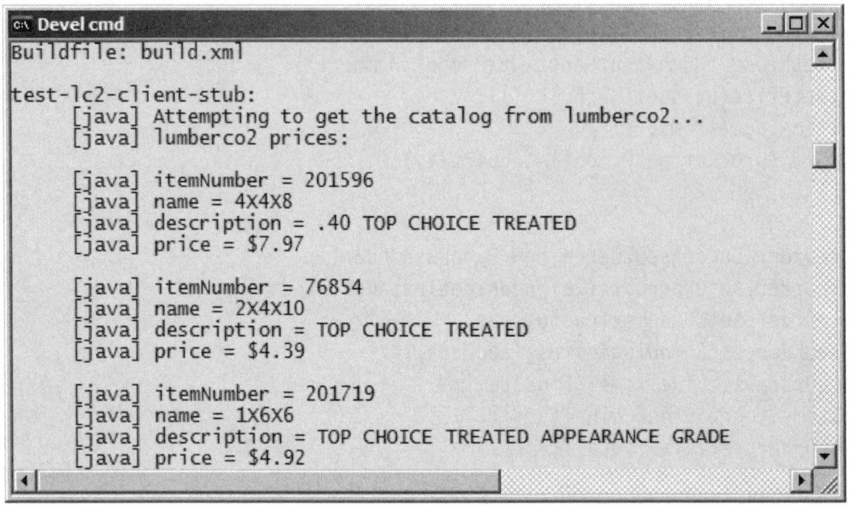

```
Devel cmd
Buildfile: build.xml

test-lc2-client-stub:
     [java] Attempting to get the catalog from lumberco2...
     [java] lumberco2 prices:

     [java] itemNumber = 201596
     [java] name = 4X4X8
     [java] description = .40 TOP CHOICE TREATED
     [java] price = $7.97

     [java] itemNumber = 76854
     [java] name = 2X4X10
     [java] description = TOP CHOICE TREATED
     [java] price = $4.39

     [java] itemNumber = 201719
     [java] name = 1X6X6
     [java] description = TOP CHOICE TREATED APPEARANCE GRADE
     [java] price = $4.92
```

Figure 8.22

Output from the lumberco2 Test

```
Devel cmd
     [java] price = $10.49

     [java] itemNumber = 21210
     [java] name = 5/4X6X8
     [java] description = STANDARD TREATED
     [java] price = $5.97

     [java] itemNumber = 84981
     [java] name = 2X6X12
     [java] description = TOP CHOICE TREATED
     [java] price = $6.97

     [java] Attempting to place an order with lumberco2
     [java] Order placed successfully.
     [java] orderNumber = 1
     [java] shipDate = 03/15/2005
     [java] total = $1236.0

BUILD SUCCESSFUL
Total time: 5 seconds
```

Figure 8.23

Output from the lumberco2 Test, Continued

We have created and deployed an EJB-based JAX-RPC service endpoint and tested it. Next we run a test to retrieve some of the data we published in the UDDI registry.

UDDI Registry Test

At this point you should have two Web services deployed on your server and their information should be published in the UDDI registry. Let us create a client to query the UDDI registry for information on the published organizations. First copy `RegistryConnection.properties` from Schemas, lumberco1, or lumberco2 and put it in the directory `lab2/client/src/generic/client`. Then create the following listing in the directory `lab2/client/src/generic/client`.

Listing 8.104 lab2/client/src/generic/client/UDDITest.java

```
package generic.client;

import java.net.PasswordAuthentication;
import java.util.*;
import javax.xml.registry.BulkResponse;
import javax.xml.registry.BusinessLifeCycleManager;
import javax.xml.registry.BusinessQueryManager;
import javax.xml.registry.Connection;
import javax.xml.registry.ConnectionFactory;
import javax.xml.registry.JAXRException;
import javax.xml.registry.JAXRResponse;
import javax.xml.registry.RegistryService;
```

```
import javax.xml.registry.infomodel.Concept;
import javax.xml.registry.infomodel.Organization;
import javax.xml.registry.infomodel.Service;
import javax.xml.registry.infomodel.ServiceBinding;

public class UDDITest {
  public static void main(String[] args) {
    Connection connection = null;

    try {
      connection = getConnection();
      RegistryService registry = connection.getRegistryService();
      BusinessLifeCycleManager lifeCycleMngr =
        registry.getBusinessLifeCycleManager();
      BusinessQueryManager queryMngr =
        registry.getBusinessQueryManager();
      System.out.println("Got RegistryService, "
        + "BusinessLifeCycleManager, and BusinessQueryManager.");

      Collection organizations =
        findOrganizations(lifeCycleMngr, queryMngr);

      for (Iterator iter = organizations.iterator(); iter.hasNext();) {
        Organization org = (Organization) iter.next();
        System.out.println();
        System.out.println("Found organization: "
          + org.getName().getValue());

        Collection services = org.getServices();

        for (Iterator iterator = services.iterator(); iterator.hasNext();) {
          Service service = (Service) iterator.next();
          System.out.println("Service name = "
            + service.getName().getValue());
          Collection bindings = service.getServiceBindings();

          for (Iterator iterator2 = bindings.iterator();
               iterator2.hasNext();) {
            ServiceBinding binding = (ServiceBinding) iterator2.next();
            String accessURI = binding.getAccessURI();
            System.out.println("AccessURI = " + accessURI);
          }
        }
      }
    }catch (JAXRException e) {
```

```
      e.printStackTrace();
      return;
    }finally {
      try {
        connection.close();
      }catch (Throwable e) {
        // Eat this one.
      }
    }
  }

  private static Collection findOrganizations(
      BusinessLifeCycleManager lifeCycleMngr,
      BusinessQueryManager queryMngr)
    throws JAXRException {
    // Find the lumber.org WSDL concept.
    Collection namePatterns = new HashSet();
    namePatterns.add("lumber.org:LumberWholesaler");
    BulkResponse response = queryMngr.findConcepts(null, namePatterns,
      null, null, null);
    Concept wsdlConcept = null;

    if (response.getStatus() == JAXRResponse.STATUS_SUCCESS) {
      Iterator iter = response.getCollection().iterator();

      if (iter.hasNext()) {
        wsdlConcept = (Concept) iter.next();
      }
    }else {
      logExceptions(response);
      throw new JAXRException(
        "Failed to find the lumber.org WSDL concept.");
    }

    Collection specifications = new ArrayList();
    specifications.add(wsdlConcept);

    response = queryMngr.findOrganizations(null, null, null,
      specifications, null, null);

    if (response.getStatus() != JAXRResponse.STATUS_SUCCESS) {
      logExceptions(response);
      throw new JAXRException("Failed to find the organizations "
        + "using the lumber.org WSDL concept.");
    }
```

```
  return response.getCollection();
}

public static Connection getConnection() throws JAXRException {
  ResourceBundle connectionProperties =
    ResourceBundle.getBundle("generic.client.RegistryConnection");

  Connection connection =
    makeRegistryConnection(
      connectionProperties.getString(
        "javax.xml.registry.lifeCycleManagerURL"),
      connectionProperties.getString(
        "javax.xml.registry.queryManagerURL"),
      connectionProperties.getString("registry.username"),
      connectionProperties.getString("registry.password"));
  return connection;
}

public static Connection makeRegistryConnection(
    String lifeCycleManagerURL, String queryManagerURL,
    String userName, String password)
  throws JAXRException {
  Connection connection = null;
  Properties props = new Properties();
  props.setProperty("javax.xml.registry.lifeCycleManagerURL",
    lifeCycleManagerURL);
  props.setProperty("javax.xml.registry.queryManagerURL",
    queryManagerURL);

  System.out.println(
    "Attempting to make a connection to the registry.");
  System.out.println("javax.xml.registry.lifeCycleManagerURL = "
    + lifeCycleManagerURL);
  System.out.println("javax.xml.registry.queryManagerURL = "
    + queryManagerURL);

  try {
    // Look up the connection factory via JNDI.
    ConnectionFactory factory = ConnectionFactory.newInstance();
    // Configure the connection factory.
    factory.setProperties(props);

    // Connect to the registry.
    connection = factory.createConnection();
```

```
    }catch (JAXRException e) {
      throw new JAXRException("Failed to connect to the registry.", e);
    }

    System.out.println("Created a connection to the registry.");

    // Log in to the registry.
    PasswordAuthentication passwordCredential =
      new PasswordAuthentication(userName, password.toCharArray());
    Set credentials = new HashSet();
    credentials.add(passwordCredential);
    connection.setCredentials(credentials);
    System.out.println("Authenticated with the registry.");

    return connection;
  }

  private static void logExceptions(BulkResponse response)
    throws JAXRException {
    System.err.println("Exceptions from bulk response:");

    for (Iterator iter = response.getExceptions().iterator();
         iter.hasNext();) {
      Exception ex = (Exception) iter.next();
      ex.printStackTrace();
    }

    System.err.println("----------");
  }
}
```

The `build.xml` file in Listing 8.87 already has code to build and run this test. To build the client, make sure your server is running with everything deployed and then open a command prompt, navigate to directory `lab2/client` where `build.xml` is located, and enter the following command:

```
ant build-generic-client
```

Then, to run the test enter the following command:

```
ant test-generic-client-uddi
```

The output should look similar to Figure 8.24.

`UDDITest` uses JAXR to connect to the registry, find organizations, and output information on the organizations. It does not output all of the information that we published, but you could always add to it. We are done! You created and deployed an industry-standard WSDL and associated XML Schemas, both a Servlet-based and an EJB-based JAX-RPC service endpoint Web service that

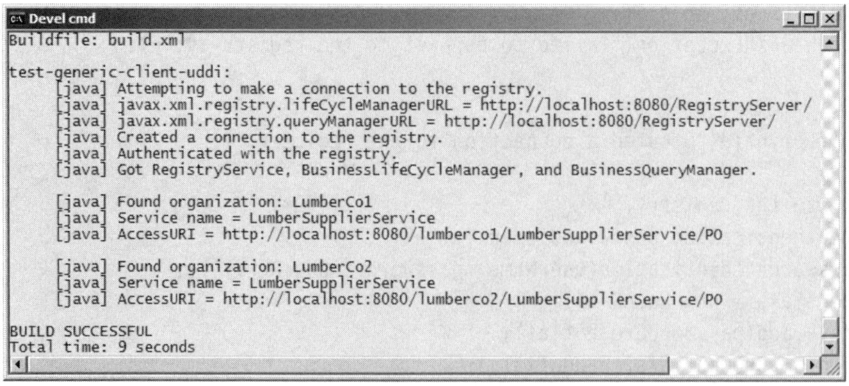

```
Buildfile: build.xml

test-generic-client-uddi:
     [java] Attempting to make a connection to the registry.
     [java] javax.xml.registry.lifeCycleManagerURL = http://localhost:8080/RegistryServer/
     [java] javax.xml.registry.queryManagerURL = http://localhost:8080/RegistryServer/
     [java] Created a connection to the registry.
     [java] Authenticated with the registry.
     [java] Got RegistryService, BusinessLifeCycleManager, and BusinessQueryManager.

     [java] Found organization: LumberCo1
     [java] Service name = LumberSupplierService
     [java] AccessURI = http://localhost:8080/lumberco1/LumberSupplierService/PO

     [java] Found organization: LumberCo2
     [java] Service name = LumberSupplierService
     [java] AccessURI = http://localhost:8080/lumberco2/LumberSupplierService/PO

BUILD SUCCESSFUL
Total time: 9 seconds
```

Figure 8.24
Output from the UDDI Test

implements the service defined by the standard WSDL, published information on everything in a UDDI registry, and wrote JAX-RPC and JAXR based clients to test it all.

8.8 Summary

Businesses have found that by exposing and distributing their applications over the Internet, they can achieve benefits in business productivity and customer satisfaction. This translates to cost savings and an increase in business transactions, which leads to higher revenues. However, software professionals have found that it is extremely cumbersome to integrate these vast worldwide disparate systems using preexisting distributed computing technologies such as DCOM, CORBA, or even J2EE. As a result, Web services were created. Web services are an implementation of the service-oriented architecture concept that uses standards-based technologies, founded on XML and Internet protocols, to achieve interoperability. Web services are considered the next evolutionary phase of distributed computing.

Web services today are based on four core standard specifications—XML, SOAP, WSDL, and UDDI. These specifications are independent of any programming language, operating system, hardware, or vendor application, which is one reason why Web services have succeded in large-scale interoperability where past attempts have failed. Additionally, the specifications SOAP, WSDL, and UDDI were designed to be independent of the underlying transport protocol. However, the primary transport protocol used for Web services today is HTTP, followed at a distant second by SMTP. This makes sense when you consider the fact that the majority of the traffic on the Internet is HTTP, followed, as you might expect, by e-mail (SMTP). Web developers are quite familiar with HTTP and Web servers already support it, so using HTTP to transport SOAP messages is a natural fit. Plus HTTP has built-in support for the request-response paradigm, which also to models another familiar concept for developers—RPC. RPC-based Web services provide a nice starting point for developers that feel at home with procedure call semantics, but are a bit overwhelmed by the document-centric nature of Web services. However, experience has shown that document-centered Web services provide better interoperability and cope with change better than RPC-based services.

The inability of a software system to effectively cope with change is often referred to as the "brittleness" of the system. The distributed systems of the past have incorporated various degrees of tight coupling between the components of the system. This tight coupling made it difficult or even impossible to change one component of the system without having to change another component with which it was integrated. Web services were designed to allow loosely coupled applications (services) to be readily integrated, thereby reducing or even eliminating the brittleness problem. Because Web services are independent of the platform, you can change the underlying operating system or vendor implementation (J2EE, .NET, Perl, etc.) for one or more services without affecting the clients or services that rely on them. Additionally, because the data transmitted between Web services is simply text data instead of binary data (as in other distributed systems), Web service implementations can be readily written for nearly any platform, including legacy systems such as mainframes based on COBOL, Pascal, or FORTRAN.

Web services written in Java are a highly effective solution to the brittleness problem. In addition to the loose coupling between distributed applications that Web services provide, Java adds loose coupling between the Web service implementation (business logic) and the underlying server and operating system. Java gives you the ability to easily swap out your operating system and/or J2EE server for systems that provide better performance, reliability, or some other quality of service, without having to rewrite your application or even change your business logic at all. The combination of Java and Web services is quite powerful at combating system brittleness, but they cannot solve the brittleness problem on their own. Bad design and improper planning can foul up any system and eliminate the inherent support for interoperbility that is built into Web services. When deciding to use Web services, you should evaluate several designs for their ability to endure changes that will inevitably be driven by business needs. And remember that Web services are not always the best solution. Web services can add a large degree of complexity to your application when it may not be necessary. If you know that the application you are developing will never interact with a different platform, then you might as well stick with the same technology on both ends of the client-server equation.

The field of Web services is complex and very large, and this chapter really just scratched the surface. In fact, several entire books have been written on the subjects in this chapter. This chapter provided an introduction to Web services and the service-oriented architecture concept, as well as knowledge in how to develop Web services with Java and J2EE. The purpose of this chapter was to give you a foundation, not to make you an expert. With a solid foundation of knowledge you can have great success in the workplace.

One of the main things about Web services to remember is that they are based on the service-oriented architecture concept, which consists of a service provider, service broker, and service requester. The role of the *service provider* is to develop the Web service, make it available on a network (intranet or the Internet), and publish information about the Web service to a service broker (UDDI registry). The information published should include a link to the location of the WSDL service description and may include some other description of the service, the name of the company providing the service, a category for the service, and links to any industry specifications that the service adheres to. The role of the *service broker* is to provide a common location for organizations to publish their services (a UDDI registry) and the ability for customers or partners to discover them (as a phone book). The role of the *service requester* is to search the UDDI registry, find a published Web service, and bind to the Web service to invoke it. Of course many Web services are developed without the use of a service broker. Once a service requester has the information about a service provider, the service broker is not needed.

XML provides Web services applications with a universal mechanism for structuring data and defining data types. SOAP provides a standard for packaging that data and exchanging it between applications over a network. WSDL provides a common method for describing Web service interfaces. UDDI enables publishing and finding information on existing Web services (service discovery).

Java provides several APIs that make creating Web services much easier than it would be if you had to manually process the XML. SAAJ is a low-level API for creating, processing, and even transmitting SOAP messages. JAX-RPC is a higher level API that allows Java developers to interact with remote Web services by simply executing method calls on remote objects. JAX-RPC handles the marshalling and unmarshalling of data between Java and XML, so that developers can concentrate on their business logic. JAXR is an API for interacting with UDDI registries, including publishing and searching. JAXR provides Java objects for each of the UDDI data structures, as well as functionality to generate SOAP messages, consisting of UDDI data structures, for invoking the UDDI inquiry and publication Web services. Under the covers, both JAX-RPC and JAXR use SAAJ to process SOAP messages.

Finally, J2EE provides specifications on how stateless session EJBs can be exposed as Web services, and plain Java objects can be deployed to a Servlet container and process Web service requests. EJB service endpoints benefit from all of the same container-managed services that are provided to traditional stateless session EJBs, and service endpoints dropped into the Servlet container get access to the same resources as ordinary Java Servlets. J2EE defines a new deployment descriptor for deploying Web services called `webservices.xml`. The purpose of this deployment descriptor is to identify which J2EE components are Web services and to link the J2EE components and their associated Web services artifacts (like WSDL).

8.9 Self-Review Questions

1. Web services can be deployed only on the Internet.
   - **a.** True
   - **b.** False
2. What is the purpose of a service broker?
   - **a.** Sales of Web services
   - **b.** Pricing of Web services
   - **c.** Service discovery
   - **d.** Implementation of Web services
3. What are the four core Web service technologies?
   - **a.** JAXP, SAAJ, JAX-RPC, and JAXR
   - **b.** XML, SOAP, WSDL, and UDDI
   - **c.** XML, SAAJ, JAX-RPC, and JAXR
   - **d.** SAAJ, JAX-RPC, SOAP, and WSDL
4. Bottom-up development typically produces Web services that are more interoperable than top-down development.

a. True

b. False

5. A WSDL `portType` is used to describe what?

a. Web service implementation

b. Web service binding

c. Web service interface

d. Web service endpoint address

6. What WSDL element defines the underlying protocols used by a Web service?

a. `binding`

b. `portType`

c. `service`

d. `message`

7. WSDL can be used only to describe services that use SOAP and HTTP.

a. True

b. False

8. What API does SAAJ extend?

a. JAX-RPC

b. JDOM

c. JAXP

d. DOM

9. What Java API was designed to allow developers to invoke Web services by simply making a method call on a remote object?

a. SAAJ

b. JAX-RPC

c. JAXR

10. JAX-RPC provides a client-side and a server-side API.

a. True

b. False

11. Servlet-based JAX-RPC service endpoints do not have access to the same resources as a Java Servlet.

    a. True

    b. False

12. In what data structure does UDDI store references to WSDL documents?

    a. `publisherAssertion`

    b. `businessEntity`

    c. `businessService`

    d. `bindingTemplate`

    e. `tModel`

13. What element in UDDI is used to define the URL for a Web service?

    a. `accessPoint`

    b. `discoveryURL`

    c. `SpecificationLink`

    d. `ExternalLink`

14. What Java API is used for interacting with XML-based registries?

    a. SAAJ

    b. JAX-RPC

    c. JAXR

15. JAXR was designed only for UDDI.

    a. True

    b. False

8.10 Keys to the Self-Review Questions

1. b 2. c 3. b 4. b 5. c 6. a 7. b 8. d 9. b 10. a 11. b 12. e 13. a 14. c 15. b

8.11 Exercises

1. Describe the service-oriented architecture concept and how Web services are related to the SOA concept.

2. What are the goals of service-oriented architectures?
3. Describe what *interoperable* means in the context of Web services.
4. What are the advantages of loosely coupled distributed systems? What are the disadvantages of tightly coupled distributed systems?
5. What are the three roles and three operations of SOA?
6. Briefly describe the four core Web service technologies.
7. Describe the interaction that occurs between the three SOA roles, and how the four core Web service technologies are used in the interaction.
8. How do the three SOA roles communicate?
9. What is the underlying technology of all the other Web service technologies and what great benefit does this technology provide?
10. List and briefly describe the three Java APIs for developing Web services that are discussed in this chapter.
11. What are the organizations that maintain the four core Web service technologies and the three Java APIs discussed in this chapter?
12. What is the benefit of using the Java APIs for developing Web services instead of working directly with the core Web service technologies?
13. Describe both top-down and bottom-up development in the context of Web services.
14. What is the purpose of a WSDL document?
15. What key information does a WSDL document provide?
16. Why do we not simply write a Web service description in plain natural language (English, Spanish, whatever)?
17. How do code generators use WSDL documents?
18. Describe the two major sections of a WSDL document and what WSDL components are contained in each section.
19. List and briefly describe the purpose of the key WSDL elements.
20. What technology is used to define data types in a WSDL document?
21. What is SAAJ used for, what other Java APIs use SAAJ under the covers, and of what design pattern is SAAJ an implementation?
22. Map each of the SOAP elements to their corresponding Java object in SAAJ.

23. Describe how the JAX-RPC API is used to develop Web services, and the benefits that it provides Java developers.

24. What are the two options for implementing a JAX-RPC service endpoint? Which option allows you to deploy a plain Java object as a Web service?

25. What Java type must you create (either by hand or with a tool) when developing both Servlet-based and EJB-based JAX-RPC service endpoints? To what WSDL element does this type correspond?

26. In Servlet-based JAX-RPC service endpoints, what class gives you access to the SOAP message? How do you access this class from a Servlet-based endpoint? How about in EJB-based endpoints?

27. List and briefly describe the three client-side programming models for JAX-RPC. Which requires you to generate classes using a JAX-RPC compiler? Which is the most dynamic in nature?

28. What is the name of the process that JAX-RPC executes to convert Java data types to XML data types. What about the reverse?

29. Describe how a WSDL interface definition is mapped into Java using the rules defined by JAX-RPC.

30. What deployment descriptors does J2EE require to deploy a Servlet-based JAX-RPC service endpoint? What deployment descriptors are needed for EJB-based endpoints?

31. What is the purpose of a UDDI registry?

32. List and briefly describe the primary UDDI data structures.

33. How does UDDI link data structures?

34. What are the two UDDI APIs and what are they used for? List the categories of operations for each API.

35. What are the three categorization schemes that all UDDI registries must support?

36. Map each of the primary UDDI data structures to their corresponding Java object in JAXR.

37. What XML-based registry was JAXR primarily designed around and why?

38. Why are all of the Java APIs in this chapter hollow, meaning they require a vendor implementation?

8.12 Programming Exercises

1. Develop and deploy your own simple Servlet-based JAX-RPC service endpoint. Test it with a generated stub client. Use a J2EE 1.4 (or later) compatible server.
2. Develop and deploy your own simple EJB-based JAX-RPC service endpoint. Test it with a generated stub client. Use a J2EE 1.4 (or later) compatible server.
3. Develop and deploy a Web service in Java on any server. Write a JAX-RPC dynamic proxy client to test the service. Write a JAX-RPC DII client to test the service.
4. Write a SAAJ client to test any Web service.
5. Write an application to publish data in a UDDI registry and then query for the data you published.
6. Write dynamic proxy and DII clients for the Web services deployed in Lab 2.

8.13 References

Basic Profile Version 1.0, Final Material, April 16, 2004. http://www.ws-i.org/Profiles/BasicProfile-1.0.html.

Basic Profile Version 1.1, Final Material, August 24, 2004. http://www.ws-i.org/Profiles/BasicProfile-1.1.html.

Deitel, Harvey M., Paul J. Deitel, Jon P. Gadzik, Kyle Lomeli, Sean E. Santry, and Su Zhang. 2003. *Java Web Services for Experienced Programmers: Deitel Developer Series.* Upper Saddle River, NJ: Pearson Education, Inc.

Extensible Markup Language (XML) 1.0 (Third Edition), W3C Recommendation, February 4, 2004. http://www.w3.org/TR/REC-xml.

Graham, Steve, Doug Davis, Simeon Simeonov, Glen Daniels, Peter Brittenham, Yuichi Nakamura, Paul Fremantle, Dieter Koenig, and Claudia Zentner. 2004. *Building Web Services with Java: Making Sense of XML, SOAP, WSDL, and UDDI.* 2nd ed. Indianapolis: Sams Publishing.

Java API for XML-based RPC (JAX-RPC) Specification, version 1.1. http://java.sun.com/webservices/reference/api/index.html.

Java API for XML Registries (JAXR) Specification, version 1.0. http://java.sun.com/webservices/reference/api/index.html.

Java 2 Enterprise Edition Specification, version 1.4. http://jcp.org/en/jsr/detail?id=151.

Monson-Haefel, Richard. 2004. *J2EE Web Services.* Boston: Addison-Wesley.

Nagappan, Ramesh, Robert Skoczylas, and Rima Patel Sriganesh. 2003. *Developing Java Web Services, Architecting and Developing Secure Web Services Using Java.* Indianapolis: Wiley Publishing Inc.

Namespaces in XML, W3C Recommendation, 1999. http://www.w3.org/TR/REC-xml-names.

Simple Object Access Protocol (SOAP) 1.1, W3C Note, May 8, 2000. http:///www.w3.org/TR/SOAP.

Singh, Inderjeet, Sean Brydon, Greg Murray, Vijay Ramachandran, Thierry Violleau, and Beth Stearns. 2004. *Designing Web Services with the J2EE 1.4 Platform: JAX-RPC, SOAP, and XML Technologies.* Boston: Addison-Wesley.

SOAP Messages with Attachments, W3C Note, December 11, 2000. http://www.w3.org/TR/SOAP-attachments.

SOAP Version 1.2 Part 0: Primer, W3C Recommendation, June 24, 2003. http://www.w3.org/TR/soap12-part0/.

SOAP Version 1.2 Part 1: Messaging Framework, W3C Recommendation, June 24, 2003. http://www.w3.org/TR/soap12-part1/.

SOAP Version 1.2 Part 2: Adjuncts, W3C Recommendation, June 24, 2003. http://www.w3.org/TR/soap12-part2/.

SOAP Version 1.2 Email Binding, W3C Note, July 3, 2002. http://www.w3.org/TR/soap12-email.

SOAP with Attachments API for Java (SAAJ) Specification, version 1.2. http://java.sun.com/webservices/reference/api/index.html.

UDDI Version 2.04 API Specification, UDDI Committee Specification, July 19, 2002. http://uddi.org/pubs/ProgrammersAPI-V2.04-Published-20020719.htm.

Web Services Description Language (WSDL) 1.1, W3C Note, March 15, 2001. http://www.w3.org/TR/wsdl.

XML Schema Part 0: Primer Second Edition, W3C Recommendation, October 28, 2004. http://www.w3.org/TR/xmlschema-0/.

XML Schema Part 1: Structures Second Edition, W3C Recommendation, October 28, 2004. http://www.w3.org/TR/xmlschema-1/.

XML Schema Part 2: Datatypes Second Edition, W3C Recommendation, October 28, 2004. http://www.w3.org/TR/xmlschema-2/.

Index

T